The SAGE
Handbook of
Social Marketing

The SAGE Handbook of
Social Marketing

Edited by

Gerard Hastings,
Kathryn Angus and
Carol Bryant

Los Angeles | London | New Delhi
Singapore | Washington DC

SAGE Publications Ltd
1 Oliver's Yard
55 City Road
London EC1Y 1SP

SAGE Publications Inc.
2455 Teller Road
Thousand Oaks, California 91320

SAGE Publications India Pvt Ltd
B 1/I 1 Mohan Cooperative Industrial Area
Mathura Road, Post Bag 7
New Delhi 110 044

SAGE Publications Asia-Pacific Pte Ltd
33 Pekin Street #02-01
Far East Square
Singapore 048763

Library of Congress Control Number: 2011922615

British Library Cataloguing in Publication data

A catalogue record for this book is available from the British Library

ISBN 978-1-84920-188-9

Typeset by Cenveo Publisher Services
Printed by MPG Books Group, Bodmin, Cornwall
Printed on paper from sustainable resources

Contents

Editorial Board and Reviewers

About the Authors

Dana L. Alden completed his PhD at the University of Texas, Austin in 1990 and joined the Marketing Department at the University of Hawaii. His research focuses on global brands, globalisation of consumer culture and healthcare marketing. In 2007, Dana received the Excellence in Global Marketing Research Award from the American Marketing Association. He conducts research on shared patient–physician decision-making and patient decision aids. His work appears in leading journals such as *Social Science & Medicine*, *Journal of Marketing*, *Journal of International Business Studies* and *Health Communications*. Dr Alden currently holds the William R. Johnson Jr Distinguished Professorship.

Kathryn Angus has been employed at the Institute for Social Marketing at the University of Stirling in the UK (formerly the Centre for Social Marketing at the University of Strathclyde) for a decade. Her research interests include the impact of commercial marketing on people's health and behaviour; the effectiveness of social marketing; and systematic review methodologies and literature search strategies. With colleagues at the Institute, Dr Angus has recently co-authored articles in the *British Medical Journal*, the *Journal of Social Marketing*, *Alcohol and Alcoholism* and *Health Education*.

Thomas Boysen Anker is lecturer in marketing at the University of Glasgow Business School. He holds a BA and MA in philosophy as well as a PhD in marketing ethics from the University of Copenhagen and has worked with the Institute for Social Marketing, University of Stirling, for two years as a visiting researcher. His research in social marketing covers primarily critical social marketing (e.g. analysing the societal impact of alcohol marketing) and social marketing ethics (e.g. ethical challenges in corporate and commercial applications of social marketing). Dr Anker has taught social marketing at the University of Copenhagen and done various workshops on social marketing for local council staff working with public health promotion.

Debra Z. Basil is an Associate Professor of Marketing and co-founder of the Centre for Socially Responsible Marketing at the University of Lethbridge, where she recently received the University Scholars Award designation. Her research interests include cause-related marketing and the use of fear appeals in social marketing. She co-edited the book *Social Marketing Advances in Research and Theory*. Recent publications include 'Using social marketing to encourage towel reuse' in the *Journal of Business Research*, 'Company support for employee volunteering: A national survey of companies in Canada' in the *Journal of Business Ethics*, and 'Guilt and giving: A process model' in *Psychology & Marketing*.

Michael D. Basil is a Professor of Marketing at the University of Lethbridge in Alberta, Canada. He received his PhD in Communication from Stanford in 1992 focused on information processing of messages, especially health communication. His interest in social marketing arose from work with Porter Novelli and the US Centers for Disease Control and Prevention where he realised that communication is more effective when it begins with an understanding of the behavioural barriers the audience faces and attempts to reduce those barriers. Professor Basil publishes in the fields of health communication, marketing, psychology and public health.

Jay M. Bernhardt is Department Chairperson and Professor of Health Education and Behavior at the University of Florida, where he serves as Director of the Center for Digital Health and Wellness. Dr. Bernhardt also is Founder and President of Digital Health Impact, Inc. From 2005 to 2010, he served as Director of the National Center for Health Marketing at the Centers for Disease Control and Prevention. Prior to that, Dr Bernhardt was Assistant Professor of Behavioral Sciences and Health Education at Emory University and Assistant Professor of Health Promotion and Behavior at the University of Georgia. He serves on three Editorial Boards and is Associate Editor of *Health Education & Behavior.*

Carol A. Bryant is a Distinguished USF Health Professor and Co-Director of the Florida Prevention Research Center at the University of South Florida College of Public Health. For 20 years, she has directed social marketing research on a wide variety of public health projects. With colleagues at the Florida Prevention Research Center, she is developing and evaluating an innovative framework – community-based prevention marketing for designing and tailoring behavior change interventions. In addition to research, Professor Bryant teaches a variety of graduate-level social marketing courses and coordinates the annual Social Marketing and Public Health Conference. Professor Bryant is also founding editor of the *Social Marketing Quarterly* and senior author of *The Cultural Feast: An Introduction to Food and Society.*

Georgina Cairns is a senior lecturer in the Institute for Social Marketing, at the University of Stirling and the Open University. She is leading the development and 2012 launch of a Masters Degree programme in social marketing. Georgina's main research interest is how marketing, public policy, food and alcohol behaviours and cultures combine and interact with one another, to impact health and well-being. Georgina's professional interest in social marketing in developing countries is based on living and working in Asia as the director of a food and health capacity building organisation and as a consultant for many years.

Robert B. Cialdini is Regents' Professor of Psychology and Marketing at Arizona State University, where he has also been named Distinguished Graduate Research Professor. He has been elected president of the Society of Personality and Social Psychology. Professor Cialdini is the recipient of the Distinguished Scientific Achievement Award of the Society for Consumer Psychology, the Donald T. Campbell Award for Distinguished Contributions to Social Psychology and the Peitho Award for Distinguished Contributions to the Science of Social Influence.

Sameer Deshpande spent his initial years in India, before moving to North America and earning his PhD from the University of Wisconsin-Madison. Currently, he is an associate professor in Marketing at the Faculty of Management and faculty member of the Centre for Socially Responsible Marketing at the University of Lethbridge. Dr Deshpande research interests include applying social marketing thought to a variety of public health issues. He also offers social marketing workshops and provides consulting to non-profit and government agencies. Dr Deshpande serves on the editorial board of the *Journal of Social Marketing.*

Timothy Dewhirst is an Associate Professor in the Department of Marketing and Consumer Studies at the University of Guelph in Canada. His research areas of interest include tobacco marketing and public policy, branding and brand management, sponsorship-linked marketing and social marketing. He has served as an invited consultant for the Attorney General's Office in the state of California, Health Canada, Physicians for a Smoke-Free Canada as well as the World Health Organization, in which he was named as an expert for the elaboration of a template for a protocol on cross-border advertising, promotion and sponsorship (with respect to the Framework Convention on Tobacco Control). Professor Dewhirst has served as an expert for the plaintiff's counsel in tobacco litigation. Additionally, he is an Associate Editor of *Tobacco Control.*

Christine Domegan is a Senior Lecturer in Marketing at the National University of Ireland, Galway. Dr Domegan researches social marketing and its application to value co-creation, public policy, strategic partnerships and marketing theory through a multi-disciplinary lens. Her current work embraces recycling, men's health, positive ageing, health literacy and science in society. Christine teaches Social Marketing at undergraduate and postgraduate levels in Ireland and the UK, including extensive PhD supervision. Recent social marketing publications, among others, appear in the *Journal of Nonprofit and Public Sector Marketing*, the *Journal of Business and Industrial Marketing* and the *Irish Journal of Management*.

Rob Donovan is Professor of Behavioural Research in the Faculty of Health Sciences, Adjunct Professor of Social Marketing in the School of Marketing and Principal of Mentally Healthy WA's Act-Belong-Commit campaign at Curtin University. After a career in commercial marketing he returned to academia in the early 1990s. He has a broad range of interests, including alcohol, tobacco and drugs, child abuse, domestic violence, racism and mental health. He is Deputy Chair of the WA Ministerial Council on Suicide Prevention, is currently a Vice-president of the Board of Relationships Australia WA, and represents the Australian government on the World Anti-Doping Agency's Education Committee.

Jeff French has extensive experience of developing, leading and evaluating behaviour change projects, social marketing programmes and the development of communication strategies at international, national, regional and local level. With over 30 years' experience at the interface between government, public, private and NGO sectors, Jeff has a broad practical and theoretical understanding of national and international health and social development issues. He has published over 80 chapters, articles and books in the fields of behaviour change, social marketing, community development, health promotion and communications. Jeff is a visiting professor at Brunel University and Brighton University and a Fellow at Kings College University London and teaches at four other universities in the UK. Jeff was the Director of Communication and Policy at the Health Development Agency for five years from 2000 to 2005. From March 2005 to July 2009, Jeff set up and managed the National Social Marketing Centre for England. In August 2009, Jeff became the Chief Executive of Strategic Social Marketing Ltd. Professor French is a member of the Editorial Board of the *Journal of Social Marketing*, the organiser of the World Social Marketing Conference and a member of the Global Social Marketing Association Executive Committee.

Fiona J. Harris is a Lecturer in Management at the Open University Business School and Deputy Director of ISM-Open. She has worked on a range of social marketing research projects in collaboration with colleagues at the Institute for Social Marketing (ISM) at Stirling in the areas of tobacco control and the impact of alcohol marketing. Dr Harris has a background in applied psychology and her current research interests, alongside social marketing, include sustainable fashion and ethical issues in marketing.

Gerard Hastings is the first UK Professor of Social Marketing and founder/director of the Institute for Social Marketing (http://www.ism.stir.ac.uk/) and Centre for Tobacco Control Research (http://www.ctcr.stir.ac.uk/) at Stirling and the Open University. He researches the applicability of marketing principles like consumer orientation, branding and strategic planning to the solution of health and social problems. Professor Hastings also conducts critical marketing research into the impact of potentially damaging marketing, such as alcohol, tobacco and fast food promotion.

Ronald Paul Hill has a PhD in business administration from the University of Maryland College Park and is the Richard J. and Barbara Naclerio Endowed Chair, Villanova School of Business and Senior Associate Dean, Intellectual Strategy. He has authored nearly 150 journal articles, book chapters and conference papers on a variety of topics. Areas include restricted consumer behaviour, marketing ethics, corporate social responsibility and public policy. Outlets for this research include *Journal of Marketing Research, Journal of Consumer Research, Business and Society, International Journal of Research in Marketing, Human Rights Quarterly, Journal of the Academy of Marketing Science, Harvard Business Review* and *Journal of Public Policy and Marketing*. Dr Hill's term as Editor of the *Journal of Public Policy and Marketing* extends from 1 July 2006 until 30 June 2012.

Janet Hoek is a professor in the Department of Marketing at the University of Otago, New Zealand. She has a long-standing interest in the marketing-public policy nexus, particularly tobacco control and food marketing. Professor Hoek has served on several government advisory groups, provided expert advice to government, and her work has appeared in *Tobacco Control*, the *Journal of Advertising Research*, the *Journal of Business Research*, the *Bulletin of the World Health Organisation* and the *Journal of Marketing and Public Policy*.

Sandra C. Jones (BA, MBA, MPH, MAssessEval, PhD) is the Director of the Centre for Health Initiatives, and a Professor in the Faculty of Health & Behavioural Sciences, University of Wollongong. Her research focuses on the relationship between media and health, including the impacts of advertising on health behaviour, and the use of social marketing to improve population health. Professor Jones has conducted extensive research into the nature and effects of alcohol advertising and marketing and has developed, implemented and evaluated a range of health-related social marketing interventions, particularly in the areas of cancer prevention and chronic disease management.

Klemens Kappel is Associate Professor in Philosophy, Division of Philosophy, Institute of Media, Cognition and Communication. Professor Kappel's current research interests are in social epistemology and general epistemology, but he has a broad range of interests, including applied philosophy, ethics, bioethics and political philosophy.

Patrick Kenny BBLS, MBS is a lecturer in Marketing in the School of Marketing, Dublin Institute of Technology, Ireland. He is pursuing a PhD at the Institute for Social Marketing in the University of Stirling, where his work focuses on the influence of alcohol marketing and social norms on young people. He is a regular commentator in the Irish media on issues relating to alcohol policy and has also given testimony in court as an expert witness on advertising regulation and ethics. Dr Kenny has been a visiting lecturer in marketing strategy in institutions across Europe and also delivers a wide range of executive training programmes in marketing and strategy to entrepreneurs and managers in the SME sector.

Philip Kotler is the S.C. Johnson Distinguished Professor of International Marketing at the Kellogg School of Management, Northwestern University. His *Marketing Management* (13th edn) is one of the world's leading textbooks on marketing, and he has published 50 other books and over 150 articles in leading journals. His research covers strategic marketing, consumer marketing, business marketing, services marketing and social marketing. He has consulted with IBM, Bank of America, Merck, General Electric and Honeywell. He has received honorary doctorate degrees from 12 major universities. Professor Kotler initiated the development of the field of social marketing which deals with environmental, health, educational and community issues.

Wonkyong Beth Lee is an Assistant Professor of Consumer Behaviour at the University of Western Ontario's DAN Management and Organizational Studies in Canada. Her research has focused on examining the relation between social influence (i.e. culture and norms) and attitudes, particularly in the domain of both consumer and health behaviour. Professor Lee's work has been published in *Health Psychology*, *Tobacco Control* and *Personality and Social Psychology Bulletin*.

Nancy R. Lee has an MBA and more than 25 years of professional marketing experience, with special expertise in Social Marketing. She is an adjunct faculty member at the University of Washington and the University of South Florida, and owns a small consulting firm, Social Marketing Services, Inc., in Seattle, Washington. She conducts seminars and workshops on social marketing and marketing in the public sector and has participated in the development of more than 100 social marketing campaigns. She has been a guest lecturer at the University of Cape Town in South Africa; the Health Promotion Board in Singapore; Victoria University in Melbourne, Australia; National University of Ireland in Galway; Yale University and Oxford University. She has conducted social marketing workshops for more than 2,000 public sector employees, including most recently for US AID in Jordan and The World Bank. She has been a keynote speaker on social marketing at local and international conferences including ones addressing Public Health, Injury Prevention, Environmental Protection and Poverty Reduction.

She has coauthored eight books on social marketing with Philip Kotler, the most recent, the 4th Edition of Social Marketing: Influencing Behaviors for Good (SAGE, 2012).

R. Craig Lefebvre is chief maven at socialShift, Research Professor in the College of Public Health at the University of South Florida, and Lead Change Designer at RTI International. Craig has over 100 publications in the areas of community health promotion, social marketing, social and mobile media and public health and serves on the Editorial Boards of the *Journal of Social Marketing* and *Social Marketing Quarterly*. His current work blends design thinking, social and mobile technologies and marketing in social change programmes. Professor Lefebvre publishes the blog *On Social Marketing and Social Change* [http://socialmarketing.blogs.com] and is on Twitter @chiefmaven.

Lynne Doner Lotenberg, is Vice President, Strategic Planning and Research at Hager Sharp. Ms Lotenberg's major research interests are effective techniques to plan and evaluate marketing and communication efforts to facilitate social change and improve public health. Ms Lotenberg is co-editor of *Social Marketing Quarterly* and co-author of the first and second editions of *Marketing Public Health: Strategies to Promote Social Change.*

Kelli McCormack Brown, PhD, CHES is a professor of health education and behaviour at the University of Florida. Professor McCormack Brown has been able to blend her health education and promotion experience with community-based prevention marketing (CBPM) and, through these efforts, has written numerous peer-reviewed articles on how health education and communities can effectively use social marketing to develop behaviour change interventions.

Robert J. McDermott has taught in higher education for 35 years. In 1998, he was part of team of scholars awarded a Prevention Research Center by the US Centers for Disease Control and Prevention (CDC). He continues to serve as co-Director of that Center. The Florida Prevention Research Center (FPRC) has created and field tested a new model for health behaviour change in communities – community-based prevention marketing (CBPM). Dr McDermott has been a member of the CDC's invited working group on defining *Health Education in the 21st Century*, a visiting professor at the University of Cologne (Germany) and at the University of Wisconsin, a consultant to the CDC's Division of Adolescent and School Health, for collaboration with the Russian Federation, and a consultant to the European Union's, *Health Promotion for Family Caregivers of People with Alzheimer's Disease and Related Mental Disorders Project* (1997), and its *Communicating AIDS Project* (1994). In addition to more than 250 scientific articles, he has written over 50 book chapters, and three books. Dr McDermott is a Fellow of the *American School Health Association* (1988), the *American Academy of Health Behavior* (1998), the *Royal Institute of Public Health* (2002), the *American Association for Health Education* (2005) and the *Royal Society for Health Promotion* (2007). In 2004, Dr McDermott founded a new E-journal for the public health community of Florida, the *Florida Public Health Review*. In 2011 he became Editor of the *Journal of School Health.*

Laura MacDonald is a research assistant based in the Institute for Social Marketing at the University of Stirling. She graduated from the London School of Hygiene and Tropical Medicine in 2009 with an MSc in Control of Infectious Diseases. Laura is interested in evidence-based health communication, particularly for the prevention and control of communicable diseases.

Bruce Mackay works for HLSP, a consulting firm in London. He did a PhD on family planning in Kenya, and then spent 15 years in the UK marketing mortgages, insurance and software. Since 1995, he has worked on social marketing of oral contraceptives, condoms and bednets, as well as broader behaviour change for HIV prevention. Dr Mackay's main interest is in how people in poor countries behave as consumers in unregulated healthcare markets – and why most governments and aid donors pretend that these markets do not exist.

Susana Marques, PhD, was involved, as a researcher, in the Evaluation of *Blueprint,* a research programme designed and funded by the British Home Office to examine the effectiveness of a multi-component approach to drug education. She concluded her doctoral studies in July 2008 at the University of Stirling, in Scotland, and since September 2009, she is Coordinator Professor in the High Institute of Administration and Management in Porto, Portugal, and a member of *iMARKE,* a Research Unit in the field of Marketing and Strategy at the University of Minho. Her main research interests are social, relationship and critical marketing.

Darren Mays is a Research Instructor in the Department of Oncology, Georgetown University Medical Center and Associate Member of the Cancer Control Program of the Lombardi Comprehensive Cancer Center. His research focuses on behavioral cancer prevention in pediatric populations, with a focus on the application of communication technology-based approaches to health behavior change intervention. Prior to that, he worked at the Agency for Healthcare Research and Quality, the Centers for Disease Control and Prevention, and completed his pre-doctoral studies in the Department of Behavioral Sciences and Health Education, Rollins School of Public Health, Emory University.

Gary Noble is Associate Dean and Director of the Centre for Social Marketing at the University of Wollongong, Australia. His research interests include the role and use of social marketing in the area of pro-environmental behaviour change, non-profit marketing and corporate social responsibility. Dr Noble has been a consultant to various government and non-profit organizations in the development of their social marketing interventions and his work has been published in numerous academic journals.

William D. Novelli is Professor in the McDonough School of Business at Georgetown University. He teaches business and publc policy, nonprofit leadership and management and corporate social responsibility. He oversees the Global Social Enterprise Initiative at the school. Previously, he was CEO of AARP, a membership organization of over 40 million people age 50 and older and the co-founder of Porter Novelli, which began as a social marketing firm and is now a worldwide public relations agency.

Guido Palazzo is Professor of Business Ethics at the University of Lausanne (Switzerland). His research interests are in corporate social responsibility and (un)ethical decision-making. He is associate editor of *Business Ethics Quarterly* and *European Management Review* and member of the editorial board of *Academy of Management Review, Journal of Management Studies* and *Business & Society.* Professor Palazzo's work has appeared in journals such as *Academy of Management Review, Journal of Management Studies, Business Ethics Quarterly* and *Journal of Business Ethics.*

Ken Peattie is Professor of Marketing and Strategy at Cardiff Business School and Director of the ESRC-funded BRASS Research Centre based at Cardiff. Ken's main research interests focus on sustainability marketing and social marketing, examining how both companies and the public sector can promote healthy and sustainable behaviours, lifestyles and communities. He has published three books and numerous book chapters and articles in leading journals on these topics. Professor Peattie's most recent book, *Sustainability Marketing: A Global Perspective*, co-authored with Professor Frank-Martin Belz, was named as the 2010 Business Book of the Year by the German Business Research Association.

Sue Peattie is a Lecturer in Marketing at Cardiff Business School and an Associate of BRASS Research Centre (www.brass.cf.ac.uk) at Cardiff University. She has taught and conducted research in social marketing for the last 20 years and regularly provides advice and expertise to a variety of national and international projects. Most recently she has been working with South Wales Fire and Rescue Service on Project Bernie, an innovative and highly successful project to reduce the incidence of deliberate grass fires in Wales. This involved providing critical guidance and direction to the project from design and delivery through to evaluation.

Petia K. Petrova is a faculty member at Dartmouth, an author of a number of articles published in the leading psychology and business journals, and a frequent speaker at national and international conferences. As an expert in persuasion, Dr Petrova has consulted for a variety of government and corporate organisations. For her work on resistance to persuasion, Dr Petrova has received the Individual Research Service Award from the National Institutes of Health.

Simone Pettigrew is Professor of Marketing at the University of Western Australia Business School. Her primary research interests are consumer education and empowerment, with a specific focus on health promotion. Current research projects relate to child obesity, alcohol consumption, ageing and mental health. She is the founder and editor of the *Journal of Research for Consumers* (www.jrconsumers.com) and a co-editor of the first handbook on Transformative Consumer Research. Professor Pettigrew has published in the *Journal of Public Policy and Marketing*, *BMC Public Health*, *International Journal of Obesity*, *Journal of Marketing Management*, *Consumption, Markets and Culture*, and *Qualitative Market Research*.

Michele Roberts is Assistant Professor of Marketing at the University of Western Australia Business School. Her primary research interests are in the areas of consumer behaviour and advertising, with a particular focus on social marketing. Dr Roberts current research relates to the effects of food marketing on children's diets.

Michael Saren is Professor of Marketing at the University of Leicester. Having conducted many research projects into various aspects of marketing, technology and consumer innovation over the last 30 years, Professor Saren's recent research has focused on the development of marketing theory, particularly marketing knowledge, culture and relationships. He was a convener of the marketing streams at the Critical Management Studies Conferences, 1999–2011; and one of the founding editors in 2001 of the journal *Marketing Theory* (Sage Publications). Professor Saren is also co-editor of books on *Rethinking Marketing* (Brownlie et al., 1999, Sage Publications), *Critical Marketing: Defining the Field* (Saren et al., 2007, Elsevier) and is author of *Marketing Graffiti: The View from the Street* (Saren, 2006, Butterworth-Heinemann).

Carol Schechter is Vice President at Abt Associates. Ms Schechter brings more than 30 years' experience to her work in health communication, behavioural science and social marketing. She received an MA in economics and an MPH in health planning from the University of Michigan.

Anne M. Smith is Reader in Marketing at the Open University Business School where she has developed social marketing courses including undergraduate, online CPD and Open-learn. Her main research interests focus on the service sector, particularly health. Her studies have examined how consumers evaluate services, the ways in which service design and service quality impact on evaluation and behaviour and how this differs across cultures. Further research by Dr Smith has focused on the nature and determinants of environmentally responsible behaviour and how an internal marketing approach can promote such behaviour within organisations. Dr Smith's work has been published in a number of international journals.

William Smith is Academy for Educational Development Executive Vice President/Senior Scientist and a Health Literacy Expert.

Martine Stead is Deputy Director of the Institute for Social Marketing (ISM) at the University of Stirling and the Open University. Established in 1979, the Institute is the UK's leading centre for the academic study of social marketing. Martine's research interests include the development and evaluation of social marketing behaviour change interventions, the effectiveness of social marketing and the processes by which interventions are implemented in real-world settings. Dr Stead also acts as a social marketing adviser to many NGO, public sector and community projects.

John Strand is Vice President and Director, FHI 360 Center for Social Marketing and Behavior Change. Over the past 25 years, Mr Strand has pursued practical ways to apply marketing and communication strategies in social change programmes in the United States, Africa and Asia. His recent interests include storytelling and framing to promote policy, system and environmental change. Mr Strand received an MEd in international education from Teachers College, Columbia University and is an Editorial Review Board member of *Social Marketing Quarterly*.

Rosemary Thackeray, PhD, MPH, is an associate professor in the Department of Health Science at Brigham Young University in Provo, Utah. Her research focuses on social marketing and health communication; she teaches an upper-division social marketing course. She has served as the co-associate editor for the journal *Health Promotion Practice*, with responsibility for the social marketing department. Prior to joining the faculty at Brigham Young University, Dr Thackeray was employed at the Utah Department of Health. During a sabbatical, Dr Thackeray worked for the Centers for Disease Control and Prevention, National Center for Health Marketing.

James B. Weaver III is a Senior Health Communications Specialist in the Office of the Associate Director for Communication, Centers for Disease Control and Prevention, US Department of Health and Human Services. Before that, he was a Professor of Communication and Psychology at Virginia Polytechnic Institute and State University. He has authored or co-authored dozens of refereed research articles and book chapters and 1 book. Recent publications have appeared in the *Journal of the American Medical Informatics Association*, the *American Journal of Preventive Medicine*, and the *American Journal of Public Health*. His program of research is currently focused on health information disparities as component causes of public health outcomes.

Boe Workman, PhD, is Senior Director of CEO Communications at AARP. He has been writing on aging, public policy and social issues for over 25 years. Dr. Workman is co-author with Bill Novelli of *Fifty Plus: Give Meaning and Purpose to the Best Time of Your Life* and editor of *Voice of an Aging Nation: Selected Speeches of Horace B. Deets* and *Voice of Social Change: Selected Speeches of Bill Novelli*, both published by AARP.

List of Figures

List of Tables

Foreword

Philip Kotler and Nancy R. Lee

In the early 1970s, I realized that marketing concepts and tools could be applied to more than goods and services to be sold for a profit. My colleague Gerald Zaltman and I published an article called 'Social Marketing: An Approach to Planned Social Change.' We chose the name 'social marketing' to show that not all marketing is commercial, that marketing could also be used to influence behaviors that would create net benefits for the individual, community, and society at large. Philip Kotler

The fact that SAGE publications has commissioned this Handbook signals just how far we've come in the past four decades. In writing this Foreword, Nancy R. Lee and I have found evidence that many of our hopes for the contribution this discipline can make have been realized. Our observations are reflected in the following section, as well as in Box A, a chronology of seminal events. We also take this opportunity to acknowledge where we can mature the field further, and imagine even greater possibilities over the next decade.

Box A Social Marketing: Seminal Events and Publications

1970s

1971: A pioneering article, 'Social Marketing: An Approach to Planned Social Change,' by Philip Kotler and Gerald Zaltman, in the July issue of *Journal of Marketing*, coins the term 'social marketing.'

More distinguished researchers and practitioners join the voice for the potential of social marketing, including Alan Andreasen (Georgetown University), James Mintz (Federal Department of Health, Canada), Bill Novelli (cofounder of Porter Novelli Associates) and Bill Smith (Academy for Educational Development).

1980s

World Bank, World Health Organization, Population Services International (PSI) and CDC start to use the term and promote interest in social marketing.

1981: An article in the *Journal of Marketing* by Paul Bloom and William Novelli reviews the first 10 years of social marketing and highlights the lack of rigor in the application of marketing principles and techniques in critical areas of the field, including research, segmentation and distribution channels.

1988: An article in the *Health Education Quarterly*, 'Social Marketing and Public Health Intervention,' by R. Craig Lefebvre and June Flora, gives social marketing widespread exposure in the field of public health.

1989: A major book, *Social Marketing: Strategies for Changing Public Behavior*, by Philip Kotler and Eduardo Roberto, lays out the application of marketing principles and techniques for influencing social change.

1990s

Academic programs are established, including the Center for Social Marketing at the University of Strathclyde in Glasgow and the Department of Community and Family Health at the University of South Florida.

(Continued)

(*Continued*)

1992: An article in the *American Psychologist* by James Prochaska, Carlo DiClemente and John Norcross presents an organizing framework for achieving behavior change considered by many as the most useful model developed to date.

1994: A publication, *Social Marketing Quarterly*, by Best Start Inc. and the Department of Public Health, University of South Florida, is launched.

1995: A book, *Marketing Social Change: Changing Behavior to Promote Health, Social Development, and the Environment*, by Alan Andreasen, makes a significant contribution to both the theory and practice of social marketing.

1999: The Social Marketing Institute is formed in Washington, DC, with Alan Andreasen from Georgetown University as interim executive director.

1999: A book, *Fostering Sustainable Behaviors*, by Doug McKenzie-Mohr and William Smith, provides an introduction to community-based social marketing.

2000s

2001: The book *Ethics in Social Marketing*, edited by Alan Andreasen, is published.

2002: Kotler and Lee's book *Social Marketing: Improving the Quality of Life* is published.

2003: A book, *Social Marketing: Principles & Practice*, by Rob Donovan, is published in Australia.

2005: The National Social Marketing Centre is formed in London, England, headed by Jeff French and Clive Blair-Stevens.

2005: The 10th annual conference for Innovations in Social Marketing is held.

2005: The 16th annual Social Marketing in Public Health conference is held.

2006: A book, *Social Marketing in the 21st Century*, by Alan Andreasen, describes an expanded role for social marketing.

2007: Gerard Hasting's *Social Marketing: Why should the Devil have all the Best Tunes?* is published.

2008: The first World Conference for Social Marketing is held in Brighton, England and CDC launches an annual conference with a social marketing emphasis.

2009: Kotler and Lee's book *UP and OUT of Poverty: The Social Marketing Solution* is published, as is *Social Marketing and Public Health: Theory and Practice*, by French, Blair-Stevens and Merritt.

2010s

2010: More books are published, including Nedra Weinreich's 2nd edition of *Hands-On Social Marketing* and Cheng, Kotler, and Lee's *Social Marketing for Public Health: Global Trends and Success Stories*, and the *Journal of Social Marketing* is launched from Australia.

2011: The 4th edition of Kotler and Lee's Social Marketing: Influencing Behaviors for Good is published, as was a new book by Doug McKenzie-Mohr, Nancy R. Lee, Wesley Schultz and Philip Kotler Social Marketing to Protect the Environment: What Works. The Social Marketing in Public Health Conference celebrates its 40th year and the second World Conference for Social Marketing will be held in Dublin, Ireland, and the Global Social Marketing Association is launched.

HOW WE'VE GROWN OVER THE PAST FOUR DECADES

- From applications almost exclusively for **public health** issues to ones contributing to injury prevention, environmental protection, community involvement and, most recently, financial well- being.
- From primarily **mass media** campaigns to the use of additional marketing tools almost always needed to reduce barriers and increase benefits including developing new products, providing incentives, increasing convenience of access, creating prompts and nudges in the environment and finding more efficient and effective media tactics including edutainment and social media.
- From a focus on influencing **voluntary** behaviors to the recognition that we have a role to play in increasing citizen compliance with existing regulations: from not drinking and driving to properly disposing of hazardous waste.

- From a primarily **academic** conversation regarding theories and models to blogs, lively discussions and postings of case studies on listserves, formal presentations at conferences and journal articles contributed by practitioners on the frontline responsible for influencing public behaviors.
- From introductory **workshops** to social marketing courses at universities to online courses and webinars to certificates in social marketing and to at least two master degree programs.
- From one annual **social marketing in public health conference in the USA** to annual conferences around the world, ones that have included keynote speakers and special sessions on applications for protecting the environment and enhancing financial well-being.
- From a few **articles** in a variety of academic journals to two exclusive journals for social marketers to more than a dozen books with social marketing in the title.
- From thinking our only targeting audiences were individuals **downstream** to a recognition that the same model can be used to influence important others midstream (e.g. friends, family members, teachers, healthcare providers), and those upstream that are critical to supportive environments (e.g. policymakers, corporations).
- From a reliance on traditional **marketing-focused theories** to integration of many traditional behavior change theories including behavioral economics, environmental psychology, community mobilization and social norms.
- From efforts primarily in **North America and the UK** to ones applying social marketing principles and techniques in most countries throughout the world. The Fostering Sustainable Behaviors listserve, for example, includes more than 8000 members worldwide.
- From proposals for contractors to provide **communications'** campaigns to some now specifying a social marketing approach and experience is required.
- From **listserves** providing primarily information exchange to a global professional association, anticipated to launch in the spring of 2011 at the second world conference for social marketers. This organization will provide members around the world with enhanced access to training opportunities, resources and professional networking.
- From **no mention of the term in CDC's (Centers for Disease Control and Prevention) Healthy People Goals** to three related objectives in the most recent 2020 goals: (1) increase the proportion of State health departments that report using social marketing in health promotion and disease prevention programs; (2) increase the proportion of schools of public health and accredited master of public health (MPH) programs that offer one or more courses in social marketing; and (3) increase the proportion of schools of public health and accredited MPH programs that offer workforce development activities in social marketing for public health practitioners.

WHAT WE WOULD LIKE TO SEE HAPPEN OVER THE NEXT DECADE

- Social marketing becomes a required course for those seeking a bachelors or masters degree in public health, public administration, environmental studies, international affairs, political science and medicine. We can't imagine a business degree without a required course in marketing. Those involved in influencing citizen or patient behaviors will benefit from this requirement as well.
- Every newly elected public official receives at least a half-day briefing on social marketing and its relevance and applications for policymakers.
- Corporations are engaged as partners with social marketers, recognizing opportunities to develop more products that will assist in influencing desired behaviors: for example, vegetables that taste better; indicators in our car that tell us how much that trip we just took cost in gas; applications to estimate our blood alcohol level; litter receptacles that say 'thank you,' sunscreen lotions that help prevent cancer but don't keep you from tanning and stickers on fruits and vegetables in the grocery store that indicate how many miles they 'traveled' to get there.
- More commercial sector marketers migrate to the field, just as they have migrated to non-profit organizations and foundations over the past two decades, finding a way to 'do more good' with their skills and experience.

- Organizations including US AID, The World Bank and the United Nations recognize even more than they do today the role that social marketing can play in influencing behaviors that reduce poverty.
- Governmental agencies create jobs with the title of social marketing; in fact, at national levels there are even Social Marketing Czars.
- The general public and the media understand the distinction between social media and social marketing.
- Debates among social marketers regarding the viability of communications-only campaigns fade away, similar to how the marketing field evolved from the sales concept to one that recognizes that in order for an exchange to take place, we must offer potential customers desired benefits that exceed perceived costs compared with competitive alternatives.

Introduction: A Movement in Social Marketing

Gerard Hastings[1]

INTRODUCTION

The tall, gaunt septuagenarian rose slowly to his feet at the back of the hall. The phrase "distinguished hippy" would probably best capture his appearance – distinguished enough to bring the hubbub of the large meeting to a respectful silence; hippy enough to defy prediction. No one could tell what was coming next, but we somehow knew it would be worth hearing. He cleared his throat and in a sonorous Californian burr declared: *"My name is Vince and I'm a veteran of the fight to stop the Vietnam War. Now, for the first time in the thirty eight years since our direct action ended that conflict, I feel able to use the 'M' word".* We were at a state-wide gathering to discuss the threat from obesity and coming to the end of a discussion on the role that social marketing might play. We had explored its capacity to empower grass roots action, enable policy change, marshal advocacy, constrain the fast food industry and mobilise the population. I thought for a gratifying moment his 'M' word was marketing, but he continued *"I mean we have a movement – and it is movements that make a difference, that change things. We needed a movement then to stop the War, and we need a movement now to fight obesity; we have one".* Vince was telling us that social marketing could help to tackle obesity because it was taking on the multi-faceted, engaging and strategic qualities of a movement. It was a profound insight.

A TIME TO BE REFLEXIVE

A Sage Handbook is an academic discipline's state of the nation address. It provides a systematic assessment of the field's development, addresses *"the key debates and issues"* and adjudicates on progress made. A handbook, like a good President, also looks forward and maps out a direction of travel.

It is an apposite time to do this for social marketing; a time when markets and marketing are themselves being questioned and called to account. Just as the great depression of the 1930s shook our faith in capitalism, so the global financial crisis of recent time has cast doubt on the fundamentals of our economic system. If a publication as august and conservative as *The Economist* can declare 2009 *"a year of sackcloth and ashes for the world's business schools"* and

state that *"the real question is not whether business schools need to change, but how"* (The Economist, 2009), marketers have to sit up and listen. These concerns are broadened by Michael Porter and Mark Kramer in the Harvard Business Review, using equally dramatic language: *"The capitalist system is under siege. In recent years business increasingly has been viewed as a major cause of social, environmental, and economic problems. Companies are widely perceived to be prospering at the expense of the broader community"* (Porter and Kramer, 2011: 64).

In this debate it helps to strip out the concepts and principles from the economics; money can muddy the waters. The massive financial value of a brand like Marlboro overshadows and distorts questions about its power and acceptability – about how it works, the effects it has and whether these are desirable. And business schools, as

The Economist goes on to argue, have had their vital senses of cynicism and scepticism dulled by a growing dependency on business and a resulting reluctance to *"to bite the hands that feed them"*.

Social marketers – and this Handbook – enter this debate from two sides. First they argue that in essence marketing is about human behaviour, not money. The core skill of commercial marketers lies in *"getting us to do things – buy their products, visit their shops, attend to their messages,* deliver *their messages* (many of us now spend our lives festooned in logos), *buy their products again"* (Hastings, 2007: 3). This skill has enormous applicability beyond the marketplace: much human tribulation – racism, criminality, ill health, global warming, aggression, accidental injury and death – is driven by our behaviour. It might be the behaviour of the individual or of a swathe of stakeholders: the teen who chooses to binge drink, the neglectful parent, the bar worker who sells her the booze, the drink producer who develops alcopops or the politician who fails to control such irresponsibility. All these behaviours, as Lefebvre emphasises in chapter 2, and numerous other authors confirm, are susceptible to the subtleties and skills of marketing.

Second, social marketers recognise that commercial marketing needs to be critiqued and controlled. This is honest to both marketing theory (Saren, chapter 6) and an essential component of effective action (see Hoek, Jones and Dewhirst and Lee in chapters 16, 17 and 26). Marketing is a very powerful mechanism with no built-in moral compass. Tobacco provides the most egregious illustration of this: given that we now know that nicotine is as addictive as heroin, smoking is overwhelmingly adopted by children rather than adults and half of those who do not manage to quit will be killed by their habit, it seems both foolish and morally repugnant to allow the marketing of tobacco. More pragmatically, from a social marketing perspective, it makes little sense to spend limited resources counteracting the predations of multinational tobacco companies; far better to prevent them happening in the first place.

This takes us into the realm of regulation, which for some seems a step too far (Rothschild, 1999). Social marketing, so the argument runs, should focus on voluntary not compulsory behaviour – on persuading not telling. But this seems too delimiting given that commercial marketers show no such circumspection. As the National Cancer Institute's (NCI) (2008) scrupulous analysis of tobacco promotion demonstrates "stakeholder marketing" is as much a part of a tobacco company's business plan as the Marlboro cowboy, and the same strategic perspective led major food companies to spend an estimated one billion Euros last year persuading the European Commission not to mandate traffic light food labelling (Hickman, 2010). Furthermore, the NCI's monograph is merely reflecting a plethora of standard marketing texts which emphasise the importance of environmental scanning and present well-established tools such as PEST and SWOT analyses (Jobber, 2009). In this way marketers recognise two simple truths. First, that consumers' freedom of choice, like the perfect market, is an unattainable ideal that will always be constrained by social and political context; so efforts can and must be made to make that context as favourable as possible. Second, that this context is greatly influenced by (voluntary) human behaviour – of policy making and other stakeholders, and indeed consumers (think of the influence of grassroots organisations like Mothers Against Drunk Driving) – and hence susceptible to marketing. Many chapters emphasise the importance of this upstream agenda – including Kenny and Hastings (chapter 4), French (chapter 24), and Novelli and Workman (chapter 25).

These different sides of the social marketing coin are encapsulated in Lazer and Kelley's seminal definition:

> Social marketing is concerned with the application of marketing knowledge, concepts and techniques to enhance social as well as economic ends. It is also concerned with analysis of the social consequence of marketing policies, decisions and activities. (1973: ix)

In adopting this definition we abut this volume with the *Handbook of Marketing and Society* (Bloom and Gundlach, 2001). Specifically, we use social marketing theory and practice as a lens to examine three of the *"paths through which marketing affects societal welfare"* (Bloom and Gundlach, 2001: xv) that the editors identify:

- Public policy decisions
- Corporate marketing decisions
- Consumer welfare decisions

To this we would add an interest in the role of civil society, where much social marketing expertise resides (see, for example, the case studies in section 6). Thus, the purview of social marketing can be illustrated as in Figure I.1, with citizens at its centre but equally cognisant of the power and influence of stakeholders in commerce, policy making and deployment and civil society.

In this way, we return to the origins of the marketing discipline and provide further answers to the vital question identified by Wilkie and Moore in their investigation of the origins of marketing thought: how the relationship between

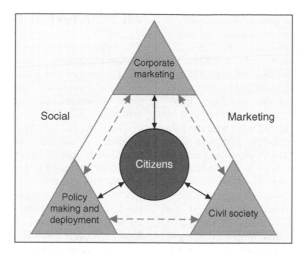

Figure I.1 'The Domain of Social Marketing'

citizens, business, civil society and government can *"facilitate the maximal operations of the system for the benefit of the host society"* (Wilkie and Moore, 2003: 118). Social marketing then uses the unique and well-tested attributes of marketing not just to analyse the minutiae of individual behaviour, but the broader functioning of society as a whole; so it can, as Hoek does in chapter 16, ask questions like: why does society permit *business interests that prosper when public health deteriorates.*

This sounds like an ambitious agenda, but then we should remember the power of our commercial cousin: the Coca-Cola Corporation has not only developed into one of the most successful economic organisations on the planet, but arguably did more to open up China than Richard Nixon – and, much more ominously, the recent banking crisis which brought the world economic system to its knees, was largely driven by bright young marketing-literate MBAs. If commercial marketing can do all this, social marketing should also be thinking big.

Taking this broader perspective on social marketing also buttresses the discipline against some perennial criticisms.

FOUR CRITICISMS

In their Foreword, Kotler and Lee explain how social marketing has emerged and developed over the last four decades. In the process they identify four areas of contention. First, the word marketing brings with it much difficult baggage for many in

the social and public sectors. It carries implications of duplicity and manipulation dating back, before the term social marketing was even coined, to the work of people like Ralph Nader and Vance Packard. This throws up the suspicion that social marketing will pollute the pure water of fields of endeavour like public health or international development with the sleazy practices of Wall Street and Soho Square. Furthermore, marketing, as practiced by tobacco or infant formula multinationals, all too often represents a very real manifestation of the competition. Marketing, it seems to many in public health, is not there to be adopted, but defeated. Donovan's reminder about the importance of moral and ethical analysis in social marketing (chapter 1) is, therefore, well taken.

The commercial origins of marketing have also created another key obstacle: to those outside the business community its full subtleties and complexities are often lost and it is traduced into a synonym for advertising. Even today, many people mistakenly equate social marketing with mass media campaigns. As a result it is, at best, seen as simply a means of flagging up the real work of service provision, professional intervention or policy change – or, at worst, a substitute for effective action, a waste of precious resources and a fig leaf for under-performing politicians. And yet this book, written by the leaders in the field, has only two chapters out of 28 that focus on communication.

The emphasis on advertising also feeds another potent social marketing myth; that it focuses only on the individual: *"Social marketing tends to reduce serious health problems to individual risk factors and ignore the proven importance of the social and economic environment as major determinants of health*" (Wallack et al., 1993: 23). In the process, the argument runs, it ignores the collective causes of so many human problems – whether it be the point of sale display that entices a child to try cigarettes or the poor public transport provision that encourages an over-reliance on the car. Thus, social marketing is hit with the twin criticisms of being ineffective (because it is blinkered and ill-targeted) and unethical (because it ends up blaming the victim for the predicament they could never realistically avoid).

Paradoxically, if it fights off all these brickbats, social marketing is finally condemned for offering nothing new. It is simply a variant on enlightened health promotion, media advocacy or community development. In reality, to use Noble and Basil's (chapter 9) phraseology, it complements these other approaches – as McDermott et al. (chapter 27), Novelli and Workman (chapter 25) and the work on Community-based Prevention Marketing by Bryant and colleagues (below) attest.

Despite these criticisms, and the ultimate Catch-22, social marketing has, as Kotler and Lee also point out, more than stood the test of time. It is the subject of numerous textbooks and many learned articles. It is being taught in graduate schools, adopted by practitioners and funded by Governments. And it is a global phenomenon. This Handbook, for example, includes contributions from three continents and nine countries – even though it is perforce limited to English language contributions.

The Handbook also confirms the widening scope and maturity of social marketing. We approached the leading thinkers in the field and, although we sometimes pointed individual authors towards certain domains, typically reflecting their particular expertise, we also gave them extensive editorial freedom to address the topics they felt were most relevant. Thus, the book is an exercise in democratic thinking – as befits a field of endeavour, which, as Jeff French (chapter 24) points out, is essentially democratic in its conception – and the scope of the chapters provides a de facto definition of the discipline. It is clear that social marketers have profound insights to share on topics as wide ranging as inequalities, international development and corporate maleficence. In the process they demonstrate that the discipline has a valuable part to play, not just in tackling micro behavioural problems such as binge drinking or teen pregnancy, but in the biggest debates of our time. It can and is answering Wilkie and Moore's (2003) vital and profound question.

THE STRUCTURE OF THE BOOK

The first three sections – Theoretical Debates; Marketing Planning; and Research: Its Roles and Techniques – examine the theory and practice of social marketing. Recurrent themes are the need for innovation, flexibility and breadth of vision.

Thus, in the first of these sections Donovan (chapter 1), calls for an eclectic approach to behavioural theory suggesting social marketers should be prepared to trawl a wide selection of models and constructs to select ones that best suit their field of endeavour, always combining this thinking with ethical vigilance. Lefebvre first on his own, and then co-authoring with Philip Kotler (chapters 2 and 5), also throws the net wide invoking design thinking, social capital, diffusion theory, behavioural economics and the rather neglected idea of demarketing, to aid social marketing strategy.

Marques and Domegan (chapter 3) emphasise the need for long-term vision through the crucial dimension of relationship marketing, and call for social marketers to analyse relationship quality, trust, perceived value, satisfaction, commitment, identification and cooperation. Kenny and Hastings (chapter 4) complement this focus on the long term, arguing for more attention to breadth, in view of the immense influence of social norms and social context on both individual and stakeholder (including commercial marketer) behaviours. Saren (chapter 6) picks up this last theme and provides a comprehensive theoretical justification for the vital role of critical thinking in social marketing.

Finally, Petrova and Cialdini bring us back to core business by taking a social psychological look at how to overcome resistance in chapter 7.

Moving into practice, Section 2, Marketing Planning, begins with a careful and revealing analysis of the fundamental role that segmentation plays in marketing; Doner Lotenberg et al. (chapter 8) remind us that, without the clarity of focus it provides, the core marketing concept of consumer orientation rapidly loses its meaning. Noble and Basil (chapter 9) bring us to a discussion of strategy and argue compellingly for competitive analysis to underpin the key construct of positioning in social marketing: standing out from the crowd is, it seems, as important for us as it is for a can of Coke or a pack of Marlboro. On the other hand, Peattie and Peattie (chapter 10) remind us that transferring thinking from the for profit to the non-profit sector can also create problems – at least if it is done in an over-literal way. Their example is the marketing mix, which they argue should not be "force-fitted" by social marketers, but carefully adapted to suit the particular circumstances.

Alden et al. and Mays et al. then bring us the thorny issue of communications. The first paper (chapter 11) again emphasises the need for breadth of vision bringing multiple communication channels into alignment with each other and other elements of the marketing effort: the focus is not on telling people what to do, as getting them to do it. Mays et al. (chapter 12) discuss the multiple innovations taking place in the digital arena, leavening the excitement with a call for caution. The question they stimulate is: do new media just add to our choice of clubs, or fundamentally change the nature of the game? It is a question we pick up below.

All this activity – segmentation, positioning, delivery – depend on research, and Section 3 picks this topic up. Stead and McDermott (chapter 13) address three major questions: why evaluate? what should be measured? and how should it be measured? In responding they remind us again that a breadth and diversity of approach is needed in research, just as much as in theory selection and programme delivery. The two subsequent chapters then go on to present the latest thinking on qualitative (Pettigrew and Roberts in chapter 14) and quantitative (Harris in chapter 15) methods. Overall, the three research chapters remind us of social marketing's abiding and very adult relationship with research – which recognises that it should act as neither overbearing judge nor a blunt substitute for decision making, but as a facilitator of intelligent action.

Section 4, Dancing with the Devil, focuses on a contentious issue for social marketers: what exactly is our relationship with commercial, and especially, corporate marketing. Demonic references tend to raise the temperature, but they do focus the mind on a crucial concern: time and again corporate marketers are on the other side of the fence from social marketers. Hoek (chapter 16) and Jones (chapter 17) (and Dewhirst and Lee in Section 6) are right to remind us that in the case of food, alcohol and tobacco – the triplets that form the foundation of public health – business interests are all too often prospering at the expense of morbidity and mortality. Palazzo and then Anker and Kappel, however, do explore the potential for working with business. Palazzo (chapter 18) argues that social marketers and those engaged in Corporate Social Responsibility *"can no longer afford to ignore each other"* as they share many agendas, and gives some consideration to what he sees as the growing field of "corporate social marketing" (CSM). Anker and Kappel (chapter 19) look into CSM in more detail, highlighting the case of Dove soap which has been promoted on an intuitively appealing anti-ageism platform.

Both chapters however acknowledge the dangers inherent in the mixed motives involved; as Anker and Kappel point out, Dove *"got their corporate pay-off: the campaign is reported to have led to a 700% increase in product sales, and increased Dove's share of firming lotions in the UK from 1% to 6%"* while *"they surely have not solved the problem of distorted beauty ideals in contemporary Western society"*.

Finally in this section, Smith (chapter 20) brings us back to a more comfortable zone, that of transferring learning between commercial and social marketing. Specifically she examines the benefits and opportunities that arise from internal marketing. In doing so she reminds us of the vast and hugely valuable services marketing literature – a point also made earlier in the book by Marques and Domegan (chapter 3).

Section 5 – Upstream and Social Change – addresses four contemporary issues in social marketing. Ronald Paul Hill (chapter 21) picks up the vital concern of inequalities; following the publication of *The Spirit Level* (Wilkinson and Pickett, 2010) it is now clear that inequity in society is harmful to everyone – rich as well as poor – and reducing disparities is a massive priority. Hill adopts a profoundly ethnographic approach, enabling the poor to tell their own stories and arguing that only when these stories are accorded at least equal value with other narratives will serious progress be made. In short, he reminds us that as good social marketers we should always seek to see the world through our customers' eyes. Cairns et al. (chapter 22) take us to another form of inequality: that between developed and developing countries. In a similar way to Hill, they argue for a coming together, a greater respect, a more profound sharing between what have effectively developed into separate arms of the social marketing movement.

French (chapter 24) then examines the relationship between social marketing and government, and commends the former to the latter. In essence he echoes a lesson long established in the business literature: that for government, as for firms, marketing is not an ad hoc add-on but core business. Finally, Peattie (chapter 23) addresses what is arguably the biggest issue of all: climate change and sustainability. Like French, he argues that progress will depend on profound and long-lasting change to our relationship with our planet – not fragmented campaigns.

Section 6 presents three Case Studies. The first two look at how social marketing has worked in practice. Novelli and Workman (chapter 25) examine its (mostly) successful combination with advocacy in the work of the AARP[2] and specifically the passage of Medicare legislation. Dewhirst and Lee (chapter 26) then look at the role of social marketing in tobacco control. The last case study by McDermott et al. (chapter 27) takes a different approach and examines the response to social marketing from the field of health promotion, arguing that there is still a lot of resistance in evidence. The authors call for health promotion to be more open to social marketing, but equally they present a prime face case for social marketing to do a better job of marketing itself.

The very last chapter is an Afterword written by an elder statesman of social marketing practice, with vast experience of direct involvement in social marketing across the globe. Very conscious that this is an academic book aimed at academics, we were anxious to see whether it had any traction in the real world of behaviour change. We might think our musings to be important, but what about someone who is used to making a real, tangible difference? Gratifyingly our efforts pass the test. We can do no better than quote Bill Smith's conclusion:

> After reflecting on the excellent chapters in this book and on my own experience across many countries and many social marketing challenges I have concluded our future lies is opening up rather than closing down. The fears that we have abandoned marketing in favor of too much communication are well founded. But I don't believe the answer is to convince people to focus. Instead if we bring in new people, think of ourselves as the specialists we are and add a cadre of integration managers we have a better chance, not only of improving the quality of our work, but of living up to the mission set for us by Adam Smith: 'the interest of the producer ought to be attended to, only so far as it may be necessary for promoting that of the consumer'.

LOOKING TO THE FUTURE

Thus, the contributing authors have provided an exposition of the current state of the social marketing nation. They confirm the vibrancy and breadth of the discipline: social marketers are innovating and continuing to learn both in theory and practice; they are challenging the status quo and, in *The Economist*'s crunchy words, biting a few hands; and they are thinking big – addressing wide scale social change, not just the minutiae of individual behaviour.

The authors also suggest a positive future for a discipline which is continuing to adapt and grow. It has been able to offer ways forward on problems such as sustainability and HIV/AIDS that were unrecognised when the idea was first conceived and labelled back in 1971, and it can

continue to do so as new challenges emerge. For us as editors, two particularly hopeful signs are the disciplines energetic engagement at the two levels illustrated in Figure 1.1: with citizens and stakeholders.

Citizens, community activism and participatory media

Community activism

Listening to and learning from the people we want to work with – whether we term them consumers, clients, target groups or just plain citizens – is, as many of the contributors underline, the sine qua non of social marketing. Kotler and Lee's Foreword notes that in the early years of the discipline this took the form of the then revolutionary idea of public health communications being pretested with audiences as well as scrutinised by medics – and then changed in response to the former as well as the latter. For the first time since the birth of modern medicine there was official recognition that the doctor did not always know best. Since then the idea has remained at the core of social marketing and continues to provide its essential strength because it recognises the power of ordinary people. This power takes two forms. First, in a conventional sense, people can and will resist change if they feel it does not meet their needs. Smokers will continue to smoke in the teeth of stark health warnings and motorists to drive too fast despite ubiquitous speed cameras not just because they are ignorant or recalcitrant (though they may be both) but because they can. More subtly, social marketing is, time and again, focussed on processes not outcomes. The concern is not so much with ad hoc behaviours but on-going lifestyles. This speaks to personal and collective empowerment and growth – and a further adjustment to the balance of power between the expert and the citizen.

Work at the Florida Prevention Research Center (FPRC) at the University of South Florida is taking this to its natural conclusion. To overcome the paternalism, Anker and Kappel (chapter 19) see as inherent in a funder-driven agenda and expert-driven planning process, the FPRC has blended elements of community organising with social marketing. Called Community-based Prevention Marketing (CBPM), this synergistic framework allows members from the affected community to select the social problems they want to tackle, set program goals, and participate in the research, strategy development, and program activities used to reach those goals. Community involvement provides valuable information about local problems and the assets available to resolve them, enhancing the fit between program strategies and local institutions and customs. By working together, network ties may be strengthened and new problem solving skills acquired, thereby enhancing the community's capacity to tackle new issues. Most importantly, communities are treated as agents and partners instead of *"passive consumers of messages and programs"* (Lefebvre, 2009a). As Marques and Domegan (chapter 3) point out, this underlines the importance of relational thinking to social marketing: *"Relationship marketing provides a new foundation for social marketing thinking, a genuine change in values and ethics and a new logic that sees consumers as the prime drivers of the value creation process"*.

In the resulting CBPM approach, social marketers teach community partners to follow a nine-step process: (1) mobilise the community; (2) develop a profile of community problems and assets; (3) select target behaviours, audiences, and when possible, existing interventions to tailor for local application; (4) build community capacity to address the priority or target problem(s); (5) conduct formative research; (6) develop a marketing strategy; (7) develop or tailor program materials and tactics; (8) implement the new or tailored intervention and (9) track and evaluate the program's impact.

One of CBPM's distinguishing characteristics is the partnership created between social marketers and community members. Communities may be based on locality, ethnicity, sexual orientation, occupation or shared interests. When based on geographic bounded localities, community boards or coalitions are formed that typically include local public health professionals, lay leaders and activists, representatives of local businesses, churches, voluntary organizations and residents. Working together, social marketers and their community partners analyse local problems, set goals, conduct consumer research, and use research results to design, implement, and evaluate social marketing interventions aimed at achieving those goals. Thus, in addition to enhancing the long lasting success of social marketing interventions, CBPM enhances community organising efforts by giving its members a more effective planning process (Bryant et al., 2000).

Another distinguishing feature is CBPM's goal to build the community's capacity to solve local problems by teaching them social marketing skills. Unlike other community organising models, community members are taught to analyse the competition, select target behaviours and priority population segments to optimise their return on investment, and use consumer research to develop a strategic plan based on marketing's 4 Ps. Through participation in all phases of the planning and implementation process, some community members gain the social marketing skills needed

to address other issues and work together to sustain and institutionalise solutions.

Experience in several settings has demonstrated that CBPM is effective in teaching communities to use marketing approaches for designing new public health interventions, tailoring evidence-based interventions for application in new settings and creating local programs to capitalise on the brand equity of national media campaigns (Bryant et al., 2009). It has also increased community coalitions' capacity to use marketing principles for policy advocacy, and service delivery improvements (Morris, 2008).

CBPM gains much of its success from the synergy between community organisation and social marketing principles and techniques. By leveraging the wisdom of local groups, and nurturing ownership of the problem-solving process, CBPM increases the likelihood interventions will succeed and changes be sustained (Minkler and Wallerstein, 1998). Community participation also enhances the validity of formative research results, strengthens participants' sense of social connectedness, control over their lives and ability to change (Minkler and Wallerstein, 1998).

The essence of CBPM is neatly encapsulated by Marques and Domegan (chapter 3) when they argue that *"first and foremost"* for social marketers *"the collaboration is with the client/consumer as a co-creator of value"*, an insight being picked up around the world. In the Netherlands the Eigen Kracht *Centrale* (Family Group Conferencing) is *"striving for a society based on participation and mutual self-reliance of citizens, where citizens remain in charge of their own life, especially when dealing with organizations and government bodies"* (Eigen Kracht *Centrale*, 2011). Similarly, Amnesty International's work in the Northern Territory of Australia shows that giving aboriginal communities greater control of their own health services in and of itself enhances outcomes (Marland, 2010). And across the Pacific in South America at least one development NGO has recognised the value of replacing external experts with indigenous citizens trained as Kamayoqs or knowledge bearers (The Open University, 2002).

Like all community-based approaches, CBPM is also challenging. Community participation and self-determination can be difficult and time-consuming. Trust and cooperation between "outsiders" (social marketing experts) and community members can be difficult to establish, especially in disenfranchised populations. Moreover, the time required to reach consensus on major program decisions can extend the planning process and delay program implementation. Nor is CBPM appropriate for all communities and problems: the social marketing expertise and/or community leadership and commitment may simply not be available (Bryant et al., 2009).

Nonetheless, CBPM is an extremely promising and quintessentially social marketing approach which takes the core notion of consumer orientation to its natural conclusion and establishes a broad social agenda for the discipline.

Participatory media[3]

The individual and community empowerment which CBPM and similar approaches engender are also being greatly facilitated by burgeoning digital media. This sector is growing fast, as Mays et al. make clear in chapter 12, with the last five years seeing an explosion in the use of internet and mobile devices for information seeking, recreation and interpersonal connectivity, especially via social networking sites.

In the USA, 85% of all Americans and 96% of young adults, 18–29 years of age, own a cell phone (Smith, 2010). Whereas disparities continue to exist in technology ownership and use, the 2010 Pew Internet Project (Smith, 2010) found changes during the last five years that underscore Mays et al.'s recommendation to monitor both attitudes and practices among specific audience segments before relying on these communication channels to reach them. For instance, while minorities in the USA still lag somewhat behind Anglo Americans in desktop computer ownership and broadband internet use, they are more likely than whites to own a mobile phone and far more likely to use their mobile devices for text messaging, visiting social networking sites, accessing the internet, and posting multimedia content online. Compared with their white counterparts, minorities also share more positive attitudes about government agencies' use of social technologies to share information with them (The Pew Research Center's Internet & American Life Project, 2010).

Cell phone use for information seeking and interconnectivity is also growing internationally. In a comparison of eight countries, overall cell phone use was highest (90%) among Indian youth, while smartphone penetration was highest (47%) among youth in Italy (Nielsen, 2010a). In the USA, cell phones are now used by more than two-thirds of youth even in the 8- to 18-year-old bracket (Rideout et al., 2010). With improved smartphones and the introduction of tablet computers, such as the iPad, that offer larger screens, we can expect to see reliance on mobile media to increase further as information seeking and internet access devices. According to Nielsen (2010b), constant interconnectivity is giving birth to an important new audience segment within the teen and 20-something age cohorts. Called "Gen C",

this segment represents a community of "digital natives" around the globe whose identities are being formed by a strong desire to 'connect' around interesting ideas, cultural objects, causes and movements" (Nielsen, 2010b). These youth gain credibility among peers by sharing their ideas and observations online, and use mobile devices to engage in constant conversations via social media platforms, where they actively participate and collaborate with others in story-telling and information creation.

The interest in digital media is becoming mainstream for social marketing. In addition to numerous for-profit products, such as wireless wellness diaries, blood-pressure monitors and medical management systems, non-profit and government agencies, such as the Centers for Disease Control and Prevention, are using new media in their health promotion efforts, and encouraging others to do likewise (Centers for Disease Control and Prevention, 2011).

Arguably it is the active, empowered engagement in digital media of Gen C – a phenomenon that has led researcher Mark Grindle to rename them "participatory media" (Grindle, 2004) – that has the most fundamental implications for social marketing. It provides an electronic and ubiquitous platform for the grassroots activism of CBPM and its cousins. This has the power to transform ordinary people and community groups from passive message recipients, into fellow storytellers, network builders and co-creators of value. They are now able to search for, or "pull" information they want instead of waiting for it to be "pushed" to them (SMLXL, 2007). As Lefebvre notes, mobile technologies provide:

> More than a communication device – they can become marketing tools that address all elements of the marketing mix when strategically considered in the context of how people use them. Cell phones are an always-on, two-way communication channel, a signal or cue for action, a resource of instant access to health information, a tool for social support and the development of social capital, a production tool, a way to engage audiences, and a data collection and feedback device. (2009b: 493–494)

And as social marketing continues to learn from its corporate counterparts, it is worth noting that the latter have reached an impasse: social media do not provide the silver bullet they seemed to promise. Human beings do not want to use participatory media to create or enter communities simply to warm their hands around the rosy glow of commercial brands: they want to meet like-minded people, help each other, develop themselves and gain status (Moran and

Gossieaux, 2010). And, they adopt a healthy and critical distance from commerce and its products, even if it is simply at the level of pointing their peers towards better deals – and/or behaviours — elsewhere. Moreover, significant rewards are made available in the form of peer approval and social status to those who do. Commerce is learning quickly that participatory media grows and speaks from the bottom up; it allows marketers to come alongside end users, listen to them, understand *their* motives and desires – and then helping *them* to co-create *their own* new products, processes, behaviours and lifestyles.

The prospects of participatory media are indeed exciting, and the greatest potential will come, Grindle (2010) argues, when we move beyond a focus on technological wizardry and begin to absorb some of the storytelling skills of traditional media (perhaps best exemplified by commercial cinema). Interactive storytelling allows people not just to participate but to perform in a journey of their own making. Cinematic storytelling has the ability to structure and evoke powerful emotions – pride, self-worth, identity, belonging, status and validation: it will make it possible for people to experiment with whole new lifestyles in safe and self-asserting, life-affirming contexts. Refusing a cigarette from your mate can be very challenging in real life – and it is unlikely to deliver any greater status or rewards – but as an avatar such possibilities can be tried out, tested and rewarded:

> By combining interactivity and reward structures – as evolved by the computer games industry – with storytelling and emotional structuring – as evolved by commercial cinema – Social Marketing can help clients to experiment outside of their local, real world familial and peer group milieu – as many young people around the world are beginning to do and enjoy. By embracing participatory media and emergent storytelling forms, Social Marketers can collaborate with and help to co-create identities, environments, behaviours and life styles. It can help participants rehearse real-life challenges, take on real-life antagonists and experience rewards and emotions unavailable anywhere else. We can be heroes. (Grindle, 2004)

The last sentiment was recognised fully by game designer Jane McGonigal who in collaboration with World Bank ran an initiative last year called *EVOKE – a crash course in changing the world* (Hawkins, 2010). Participants were given the opportunity to take on the role of hero and experiment with the challenges of real-world development scenarios played out online. Real world financial rewards and opportunities were given to those who were able to empower others

and collaborate to collect real world evidence. No formal evaluation has been released at the time of writing, but the weblogs are certainly very positive. Participatory media clearly have much social marketing potential, offering as they do the opportunity to take value creation and the Kamayoqs to scale. In addition, they give more power to the people and push towards a further rebalancing between expert and citizen.

Stakeholders: the case for critical analysis

As the University of South Florida work demonstrates, progress depends on movement not just by the individual citizen but by community groups, and civil society. This takes us back to Figure 1.1 and reminds us that successful social change is also influenced by the wider social context and specifically by the actions of other stakeholders – as well as individuals. For us social marketers, our alter egos in the commercial sector loom especially large and many of the chapters, as we have noted, provide valuable critical assessments here. As Marques and Domegan point out, "*social marketers' legitimacy is greater if social marketers are critical about themselves: their own processes and outcomes but especially about their assumptions or taken for granted 'truths'. From a critical perspective, the challenge is to make those assumptions explicit so they can be contested on other grounds than are provided for by the prevailing paradigm*" (Eakin et al., 1996). This last sentiment captures the crucial role of critical thinking – and, indeed, this Handbook: to uncover the taken for granted and test it in the courtroom of academic and public debate. And as Jones, Hoek, Dewhirst and Lee, and numerous other contributors to this Handbook make clear, an open and frank debate about the role of commercial marketing is an essential part of this rigour. This book is testament to the power of marketing and its potential to do good if used in by the right people in the right way. It would be derelict – and profoundly damaging to social marketing – if we did not also recognise and point up its capacity to do harm. Speaking truth to power is a crucial part of the social marketer's role.

Scottish tobacco control, and specifically the move to smokefree public places – which Scotland did ahead of all its UK and European neighbours, excepting only Ireland – provides an instructive case study. The aim was extremely challenging, its fulcrum the public house (pub) or bar: Glasgow pubs in particular were a byword for unhealthy behaviours played out in a perpetual and acrid fug. Making them the spearhead of public health policy in Scotland (whose sobriquet was then "the sick man of Europe") seemed improbable to the point of foolishness. But it was done; came in without demure (mostly) and was probably the single most popular achievement of the then McConnell Government. A public opinion survey a few days after the law's introduction showed that no fewer than 84% of 16–24 year olds not only approved of the measure, but thought it one "that Scotland could be proud of" – praise indeed from a fiercely nationalistic populace (Cancer Research UK, 2006).

This success depended on multiple actions. The attention of politicians was engaged by a carefully marshalled evidence base showing that (a) second hand smoke is extremely toxic and (b) making hospitality venues smokefree does not harm business. This attention turned to commitment when the First Minister met with Micheál Martin, the Irish Health Minister who had already brought in similar legislation in Eire, who convinced him of the political, as well as the public health, advantages. Reputedly, when asked by Jack McConnell what he would do differently if he had his time over, Martin replied simply: "*I would have done more sooner*". McConnell was won over: he had gone over to Ireland on the Friday night set against going smokefree and he returned on the Monday all in favour; one of the clearest examples of source effect ever recorded. Other key stakeholders, including the hospitality trade unions, the health and safety professionals and, of course, the medics were recruited to the cause be elucidating the benefits both through their professional bodies (more helpful source effects) and concerted press and PR activity. The Scottish people were engaged through a mass media campaign emphasising the harmful effects of second hand smoke that reinforced an existing dislike of the aesthetic unpleasantness of smoke-filled pubs. Cancer clearly had the biggest shroud to wave, but the discomfort and laundry bills that resulted from being kippered at the pub added a perhaps more powerful everyday resonance.

There was, however, also loud and very active opposition from much of the hospitality sector, their genuine anxieties inflamed by unscrupulous and self-serving interference by the tobacco industry. The tobacco companies themselves had long been persona non-grata, but they stirred things up from afar. Perhaps the best documented evidence of their dissembling was revealed in a paper published in the journal *Tobacco Control* (Scollo et al., 2003), which showed that out of 97 studies on the economic impact of smokefree ordinances, some 35 showed it had a bad effect on bars and restaurants. Thirty-one of these studies had two things in common, as the paper demonstrates: first, they were generally of poor quality (e.g. they lacked control groups or objective outcome

measures) and second, every single one was supported in some way by the tobacco industry. (The funding sources for the other four studies were unknown.) The higher quality independent studies all showed that smokefree had no negative commercial impact. Despite the revelation of this and other trickery, however, most of the hospitality sector remained adamantly opposed to going smokefree – and an excellent public health intervention had to proceed in the teeth of their opposition. For the most part, this group remains implacably opposed, and smokefree is still being blamed when pubs get into financial difficulty – despite the want of any reliable evidence to support this position.

The case reminds us that social marketing success is built on understanding who needs to do what; identifying their motivations for doing it and catering for these; recognising that both the who and the why are likely to be many and various; accepting that emotions, irrelevances and seeming trivialities often win out over what the experts perceive to be the important things; acknowledging that while evidence matters it will frequently get trumped by what a mate says; and being realistic enough to concede that sometimes the competition is exactly that, and has to be defeated rather than courted. In short, it shows that effective social change and social marketing depends on multi-faceted, multi-stakeholder sensitivity – combined with strong-minded critical appraisal and action.

CONCLUSION

The commissioning of this handbook is a landmark in the development of social marketing. It has provided a chance to assess progress and look forward. The response of the contributors has been heartening and impressive; leading thinkers from across the world have welcomed the opportunity discuss and analyse the theory, practice and above all, potential of a discipline that was only christened 40 years ago. They demonstrate that Kotler and Zaltman's profound insight back in 1971 marked the start of long and complex journey which has generated much learning and culminated in a rounded and mature discipline. In the process, to use Wallack et al's (1993) metaphor, social marketers are not just able to help with the loose threads of individual behaviour change, but also with the flaws in the fabric of society. Thus, social marketing has come of age and, as any established and rounded discipline should, is now busy addressing the major concerns of our age. It is helping "*facilitate the maximal operations of the system for the benefit of the host society*". Or, as Vince, the veteran of the fight against the Vietnam war who began this chapter would say, it has succeeded in becoming a movement.

NOTES

1 I would like to thank Carol Bryant and Kathryn Angus for their enormous help with writing this chapter and their patience in reading and commenting on drafts.

2 Founded in 1958, AARP is a non-profit, non-partisan membership organisation that helps people aged 50 years and over to improve the quality of their lives.

3 I would like to thank Mark Grindle for his enormous assistance with drafting this section.

REFERENCES

Bloom, P.N. and Gundlach, G.T. (2001) *Handbook of Marketing and Society*. Thousand Oaks, CA: Sage Publications.

Bryant, C.A., Forthofer, M., McCormack Brown, K., Landis, D. and McDermott, R.J. (2000) 'Community-based prevention marketing: the next steps in disseminating behavior change', *American Journal of Health Behavior*, 24: 61–68.

Bryant, C.A., McCormack Brown, K., McDermott, R.J., Debate, R.D., Alfonso, M.A., Baldwin, J.L., Monaghan, P. and Phillips, L.M. (2009) 'Community-based prevention marketing: a new planning framework for designing and tailoring health promotion interventions', in R. DiClemente, R.A. Crosby, M.C. Kegler (eds), *Emerging Theories in Health Promotion Practice and Research: Strategies for Improving Public Health*, 2nd edn. San Francisco, CA: Jossey-Bass, pp. 331–356.

Cancer Research UK (2006) *Young Scots 'most proud' to be smoke-free as iconic image unveiled*. Cancer Research UK Press Release, 14 March. Online: http://info.cancerresearchuk.org/news/archive/pressrelease/2006-03-14-young-scots-most-proud-to-be-smoketree-as-iconic-image-unveiled [accessed 27 January 2011].

Centers for Disease Control and Prevention (2011) *CDC Social Media Tools Guidelines & Best Practices*. 24 January. Online: http://www.cdc.gov/SocialMedia/Tools/guidelines/ [accessed 27 January 2011].

Eakin, J., Robertson, A., Poland, B., Coburn, D. and Edwards, R. (1996) 'Towards a critical social science perspective on health promotion research', *Health Promotion International*, 11(2): 157–165.

The Economist (2009) 'The pedagogy of the privileged', *The Economist* (online edition), 24 September. Online: http://www.economist.com/node/14493183/print [accessed 26 January 2011].

Eigen Kracht *Centrale* (2011) 'What we do'. Online: http://www.eigen-kracht.nl/en/inhoud/what-we-do [accessed 26 January 2011].

Grindle, M. (2004) 'At what stage is our understanding of the interactive entertainment development industry in Scotland?', paper presented at *The Scottish Media and Communication Association Annual Conference*, 3 December. Dundee: University of Abertay.

Grindle, M. (2010) 'Can computer games save the planet? The role interactive entertainment might play in marketing sustainable consumption', paper presented at the *ISM-Open Conference Changing Times, New Challenges*, 3 November. Milton Keynes: The Open University.

Hastings, G. (2007) *Social Marketing: Why Should the Devil Have All the Best Tunes?* Oxford: Butterworth-Heinemann.

Hawkins, R. (2010) 'EVOKE - a crash course in changing the world', *EduTech - a World Bank Blog on ICT use in Education* (Weblog), Online: http://blogs.worldbank.org/edutech/evoke-a-crash-course-in-changing-the-world [accessed 27 January 2011].

Hickman, M. (2010) 'Food companies in massive lobby to block colour-coded warnings', *The Independent* (online edition), 15 June. Online: http://www.independent.co.uk/life-style/food-and-drink/news/food-companies-in-massivelobby-to-block-colourcoded-warnings-2000523.html [accessed 26 January 2011].

Jobber, D. (2009) *Principles and Practice of Marketing*, 6th edn. London: McGraw-Hill Education (1st edn, 1995).

Lazer, W. and Kelley, E. (1973) *Social Marketing: Perspectives and Viewpoints*. Homewood, IL: Richard D. Irwin.

Lefebvre, R.C. (2009a) 'Social Models for Marketing: Building Communities' *On Social Marketing and Social Change* (Weblog), 20 October. Online: http://socialmarketing.blogs.com/r_craiig_lefebvres_social/2009/10/social-models-formarketing-building-communities.html [accessed 26 January 2011].

Lefebvre, R.C. (2009b) 'Integrating cell phones and mobile technologies into public health practice: a social marketing perspective', *Health Promotion Practice*, 10(4): 490–494.

Marland, S. (2010) 'Healthy homelands' *Amnesty International > Our work > Demand Dignity*. Online: http://www.amnesty.org.au/poverty/comments/22681/ [accessed 26 January 2011].

Minkler, M. and Wallerstein, N. (1998) 'Improving health through community organization and community building: a health education perspective', in M. Minkler (ed), *Community Organizing and Community Building for Health*. New Brunswick, NJ: Rutgers University Press, pp. 26–50.

Moran, E.K. and Gossieaux, F. (2010) 'Marketing in a hyper-social world: the tribalization of business study and characteristics of successful online communities', *Journal of Advertising Research*, 50(3): 232–239.

Morris, C. (2008) *Achieving Diverse Participation and Improved Idea Exchange in the Community-Based Public Health Coalition*. Report to the Florida Prevention Research Center. Lexington, KY: unpublished document.

National Cancer Institute (2008) *The Role of the Media in Promoting and Reducing Tobacco Use. Tobacco Control Monograph No. 19*. Bethesda, MD: US Department of Health and Human Services, National Institutes of Health, National Cancer Institute.

Nielsen (2010a) *Mobile Youth around the World*. New York: The Nielsen Company. Online: http://no.nielsen.com/site/documents/Nielsen-Mobile-Youth-Around-The-World-Dec-2010.pdf [accessed 27 January 2011].

Nielsen (2010b) *Introducing Generation C: The Connected Collective Consumer*. 27 October. Online: http://blog.nielsen.com/nielsenwire/consumer/introducing-gen-c-%E2%80%93-the-connected-collective-consumer/ [accessed 27 January 2011].

The Open University (2002) *International Development: Challenges for a World in Transition. Sustainability*. Milton Keynes: The Open University.

The Pew Research Center's Internet & American Life Project (2010) *Technology Trends Among People of Color*. 17 September. Online: http://pewinternet.org/Commentary/2010/September/Technology-Trends-Among-People-of-Color.aspx [accessed 27 January 2011].

Porter, M.E. and Kramer, M.R. (2011) 'Creating shared value: How to reinvent capitalism - and unleash a wave of innovation and growth', *Harvard Business Review*, (Jan -Feb): 62–77.

Rideout, V.J., Foehr, U.G. and Roberts, D.F. (2010) *Generation M2: Media in the Lives of 8- to 18-Year-Olds. A Kaiser Family Foundation Study*. Menlo Park, CA: The Henry J. Kaiser Family Foundation. Online: http://www.kff.org/entmedia/upload/8010.pdf [accessed 27 January 2011].

Rothschild, M. (1999) 'Carrots, sticks and promises: a conceptual framework for the management of public health and social issue behaviors', *Journal of Marketing*, 63(4): 24–37.

Scollo, M., Lal, A., Hyland, A. and Glantz, S. (2003) 'Review of the quality of studies on the economic effects of smoke-free policies on the hospitality industry', *Tobacco Control*, 12: 13–20.

Smith, A. (2010) *Americans and Their Gadgets*. Washington, DC: Pew Research Center's Internet & American Life Project. Online: http://pewinternet.org/Reports/2010/Gadgets.aspx [accessed 27 January 2011].

SMLXL (2007) *Mobile as the 7th Mass Media: An Evolving Story*. SMLXLWhite Paper. Online: http://smlxtralarge.com/wp-content/uploads/2008/03/smlxl-m7mm-copy.pdf [accessed 10 December 2010].

Wallack, L., Dorfman, L., Jerngian, D. and Themba, M. (1993) *Media Advocacy and Public Health: Power for Prevention*. Newbury Park, CA: Sage Publications.

Wilkie, W.L. and Moore, E.S. (2003) 'Scholarly research in marketing: exploring the '4 eras' of thought development', *Journal of Public Policy and Marketing*, 22(2): 116–146.

Wilkinson, R. and Pickett, K. (2010) *The Spirit Level: Why Equality is Better for Everyone*. London: Penguin.

Theoretical Debates

1. THEORETICAL MODELS OF BEHAVIOUR CHANGE – R. DONOVAN

Donovan's chapter opens with a discussion of the reasons why theory is important to social marketers and an overview of theoretical foundations relevant to the field. The chapter describes 'cognitive decision models' (e.g. the health belief model, protection motivation theory, social learning theory, and the theory of reasoned action) as well as social change models (community-readiness model, stages of change, diffusion theory, social ecology model). It also includes a brief discussion of two concepts largely often overlooked by social change theorists: morality and legitimacy. Behaviour modification (or applied behaviour analysis) principles are also presented to underscore the importance of considering environmental factors and skills when translating people's beliefs, attitudes and intentions into action. Donovan ends with a reminder that these models are useful for targeting policymakers as well as individuals, and a call for future research to enhance the predictability of health behaviour theories.

2. SOCIAL MODELS FOR SOCIAL MARKETING: MARKETING: SOCIAL DIFFUSION, SOCIAL NETWORKS, SOCIAL CAPITAL, SOCIAL DETERMINANTS AND SOCIAL FRANCHISING – R. C. LEFEBVRE

In this chapter, Lefebvre reviews theoretical models that focus beyond the individual. To equip social marketers to tackle social needs such as poverty and policy change, he reviews key elements of social determinants, social diffusion, social networks, social capital, building communities and social franchising. Lefebvre makes a compelling argument that a 'more comprehensive perspective on how social marketing can be applied to the work of social innovation and change can provide new opportunities and tools to realise its potential and our ability to do good for the world'.

3. RELATIONSHIP MARKETING AND SOCIAL MARKETING – S. MARQUES AND C. DOMEGAN

Marques and Domegan note that social marketing can be undermined by an underuse of relationship marketing. From three differing definitions, they propose that the Nordic school of thought has the most to offer social marketing, where relationship marketing defines the organisation as a service governed from a process management perspective with developed active networks and partnerships. The authors present the three key processes underlying relationship marketing as: the interaction process of the established relationship(s); the two- or multi-way communication process; and the value creation process, or how customers strive to fulfil their needs. These processes are supported by six psychological and one behavioural construct which social marketers should address and explore: relationship quality, trust, perceived value, satisfaction, commitment, identification and cooperation.

4. UNDERSTANDING SOCIAL NORMS: UPSTREAM AND DOWNSTREAM APPLICATIONS FOR SOCIAL MARKETERS – P. KENNY AND G. HASTINGS

Social norms perceptions, part of the peer influence field, are a powerful influence on human behaviour, especially amongst the young and vulnerable. In their chapter, Kenny and Hastings describe how social norms' formation, influence and how marketing campaigns can manipulate them, are important to social marketers, as is an awareness of the categories of prescriptive and descriptive norms. Using the illustration of alcohol consumption, the authors demonstrate why an understanding of social norms is required for 'downstream' applications, such as social norms marketing campaigns, and for 'upstream' applications, such as regulations for the marketing of harmful products.

5. DESIGN THINKING, DEMARKETING AND BEHAVIORAL ECONOMICS: FOSTERING INTERDISCIPLINARY GROWTH IN SOCIAL MARKETING – R. C. LEFEBVRE AND P. KOTLER

Lefebvre and Kotler encourage us to look outside the social marketing literature for innovative ideas that can improve our practice. Their chapter introduces us to ideas from two emerging disciplines, behavioural economics and design thinking, and a decades old commercial marketing approach, demarketing, that has been underutilised by social marketers. Their thought-provoking summaries of relevant principles and applications from these three idea sets are designed to provide social marketers with alternative ways to think about social problems and to develop more effective solutions for individual behaviour change interventions and organisational, policy and cultural shifts. While acknowledging that evidence to support the efficacy of these approaches is still lacking, they make a compelling case for exploration of their utility in designing social marketing interventions.

6. CRITICAL MARKETING: THEORETICAL UNDERPINNINGS – M. SAREN

Saren describes the role and importance of critical marketing and why it provides support for the social marketing discipline. A range of mainstream marketing topics challenged by critical assessment are reviewed from this stance, including the core marketing concept, critical theory, the role of markets, consumer behaviour, and marketing assumptions, knowledge and philosophy. Saren proposes that social marketers can use and develop critical research methodologies to study underlying social and behavioural phenomena from a more holistic perspective than commercial market research methods and consumption theories may permit.

7. NOVEL APPROACHES TOWARDS RESISTANCE TO PERSUASION – P. K. PETROVA AND R. B. CIALDINI

Petrova and Cialdini review recent research about creating and overcoming resistance to persuasive messages. They first answer the question: 'What constitutes an effective counterargument? They then examine how social marketing campaigns can increase resistance to persuasive messages promoting risky behaviours and reduce resistance to messages promoting healthy behaviours. They give special attention to overcoming three types of resistance to social marketing interventions: reactance, scepticism and inertia. Also of interest to social marketers are their insights into alignment of counterarguments, revelation of manipulative intent and undermining the credibility of stronger opponents.

Theoretical Models of Behaviour Change

Rob Donovan

'There's nothing so practical as a good theory' said the father of social psychology Kurt Lewin way back in 1952. These words were true then and are still true today.

While the word 'theory' has a number of lay and technical reasons, it is used here in its scientific meaning: that is, a theory about some phenomenon is a set of concepts and their interrelationships that attempts to explain the occurrence of or changes in the phenomenon under question. What distinguishes theory in this sense from other meanings, is that the concepts can be operationalised and hence the theory is empirically testable.

Theoretical models of behaviour change are useful for a number of reasons:

- First and foremost, generating a theory or model of the behaviour or issue under consideration makes us think more deeply and more creatively about that behaviour, its causes, influencers, and so on.
- Second, such thinking results in the identification of a variety of factors that may influence that behaviour.
- Third, the identification of factors potentially influencing a behaviour provides hypotheses for testing and guidelines for conducting qualitative and quantitative research into how the various factors influence the behaviour both independently as well as how they might interact.

- Fourth, a model of influencing factors provides direction for developing interventions to change the behaviour in question by changing the influencing factors.
- Fifth, evaluation of such interventions then provides feedback for further refinement of the model.

The value of iterative feedback from interventions to theories, and from theories to interventions, is summed up in further words of wisdom attributed to Lewin: 'If you want to truly understand something, try to change it.'

There are numerous models of behaviour change, from individual to organisational to system perspectives. Darnton (2008) identified some 60 models with approximately half of those having some presence in the literature. Not unexpectedly, there is considerable overlap between many models. Drawing from Donovan and Henley (2010), this chapter presents the major theoretical models used in social marketing, public health and social policy campaigns, across different countries and cultures, concentrating on those either most widely used or of most potential utility.

A useful binary classification of such models is that some (the vast majority) emphasise how beliefs and attitudes influence individual decision making and behaviour change, while others emphasise how behaviour change occurs over time for individuals or populations. The former are generally known as 'cognitive decision models' or knowledge–attitude–behaviour (KAB) models, while the latter are known as stage of change models when referring to changes in individuals' beliefs and attitudes over time, and as diffusion models when related to how ideas and behaviours are adopted and spread throughout a community or population.

This chapter begins with cognitive decision models and includes a brief discussion of two concepts generally ignored by the KAB models: morality and legitimacy. Behaviour modification (or applied behaviour analysis) principles are also included to further emphasise that we must translate people's beliefs, attitudes and intentions into action, and that to do this, we must be aware of the necessary environmental factors and skills that will facilitate this translation.

COGNITIVE DECISION MODELS

Most of these models are based on the assumption that an individual's beliefs about some person, group, issue, object or behaviour will determine the individual's attitude with respect to that person, group, issue, object or behaviour. Subject to social norms and self-efficacy, these attitudes in turn predict how the individual intends to act with regard to that person, group, issue, object or behaviour. Finally, whether or not these intentions result in behaviour will depend on environmental facilitators and inhibitors, both perceived and actual, and both situational (temporary) and structural (enduring). In short, favourable attitudes and intentions towards purchasing and consuming more fruit and vegetables will only translate into behaviour where good quality fruit and vegetables are readily available at a competitive price.

The KAB or 'social cognition' models conceptualise the influences on behaviour, and hence provide a framework for formative research, strategy development and campaign evaluation. In general, changes in the major components in these models, such as attitudes, norms and efficacy, have been found to be good predictors of changes in behaviours and intentions (Webb and Sheeran, 2006).

The health belief model

The health belief model (HBM) was perhaps the first behavioural model in health education. It was developed in the 1950s by US Public Health Service workers in an attempt to explain participation and non-participation in screening

programmes for tuberculosis (Becker, 1974; Rosenstock, 1974; Rosenstock et al., 1988). As the oldest model, the HBM has been used in planning programmes in a wide variety of health areas and is still widely used today in a broad variety of areas (see Darnton, 2008).

The model lists the following factors that are presumed to influence behaviour change in response to a potential health threat:

- Perceived susceptibility: the individual's perceived likelihood of the threat occurring to them (e.g. contracting HIV and AIDS).
- Perceived severity: the individual's beliefs about the negative consequences of the threat occurring to them (e.g. how severe HIV/AIDS is seen to be).
- Perceived benefits of the recommended behaviour: the individual's perceptions that the recommended behaviour will avert the threat (and any other additional benefits) (e.g. perceived likelihood of condoms reducing risk of transmission of HIV).
- Perceived costs and barriers: the individual's perceptions of the costs of, and perceived barriers to, adopting the recommended behaviour (e.g. perceived reaction of potential partners, etc.).
- Cues to action: individual, situational or enduring events or activities that prompt the individual to act (internal such as symptoms; external such as advertising or word-of-mouth recommendations).

It is also assumed that demographic and psychosocial variables will moderate the above variables.

Hence, an individual is more likely to take up exercise if they consider they are at high risk for diabetes, if they perceive diabetes as a serious disease, if they believe that increased exercise is effective in reducing the risk of diabetes, if they perceive no major barriers or costs (financial, social or physical) to increasing their level of exercise, and if a friend draws their attention to a physical activity programme commencing at a nearby community recreation centre.

Protection motivation theory

Rogers' (1975) protection motivation theory (PMT) was developed originally as a model of fear arousal to explain the motivational effect resulting from physical, social or psychological threats. PMT incorporates the concept of self-efficacy from Bandura's (1986) social learning theory. PMT postulates that individuals undertake two major appraisals when confronted with a threat: a threat appraisal and a coping appraisal. Similar to the HBM, a threat is appraised on two major factors: the individual's perceived *vulnerability* to the threat and a *coping* appraisal.

Vulnerability is assessed on these two factors:

- The perceived severity of the threatened harmful event if it occurs.
- The perceived likelihood of the threatened outcome occurring if the recommended behaviour is not adopted.

The coping appraisal consists of an appraisal of the recommended behaviour on the following two factors:

- The perceived effectiveness of the promoted behaviour to avoid or reduce the likelihood of occurrence of the threat (i.e. response efficacy).
- The individual's belief in their own ability to perform the recommended behaviour (i.e. self-efficacy).

If an individual (e.g. a corporate executive) determines that they are vulnerable to a threat (e.g. a boycott of the company's products by 'green' consumers), that the recommended behaviour (e.g. adopting recyclable packaging) would be effective in removing the threat, and that they are able to carry out the recommended behaviour (i.e. the recyclable packaging and technology are available and affordable), then the recommended behaviour is likely to occur. If the threat appraisal is low, either because it is extremely unlikely to occur or not severe enough to worry about, or if the threat is seen to be significant but the recommended behaviour is not seen to be effective or within the individual's capabilities (e.g. a hostile board of directors), the recommended behaviour will not occur.

Rogers later added two further factors: response costs (perceived and actual) that inhibit adoption of the desired behaviour; and perceived rewards of continuing the undesirable behaviour that facilitate its continuation.

The PMT has been applied in a number of health areas, including exercise, alcohol consumption, smoking, breast cancer screening and sexually transmitted diseases, predicting intentions to engage in anti-nuclear war behaviours, earthquake preparedness and burglary prevention. In general, the concepts of vulnerability and coping appraisal – particularly self-efficacy – have been found to be significant predictors of intention and behaviour change. For example, a University of Utrecht study in the Netherlands of obese subjects in a weight-loss programme found that those who at the start perceived themselves

better able to control their weight and eating behaviour lost significantly more weight than the others. Strong self-efficacy was in fact the best predictor of weight-loss success (Squires, 2005). The implication is that such interventions must include ways of building people's perceived (and actual) self-efficacy.

Social learning theory

At a basic level, learning occurs via a process of reinforcement: behaviours that are rewarded tend to be repeated, while behaviours that are punished tend not to be repeated. Social learning theorists, such as Albert Bandura (1977), believe that many learned behaviours depend on social reinforcement: for example, peer pressure influencing illicit drug use and social norms influencing recycling. However, social learning theorists also believe that new behaviours can be learned not only by actually experiencing reinforcements, but also by *observing* reinforcements delivered to others. This is the basis of 'modelling': adopting behaviours through imitating the behaviours of others. Hence there has always been concern about how elite athletes, football stars and other celebrities serve as 'role models' for young people.

The power of a model to induce attitude and behaviour change depends on such things as the model's credibility, attractiveness (physical in particular), expertise (in a technical area) and empathy with the audience. It also depends on how clearly and credibly the model's behaviour is seen to be rewarded. Social learning theory is the primary rationale for testimonial-type communications, and for the modelling of desirable health behaviours in television advertising and entertainment vehicles such as soap operas ('edutainment'; see Singhal et al., 2004 for examples from around the world).

Bandura (1986) expanded his social learning theory to a comprehensive 'social-cognitive' model. Many of the constructs in this model are similar to those of the health belief model with the addition of the concept of self-efficacy with regard to performing a particular behaviour. Perceived self-efficacy reflects the individual's ability and self-confidence in performing the recommended behaviour. The concept of self-efficacy is perhaps Bandura's major contribution to social-cognition models (considered separately as 'self-efficacy theory' by some writers: e.g. Godin, 1994) As noted above, self-efficacy has been found to be a major predictor of outcomes in a large number of studies, across a broad range of behaviours and models, as well as independently of any particular model. It is particularly relevant for addictive behaviours, where it is crucial to offer the target audience help in dealing with their addiction. Efficacy is also important when considering the use of threat appeals, where it is argued that if an individual experiences high anxiety as a result of the threat, but considers themselves helpless to avoid the threat, then the maladaptive behaviour (e.g. smoking, drug-taking, violence) might in fact increase. The CABWISE campaign in the UK used fear-arousal to motivate young women to call for a licensed cab rather than accepting a ride from unlicenced cabs after a night out. Unlicenced cab drivers were responsible for a large number of sexual assaults on young women in such circumstances. The campaign ensured that young women had a simple way to get the phone numbers of local licensed cabs and hence avoid a possible sexual assault. Posters of the number to text for these local numbers were placed in strategic travel locations around the city of London – and particularly in nightlife areas, including the venues (Okin et al., 2009).

The theory of reasoned action

The theory of reasoned action (TRA) is perhaps the most developed of this type of model and is widely used in social psychology and the consumer purchasing behaviour literature. It has more recently been applied to a variety of health and environmental behaviours.

Fishbein and Ajzen (1975) proposed that behaviour is predicted by an individual's *intention* to perform the behaviour, which, in turn, is a function of *attitude* towards that behaviour and *subjective norms* with regard to that behaviour. Attitude is a function of *beliefs* about the consequences of the behaviour weighted by an evaluation of each outcome. Subjective norms are a function of how significant others view the behaviour, weighted by the motivation to conform with each. Hence, an individual might have a positive attitude towards binge drinking, but not engage in the behaviour because their football teammates are opposed to it as it affects their chances of winning. Similarly, an individual might have a negative or neutral attitude towards separating glass, paper and metal in their garbage, but do so because their children encourage it and all the neighbours are seen to be doing it.

Formative research (usually qualitative) is necessary to identify all of the relevant beliefs with regard to the consequences of adopting or not adopting the recommended behaviour, and whether these consequences are viewed negatively, positively or neutrally. To accurately predict intentions, it is necessary to ensure that *all* relevant beliefs are identified and assessed.

For example, favourable attitudes towards recycling might be overestimated because only beliefs that were evaluated positively were included, while many beliefs that would be evaluated negatively were unintentionally omitted. Similarly, to gain an accurate measure of subjective norm, research is necessary to identify all relevant others, how these others are perceived to feel about the recommended behaviour, and the extent to which the individual feels motivated to comply with these others. For example, there are a number of relevant others who might influence an athlete's attitude towards using illegal performance-enhancing drugs: parents; friends; team members; coach; trainer; sports psychologist; team physician; sponsor (or potential sponsor); sporting federation administrators; current and past leading athletes in that sport; and fans of that sport.

Fishbein's model introduced two important features. First, the model makes a clear distinction between attitudes towards objects, issues or events per se, and attitudes towards behaving in a certain way towards these objects, issues, events, etc. For example, an individual may have a favourable attitude towards low carbon print electric cars, but a negative attitude towards actually buying one because of their higher price and perceived low power. Similarly, an individual may have a favourable attitude towards condoms per se, but a negative attitude towards actually buying or carrying condoms. Hence, when exploring beliefs and attitudes to predict intentions and behaviour, it is necessary to be precise in terms of whether one is measuring attitudes towards an issue per se (e.g. exercise), or attitudes towards engaging in a behaviour (e.g. exercising). This aspect of the TRA forces interventionists to more precisely determine what specific behaviour they wish to change, in what context and in what time frame (called the principle of compatibility; Ajzen, 1988).

Second, the TRA distinguishes between the individual's beliefs related to the object or issue per se, and the individual's beliefs about what other people think about the issue, and how others think they should behave towards the issue (i.e. normative beliefs). Hence, the Fishbein model incorporates social *norms* as an influence on attitudes and behaviour.

For example, consider planning an intervention to increase young males' consumption of lower alcohol beer rather than full strength beer. *Attitude* would be measured by first identifying the individual's *beliefs* about the likely consequences of drinking reduced-alcohol beer, which might be less intoxicating, cause fewer hangovers, increased alertness, less risk of exceeding the legal blood alcohol limit if randomly breath tested, less enjoyment of full-bodied taste, less variety of beer type, less brand imagery, and so on. In research terms, individuals are asked to state *how likely* is it that each of these consequences would occur if they switched to reduced-alcohol beer. This is followed by an *evaluation* of the beliefs (how positively or negatively the consequences of fewer hangovers, increased alertness, less taste, etc.) are viewed. Attitude is then the sum of the likelihood multiplied by evaluation scores for each belief.

Social norms would be measured by first identifying all relevant others (i.e. friends, workmates, family, sporting club mates, partner, etc.), and then establishing how likely it is that each of these would endorse the individual switching to reduced-alcohol beer (normative *beliefs*). These scores are then weighted by how likely the individual would be to comply with each relevant other (e.g. workmates' opinions might be far more important than a spouse's opinion – or vice versa). This last point shows that the behaviour to be predicted should also be defined with regard to situation, particularly in terms of the social environment. An individual might behave quite differently depending on who else is present. Young males often moderate their drinking behaviour in the presence of young women (and perhaps stern parents), and brand choices are far more important in some bars and among some groups than others.

Fishbein and Ajzen's model has spawned a number of extensions, most notably the theory of planned behavior (TPB; Ajzen, 1988) and the theory of trying (TT; Bagozzi and Warshaw, 1990). The TPB extended the TRA by adding perceived behavioural control – the extent to which the individual perceived the recommended behaviour to be easy or difficult to do (similar to self-efficacy in other models).

Both the TRA and TPB have been used quite extensively across a number of consumer purchasing, lifestyle and health behaviours (particularly smoking, exercise and STD prevention), with generally good results for all of the major variables in the models in terms of predicting intentions or behaviours. For example, the '1% or less' milk campaign in Wheeling, West Virginia was based on the TRA and the compatibility principle. It resulted in a significant increase in low-fat milk share (29–46%), with 34% of a Wheeling sample reporting switching versus 4% of a comparison community. Analysis of the data showed that the intervention increased intention and attitude (but not subjective norm), and there were significant increases in beliefs about the healthiness, taste and cost of low-fat milk (Booth-Butterfield and Reger, 2004). More recent research has provided support for the usefulness of the TPB

in predicting adolescent athletes' intentions to use doping substances (Lucidi et al., 2008).

The theory of trying

The theory of trying has two major elements of interest (Bagozzi and Warshaw, 1990). First, TT's focus is on end-goals (e.g. weight loss) rather than on behaviour choices in specific situations, and hence is directly applicable to most issues in health promotion and social marketing. Second, the theory focuses on *trying* to achieve these goals (i.e. attempting to quit smoking) rather than *actual attainment* of the goals (i.e. successfully quitting smoking). This is a far more realistic focus. For example, rather than attempting to determine the predictors of (successful) quitting, we should first determine the predictors of *trying* to quit. Many studies have failed to show a relationship between attitudes or intentions and behaviours, because the behaviours have been defined as successful outcomes (e.g. loss of weight; adoption of regular exercise; introduction of policy changes), rather than *trying* to achieve these goals. Separating trying from achieving also forces the campaign planner to separately consider what leads to trying and what factors then come into play to facilitate or inhibit a successful outcome.

An individual's overall *attitude towards trying* some behaviour (e.g. to lose weight) is a function of three factors:

- Attitude towards succeeding and the perceived likelihood (or expectation) of success.
- Attitude towards failing and the perceived likelihood (or expectation) of failing.
- Attitude towards the actual process of trying to lose weight.

Each of the above attitudes is measured by assessing the likelihood of various consequences occurring as a result of succeeding, failing, and engaging in the process, weighted by the evaluation of these consequences. For example, the consequences of successfully losing weight might be feeling healthier, looking better, increased self-esteem, reduced risk of diabetes or reduced cardiovascular risk. The consequences of not losing weight might be feeling unhappy, feeling uncomfortable in one's clothes, increased risk of diabetes and heart disease, and so on. Beliefs about the consequences of the process of losing weight might include often feeling hungry, having to go without the foods one really likes, having to avoid restaurants and take-away food, more time in preparation of food and less choice of foods. Each of these beliefs is weighted by an evaluation of these consequences and summed to provide an overall attitude.

An individual's *intention to try* to lose weight will be determined by:

- The individual's overall attitude towards trying to lose weight as assessed above.
- Social norms about trying to lose weight (i.e. beliefs about important others' attitudes towards the individual losing weight).
- The number of times the individual has previously tried to lose weight.

Actually *trying* to lose weight will be determined by:

- The individual's intention to try to lose weight.
- The number of times the individual has previously tried to lose weight.
- The time since the last try.

Bagozzi and Warshaw (1990) showed that their model significantly and substantially predicted trying to lose weight (and was a better predictor than the TPB), although frequency of past trying was not a significant predictor of trying. On the other hand, some quitting studies have shown that frequency of past trying is a significant predictor of attempts to quit and successful quitting.

A major positive about this theory is that it draws attention to the sorts of things people go through in trying to cease an unhealthy behaviour and adopt a healthy one. This suggests that the messages should demonstrate empathy with the target audience and ensure that the intervention accommodates or minimises people's discomforts.

Cognitive dissonance

Many campaigns aim to generate a state of dissonance in the individual, with the recommended behaviour as the means of eliminating this uncomfortable state. Cognitive dissonance occurs when an individual holds beliefs that are inconsistent, or when the individual's actions are inconsistent with their beliefs or values (Festinger, 1957). For example, a politician would experience dissonance if they believed that mandatory sentencing unfairly discriminated against lower socio-economic groups or a particular ethnic group, but their party was introducing such legislation; a smoker would experience dissonance if they believed that smoking affected their pet's health; and an illicit drug user would experience dissonance if they believed that such use was morally wrong.

Dissonance is considered psychologically uncomfortable and anxiety arousing. The degree of dissonance, and hence the degree of discomfort, is a function of how strongly held are the various beliefs. Individuals experiencing dissonance are assumed to be motivated to reduce this dissonance, either by changing beliefs or actions so as to be consistent (e.g. the smoker quits; or the smoker discounts the evidence that smoking causes cancer), or by generating a set of beliefs that overpower the dissonant belief (e.g. the smoker thinks of a large number of positives about smoking so as to convince himself that the benefits outweigh the negatives) (O'Keefe, 1990).

Dissonance tactics are particularly appropriate for interpersonal interactions, such as workshops and lobbying. Similarly, forced behaviour adoption can result in attitude changes to be consistent with the behaviour – as happened in several countries with regard to legislation making wearing seat belts compulsory. On the other hand, in the politician's situation above, if a conscience vote is disallowed, voting for the legislation may lead to a change in beliefs in favour of the legislation.

There has been little published work on the use of this model in health and social marketing. However, it is often implied in the strategy of many campaigns and is useful for understanding psychological processes and complements the more comprehensive attitude/behaviour-change models.

Theory of interpersonal behaviour

Triandis' (1977) theory of interpersonal behaviour (TIB) is similar in many respects to the theory of reasoned action, but has not received much attention outside of psychology and hence little systematic use in health and social marketing.

The TIB includes two concepts of particular interest not included or given little weight in other models: the influence of habit and personal normative beliefs. The inclusion of habit demands that the social marketing practitioner distinguish between 'new' behaviours versus established behaviours, while the concept of personal normative beliefs recognizes that individuals' morals and internalized values are important predictors in addition to *social* norms.

Triandis states that the likelihood of an individual performing a given behaviour is a function of:

- The degree to which the behaviour is already habitual.
- Intentions to perform the behaviour.
- Conditions facilitating or inhibiting carrying out the behaviour.

Intentions in turn are influenced by four elements:

- The individual's anticipated emotional response to performing the behaviour (i.e. pleasure/disliking; bored/interested; etc.).
- A cognitive summing up of the positive and negative consequences of performing the behaviour (cost–benefit analysis).
- Perceived social norms and whether that behaviour is appropriate to the individual's social role(s).
- Felt obligation to perform the behaviour according to the individual's internalised values.

Hence, hospital doctors and nurses could be persuaded to increase their hand washing with antiseptic activity if they had positive expectations – or memories – about the proposed activity; if they considered the benefits outweighed the costs; if social norms reinforced the activity and it was considered appropriate for their age, gender and social status; and if they considered it the right thing to do (Nicol et al., 2009). The inclusion of role beliefs (or self-identity) is a valuable yet little explored concept. However, the concept may be particularly relevant for stimulating community action on environmental and planning issues. It is likely that many people do not take part in advocacy activities because they see these roles as inappropriate for them.

One of the major points from the Triandis model is the drawing of attention to the emotional aspects of the desired behaviour change. The 'truly clean' hand-washing campaign in Ghana targeted mothers in particular to increase hand washing with soap before eating and after toilet use to lessen diarrhoeal diseases in children. The campaign used a mix of media and interpersonal communication channels. Research indicated that 'disgust' via a fear of contamination drove other hygiene behaviours, so the television advertising attempted to associate disgust with unclean hands after toilet use, showing that water alone was not sufficient. The campaign significantly increased self-reported hand washing with soap (Scott et al., 2008).

Behaviour modification (applied behavioural analysis)

Many social marketing campaigns, particularly in road safety and public health, are aimed at *ceasing* or *decreasing undesired* behaviours (e.g., don't drink and drive; don't exceed the speed limit; reduce speed; eat less fat; quit smoking; reduce alcohol consumption; and so on), while others are aimed at *adopting* or *increasing desired* behaviours (e.g. drink reduced-alcohol beer more frequently; use a condom; eat more fruit and vegetables; walk to the bus stop/up the stairs/to the shop; and so on).

The question in many situations therefore is whether the emphasis should be on increasing the desired behaviour or on decreasing the undesired behaviour. For example, for targeting reduced obesity in children, should we focus on reducing the time spent watching TV and playing video games (i.e. reduce inactivity) or focus on increasing the children's level of physical activity? Regardless of the answer, learning theory draws our attention to the fact that different strategies might be more appropriate for decreasing or ceasing a particular behaviour versus increasing or adopting a behaviour. This has significant implications for message strategies in communication materials and for direct behavioural interventions.

Behaviour modification (the terms 'behaviour modification' and 'applied behaviour analysis' are generally interchangeable) is defined as the systematic application of principles derived from learning theory to altering environment–behaviour relationships in order to strengthen adaptive behaviours and weaken maladaptive behaviours (Elder et al., 1994). Behaviour modification is based on the assumption that behaviour is determined by environmental antecedents and consequences. Hence interventions are designed on the 'ABC' model: **a**ntecedents; **b**ehaviour; **c**onsequences (Elder et al., 1994; Geller, 1989)

Table 1.1 delineates two ways of *increasing* a behaviour and two ways of *decreasing* a behaviour. The former are termed *reinforcement* strategies, whereas the latter are termed *punishment* strategies. Table 1.1 is an elaboration of the simple principle that a behaviour followed by a positive outcome will tend to be repeated, whereas a behaviour that attracts a negative outcome will tend to cease. In Table 1.1, the impact on a behaviour is shown to be a function of two binary dimensions: (a) whether the behaviour results in the removal or delivery of a consequence; and (b) whether that consequence is a positive or negative consequence.

The two ways of increasing or reinforcing a behaviour are:

- Positive reinforcement: the behaviour is followed by a pleasant consequence (e.g. group socialising after exercise).
- Negative reinforcement: the behaviour is followed by removal of an unpleasant situation (e.g. headache and tension gone after meditation).

Tables 1.1 Behaviour modification strategies

Consequence type	Procedure following behaviour ...	
	Deliver consequence	Remove consequence
Good/Pleasant	Positive reinforcement (increases behaviour)	Negative punishment (decreases behaviour)
Bad/Unpleasant	Positive punishment (decreases behaviour)	Negative reinforcement (increases behaviour)

The two ways of decreasing or punishing a behaviour are:

- Positive punishment: the behaviour is followed by an unpleasant consequence (e.g. speeding is followed by a fine).
- Negative punishment (or 'response cost'): the behaviour is followed by removal of a pleasant situation (e.g. drunk driving is followed by a loss of licence and hence limitations on mobility and socialising).

Two other processes are also relevant:

- Extinction: a behaviour will decrease and eventually cease (extinguish) if previously applied positive consequences are discontinued or barriers prevent them being obtained. For example, walking may decrease if aesthetic features of the environment are removed or friends are no longer available to walk with; blood-donating behaviour will decline if donors have to visit a central location rather than donating at the worksite.
- Response facilitation: a behaviour will strengthen or re-emerge if a punishment is discontinued. For example, an athlete may revert to using performance-enhancing drugs when the level of random testing is reduced; speeding behaviour returns after speed camera use declines.

In designing interventions, formative research is necessary to determine the appropriate reinforcers and punishments for the various target groups. Some people may be motivated primarily by social recognition rewards, others by financial incentives, and others by gifts. Young males fear the loss of their driving licence more than the threat of physical harm to themselves, and the GutBusters® programme for men emphasized the 'looking good' benefit of weight loss and increased physical activity rather than health benefits.

Feedback on positive results, such as number of accident-free days in a workplace, is an important reinforcer. Advocates should remember that as well as writing to politicians and policymakers whom they wish to persuade, they should also write to those already onside, with reinforcing messages thanking them for their support.

Another lesson from behaviour modification is to identify the reinforcers of the behaviours we wish to reduce or eliminate. Such an understanding is liable to lead to more sustained change if attempts are then made to either substitute benign reinforcers or take away the need for the reinforcers in the first place. For example, much alcohol and drug abuse is related to escaping from reality. Hence, interventions making reality more tolerable, or indeed enjoyable, are required.

Conditional cash incentives to the poor, in several countries, have resulted in positive health outcomes – especially for children. Kane et al. (2004) analysed 47 trials of cash incentives for preventive health behaviours such as immunization, cancer screening, condom purchase, education session attendance, prenatal care, weight loss and tuberculosis screening. They found that these incentives were generally successful in that they worked for around 73% of the cases studied. However, there are some ethical and sustainability issues around offering financial incentives, and there are clearly problems in determining how much the incentive should be and for how long it should be paid.

Most of the above deals with the behaviour–consequence link. Interventions can also facilitate the desired behavioural response by looking at the antecedent–behaviour link:

- Environments should be designed to make the behaviour change easy, such as worksite exercise rooms and showers; smaller plates in restaurants to limit food portions.
- Reminder signs can be very effective. A 'take the stairs' sign placed near a elevator increased use of the stairs dramatically; 'belt up' signs at car park exits increase seat-belt use; nutrition information on menus increases healthy food selections.
- Opinion leaders, experts and celebrities can be used to demonstrate the behaviour or wear clothing promoting the behaviour.

- Target individuals can be encouraged to make public commitments to adopt the desired behaviour.
- Educational materials with behavioural tips are also useful; quitting smokers are encouraged to identify environmental cues that trigger smoking and to remove them.
- Education sessions should include interactive demonstrations rather than just passive lecturing (*'Tell them and they'll forget – Demonstrate and they'll remember – Involve them and they'll understand'*).

Much of the above can be termed 'choice architecture', introduced in the book *Nudge* (Thaler and Sunstein, 2008). The premise of the book is that the environment can be designed to reduce opportunities for 'bad' choices and to 'nudge' people into desirable choices while retaining 'freedom of choice'. While this concept is hardly novel, the book reminds us that we can extend these ideas into better decision making in neglected economic areas such as savings plans, insurance and retirement planning decisions.

Morality and legitimacy

Morality refers to the individual's beliefs about whether certain actions are 'right or wrong', or whether they 'should or should not' take that action. Legitimacy refers to individuals' beliefs about whether laws are justified, whether these laws are applied equally and whether punishments for transgressions are fair (Tyler, 1990, 1997). The concept of legitimacy applies not only to judicial legislation but also to rules, regulations and policies of organisations. In general, people are more likely to obey rules that they believe are justified and that are enforced in a fair and unbiased manner.

With some reflection, and given the use of 'laws' to regulate and influence behaviour, both concepts clearly have considerable relevance in some areas of social marketing. However, they have been largely neglected in social change models, and particularly in public health research and intervention strategies. This neglect is surprising given the historical links between health and (religious) morality (Thomas, 1997), and the fact that Fishbein's theory of reasoned action originally included the concept of moral or personal norms. Triandis' model included personal normative beliefs, but, as mentioned above, his model has attracted limited attention in health and social interventions. Furthermore, legislation is widely used to regulate a broad range of activities, such as driving behaviours, under-age alcohol and tobacco consumption, drug use, land degradation and toxic waste disposal, lighting fires in forests, littering behaviour, physical abuse, child abuse and neglect and so on.

Hence, it is important to assess people's perceived legitimacy of the laws and the authorities behind the laws in these areas. In fact, crime prevention is one area where public health and anti-violence professionals are beginning to come together (WHO, 2002) and some social marketers are also taking an interest (e.g. Hastings et al., 2002). Criminologists have been developing conceptual frameworks in these areas, with striking similarities to concepts in cognitive decision models, as described in this chapter (e.g. Vila, 1994).

Norman and Connor (1996) found only a few studies that incorporated measures of moral norms within the public health domain. Such studies include explaining altruism and helping behaviour such as donating blood and intentions to donate organs. Other studies have found measures of moral norms to be predictive of recycling behaviour, eating genetically produced food, buying milk, using condoms and committing driving violations (see Donovan and Henley, 2010).

Other than road safety and doping in sport (Donovan et al., 2002; Donovan, 2009), few public health and public policy campaigns have considered the use of moral or legitimacy appeals. Road safety campaigns have emphasised that drinking and driving is a danger to others and hence morally unacceptable. Legitimacy has also been part of road safety campaigns. For example, 'Buckle Up. It's the Law' in the USA appeals directly to compliance because it is a legal requirement, while the UK's 'It's 30 for a reason' can be seen as an attempt to increase people's perceived justification (legitimacy) for that speed limit in built-up areas.

An interesting study in light of 'situational prompts' noted elsewhere in this chapter is that of Shu et al.'s (2009) studies of choices in ethical-dilemma-type scenarios where subjects had the opportunity to carry out an unethical behaviour undetected. They found that many people almost unthinkingly chose the unethical behaviour. However, they also found that increasing moral salience by simply having people read or sign an honour code significantly reduced or eliminated unethical behaviour.

CHANGE MODELS

The transtheoretical stages of change model

The transtheoretical model (TTM) of behaviour change derives from Prochaska's clinical work with cigarette and drug addiction (Prochaska and DiClemente, 1984, 1986). This model now forms the fundamental basis of some social marketing frameworks (Andreasen, 1995).

The stages-of-change concept not only delineates the stages an individual goes through during a behaviour change but also is used to divide the target population (e.g. smokers, non-exercisers, coercive parents, men who use violence, drug users) into sub-segments depending on their stage in progression towards adoption of the desired behaviour (i.e. quitting; taking up exercise, using positive parenting practices, ceasing violent behaviour, stopping drug use) (see Prochaska et al., 2005, 2007).

The stages are:

1. **Precontemplation** – where the individual is not considering modifying their undesired behaviour.
2. **Contemplation** – where the individual is considering changing an undesired behaviour, but not in the immediate future.
3. **Preparation** – where the individual plans to try to change the undesired behaviour in the immediate future (i.e. in the next two weeks or an appropriate time frame).
4. **Action** – the immediate (six-month) period following trial and adoption of the recommended behaviour and cessation of the undesired behaviour.
5. **Maintenance** – the period following the action stage until the undesired behaviour is fully extinguished.
6. **Termination** – when the problem behaviour is completely eliminated, that is, 'zero temptation across all problem situations'.

It is claimed that individuals at different stages of change would have different attitudes, beliefs and motivations with respect to the (desired) new behaviour, and hence different treatment approaches and communication strategies may be necessary for individuals in the different stages of change. There is some support for these claims over a variety of areas, but particularly smoking, nutrition and exercise (de Vet et al., 2008; Oman and King, 1998; Spencer et al., 2006). Donovan and Henley (2010) report that the model has also been applied across a variety of countries and subgroups, including the UK, African-American and Hispanic sub-populations in the USA, Holland, Sweden, Spain and 15 European Union states.

Prochaska et al. (1994) describe nine activities or processes of change that individuals use to proceed through the stages of change:

• Consciousness raising – increasing awareness about the problem.

• Emotional arousal – dramatic expressions of the problem and consequences.
• Self-re-evaluation – reappraisal of the problem and its inconsistency with self-values.
• Commitment – choosing to change and making a public commitment to do so.
• Social liberation – choosing social environments that foster or facilitate change.
• Relationship fostering – getting help from others, professional or otherwise.
• Counter-conditioning – substituting alternatives.
• Reward – administering self-praise or other positive experiences for dealing with the problem.
• Environmental control – restructuring of the environment to reduce temptations and opportunities.

The processes at the top of the list are experiential, whereas those lower in the list are behavioural. The former occur more in the earlier stages of change, the latter in the later stages. The TTM also incorporates the notion of decisional balance: that an evaluation of the costs (cons) and benefits (pros) of making the change varies over the stages, with cons outweighing pros in precontemplation, pros outweighing cons in the action stage, with crossing over occurring during contemplation.

Donovan et al. (1999) tested three anti-smoking ads and analysed the results for precontemplators, contemplators and those in the ready-for-action and action stages. Figure 1.1 shows a significant relationship between the stages of change and the ads' impact on intentions to quit or cut down the amount smoked. These results confirm that smokers in the different stages of change react quite differently to anti-smoking communications.

The stages-of-change concept is similar to marketing's 'buyer-readiness' concept, which states that, at any particular point in time, the market can be described in terms of those unaware

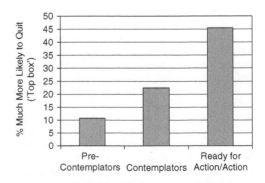

Figure 1.1   Impact of quit ads on likelihood of quitting or cutting down by smokers' stage of change (from Donovan et al 1999)

of the product, those aware of the product, those informed about the product, those interested in the product, those motivated to buy the product and those who have formed an intention to buy the product (Kotler, 1988) (the AIDA model: awareness; interest; desire; action). The implications of this are that marketing objectives and strategy will vary according to the relative proportions of the total market in each of these different stages.

The stages-of-change concept is widely used but perhaps not always properly understood, especially with regard to the various processes applicable to each of the stages (Whitelaw et al., 1999). Nevertheless, regardless of whether one adopts Prochaska's recommended intervention processes for the various stages, the model is very useful as a segmentation method for recruiting subsamples for formative research and for targeting in those areas most related to addictive behaviours from whence it was derived. Furthermore, regardless of the finer points of these models, the concept of 'buyer readiness' or 'readiness to change' is a useful one in a practical sense. The Western Australian' Freedom From Fear' domestic violence campaign targets 'men who are aware of their problem with violence and want to change'. In stages terminology, that means violent men in the contemplator and ready-for-action stages (Donovan et al., 2000). In fact, the booklet for men explicitly states on the cover: 'For men who want to change'.

Stages of change for public opinion

At a broader level, the much respected public opinion tracker Daniel Yankelovich (1992 has delineated seven stages of public opinion change. Yankelovich's seven stages are:

1. **Dawning awareness**: this is when people first begin to become aware of an issue, usually through mass-media news reports.
2. **A sense of urgency**: people move from simple awareness of an issue to developing a sense of urgency about needing to form an opinion about it.
3. **Discovering the choices**: people start to explore choices and look at the pros and cons about the issue, although there is widespread variation in the population in depth of understanding.
4. **Resistance**: at this stage many people – through misunderstanding (or wishful thinking) – tend to opt for easy options rather than look more closely at benefits and trade-offs.
5. **Weighing the choices**: in this stage, people more rationally and realistically weigh the pros and cons of alternatives.

6. **Taking a stand intellectually**: at this stage, many people endorse an option in theory but do not necessarily make any personal behavioural changes (as where people accept the need for carbon emission controls but do little about their behaviours).
7. **Making a responsible judgement morally and emotionally**: in the final stage, people not only endorse an option but also accept the full implications of that option and modify their own behaviours to be consistent with that option.

Yankelovich's model is particularly useful for those planning advocacy campaigns based on mobilising public opinion.

Community readiness model

Another useful model, particularly for community-based interventions in developing countries or remote/rural communities in developed countries, is the community readiness model (Kelly et al., 2003). This model – as its name suggests – is concerned with the stages a community must go through to be ready for an intervention, rather than the stages of progression after an intervention occurs. The model first looks at factors such as the community's current knowledge, actions and attitudes towards the issue in question, leadership in the community and community resources. It then delineates nine stages from 'no awareness' through various stages of denial, pre-planning, preparation and training, through to implementation of the intervention with 'high level of community ownership'.

Diffusion theory

Everett Rogers first published his book *Diffusion of Innovations* in 1962. The concept has been readily adopted in commercial marketing (to predict new product adoption) and is widely used to explain the adoption of public health and agricultural processes, in particular, in developing countries. However, it is only in the past 15 years or so that it has attracted much attention in the public health area in developed countries. The general concept no doubt also received an impetus from Gladwell's (2000) book *The Tipping Point*.

Rogers (1983; 1995) defines 'diffusion' as the process by which an innovation is communicated through certain channels over time among the members of a social system. Diffusion theory applies to both planned and unplanned diffusions, and to both desirable and undesirable innovations (e.g. the rapid adoption of the cocaine variant 'crack' in the USA).

Many innovations 'take off' at about the 20% adoption mark, when, according to Rogers (1995), interpersonal networks become activated so that a critical mass of adopters begins using an innovation. From the social marketing practitioner's point of view, one of the major issues is how the rate of adoption of the new idea, product or behaviour can be accelerated. This can be assessed via an analysis of each of the four main elements in diffusion: the innovation, communication channels, time and the social system.

The innovation

An innovation is an idea, product or practice that is perceived as new by the adopting population; that is, it need not be objectively 'new'. The attributes of the innovation that influence its rate of adoption are:

- *Relative advantage.* If the new product or practice is clearly seen to be 'better' than the old, then it will be adopted more readily. Relative advantage can be assessed in a variety of ways, including convenience, economy, prestige and time. Email is much faster than postal mail; automated garbage trucks are perceived to be more economical than manned trucks.
- *Compatibility.* The more the new product or practice is consistent with current values and past experiences, the more readily it will be adopted. Family planning and STD prevention practices face a barrier in countries where cultural and religious values are opposed to these practices. Automated teller machines are incompatible with many people's desire for interpersonal interactions.
- *Complexity.* New practices and ideas that are easy to understand are more readily adopted than those difficult to understand or that require special skills and training. User-friendly software was a major factor in the rates of adoption of office and home computers and the new social media.
- *Trialability.* Being able to trial a new product or practice reduces the risk of the new product not delivering the promised benefits and allows the adopter to learn about the innovation before adoption. New grains can be trialled in limited agricultural plots. Copy machines were initially placed in offices and the owners were charged on a per-copy basis. The more a product or practice can be trialled before 'purchase', the greater the rate of adoption.
- *Observability.* The more the innovation and its results are publicly visible, the greater the rate of adoption. Observability provides greater exposure as well as stimulating social discussion. Mobile phone adoption was clearly helped by visibility of use – and clear demonstration of effectiveness in communication.

Communication channels

Rogers (1995) suggests that mass media channels are the most effective way of creating awareness for a new idea, product or practice, whereas interpersonal channels are the most effective way of getting the target audience to accept and adopt the new idea. Rogers states that a major impediment to most planned social diffusions is that the change agent and the target are quite dissimilar ('heterophilus'). Tupperware's use of party hosts to sell products to their friends is a very good example of acknowledging that persuasion occurs best between people of similar interests. The importance of interpersonal networks in the diffusion process is one of the most important concepts of the diffusion process, and hence for community development interventions.

Time

Time can be noted on an individual basis in the sense of the time taken to move from awareness, through persuasion, to decision, and adoption. Some decision processes are relatively brief, while others may take several months.

Time also can be considered in the sense of some people adopting the innovation soon after its introduction (early adopters), while others adopt only after the vast majority have adopted ('laggards'). In general, five groups are noted: innovators (the first 2–3%); early adopters (the next 10–15%); the early majority (the next 30–33%); the late majority (the next 30–33%) and the laggards (the final 17–20%). Effort expended on identifying the innovators and early adopters can result in a more efficiently planned diffusion.

The social system

The social structure also influences the rate of adoption. Variables here include: the extent to which communication channels exist; the presence or absence of strong opinion leaders; the prevailing social norms and their variation between parts of the system; whether the adoption decision is an individual one or must involve collective decision-making, or a single authority's decision; and whether adoption of the innovation has desirable and undesirable consequences, not only for the individual but also for the social system as a whole. Rudd (2003) analyses how health policies diffuse through to general practice, given the nature of general practice and the attitudes and beliefs of general practitioners about their role in the health system. Social system factors appear particularly important in developing countries (McKee, 1992), and, for example, in Indigenous communities in Australia.

Social ecology

The theory of social ecology in health promotion is another example of the shift from the downstream, individual-focused, lifestyle modification approach to a broader understanding of health protective factors. Stokols (1996) advocated the theory of social ecology as one of three complementary perspectives on health promotion:

- Targeting the individual with behaviour change recommendations relating to lifestyle issues such as smoking, substance use, diet, exercise and safety.
- Changing the environment to maximise health protective factors by creating a safe place, free from contagious disease and unhealthy levels of stress (caused by environmental factors such as pollution, racism or violence), in which healthy behaviours are actively facilitated and where people have access to health care.
- Social ecological analyses that attempt to understand the interplay between the environment and the individual, emphasising the interdependence of multiple environments and the contributions of many, diverse disciplines.

Thus, while the individual behaviour change approach may be concerned with persuasion theories and health communication, and the environmental change approach may consider urban planning and injury control, the social ecological approach focuses on aspects such as cultural change models of health, medical sociology, community health and public policy (Stokols, 1996). The major contribution of the social ecological approach is that it provides a systems framework within which behavioural and environmental factors can be integrated, thereby eliminating the claimed 'blind spots' inherent in focusing on either the individual or the environmental approach. A typical ecological health evaluation involves different levels of analysis and multiple methodologies, from individual medical examinations to environmental assessments to epidemiological analyses.

Cohen et al. (2000) provide a useful framework based on ecological theory. They postulate four categories of structural factors that influence individuals' behaviours: the availability of protective or harmful consumer products (e.g. tobacco; alcohol; guns; fatty foods; condoms; fruit and vegetables); physical structures and physical characteristics of products (e.g. buildings; neighbourhood design; lighting; seat belts; childproof medicine containers); social structures and policies (e.g. strict vs lax enforcement of laws and policies; unsupervised youth; social norms); and media and cultural messages (e.g. advertising messages re materialism; depictions of violence, racism, etc.). Hence, with regard to firearms in the USA, there is relatively easy availability, fear and perceived likelihood of crime facilitate purchasing, safety locks can make guns safer while other modifications make them more lethal, and television shows and movies suggest that guns are a good – and normative – way to resolve conflicts.

SYNTHESISING THE MODELS

Behavioural scientists have now generally come to the following set of principles with respect to an individual performing a recommended behaviour.

- The individual must have formed an intention to perform the behaviour or made a (public) commitment to do so.
- There are no physical or structural environmental constraints that prevent the behaviour being performed.
- The individual has the skills and equipment necessary to perform the behaviour.
- Individuals perceive themselves to be capable of performing the behaviour.
- The individual considers that the benefits/rewards of performing the behaviour outweigh the costs/disbenefits associated with performing the behaviour, including the rewards associated with *not* performing the behaviour (i.e. a positive attitude towards performing the behaviour).
- Social normative pressure to perform the behaviour is perceived to be greater than social normative pressure not to perform the behaviour.
- Individuals perceive the behaviour to be consistent with their self-image and internalised values (i.e. morally acceptable).
- Individuals perceive the behaviour to be consistent with their social roles.
- The individual's emotional reaction (or expectation) in performing the behaviour is more positive than negative.

Hence, if a violent man has formed a strong intention to call a helpline about his violence, if a telephone is easily accessible, and if the call can be made in private and with assured confidentiality, it is likely that the behaviour will occur. The remainder of the above variables primarily influence intention or facilitate/inhibit translating the intention into action.

Overall, it is clear that many of the above models, particularly the KAB models, have similar concepts, but that no one model includes all relevant concepts. Therefore, a pragmatic, eclectic approach is advocated in practice, selecting concepts from each of the models depending on which are more or less applicable to the behaviour in question. For example, Donovan and Henley (2010) suggest the following questions need answering to develop appropriate interventions for an adult at risk of type 2 diabetes:

1. What is the individual's perceived likelihood of contracting diabetes, given no change in his current behaviour?
   What beliefs or perceptions underlie this perceived likelihood?
   If the perceived likelihood is unrealistically low, what sort of information, presented in what way, and by whom, might increase this likelihood?
   What is their knowledge of the causes of diabetes?
2. What is the individual's perceived severity of contracting diabetes?
   Is this realistic? If not, what sort of information, presented in what way and by whom might change this perception?
3. What is the individual's attitude toward adopting the recommended alternative behaviours such as a change in diet or adoption of exercise?
   Are some behaviours more acceptable than others? Why?
   What are the perceived benefits of continuing the risk behaviours?
   What are the perceived benefits and the disbenefits of the alternative behaviours?
   What social and physical environment barriers inhibit adoption of the recommended dietary and exercise behaviours? What facilitators exist?
4. What is the individual's perceived likelihood of averting the threat if the recommended behaviours are adopted?
   If this is low, on what beliefs is this perception based? What information might change this perception?
5. What are the individual's beliefs about their ability to adopt the recommended behaviours?
   On what beliefs are these efficacy perceptions based?
   Is skills training required?

What intermediate goals can be set to induce trial?
6. What appear to be the major motivations that would induce trial of the recommended behaviours?
   Are positive benefits (e.g. feelings of wellness, increased capacity for physical activity) more motivating than negative benefits (e.g. avoidance of disease) for some individuals or groups, and vice versa for others?
7. What are the individual's main sources of information and advice for health?
   Who are their major influencers?
8. How do the individual's social interactions, including his extended family, club memberships, employment and home-care role influence his health beliefs and behaviours?
9. Does the individual exhibit any personality characteristics that might inhibit or facilitate the adoption of healthy behaviours?
10. What are the individual's perceptions of social norms with regard to the recommended behaviours?
    Who are their relevant reference groups and their relative influence?
    Does the individual see the recommended behaviours as compatible with their social roles and self-image?
11. What are the individual's perceptions of the morality of non-compliance with the recommended behaviour and consistency with internalized values?
12. What are medical practitioners' and other primary healthcare workers' knowledge of diabetes risk factors and their willingness to undertake preventative measures with patients exhibiting these risk factors?
13. What factors exist in the individual's social, economic, work and physical environment that facilitate and inhibit attendance at diabetes screening?
14. What factors exist in the individual's social, economic, work and physical environment that facilitate and inhibit healthy eating and exercise habits?
15. What are health bureaucrats' knowledge of diabetes and their attitudes towards allocating funds to prevention?

CONCLUSION

As the above questions show, the models described in this chapter apply to an individual's beliefs and attitudes about the risky or unhealthy behaviours in question, as well as to their beliefs and attitudes about broader environmental influences related to those behaviours. The last five questions are a reminder that these models are useful not only for developing campaigns targeting individuals to promote adoption or maintenance of desired behaviours and cessation of undesired behaviours but also for developing advocacy campaigns targeting policymakers and legislators to introduce policies, regulations and legislation that will not only remove barriers to, but provide conditions that facilitate the adoption of, desired behaviours by individuals. For example, if a politician is shown survey evidence that her constituents are overwhelmingly in favour of reduced liquor outlet hours, if she is aware of considerable media publicity supporting such a move, if she is experienced at tabling motions at party and committee meetings, and if she is personally aware of the effects of excess alcohol consumption due to extended trading hours, then it is likely that she will comply with an advocacy group's request to have the issue of liquor outlet trading hours included on the agenda of her party's next meeting. The key is to carry out appropriate additional research in advocacy areas to identify the beliefs, attitudes and skills relevant to political behaviours. It may well be that a 'new' model, or, more likely, an existing model with 'new' additional concepts would result from such an effort.

It has been suggested that some of these models might be more or less appropriate for different behaviours, and that this could be a fruitful area for future research. However, this author recommends an eclectic approach, as indicated in the above synthesis of the models. It is considered that a more fruitful area for research is not so much about which model best explains a particular phenomenon, but what concepts from all or any of the models are more or less relevant to particular phenomena. Related to that approach, is that future research could also attempt to identify new (or abandoned) concepts (such as morality and legitimacy) that would enhance the predictability of attitudes and behaviours in particular domains. It is likely that monitoring the development and use of models in areas such as criminology, consumer behaviour, political science, social geography and sociology could be beneficial in this regard.

KEY WORDS: Theory; behaviour change models; persuasion; attitudes; morality and health behaviour.

Key insights

- Theory informs practice – and practice informs theory.
- Theoretical models guide formative research, intervention design and evaluation.
- Evaluation guides intervention modification and model refinement.
- No one model explains all behaviours or the same behaviour for all individuals. Be eclectic. Use concepts from all the models.
- The environment is crucial. Homicide detectives ask themselves the following: Did the suspect have a motive? Did the suspect have the means? And, most importantly, did the suspect have the opportunity?

REFERENCES

Ajzen, I. (1988) *Attitudes, Personality, and Behavior.* Chicago, IL: The Dorsey Press.

Andreasen, A. (1995) *Marketing Social Change: Changing Behavior to Promote Health, Social Development, and the Environment.* San Francisco, CA: Jossey-Bass Publishers.

Bagozzi, R.P. and Warshaw, P.R. (1990) 'Trying to consume', *Journal of Consumer Research,* 17: 127–140.

Bandura, A. (1977) *Social Learning Theory.* Englewood Cliffs, NJ: Prentice-Hall.

Bandura, A. (1986) *Social Foundations of Thought & Action: A Social Cognitive Theory.* Englewood Cliffs, NJ: Prentice-Hall.

Becker, M.H. (1974) 'The health belief model and personal health behaviour', *Health Education Monographs,* 2: 324–473.

Booth-Butterfield, S. and Reger, B. (2004) 'The message changes belief and the rest is theory: the "1% or less" milk campaign and reasoned action', *Preventive Medicine,* 39(3): 581–588.

Cohen, D., Scribner, R., and Farley, T. (2000) 'A structural model of health behavior: a pragmatic approach to explain and influence health behaviors at the population level', *Preventative Medicine,* 30(2): 146–154.

Darnton, A. (2008) Reference report: an overview of behaviour change models and their uses. GSR: Government Social Research.

de Vet, E., de Nooijer, J., de Vries, N. and Brug, J. (2008) 'Testing the transtheoretical model for fruit intake: comparing web-based tailored stage-matched and stage-mismatched feedback', *Health Education Research,* 23(2): 218–227.

Donovan, R.J. (2009) 'Towards an understanding of factors influencing athletes' attitudes towards performance-enhancing technologies: implications for ethics education', in T.H. Murray, K.J. Maschke and P. Wasunna (eds), *Enhancing Technologies in Sport: Ethical, Conceptual and Scientific Issues.* Baltimore, MD: The Johns Hopkins University Press.

Donovan, R.J. and Henley, N. (2010) *Social Marketing: An International Perspective.* Cambridge: Cambridge University Press.

Donovan, R.J., Leivers, S. and Hannaby, L. (1999) 'Smokers' responses to anti-smoking advertisements by stage of change', *Social Marketing Quarterly,* 5(2): 56–63.

Donovan, R.J., Francas, M., Paterson, D. and Zappelli, R. (2000) 'Formative research for mass media-based campaigns: Western Australia's 'Freedom From Fear' campaign targeting male perpetrators of intimate partner violence', *Health Promotion Journal of Australia*, 10(2), 78–83.

Donovan, R.J., Egger, G., Kapernick, V. and Mendoza, J. A. (2002). 'A conceptual framework for achieving drug compliance in sport', *Sports Medicine*, 32(4): 269–284.

Elder, J.P., Geller, E.S., Hovell, M.F. and Mayer, J.A. (1994) *Motivating Health Behaviour*. New York: Delmar.

Festinger, L. (1957) *A Theory of Cognitive Dissonance*. Stanford, CA: Stanford University Press.

Fishbein, M. and Ajzen, I. (1975) *Belief, Attitude, Intention and Behaviour: an Introduction to Theory and Research*. Reading, MA: Addison-Wesley.

Geller, E.S. (1989) 'Applied behavior analysis and social marketing: an integration for environmental preservation', *Journal of Social Issues*, 45: 17–36.

Gladwell, M. (2000) *The Tipping Point: How Little Things can Make a Big Difference*. London: Little Brown & Company.

Godin, G. (1994) 'Social cognitive models', in R.K. Dishman (ed.), *Advances in Exercise Adherence*, 2nd edn. Champaign, IL: Human Kinetics, pp. 113–136.

Hastings, G., Stead, M. and MacFadyen, L. (2002) 'Reducing prison numbers: does marketing hold the key? ' *Criminal Justice Matters*, 49: 20–25.

Kane, R.L., Johnson, P.E., Town, R.J. and Butler, M. (2004) 'A structured review of the effect of economic incentives on consumers' preventive behavior', *American Journal of Preventive Medicine*, 27(4): 327–352.

Kelly, K.J., Edwards, W., Comello, M., et al. (2003) 'The Community Readiness Model: a complementary approach to social marketing', *Marketing Theory*, 3(4): 411–426.

Kotler, P. (1988) *Marketing Management: Analysis, Planning, Implementation and Ccontrol*. Englewood Cliffs, NJ: Prentice-Hall.

Lucidi, F., Zelli, A., Mallia, L., et al. (2008) 'The social-coginitive mechanism regulating adolescents' use of doping substances', *Journal of Sports Sciences*, 26: 447–456.

McKee, N. (1992) *Social Mobilisation and Social Marketing*. Pennang, Malaysia: Southbound.

Nicol, P.W., Watkins, R.E., Donovan, R.J., Wynaden, D. and Cadwallader, H. (2009) 'The power of vivid experience in hand hygiene compliance', *Journal of Infection Control*, 72: 36–42.

Norman, P. and Connor, M. (1996) 'The role of social cognition models in predicting health behaviours: future directions', in M. Conner, and P. Norman (eds), *Predicting Health Behaviour*. Buckingham: Open University Press, pp. 197–225.

O'Keefe, D.J. (1990) *Persuasion: Theory and Research*. San Francisco, CA: Sage Publications.

Okin, G., Sangster, V., Thurner, R. and Adam, F. (2009) 'CABWISE: creating a brand to help prevent rapes', in N. Dawson (ed), *Advertising Works 17: Proving the Payback on Marketing Investment*. Henley-on-Thames: World Advertising Research Centre.

Oman, R.F. and King, A.C. (1998) 'Predicting the adoption and maintenance of exercise participation using self-efficacy and previous exercise participation rates', *American Journal of Health Promotion*, 12(3): 154–161.

Prochaska, J.O. and DiClemente, C.C. (1984) *The Transtheoretical Approach: Crossing the Traditional Boundaries of Therapy*. Homewood, IL: Dow-Jones/Irwin.

Prochaska, J.O. and DiClemente, C.C. (1986) 'Toward a comprehensive model of change', in W.R. Miller, and N. Heather (eds), *Treating Addictive Behaviours: Processes of Change*. New York: Plenum Press.

Prochaska, J.O., Norcross, J.C. and DiClemente, C.C. (1994) *Changing for Good*. New York: Avon Books.

Prochaska, J.O., Velicer, W.F., Redding, C., et al. (2005) 'Stage-based expert systems to guide a population of primary care patients to quit smoking, eat healthier, prevent skin cancer, and receive regular mammograms', *Preventive Medicine*, 41: 406–416.

Prochaska J.O., Evers K.E., Prochaska J.M., Van Marter, D. and Johnson J.L. (2007) 'Efficacy and effectiveness trials: examples from smoking cessation and bullying prevention', *Journal of Health Psychology*, 12: 170–178.

Rogers, R.W. (1975) 'A protection motivation theory of fear appeals and attitude change', *Journal of Psychology*, 91: 93–114.

Rogers, R.W. (1983) 'Cognitive and physiological process in fear appeals and attitude change: a revised theory of protection motivation', in J. Cacioppo, and R. Petty (eds), *Social Psychophysiology*. New York: Guilford Press.

Rogers, E.M. (1995) *Diffusion of Innovations*, 4th edn. New York: The Free Press.

Rosenstock, I.M. (1974) 'Historical models of the health belief model', in M.H. Becker and N.J. Thorofare (eds), *The Health Belief model and Personal Health Behavior*. Thorofare, NJ: Charles B. Slack.

Rosenstock, I., Strecher, V. and Becker, M. (1988) 'Social learning theory and the health belief model', *Health Education Quarterly*, 15: 175–183.

Rudd, C. (2003) 'Merging general practice-driven reforms and public sector strategies in the 1990s: a framework for health policy', Unpublished doctoral dissertation, University of Western Australia, Perth.

Scott, B.E., Schmidt, W.P., Aunger, R., Garbrah-Aidoo, N. and Animashaun, R. (2008) 'Marketing hygiene behaviours: the impact of different communication channels on reported handwashing behaviour of women in Ghana', *Health Education Research*, 23(3): 392–401.

Shu, L.L., Gino, F. and Bazerman, M.H. (2009) *Dishonest Deed, Clear Conscience: Self-Preservation through Moral Disengagement and Motivated Forgetting (Working Paper)*, Boston, MA: Harvard Business School.

Singhal, A., Cody, M.J., Rogers, E.M. and Sabido, M. (eds) (2004) *Entertainment-Education and Social Change: History, Research, and Practice*. Hillsdale, NJ: Lawrence Erlbaum.

Spencer, L., Adams, T.B., Malone, S., Roy, L. and Yost, E. (2006) 'Applying the transtheoretical model to exercise: a systematic and comprehensive review of the literature', *Health Promotion Practice*, 7(4): 428–443.

Squires, S. (2005) To lose well, think positive. *The Washington Post*, p. HE01. Retrieved 23 March, 2005, from: http://www.washingtonpost.com/wp-dyn/articles/A55828-2005Mar22.html.

Stokols, D. (1996) 'Translating social ecological theory into guidelines for community health promotion', *American Journal of Health Promotion*, 10(4): 282–298.

Thaler, R. and Sunstein, C. (2008) *Nudge: Improving Decisions about Health, Wealth, and Happiness*. New York: Yale University Press.

Thomas, K. (1997) 'Health and morality in early modern England', in A.M. Brandt, and P. Rozin (eds), *Morality and Health*. New York: Routledge, pp. 15–34.

Triandis, H.C. (1977) *Interpersonal Behavior*. Monterey, CA: Brooks/Cole Publishing Company.

Tyler, T.R. (1990) *Why People Obey the Law*. New Haven, CT: Yale University Press.

Tyler, T.R. (1997) 'Misconceptions about why people obey laws and accept judicial decisions', *American Psychological Society Observer*, September: 12–46.

Vila, B. (1994). 'A general paradigm for understanding criminal behavior: extending evolutionary ecological theory', *Criminology*, 32: 311–360.

Webb, T. and Sheeran, P. (2006) 'Does changing behavioral intentions engender behavior change? A meta-analysis of the experimental evidence', *Psychological Bulletin*, 132(2): 249–268.

Whitelaw, S., MacHardy, L., Reid, W., and Duffy, M. (1999) 'The stages of change model and its use in health promotion: a critical review', *Health Education Board of Scotland Research Centre*.

WHO (2002) *World Report on Violence and Health: Summary*. Geneva: World Health Organization.

Yankelovich, D. (1992) 'How public opinion really works', *Fortune*, 126(7): 102–105.

2

Social Models for Social Marketing: Social Diffusion, Social Networks, Social Capital, Social Determinants and Social Franchising

R . C r a i g L e f e b v r e

Despite early calls for social marketing to be concerned with social and population-based behavior change (Kotler and Zaltman, 1971; Lefebvre and Flora, 1988; Walsh et al., 1993), many definitions of social marketing that emerged over the next two decades have promoted a variation of the theme 'individual behavior change for the common good' (cf. Andreasen, 1995; Kotler and Lee, 2008; Siegel and Lotenberg, 2007). This perspective on social marketing has led to the adoption of a variety of behavior change theories to guide social marketing programs, most notably the transtheoretical stages of change model, social cognitive theory, the health belief model and the theory of reasoned action (Lefebvre, 2001). More recently, Hastings (2007) has embraced the notion of social marketing as a way to enhance social goals and also to analyze the social consequences of marketing policies, decisions and activities. Similarly, Donovan and Henley (2003) take issue with the prevailing individually focused frames for change in social marketing and call for a focus on social determinants seeing 'the primary future goal of

social marketing as achieving changes in these social determinants of health and well-being' (p. 6). In this chapter we share this perspective on looking beyond the individual. What we explore in this chapter is the need to incorporate more social perspectives into social marketing. Among the more salient social models we cover are social diffusion, social networks, social determinants, social capital, building communities and social franchising. We end with a look forward for how social marketing can become an important lever in the arena of social policy development and implementation.

SOCIAL DETERMINANTS

For many years, some social marketers were haunted by the idea that they 'did not go upstream' – that is, they focused on individual actions and responsibilities and did not consider, or target, social determinants of behavior (though the charge had been leveled more generally against health educators; Crawford, 1977). The focus on individual behaviors and determinants was attacked by some as 'victim-blaming' who then proposed upstream approaches that focused on structural, economic, policy and social determinants such as media advocacy as an alternative to social marketing (Wallack, 1990). Only recently have some social marketers finally changed their frame of reference to accommodate this broader view of social determinants and health (cf. Andreasen, 2006). Other researchers have documented how the social marketing approach can enhance the understanding of social forces from the audience point of view and can be used as a tool to foster citizen participation in community-based planning for health promotion (Higgins et al., 1999).

This shift of social marketing to focus on social determinants must be accelerated. The recent World Health Organization (WHO) Commission on Social Determinants of Health (2008) called for:

> ... the WHO and all governments to lead global action on the social determinants of health with the aim of achieving health equity. It is essential that governments, civil society, WHO, and other global organizations now come together in taking action to improve the lives of the world's citizens. Achieving health equity within a generation is achievable, it is the right thing to do, and now is the right time to do it.

Various authors and governments offer lists of what are these social determinants (see Table 2.1 for examples). Our point here is to call attention to the role social marketing can play not only in addressing social determinants but also in making the ideas relevant to various groups of people. For example, shifting the perspective of public health policymakers, researchers and practitioners from genetic, biologic and behavioral determinants to physical environment and social ones will be one set of challenges. An equally important group of questions will focus on how to communicate about social determinants with the public in ways that make it relevant to them and offer opportunities to improve their own health. After decades of public health messages and programs that have focused on individual knowledge, attitudes and behaviors, initial research suggests this will also be no easy task (see Niederdeppe et al., 2008).

The shift in thinking about what the determinants of health and disease are, from ones that are individually based to ones that are social in nature, challenges social marketers to awake to the idea that we are in the business of social change and

Table 2.1 Examples of social determinants of health

Early life
Social exclusion
Addictions
Social support
Transportation policy
Aboriginal status
Education
Employment and working conditions
Food security
Healthcare services
Housing
Income and its distribution
Social safety net
Social exclusion
Unemployment and employment security
Socioeconomic status
Access to services
Discrimination by social grouping (e.g. race, gender, or class)
Social or environmental stressors

not simply changing the behavior of individuals. It also points to the important perspective and role we can bring in engaging with policymaking bodies, organizations and programs to broaden their ideas and activities about what is important to focus on to improve the health of all people everywhere. The remainder of this chapter focuses on theories and models to help us better conceptualize and influence large-scale change that moves beyond individuals to groups, communities, populations and policies.

SOCIAL DIFFUSION

Among the most data-driven models for behavior change at a group or population level is diffusion of innovations (Rogers, 1995). Lefebvre (2001), in a review of theoretical models used in social marketing programs, asserted that 'Diffusion of innovations research and concepts offer a tremendous amount of insight for social marketers to use in designing their programs, yet we see very little active discussion of it in social marketing circles.' *Social diffusion offers one of the most robust theoretical platforms for taking innovations in ideas, behaviors and practice to scale.* Yet, though the calls for scaling up successful behavioral interventions for such things as HIV prevention are reverberating around the globe (Global HIV Prevention Working Group, 2007), we see little discussion or application of the model by social marketers or, for that matter, anyone else. Social marketing needs to focus on 'pushing the curve' of adoption of health practices among individuals, the adoption of effective interventions among practitioners, and the adoption of health-promoting and supportive policies among policymakers.

Adopting diffusion of innovations explicitly into social marketing programs means that models of individual behavior change that are central to the ideas of social marketing espoused by Andreasen (1995), Kotler and Lee (2008) and others must be replaced with an understanding of the characteristics of groups of people who adopt (or fail to adopt) healthier, environmentally conscious or socially beneficial behaviors. These characteristics include (a) the contextual factors that surround the adoption of new practices and policies, (b) people's perceptions of the innovation as a normative behavior among their reference group or peers (which studies suggest account for anywhere from 50 to 86% of the variance in the rate of diffusion of new behaviors) and (c) a risk–benefit analysis that substitutes certainty of outcomes and familiarity with the new behavior over costs and benefits of changing current ones. Social marketers need to design their behavior, product and service offerings to answer the questions that are associated with adoption or termination:

- How is this better than what I currently do (relative advantage)?
- How is it relevant to the way I go about my everyday life (compatibility)?
- Is it simple enough for me to do (complexity)?
- Can I try it first (trialability)?
- Can I watch others do it and see the consequences of their actions (observability)?

Social marketing for behavior change at scale also needs to explore more extensively the use of such audience segments as

Innovators: who have a high tolerance of risk; are fascinated with novelty; usually viewed by others in their community as mavericks, not opinion leaders and whose social networks transcend geographic boundaries.

Early Adopters: who are the community opinion leaders and well-connected socially and locally; have the resources and risk tolerance to try new things and are the people who are watched by others – and they know it.

Early Majority: the people who are very engaged in local peer networks; rely on personal familiarity before adoption and continually ask the question, 'How does this new behavior, product or service help me?'

Late Majority: the group of people who are most sensitive to peer pressure and norms, yet very cautious about change of any kind; they seek to minimize uncertainty of outcomes and want to see the proof of relative advantage locally – not read about it on websites or see it on television.

Laggards: these are the traditionalists who believe in the tried and true; they are near isolates in their social networks which explains why they can be so difficult to reach and influence (vs having individual deficits); they are often suspicious of innovation and change agents; and they are seeking assurances that adoption of new behaviors (such as stopping smoking, driving a low carbon emission vehicle) will not fail.

The diffusion of innovations literature is immense and is beyond our ability to adequately cover here (some excellent sources for more detailed exploration of this area include Maibach et al., 2006; Strang and Soule, 1998). Yet, there are some lessons we have drawn from this work over the years that are proposed as new ways to conceptualize social marketing strategy.

1. Find sound innovations/solutions: ones that meet the criteria noted earlier and are relevant to people's everyday lives.
2. Provide opportunities for Innovators to discover them.
3. Engage the curiosity of the Early Adopters.
4. Target the weak ties between Innovators and Early Adopters through identifying the 'boundary spanners' who interact with multiple networks.
5. Promote the work of Early Adopters.
6. Create spanable social distances between groups through various means, including using social media such as social network sites and blogs, and convening meetings of the 'unlike' rather than the usual host of like-minded agents.
7. Enhance salience and attractiveness of the 'positive deviants' – the people who are already practicing the target behavior or using the product and service; put the practitioners of 'new' behaviors in contexts and situations that attract imitation or modeling.
8. 'If you can't imitate them, don't copy them.' Expect and encourage reinvention.
9. Support time and energy for discovery, testing, networking, adapting, monitoring and preserving the past. Do not write off the traditionalists, especially when encouraging organizational change.
10. Start with yourselves and your partners.

With respect to this last point, a recent study highlights that strongly linked and centralized coalitions are less likely to adopt new evidence-based public health programs than ones that are less dense and have more decentralized structures (Valente et al., 2007). Their results are based on a study involving 24 communities targeted for interventions to promote the adoption of substance abuse prevention programs. In interpreting their data, the authors conclude: 'Our results suggest that simply increasing network communication or connectedness, or both, among coalition members will not result in improved adoption of evidenced-based practices.' What was important was the presence of the 'boundary spanners' or individuals from organizations who were not part of the clique that had developed around substance abuse. These were the people more likely to be open to innovation; the traditionalists had their own point of view.

Our challenge in the years ahead, whether it is in HIV prevention or the prevention of childhood obesity, is to apply the evidence base of diffusion research to social marketing programs to achieve broad and sustainable change. To do so, researchers, their funders and policymakers must appreciate that developing and testing programs meant to achieve scale need to be designed that way to begin with; not by answering circumscribed research questions in highly controlled or contrived circumstances with little chance of replication in the field. Program designers and implementing agents must also be cognizant of the ways in which population groups adopt new behaviors and practices and factor these into their thinking and efforts. It seems that very few social marketers know how to transform programs focused on individual behavior change into ones scaled for population impact. And few program directors and donors seem willing to take the risk that is inherent in moving from 'the zoo' of controlled experiments to 'the jungle' of people's real lives (see especially #8 above).

This state of affairs must change if social marketing is to have the impact we aspire to. 'The Failure to Scale' paper by the Global HIV Prevention Working Group (2007) starkly lays out the picture for over 20 years of research and work in HIV prevention:

Despite the extraordinary potential of available prevention strategies, most people at risk of HIV infection have little or no access to basic prevention tools. Although necessary coverage levels vary depending on national circumstances, current coverage levels for essential prevention strategies are woefully inadequate for any national epidemic.

* Condoms. Only 9% of risky sex acts worldwide are undertaken while using a condom, and the global supply of condoms is millions short of what is needed.

* HIV Testing. In the most heavily affected countries of sub-Saharan Africa, only 12% of men and 10% of women know their HIV status.

* Treatment for Sexually Transmitted Infections. It is estimated that fewer than 20% of people with a sexually transmitted infection are able to obtain treatment, even though untreated STIs increase the risk of HIV acquisition and transmission by several orders of magnitude.

* Prevention of Mother-to-Child Transmission. Years after clinical trials demonstrated that a brief, inexpensive antiretroviral regimen could reduce the risk of mother-to-child HIV transmission by 50%, only 11% of HIV-infected pregnant women in low- and middle-income countries receive antiretroviral prophylaxis.

* Prevention for Vulnerable Populations. Prevention services reach only 9% of men who have sex with men, 8% of injection drug users, and fewer than 20% of sex workers.

* Prevention in Health Care Settings. An estimated 6 million units of unscreened blood are transfused yearly in developing countries, and 40% of injections administered in health care settings are unsafe.

The list of health topics and issues around 'barriers to broad adoption and diffusion' could continue for pages. Our suggestion here is that *social marketing should focus on achieving success at scale as a primary point of differentiation from other approaches to behavior and social change.*

SOCIAL NETWORKS

Over the past decade there has been a dramatic shift in the emphasis of determinants of health and social behaviors from individuals to networks and communities. For example, in three major areas of interest for public health officials and social marketers – HIV prevention (Adimora et al., 2007; Helleringer and Kohler, 2007; Mah and Halperin, 2008), obesity (Christakis and Fowler, 2007) and tobacco use (Christakis and Fowler, 2008) – the role of social networks in disease transmission and the prevalence of risk behaviors is challenging us to adopt concepts and practices that focus on social units of analysis, change and outcome. Concurrent sexual partnerships, that is having two or more stable sexual partners over time, is being seen as one of the previously hidden drivers of the HIV epidemic (Halperin and Epstein, 2004). Concurrency, especially when the partners are sexually active with others in a small world network (see below), heightens the risk of HIV transmission because these relationships are not casual or one-off sexual encounters, but are maintained over time where a level of trust develops that diminishes their perceived riskiness. Thus, when one partner becomes infected, they are highly likely to have sex with one or more other partners during the window of greatest HIV infectivity. Developing interventions to address the network effects of sexual activity are only just beginning. Similarly, the work of Christakis and Fowler (2007, 2008) provides descriptive evidence that the likelihood of becoming obese rises as close members of one's social network become overweight and obese and that stopping smoking is also highly susceptible to the smoking status of others. Again, the implications for interventions that address these disease risk factors are only now being explored. However, it is clear that simply focusing on individual determinants of these conditions can no longer be a singular pursuit for social marketing or any other types of risk reduction programs.

A comprehensive review of research on social networks is beyond the scope of this chapter, and several recent reviews are available (Goyal, 2007; Valente, 2010). Yet, a quick glance introduces us to an entirely new set of concepts and ways of thinking about human behavior and the social forces that directly influence it. Goyal (2007), for example, posits that how individuals gather information for making behavioral choices is shaped by the pattern of connections between people in a society. Three core network properties he discusses are (1) *degrees* or how many links each member in a network has with others; (2) *clustering* – how dense the connections between members of a network are (recall the Valente et al. study on community coalitions and substance abuse program adoption) and (3) *average distances* or how far away each person in a network is from another in terms of the number of links necessary to reach them (popularized as '6 degrees of separation' or 'the Kevin Bacon game'; Watts, 2003). Networks that are characterized with small average degrees (everyone has at least a few connections with others), high clustering (they mostly connect with others in the network) and small average distances (there are few degrees of separation between them so that most people know or are at least acquainted with most of the others) are referred to as small world networks (Watts and Strogatz, 1998).

One of the implications of this work in social networks is that people learn about and choose among behavioral options by directly observing others in their social circle engaging in behaviors and the consequences they experience. A second

point is that they also learn about new behaviors through their friends and associates who connect with other networks (boundary spanners) and bring that information or those practices back to the immediate network. Goyal (2007) concludes from his review of empirical work in economics and social networks that variations in behaviors among individuals are related not only to the connections people have within the same social group but also to their being members of different groups. The implications for social marketers seem clear: who people associate with, or are connected to, must be considered and addressed by intervention efforts. These network variables, in turn, might also serve as intervention points by, for instance, focusing on people with high degrees of connections within a network (connectors, influentials or opinion leaders), reducing the density of a network in which risk behaviors are concentrated by introducing more boundary spanners or increasing social connections of members of the group outside their immediate network, understanding the members of a network who are most attentive and responsive to the behaviors of others and enhancing the salience and attractiveness of 'positive deviants' by positioning these practitioners of desired behaviors in a light that attracts imitation or modeling.

These types of social network analyses must also be sensitive to information asymmetries that will exist among individuals within a group as well as between groups. Indeed, Viswanath and Kreuter (2007) point to the existence of communication inequalities as possibly underlying many of the social inequalities we see in health risks and conditions. These communication inequalities are manifested as differences among social classes in the generation, manipulation and distribution of information at the group level and differences in access to and ability to take advantage of information at the individual level. As a consequence, communication inequalities may act as a significant deterrent to obtaining and processing information; in using the information to make prevention, treatment and survivorship-related decisions; and in establishing relationships with providers.

Social networks have also played a major role in the development of the so-called Web 2.0 in which collaborative and dynamic models of communication underlie the philosophy, software development and user behaviors (Lefebvre, 2007). The ubiquity and popularity of blogs, social network sites, social sharing sites for photos and videos, wikis and virtual worlds have made the network connections among people more obvious. And, more importantly, these social media have unleashed a set of tools and resources that allow the people formerly known as the audience to create content for themselves and to tap into pools of collective wisdom. Social marketing programs must adapt to be both relevant to people's (new) lives and to harness this collective wisdom and power for social change. Similarly, the explosion in the adoption of wireless communication technologies, notably mobile telephones and smart phones (that connect wirelessly to the internet), are enabling communications that transcend place-based methods ('we call to individuals, not places'; Ling, 2008) and are further driving home the idea that people are communities, not individuals (Ahonen and Moore, 2005). As Lefebvre (2007) noted, while we have always been aware that there are social influences for many of the individual behaviors we seek to influence for environmental protection and the improvement of public health and social conditions, these social technologies are changing the weights we use in our models of determinants of behavior and the ways in which we approach modifying them.

We conclude this section by posing the questions Lefebvre (2007) asked about the consequences and implications of adopting a social networking perspective into our work as social marketers:

- How can we enhance linkages that already exist among people, organizations and communities to allow them to access, exchange, utilize and leverage the knowledge and resources of the others?
- How do we help develop, nurture and sustain new types of linkages that bring together like-minded people, mission-focused organizations and communities that share interests to address common problems and achieve positive health and social change?
- How do we identify, encourage and enable the many different types of indigenous helpers that are found in social networks so that they can be more effective in promoting positive health, environmental and social behaviors and policies?
- What do we do to better engage communities in monitoring, problem analysis and problem solving; striving to health and social equity; and increasing social capital?
- How do we go about weaving together existing social networks of individuals, organizations and communities to create new sources of power and inspiration to address health and social issues?
- How does a networked view of the world disrupt our usual ways of thinking about and engaging the people, organizations and communities with which we usually work? What are the insights we can gain from this perspective?

Where information and communication technologies may evolve to in the next few years is an open question. We see the blending of social media marketing techniques and mobile technologies with social marketing as a fertile area for exploration and achieving scalable results.

SOCIAL CAPITAL

Social capital is at the nexus of social determinants, social networks and community assets models or community building (see Section 'Building Communities'). It has become a popular and influential idea in social science and public health research, though it is not without its detractors who regard it as simplistic or divorced from economic and power relationships in communities (DeFilippis, 2001; Muntaner et al., 2001). A distinguishing feature of social capital from a social marketing point of view is that it is not merely structural – it has *value* to the individual, family, neighborhood or community to which it refers (Putnam, 2000). Putnam (2000) outlines the defining characteristics of social capital as including:

- The existence of *community networks*.
- *Civic engagement* (participation in these community networks).
- Local *identity* and a sense of solidarity and equality with other community members.
- Norms of *trust* and *reciprocal help and support*.

Perry (2000) identifies the important components of social capital to include 'social structures that effectively promote positive social norms and appropriate role models, provide useful information, are trustworthy in meeting obligations, and have definite expectations.'

Wallack (2000) offers a comprehensive review of the research linking social capital to health. He identifies the pathways through which low social capital may contribute to poor health status and health disparities to include: (1) systematic underinvestments in health and social infrastructure, (2) inhibition of the flow of health information (see the discussion of communication inequalities earlier), (3) an increase in one's sense of isolation and (4) lowered individual and collective efficacy. In proposing interventions that seek to increase social capital, he suggests these questions for us to consider in selecting strategies:

- Does the approach increase the capacity of individuals or small groups to participate in collective action by (a) providing participatory skills and (b) creating a structure or network through which individuals, groups and organizations can act?

- Does the approach connect the problems or issues to broader social forces?
- Does the approach increase the community's capacity to collaborate and cooperate by strengthening existing groups (create bonding capital) and connect various groups (create bridging capital)?
- Does the approach reflect a social justice orientation – the idea that each member of the community owes something to all the rest, and the community owes something to each of its members?

Social capital offers a bridging idea and a focal point for social marketers who aim to address social determinants through the application of social diffusion and social networks (see Glenane-Antoniadis et al., 2003). It may, for example, be one strategy to decrease rates of concurrent sexual partnerships. It might also prove useful in addressing community-level factors that are implicated in obesity (Cohen et al., 2006). And we have yet to explore in any depth how social media might be employed as a tactic to build social capital for health in communities and to eliminate health disparities (Bolam et al., 2006).

BUILDING COMMUNITIES

For many years communities were inextricably linked with social marketing. Lefebvre and Flora (1988) laid out the defining features of the social marketing approach based on experiences they shared directing community interventions aimed at reducing cardiovascular diseases. Yet, there has been a marked separation between social marketers and community change agents so that even by the early 1990s, we can recall where social marketing and community development components of Health Canada could not find common ground for collaboration. As more practitioners appropriated social marketing as the basis for the development of 'new' health communication campaigns, the term became associated (and in some quarters still is) with mass media campaigns that segmented their audience, pretested materials and considered the 4Ps only in the context of communication planning, not marketing. This approach was best embodied in *The Pink Book –Making Health Communication Programs Work*, first printed in 1989 (and available now as a revised online version at www.cancer.gov/pinkbook).

The differences in the social marketing approach became even more pronounced in the international community where social marketing became synonymous with the marketing of products for family planning, HIV prevention and

malaria control while various other groups organized themselves around concepts such as behavior change communication, health communication, development communication and community mobilization to name a few. Responding to this fracturing of resources and talent, McKee (1992) wrote a book that he hoped would 'enhance the understanding of social mobilization, social marketing and community participation among communicators who sometimes set up unnecessary barriers between their various fields.' Few seem to have heeded his call.

A hybrid approach developed independently in North America to reunite community with social marketing was coined as community-based social marketing (CBSM; McKenzie-Mohr, 2000). McKenzie-Mohr and Smith (1999) described CBSM as a process of identifying the barriers and benefits to engaging in behaviors and then organizing the public into groups with shared characteristics in order to more efficiently deliver programs (p. 3). Bryant and associates (2000) used the term 'community-based prevention marketing' to refer to programs with similar strategies that combine community participation with social marketing approaches.

The community-based approach as a context for implementing social marketing programs has much to commend it. Drawing from our experience and those of McKee (1992), these advantages include:

- Gaining community insight into problems and their support for proposed solution.
- Ensuring the use of indigenous knowledge and expertise.
- Mobilizing and employing local communication channels including local mass media and local social and interpersonal communication networks.
- Localizing distribution of products and services and improving access and opportunities to engage in new behaviors.
- Helping build sustainable solutions.

Engaging the community is also not without its drawbacks. McKee (1992) notes that community participation can also mean cursory consultation with the community rather than full engagement in a dialogue about problems and solutions. Participation from the community may develop into a 'participating elite' who may, or may not, represent broader community viewpoints. Program planners can fail to recognize the opportunity costs for people who are approached to participate in the development and oversight of the program. Open participation also can lead to manipulation and conflict by and among different parties or stakeholders. And local agendas may not match those of the donor or lead agency. Finally, he also notes that to truly move from a social marketing 'shell' of a program to a community-driven one, there is a need for partnership development and to gain strong public advocacy and political commitment to create a culture in which to embed and support social goals. These are skills many social marketers are in need of learning.

Given much of the discussion in this chapter, it should be clear that these community-based approaches could benefit from the insights provided by a social determinants frame and research on social capital, social networks and using social media. We also suggest that future marketing efforts need to work from asset-based models of community development rather than ones solely based on mapping and addressing deficits or needs. Kretzmann and McKnight (1993) list several arguments against relying on needs assessments and mapping in community projects including:

- It provides a nearly endless list of problems and needs that leads to a fragmentation of efforts to provide solutions.
- Targeting resources based on a needs assessment directs funding not to residents but to service providers, a consequence not always either planned for or effective.
- Making resources available on the basis of the needs map can have negative effects on the nature of local community leadership by forcing them to highlight their problems and deficiencies, and ignoring their capacities and strengths.
- Providing resources on the basis of the needs map underlines the perception that only outside experts can provide real help.

These authors argue that a needs-based strategy will inevitably focus on community survival rather than shift to serious change or community development. As an alternative approach, they propose an 'asset-based community development' approach that involves three interrelated characteristics:

- The strategy starts with what is present in the community, the capacities of its residents and workers, the associational and institutional base of the area – not with what is absent, problematic or what the community needs.
- The development strategy concentrates on the agenda-building and problem-solving capacities of local residents, local associations and local institutions to stress the primacy of local definition, investment, creativity, hope and control.
- Implementation of the resulting strategy will be relationship driven. Thus, one of the central challenges for asset-based community developers is to constantly build and rebuild the relationships between and among local residents, local associations and local institutions.

This look at the asset-based model is intended to reinforce the need for social marketers, particularly those who work in resource-constrained contexts and with disadvantaged populations, to view their *work in communities as needing to expand to working* **with** *communities*. Through these programs, community strengths and competencies should receive at least equal attention in marketing plans as do needs and barriers. Indeed, one of the potential unintended effects of well-done social marketing programs done IN communities is that they result in lowered social capital, self-efficacy and collective efficacy and increased dependency among citizens on experts. An asset-based approach to community programs reinforces two core values of the social marketing approach: the audience orientation and the engagement of people in the process as co-creators of the program rather than treating them as passive consumers of messages and programs.

SOCIAL FRANCHISING

Applying commercial marketing practices to public health services has been a natural progression of social marketing in developing countries. Its first use was to develop franchise procedures to increase awareness of family planning services, improve availability and accessibility of contraceptive supplies and services, and promote cost recovery from retailers and fee-paying clients through the application of commercial strategies to the promotion of contraceptive methods (Ruster et al., 2003). Since these initial efforts, social franchising has expanded to include many different types of health services and products.

In the prototype of family planning services, social franchising supports long-term contraceptive methods and broader reproductive health care and requires the participation of trained health providers. Networks of providers, or franchisees, are service producers in the clinic franchise system; they create standardized services under a franchise name. The result is a network of service providers offering a uniform set of services at predefined costs and quality of care (Stephenson et al., 2004). In their analysis of successful strategies for the base of the pyramid (BOP, or the poorest people in the world – often determined as living on less than $2 USD a day), Hammond et al. (2007) find support for localizing value creation through franchising, agent strategies that involve building local ecosystems of vendors or suppliers, or by treating the community as the customer. Successful franchising models now exist in numerous sectors of the BOP market including health care (franchise and agent-based direct marketing), information and communication technologies (local phone entrepreneurs and resellers), food (agent-based distribution systems), water (community-based treatment systems) and energy (mini-hydro-power systems).

Franchisers in the health sector, often supported by international donors and non-governmental organizations (NGOs), establish protocols, provide training for health workers, certify those who qualify, monitor the performance of franchisees and provide bulk procurement and brand marketing. Stephenson and colleagues (2004) found that reproductive health service providers may be motivated to join a franchise network for their perceived operating advantages of increasing their revenue, providing staff training opportunities and expanding their service capabilities and ability to reach more and poorer people with their services. Their data also support the notion that franchises can result in increased client volumes and range of family planning brands, and perhaps achieve greater efficiencies as demonstrated by the lower staff: client ratios in franchise clinics in comparison with private ones.

Social franchising can also be a strategy for improving health service delivery to priority populations. For example, Lönnroth et al. (2007) have reported that highly subsidized tuberculosis care delivered through a private sector social franchise in Myanmar could reach the poor with quality services, while Decker and Montagu (2007) have noted the potential of social franchises to provide services particularly tailored to youth in Western Kenya. Several health franchising operations (Greenstar in Pakistan, Kirsunu Medical Education Trust in Kenya, Well family Midwife Clinic Network in the Philippines) have demonstrated that they can rapidly expand basic health services to poor people, capture economies of scale and reduce the information asymmetries that often adversely affect the quality of care. Whether these programs can be financially sustained in the longer term is still an open question. What Stephenson et al. (2004) suggest, and one strategy that is actively pursued by a number of NGOs, is to expand service offerings to include the treatment of malaria, tuberculosis, provision of point-of-use water products and other essential products and medicines. Yet, despite their promise, a review of evidence for the effectiveness of social franchises to improve access and quality of care in low- and middle-income countries concluded that there was currently a lack of rigorous studies from which to draw any conclusions (Koehlmoos et al., 2009).

A LOOK FORWARD

Social marketing must embrace social models of health determinants, health behavior change and diffusion, community participation and service delivery to achieve greater scale in what it does best and improve the effectiveness and efficiency of programs in general. Innovation in these and other areas will allow researchers and practitioners to move beyond the echo chamber of what passes for conversations about social marketing and recurring drifts back to what is rather than what it should aspire to become. In large part, embracing the 'social' of social marketing positions us much better to have a place at the table of social policy. Enlarging the scope of social marketing also allows us to consider the broader application of social marketing to basic social needs such as poverty alleviation (Kotler and Lee, 2009; Melnick, 2007) and shifting cultures from ones of consumerism to sustainability (Sachs and Finkelpearl, 2010).

Coping with the many challenges confronting our world requires innovation in how we think about them and design solutions to solve them. Economic and policy initiatives are only partial solutions to issues as diverse as safer neighborhoods, childhood obesity and energy conservation. Education and information campaigns only go so far in reducing the use of tobacco products, increasing the use of preventive health services and expanding sustainable agricultural practices. Laws and regulations improve the safety of our food supply, reduce environmental pollutants and protect against unintentional injuries involving all types of consumer products – yet they too are only partial solutions.

Social innovations may be best achieved through a set of integrated activities that analyze, design for, implement and evaluate programs that specifically address (1) products, services and behaviors that will improve individual and social well-being; (2) realign incentives and costs to facilitate and sustain products, services and behaviors for the individual and social good; (3) create opportunities and improve access to beneficial products, services and places that encourage and support behavior change and (4) employ state-of-the-science communication strategies and tools to promote and support positive change at all levels of society – individuals, families and other social networks, organizations and communities (Lefebvre, 2009a,b). A more comprehensive perspective on how social marketing can be applied to the work of social innovation and change can provide new opportunities and tools to realize its potential and our ability to do good for the world.

KEY WORDS: Community development; diffusion of innovation; social capital; social determinants; social franchising; social innovation; social networks.

Key insights

- Global health actions to improve people's lives must focus on social determinants of behavior. Social marketing should be used to facilitate the adoption of approaches to individual and social change that incorporate social determinants among policymakers and other segments of the public.
- Models of social diffusion offer one of the most robust theoretical platforms for taking innovations in ideas, behaviors and practice to scale.
- Social network analysis and action, especially as they are enabled by social media and mobile technologies, offer frameworks for applying social marketing to enhance and expand networks for health and social improvement and increase social capital in communities.
- Social marketing provides a strategic array of insights and approaches that can be used to co-create change in communities.
- The emergence of social franchising models can be adopted as a strategy for improving health and social service delivery in many different contexts and cultures.
- Social marketing can be an organizing framework for social innovations needed to frame and design solutions to problems such as poverty and sustainability.

REFERENCES

Adimora, A.A., Schoenbach, V.J. and Doherty, I.A. (2007) 'Concurrent sexual partnerships among men in the United States', *American Journal of Public Health*, 97: 2230–2237.

Ahonen, T.T. and Moore, A. (2005) *Communities Dominate Brands*. London, UK: Futuretext.

Andreasen, A.R. (1995) *Marketing Social Change: Changing Behavior to Promote Health, Social Development, and the Environment*. San Francisco, CA: Jossey-Bass.

Andreasen, A.R. (2006) *Social Marketing in the 21st Century*. Thousand Oaks, CA: Sage Publications.

Bolam, B., McLean, C., Pennington, A. and Gillies, P. (2006) 'Using new media to build social capital for health: A qualitative process evaluation study of participation in the CityNet Project', *Journal of Health Psychology*, 11: 297–308.

Bryant, C.A., Forthofer, M.S., McCormack Brown, K.R., Landis, D.C. and McDermott, R.J. (2000) 'Community-based prevention marketing: The next steps in disseminating behavior change', *American Journal of Health Behavior*, 24: 61–68.

Christakis, N.A. and Fowler, J.H. (2007) 'The spread of obesity in a large social network over 32 years', *New England Journal of Medicine*, 357: 370–379.

Christakis, N.A. and Fowler, J.H. (2008) 'The collective dynamics of smoking in a large social network', *New England Journal of Medicine*, 358: 2249–2258.

Cohen, D.A., Finch, B.K., Bower, A. and Sastry, N. (2006) 'Collective efficacy and obesity: The potential influence of social factors on health', *Social Science and Medicine*, 62: 769–778.

Commission on Social Determinants of Health (2008) *Closing the Gap in a Generation: Health Equity through Action on the Social Determinants of Health, Final Report*. Geneva: World Health Organization.

Crawford, R. (1977) 'You are dangerous to your health: The ideology and politics of victim blaming', *Journal of Health Services*, 7: 663–680.

Decker, M. and Montagu, D. (2007) 'Reaching youth through franchise clinics: Assessment of Kenyan private sector involvement in youth services', *Journal of Adolescent Health*, 40: 280–282.

DeFilippis, J. (2001) 'The myth of social capital in community development', *Housing Policy Debate*, 12: 781–806.

Donovan, R. and Henley, N. (2003) *Social Marketing: Principles and Practice*. Melbourne, Australia: IP Communications.

Glenane-Antoniadis, A., Whitwell, G., Bell, S.J. and Menguc, B. (2003) 'Social marketing and social capital', *Marketing Theory*, 3: 323–343.

Global HIV Prevention Working Group. (2007) *Bringing HIV Prevention to Scale: An Urgent Global Priority* [accessed 5 March 2009 at http://globalhivprevention.org/pdfs/PWG-HIV_prevention_report_FINAL.pdf].

Goyal, S. (2007) *Connections: An Introduction to the Economics of Networks*. Princeton, NJ: Princeton University Press.

Halperin, D.T. and Epstein, H. (2004) Concurrent sexual partnerships help to explain Africa's high HIV prevalence: Implications for prevention. *Lancet*, 364 (9428): 4–6.

Hammond, A., Kramer, W.J., Tran, J., Katz, R. and Walker, C. (2007) *The Next 4 Billion: Market Size and Business Strategy and the Base of the Pyramid*. Washington, DC: World Resources Institute.

Hastings, G. (2007) *Social Marketing: Why Should the Devil Have All the Best Tunes?* Oxford, England: Elsevier.

Helleringer, S. and Kohler, H-P. (2007) 'Sexual network structure and the spread of HIV in Africa: Evidence from Likoma Island, Malawi', *AIDS*, 21: 2323–2332.

Higgins, J.W., Vertinsky, P., Cutt, J. and Green, L.W. (1999) 'Using social marketing as a theoretical framework to understand citizen participation in health promotion', *Social Marketing Quarterly*, 5: 42–55.

Koehlmoos, T.P., Gazi, R., Hossain, S.S. and Zaman, K. (2009) 'The effect of social franchising on access to and quality of health services in low- and middle-income countries', *Cochrane Database of Systematic Reviews*, Issue 1. Art. No.: CD007136. DOI: 10.1002/14651858.CD007136.pub2.

Kotler, P. and Lee, N.R. (2008) *Social Marketing: Influencing Behaviors for Good*, 3rd edn. Thousand Oaks, CA: Sage Publications.

Kotler, P. and Lee, N.R. (2009) *Out of Poverty: Social Marketing Solutions to Fight the Cycle of Poverty*. Upper Saddle Back, NJ: Wharton School Publishing.

Kotler, P. and Zaltman, G. (1971) 'Social marketing: An approach to planned social change', *Journal of Marketing*, 35: 3–12.

Kretzmann, J.P. and McKnight, J.L. (1993) *Building Communities from the Inside Out: A Path toward Finding and Mobilizing a Community's Assets*. Evanston, IL: Institute for Policy Research.

Lefebvre, R.C. (2001) 'Theories and models in social marketing', in P.N. Bloom and G.T. Gundlach (eds), *Handbook of Marketing and Society*. Newbury Park, CA: Sage Publications, pp. 506–518.

Lefebvre, R.C. (2007) 'The new technology: The consumer as participant rather than target audience', *Social Marketing Quarterly*, 13: 31–42.

Lefebvre, R.C. (2009a). 'The change we need: New ways of thinking about social issues', *Social Marketing Quarterly*, 15: 142–144.

Lefebvre, R.C. (2009b) 'The change we need: New ways of thinking about social issues,' *On Social Marketing and Social Change*. Posted on 29 January 2009. Available from: http://socialmarketing.blogs.com.

Lefebvre, R.C. and Flora, J.A. (1988) 'Social marketing and public health intervention', *Health Education Quarterly*, 15: 299–315.

Ling, R. (2008) *New Tech, New Ties: How Mobile Communication is Reshaping Social Cohesion*. Cambridge, MA: MIT Press.

Lönnroth, K., Aung, T., Maung, W., Kluge, H. and Uplekar, M. (2007) 'Social franchising of TB care through private GPs in Myanmar: An assessment of treatment results, access, equity and financial protection', *Health Policy and Planning*, 22: 156–166.

Mah, T.L. and Halperin, D.T. (2008) 'Concurrent sexual partnerships and the HIV epidemics in Africa: Evidence to move forward', *AIDS and Behavior*. Published online: 22 July 2008. [cited 5 March 2009]. Available from: http://www.springerlink.com/content/aq8244262614q762/

Maibach, E.W., Van Duyn, M.A. and Bloodgood, B. (2006) 'A marketing perspective on disseminating evidence-based approaches to disease prevention and health promotion', *Preventing Chronic Disease* [serial online] July [cited 5 March 2009]. Available from: http://www.cdc.gov/pcd/issues/2006/jul/05_0154.htm.

McKee, N. (1992) *Social Mobilization and Social Marketing in Developing Communities: Lessons for Communicators*. Panang, Malaysia: Southbound.

McKenzie-Mohr, D. (2000) 'Fostering sustainable behavior through community-based social marketing', *American Psychologist*, 55: 531–537.

McKenzie-Mohr, D. and Smith, W. (1999) *Fostering Sustainable Behavior: An Introduction to Community-Based Social Marketing*. Washington, DC: Academy for Educational Development and Gabriola Island, BC, Canada: New Society Publishers.

Melnick, G.A. (2007) 'From family planning to HIV/AIDS prevention to poverty alleviation: A conversation with Mechai Viravaidya', *Health Affairs*, 26: 670–677.

Muntaner, C., Lynch, J. and Smith, G.D. (2001) 'Social capital, disorganized communities, and the third way: Understanding the retreat from structural inequalities in epidemiology and public health', *International Journal of Health Services*, 31: 213–237.

Niederdeppe, J., Bu, Q., Borah, P., Kindig, D.A. and Robert, S.A. (2008) 'Message design strategies to raise public awareness of social determinants of health and population health disparities', *Millbank Quarterly*, 86: 481–513.

Perry, C.L. (2000) 'Preadolescent and adolescent influences on health', in B.D. Smedley and S.L.Syme (eds), *Promoting Health: Intervention Strategies for Social and Behavioral Research*. Washington, DC: National Academy Press, pp. 217–253.

Putnam, R.D. (2000) *Bowling Alone: The Collapse and Revival of American Community*. New York: Simon and Schuster.

Rogers, E. (1995) *Diffusion of Innovations*, 4th edn. New York: The Free Press.

Ruster, J., Yamamoto, C. and Rogo, R. (2003) 'Franchising in health emerging models, experiences, and challenges in primary care', Viewpoint (June). Washington, DC: The World Bank,

Sachs, J. and Finkelpearl, S. (2010) From selling soap to selling sustainability: Social marketing, in The Worldwatch Institute, *2010 State of the World: Transforming Cultures from Consumerism to Sustainability*. New York: W.W. Norton and Company.

Siegel, M. and Lotenberg, L.D. (2007) *Marketing Public Health: Strategies to Promote Social Change*, 2nd edn. Sudbury, MA: Jones and Bartlett Publishers.

Stephenson, R., Tsui, A.O., Sulzbach, S., et al. (2004) 'Reproductive health in today's world: Franchising reproductive health services', *Health Services Research*, 39: 2053–2080.

Strang, D. and Soule, S.A. (1998) 'Diffusion in organizations and social movements: From hybrid corn to poison pills', *Annual Review of Sociology*, 24: 265–290.

Valente, T.W. (2010) *Social Networks and Health: Models, Methods, and Applications*. New York: Oxford Press.

Valente, T.W., Chou, C.P. and Pentz, M.A. (2007) 'Community coalition networks as systems: Effects of network change on adoption of evidence-based prevention', *American Journal of Public Health*, 97: 880–886.

Viswanath, K. and Kreuter, M.W. (2007) 'Health disparities, communication inequalities, and e-Health: A commentary',

American Journal of Preventive Medicine, 32(5 Suppl): S131–S133.

Wallack, L. (1990) 'Two approaches to health promotion in the mass media', *World Health Forum*, 11: 143–154.

Wallack, L. (2000) 'The role of the mass media in creating social capital: A new direction for pubic health', in B.D. Smedley and S.L. Syme (eds), *Promoting Health: Intervention Strategies for Social and Behavioral Research*. Washington, DC: National Academy Press, pp. 337–365.

Walsh, D.C., Rudd, R.E., Moeykens, B.A. and Moloney, T.W. (1993) 'Social marketing for public health', *Health Affairs*, 12: 104–119.

Watts, D.J. (2003) *Six Degrees: The Science of a Connected Age*. New York: W.W. Norton and Company.

Watts, D.J. and Strogatz, S.H. (1998) 'Collective dynamics of "small-world" networks', *Nature*, 393(June): 440–442.

3

Relationship Marketing and Social Marketing

Susana Marques and Christine Domegan

INTRODUCTION

Relationship marketing (RM) provides a new foundation for social marketing thinking, genuine change in values and ethics and a new logic that sees consumers as the prime drivers of the value creation process. The term 'relationship marketing' was first introduced by Berry in the services marketing in 1983. Since then, RM has been significantly embraced by several subdisciplines of marketing – business-to-business marketing, marketing channels, retailing, consumer marketing and non-profits – to the point of a paradigm shift.

This alone would suggest RM has significant rewards to offer social marketing and there is convergence about the promise of the RM school of thought for social marketing (Andreasen, 2001; Glenane-Antoniadis et al., 2003; Hastings et al., 2002; Peattie and Peattie, 2003; Hastings, 2003). Social marketing has particular characteristics that make RM potentially applicable: the absence of the profit motive; the focus on high-involvement decisions; complex and multifaceted behaviors; changes that take a long time; the relevance of trust and the need to target the most needy and hard-to-reach groups in society (Hastings, 2003). The relational approach is advocated in the literature as an alternative to the 'intervention mentality' (Hastings et al., 2002). Despite its potential, the social marketing field has been slow, if not resistant, to absorb relational thinking. It may be, as Rothschild (2001b) argues, that social

marketers have been more concerned with telling people how to behave and less concerned with building relationships.

This chapter demonstrates that RM helps social marketing and that its absence seriously undermines the field. It also argues that RM is more capable of responding to the complexities of contemporary pluralist societies, in which there is no universal agreement on a single way of life. From the literature, we have identified the key processes and constructs of RM that are most applicable, relevant and transferable to social marketing. Furthermore, we have identified the challenges of that transference, given the particular characteristics of social marketing. Our explicit objectives are to, first, examine the key RM processes and constructs for social marketing and, second, discuss the challenges raised by the transference.

We begin this chapter by defining RM and what the term means. As part of this, three broad approaches to RM are presented: namely, the North-American, Anglo-Australian and Nordic schools of thought. That done, we then detail three key RM processes (communication/dialogue; interaction and value creation) and seven critical RM constructs (relationship quality, trust, commitment, satisfaction, identification, perceived value and cooperation), together with the conceptual and operational implications they pose for social marketing. We conclude with the challenges RM raises for social marketing as a new way of thinking about social issues.

RELATIONSHIP MARKETING: ITS THEORETICAL UNDERPINNINGS

Currently, there are wide variations in understandings of, and approaches to, RM, with no universal agreement on a definition. Different authors have different perspectives (Christopher et al., 1991; McKenna, 1991; Sheth, 1994). Gummesson (1994) sees RM as a marketing approach that is based on relationships, interactions and networks. As he explains, the shift in the marketing paradigm means that the 4Ps develop their role from being founding parameters of marketing to that of being contributing parameters to relationships, networks and interaction. RM identifies, establishes, maintains and enhances relationships with customers and other stakeholders, at a profit, so that the objectives of all parts involved are met, and that is done by mutual exchange and fulfilment of promises (Grönroos, 1994a). Morgan and Hunt (1994) posit that RM refers to all marketing activities directed toward establishing, developing and maintaining successful relationships.

Payne (2000) identifies three broad approaches to RM: the Anglo-Australian approach (Christopher et al., 1991); the Nordic approach (Grönroos, 1994ab, 1996, 2000a, 2004; Gummesson, 1994, 1997, 1998, 2002) and the North American approach (Sheth and Parvatyar, 1995; Parvatyar and Sheth, 2000). In general, and as explained by Payne (2000), the Anglo-American and the Nordic groups define RM more broadly, going beyond customer relationships to include other specific markets or stakeholders, whereas the North American argues for a narrow definition at the customer–supplier dyad level. We think the Nordic school of thought of RM is the one that best captures the essence and strategic implications of a paradigm shift and, in that sense, it has a lot to offer to social marketing. Furthermore, it contextualizes RM in society as a whole and stimulates critical thinking through its emphasis on the need to re-examine marketers' assumptions. We now examine the specificities of the different approaches identified by Payne (2000).

The North American approach

Parvatyar and Sheth (2000) define RM as the ongoing process of engaging in cooperative and collaborative activities and programs with immediate and end-user customers to create or enhance mutual economic value at reduced cost. Sheth and Parvatyar (2002) demonstrate the uniqueness of the RM concept and its distinct properties as:

- A one-to-one relationship between the marketer and the customer.
- An interactive process, not a transaction.
- A value-added activity through mutual interdependence and collaboration between suppliers and customers.

For Sheth and Parvatyar (1995), in RM, the roles of producers, sellers, buyers and consumers are blurring, compared with traditional marketing where the seller and the buyer (marketing actors) have well-defined roles, where they independently create values and there is a place and time of transaction that can be easily articulated for exchange. The relationship is, instead, a process of value creation through cooperative and collaborative effort (Parvatyar and Sheth, 2000). Therefore, RM is an alternative paradigm where *value creation replaces value distribution*; the focus is on the processes of relationship engagement and not on the outcome or consequence of relationship.

The Anglo-Australian approach

Christopher et al. (1991) emphasize three issues in their approach:

- RM strategies are concerned with a broader scope of external 'market' relationships which include suppliers, business referral and 'influence' sources.
- RM also focuses on the internal (staff) relationships critical to the success of (external) marketing plans.
- Improving marketing performance ultimately requires a resolution (or realignment) of the competing interests of customers, staff and shareholders, by changing the way managers 'manage' the activities of the business.

They theorize that marketing is concerned with exchange relationships between the organization and its customers, with quality and customer services as the key linkages in this relationship. The challenge to the organization is to bring these three critical areas into closer alignment. As a result of this lack of alignment in traditional marketing, the RM concept emerges as the new focal point integrating customer service and quality with a market orientation. Christopher et al. (1991) point out some important differences between transaction marketing and relationship marketing (Table 3.1).

These differences are convergent with the North American school. Parvatyar and Sheth (2000) explain the emergence of RM practice with the growing de-intermediation process due to the advent of sophisticated computer and telecommunication technologies; the growth of the service economy; the total quality movement; the hyper-competition and consequent need for

Table 3.1 Transaction vs relationship marketing

Transaction marketing	Relationship marketing
• Focusing on single sale	• Focus on consumer retention
• Orientation on product features	• Orientation on product benefits
• Short time scale	• Long time scale
• Little customer service	• High customer service
• Limited customer commitment	• High customer commitment
• Moderate customer contact	• High customer contact
• Quality is a production focus	• Quality is the concern of all

Source: Christopher, M., Payne, A. and Ballantyne, D. (1991) *Relationship Marketing*. Oxford: Butterworth-Heinemann.

customer retention and loyalty and the rapid change of customer expectations and globalization. The comparison between transaction and RM elaborated by Christopher et al. (1991) is very useful, but we think that the Nordic school approach points more clearly to the fundamental differences.

The Nordic school approach

The main role and contribution of the Nordic school (Grönroos, 1994ab, 1996, 2000a, 2004; Gummesson, 1994, 1997, 1998, 2002) has been in helping to extend the notion of RM from service marketing to general marketing, to the point of defining RM as the new marketing paradigm: the customer is an integral part of the marketing and delivery process and this demands a close relationship between the provider and the customer (Aijo, 1996). The Nordic school also sees marketing more as a marketing-oriented management than as a separate function. Hence, relationship building and maintenance is at the core of managing. Grönroos (1996, p. 12) emphasizes that 'common mistakes when discussing RM follow from a failure to understand this philosophical shift'. It represents a new foundation for thinking, a new logic to deal with complexity and a genuine change in values and ethics (Gummesson, 1997). One of the main contributions of the Nordic school researchers is their conceptualization of RM as a value creation process and their call to make sure that marketers should not confuse/mix strategic with tactical implications of RM (Grönroos, 1996).

Grönroos (1996) emphasizes that a key requirement in RM is that the firm is defined as a *service* business. Customers do not only look for goods or services, they demand a much more holistic service offering that includes information, delivering, updating and repairing. Competing with the core offering is not enough. Instead, firms have to compete with the total service offering. This requires a transition from the product as the dominating element of the offering to the management of human resources, technology, knowledge and time. This means that competences and resources are crucial.

An ongoing relationship with customers, where customers look for value in the total service offering, also requires managing the firm from a *process management perspective* (Grönroos, 1996). It requires internal collaboration among functions and departments which are responsible for different elements of the offering: for example, the core product itself, advertising the product, delivering the product and taking care of complaints. 'The whole chain of activities has to be coordinated and managed as one total process' (Grönroos, 1996, p. 10). As Grönroos (1996) emphasizes, the process management perspective is very different from the functionalistic management approach based on scientific management. Functionalistic management allows for 'sub-optimization because each function and corresponding department is more oriented toward specialization within its function than collaboration between functions' (Grönroos, 1996, p. 10). The result is the creation of sub-values but not total value.

Finally, from the Nordic school perspective, RM requires developing *active partnerships and networks*. RM is based on cooperation with customers, other stakeholders and network partners. This means firms will not view one another from a win–lose perspective but will rather benefit from a win–win situation, where the parties work as partners. This demands trust and commitment.

To define the organization as a service, utilizing a process perspective and developing networks, there are three underlying key RM processes required: interaction, communication/dialogue and value creation (Grönroos, 2000a). We now turn our attention to a discussion of these key RM processes, together with their underlying constructs, and the implications they pose for social marketing.

KEY RM PROCESSES AND SOCIAL MARKETING CONSEQUENCES

The interaction process

The relationship, once it has established, proceeds in an interaction process where various types of contacts occur over time. In order to understand the interaction process one must divide it into logical parts (Grönroos, 2000a). In a relationship marketing context, it has been studied in terms of acts (moments of truth), episodes (social encounters; interrelated acts), sequences (interrelated episodes) and relationships (e.g. Holmlund, 1996). As Storbacka (2000, p. 566) explains, 'episodes are events that represent complete functions from the customer's point of view'. The word relationship implies that the link between the provider and the customer lasts longer than one episode. 'A long-term relationship with one provider can be described as a string of episodes and the total benefit or value that the customer receives during the relationship is not provided in one episode'. Rather, the benefits are delivered in 'smaller portions' during the relationship (Storbacka, 2000, p. 566). Some relationships are built from series of discrete episodes in which customers make repetitive purchase decisions. There are, however, also relationships that are continuous, in which customers make contracts (implicit or explicit) with providers and receive offerings on demand. As explained by Storbacka, in a continuous relationship context, customers, by definition, use a large variety of different episode types, ranging from simple routine episodes to complex episodes.

In social marketing, because of its unique characteristics, interaction can play a major role. This role is demonstrated in a study by Velleman et al. (2000) who concluded interaction was vital to the work with parents, rather than teaching drugs prevention to them. Considerable interaction occurred: project workers actively consulted numerous agencies, including community groups, parents and parents of children with dependent drug problems. This interaction was a collaborative endeavor, done 'with' parents, not 'to' them. Furthermore, keeping regular contact between parents' initial interest and the start of the course resulted in improved attendance rates (Velleman et al., 2000).

Another important interaction inference for social marketers is the willingness to change the offer because sometimes marketers have to reposition it in order to change consumers' understanding of the product and its benefits (Andreasen, 1995). Without this type of flexibility, social marketing becomes meaningless (Hastings, 2003)

and, consequently, unable to truly interact with consumers.

This has one further challenge for social marketing – programs need longer time frames. According to Hastings (2003), a minimum of five years is needed, as interaction and RM are not compatible with short time frames.

From this perspective, relationship building in social marketing is complex, on a practical level, because there is rarely one single organization involved. Social marketing programs are normally funded, developed and delivered by different organizations. The delivery, in particular, can get even more complex when it is devolved to numerous organizations: for example, schools, doctors or community partners. Furthermore, some delivery agents may not approve or have any allegiance to the funder or the developer. This raises different sorts of challenges: the need to define who is responsible for the relationship and the need to focus on developing consistency and integration of the 'collective'. *Blueprint program* – a major research program designed to examine the effectiveness of a multi-component approach to drug education in England – is a good illustration of these challenges. The parent component, for example, one element of the program, involved different people and organizations in the design, recruitment and delivery. The links between the different parts of the parent program were weak and operated as a sum of isolated parts rather than as a whole – a sum of episodes rather than a string of episodes (Marques, 2008).

The multiplicity of potential relationships in social marketing presents opportunities as well as challenges: one of them is how to prioritize, handle and create synergies between them. The form that these relationships take may vary – at least in terms of whom the relationship is built with – but, as Hastings (2003) explains, the principle of relational thinking holds true throughout.

The communication/dialogue process

The Nordic school follows the view that if relationship marketing is to be successful, an integration of all marketing communications messages is needed to support the establishment, maintenance and enhancement of relationships with customers. The interaction and planned communication processes indeed parallel one another, which means they should support and not counteract one another.

The characteristic aspect of marketing communication in an RM context is an attempt to create a two-way or sometimes multi-way communication process. The communication support to RM is called a dialogue process. This process includes a variety of elements: sales activities, mass communication activities, direct communication and public relations. A dialogue can be seen as an interactive process of reasoning together (Ballantyne, 2000) so a common knowledge platform is possible. The intent is to build shared meanings and get insights in what the two parties can do together and for one another. Customers should feel that the firm which communicates with them shows a genuine interest in them and their needs, requirements and value systems. They should see that the firm appreciates feedback and makes use of it. Therefore, as Grönroos (2000b, 2004) emphasizes, planned communication messages per se do not lead to a dialogue. They may initiate it but interaction-based messages are required. Furthermore, and according to the Nordic school, the dialogue process starts before the interaction process: this is the stage in which the relationship is established. Only the integration of the dialogue and the interaction processes into one strategy that is systematically implemented creates RM (Grönroos, 2000b, p. 107).

The relevance of dialogue is emphasized by Tzokas and Saren (1997) to the point of defining RM as 'the process of planning, developing and nurturing a relationship climate that will promote a dialogue between a firm and its customers which aims to imbue an understanding, confidence and respect of each others' capabilities and concerns when enacting their role in the market place and in society' (p. 106). As Elinor and Gerard (1998) suggest 'dialogue moves us beyond the individual to a focus on the larger social and cultural context in which we live: it works to bring integration and wholeness perspective into the day-to-day decisions we make' (p. 14). RM researchers have approached dialogue as a means of appreciating the broader dimensions in which actors from the production and consumption systems are associated.

To open channels of communication and nurture dialogue between upstream and downstream stakeholders, Safefood, the Food Safety Promotion Board of Ireland, utilized systematic reviews. The rigorous standards of systematic reviews (replication, revisable and credible) assisted in building trust and cooperation between social marketing researchers and policymakers. The interactive process of the systematic review changed the role of the stakeholders from being isolated, passive and unaware to being strategically connected, active and engaged (McHugh and Domegan, 2009).

Tzokas and Saren (1997, 1999) emphasize that one of the challenges faced by contemporary organizations has to do with the development of mechanisms to assist organizations-wide co-learning about their customer base: this, they suggest, can be conceived as organizational learning about how customers perceive or attribute value and their attributions. From a relationship marketing management perspective, they see dialogue as an opportunity for value transformation and an avenue for competitive advantage. By creating unique co-experiences and a new way of being in a relationship, dialogue transforms perceptions to co-perceptions about what defines, creates and delivers value for both the firm and its customers.

In transferring RM's communication/dialogue lessons to social marketing, the main issues are (1) to overcome the fear logic and (2) to use branding as a relational strategy.

An important debate in the social marketing literature is about the effectiveness of using fear appeals. MacFadyen et al. (2000) criticize the over-reliance on threats, as these may be ineffective, disempowering and damaging. Henley et al. (1998) argue that positive appeals are underutilized. Despite some evidence that fear messages are persuasive, Hastings et al. (2004) suggest that marketers in both the commercial and social sector should be cautious about their use. As they explain, most studies are laboratorial; therefore, marketing questions concerning the use of fear in the real world remains unexplored.

If consumers' feelings of self-esteem and personal comfort are threatened by fear messages it is likely that they will not be receptive to building long-term relationships with the communicator or, if they do, that it will probably be a patronizing relationship rather than one of mutual respect. Long-term effects of fear messages and their impact on relationships are important and that is why there is a need to compare fear approaches with alternative, more creative approaches (Hastings et al., 2004). Alternatives to fear messages include, as suggested by Hastings et al., 'empathy strategies', use of humor, irony and supportive messages, positive role models, empowerment and postmodernism (treating the consumer as knowing and worldly wise).

Another relevant implication of communication/dialogue for social marketing is branding. RM terms, branding has the potential to communicate in a more positive and empathetic way. Peattie and Peattie (2003) consider that the power of branding and the ability to connect with consumers' emotions demonstrate an area where social marketing can still learn with commercial marketing. Branding may provide an important function in social marketing programs by helping individuals to communicate and signal to themselves as well others that they are engaging in desirable behaviors so that they are better able to realize more immediate benefits and receive more positive reinforcement (Keller, 1998). Instead, social marketers need to provide unique benefits and meanings that can be extended to the development of social marketing brand images and the enhancement of the target's self-image. As pointed out by Rothschild (2001b), one of the challenges is that when asking a target to stop exhibiting a current behavior, social marketers have to realize that the current behavior has a relationship to a brand that may have a powerful meaning for the self-image of the target population.

Recent neurosciences research (Damásio, 2004) shows that emotions are extremely valuable, but it is the process of 'feeling the knowledge that we feel' – the conscience – that assures that the immediate gains of emotions are maintained over time. This implies a deep and long process which social marketers can't ignore. If social marketers want to develop long-term relationships they have to help consumers to understand their own process of feeling rather that just appeal to superficial emotional responses.

Despite the power of branding, some are cautious about its application in the social sector. A strong brand identity can amplify the impact of a campaign, but it can also be perceived as authoritarian (Stead and Hastings, 2003).

From the dialogue process, the social marketing's concern is to see dialogue as a co-learning process, as an opportunity for value definition and transformation (Tzokas and Saren, 1997). The study of Velleman et al. (2000) about the process of involving parents in drugs prevention in the UK illustrates the potential of dialogue for social marketers. They don't explicitly conceptualize the process as a dialogue but the logic is similar. They explain how parents' needs and wants changed throughout several drug prevention programs. Project workers noted a difference between parents' needs and their initial wants. Needs (e.g. skills in communication) were, at first, often not recognized by parents. On the other hand, some wants (e.g. a simple answer to a problem or reassurance that their children would not become involved in drugs) were requested, although parents later often came to view them as unrealistic. As they progressed, their needs became more sophisticated and a great deal of flexibility was necessary. Through interacting with parents, project workers also opened up their own perspectives: they realized that drug problems do not exist in isolation and prevention should not be pursued independently of wider issues relating to parenting, family life and wider social issues. Therefore, projects had to be seen as instigators of a developmental process. Project workers indicated that if parents saw the relevance of what they were learning they became enthusiastic and wanted to go on

further learning or activities. Several project workers commented that this further learning was not necessarily directly related to drugs prevention but formed part of the individual's personal development, and points to the power of dialogue to re-contextualize specific problems in wider social issues.

The implications are that social marketers have to understand the power of dialogue as a process of co-learning and co-defining value; to interact with consumers from the very beginning of programs, so co-meanings and co-experiences emerge and to be flexible, offer different routes of engagement, address continuity and build alternative progression routes and opportunities for further learning with consumers.

The value creation process

The Nordic school emphasizes that it is not enough to understand the needs of customers: one must also know how they strive to achieve the results required to fulfill these needs. This can be labeled the customer's value-generating process (Grönroos, 2004). Because a relationship is a process over time, value for customers also emerges from a process overtime. In a relationship context, the offering includes both a core product and additional services. On top of the value created by singular episodes (e.g. exchange of information) customer perceived value can be expected to include an explicit value component related to the mere fact that a relationship with a service provider/firm exists (Ravald and Grönroos, 1996). This value component includes, for example, a feeling of security and a sense of trust. The Nordic authors argue that it is easy to see how the value of the core of the offering becomes highly questionable if the additional services are missing or not good enough.

A successful RM strategy requires that all processes are integrated: interaction process is the core; dialogue is the communications aspect of RM, value is the outcome of RM. This debate deepens our understanding of the concepts of interaction and value creation. It is very important to the social marketing context and converges with the idea that RM is capable of responding to the requirements of contemporary pluralist societies; there are no single/ideal answers to social problems, so social marketers need time, resources and flexibility. The major concern for social marketers is to explore opportunities for value co-creation, which implies that they need to understand and incorporate in their programs the customers' value-generating process (Grönroos, 2004). Consumers build their own unique consumption experiences and these are hard to be predetermined by marketers. For example, parents may opt for different types on engagement in drugs prevention programs and 'build their own program'. In Food Dudes – a healthy eating school-based program designed to increase 4- to 11-year-old children's consumption of fruit and vegetables – the traditional approach of telling children what to eat was unsuccessful. Actionable insights showed that children are motivated by praise, recognition and rewards and positive role models have a powerful influence over children's learning and value system. As a result, two key elements of the program include video adventures featuring hero figures, 'the Food Dudes', who like fruit and vegetables and small rewards, for example, stickers to ensure children begin to taste new foods (Maloney, 2006). This also points to the concept of value in use, further examined below, when examining the construct of perceived value.

Relationship marketing provides a whole new way of thinking about social issues. One of the main contributions of RM is that it helps to uncover fundamental contradictions in, and challenges to, current social marketing thinking. For example, despite confirmation that the concept of choice is crucial, the field is dominated by prescriptive interventions (Hastings, 2003). The significant conceptual contribution of RM to social marketing is the emphasis RM puts on the process of value co-creation through collaboration and cooperation. First and foremost, the collaboration is with the client/consumer as a co-creator of value. Andreasen (1995) emphasizes that social marketers work at a deep level – dealing with high involvement behavior – and this demands that they understand the complex motivations involved. However, as Andreasen points out, many organizations are caught up in a social service/intervention mentality that sees customers as the problem and resistant to marketing research. The right mindset is, he suggests, a customer-centered mindset: the organization is led by its customers and does not try to make customers serve the organization's purpose. The organization starts with the customer and where their behavior is and not where the organization wants their behavior to be.

In line with this thinking, Brenkert (2002) suggests social marketers have to invite people to become part of a process of change to enhance their welfare rather than treat them as recipients or targets of efforts to change their behaviors. Social marketing must focus on the social problems of the people who have them, not on the desires of those who hire them. There is a major difference between the logic of persuasion and the logic of engaging, This demands a broader contextualization of programs, and has profound practical implications. For example, when recruiting parents to a drugs education program, it is necessary to take into consideration that parents often underestimate the extent of their own influence. Therefore, rather than just persuading them to attend parents' workshops, it is necessary to work with parents to understand how they perceive their role, what makes them underestimate their level of influence and what barriers exist to attendance. This seems quite obvious, but, as demonstrated by *Blueprint*, the assumptions of experience and expertise in working with parents are not compatible with relational thinking and its core principle of co-creation.

Embracing the client as the co-creator of value is about balancing the individual with the social. As MacFadyen et al. (2000) explain, 'social marketing is in the business of entrenched, taboo or even illegal behaviors and their resolution may involve the conflicting interests of the social marketing, the consumer and wider society' (p. 719). Social marketers must decide which behaviors to address, define priorities and advocate certain lifestyles or habits. This is a relevant ethical challenge that social marketers have to face. A complementary ethical challenge raised by Brenkert (2002) is that to be effective, not simply in some temporary manner but in the long run, social marketers must consider the social context of the problem they seek to resolve. He emphasizes that targets must be motivated to change, but', for this to be ethically grounded, social marketers must seek not only incentives for those they target but also justifications set within the larger contexts they inhabit' (p. 24). Consequently, theories of individual and social change that take a broader, more inclusive perspective may be relevant for social marketing as they understand people's lives in an everyday sense.

Theoretically, for social marketing, the value co-creation of RM is a partnership concept, not just downstream, but also mid- and upstream. Social marketing, in seeking to resolve conditions and forces that cause social problems, identifies a total market dimension to social change, seeing four partnership levels in a democracy for behavioral influence: micro level, group level, macro society level and macro international/global level, shown in Table 3.2, that are affected by the value creation sought by social marketing (Domegan and Bringle, 2010).

The application of social marketing at *all four* of these levels results in a conceptual maturing toward the 'market with' and 'relational' approach for social marketing (Hastings, 2003; Hastings and Saren, 2003; Lusch and Vargo, 2006; Grönroos, 2006; Wilkie and Moore, 2003). This 'market with' approach of social marketing embraces upstream stakeholders, partnerships,

Table 3.2 Types of social change, by time and level of partnership

Change	Micro level (individual)	Group level (group/community/ organization)	Macro level (society/nation)	Macro level (international or global)
Short term	Behavior change	Changes in norms/ Administrative change	Policy change	Policy change
Example:	Attendance at stop-smoking clinic	Removal of tobacco advertising from outside a school	Banning of all forms of tobacco marketing	Banning of all forms of tobacco marketing: e.g. in all EU countries
Long term	Lifestyle change	Organizational change	'Socio-cultural evolution'	'Socio-cultural evolution across societies'
Example:	Smoking cessation	Deter retailers from selling cigarettes to minors	Eradication of all tobacco-related disease	Eradication of all tobacco-related disease in the EU

Adapted from MacFadyen, L., Stead, M. and Hastings, G. (1999) *A Synopsis of Social Marketing*. Available at: www.social-marketing.com.html, p. 4.

multiple exchanges and the co-creation of value at all levels including that of the whole system – a macro society level constituting those who control the social context influencing the other two units (Brenkert, 2002). This is attributable to the fact that individuals influence, and are influenced by, those surrounding them, thereby requiring this four-tiered approach to the exchange process building upon both economic and social dimensions. This multiple exchange process results in social marketing having an extensive constellation of co-creating value stakeholders and relationships to satisfy and manage. The relationships are simultaneously active and engaged at all levels with the customers, communities and policymakers. This, in turn, achieves synergy between the multiple change agents to bring about the desired behavioral change of benefit for the individual and society (Lusch et al., 2010).

These conceptual aspects of relational thinking have important critical marketing implications. In particular, the effects of marketing on issues like social exclusion, the creation of false needs and identities affect health and consumer behavior (Hastings and Saren, 2003). Social marketers' legitimacy is greater if social marketers are critical about themselves: their own processes and outcomes, but especially about their assumptions or taken-for-granted 'truths'. From a critical perspective, the challenge is to make those assumptions explicit so they can be contested on other grounds than are provided for by the prevailing paradigm (Eakin et al., 1996). Critical thinking is fundamental to deconstruct the transactional paradigm, its assumptions of expertise and the subsequent implications in the design, implementation and evaluation of programs. The shift to relational

thinking demands a more self-reflective social marketing and a re-contextualization of the field in the value pluralist societies. The *Blueprint* evaluation is a good illustration of how relational thinking can enhance the critical power of evaluation (Marques, 2008).

The operational and tactical implications of client and partnership value co-creation for social marketing are just as far reaching. Just because a program does not result in behavior change it does not mean it failed (Hastings et al., 2002; Hastings, 2003). The focus on behavior change needs to be combined with a focus on relationships, otherwise programs that do not result in behavior change will be labeled as failures. Hastings (2003) discusses the case of *NE Choices* to illustrate and elaborate his argument. As he explains, the intervention had everything to work: a strong theoretical underpinning (social-influences approach backed by social marketing); a multi-component design (built around a high school drama initiative, with additional community, school governor and parent components); extensive, long-term resources; a comprehensive bank of formative, process and impact evaluations to inform its development and implementation and a quasi-experimental design to measure its effects on behavior (outcomes). The result was therefore extremely consumer and stakeholder oriented. However, despite all these strengths, it was perceived as unsuccessful. As emphasized by Hastings (2003), the case of NE Choices evaluation demonstrates that social marketers need to change the way programs are evaluated and attribute much more importance to intermediate measures. There are already some indicators of RM in health promotion evaluation literature, particularly in what concerns typical community-based programs. Some of those indicators are included in the set of main principles of the health promotion initiatives defined by the World Health Organization (WHO): empowerment, participation, inter-sectoral collaboration, capacity-building and sustainability. However, a true shift to relational thinking requires more than this. In particular, process evaluation is very well suited to study RM as it focuses on how programs operate rather than on behavior objectives. From a relational perspective, process evaluation has to explicitly approach recruitment and delivery as value-creation processes and overcome the limitations of transactional frameworks. In *Blueprint,* evaluation of the parent program a first step toward this shift was achieved (Marques, 2008).

The three RM processes of interaction, communication/dialogue and value creation and their consequences for repositioning social marketing in the center of the broader social context are summarized in Table 3.3.

KEY RM CONSTRUCTS AND SOCIAL MARKETING IMPLICATIONS

Going deeper into these RM processes, we find relationship quality, trust, commitment, satisfaction, perceived value, identification and cooperation as the key variables that are at the center of the meaning of relationalism. They are complex, often overlapping and ambiguous concepts (Gundlach et al., 1995), but at the same time full of potential. Social marketers have to address and explore them. We now examine psychological (relationship quality, trust, commitment, satisfaction, perceived value and identification) and behavioral (cooperation) key RM constructs.

Relationship quality

Relationship quality can be considered an overall assessment of the strength of a relationship (Garbarino and Johnson, 1999). To Roberts et al. (2003), relationship quality is a higher-order construct made of several distinct, though related, dimensions. Most conceptualizations of relationship quality in consumer markets build on Morgan and Hunt's (1994) theory of trust and commitment by including satisfaction as a key concept (e.g. Crosby et al., 1990; Gruen, 1995; Garbarino and Johnson, 1999; De and Odekerken-Schroder, 2001; Hennig-Thurau et al., 2002; Roberts et al., 2003). It is important to distinguish and compare the concepts of relationship quality and service quality. There is a consensus that relationship quality and service quality are different constructs, which means that what people value in a relationship does not necessarily correspond to what people value in a service. Crosby et al. (1990) state that service quality is a necessary but not sufficient condition for relationship quality. To illustrate this argument, Roberts et al. (2003) explain that one may be very satisfied with the service provided by the hairdresser, but may not feel that one has a personal relationship with the hairdresser. Nevertheless, they continue, it is impossible for a person to have a relationship with a hairdresser in the absence of a good service, as that is the basic foundation for the relationship to exist. However, there are different views in the literature around this issue. For example, Rosen and Suprenant (1998) and Bennett and Barkensjo (2005) admit that it is possible to have a good relationship with a service provider even if the quality of the service provided by an organization might not, of itself, be satisfactory. Similarly, Gwinner et al. (1998) demonstrated that customers might remain in the relationship even if they perceive the core service attributes to be less than superior provided they are receiving important relational benefits. Roberts et al. (2003) suggest that, despite the unavoidable overlap in the operationalization of the two constructs, it needs to be kept in mind that service quality in essence seeks to measure firm performance along transactional dimensions, whereas relationship quality emphasizes the intangible aspects of ongoing interactions over one of encounters. But, as proposed by Roberts et al. (2003), more research is needed to

Table 3.3 RM key processes and social marketing consequences

Interaction	Partnerships, co-learning, cooperation, collaborative, longer time frames
Communication/ dialogue	Critical marketing, two-way, shared meanings, positive appeals, branding, flexibility
Value creation	Co-creation, co-meaning, co-contextualization, networks, perceived value, experiences, integration

examine whether it is better to improve the service or the relationship.

Trust

There is a consensus in the literature that trust is a very relevant indicator of relationship quality. Trust has received a great deal of attention in social psychology (Deutsch, 1960; Lewicki and Bunker, 1996), sociology (Lewis and Weigert, 1985) economics (Dasgupta, 1990; Williamson, 1993) and organizational behavior (Hosmer, 1995; Rousscau et al., 1998; Wicks et al., 1999).

Moorman et al. (1992) define trust as *a willingness to rely on an exchange partner in whom one has confidence.* Their definition, they explain, spans the two general approaches to trust in the literature (Moorman et al., 1993, p. 82). One of them views trust as a belief, confidence or expectation about an exchange partner's trustworthiness that results from the partner's expertise, reliability or intentionality (e.g. Blau, 1964; Rotter, 1967). The other approach views trust as a behavioral intention or behaviour that reflects a reliance on a partner and involves vulnerability and uncertainty on the part of the trustor (Deutsch, 1962; Coleman, 1990). This view suggests that, without vulnerability, trust is unnecessary because outcomes are inconsequential for the trustor (Moorman et al., 1993, p. 82). Uncertainty is also critical because trust is unnecessary if the trustor can control an exchange partner's actions. In line with Moorman et al. (1993), Morgan and Hunt (1994) conceptualize trust as existing when one party has confidence in an exchange's partner's reliability and integrity. For Gundlach and Murphy (1993), trust is the variable most universally accepted as a basis for any human interaction or exchange. It is one dimension of ethical exchange therefore required for fair and open exchanges to occur.

This moral dimension of trust is also addressed in the organizational behavior literature (Hosmer, 1995; Wicks et al., 1999). Hosmer (1995) defines trust as 'the expectation by one person, group or firm of ethically justifiable behavior – that is morally correct decisions and actions based upon ethical principles of analysis – on the part of other person, group, or a firm in a joint endeavour or economic exchange' (p. 145). This definition makes trust's moral duty explicit and puts together organizational theory and moral philosophy. Wicks et al. (1999) write that, although rational prediction is clearly an important part of trust, affect, that is emotion, also needs to be considered. The affective element has a clear moral element; thus, the emotional bond is not just in the relationship but a belief in the moral character of the trustee. Similarly, McAllister (1995) suggests that trust based on emotional states such as care and concern are deeper than trust based primarily on cognitive perceptions of predictable dependable behaviors.

Social marketing is founded on trust (Hastings, 2003). It is not driven by profit but a desire to benefit the target audience. Social marketers are motivated to place the consumer's interest ahead of self-interest. Therefore, they are expected to have benevolent behaviors and practices which are often regarded as extra role action and valued by consumers. The affective dimension of trust, and its moral element, is well supported. The affective element is crucial for relationships. All this plays in favor of social marketing but there are issues that pose particular concerns to social marketers: there might be a negative side to contacts with authority (Gummesson, 2002); many times people are cynical and sceptical about authorities; the relationship is many times indirect and asymmetrical (Brenkert, 2002); when health becomes synonymous with the moral good, the potential for resistance is created (Crossley, 2002). Furthermore, in the field of social change, the issue of vulnerability is very important and social marketers have to work with consumers to find ways of dealing with it. Naturally, this is not compatible with a patronizing logic.

Perceived value

When talking about value, it is important to distinguish the value-in-exchange concept from the value-in-use concept. As pointed out by Grönroos (2006), traditionally, value is viewed in the literature as embedded in the product that is exchanged – the value-in-exchange notion – but, according to a more recent view in the literature of how value for customers emerges, value is created when products, goods or services are used by customers. This is value-in-use notion (Woodruff and Gardial, 1996; Vargo and Lusch, 2004). According to this view, 'Suppliers and service providers do not create value in their planning, designing and production processes. The customers do it themselves in their value-creating processes, in other words, in their daily activities when products are needed by them for them to perform activities' (Grönroos, 2006, p. 323). Suppliers only create the resources or means required to make it possible for customers to create value for themselves. In this sense, at least when suppliers and customers interact, they are engaged in co-creation of value. However, as Grönroos (2006) explains, customers are also sole creators of value. Goods are resources and the firm makes them available for money so that the customers in their own processes will be able to use them in a way that creates value for them. In social marketing, because we are dealing with complex and long-term behaviors, the concept of value in use is extremely important. For example, by itself, information for parents about drugs might have limited value unless parents are able to do something with it.

Ravald and Grönroos (1996) emphasize that the value concept is multifaceted and complicated. They argue that adding value can be done in several ways: one of them is adding benefits; the other might be to reduce the customer-perceived sacrifice by minimizing the relationship costs for the customer. Andreasen (1995) discusses and compares benefit-based strategies with cost-based strategies in the context of social marketing. This comparison refers to behavior, but we believe it can be extended to relationships. Perceived value is a very important concept to social marketers. The benefits and costs have to be related with consumers' values, which might be challenging due to their dynamic and contingent nature.

Satisfaction

Satisfaction is considered to be crucial for organizations that strive for long-term relationships with customers (Oliver and Swan, 1989). Satisfaction is a construct almost absent in business-to-business literature, but considered very important in consumer contexts. Gruen (1995) argues that the psychological construct of satisfaction is a critical central outcome of relationship marketing. Business-to-consumer (BTC) relationships may be more tenuous than business-to-business (BTB); as a result, the construct of commitment is likely to play a lesser role, while constructs like satisfaction and trust will be more important in BTC than BTB. Using social psychology theory as a guide, Gruen (1995) argues that the aspect of a BTC relationship to which the member's satisfaction will be related is the perceived value of the benefits or rewards received from the exchanges with the organization (Thibaut and Kelly, 1959). It is the member's assessment of the relative value of the basic exchanges in relationship. As the services marketing literature continually suggests, customers (members) must be satisfied with the basic services of the organization. 'Satisfaction is somewhat volatile, as it often depends on a member's most recent exchanges with the organization' (Gruen, 2000, p. 369). It has positive effects in trust and in commitment and it is likely to have some impact on retention and co-production (Gruen, 2000). Bennett and Barkensjo (2005) suggest that the level of client need has the potential to affect satisfaction. In the charity context, beneficiaries often place critical dimensions of their lives in a charity's hands and want desperately to be assisted.

Satisfaction is the assessment of the relative value of the basic exchanges; it concerns the way benefits/rewards are perceived. In social marketing the benefits are many times ambiguous and invisible, which makes the job of social marketing difficult. Furthermore, satisfaction is somewhat unstable, as it often depends on the consumer's most recent exchanges with the organization (Gruen, 1995). The issues here social marketers have to be careful about are the expectations they create and making sure they are capable of fulfilling them in a consistent and continuous way.

Commitment

Commitment is an important indicator of relationship quality. It is recognized as an essential ingredient for successful relationships and is considered to be central to all relational exchanges between the firm and its various partners (Dwyer et al., 1987; Morgan and Hunt, 1994; Gundlach et al., 1995).

As discussed by Morgan and Hunt (1994), commitment has been central in the social exchange literature (Thibaut and Kelly, 1959; Blau, 1964; Cook and Emerson, 1978), which characterizes commitment as a variable that is core in distinguishing social from economic exchange. Drawing on the conceptualizations of commitment in social exchange (Cook and Emerson, 1978), marriage (Thompson and Spanier, 1983) and organizations (Meyer and Allen, 1984), Morgan and Hunt (1994) define relationship commitment as an exchange partner believing the relationship is worth working on to ensure that endures indefinitely. Their definition corresponds to the one developed by Moorman et al. (1993). Equally inspired by social exchange theory, Dwyer et al. (1987) define commitment as 'an implicit or explicit pledge of relational continuity between exchange partners' (p. 19). It implies a willingness to make short-term sacrifices to realize longer-term benefits (Dwyer et al., 1987). Similarly, Gundlach and Murphy (1993) say that the characteristics of commitment are thought to be sacrifice, stability and loyalty.

Gundlach et al. (1995) posit that the structure of commitment is constituted by its credibility – the magnitude of the parties' combined commitments – and its proportionality or mutualness. They conceptualize commitment through a three-component model (p. 79):

- *Instrumental component:* an affirmative action taken by one party that creates a self-interest stake in the relationship; it is like a calculative act.

- *Attitudinal component*: an enduring intention by the parties to develop and maintain a stable long-term relationship.
- *Temporal dynamics*: they are at the very heart of the construct and correspond to consistent lines of activity. Two of its important elements are durability and consistency over time. Durability presumes the parties can discern the benefits attributable to the exchange relation and anticipate an environment that will abet continued affective exchange. Consistency is very important because when a party's input levels fluctuate, the other party will have difficulty predicting the outcomes from exchange.

In the charity context, commitment is considered to be deeply related to the concept of bonding. Bonding should occur as beneficiaries come to believe that a charity is motivated by a genuine concern for their welfare (Bennett and Barkensjo, 2005). Various but similar descriptions of loyalty and commitment are found. In empirical research, the term 'loyalty' often refers to repeat patronage, while 'commitment' is used to denote customers' affective preferences (Oderkerken-Schroder, 1999).

Commitment to the relationship is crucial to social marketing. The complex and long-term behaviors addressed by social marketers demand continuity and consistency and, without commitment, individuals/consumers' involvement and participation will not be genuine. Commitment implies a willingness to make short-term sacrifices to realize longer-term benefits (Dwyer et al., 1987). It presumes durability and consistency.

In social marketing, the tyranny of small decisions (Rothschild, 2001a) raises particular challenges to social marketers. Furthermore, because of the need to articulate the work of different people and organizations involved in social marketing programs, it is very important to assure consistent levels of commitment of all relevant actors.

Identification

The phenomenon of identification is the perception of belonging to a group with the result that a person identifies with that group (*I am a member*). With increasing interest in RM strategies, there has been growing interest in organizational identification and the way it relates to customer behavior (Bhattacharya et al., 1995; Bhattacharya and Bolton, 2000; Arnett et al., 2003; Bhattacharya and Sen, 2003).

Similar to commitment, identification is considered as a type of bond connecting the individual with the organization. The key difference is that in identification organizational images are linked to members' self-concepts (Battacharya et al., 1995). Gruen (2000) argues that increased levels of identification will lead to increased levels of retention, participation/loyalty and co-production. He also points that whereas satisfaction and commitment have been examined in virtually all types of RM, the concept of identification is generally reserved for situations involving memberships. Bhattacharya et al. (1995) suggest that corporate philanthropy and cause-related marketing programs can better enhance identification if they draw consumers inside the organization as members. However, more recently, Bhattacharya and Sen (2003) extended research on social identity (Tajfel and Turner, 1979) and organizational identification (Bergami and Bagozzi, 2000), and proposed that identification with organizations can also occur in the absence of formal membership, as with the case of consumers and companies both for and non-profit. They also enlarge the view of the 'extended self' (Belk, 1988), suggesting that it seems to stem not only from material possessions or even memberships but also from people's positive and negative psychological connections with organizations. This view assumes that identification has both cognitive and affective dimensions (Bergami and Bagozzi, 2000).

Bhattacharya and Sen (2003) suggest that consumers will identify with an attractive company identity only when their interactions with that company are significant, sustained and meaningful enough to embed them in the organizational network. As they explain, 'embedded relationships arise when consumers engage in company-related rites, rituals and routines' (p. 82). They also increase when consumers network with other company stakeholders and other consumers through on- and offline communities (e.g. discussions forums hosted by the American Cancer Society) or get involved in company decision making. Embedded relationships are more likely to occur when the company and its products/services contribute to the satisfaction of idiosyncratic, important interests and provide opportunities for self-expression (Bhattacharya and Sen, 2003).

Applying identity theory in the non-profit marketing context, Arnett et al. (2003) argue that identity theory captures the social nature of an exchange relationship as it explicitly incorporates many of the social benefits that are derived from the relationship: for example, self-esteem. 'Identity theory posits that identities are arranged hierarchically and that salient identities are more likely to affect behavior than those that are less important' (p. 89).

In addition, these identities often compete against one another. As Bhattacharya et al. (1995) suggest, identification is not simply a bilateral relationship between a person and an organization, isolated from other organizations, but a process in a competitive arena, so it is important to think about identification but also about desidentification. Bhattacharya and Elsbach (2002) discuss this in social marketing initiatives – for example, the California Anti-Tobacco Coalition tries to influence consumers to desidentify with Philip Morris – and argue that these do not only lead to individual-level behavior change but also could lead to related macro- or population-level changes.

Social marketing programs often deal with existent identities which can create resistances from the target/individuals. Coupled with this, many times, social marketing programs involve a collective of people, rather than a single organization, which makes identification particularly challenging but also especially relevant.

Cooperation

Cooperation is considered to be one of the main values of the RM paradigm and a crucial condition of the value creation process (Grönroos, 1994a, 2000a; Parvatyar and Sheth, 2000; Gummesson, 2002). As a construct, it is normally considered to be a desired behavior in RM (Morgan and Hunt, 1994; Gruen, 1995; Sheth and Parvatyar, 1995). Morgan and Hunt (1994) propose that cooperation is one of the main indicators of success and it arises directly from both relationship commitment and trust. As they explain, cooperation means working together to achieve mutual goals. Because conflictual behavior can coexist temporarily with cooperative actions, cooperation is not simply the absence of conflict. Nor, they emphasize, is cooperation the same thing as acquiescence: cooperation is proactive; acquiescence is reactive.

Morgan and Hunt (1994) show empirical evidence to posit that trust has the strongest effect in cooperation and suggest further research about possible forms of cooperation that are more conducive to success. One possible form – citizenship behaviors/extra role behaviors – is, as they demonstrate, well studied in the organizational behavior literature (Organ, 1988). Organ (1988) suggests that citizenship behaviors can be exhibited in a variety of forms, such as altruism, civic virtue and by word of mouth. In the beneficiary RM context, beneficiaries cooperated, recommending the charity to other people and engaging in positive word of mouth (Bennett and Barkensjo, 2005).

By encouraging cooperation, RM gives firms access to improved customer information and input from the consumer. One such example is the

Heart Truth, the National Heart, Lung and Blood Institute initiative to create awareness about women and heart disease; cooperation with America's fashion industry was essential to access the 'considerable promotional and communication capabilities and distribution channels of the fashion industry… and opening doors to opportunities with the corporate and media sectors' (Temple et al., 2008, p. 68). Furthermore, this cooperation can extend to the product development process, involving consumers early on in product development and testing (Roberts et al., 2003). Sheth and Parvatyar (1995) argue that RM is likely to make marketing practices more effective because, on the one hand, the individual customer's needs are better addressed, and on the other hand, consumer involvement in the development of the marketing processes and practices leads to greater commitment. Relationship marketing also leads to a greater efficiency because with cooperative and efficient consumer response marketers will be able to reduce many unproductive resources wasted in the system. And, as cooperation develops, the consumer will be willing to undertake some of the value creation activities such as co-production. Examining BTC relationships, Gruen (2000) argues that co-production behaviors create value both for the organization and for the members. It can take many forms, such as word of mouth and participation in activities of the organization. He sees co-production as a consequence of satisfaction, commitment, identification and member interdependence. Regarding member interdependence, Gruen (2000) explains that a large portion of the value of belonging to a membership organization comes through the relationships that members establish with other members; although the membership organization seeks to provide value to the individual members, they often obtain value through exchanges among themselves, for example, using informal networks. 'Relationship interdependence is viewed as the extent of the mutual value of the exchanges between members' and it 'can be characterized by both the breadth of the network and the quality of exchanges' (p. 371–372).

Cooperation is very relevant to social marketing. The challenge is to develop and stimulate innovative, creative and efficient forms of cooperation. These key RM processes and constructs, coupled with their social marketing implications, are captured in Table 3.4.

CONCLUSION

Relationship marketing has had a major impact upon generic marketing. Its implications for social

Table 3.4 Key RM processes and constructs and social marketing implications

Relationship quality	Trust, commitment, satisfaction
Trust	Confidence, reliability, uncertainty, integrity, ethics
Commitment	Bonding, relational continuity, sacrifice, loyalty
Satisfaction	Relative value, recent exchanges
Identification	Bonding, membership; disidentification
Perceived value	Mutual, in-use, costs/benefits
Cooperation	Mutual goals, co-learning and knowledge, proactive

marketing are even more profound. Behavior change remains a key goal, but progress toward this goal demands the inclusive and strategic vision of relational thinking (Hastings, 2003). Ultimately, this requires that social marketers redefine their role in society: behavior change experts as relationship managers.

The key challenges are the following: to re-question and make assumptions explicit, to overcome the persuasion logic and really see consumers as the main drivers of the value creation process; to overcome the product logic and invest in resources and competences; to move from a functionalistic to a process management perspective and find more flexible organizational structures and to develop networks and identify priority partnerships. Additional challenges are to recognize that relationship marketing is not a 'lip service' (Grönroos, 1996) and to see beyond

Table 3.5 Key RM insights/lessons for social marketing

- RM has profound conceptual, strategic and operational implications for social marketing
- RM demands on social marketers to see the client as a co-creator of value
- RM calls on social marketers to adopt partnerships, networks, cooperation and collaboration
- RM requires social marketing to integrate three key RM processes of interaction; communication/dialogue and value creation
- Social marketers need to exploit RM key constructs of relationship quality, trust, commitment, satisfaction, identification and perceived value and cooperation
- RM emphasizes long-term vision and strategies for social marketing

its technical potentialities. This implies that recruitment and delivery are re-conceptualized as dialogue, interaction and value creating processes, which, in turn, will optimize the integrative potential of RM.

Relationship marketing is much more than a sum of exchanges in isolated transactions and it is much more than a set of techniques. It is a new foundation for thinking that requires strategic vision and a sense of the whole. These insights and lessons from RM for social marketing are summarized in Table 3.5.

KEY WORDS: Relationship marketing; interaction; communication/dialogue; value creation; relationship quality; trust; commitment; satisfaction; identification; perceived value; cooperation.

REFERENCES

Aijo, T.S. (1996) 'The theoretical and philosophical underpinnings of relationship marketing: Environmental factors behind the changing marketing paradigm', *European Journal of Marketing*, 30(2): 8–18.

Andreasen, A.R. (1995) *Marketing Social Change: Changing Behaviour to Promote Health, Social Development and the Environment*. San Francisco, CA: Jossey-Bass.

Andreasen, A.R. (2001) 'Intersector transfer of marketing knowledge', in P. Boom and G. Gundlach (eds), *Handbook of Marketing and Society*. Thousand Oaks, CA: Sage Publications.

Arnett, D.B., German S.D. and Hunt, S.D. (2003) 'The identity salience model of relationship marketing success: The case of non-profit marketing', *Journal of Marketing*, April: 89–105.

Ballantyne, D. (2000) 'Dialogue and knowledge generation: Two sides of the same coin in relationship marketing', in *Proceedings of the 2nd WWW Conference on Relationship Marketing*. Monash University and MCB University Press. Available online at: www.mcb.co.uk/services/conferen/nov99/rm/paper3.html.

Belk, R.W. (1988) 'Possessions and the extended self', *Journal of Consumer Research*, 15(2): 139–168.

Bennett, R. and Barkensjo, A. (2005) 'Relationship quality, relationship marketing and client perceptions of the levels of service quality of charitable organizations', *International Journal of Service Industry Management*, 16: 81–106.

Bergami, M. and Bagozzi R.P. (2000) 'Self-categorization and commitment as distinct aspects of social identity in the organization: Conceptualization, measurement, and relation to antecedents and consequences', *British Journal of Social Psychology*, 39: 555–577.

Berry, L.L. (1983) 'Relationship marketing', in L.L. Berry, G.L. Shostack and G.D. Upah (eds), *Emerging Perspectives of*

Services Marketing. Chicago, IL: American Marketing Association, pp. 25–28.

Bhattacharya, C.B. and Bolton, R.N. (2000) 'Relationship marketing in mass markets', in J.N. Sheth and A. Parvatyar (eds), *Handbook of Relationship Marketing.* Thousand Oaks, CA: Sage Publications, pp. 327–354.

Bhattacharya, C.B. and Elsbach, K.D. (2002) 'Us versus them: The roles of organizational identification and disidentification in social marketing initiatives', *Journal of Public Policy & Marketing,* 21: 26–36.

Bhattacharya, C.B. and Sen, A. (2003) 'Consumer–company identification: A framework for understanding consumers' relationships with companies', *Journal of Marketing,* 67(2): 76–88.

Bhattacharya, C.B., Rao, H. and Glynn, M.A. (1995) 'Understanding the bond of identification: An investigation of its correlates among art museum members', *Journal of Marketing,* 59(4): 46–57.

Blau, P.M. (1964) *Exchange and Power in Social Life.* New York: John Wiley & Sons, Inc.

Brenkert, G. (2002) 'Ethical challenges of social marketing', *Journal of Public Policy & Marketing,* 21: 14–25.

Christopher, M., Payne, A. and Ballantyne, D. (1991) *Relationship Marketing.* Oxford: Butterworth-Heinemann.

Coleman, J. (1990) *Foundations of Social Theory.* Cambridge, MA: Harvard University Press.

Cook, K.S. and Emerson, R.M. (1978) 'Power, equity and commitment in exchange networks', *American Sociological Review,* 43(October): 721–739.

Crosby, L.A., Evans, K.R. and Cowles, D. (1990) 'Relationship quality in services selling: An interpersonal influence perspective', *Journal of Marketing,* 54(3): 68–81.

Crossley, M. (2002) 'Introduction to the Symposium *Health Resistance* – The limits of contemporary health promotion', *Health Education Journal,* 61(2): 101–112.

Damásio, A.R. (2004) 'Emotions and feelings: A neurobiological perspective', in A.S.R. Manstead, N. Frijda and A. Fischer (eds), *Feelings and Emotions: The Amsterdam Symposium.* New York: Cambridge University Press, pp. 49–57.

Dasgupta, P. (1990) 'Trust as a commodity', in D. Gambetta (ed), *Trust: Making and Breaking Cooperative Relations.* Oxford: Basil Blackwell , pp. 49–72.

Deutsch, M. (1960) 'The effect of motivational orientation on trust and suspicion', *Human Relations,* 13: 123–139.

Deutsch, M. (1962) 'Cooperation and trust: Some theoretical notes', in *Nebraska Symposium on Motivation.* Lincoln, NE: Nebraska University Press, pp. 275–320.

De Wulf, K. and Odekerken-Schroder, G. (2001) 'A critical review of theories underlying relationship marketing in the context of explaining consumer relationships', *Journal for the Theory of Social Behavior,* 31: 73–102.

Domegan, C. and Bringle, R. (2010) 'Charting social marketing's implications for service learning', *Journal of Non-profit and Public Sector Marketing,* 22(3): 198–215.

Dwyer, F.R., Schurr, P.H. and Oh, S. (1987) 'Developing buyer–seller relationships', *Journal of Marketing,* 51: 11–27.

Eakin, J., Robertson, A., Poland, B., Coburn, D. and Edwards, R. (1996) 'Towards a critical social science perspective on health promotion research', *Health Promotion International,* 11(2): 157–165.

Elinor, L. and Gerard, G. (1998) *Dialogue: Rediscovering the Transforming Power of Conversations.* New York: John Wiley & Sons, Inc.

Garbarino, E. and Johnson, M. (1999) 'The different roles of satisfaction, trust and commitment in customer relationships', *Journal of Marketing,* 63(April): 70–87.

Glenane-Antoniadis, A., Whitwell, G., Bell, S.J. and Menguc, B. (2003) 'Extending the vision of social marketing through social capital theory', *Marketing Theory,* 3(3): 323–343.

Grönroos, C. (1994a) 'Quo vadis, marketing? Toward a relationship marketing paradigm', *Journal of Marketing Management,* 10: 347–360.

Grönroos, C. (1994b) 'From marketing mix to relationship marketing: Towards a paradigm shift in marketing', *Management Decision,* 32(2): 4–20.

Grönroos, C. (1996) 'Relationship marketing: Strategic and tactical implications', *Management Decision,* 34(3): 5–14.

Grönroos, C. (2000a) 'Relationship marketing: The Nordic School perspective', in J.N. Sheth and A. Parvatyar (eds), *Handbook of Relationship Marketing.* Thousand Oaks, CA: Sage Publications.

Grönroos, C. (2000b) 'Creating a relationship dialogue', *The Marketing Review,* 1: 5–14.

Grönroos, C. (2004) 'The relationship marketing process: Communication, interaction, dialogue, value', *Journal of Business & Industrial Marketing,* 19(2): 99–113.

Grönroos, C. (2006) 'Adopting a service logic for marketing', *Marketing Theory,* 6(3): 317–333.

Gruen, T.W. (1995) 'The outcome set of relationship marketing in consumer markets', *International Business Review,* 4(4): 447–469.

Gruen, T.W. (2000) 'Membership customers and relationship marketing', in J.N. Sheth and A. Parvatyar (eds), *Handbook of Relationship Marketing.* Thousand Oaks, CA: Sage Publications.

Gummesson, E. (1994) 'Making relationship marketing operational', *International Journal of Service and Industry Management,* 5(5): 5–20.

Gummesson, E. (1997) 'Relationship marketing as a paradigm shift: Some conclusions from the 30R approach', *Management Decision,* 35(4): 267–272.

Gummesson, E. (1998) 'Implementation requires a relationship marketing paradigm', *Journal of the Academy of Marketing Science,* 26(3): 242–249.

Gummesson, E. (2002) *Total Relationship Marketing, Rethinking Marketing Management: From 4Ps to 30Rs,* 2nd edn. Oxford: Butterworth-Heinemann.

Gundlach, G.T. and Murphy, P.E. (1993) 'Ethical and legal foundations of relational marketing exchanges', *Journal of Marketing,* 57: 35–46.

Gundlach, G.T., Achrol, R.S. and Mentzer, J. (1995) 'The structure of commitment in exchange', *Journal of Marketing,* 59: 78–92.

Gwinner, K.P., Gremler, D.D. and Bitner, M.J. (1998) 'Relational benefits in services industries: The customer's perspective', *Journal of the Academy of Marketing Science*, 26(2): 101–114.

Hastings, G. (2003) 'Relational paradigms in social marketing', *Journal of Macromarketing*, 23: 6–15.

Hastings, G. and Saren, M. (2003) 'The critical contribution of social marketing, theory and application', *Marketing Theory*, 3(3): 305–322.

Hastings, G., Stead, M. and Mackintosh, A.M. (2002) 'Rethinking drugs prevention: Radical thoughts from social marketing', *Health Education Journal*, 61(4): 347–364.

Hastings, G., Stead, M. and Webb, J. (2004) 'Fear appeals in social marketing: Strategical and ethical reasons for concern', *Psychology & Marketing*, 21(11): 961–986.

Henley, N., Donovan, R.J. and Moorhead, H. (1998) 'Appealing to positive motivations and emotions in social marketing: Example of a positive parenting campaign', *Social Marketing Quarterly*, Summer: 48–53.

Hennig-Thurau, T., Gwinner, K.-P. and Gremler, D.D. (2002) 'Understanding relationship marketing outcomes. An integration of relational benefits and relationship quality', *Journal of Services Research*, 4(3): 230–247.

Holmlund, M. (1996) A Theoretical framework of perceived quality in business relationships (Research Rep.). Helsinki, Finland: Swedish School of Economics and Business Administration.

Hosmer, L.T. (1995) 'Trust: The connecting link between organizational theory and philosophical ethics', *Academy of Management Review*, 20(2): 379–340.

Keller, K.L. (1998) 'Branding perspectives on social marketing', *Advances in Consumer Research*, 25: 299–302.

Lewicki, R. and Bunker, B. (1996) 'Developing and maintaining trust in work relationships', in R.M. Kramer and T.R. Tyler (eds), *Trust in Organizations: Frontiers of Theory and Research*. London: Sage Publications, pp. 114–139.

Lewis, J.D. and Weigert, A. (1985) 'Trust as a social reality', *Social Forces*, 63(4): 967–985.

Lusch, R.F. and Vargo, S.L. (2006) 'Service-dominant logic: Reactions, reflections and refinements', *Marketing Theory*, 6(3): 281–288.

Lusch, R.F., Vargo, S.L. and Tanniru, M. (2010) 'Service, value networks and learning', *Journal of the Academy of Marketing Science*, 38: 19–31.

McAllister, D. (1995) 'Affect and cognition based trust as foundations for interpersonal cooperation in organization', *Academy of Management Journal*, 38: 24–59.

MacFadyen, L., Stead, M. and Hastings, G. (2000) 'Social marketing', in M.J. Baker (ed), *The Marketing Book*, 5th edn. Oxford: Butterworth-Heinemann, pp. 694–725.

McHugh, P. and Domegan, C. (2009) 'Systematic reviews: Their emerging role in connecting theory and policy', Irish Social Sciences Conference, 1 December, Galway, Ireland.

McKenna, R. (1991) *Relationship Marketing. Successful Strategies for the Age of Customer*. New York: Addison-Wesley.

Maloney, M. (2006) 'Food Dudes Programme in Ireland', 5th International Symposium of the International Fruit and Vegetable Alliance, October, Dublin, Ireland.

Marques, S. (2008) 'Creating value through relationships: A critical contribution from Social Marketing, Doctoral Dissertation'. University of Stirling, Scotland.

Meyer, J.P. and Allen, N.J. (1984) 'Testing the side-bet theory of organizational commitment: Some methodological considerations', *Journal of Applied Psychology*, 69(3): 372–378.

Moorman, C., Deshpande, R. and Zaltman, G. (1993) 'Factors affecting trust in market research relationships', *Journal of Marketing*, 57: 81–101.

Moorman, C., Zaltman, G. and Deshpandé, R. (1992) 'Relationships between Providers and Users of Market Research: The Dynamics of Trust Within and Between Organizations', *Journal of Marketing Research*, 29 (August): 314–328.

Morgan, R.M. and Hunt, S.D. (1994) 'The commitment-trust theory of relationship marketing', *Journal of Marketing*, 58(3): 20–38.

Oderkerken-Schroder, G. (1999) 'The role of the buyer in affecting buyer–seller relationships. Empirical studies in a retail context. Doctoral dissertation, University of Maastricht.

Oliver, R.L. and Swan, I.F. (1989) 'Consumer perceptions of interpersonal equity and satisfaction in transactions: A field survey approach', *Journal of Marketing*, 53(April): 21–35.

Organ, D. (1988) *Organizational Citizenship Behaviour*. Lexington, MA: Lexington Books.

Parvatyar, A. and Sheth, J.N. (2000) 'The domain and conceptual foundations of relationship marketing', in J.N. Sheth and A. Parvatyar (eds), *Handbook of Relationship Marketing*. Thousand Oaks, CA: Sage Publications, pp. 3–38.

Payne, C. (2000) 'Relationship marketing, the UK perspective', in J.N. Sheth and A. Parvatyar (eds), *Handbook of Relationship Marketing*. Thousand Oaks, CA: Sage Publications, pp. 39–60.

Peattie, S. and Peattie, K. (2003) 'Ready to fly solo? Reducing social marketing's dependence on commercial marketing theory', *Marketing Theory*, 3(3): 365–385.

Ravald, A. and Grönroos, C. (1996) 'The value concept and relationship marketing', *European Journal of Marketing*, 30(2): 19–30.

Roberts, K., Varki, S. and Brodie, R. (2003) 'Measuring the quality of relationships in consumer services: An empirical study', *European Journal of Marketing*, 37(1/2): 169–196.

Rosen, D.E. and Surprenant, C. (1998) 'Evaluating relationships: Are satisfaction and quality enough? ', *International Journal of Service Industry Management*, 9(2): 103–125.

Rothschild, M.L. (2001a) 'A few behavioural economics insights for social marketers', *Social Marketing Quarterly*, 7(3): 9–13.

Rothschild, M.L. (2001b) 'Book review: Aaker, DA, 1995, *Building Strong Brands*', *Social Marketing Quarterly*, 7(2): 36–40.

Rotter, J.B. (1967) 'A new scale for the measurement of inter-personal trust', *Journal of Personality*, 35(4): 651–665.

Rousseau, D.M., Sikin, S.B., Burt, R.S. and Camerer, C. (1998) 'Not so different after all: A cross discipline view of trust', *Academy of Management Review*, 23: 393–404.

Sheth, J.N. (1994) 'A normative model of retaining customer satisfaction', *Gamma News Journal*, July–August: 4–7.

Sheth, J.N. and Parvatyar, A. (1995) 'Relationship marketing in consumer markets: Antecedents and consequences', *Journal of the Academy of Marketing Science*, 23(4): 255–271.

Sheth, J.N. and Parvatyar, A. (2002) 'Evolving relationship marketing into a discipline', *Journal of Relationship Marketing*, 1: 3–16.

Stead, M. and Hastings, G. (2003) *Using the media for drugs prevention: An overview of literature on effectiveness and good practice*, Report produced for COI, Centre for Social Marketing, University of Strathclyde

Storbacka, K. (2000) 'Customer profitability: Analysis and design issues', in J.N. Sheth and A. Parvatyar (eds), *Handbook of Relationship Marketing*. Thousand Oaks, CA: Sage.

Tajfel, H. and Turner, J.C. (1985) 'The Social Identity Theory of Intergroup Behavior', in S. Worchel and W. G. Austin (eds), *Psychology of Intergroup Relations*, Chicago Nelson-Hall, pp. 6–24.

Temple, S., Long, T., Wayman, J., Taubenheim, A. and Patterson, J. (2008) 'Alliance building: Mobilizing partners to share the Heart Truth with American Women', *Social Marketing Quarterly*, 14(3): 68–78.

Thibaut, J.W. and Kelly, H.H. (1959) *The Social Psychology of Groups*. New York: John Wiley & Sons, Inc.

Thompson, L. and Spanier, G.B. (1983) 'The end of marriage and acceptance of marital termination', *Journal of Marriage and the Family*, 45(February): 103–113.

Tzokas, N. and Saren, M. (1997) 'Building relationship platforms in consumer markets: A value chain approach', *Journal of Strategic Marketing*, 5(2): 105–120.

Tzokas, N. and Saren, M. (1999) 'Value transformation in relationship marketing', *Australasian Marketing Journal*, 7: 52–62.

Vargo, S.L. and Lusch, R.F. (2004) 'Evolving to a new dominant logic for marketing', *Journal of Marketing* 68: 1–17.

Velleman, R., Mistral, W. and Sanderling, L. (2000) *Taking the Message Home: Involving Parents in Drugs Prevention*. Drugs Prevention Advisory Service, Home Office.

Wicks, A.C., Berman, S.L. and Jones, T.M. (1999) 'The structure of optimal trust: Moral and strategic implications', *Academy of Management Review*, 24: 99–116.

Wilkie, W. and Moore, E. (2003) 'Scholarly research in marketing: Exploring the "four eras" of thought develop-ment', *Journal of Public Policy and Marketing*, 22(2): 116–146.

Williamson, O.E. (1993) 'Calculativeness, trust and economic organization', *Journal of Law & Economics,* 36: 453–486.

Woodruff, R.B. and Gardial, S. (1996) *Know Your Customers – New Approaches to Understand Customer Value and Satisfaction*, Oxford: Blackwell.

4

Understanding Social Norms: Upstream and Downstream Applications for Social Marketers

Patrick Kenny and Gerard Hastings

INTRODUCTION

A solid appreciation of social norm perceptions – and specifically their formation, their influence on behavior and the effects of manipulating them through marketing campaigns – is important for social marketers. This understanding is of equal importance for social marketers engaged in both 'upstream' and 'downstream' (Goldberg, 1995) efforts to bring about behavior change. Social marketers engaged in traditional 'downstream' initiatives aimed at encouraging change on the part of those who have already developed unhealthy behavioral habits (rescuing those who have already fallen into the river in Goldberg's analogy) can benefit from understanding how the manipulation of social norm perceptions can bring about positive change on the part of both individuals and groups. Most research in the field focuses on this task of changing the habits of those who are already engaged in harmful activity. However, those with an interest in 'upstream' social marketing, who want to prevent people developing unhealthy habits (or jumping into the river, as Goldberg would put it) in the first place, may also find the insights garnered from the social norms literature to be beneficial for their work.

This chapter reviews the diverse literature on social norms, arguing that norms are a powerful influence on human behavior, especially among the young and vulnerable. In particular, the chapter examines the somewhat controversial 'downstream' applications of normative influence in the so called social norms approach, critically examining some of the weaknesses of this work. It then examines the comparatively less researched, but significant, upstream applications of social norms by examining sources of normative influence. Suggestions for social marketing practitioners and researchers are then presented.

THE NATURE OF SOCIAL NORMS

Social norm influences are situated within the wider field of peer influence, a topic on which there is a broad consensus in the empirical literature. Peers are generally acknowledged as one of the most significant influences on a variety of behaviors throughout adolescence (Borsari and Carey, 2001), and often overtake parents in importance as sources of influence as children progress through their teenage years (Csikszentmihalyi and Larson, 1984). Peers exert influence both directly and indirectly (Borsari and Carey, 2001). Direct peer influence has been subject to considerably less empirical investigation, but the evidence that exists indicates that direct offers to engage in, for example, drinking, smoking and sexual relations, exert a strong influence on behavior (Klein, 1992; Rabow and Duncan-Schill, 1994; Shore et al., 1983; Wood et al., 2001), particularly in the case of those who are less socially established and personally mature.

Significantly more research has focused on indirect peer influences, of which there are two types: modeling and social norms. For methodological reasons, most modeling research has focused on drinking behavior in quasi-experimental settings in which subjects are paired with confederates in a bar. This body of research shows that models influence concurrent, but not future drinking (Caudill and Kong, 2001; Caudill and Marlatt, 1975; Collins et al., 1985; Dericco and Garlington, 1977). Interest in the modeling explanation for peer influence has declined in recent years, in part because of the significant methodological challenges inherent in the experimental approach to modeling research (Borsari and Carey, 2001).

By contrast, social norms have consistently been seen as important drivers of human behavior, with some of the earliest work on social norms being published in the early part of the last century. Sumner (1906) understood norms to be the customs adopted by a group in order to effectively meet their basic needs, while Sherif (1936) conducted some of the earliest experiments on norm formation and transmission.

Since these early works, norms, variously defined, have played an important role in a variety of sociological and communication theories which either use norms as explanatory variables or seek to determine their influence on behavior. These theories include, among others, the theory of reasoned action (Fishbein and Ajzen, 1975); the theory of planned behavior (Ajzen, 1991); attribution theory (Heider, 1958); social learning theory (Bandura, 1986); problem behavior theory (Donovan et al., 1983); social comparison theory (Festinger, 1954); spiral of silence theory (Noelle-Neumann, 1973); peer cluster theory (Oetting and Beauvais, 1987); cultivation theory (Gerbner and Gross, 1976); the theory of presumed influence (Gunther and Storey, 2003); symbolic interactionism (Mead, 1934); differential association theory (Sutherland and Cressey, 1955); social identity theory (Turner, 1982); self-categorization theory (Turner et al., 1987); primary socialization theory (Oetting and Donnermeyer, 1998) and social network theory (Granovetter, 1973).

There has been a significant expansion in the research base on norms since the early 1990s, particularly as a result of the discovery that people tend to overestimate peer norms (Perkins and Berkowitz, 1986), that these overestimations

influence behavior (Cialdini et al., 2006), and that behaviors can be changed when these overestimations are corrected (Perkins et al., 2010). However, despite this extensive background and the growing interest in social norms research, there remain significant conceptual and methodological difficulties within the field.

Types and characteristics of social norms

Perhaps one of the greatest challenges hampering the development of social norms studies has been the inconsistent use of terminology, which is both a contributor to, and a symptom of, conceptual confusion in the field (Larimer et al., 2004; Rimal and Real, 2003). Researchers have examined the influence of social norms under such diverse terms as local and global norms (Miller and Prentice, 1994), proximal normative beliefs (Maddock and Glanz, 2005), normative beliefs and modeling (Oostveen et al., 1996), social modeling (Wood et al., 2001), peer norms and adult norms (Epstein et al., 1999) and perceived social influences (Dusenbury et al., 1994).

This general confusion has hampered the development of the field and frustrated attempts to coherently unpack the relative importance of normative social influences in different behavioral contexts. However, it does seem that the persuasive conceptual and empirical work of Rimal and colleagues in developing the Theory of Normative Social Behavior (Lapinski and Rimal, 2005; Rimal, 2008; Rimal and Real, 2003, 2005; Rimal et al., 2005), as well as the experimental work of Cialdini (Chapter 7) and colleagues in developing the Focus Theory of Normative Conduct (Cialdini, 2003; Cialdini et al., 1990, 2006; Kallgren et al., 2000; Reno et al., 1993) is beginning to bring greater consensus and coherence to the field.

Notwithstanding the development of this consensus, there remain significant conceptual and definitional challenges in the social norm literature. In order to utilize normative influences effectively, social marketers must be able to distinguish between the different types of norms, their formation and their different impacts upon behavior (Lee et al., 2007). Perhaps the simplest way to classify the different types of norms is in two broad categories: namely descriptive and prescriptive norms. Prescriptive norms, in turn, can be categorized as being either injunctive norms or subjective norms. A third overall category – that of personal norms – is also of note. Although sometimes considered to be another type of social norm (Bobek et al., 2007), personal norms are technically not *social* in nature, although they are almost certainly influenced by, and moderate the influence of, the other types of social norms.

Descriptive norms operate by way of example (Cialdini et al., 2006) and refer to perceptions of what others actually do in a given situation. They are a powerful influence on behavior, especially in novel or ambiguous contexts (Lapinski and Rimal, 2005) and among those who are susceptible to social anxiety (Neighbors et al., 2007a). Following the descriptive norms we observe in our surroundings requires little cognitive processing – even birds and fish and insects follow the descriptive norms of their peers (Cialdini, 2003). These norms broadly influence behavior because individuals perceive that others, especially those who are similar, are effective guides to behavior (Deutsch and Gerard, 1955; Fekadu and Kraft, 2002). Many of the 'social norms' interventions which have become popular in recent years are actually really only 'descriptive norms' interventions as they generally only focus on this source of influence (Rimal and Real, 2005).

Prescriptive norms are based on opinions and values rather than on the behavior of others, and refer to how individuals 'ought' to behave (Cialdini et al., 1990). The term is rarely used in the literature (see Yanovitzky et al., 2006 for an exception). Instead, prior research has used the terms *injunctive* and *subjective* norms, although these constructs could more usefully be seen as categories of prescriptive norms.

Subjective norms are an important component of the theory of reasoned action (Ajzen and Fishbein, 1980; Fishbein and Ajzen, 1975) and the theory of planned behavior (Ajzen, 1991) and refer to perceptions of whether 'most people who are important to him think he should or should not perform the behavior in question' (Fishbein and Ajzen, 1975: 302). *Injunctive norms,* on the other hand, refer to what is approved, or otherwise, by most people (Cialdini et al., 1991).

Many theorists view injunctive and subjective norms as analogous to each other (Neighbors et al., 2007b; Rimal and Real, 2005), although it seems more appropriate to view them as distinct, although often related, sources of influence (Bobek et al., 2007; Cialdini and Trost, 1998; van den Putte et al., 2005). Depending on the circumstances, injunctive and subjective norms may be congruent with each other. For example, in most situations both the subjective norms of important others, and the injunctive norms of society at large, may be opposed to the use of extreme violence. But in other circumstances clear conflicts can arise. The important reference group of parents (subjective norm) might prefer adolescents to delay sexual initiation but the wider cultural values (injunctive norm) could encourage early sexualization. Similarly, the close reference group of peers (subjective norm) may encourage illegal drug use, but society at large (injunctive norm) communicates disapproval of this behavior through its laws. There may even be conflicting subjective and injunctive norms at work simultaneously, whereby parents and peers (both sources of subjective norms in this example) could differ with respect to their views on alcohol consumption, while society in general (injunctive norm) also communicates confused messages with respect to restrictions on underage consumption on the one hand and the simultaneous glamorization of drinking communicated through pervasive marketing messages. These simple hypothetical examples illustrate the importance of separating out injunctive and subjective norms and serve to highlight the theoretical complexity of normative influences which can sometimes be mutually reinforcing or contradictory in nature. The examples also raise important issues about the salience of the reference group (Berkowitz, 2005; Borsari and Carey, 2001; Linkenbach et al., 2003) which will be examined later in the chapter.

Personal norms, on the other hand, despite occasionally being labeled as social norms (Bobek et al., 2007; Reno et al., 1993), are not principally social in nature, and could more usefully be understood as self-based standards of behavior that derive from deeply held personal or moral values (Schwartz, 1977; Schwartz and Howard, 1982). As suggested by research in the field of opinion formation and communication, such personal norms may be shaped by normative social influences (Neuwirth and Frederick, 2004; Newcomb, 1943; Noelle-Neumann, 1973). Perhaps one of the most important sources of personal norms is religious belief, but the extent to which such moral values are based on carefully thought-out principles – analogous to the intrinsic religiosity referred to by Galen and Rogers (2004) – or are simply a reflection of the prevailing norms of the salient religious reference group, and thus liable to change in different contexts, will vary with each individual case. Similarly, the relative influence of personal norms versus other types of norms will be situationally dependent (Kallgren et al., 2000).

The failure to comply with social norms generally involves some form of informal social sanction (Bendor and Swistak, 2001). The presence of such sanctions are somewhat inherent in the concept of prescriptive norms (Rimal and Real, 2005) and, despite Lapinski and Rimal's (2005) suggestion to the contrary, sanctions can also operate in the case of descriptive norms where failure to comply can lead to a potential loss of popularity or exclusion from the social network (Crandall, 1988; Schachter, 1951).

Sanctions may also apply in the case of personal norms, manifesting themselves as a loss of self-esteem or self-approval (Schwartz, 1977), otherwise known as a guilty conscience.

SOCIAL NORMS INFLUENCE BEHAVIOR

The substantial empirical literature of the past two decades provides significant evidence that normative perceptions, variously defined, influence many different types of human behavior. By far the largest body of work has focused on the influence of normative perceptions on alcohol consumption, where social norms are generally held to be amongst the strongest influencers of drinking behavior (Homish and Leonard, 2008; Lee et al., 2007; McAlaney and McMahon, 2007; Maddock and Glanz, 2005; Mallett et al., 2009; Mattern and Neighbors, 2004; Neighbors et al., 2007ab; Perkins et al., 2005; Read et al., 2005; Reed et al., 2007; Spijkerman et al., 2007; Yanovitzky et al., 2006). See also Borsari and Carey (2003) for a review of pre-2003 studies.

The evidence for normative influences on behavior is not limited to drinking behavior alone. Several studies have illustrated a relationship between social norms and smoking (Abroms et al., 2005; Andrews et al., 2008; Botvin et al., 1992; Chen et al., 2006; Gunther et al., 2006; Nichols et al; 2006; Slomkowski et al., 2005; van den Putte et al., 2005); littering and environmental protection (Cialdini, 2003; Cialdini et al., 1990; Kallgren et al., 2000; Reno et al., 1993; Schultz et al., 2007); sexual behavior (Albarracin et al., 2004; Bearman and Brückner, 2001; Bersamin et al., 2005; Chia, 2006; Fekadu and Kraft, 2002; Flores et al., 2002); gambling (Larimer and Neighbors, 2003; Moore and Ohtsuka, 1999; Neighbors et al., 2007c; Sheeran and Orbell, 1999); tax compliance (Bobek et al., 2007; Webley et al., 2001; Wenzel, 2005); eating and dieting behaviors (Crandall, 1988; Eisenberg et al., 2005; Field et al., 1999, 2001; Huon et al., 2000; Paxton et al., 1999); video pirating (Wang, 2005); opinion formation in childhood (Rutland et al., 2005); pre-marital counseling (Sullivan et al., 2004); voting intentions (Glynn et al., 2009); workplace health and safety (Linnan et al., 2005); the purchase of luxury products (Makgosa and Mohube, 2007); subject enrolment choices in schools (Dalgety and Coll, 2004) and approaches to parenting (Linkenbach et al., 2003).

It is worth noting that there is not complete consensus on the power of norms to influence behavior. For instance, in a study of students at two different universities, Cameron and Campo (2006), contrary to much of the previous research, found that across a variety of different behaviors normative influences were not significant predictors of behavior and that demographic factors, as well as actually liking the behavior in question, was a more significant predictor than normative perceptions. However, this finding may be explained by the Theory of Normative Social Behavior (Rimal and Real, 2005), which holds that positive behavioral expectancies are related to normative perceptions and mediate their influence on behavior. Cameron and Campo's finding of a weak influence of norms on behavior in a sample of 393 students in two universities also has to be set against Perkins et al.'s (2005) study of 76,145 students across 130 college campuses in which normative perceptions were a far more significant driver of drinking behavior than any other personal or demographic factors.

It must be admitted that most of the previously mentioned work on norms and behavior is cross-sectional in nature and provides indications of correlation rather than causation. However, the work Cialdini and colleagues in developing the Focus Theory of Normative Conduct (Cialdini, 2003; Cialdini et al., 1990, 2006; Kallgren et al., 2000; Reno et al., 1993), some of the work developing and testing the Theory of Normative Social Behavior (Rimal, 2008; Rimal et al., 2005), as well as the work by Glynn (2009) on voting behavior and Wenzel (2005) on tax compliance, provide an experimental evidence base for the argument that norms influence behavior. In addition to this, the quasi-experimental nature of the social norms marketing approach, which seeks to change behavior by correcting normative misperceptions, provides some indirect experimental evidence that norms shape behavior (Perkins et al., 2010). On the balance of evidence currently available – a large array of cross-sectional studies across a very wide spectrum of behavioral actions with diverse populations, supported by a smaller number of experimental studies – it seems safe to conclude that norms play a very significant role in driving human behavior, especially in ambiguous situations typically experienced by the young (Moscovi, 1976) and among those who are generally susceptible to social influence (Park and Lessig, 1977).

Explanatory theories of normative influence

Of course, the mere fact that people behave, or believe, in a certain way does not mean that others blindly follow. If this were the case there would be no outstanding bravery or selflessness or politically unpopular opinions (Lapinski and Rimal,

2005). The influence of norms is considerably more complex than the mere copying of others.

A number of attempts have been made to develop an explanatory framework for the influence of social norms. Some of this work draws upon such previously mentioned sociological theories as social learning theory (Bandura, 1986), social identity theory (Turner, 1982) and social network theory (Granovetter, 1973) and, as such, is largely beyond the scope of this chapter.

Pool and Schwegler (2007) proposed three different motivations for norm compliance. First, they argue that individuals comply with norms because they believe that the actions of others provide a clue to successful behavior, especially in ambiguous situations. These are known as accuracy-related reasons for compliance. Self-related reasons for compliance include the positive social identity associated with following a particular norm, while other-related motives imply a concern for acceptance within a group and the desire to avoid being ostracized for non-compliance with the group norm. While it is likely that individuals will primarily conform to descriptive norms for accuracy-related motives, personal norms for self-related motives and prescriptive norms for other-related motives, numerous motives are likely to be at work simultaneously.

Two general theories of normative influence have been developed and tested with a view to explaining the behavioral influence of social norms.

The Focus Theory of Normative Conduct was developed and tested across a variety of innovative littering experiments by Cialdini and colleagues (Cialdini, 2003; Cialdini et al., 1990, 2006; Kallgren et al., 2000; Reno et al., 1993) in an attempt to delineate the respective influence of descriptive and injunctive norms and to better understand the potential for harnessing these norms in behavior change campaigns.

The earliest experiments on the Focus Theory involved experimental manipulations to investigate the conditions that would increase the likelihood that visitors to a hospital would drop litter in the car park (Cialdini et al., 1990). In the first experiment, subjects exiting the elevator to return to their car encountered a confederate reading a handbill, who in half of the cases clearly dropped this handbill on the floor in view of the subject. In the remaining cases he walked past holding the leaflet. Most of the participants noticed this littering episode and momentarily deflected their attention to the garage floor; those who did not notice were excluded from the analysis. The purpose of the littering episode was to focus attention on the manipulated condition of the garage floor and to make this salient in the mind of the participants. The state of the floor indicated a

pre-existing descriptive norm – in some cases the floor was significantly littered and in others it was clean, apart from the recently dropped handbill. When the participants returned to their cars they found an identical handbill to that which was littered by the confederate underneath their windscreen wipers. The leaflet contained a short, bland message about car safety and did not refer to littering. There were no bins in the vicinity and participants faced the choice of throwing the leaflet on the ground or taking it away with them. As hypothesized by the researchers, there was less littering in those circumstances in which participants saw the confederate drop litter in an already clean environment, although the difference was not significant. The researchers concluded that the effect of dropping litter onto a clean floor was to make the anti-littering descriptive norm salient, which in turn leads to less littering. The fact that participants did not automatically copy the behavior of the littering confederate, but instead seemed to be influenced by the salient descriptive norm, indicates a normative, as opposed to a modeling, influence.

These findings were developed by the same researchers through two similar experimental manipulations (Cialdini et al., 1990). These subsequent experiments indicated that the confederate littering in a clean environment lead to less littering than when the confederate did not litter in a clean environment; in other words, focusing attention to the anti-littering descriptive norm leads to less littering. However, there was an increasingly greater propensity for subjects to litter as the descriptive norm of the manipulated environment became successively more pro-litter.

Cialdini et al. (1990) further developed these experiments by introducing an injunctive norm component in two subsequent manipulations. In the first of these the confederate either did or did not litter in an environment that was either very littered or where litter had been carefully swept up into a corner. The sweeping of litter was felt to signify an injunctive norm against littering. The results of the experiment indicated that in the absence of a norm-focus trigger, there was a minimal difference between the swept and unswept condition, but that focusing attention on the anti-littering injunctive norm magnified these differences and led to reduced littering in an anti-littering injunctive norm environment. Thus, temporarily drawing attention to a restrictive injunctive norm would seem to have the potential to outweigh the influence of a more permissive descriptive norm. The importance of focusing on injunctive norms was further emphasized in a fifth experiment in which descriptive norms were not considered or manipulated, but which found that subjects were less likely to litter when presented with an anti-littering injunctive norm message, and that presenting the subjects with injunctive norm messages that were progressively less relevant to the issue of littering resulted in progressively more littering behavior.

The power of injunctive norms was highlighted in subsequent experiments by the same research team (Reno et al., 1993). In the first of these experiments, consistent with the prior work, both injunctive and descriptive norms suppressed littering when the environment was clean but only injunctive norms did so when the environment was littered. The researchers also uncovered what might be termed a trans-situational influence of injunctive norms. In subsequent experiments in which attention was drawn to an anti-littering injunctive norm, subjects complied with this anti-littering norm by littering less frequently in an environment different to that in which they received the injunctive norm message. However, descriptive norms were found to lack this trans-situational influence, with subjects only complying with the descriptive norm when in the same context or environment in which the descriptive norm had been made salient. There is a sound theoretical rationale for these findings. Descriptive norms seem to communicate effective behavior in a particular setting. However, because injunctive norms communicate generalized values or indicate what is generally socially acceptable within a particular culture, these norms have a trans-situational relevance. Subsequent experiments have reinforced these findings and also presented evidence that personal norms can also strongly guide behavior, but only when made salient for the individual at the time of the behavior (Kallgren et al., 2000).

An alternative and complementary approach, the Theory of Normative Social Behavior, has been developed by Rimal and colleagues in an attempt to understand more clearly the precise mechanisms through which norms influence behavior (Lapinski and Rimal, 2005; Real and Rimal, 2007; Rimal, 2008; Rimal and Real, 2003, 2005; Rimal et al., 2005).

The theory suggests that the relationship between descriptive norms and behavior is extremely complex and that injunctive norms, outcome expectancies, group identity, behavioral identity (Rimal, 2008) and peer communication (Real and Rimal, 2007) moderate the relationship between descriptive norms and behavior and that injunctive norms and outcome expectancies partially mediate the relationship.

The importance of injunctive norms in the relationship between descriptive norms and behavior is intuitive. Perceiving that many peers engage in a particular behavior sends a strong cue that the behavior is socially acceptable and that the behavior may be important for peer group membership. Behavioral expectancies, the other mediating variable between descriptive norms and behavior, are defined as beliefs that one's actions will lead to benefits that one seeks (Bandura, 1986). There is a significant literature indicating that outcome expectancies strongly influence behavior (Brown et al., 1980; Neighbors et al., 2003; Read et al., 2004; Wood et al., 2001). The importance of outcome expectancies in the norms–behavior relationship is also axiomatic. If individuals perceive that a particular behavior is common, then it is likely that it is a behavior that provides benefits to those who practice it and one is likely motivated to practice that behavior in order not to miss out on the perceived benefits (Abrams and Niaura, 1987). Of course, part of the benefits associated with a behavior may be peer-oriented rather than behavior-oriented: for instance, positive emotions can result from peer acceptance (Christensen et al., 2004) and sanctions (real or imagined) can be avoided by complying with norms (Bendor and Swistak, 2001).

Group identity refers to the degree to which one considers oneself to be, or aspires to be, similar to a particular reference group. In the absence of some affinity with the group, there is no reason to believe that it would exert any influence on personal behavior. Any one individual may have numerous different reference groups and Borsari and Carey (2001) have identified 18 such groups that have frequently been used in social norms research. Each reference group may have different descriptive and prescriptive norms and will exert a different type of influence on behavior, depending on how closely one identifies with the group (Thombs et al., 1997).

The behavioral identity construct measures the degree to which one's self-identity is based around a particular behavior and the stronger this identification the more likely one is to engage in the behavior. In one test of the Theory of Normative Social Behavior, behavioral identity alone accounted for almost 40% of the variance in drinking intentions (Rimal, 2008). Thus, permissive descriptive norms will have a more significant impact on those for whom the behavior in question is an important part of their self-identity. In practice, however, it is likely that those who are heavily invested in a particular activity will select their peer groups on the basis of this behavior and thus the most salient descriptive norm will reinforce the behavior. While not tested in the literature, it would logically appear that behavioral identity and personal norms are closely related – where personal norms are important and are resistant to social influences, the behavior in question is likely to play an important role in the individual's self-identity.

The final component of the Theory of Normative Social Behavior is peer communication, which refers to the degree of frequency with which one discusses a particular behavior with peers. Interpersonal communication has been shown to be highly predictive of alcohol consumption and to moderate the influence of descriptive norms on behavior (Real and Rimal, 2007). As such, peer communication appears to be an important mechanism for the transmission and reinforcement of norms.

Social norms and behavior: conclusions

While the Theory of Normative Social Behavior reaffirms the importance of norms in influencing behavior, it also proposes a complex and incompletely understood set of interactions in the relationship and indicates the inadequacy of any approach that would suggest a one-to-one relationship between norms and behavior.

Based on both the Focus Theory of Normative Conduct and the Theory of Normative Social Behavior, a number of conclusions can be drawn about the relationship between norms and behavior. First, norms do exert an influence on behavior and the strength of this impact will vary according to the circumstances. For instance, when the norm in question is highlighted or made salient to the individual it will exert a more powerful influence. The two theories also reaffirm that there are distinct types of norms, with distinct influences on behavior. Sometimes these norms can be in conflict with each other, depending on the context, although descriptive and injunctive norms will very often be in alignment with each other, in which case the normative influence on behavior will be even more significant. Injunctive norms, once they are made salient, seem to have a transsituational influence, whereas descriptive norms seem to be more context-specific.

The relationship between norms and behavior is not a simple one and individuals do not automatically copy the behavior they see around them or immediately comply with what they perceive to be socially acceptable. The complex nature of this relationship has important implications for social norm marketing campaigns designed to elicit behavior change.

DOWNSTREAM SOCIAL MARKETING: SOCIAL NORMS MARKETING CAMPAIGNS

The fairly settled consensus that social norm perceptions influence behavior creates an interesting opportunity for public health advocates to manipulate these perceptions with a view to changing behavior. There has been considerable growth in the use of these social norm manipulations in the United States since the turn of the century, and the approach has begun to attract attention in Europe and elsewhere.

Normative misperceptions

The basic premise behind the social norms approach is that individuals regularly misperceive the social norm; that it is the misperception – rather than the actual norm – that influences behavior and that correcting this misperception results in consequent behavior change.

There is significant evidence from a variety of domains that individuals misperceive the descriptive norms relating to many different behaviors. Most of the work in the field has been focused on student drinking, where significant overestimations have been found relating to the frequency, and amounts, of consumption among student peers (Kypri and Langley, 2003; McAlaney and McMahon, 2007; Neighbors et al., 2007a; Perkins et al., 2005; Yanovitzky et al., 2006; see also Borsari and Carey, 2003 for a meta-analysis of almost two dozen older studies). Evidence also exists to indicate that people overestimate descriptive norms around smoking (Agostinelli and Grube, 2005; Bauman et al., 1992; Graham et al., 1991; Shanahan et al., 2004) as well as sexual behavior (Lamber et al., 2003; Scholly et al., 2005) and illegal drug use (Hansen and Graham, 1991; Wolfson, 2000). Recent studies have also indicated a misperception of both descriptive and injunctive norms relating to gambling (Larimer and Neighbors, 2003; Neighbors et al., 2007c) and tax evasion (Wenzel, 2005).

One study on student alcohol consumption failed to find any evidence of misperception (Wechsler and Kuo, 2000), although this study has been criticized for using different measures to compare individual and perceived peer norms (DeJong, 2003). It also determined that perceptions of peer behavior were accurate if they were within 10% of the actual peer norm, although it is not immediately clear why a 10% margin of error should be considered accurate.

In some instances the extent of the misperception can be very significant. In an analysis of the drinking norms of Scottish students, McAlaney and McMahon (2007) reported that 52% of respondents perceived that the majority of the student population got drunk at least twice per week, whereas only 12% of students reported this level of drunkenness. In a large-scale survey of 76,145 students from 130 colleges across the

USA, Perkins et al. (2005) found that most students significantly overestimated the drinking norm on their college campus and that this pattern held even where the norm was a heavy drinking one. For instance, on college campuses where the norm was to consume four drinks per drinking occasion, 15.4% of students underestimated the norm, 12.6% had accurate perceptions but more than 70% overestimated the norm, with almost 35% of students perceiving that the norm was to consume seven or more drinks per drinking occasion. Similar patterns of gross overestimation can be found in studies of sexual behavior. A survey of more than 28,000 college students in the USA found that 71% of the respondents either abstained from sexual intercourse or had one sexual partner within the previous year but the student population itself perceived that most students had at least three sexual partners during this time frame (American College Health Association, 2003). Similarly, Scholly et al. (2005) found that students significantly overestimated the prevalence of risky sexual activity and underestimated the frequency of responsible behavior: 80% of respondents had either zero or one sexual partner within the previous year, but thought that only 22% of the student population were similarly abstemious.

Individuals who misperceive the norm may fall into one of three broad categories of misperception, depending on how they view their own behavior with respect to the perceived norm. The most common type of misperception is that of *pluralistic ignorance*. This occurs when individuals incorrectly perceive that others behave or believe differently than they themselves do (Prentice and Miller, 1993). Thus, the 71% of students in the previously mentioned American College Health Association (2003) study who had at most one sexual partner in the previous year were afflicted with pluralistic ignorance in their belief that most students had three or more sexual partners within this time frame. The effect of pluralistic ignorance is to suppress behaviors and opinions that are incorrectly perceived as counter-normative; it also exerts a subtle pressure on individuals to engage more frequently or publicly in the misperceived behavior. A more unusual type of misperception, *false uniqueness*, can be viewed as a variant of pluralistic ignorance and occurs when individuals who abstain from a particular behavior incorrectly perceive that their abstention is more unique than it in fact is (Suls and Wan, 1987), perhaps because those who possess desirable attributes tend to underestimate the prevalence of those attributes (Tabachnik et al., 1983). The effect of this misperception could be to cause these individuals to withdraw from interaction with others, the result of which would lead to even

more distorted normative perceptions on the part of the rest of the population, somewhat similar to the process envisaged by the spiral of silence theory (Noelle-Neumann, 1973). *False consensus* occurs when individuals incorrectly perceive that others are like them, when in reality they are not (Ross et al., 1977). Those who possess negative characteristics tend to overestimate the prevalence of those characteristics via a process of attributive-projection (Sanders and Mullen, 1983). This is most likely to occur in situations in which individuals have a vested interest in believing that 'everyone' behaves as they do in an effort to justify their own behavior. Thus, heavy drinkers, who are more likely to select other heavy drinkers as friends, incorrectly generalize the heavy drinking norm of their close peer group to the wider society.

There are a number of reasons why misperceptions occur in the first instance. Clearly, the wider media culture plays a role in shaping our perception of reality; this matter will be discussed in more length in our discussion of 'upstream' social marketing issues. In addition to the media, Perkins (2003) points to the sheer visibility and vividness of those who engage in problematic behavior relative to their more abstemious peers. Those who are, for instance, obviously drunk or violent are very noticeable and the memory of their behavior sticks in the mind, encouraging us to perceive it as being more normative than it in fact is. On the other hand, those who behave 'normally' – those who are sober and well ordered – do not attract our attention in the same way. A somewhat different process can account for false consensus effect misperceptions, where, in the case of alcohol consumption, it seems that a form of cognitive dissonance encourages individuals to develop attitudes and beliefs that are consistent with their behavior (Kypri and Langley, 2003; Larimer et al., 2004). It may also be the case that ill-conceived social marketing campaigns which stress the extent of the problem contribute to the normalization of the very ill they were designed to cure (Cialdini et al., 2006).

Correcting misperceptions

The fact that misperceptions of the norm occur is of capital importance for public health advocates and others concerned about behavior change. Previously we have examined an extensive literature demonstrating that social norms influence behavior. This, of course, is only partly correct. Most people are unaware of what the *real* social norm actually is. Rather it is an individual's *perception* of the norm – which in a sense, is 'real' for them (Perkins and Wechsler, 1996) – that influences behavior. If the norm is misperceived, it is this misperception which is the key driver of behavior (Andrews et al., 2008; Eisenberg and Forster, 2003; McAlaney and McMahon, 2007). Thus, in Perkins et al.'s (2005) study of more than 75,000 students across the USA, a 1 drink increase in the actual norm was associated with a 0.37 drink increase in individual consumption, whereas a 1 drink increase in the perceived drinking norm was associated with a 0.48 drink increase in personal consumption. While the actual drinking norm was an important predictor of behavior, the perceived campus norm was even more significant and indeed was more important than all other demographic control variables.

The knowledge that normative perceptions impact behavior and that these norms are often misperceived has given rise to the so-called social norms approach to solving social problems. The basic tenet of this approach is that if overestimations of problem behavior can be corrected and lowered – normally through either a social norms marketing campaign or an intervention with individuals (Moreira et al., 2009) – then behavior will follow.

Advocates of the social norms approach point to a significant body of research which seems to indicate the effectiveness of the method with diverse populations in a variety of behavioral contexts, including alcohol consumption (Perkins et al., 2005, 2010), smoking (Linkenbach and Perkins, 2003), tax compliance (Wenzel, 2005) and adolescent sexual behavior (Bersamin et al., 2005). Borsari and Carey (2003) and Berkowitz (2005) provide extensive overviews of older studies which indicate successful behavior change following social norm interventions.

More recently, Moreira et al. (2009) conducted a systematic review of 22 social norm intervention random control trials. These studies involved 7275 college students and were aimed at assessing the effectiveness of social norm interventions in reducing alcohol consumption. On the basis of their analysis, they concluded that the effectiveness of social norms campaigns depends on the mechanism through which the normative correction is delivered. They found that interventions using the internet or other computer software were more effective at reducing alcohol misuse than the control condition (which often included more traditional educational approaches such as the delivery of an alcohol education leaflet). These effects were more evident over the short term, although there were some residual effects over the medium term (4–6 months). There was less evidence of an effect on behavior if the intervention was delivered in a group or individual face-to-face setting and the results of the review were inconclusive on the effectiveness of marketing campaigns to correct normative perceptions.

Criticisms of the social norms approach

Despite the robustness of the link between normative perceptions and behavior and the rapid growth in the use of social norms marketing campaigns, the field is not without its critics. The approach was first developed in the context of student drinking (Perkins and Berkowitz, 1986). The basic message of the approach – that most students drink moderately – was instantly attractive to the alcohol industry, and it provided them with a way of being seen to be proactive in encouraging responsible drinking without having to highlight the negative consequences of alcohol consumption. The fact that the alcohol industry has been involved in funding both social norms research and normative intervention campaigns has made some public health advocates inherently suspicious of the approach. Critics also point to a number of failed social norms campaigns in support of their case (Blumenthal et al., 2001; Clapp et al., 2003, Scholly et al., 2005; Werch et al., 2000), although proponents of the approach argue that such failures have occurred because of poor planning or implementation of the social norms campaign and a consequent failure to correct the underlying misperception in question (Perkins et al., 2005). The evidence supporting the effectiveness of normative interventions is also open to criticism due to the lack of control groups in many instances (Jung, 2003), although more recent studies have incorporated such controls (Perkins et al., 2010).

There are three substantial criticisms of the approach which deserve careful consideration. The first of these relates to the ethics surrounding the so-called boomerang effect, whereby the minority of individuals who *underestimate* the norm have their misperception corrected, but in an upward fashion, with the potential consequence that they could engage in more risky behavior. This is not necessarily an insignificant problem – despite the pattern of gross overestimation of the norm by most students found in the large-scale survey of American college students conducted by Perkins et al. (2005), as many as one-fifth of the students in some colleges underestimated the drinking norms of their peers. This problem may be especially acute in contexts where the actual norm in question is itself unhealthy or otherwise problematic, in which case a social norms marketing campaign could conceivably have to promote binge drinking as normative. Indeed, there is a debate about whether misperceptions even exist in normatively unhealthy environments, although proponents of the approach argue that misperceptions will still exist in such contexts (Perkins, 2003), a position supported by the finding of drinking misperceptions amongst Scottish students (McAlaney and McMahon, 2007), a population in which heavy drinking is more normative than in the USA where the theory was first developed.

Schultz et al. (2007) discovered evidence for the boomerang effect in their experimental social norm intervention aimed at reducing energy use amongst householders in California. The householders received information detailing how much energy they had used in recent weeks, as well as descriptive norm information detailing how much the average house had used in their neighborhood. As expected, over time, those whose energy consumption was above the norm reduced their energy use, but those who were originally below the norm actually increased energy consumption.

The solution to the boomerang effect may be found by resolving the second major criticism of the social norms approach: namely, its almost total neglect of power of prescriptive norms and its over-reliance on descriptive norms (Rimal and Real, 2005). Despite the significant progress that has been made in understanding the complex relationship between different types of norms and behavior, particularly with the development of the Focus Theory of Normative Conduct and the Theory of Normative Social Behavior, social norm interventions – with few exceptions (Barnett et al., 1996; Schroeder and Prentice, 1998; Wenzel, 2005) – tend to utilize descriptive norm manipulations only.

Thus, in a context in which descriptive norms may be unhealthy or problematic, it may be possible to incorporate a positive prescriptive norm appeal in order to counteract the boomerang effect. This is precisely what Schultz et al. (2007) did in their experiment with Californian homeowners. A third group in their experiment received, in addition to the previously described descriptive norm message, a prescriptive norm message either conveying approval or disapproval of that householders energy use. Those who consumed below the norm and also received a prescriptive norm message were not subject to a boomerang effect, whereas those who did not receive the prescriptive norm message increased their energy use in line with the descriptive norm.

The use of prescriptive norms in normative intervention campaigns has several benefits, building as it does on the finding from the Theory of Normative Social Behavior that descriptive norms are mediated via injunctive norms (Rimal et al., 2005) and the insight from the Focus Theory of Normative Conduct that the power of social norms

in greatly enhanced when descriptive and injunctive norms are in alignment (Cialdini et al., 2006). Such an approach also avoids the potential ethical dilemma of inadvertently encouraging the adoption of unhealthy behavior (Larimer et al., 2004) and may satisfy the concerns of public health advocates uncomfortable with labeling any level of drinking or smoking, for instance, as normative.

The level of misperception, and the relative power of that misperception in influencing behavior, also varies significantly from case to case, and the third major criticism of the social norms approach relates to the practicality of harnessing a salient norm which can influence behavior. There are numerous reference groups that can be used in social norms campaigns; as noted previously, Borsari and Carey (2001) have identified 18 different reference groups common in social norms research, and others can be added to that list. The extent of the misperception increases as social distance increases, while the influence of the misperception decreases with social distance (Borsari and Carey, 2003; McAlaney and McMahon, 2007). This finding is intuitive in the light of the importance of group identity in the Theory of Normative Social Behavior (Rimal, 2008).

This leaves a dilemma for those trying to harness the power of norms to bring about behavior change: Which peer group misperceptions should be changed in a normative intervention? The search for the most salient reference group is not an easy one. Social marketers will lack credibility if they try to correct misperceptions about close friends and these groups are so diverse as to make it practically impossible to develop a marketing campaign to correct these misperceptions (Reed et al., 2007). On the other hand, the more general norms which marketers can manipulate exert a considerably weaker influence on behavior to begin with. Perhaps this is why the systematic review conducted by Moreira et al. (2009) found more promising results for online social norms interventions, which can be tailored to individuals more readily than a marketing campaign can.

More research is needed to understand the role of group salience in normative campaigns and how they can be harnessed to bring about behavior change.

UPSTREAM SOCIAL MARKETING: SOCIAL NORMS AND MARKETING REGULATION

Social marketers and others concerned about public health are rightfully intrigued about the possibilities of harnessing the power of normative perceptions to bring about positive change. But social norms have implications that go far beyond these downstream applications. As Goldberg (1995) suggests, social marketers must not confine themselves to fishing people out of the water after they have fallen in; there comes a time when social marketers must move upstream to investigate, and indeed challenge, those influences that encourage people to jump into the water in the first instance.

Such a move upstream would uncover a variety of ecological factors, including laws and social policies, peer, community and family relationships, as well as media and marketing influences, which seem to conspire together to encourage people to 'jump into' the river (Taylor and Sorenson, 2004). Taking just one of these factors, there has been much debate about how marketing, and, more generally, the media, influence potentially unhealthy or socially damaging behaviors such as alcohol consumption (Anderson et al., 2009), smoking (Wellman et al., 2006), risky sexual behavior (Brown et al., 2006) and unhealthy food consumption (Hastings et al., 2006), among others. In order to shape the policy debate about the regulation of marketing from a public health perspective, much of this research has attempted to examine the relationship between exposure to marketing and subsequent behavior. By contrast, the reasons why marketing should have such an influence are considered with relative infrequency. Marketing does not operate like a 'magic bullet' whereby individuals automatically adopt the behavior presented to them; other intervening cognitive mechanisms are at play (Bandura, 2001). Normative perceptions provide a potentially powerful insight in this regard.

Looking at the issue from another perspective, we now have some degree of certainty that normative perceptions, accurate or otherwise, influence behavior, but we have much less certainty about where these perceptions come from in the first instance. It is generally accepted that interpersonal communication (Lapinski and Rimal, 2005) and observation (Gunther et al., 2006; Perkins, 2003) contribute to norm formation. While the role of the media in general, and marketing in particular, in norm generation and transmission has been curiously under-researched, it is intuitive that the existence, pervasiveness and content of behavioral portrayals in the media environment helps shape perceptions of reality (Conley Thomson et al., 2005).

Media and marketing may shape social norms

There are two major contrasting theories as to how marketing and the media contribute to norm formation. The first perspective broadly rests on cultivation theory (Gerbner and Gross, 1976), which proposes that media depictions of behavior, which in practice are often exaggerated distortions of reality designed to entertain and hold attention, shape people's perceptions, often without them realizing it (Bandura, 2001; Lederman et al., 2004). These effects persist even when individuals consciously deny that the media reliably depicts reality (Shrum, 1999; Shrum et al., 1998). The impact of these media effects, in which almost everyone is immersed to some degree or other, is often obscured by their pervasiveness (O'Guinn and Shrum, 1997). Research on cultivation theory has tended not to analyze media effects through a normative perspective or to use the conceptualizations adopted by researchers in the social norms field. Nevertheless, cultivation theory provides some evidence that the media influences perceptions of behavior prevalence. Researchers have found that heavy television viewing was positively correlated with perceptions of the prevalence of professions frequently depicted in the media (Gerbner et al., 1994): with greater faith in the medical profession (Volgy and Schwartz, 1980); with higher estimates of the frequency of crime (Gerbner et al., 1977) and with frequency of drug use (Coomber, 1999; Fan, 1996); with perceptions of societal affluence (O'Guinn and Shrum, 1997); and with misperceptions about the frequency of divorce (Carveth and Alexander, 1985). The cultivation approach may also operate to effect prescriptive norms – Shanahan (2004) reports that heavy television viewers have more positive attitudes toward homosexuality and argues that this is in part because of the mainstreaming of homosexuality on television.

The availability heuristic provides one possible explanation for cultivation effects (Tversky and Kahneman, 1973). This perspective suggests that individuals rely on easily accessible information when asked to make social judgments and that they infer that behaviors must be common if they are easily remembered. Relying on this theory, O'Guinn and Shrum (1997) showed that not only did heavy television viewers provide higher estimates of social affluence, but they also responded to the questions more rapidly than light viewers who made lower estimates of affluence, presumably because they were relying on the more cognitively available consumer images which are easily retrieved from their heavy television viewing. An alternative explanation of cultivation effects is that of the simulation heuristic which suggests that individuals will estimate the prevalence of an event from the ease with which they can imagine it (Kahneman and Tversky, 1982). Given the widespread and often graphic depictions of violence, sex and drug and alcohol use in the media environment, and the vividness of drunken behavior on public streets in comparison the relative 'invisibility' of the sober (Perkins, 2003), the simulation heuristic presents a theoretically plausible explanation of norm formation pathways.

An alternative explanation to that of cultivation theory is the theory of presumed influence. This is largely based on the third-person effect whereby individuals assume that the media will influence others much more powerfully than it will influence themselves (Perloff, 1993), especially when the effect is likely to be negative in nature (Gunther and Mundy, 1993). This presumption of influence on others elicits a behavior change in order to bring personal behavior into line with the media's presumed influence on others.

Gunther et al. (2006) conducted a study of smoking-related media to test the presumed influence theory. They found that the more respondents were exposed to pro-smoking media content, the more they thought that their peers were subjected to similar influences. This presumption was linked with higher estimates of peer smoking. There are two pathways of influence by which this relationship can be explained. The most logical, and intuitively satisfactory path, is similar to cultivation theory and suggests that the media provides a set of representative cues indicating peer norms on smoking. However, the researchers found that this pathway was not significant for the relationship between anti-smoking messages and perceptions of prevalence, although the relationship between pro-smoking messages and prevalence was significant. On the other hand, it was the presumed influence pathway, whereby respondents matched their perceptions with their presumption of the influence of the media on peers, that most closely fit the data. The two pathways, although similar, are different in subtle and important ways. The presumed influence pathway proposes what appears to be an unlikely approach through which individuals estimate the effects of the media on others and adapt their normative estimates, and ultimately their behavior, to match this. This latter approach was supported in two subsequent studies on the relationship between media exposure and sexual behavior in which the presumed influence pathway was more significant than the cultivation approach (Chia, 2006; Chia and Gunther, 2006) as well as in a study of advertising exposure and materialistic values among adolescents in Singapore (Chia, 2010).

As previously noted, a considerable body of evidence suggests that marketing influences both smoking (Wellman et al., 2006) and alcohol consumption (Anderson et al., 2009). That carefully designed commercial communications should achieve its objective of persuading its target audience to consume is unsurprising. However, there is also a growing literature indicating that movies and other forms of entertainment exert an influence similar to that of commercial advertising (Distefan et al., 2004; Hanewinkel et al., 2008; Sargent et al., 2006; van den Bulck and Beullens 2005; Wills et al., 2009). Some of this influence may be explained by product placement strategies, which are deliberately designed to influence consumption (Wasko et al., 1993). However, it seems probable that this influence can also be explained through normative mechanisms. In other words, media and marketing depictions provide clues to the prevalence and/or social acceptability of certain behaviors in the real world and may mediate the relationship between marketing and behavior. With few exceptions (Brown and Moodie, 2009; Chen et al., 2006; and the previously cited work on the Theory of Presumed Influence), this issue has rarely been formally assessed with the generally accepted conceptualizations and definitions of norms outlined in this chapter. However, many theorists have hinted at the probability of such a link between marketing and norms (Beck and Treiman, 1996; Lapinski and Rimal, 2005; Lederman et al., 2004; Spijkerman et al., 2007; Taylor and Sorenson, 2004; Wakefield et al., 2003; Yanovitzky and Stryker, 2001). As Chen et al. (2006: 360) cogently argue in the context of tobacco advertising:

> In addition to their direct effects on tobacco use, tobacco advertisements and promotion activities may also serve as data for adolescents to modify their perceived smoking norms, which in turn, may affect their smoking behavior. If this were the case, adolescents who have been exposed or have increased receptivity of pro-tobacco media may be more likely to perceive that there are more peer smokers around them: therefore, these adolescents would be more likely to smoke themselves. Thus, there may be a linkage from pro-tobacco media to perceived smoking norms, and further, to actual tobacco use among adolescents.

The power of the norms–behavior link is not lost on commercial marketers. Alcohol marketers have long understood the importance of social networks and relationships. For this reason, alcohol is regularly advertised, directly and indirectly, as a social lubricant. One brand, Carling, has even gone as far as to make powerful appeals to the concept of 'belonging' to a group, prominently using the word 'Belong' in the same format and style as its logo (Hastings et al., 2010).

This effect may not be limited only to the influence of marketing on descriptive norms. The mere fact that a product can be openly marketed communicates something about its social acceptability, and thus may help to shape injunctive norm perceptions (Brown et al., 2009; Lapinski and Rimal, 2005; Wakefield et al., 2003). The potential for impacting injunctive norms is also apparent when commercial operators get involved in social marketing – such as tobacco companies running youth prevention campaigns or drinks companies funding moderate drinking initiatives. In the latter case, there is good evidence to show that such efforts benefit the reputation of the sponsoring company more than they do public health (Hastings and Liberman, 2009; Hastings and Angus, in press; Wakefield et al., 2005, 2006). In the process there is a clear danger that impressionable youngsters become confused about the rights and wrongs of particular behaviors: if the people producing the beer are also the guardians of public health then it is easy to mistakenly assume that they have our best interests at heart.

CONCLUSION

Social norms have important implications for social marketers which are unfortunately commonly overlooked. Based on the evidence we have to date, we can conclude with reasonable certainty: that norms powerfully influence behavior, often to a greater extent than other important demographic factors; that norms are regularly misperceived; and, finally, that correcting these misperceptions has the potential to bring about positive behavior change. The last conclusion, about the power of harnessing norms, is of great significance for social marketers engaged in typical 'downstream' activity. Too often, norms have been harnessed in precisely the wrong fashion by social marketers. Too much emphasis on the extent of a problem, rather than on positive role models, may inadvertently reinforce the unhealthy behavior by implying that 'everyone' is doing it.

Perhaps norm-based campaigns have been ignored by some social marketers because of a legitimate concern about the role of commercial marketers in funding both research and normative campaigns to change behavior. It is understandable that public health advocates are inherently uncomfortable supporting a campaign that tells young people that drinking alcohol or smoking, for example, are normative.

This is why the most recent theoretical advances in social norm research, and particularly the Focus Theory of Normative Conduct and the Theory of Normative Social Behavior, are of such significance. This work makes clear that it is only by using *both* descriptive and prescriptive norms that we can best harness their power. It is understandable that the alcohol industry, for example, is less interested in sponsoring campaigns that communicate social disapproval of binge drinking than it is of paying for campaigns informing the public that consumption is normative amongst their peers. The capacity to align norms relating to prevalence with norms relating to social acceptability should renew the interest of social marketers in the downstream applications of norms.

There are perhaps even more exciting opportunities in the field of normative perceptions for social marketers concerned with 'upstream' interventions and research. While much work has been done in examining the influence of marketing and the media on a variety of socially problematic behaviors, most of this has been at the level of dose–response relationships. Examining social norm perceptions, their origins and formation pathways via media exposure presents a potentially fruitful field of research. Even at a basic commonsense level the importance of the relationship between norms and marketing is quite clear – the mere fact that it is legally and socially acceptable to market certain products, irrespective of the content, timing or targeting of that marketing, clearly communicates the social acceptability of the product in question. This acceptability is likely to be reinforced when the makers of these products also get involved in educating people about public health, with concomitant benefits for their corporate reputations. Serious policy implications with respect to the regulation and control of marketing may flow from innovative and creative research on these upstream aspects of social norms.

KEY WORDS: Social norms; cultivation theory; group salience; outcome expectancies; pluralistic ignorance; false uniqueness; false consensus; normative misperceptions; Focus Theory of Normative Conduct, Theory of Normative Social Behavior.

Key insights

- A significant body of research shows that social norm perceptions are a powerful driver of human behavior.
- Social norms have important implications for both 'upstream' and 'downstream' social marketers.
- Social norm perceptions have been successfully manipulated through marketing initiatives. There is evidence that these campaigns have contributed to behavior change.
- Normative perceptions are one mechanism that may help explain the impact of marketing on behavior.

REFERENCES

Abrams, D.B. and Niaura, R.S. (1987) 'Social learning theory', in H.T. Blane and K.E. Leonard (eds), *Psychological Theories of Drinking and Alcoholism.* New York: Guilford Press, pp. 131–178.

Abroms, L.B., Simons-Morton, B., Haynie, D.L. and Chen, R. (2005) 'Psychosocial predictors of smoking trajectories during middle and high school', *Addiction,* 100(6): 852–861.

Agostinelli, G. and Grube, J. (2005) 'Effects of presenting heavy drinking norms on adolescents' prevalence estimates, evaluative judgments, and perceived standards', *Prevention Science,* 6(2): 89–99.

Ajzen, I. (1991) 'The theory of planned behavior', *Organizational Behavior and Human Decision Processes,* 50(2): 179–211.

Ajzen, I. and Fishbein, M. (1980) *Understanding Attitudes and Predicting Social Behavior.* Englewood Cliffs, NJ: Prentice-Hall.

Albarracin, D., Kumkale, G.T. and Johnson, B.T. (2004) 'Influences of social power and normative support on condom use decisions: A research synthesis', *AIDS Care,* 16(6): 700–723.

American College Health Association (2003) *National College Health Assessment: Reference Group Data Base Spring 2002.* Baltimore, MD: American College Health Association.

Anderson, P., de Bruijn, A., Angus, K., Gordon, R. and Hastings, G. (2009) 'Impact of alcohol advertising and media exposure on adolescent alcohol use: A systematic review of longitudinal studies', *Alcohol and Alcoholism,* 44(3): 229–243.

Andrews, J.A., Hampson, S. and Barckley, M. (2008) 'The effect of subjective normative social images of smokers on children's intentions to smoke', *Nicotine and Tobacco Research,* 10(4): 589–597.

Bandura, A. (1986) *Social Foundations of Thought and Action: A Social Cognitive Theory.* Englewood Cliffs, NJ: Prentice-Hall.

Bandura, A. (2001) 'Social cognitive theory of mass communication', *Media Psychology,* 3(3): 265–299.

Barnett, L.A., Far, J.M., Mauss, A.L. and Miller, J.A. (1996) 'Changing perceptions of peer norms as a drinking reduction program for college students', *Journal of Alcohol and Drug Education,* 41(2): 39–62.

Bauman, K.E., Botvin, G.J., Botvin, E.M. and Baker, E. (1992) 'Normative expectations and the behavior of significant others: An integration of traditions in research on adolescents' cigarette smoking', *Psychological Reports,* 71(2): 568–570.

Bearman, P.S. and Brückner, H. (2001) 'Promising the future: Virginity pledges and first intercourse', *American Journal of Sociology,* 106(4): 859–911.

Beck, K.H. and Treiman, K.A. (1996) 'The relationship of social context of drinking, perceived social norms, and parental influence to various drinking patterns of adolescents', *Addictive Behaviors,* 21(5): 633–644.

Bendor, J. and Swistak, P. (2001) 'The evolution of norms', *American Journal of Sociology,* 106(6): 1493–1545.

Berkowitz, A.D. (2005) 'An overview of the social norms approach', in L.C. Lederman and L.P. Stewart (eds), *Changing the Culture of College Drinking: A Socially Situated Health Communication Campaign.* Cresskill, NJ: Hampton Press, pp. 193–214.

Bersamin, M.M., Walker, S., Waiters, E.D., Fisher, D.A. and Grube, J.W. (2005) 'Promising to wait: Virginity pledges and adolescent sexual behavior', *Journal of Adolescent Health,* 36(5): 428–436.

Blumenthal, M., Christian, C. and Slemrod, J. (2001) 'Do normative appeals affect tax compliance? Evidence from a controlled experiment in Minnesota', *National Tax Journal,* 54: 125–138.

Bobek, D., Roberts, R. and Sweeney, J. (2007) 'The social norms of tax compliance: Evidence from Australia, Singapore, and the United States', *Journal of Business Ethics,* 74: 49–64.

Borsari, B. and Carey, K.B. (2001) 'Peer influences on college drinking: A review of the research'. *Journal of Substance Abuse,* 13(4): 391–424.

Borsari, B. and Carey, K.B. (2003) 'Descriptive and injunctive norms in college drinking: A meta-analytic integration'. *Journal of Studies on Alcohol,* 64(3): 331–341.

Botvin, G.J., Botvin, E.M., Baker, E., Dusenbury, L. and Goldberg, C.J. (1992) 'The false consensus effect: Predicting adolescents' tobacco use from normative expectations', *Psychological Reports,* 70(1): 171–178.

Brown, A. and Moodie, C. (2009) 'The influence of tobacco marketing on adolescent smoking intentions via normative beliefs', *Health Education Research,* 24(4): 721–733.

Brown, A., Moodie, C. and Hastings, G. (2009) 'A longitudinal study of policy effect (smoke-free legislation) on smoking norms: ITC Scotland/United Kingdom', *Nicotine and Tobacco Research,* 11(8): 924–932.

Brown, J.D., L'Engle, K.L., Pardun, C.J., et al. (2006) 'Sexy media matter: Exposure to sexual content in music, movies, television, and magazines predicts black and white adolescents' sexual behavior', *Pediatrics,* 117(4): 1018–1027.

Brown, S.A., Goldman, M.S., Inn, A. and Anderson, L.R. (1980) 'Expectations reinforcement from alcohol: Their domain and relation to drinking patterns', *Journal of Consulting and Clinical Psychology,* 48(4): 419–426.

Cameron, K.A. and Campo, S. (2006) 'Stepping back from social norms campaigns: Comparing normative influences to other predictors of health behaviors', *Health Communication,* 20(3): 277–88.

Carveth, R. and Alexander, A. (1985) 'Soap opera viewing motivations and the cultivation process', *Journal of Broadcasting and Electronic Media,* 29(3): 259–273.

Caudill, B.D. and Kong, F.H. (2001) 'Social approval and facilitation in predicting modeling effects in alcohol consumption', *Journal of Substance Abuse,* 13(4): 425–441.

Caudill, B.D. and Marlatt, G.A. (1975) 'Modeling influences in social drinking: An experimental analogue', *Journal of Consulting and Clinical Psychology,* 43(3): 405–415.

Chen, X., Stanton, B., Fang, X., et al. (2006) 'Perceived smoking norms, socioenvironmental factors, personal attitudes and adolescent smoking in China: A mediation analysis with longitudinal data', *Journal of Adolescent Health*, 38(4): 359–368.

Chia, S.C. (2006) 'How peers mediate media influence on adolescents sexual attitudes and sexual behavior', *Journal of Communication*, 56(3): 585–606.

Chia, S.C. (2010) 'How social influence mediates media effects on adolescents' materialism', *Communication Research*, 37(3): 400–419.

Chia, S.C. and Gunther, A.C. (2006) 'How media contribute to misperceptions of social norms about sex', *Mass Communication and Society*, 9(3): 301–320.

Christensen, P.N., Rothgerber, H., Wood, W. and Matz, D.C. (2004) 'Social norms and identity relevance: A motivational approach to normative behavior', *Personality and Social Psychology Bulletin*, 30(10): 1295–1309.

Cialdini, R.B. (2003) 'Crafting normative messages to protect the environment', *Current Directions in Psychological Science*, 12(4): 105–109.

Cialdini, R.B. and Trost, M.R. (1998) 'Social influence: Social norms, conformity and compliance', in D. Gilbert, S. Fiske and G. Lindzey (eds), *The Handbook of Social Psychology*, 4th edn, Vol. 2. New York: McGraw-Hill, pp. 151–192.

Cialdini, R.B., Reno, R.R. and Kallgren, C.A. (1990) 'A focus theory of normative conduct: Recycling the concept of norms to reduce littering in public places', *Journal of Personality and Social Psychology*, 58(6): 1015–1026.

Cialdini, R.B., Kallgren, C.A. and Reno, R.R. (1991) 'A focus theory of normative conduct: A theoretical refinement and reevaluation of the role of norms in human behavior', *Advances in Experimental Social Psychology*, 24(20): 201–234.

Cialdini, R.B., Demaine, L.J., Sagarin, B.J., Barrett, D.W. et al. (2006) 'Managing social norms for persuasive impact', *Social Influence*, 1(1): 3–15.

Clapp, J.D., Lange, J.E., Russell, C., Shillington, A. and Voas, R.B. (2003) 'A failed social norms campaign', *Journal of Studies on Alcohol*, 64(3): 409–414.

Collins, R.L., Parks, G.A. and Marlatt, G.A. (1985) 'Social determinants of alcohol consumption: The effects of social ilnteraction and model status on the self-administration of alcohol', *Journal of Consulting and Clinical Psychology*, 53(2): 189–200.

Conley Thomson, C., Siegel, M., Winickoff, J., Biener, L. and Rigotti, N.A. (2005) 'Household smoking bans and adolescents' perceived prevalence of smoking and social acceptability of smoking', *Preventive Medicine*, 41(2): 349–356.

Coomber, R. (1999) 'Lay perceptions and beliefs about the adulteration of illicit drugs in the 1990s – A student sample', *Addiction Research and Theory*, 7(4): 323–338.

Crandall, C.S. (1988) 'Social contagion of binge eating', *Journal of Personality and Social Psychology*, 55(4): 588–598.

Csikszentmihalyi, M. and Larson, R. (1984) *Being Adolescent*. New York: Basic Books.

Dalgety, J. and Coll, R.K. (2004) 'The influence of normative beliefs on students' enrolment choices', *Research in Science and Technological Education*, 22: 59–80.

DeJong, W. (2003) 'Report to the field: The case of the missing misperception', *HEC News (Online News Service)* October 13, Washington, DC: Higher Education Center for Alcohol and Other Drug Prevention, Department of Education.

Dericco, D.A. and Garlington, W.K. (1977) 'The effect of modeling and disclosure of experimenter's intent on drinking rate of college students', *Addictive Behaviors*, 2(2–3): 135–139.

Deutsch, M. and Gerard, H.B. (1955) 'A study of normative and informational social influences upon individual judgment', *The Journal of Abnormal and Social Psychology*, 51(3): 629–636.

Distefan, J.M., Pierce, J.P. and Gilpin, E.A. (2004) 'Do favorite movie stars influence adolescent smoking initiation?' *American Journal of Public Health*, 94(7): 1239–1244.

Donovan, J.E., Jessor, R. and Jessor, L. (1983) 'Problem drinking in adolescence and young adulthood: A follow-up study', *Journal of Studies on Alcohol*, 44: 109–137.

Dusenbury, L., Epstein, J.A., Botvin, G.J. and Diaz, T. (1994) 'Social influence predictors of alcohol use among New York Latino youth', *Addictive Behaviors*, 19(4): 363–372.

Eisenberg, M.E. and Forster, J.L. (2003) 'Adolescent smoking behavior: Measures of social norms', *American Journal of Preventive Medicine*, 25(2): 122–128.

Eisenberg, M.E., Neumark-Sztainer, D., Story, M. and Cheryl, P. (2005) 'The role of social norms and friends' influences on unhealthy weight-control behaviors among adolescent girls', *Social Science and Medicine* 60(6): 1165–1173.

Epstein, J.A., Botvin, G.J., Baker, E. and Diaz, T. (1999) 'Impact of social influences and problem behavior on alcohol use among inner-city Hispanic and Black adolescents', *Journal of Studies on Alcohol*, 60(5): 595–604.

Fan, D.P. (1996) 'News media framing sets public opinion that drugs is the country's most important problem', *Substance Use and Misuse*, 31(10): 1413–1421.

Fekadu, Z. and Kraft, P. (2002) 'Expanding the theory of planned behaviour: The role of social norms and group identification', *Journal of Health Psychology*, 7: 33–43.

Festinger, L. (1954) 'A theory of social comparison processes', *Human Relations*, 7(2): 117–140.

Field, A.E., Cheung, L., Wolf, A.M., Herzog, et al. (1999) 'Exposure to the mass media and weight concerns among girls', *Pediatrics*, 103(3): e36.

Field, A.E., Camargo, C.A., Taylor, C.B., et al. (2001) 'Peer–parent, and media influences on the development of weight concerns and frequent dieting among preadolescent and adolescent girls and boys', *Pediatrics*, 107: 54–60.

Fishbein, M. and Ajzen, I. (1975) *Belief, Attitude, Intention, and Behavior: An Introduction to Theory and Research*. Reading, MA: Addison-Wesley.

Flores, E., Tschann, J.M. and Marin, B.V. (2002) 'Latina adolescents: Predicting intentions to have sex', *Adolescence*, 37(148): 659–679.

Galen, L.W. and Rogers, W.M. (2004) 'Religiosity, alcohol expectancies, drinking motives and their interaction in the prediction of drinking among college students', *Journal of Studies on Alcohol,* 65(4): 469–477.

Gerbner, G. and Gross, L. (1976) 'Living with television: The violence profile', *Journal of Communication,* 26(2): 172–194.

Gerbner, G., Gross, L., Elee M.F., et al. (1977) 'TV violence profile No. 8: The highlights', *Journal of Communication,* 27(2): 171–180.

Gerbner, G., Gross, L., Morgan, M. and Signorielli, N. (1994) 'Growing up with television: The cultivation perspective', in J. Bryant and D. Zillmann (eds), *Media Effects: Advances in Theory and Research.* Hillsdale, NJ: Erlbaum, pp. 17–41.

Glynn, C.J., Huge, M.E. and Lunney, C.A. (2009) 'The influence of perceived social norms on college students' intention to vote', *Political Communication,* 26(1): 48–64.

Goldberg, M.E. (1995) 'Social marketing: Are we fiddling while Rome burns?', *Journal of Consumer Psychology,* 4(4): 347–370.

Graham, J.W., Marks, G. and Hansen, W.B. (1991) 'Social influence processes affecting adolescent substance use', *Journal of Applied Psychology,* 76(2): 291–298.

Granovetter, M.S. (1973) 'The strength of weak ties', *American Journal of Sociology,* 78(6): 1360–1380.

Gunther, A.C. and Mundy, P. (1993) 'Biased optimism and the third-person effect', *Journalism Quarterly,* 70: 58–67.

Gunther, A.C. and Storey, J.D. (2003) 'The influence of presumed influence', *Journal of Communication,* 53(2): 199–215.

Gunther, A.C., Bolt, D., Borzekowski, D.L.G, Liebhart, J.L. and Dillard, J.P. (2006) 'Presumed influence on peer norms: How mass media indirectly affect adolescent smoking', *Journal of Communication,* 56: 52–68.

Hanewinkel, R., Morgenstern, M. and Tanski, S.E. (2008) 'Longitudinal study of parental movie restrictions on teen smoking and drinking in Germany', *Addiction,* 103(10): 1722–1730.

Hansen, W.B. and Graham, J.W. (1991) 'Preventing alcohol, marijuana and cigarette use among adolescents: Peer pressure resistance training versus establishing conservative norms', *Preventive Medicine,* 20(3): 414–430.

Hastings, G. and Angus, K. (in press) 'When is social marketing not social marketing?', *Social Marketing*

Hastings, G. and Liberman, J. (2009) 'Tobacco corporate social responsibility and fairy godmothers: The framework convention on tobacco control slays a modern myth', *Tobacco Control,* 18(2): 73–74.

Hastings, G., McDermott, L., Angus, K., Stead, M., Thomson, S. (2006) *The Extent, Nature and Effects of Food Promotion to Children: A Review of the Evidence: Technical Paper Prepared for the World Health Organization.* Geneva: World Health Organization.

Hastings, G., Brooks, O., Stead, M., et al. (2010) 'Failure of self regulation of UK alcohol advertising (Alcohol advertising: The last chance saloon)', *British Medical Journal,* 340: 184–186.

Heider, F. (1958) *The Psychology of Interpersonal Relations.* New York: John Wiley and Sons.

Homish, G.G. and Leonard, K.E. (2008) 'The social network and alcohol use', *Journal of Studies on Alcohol and Drugs,* 69(6): 906–914.

Huon, G., Lim, J. and Gunewardene, A. (2000) 'Social influences and female adolescent dieting', *Journal of Adolescence,* 23(2): 229–232.

Jung, J.R. (2003) 'Changing the focus of college alcohol prevention programs', *Journal of American College Health,* 52(2): 92–95.

Kahneman, D. and Tversky, A. (1982) 'The simulation heuristic', in D. Kahneman, P. Slovic and A. Tversky (eds), *Judgment Under Uncertainty: Heuristics and Biases.* New York: Cambridge University Press, pp. 201–208.

Kallgren, C.A., Reno, R.R. and Cialdini, R.B. (2000). 'A focus theory of normative conduct: When norms do and do not affect behavior', *Personality and Social Psychology Bulletin,* 26(8): 1002–1012.

Klein, H. (1992) 'College student's attitudes toward the use of alcoholic beverages', *Journal of Alcohol and Drug and Education,* 37(3): 35–52.

Kypri, K. and Langley, J.D. (2003) 'Perceived social norms and their relation to university student drinking', *Journal of Studies on Alcohol,* 64(6): 829–835.

Lamber, T.A., Kahn, A.S. and Apple, K.L. (2003) 'Pluralistic ignorance and hooking up', *The Journal of Sex Research,* 40(2): 129–133.

Lapinski, M.K. and Rimal, R.N. (2005) 'An explication of social norms', *Communication Theory,* 15(2): 127–147.

Larimer, M.E. and Neighbors, C. (2003) 'Normative misperception and the impact of descriptive and injunctive norms on college student gambling', *Psychology of Addictive Behaviors,* 17(3): 235–243.

Larimer, M.E., Turner, A.P., Mallett, K.A. and Geisner, I.M. (2004) 'Predicting drinking behavior and alcohol-related problems among fraternity and sorority members: Examining the role of descriptive and injunctive norms', *Psychology of Addictive Behaviors,* 18(3): 203–212.

Lee, C.M., Geisner, I.M., Lewis, M.A., Neighbors, C. and Larimer, M.E. (2007) 'Social motives and the interaction between descriptive and injunctive norms in college student drinking', *Journal of Studies on Alcohol and Drugs,* 68(5): 714–721.

Lederman, L.C., Lederman, J.B. and Kully, R.D. (2004) 'Believing is seeing: The co-construction of everyday myths in the media about college drinking', *American Behavioral Scientist,* 48: 130–136.

Linkenbach, J. and Perkins, H.W. (2003) 'Most of us are tobacco free: An eight-month social norms campaign reducing youth initiation of smoking in Montana', in H.W. Perkins (ed), *The Social Norms Approach to Preventing School and College Age Substance Abuse: A Handbook for Educators, Counselors, Clinicians.* San Francisco, CA: Jossey-Bass, pp. 224–234.

Linkenbach, J.W., Perkins, H.W. and DeJong, W. (2003) 'Parents' perceptions of parenting norms: Using the social norms approach to reinforce effective parenting', in H.W. Perkins (ed), *The Social Norms Approach to Preventing School and College Age Substance Abuse: A Handbook for*

Educators, Counselors, Clinicians. San Francisco, CA: Jossey-Bass, pp. 247–258.

Linnan, L., LaMontagne, A.D., Stoddard, A., Emmons, K.M. and Sorensen, G. (2005) 'Norms and their relationship to behavior in worksite settings: An application of the Jackson return potential model', *American Journal of Health Behavior,* 29(3): 258–268.

McAlaney, J. and McMahon, J. (2007) 'Normative beliefs, misperceptions, and heavy episodic drinking in a British student sample', *Journal of Studies on Alcohol and Drugs,* 68(3): 385–392.

Maddock, J. and Glanz, K. (2005) 'The relationship of proximal normative beliefs and global subjective norms to college students' alcohol consumption', *Addictive Behaviors,* 30(2): 315–323.

Makgosa, R. and Mohube, K. (2007) 'Peer influence on young adults' products purchase decisions', *African Journal of Business Management,* 1(3): 64–71.

Mallett, K.A., Bachrach, R.L. and Turrisi, R. (2009) 'Examining the unique influence of interpersonal and intrapersonal drinking perceptions on alcohol consumption among college students', *Journal of Studies on Alcohol and Drugs,* 7(2): 178–185.

Mattern, J.L. and Neighbors, C. (2004) 'Social norms campaigns: Examining the relationship between changes in perceived norms and changes in drinking levels', *Journal of Studies on Alcohol,* 65(4): 489–493.

Mead, G.H. (1934) *Mind, Self and Society.* Chicago, IL: University of Chicago Press.

Miller, D.T. and Prentice, D.A. (1994) 'Collective errors and errors about the collective', *Personality and Social Psychology Bulletin,* 20(5): 541–550.

Moore, S.M. and Ohtsuka, K. (1999) 'The prediction of gambling behavior and problem gambling from attitudes and perceived norms', *Social Behavior and Personality,* 27(5): 455–466.

Moreira, M.T., Smith, L.A. and Foxcroft, D. (2009) 'Social norms interventions to reduce alcohol misuse in university or college students', *Cochrane Database of Systematic Reviews,* Issue 3.

Moscovi, S. (1976) *Social Influence and Social Change.* London: Academic Press.

Neighbors, C., Walker, D.D. and Larimer, M.E. (2003) 'Expectancies and evaluations of alcohol effects among college students: Self-determination as a moderator', *Journal of Studies on Alcohol,* 64(2): 292–300.

Neighbors, C., Fossos, N., Woods, B.A., et al. (2007a) 'Social anxiety as a moderator of the relationship between perceived norms and drinking', *Journal of Studies on Alcohol and Drugs,* 68: 91–96.

Neighbors, C., Lee, M.L., Lewis, M.A., Fossos, N. and Larimer, M.E. (2007b) 'Are social norms the best predictor of outcomes among heavy-drinking college students?', *Journal of Studies on Alcohol and Drugs,* 68(4): 556–565.

Neighbors, C., Lostutter, T., Whiteside, U., et al. (2007c) 'Injunctive norms and problem gambling among college students', *Journal of Gambling Studies,* 23(3): 259–273.

Neuwirth, K. and Frederick, E. (2004) 'Peer and social influence on opinion expression: Combining the theories of planned behavior and the spiral of silence', *Communication Research,* 31(6): 669–703.

Newcomb, T.M. (1943) *Personality and Social Change: Attitude Formation in a Student Community.* New York: John Wiley and Sons.

Nichols, T.R., Birnbaum, A.S., Birnel, S. and Botvin, G.J. (2006) 'Perceived smoking environment and smoking initiation among multi-ethnic urban girls', *Journal of Adolescent Health,* 38(4): 369–375.

Noelle-Neumann, E. (1973) 'Return to the concept of powerful mass media', *Studies in Broadcasting,* 12: 67–112.

Oetting, E.R. and Beauvais, F. (1987) 'Peer cluster theory, socialization characteristics, and adolescent drug use: A path analysis', *Journal of Counseling Psychology,* 34(2): 205–213.

Oetting, E.R. and Donnermeyer, J. (1998) 'Primary socialization theory: The etiology of drug use and deviance', *Substance Use and Misuse,* 33(4): 995–1026.

O'Guinn, T.C. and Shrum, L.J. (1997) 'The role of television in the construction of consumer reality', *Journal of Consumer Research,* 23(4): 278–294.

Oostveen, T., Knibbe, R. and de Vries, H. (1996) 'Social influences on young adults' alcohol consumption: Norms, modeling, pressure, socializing, and conformity', *Addictive Behaviors,* 21(2): 187–197.

Park, C.W. and Lessig, V.P. (1977) 'Students and housewives: Differences in susceptibility to reference group influence', *Journal of Consumer Research,* 4(2): 102–110.

Paxton, S.J., Schutz, H.K., Wertheim, E.H. and Muir, S.L. (1999) 'Friendship clique and peer influences on body image concerns, dietary restraint, extreme weight-loss behaviors and binge eating in adolescent girls', *Journal of Abnormal Psychology,* 108(2): 255–266.

Perkins, H.W. (2003) 'The emergence and evolution of the social norms approach to substance abuse prevention', in H.W. Perkins (ed) *The Social Norms Approach to Preventing School and College Age Substance Abuse: A Handbook for Educators, Counselors, Clinicians.* San Francisco, CA: Jossey-Bass, pp. 3–17.

Perkins, H.W. and Berkowitz, A.D. (1986) 'Perceiving the community norms of alcohol use among students: Some research implications for campus alcohol education programming', *Substance Use and Misuse,* 21(9): 961–976.

Perkins, H.W. and Wechsler, H. (1996) 'Variation in perceived college drinking norms and its impact on alcohol abuse: A nationwide study', *Journal of Drug Issues,* 26(4): 961–974.

Perkins, H.W., Haines, M.P. and Rice, R. (2005) 'Misperceiving the college drinking norm and related problems: A nationwide study of exposure to prevention information, perceived norms and student alcohol misuse', *Journal of Studies on Alcohol,* 66(4): 470–478.

Perkins, H.W., Linkenbach, J.W., Lewis, M.A. and Neighbors, C. (2010) 'Effectiveness of social norms media marketing in reducing drinking and driving: A statewide campaign', *Addictive Behaviors,* 35(10): 866–874.

Perloff, R.M. (1993) 'Third-person effect research 1983–1992: A review and synthesis', *International Journal of Public Opinion Research*, 5(2): 167–184.

Pool, G.J. and Schwegler, A.F. (2007) 'Differentiating among motives for norm conformity', *Basic and Applied Social Psychology*, 29: 47–60.

Prentice, D.A. and Miller, D.T. (1993) 'Pluralistic ignorance and alcohol use on campus: Some consequences of misperceiving the social norm', *Journal of Personality and Social Psychology*, 64(2): 243–256.

Rabow, J. and Duncan-Schill, M. (1994) 'Drinking among college students', *Journal of Alcohol and Drug Education*, 40(3): 52–64.

Read, J.P., Wood, M.D., Lejuez, C.W., Palfai, T.P. and Slack, M. (2004) 'Gender, alcohol consumption and differing alcohol expectancy dimensions in college drinkers', *Experimental and Clinical Psychopharmacology*, 12(4): 298–308.

Read, J.P., Wood, M.D. and Capone, C. (2005) 'A prospective investigation of relations between social influences and alcohol involvement during the transition into college', *Journal of Studies on Alcohol*, 66: 23–35.

Real, K. and Rimal, R.N. (2007) 'Friends talk to friends about drinking: Exploring the role of peer communication in the theory of normative social behavior', *Health Communication* 22(2): 169–180.

Reed, M.B., Lange, J.E., Ketchie, J.M. and Clapp, J.D. (2007) 'The relationship between social identity, normative information, and college student drinking', *Social Influence*, 2(4): 269–294.

Reno, R.R., Cialdini, R.B. and Kallgren, C.A. (1993) 'The trans-situational influence of social norms', *Journal of Personality and Social Psychology*, 64: 104–112.

Rimal, R.N. (2008) 'Modeling the relationship between descriptive norms and behaviors: A test and extension of the Theory of Normative Social Behavior (TNSB)', *Health Communication*, 23(2): 103–116.

Rimal, R.N. and Real, K. (2003) 'Understanding the influence of perceived norms on behaviors', *Communication Theory*, 13(2): 184–203.

Rimal, R.N. and Real, K. (2005) 'How behaviors are influenced by perceived norms: A test of the Theory of Normative Social Behavior', *Communication Research*, 32(3): 389–414.

Rimal, R.N., Lapinski, M.K., Cook, R.J. and Real, K. (2005) 'Moving toward a theory of normative influences: How perceived benefits and similarity moderate the impact of descriptive norms on behaviors', *Journal of Health Communication*, 10(5): 433–450.

Ross, L., Greene, D. and House, P. (1977) 'The false consensus effect: An egocentric bias in social perception and attribution processes', *Journal of Experimental Social Psychology*, 13(3): 279–301.

Rutland, A., Cameron, L., Milne, A. and McGeorge, P. (2005) 'Social norms and self-presentation: Children's implicit and explicit intergroup attitudes', *Child Development*, 76(2): 451–466.

Sanders, G.S. and Mullen, B. (1983) 'Accuracy in perceptions of consensus: Differential tendencies of people with majority and minority positions', *European Journal of Social Psychology*, 13: 57–70.

Sargent, J.D., Wills, T.A., Stoolmiller, M., Gibson, J. and Gibbons, F.X. (2006) 'Alcohol use in motion pictures and its relation with early-onset teen drinking', *Journal of Studies on Alcohol*, 67: 54–65.

Schachter, S. (1951) 'Deviation, rejection, and communication', *The Journal of Abnormal and Social Psychology*, 46(2): 190–207.

Scholly, K., Katz, A.R., Gascpoigne, J. and Holck, P.S. (2005) 'Using social norms theory to explain perceptions and sexual health behaviors of undergraduate college students: An exploratory study', *Journal of American College Health*, 53(4): 159–166.

Schroeder, C.M. and Prentice, D.A. (1998) 'Exposing pluralistic ignorance to reduce alcohol use among college students', *Journal of Applied Social Psychology*, 28(23): 2150–2180.

Schultz, P.W., Nolan, J.M., Cialdini, R.B., Goldstein, N.J. and Griskevicius, V. (2007) 'The constructive, destructive, and reconstructive power of social norms', *Psychological Science*, 18(5): 429–434.

Schwartz, S.H. (1977) 'Normative influence on altruism', in L. Berkowitz (ed), *Advances in Experimental Social Psychology*, Vol. 10. New York: Academic Press, pp. 221–279.

Schwartz, S.H. and Howard, J.A. (1982) 'Helping and cooperation: A self-based motivational model', in V. Derlega and H. Grezlak (eds), *Cooperation and Helping Behavior: Theories and Research*. New York: Academic Press, pp. 327–353.

Shanahan, J. (2004) 'A return to cultural indicators', *Communications*, 29(3): 277–294.

Shanahan, J., Scheufele, D., Yang, F. and Hizi, S. (2004) 'Cultivation and spiral of silence effects: The case of smoking', *Mass Communication and Society*, 7(4): 413–428.

Sheeran, P. and Orbell, S. (1999) 'Augmenting the theory of planned behavior: Roles for anticipated regret and descriptive norms', *Journal of Applied Social Psychology*, 29(10): 2107–2142.

Sherif, M. (1936) *The Psychology of Social Norms*. New York: Harper Collins.

Shore, E.R., Rivers, P.C. and Berman, J.J. (1983) 'Resistance by college students to peer pressure to drink', *Journal of Studies on Alcohol*, 44(2): 352–361.

Shrum, L.J. (1999) 'Television and persuasion: Effects of the programs between the ads', *Psychology and Marketing*, 16(2): 119–140.

Shrum, L.J., Wyer, R.S. and O'Guinn, T.C. (1998) 'The effects of television consumption on social perceptions: The use of priming procedures to investigate psychological processes', *Journal of Consumer Research*, 24(4): 447–458.

Slomkowski, C., Rende, R., Novak, S., Lloyd-Richardson, E. and Niaura, R. (2005) 'Sibling effects on smoking in adolescence: Evidence for social influence from a genetically informative design', *Addiction*, 100(4): 430–438.

Spijkerman, R., Van den Eijnden R.J.J.M., Overbeek, G. and Engels, R.C.M.E. (2007) 'The impact of peer and parental norms and behavior on adolescent drinking: The role of drinker prototypes', *Psychology and Health*, 22: 7–29.

Sullivan, K.T., Pasch, L.A., Cornelius, T. and Cirigliano, E. (2004) 'Predicting participation in premarital prevention programs: The health belief model and social norms', *Family Process*, 43(2): 175–193.

Suls, J. and Wan, C.K. (1987) 'In search of the false-uniqueness phenomenon: Fear and estimates of social consensus', *Journal of Personality and Social Psychology*, 52: 211–217.

Sumner, W.G. (1906) *Folkways*. Boston: Ginn.

Sutherland, E.H. and Cressey, D.R. (1955) *Principles of Criminology*, 5th edn. Philadelphia: J.B. Lippincott.

Tabachnik, N., Crocker, J. and Alloy, L. (1983) 'Depression, social comparison, and the false consensus effect', *Journal of Personality and Social Psychology*, 45(3): 688–699.

Taylor, C.A. and Sorenson, S.B. (2004) 'Injunctive social norms of adults regarding teen dating violence', *Journal of Adolescent Health*, 34(6): 468–479.

Thombs, D.L., Wolcott, B.J. and Farkash, L.G.E. (1997) 'Social context, perceived norms and drinking behavior in young people', *Journal of Substance Abuse*, 9: 257–267.

Turner, J.C. (1982) 'Towards a cognitive redefinition of the social group', in H. Tajfel (ed), *Social Identity and Intergroup Relations*. Cambridge: Cambridge University Press, pp. 15–40.

Turner, J.C., Hogg, M.A., Oakes, P.J., Reicher, S.D. and Wetherell, M.S. (1987) *Rediscovering The Social Group: A Self-categorization Theory*. Oxford: Blackwell.

Tversky, A. and Kahneman, D. (1973) 'Availability: A heuristic for judging frequency and probability', *Cognitive Psychology*, 5(2): 207–232.

Van den Bulck, J. and Beullens, K. (2005) 'Television and music video exposure and adolescent alcohol use while going out', *Alcohol and Alcoholism*, 40(3): 249–253.

van den Putte, B., Yzer, M.C. and Brunsting, S. (2005) 'Social influences on smoking cessation: A comparison of the effect of six social influence variables', *Preventive Medicine*, 41: 186–193.

Volgy, T.J. and Schwarz, J.E. (1980) 'TV entertainment programming and sociopolitical attitudes', *Journalism Quarterly*, 57: 150–155.

Wakefield, M., Flay, B., Nichter, M. and Giovino, G. (2003) 'Role of the media in Influencing trajectories of youth smoking', *Addiction*, 98(s1): 79–103.

Wakefield, M., Balch, G.I., Ruel, E., et al. (2005) 'Youth responses to anti-smoking advertisements from tobacco-control agencies, tobacco companies, and pharmaceutical companies', *Journal of Applied Social Psychology*, 35(9): 1894–1911.

Wakefield, M., Terry-McElrath, Y., Emery, S., et al. (2006) 'Effect of televised, tobacco company-funded smoking prevention advertising on youth smoking-related beliefs, intentions, and behavior', *American Journal of Public Health*, 96(12): 2154–2160.

Wang, C.C. (2005) 'Factors that influence the piracy of DVD/VCD motion pictures', *Journal of American Academy of Business*, 6: 231–237.

Wasko, J., Phillips, M. and Purdie, C. (1993) 'Hollywood meets Madison Avenue: The commercialization of US films', *Media Culture and Society*, 15(2): 271–293.

Webley, P., Cole, M. and Eidjar, O.P. (2001) 'The prediction of self-reported and hypothetical tax-evasion: Evidence from England, France and Norway', *Journal of Economic Psychology*, 22(2): 141–155.

Wechsler, H. and Kuo, M. (2000) 'College students define binge drinking and estimate its prevalence: Results of a national survey', *Journal of American College Health*, 49(2): 57–64.

Wellman, R.J., Sugarman, D.B., DiFranza, J.R. and Winickoff, J.P. (2006) 'The extent to which tobacco marketing and tobacco use in films contribute to children's use of tobacco: A meta-analysis', *Archives of Pediatrics and Adolescent Medicine*, 160(12): 1285–1296.

Wenzel, M. (2005) 'Misperceptions of social norms about tax compliance: From theory to intervention', *Journal of Economic Psychology* 26(6): 862–883.

Werch, C.E., Pappas, D.M., Carlson, J.M., et al. (2000) 'Results of a social norm intervention to prevent binge drinking among first year residential college students', *Journal of American College Health*, 49(2): 85–92.

Wills, T.A., Sargent, J.D., Gibbons, F.X., Gerrard, M. and Stoolmiller, M. (2009) 'Movie exposure to alcohol cues and adolescent alcohol problems: A longitudinal analysis in a national sample', *Psychology of Addictive Behaviors*, 23: 23–35.

Wolfson, S. (2000) 'Students' estimates of the prevalence of drug use: Evidence for a false consensus effect', *Psychology of Addictive Behaviors*, 14(3): 295–298.

Wood, M.D., Read, J.P., Palfai, T.B. and Stevenson, J.F. (2001) 'Social influence processes and college student drinking: The mediational role of alcohol outcome expectancies', *Journal of Studies on Alcohol*, 62: 32–43.

Yanovitzky, I. and Stryker, J. (2001) 'Mass media, social norms and health Promotion efforts', *Communication Research*, 28(2): 208–239.

Yanovitzky, I., Stewart, L.P. and Lederman, L.C. (2006) 'Social distance, perceived drinking by peers, and alcohol use by college students', *Health Communication* 19: 1–10.

5

Design Thinking, Demarketing and Behavioral Economics: Fostering Interdisciplinary Growth in Social Marketing

R. Craig Lefebvre and Philip Kotler

In this chapter, we introduce three sets of ideas that can bring more innovation and impact into social marketing research and practice. Two of these ideas, behavioral economics and design thinking, come from outside the traditional marketing framework. However, as we will see, the principles and implications of both of these disciplines overlap with many social marketing issues. The third idea, demarketing, was introduced into marketing thought several decades ago but has seen little adoption in social marketing programs despite its relevance to any number of public health and social concerns that involve excessive consumption – whether it is consumption of products, services or natural resources.

BEHAVIORAL ECONOMICS

Behavioral economics is concerned with understanding and influencing the cognitive, emotional and social factors that influence the economic decisions made by consumers, borrowers and investors and how these decisions ultimately affect market prices, investment returns and the allocation of resources (Wikipedia: accessed 28 December 2010). Behavioral economics grew out of the interest in how token economies

developed by practitioners of operant psychology to manage behaviors in a variety of situations – notably school classrooms and inpatient psychiatric wards – could be extended into economic theory (Kagel and Winkler, 1972). Behavioral economics burst into the awareness of policymakers and the general public through the publication of such books as *Freakonomics* (Levitt and Dubner, 2005), *Nudge* (Thaler and Sunstein, 2009) and *Predictably Irrational* (Ariely, 2008). The field of behavioral economics is particularly important to social marketers in how it has successfully unseated what had been the prevailing economic model of the 'rational man' that underlies much economic and marketing thought (cf. Andreasen, 1995; Zaltman, 2003). In brief, classic economic theory held that people were motivated primarily by material incentives and made decisions in a rational way. People were assumed to be conscious, deliberate and rational entities who made decisions based on their consideration and unbiased weighting of the benefits and costs (or pros and cons) of making certain decisions or engaging in specific behaviors, ranging from what companies to invest in the stock market to how much they would pay for branded versus unbranded soft drinks. As Zaltman (2003, p. 9) notes, the extension of this 'fallacy' is that marketers assume that people can readily explain their thinking and behavior, though 95% of thinking takes place in our unconscious minds. The magnitude of the impact of the findings of behavioral economists – that many decisions people make are not rational ones – should not be underestimated. Indeed, seminal scientists in this area were awarded the Nobel Prize in Economics for their work on psychological and experimental economics.

Some of the primary features of behavioral economics are now considered.

Heuristics

The notion is that people often make decisions based on approximate rules of thumb and not strictly rational analysis. The area of heuristics is also concerned with the ideas of cognitive biases as well as bounded rationality that influence the kinds of information people are exposed to, the decisions they make and the behaviors they then choose to engage in. Some of the ways in which these personal biases are expressed include:

- *Loss Aversion* – people are more averse to losing things than they are inclined to gaining things (that helps explain why people prefer short-term vs long-term consequences for engaging in behaviors; it also addresses the common occurrence of people and organizations preferring to continue to engage in their usual practices rather than risk change or innovation).
- *Status Quo Bias* – inertia is powerful. A consistent finding in the psychological and behavioral economics research is that the best predictor of our future behavior is our current behavior. Evidence of status quo bias in social marketing includes acknowledging cultural traditions that root food consumption and sexual practices, for example (Mintz and Du Bois, 2002; Parker, 2001). The preferences of people who are referred to as laggards or traditionalists in the diffusion of innovations literature (Rogers, 1995) as well as the psychological forces that operate within bureaucracies are often attributed to this bias.
- *The Dual Self* – the recognition that people do not have a consistent 'personality' but rather their behavior is largely contingent on the circumstances they find themselves in. Aspects of 'this dual self' manifest themselves in situations where a person understands and endorses the value of engaging in protected sexual acts, but when in a situation in which emotions and interpersonal attraction become more salient, these competing preferences for acceptance, sexual satisfaction and other motives lead to decisions to not use any form of protection – 'at least

this time.' Economists and social marketers may be puzzled by this seeming contradiction; yet in psychology and behavioral economics, this is recognized as the usual state of affairs.

- *Attention Constraints* – the realization that people get distracted, sometimes despite their best intentions. One implication of this finding is to help people pay regular attention to their goals in order to ultimately meet them. Regularly paying attention to goals can be important in diverse activities, from financial and retirement planning to weight-loss efforts to coalition and organizational effectiveness.
- *Resource Slack* – the finding that when planning for the future, people realistically assume that resources will be tight, but they often expect free time to magically materialize. We often see this when people, for example, talk about the need for taking a vacation, spending more time with the family, having organizational strategic planning retreats, and the like, yet postpone them to 'when we will have more time.'

Framing

The way a problem or decision is presented to a decision-maker will affect their action. We note that this idea of framing is not new to people familiar with the area of media advocacy (Wallack, 1990) or political communication (Lakoff, 2004). However, for behavioral economists and policy-makers, the reality of the effects of framing strips away the veneer that public policy decisions are made solely on the merits of the facts and rationality (cf. Stone, 1997).

Market inefficiencies

Many economists subscribe to the idea that, when left to their own devices, markets will evolve to a point where buyers and sellers, prices and costs are in a state of equilibrium. What cannot be ignored is that in most cases there are many observed market outcomes that are contrary to rational expectations, market efficiency and social needs (the global financial crisis of 2009, the insufficient supply of condoms in southern Africa for HIV prevention and family planning). Among identified market inefficiencies that may be relevant to social marketers are:

- Inequity aversion, or the preference for fairness and resistance to inequitable outcomes (e.g., notions of social justice and health equity).
- Dynamic inconsistencies, such as when decision-makers' preferences at one point in time are inconsistent with what they prefer at another

point in time (also known as 'changing one's mind as the facts change').

- Sunk costs, a term that refers to costs that cannot be recovered once they have been incurred. The idea of sunk costs are relevant to everything from infrastructure construction projects to the development of a social marketing program where decisions may be based on not wasting already invested resources, despite other evidence that the project should be modified or discontinued.
- Finally, herd behavior describes how individuals in a group can act together without planned direction.

Defaults, or what happens to a person when they do not actively make a choice, is one of the more popular behavioral economic principles currently being applied in marketing, medical care and public policymaking of all types. How default options are constructed, known as choice architecture (Thaler and Sunstein, 2009), has been shown to increase the percent of people who enroll in retirement accounts or become organ donors (Amir et al., 2005). The research suggests that defaults work best when decision-makers are indifferent, confused or conflicted about the choice, or overwhelmed by the multitude of choices they are presented. Indeed, a finding of decision-making research is that presenting people with too many choices results in 'choice overload.' In the face of such overload, many people simply choose to avoid any decision. A practical implication of these findings is for the 200 eating choices people are faced with every day in the USA (Wansink and Sobal, 2007). One approach would be to modify cues at the place-of-choice (or desire) to create healthy default options for main courses and side items by prearranging them to be more visible, the first choice and the easiest one, as opposed to just implementing a nutrition labeling (promotion) program (Wansink et al., 2010). In the same vein, simply presenting people with lists of various ways that they might eat more fruits and vegetables can viewed by them as overwhelming, and the decision might be to 'maintain the status quo' because the decisions look too complicated or overwhelming.

INTEGRATING BEHAVIORAL ECONOMICS AND SOCIAL MARKETING

Young and Caisey (2010) provide a thoughtful approach to integrating behavioral economics and social marketing approaches through the lens of reducing car ownership. In their discussion they use the behavioral economic framework for the identification of the motivations that maintain car ownership and view social marketing as a way to use these insights as a platform for program development.

In his call for the inclusion of behavioral economics into the social marketing toolbox, Smith (2010) noted three ideas for integration:

1. The recognition of the dual self, or what he referred to as the 'hot and cold self,' should be incorporated into how we plan and implement market and formative research studies.
2. Similarly, how we segment people might also benefit from this 'hot/cold' perspective. Such segmentation schemes would recognize that some people might change preferences more readily as their 'state' or context changes. The marketing challenge could then be to provide people with more skills to inoculate themselves from changing so easily, or create new circumstances where the preferred healthy choices are more easily made.
3. The idea of defaults and choice architecture should move social marketing more towards the creation and design of policies, products and services to optimize trial behaviors and sustained adoption of them.

Bertrand et al. (2006) examined how behavioral economics and marketing could be used to improve decision-making among the poor, for whom they saw narrower margins of error given the environments in which they live as compared with more affluent people. Among their recommendations we have adapted to social marketing practice are:

1. Improve the ease of access and opportunities to products, services and information that are too often taken for granted by policymakers and program planners (what the authors labeled 'creating the right channel factors').
2. Expand beyond the dual self or 'hot–cold' idea and appeal to the right identity, recognizing that people may refer to a variety of social groups in how they think about themselves and identify with others (in the social media marketing world, an analogous idea in the market of <1, where even as a person explores the internet or participates on various social network sites, their preferences and behaviors may be very different depending on which site they are currently on).
3. Create opportunities to improve people's ability to process information to compensate for having too many choices or the complexity of the information. They also note that when information is presented to people in small groups, they are more likely to adopt the recommendations because the group interaction allows for social norms to be addressed as well.

4. Incorporate time management and planning into change programs to address the resource slack bias many people bring to these challenges.
5. Focus on the nuances of policy and program design, including having clear incentives that are offered in the right context; offering natural and desirable defaults and not too many options; framing options as gains or losses and as injunctive or popular norms; selecting the right format for communications to enhance its persuasive ability; and appealing to the right 'identity' for the program purpose or behavior to be adopted.

We close by noting that we would likely not be writing about behavioral economics here were it not for its recognition and adoption by public policymakers worldwide. For example, in the UK the Institute for Government recently published a monograph entitled 'MINDSPACE: Influencing behaviour through public policy,' the foreword of which began:

> This report... shows how behavioural theory could help achieve better outcomes for citizens, by complementing more established policy tools, or by suggesting more innovative interventions (Dolan et al., 2010).

Many of the elements of the MINDSPACE model are drawn directly from the behavioral economics literature. In the end, we believe that behavioral economics provides social marketers with more tools and frameworks within which to analyze and devise methods to alter individual, organizational and social change activities. Moreover, there are aspects of behavioral economics that support the social marketing approach, including the distrust of rational-based approaches to change, the focus on situational determinants of behavior, the need to increase access and opportunities for change, and greater attention to how price (as both an incentive and a cost) contribute to the decisions people make about what they do and how they do it in everyday life.

DESIGN THINKING

For many social marketers, the idea of design may conjure up the tasks associated with creating posters, brochures and other types of print material. Others may think of design as the aesthetics they see in fashion magazines, home decorating catalogues and high-end department stores. And while they are likely to ascribe design elements to their experience with various technology products (Apple being a prime example), their application might be less obvious in such places

as re-engineering nursing staff shift changes at Kaiser Permanante or developing the Aravind eye care system in India. As Tim Brown, CEO of IDEO, one of the leaders in the design thinking movement, has noted, design has been shifting from an interest in 'posters and toasters' to services and processes. He describes design thinking as: '... a human-centered design ethos ... [by which] innovation is powered by a thorough understanding, through direct observation, of what people want and need in their lives and what they like or dislike about the way particular products are made, packaged, marketed, sold, and supported.' This shift in design focus can be characterized from making ideas 'pretty and appealing' to developing ideas themselves that are desirable to people, technically feasible and financially viable for the organization (Brown, 2008).

Championed by organizations including IDEO and the Rotman School of Management, design thinking focuses on the process for practical, creative resolution of problems or issues that might lead to a new or improved product or service, new processes or experiences for consumers or users, or new social and organizational systems. Businesses are incorporating design thinking as a way to stimulate more innovation in the products and services they offer. Brown and Wyatt (2010) suggest that many non-profit organizations are also adopting design thinking for developing social innovations in the face of chronic, ongoing social problems.

Design thinking has grown in recognition and prominence among business leaders in the past few years. Roger Martin, Dean of the Rotman School of Management at the University of Toronto, views design thinking as leading a movement that looks at wicked problems, or social mysteries such as how to make healthcare systems work or why some cities seem to 'work' better than others, to come up with new heuristics or guidelines for an organized exploration of the possibilities (Martin, 2009). For example, social marketing offer a set of heuristics for thinking about social problems and social change by invoking the 4Ps to analyze and create solutions to social problems.

A distinguishing mark of design thinkers is abductive reasoning: that no new idea or innovation can be proven deductively or inductively from past data, but by 'logical leaps of the mind' when observed data, or outcomes, do not fit with existing models or explanations (Martin, 2009). Abductive reasoning is, simply, wondering how something might be done differently, or made better (Berger, 2009). As Martin (2009, p. 37) argues, the abductive reasoning approach offers a way to move beyond the reliability bias of attempting to produce consistent, predictable outcomes but which may not be valid in meeting a desired objective. In the public health space, an example would be mandating many different types of organizations to implement interventions with known parameters and explicit protocols (i.e., they can be reliably reproduced) yet may have little external validity (e.g., the desired results have only been achieved in highly controlled and well-resourced circumstances).

In the practice of design thinking, this abductive reasoning process is characterized by looking for new data points (instead of unquestionably accepting the data that are available), challenging accepted explanations by continually asking 'Why?' and imagining new worlds or possibilities (What if...?). Berger (2009, p. 73) calls this 'making hope visible.' By this he means that designers bring future possibilities into view for people we work with in ways that are compelling, accessible and clear. In practice, this leads us to work with people to understand the specific nature of what they want to achieve ('a better world for all' is not precise or clear). Unlike the 'evidence-based approach' that applies old solutions to similar problems, design thinking focuses on developing innovative approaches for the problems that defy easy solutions.

What lies at the core of the design thinking approach is the unwavering focus on people as not only the judge and jury for how we should think about problems and design for their solution but also as the co-creators of solutions whenever possible. Designers encourage the 'beginner's mindset' to put aside perceptions, assumptions and stereotypes that may cloud or block the amount of empathy one has with the people we are working with.

This human-centeredness is expressed not just as empathy for people, but the use of innovative qualitative methods to get below the superficial and artificial understandings that surveys and focus groups provide and develop a deeper level of understanding of who the people are we intend to serve and what is important to them. Some of these techniques include the use of journey maps, photo captures, cultural probes and personas development; conversations with positive deviants or extreme users and participatory methods. These techniques are intended to move beyond the obvious and spoken to get a view of people's lives as they experience them. From these insights comes an understanding from which alternative frames and solutions to the problem can be developed, tested and implemented. The value of design research is judged by its 'world-changing' impact on the designers (or social marketers) in how it inspires them and the results that follow (cf. Laurel, 2003).

Reflecting their roots in industrial design and engineering, many design thinkers highlight prototyping solutions as part of their approach. Expressing ideas visually; with your hands; and with models, scenarios, simulations and role-plays are an essential part of the process. These prototypes do not demand much investment in resources; they are necessary only to generate feedback and drive an idea forward (Brown, 2009, p. 91). Prototypes use materials ready for a 'pre-test' with an audience; prototypes rarely see the light of day, or extend beyond the core project team. The power of prototyping is in making the abstract conversations and ideas into something tangible (or as one of our students succinctly stated it: 'When in doubt, draw it out!'). They provide the team with multiple ways of working through a new idea for behavior change, product development or service delivery process (and as some people in disaster preparedness know, response coordination) from multiple points of view and in rapid succession. The objective is to thoroughly explore and vet what might be many 'wonder-ful' approaches to a problem through hard-headed analysis, working with the known (and anticipated) constraints, trial and error, and learning by failing, so that what emerges are the most desirable, feasible and viable approaches to improving social and personal well-being (Brown, 2009, p. 18).

Berger (2009) studied a number of designers, and the cross-cutting design principles he detected are summarized in Table 5.1. All of these principles have relevance and application in social marketing, from 'Going Deep' to better understand the people we wish to serve to 'Starting Anywhere' in order to begin bringing improvements to our programs and activities now – not after some far-off evaluation or when the next project is funded.

THE PROCESS OF DESIGN THINKING

Lombardi (2005) summarizes a number of writings about the design thinking process as being:

- Collaborative, especially with others having different and complementary experience, to generate better work and form agreement.
- Abductive, inventing new options to find new and better solutions to new problems.
- Experimental, building prototypes and posing hypotheses, testing them, and iterating this activity to find what works and what doesn't work to manage risk.
- Personal, considering the unique context of each problem and the people involved.

Table 5.1 Principles of design thinking

1. **Ask stupid questions** – What is design? Who is Bruce Mau? And, by the way, does it have to be a light bulb?
2. **Jump fences** – How do designers connect, reinvent and recombine? And what makes them think they can do all these things?
3. **Make hope visible** – The importance of picturing possibilities and drawing conclusions
4. **Go deep** – How do we figure out what people need – before they know they need it?
5. **Work the metaphor** – Realizing what a brand or business is really about – then bringing it to life through designed experiences
6. **Design what you do** – Can the way an organization behaves be designed?
7. **Face consequences** – Coming to terms with the responsibility to design well. And recognizing what will happen if we don't
8. **Embrace constraints** – Design that does 'more with less' is needed more than ever in today's world
9. **Design for emergence** – Applying the principles of transformation design to everyday life
10. **Begin anywhere** – Why small actions are more important than big plans

Adapted from Berger (2009).

• Integrative, perceiving an entire system and its linkages.
• Interpretive, devising how to frame the problem and judge the possible solutions.

A core approach to the design process is taught by George Kemble, a design methodologist at Stanford University, as a 'begin anywhere process' that has five essential requirements (Berger, 2009).

1. Empathy – gain an understanding and expertise with the problem primarily through experiencing it with the people directly involved with it.
2. Framing – be sure that you are asking and answering the right questions (see Table 5.1 for ideas) and not reflexively resorting to established theories or research as the only sources of data. Develop a point of view about the problem that best reflects the empathy and understanding you develop about the people and the problem.
3. Generating options and ideas – using brainstorming and other techniques, create the plausible and implausible ideas that might actually lead to a breakthrough, a new way to approach the problem, or a twist on an old idea.
4. Prototypes – the practical heart of design is to quickly move into prototyping solutions based on the ideas that were created. It is much less deliberative than most social marketers and others are used to. 'Let's role play how that might work right now!' 'Let's sketch out all the ways this could possibly work.' 'What if we made it look like this – or this – or this?' Take it out, try it and throw it away, modify it or run with it. This is a very different and fast-forward approach from bludgeoning concepts and 'pretest materials' to oblivion in focus groups.

5. Iterations – keep moving the process forward by introducing slight improvements and modifications based on feedback from people, practical use and more formal tests.

It is by working through and around these steps, not just sequentially but as the solution process takes you, that designers seek to redesign their world.

INTEGRATING DESIGN THINKING AND SOCIAL MARKETING

While design thinking is gaining more prominence in public health (e.g., the identification of consumer-centered design principles for enhancing smokers' experiences with cessation treatments; Backinger et al., 2010), the use of design principles in public health have been around for decades, though they have been described with different terms. We look at three very different examples from public education campaigns, organizational innovation in health agencies and clinical health care.

'5 A Day for Better Health'

The US national campaign to increase the number of servings of fruits and vegetables that adults eat each day began with a very tight focus on defining and characterizing the priority consumer segment to which the media campaign would be directed (cf. Lefebvre, 2010; Lefebvre et al., 1995; Sutton et al., 1995). The program designers then spent a great amount of time understanding fruit and vegetable consumption from the consumers' point of view rather than only sifting through the scientific evidence. One finding that emerged from the priority consumer segment was the different ways they described people who ate five servings a day (the models or 'positive deviants') who were 'sensible, healthy, disciplined and fit,' while they described themselves (people who ate far fewer servings a day) as 'dependable, capable, sensible and careful.' The differences the audience drew between the model and the status quo helped shape an approach to the campaign messages and suggested behaviors that were tested to be sure they fit with the peoples' sense of themselves and their daily life patterns.

In focus group sessions, the program designers also found that many people were put off by what they called 'boring' presentations of fruits and vegetables at meals, that some described themselves as 'finicky' eaters, found it inconvenient or too time-consuming to prepare and cook fresh vegetables, did not know how to pick and store ripe produce, and usually overestimated what a serving size actually was (thinking 'How could I ever eat THAT much?'). These and other consumer research findings led to an emphasis on adding two or more servings of fruits and vegetables a day, 'the easy way' – what was seen by people as an achievable goal. The tone of the campaign was established to reflect an empathy and link to the audience that reflected their busy and hectic lives. Their limited attention was respected and the campaign tactics focused on times, places and states of mind when they were most likely already thinking about food choices and making these decisions rather than trying to interrupt their day at inconsequential times to pay attention to campaign messages.

The media campaign also focused on things the audience really wanted to know: messages and offerings were designed to solve their problems of 'How do I fit fruits and vegetables easily and conveniently into my day?' (try a glass of fruit or vegetable juice before you leave the house/apartment in the morning), 'How do I get more fruits and vegetables into meals or when eating out?' (add frozen vegetables to soup or stews, have a ready list of places to eat that offer a lot of choices) and 'Who has the time to cook vegetables?' (here are some easy and attractive ways to prepare vegetables using a microwave oven). Many of these suggestions were drawn from the focus groups with people who ate five servings a day to add more authenticity and experience to the campaign components.

This focus on helping people learn new behaviors, rather than changing them, reflects a design approach that respects the individual rather than attempting to overpower them in some way (e.g., through persuasive or emotional appeals with vivid imagery; Lefebvre, 2010).

While the 5 A Day did not explicitly use design thinking as it is being described here, it presaged the fundamental elements of a people-driven perspective rather than an expert-driven one – in this case coming from a social marketing perspective embodied in the consumer-based health communication model (Sutton et al., 1995). Indeed, the commonly shared elements between marketing and design approaches of focusing and learning from people explains some of the attraction that design thinking already has among some public health professionals.

The National Health Service and organizational innovation

The English National Health Service (NHS) used design thinking and principles in its efforts to 'create a revolution in health care' (Bevan et al., 2007). The process is a systemic reorienting of the national healthcare system to be more accessible, effective and safe. The group within the NHS responsible for directing this organizational change realized that existing models of diffusion of best practices and quality improvement were not sufficient for the scope and scale of change imagined by the NHS and the government. The authors also noted that the pragmatic approach of design, *searching for solutions rather than analyzing problems*, fit with the practical knowledge and experimentation that practitioners and action researchers favor while also appealing to people in the healthcare context where moving from research to action is highly desirable.

The project's main goal was to create an improvement 'product' that would appeal to chief executives and senior leaders of NHS hospitals and primary care organizations. A second important objective was to establish a set of design principles that could be utilized in future improvement activities.

The authors describe using a four-stage design approach that included:

1. Reflection, analysis, diagnosis and description: looking back, establishing and codifying what they knew and looking for patterns in the data.
2. Imagination and visualization: looking forward, hypothesis formulation, imagining what may be possible.
3. Modeling, planning and prototyping: identifying alternative solutions and, through prototyping and testing, coming up with something that might work.

4. Action and implementation: building, testing and modifying what works.

Through Step 1, the initiative focused on local development plans (LDPs) that specified service priorities for the next year and how they would be met. Their research discovered that, although there were any number of ongoing NHS improvement priorities, very few made their way into LDPs. There was, in short, a gap between organizational change efforts and local adoption of them. And when such improvements were approached in the LDPs, it was through trying to make a process 'more efficient' rather than to redesign the service process itself. Most revealing during this discovery phase was an audit of all the ongoing improvement initiatives from the point of view of the chief executives and senior leaders. The authors were surprised to find that more than 1,000 different best practices were being promulgated and this overwhelming 'advice' was a leading contributor to the disengagement of many local executives and leaders from the entire effort.

Taking this knowledge forward, and with additional insights gained through imagining different scenarios and reactions to improvement efforts, the team decided to stake out what they referred to as '10 high-impact changes' that would resonate and be acceptable to the executives. The process of winnowing down over 1000 possibilities for this list to the final 10 was done through a series of expert meetings and other interactive sessions with experts, executives and leaders in the prototyping phase. The final 'top 10' included:

- Improve patient flow across the whole NHS by improving access to key diagnostic tests.
- Avoid unnecessary follow-ups for patients and provide necessary follow-ups in the right care setting.
- Apply a systematic approach to care for people with long-term conditions.
- Redesign and extend roles in line with efficient patient pathways to attract and retain an effective workforce.

Two of the 10 items were then further elaborated and tested with the chief executives. Based on the reactions to these two prototypes, further modifications were made to the template and then applied to all 10 of the high-impact change targets. The final implementation effort was awarded the prize for the best productivity improvement in the public sector and was projected by independent auditors of having the capability of producing over £1 billion in savings. And, the authors note, the design process may have had its most important impact on narrowing the 'engagement gap'

between the central NHS offices and chief executives and leaders at the local level.

Patient-centered care

Donald Berwick begins his 'confessions of an extremist' (2009) with a story of accompanying a friend who was having chest pain to the hospital. When the doctors wanted to send her for a cardiac catheterization, she asked if her friend, Dr Berwick, could come in with her. They were firmly told 'No.' He continues:

> Moments later, my friend was wheeled away, shaking in fear and sobbing.
>
> What's wrong with that picture?
>
> Most doctors and nurses, I fear, would answer that what is wrong with that picture is the unreasonableness of my friend's demand and mine, our expecting special treatment, our failure to understand standard procedures and wise restrictions, and our unwillingness to defer to the judgment of skilled professionals.
>
> I disagree. I find a lot wrong with that picture, but none of it is related to unreasonable expectations, special pleading, or disrespect of professionals. What is wrong is that the system exerted its power over reason, respect, and even logic in order to serve its own needs, not the patient's. What is wrong was the exercise of a form of violence and tolerance for untruth, and – worse for a profession dedicated to healing – needless harm.
>
> The violence lies in the forced separation of an adult from a loved companion. The untruth lies in the appeal to nonexistent rules, the statement of opinion as fact, and the false claim of professional helplessness: 'impossibility.' The harm lies in increasing fear when fear could have been assuaged with a single word: 'Yes.'

Patient-centered care, in all of its manifestations, is a design problem. It starts with the perspective of the patient, not the healthcare provider, institution or payer. Designing health care that is patient-centered asks how do we improve delivery of services that delight our customers, rather than focusing on improving health care to make it more safe, timely, effective, efficient and equitable. Indeed, the dynamic interplay among proponents of patient-centered care and classic professionalism played a significant role in the debates over the Institute of Medicine's recommendations in *Crossing the Quality Chasm* (Berwick, 2002). Berwick reminds us that the quality of care at medical institutions such as the Mayo Clinic is determined by adherence to core promises such as

'The best interest of the patient is the only interest to be considered.' Two other patient centers' 'design ideas' he notes are 'Nothing about me without me' and 'Every patient is the only patient.'

Berwick formulates his definition of patient-centered care as:

> The experience (to the extent the informed, individual patient desires it) of transparency, individualization, recognition, respect, dignity, and choice in all matters, without exception, related to one's person, circumstances, and relationships in health care.'

And while he lists a variety of practices that would be changed if patient-centered care truly drove healthcare practice and norms, he also anticipates the challenges of situations where evidence-based medicine would have to bow to patient (and family) decision-making: shared decision-making about surgical procedures may lower costs, and perhaps even making the healthcare profession more humane.

Leading healthcare institutions in the USA are already engaged in using design thinking to transform health care. Kaiser Permanente had their staff learn design thinking principles and then apply them to problems they identified. One example shared by Brown (2009, pp. 172–174) involved the problems that occur during nursing shift changes when departing nurses are attempting to debrief oncoming nurses, a process that required about 45 minutes, was unsystematically done in four different Kaiser hospitals and left patients feeling a gap in their care. Through the application of the framing–options–prototyping–ideation process, the systemic problems were addressed. This success led to the creation of an Innovation Consultancy Team that was charged with spreading design thinking as an innovation process throughout the Kaiser Permanente system. The Mayo Clinic has also established the Center for Innovation, which includes a Design Research Studio that visualizes, models, prototypes and tests healthcare delivery solutions (http://centerforinnovation.mayo.edu/design-thinking.html).

All of this is a prelude to the challenge: Why aren't we applying design thinking more often to behavior change and social marketing? As an example, knowing that there may be as many as 200 opportunities a day to influence what, and *how*, people eat (Wansink and Sobal, 2007), the behavior design and social marketing implications become both clearer and more focused. And then we might target places and situations such as people's proximity and access to vending machines, the features of product packaging in which 'more for your money' is either the implicit or explicit appeal, and who we eat with.

The challenge that design thinking poses for social marketers and the issues we work with is its insistence on breaking out of the 'heuristic bias' – the inclination (see status quo discussion earlier in this chapter) to think and act in ways that are familiar and already mapped out (Brown, 2009, p. 8). One should ask the question: Is social marketing a method to primarily disseminate and apply evidence-based practices (see, e.g., the discussion of physical activity and social marketing by Dearing et al., 2006) or is it a method to develop innovative approaches to solving wicked problems (Lefebvre, 2009)? The focus of the former approach is clearly much more constrained when compared with one that seeks the intersection of observation and imagination. Yet, design thinking can play an integral role for how to best shape and tailor (design) best practices to fit the contours of the people, organizations and context in each unique situation.

WHAT IF?

Staff from IDEO at the 2007 Innovations in Social Marketing Conference posed some questions they had as designers about social marketing (Lefebvre, 2007). We leave this section by offering them to you to ponder as well:

What if we called ourselves storytellers – what if we called them creators instead of consumers?
What if our brand was about helping people reach their goals?
What if a social change movement could be successful with little to no promotion?
What if we embraced experiments (or prototyping) instead of waiting for the perfect answer?
What if the people we served created the messages?
What if we invited people at the extremes to put our messages in surprising places?
What if people were clamoring to play with us?
What if we understood our stakeholders as well as the people we serve?
What if social marketers were synonymous with trusted advisors?

DEMARKETING

In the commercial sphere, marketing has always been associated with increasing the demand for goods and services by making them as attractive, affordable, conveniently available and desirable as possible. And until the past few years, these activities have occurred with little thought to their impact on the environment.

But now we are beginning to recognize the specter of finite resources and negative impacts on our planet. The expression 'running out of steam' may well express the concern of many people about the planet's 'carrying capacity' to provide the resources on the scale needed to support the growing population and the needs of this and the next generation. It is entirely possible for one generation to exploit the existing resources – oil, water, air, timber, fish – so intensely that the next generation is doomed to accept a lower standard of living. Much talk is heard by families in advanced economies about whether their children will be able to live as well and as healthy as they have.

As we move into a world marked by a growing awareness of limited resources and negative impacts from industrial activity on our air and water, we confront the problem of the planet's sustainability. Christopher Flavin, the president of the Worldwatch Institute (2010) writes:

Since 2005, thousands of new government policies have been enacted, hundreds of billions of dollars have been invested in green businesses and infrastructure, scientists and engineers have greatly accelerated development of a new generation of 'green' technologies, and the mass media have turned environmental problems into a mainstream concern (p. xvii).

He goes on then to note: 'Amid this flurry of activity, one dimension of our environmental dilemma remains largely neglected: its cultural roots.' Indeed, beginning from this preface of their 2010 State of the World report entitled 'Transforming Cultures: From Consumerism to Sustainability,' The Worldwatch Institute compiled a series of essays exploring how to revitalize religious values, transform business models, reform educational paradigms and tap the skills of professionals from advertisers to musicians to social marketers in order to create cultural shifts that contribute to sustainability.

For social marketers who work on consumer and environmental issues, the recognition and welcome of our work into a transdisciplinary sustainability movement is gratifying. And the vision of achieving cultural shifts, not only individual behavioral changes, poses an exhilarating set of challenges for the years ahead.

Although we began this section focusing on environmental sustainability, the strategic marketing issues it raises are similar to those faced by social marketers who deal with such public health issues as addictions, tobacco use and obesity, where the aim is to reduce unhealthy behaviors and/or excesses. In the area of health care, the overutilization of services and the practice of medicine with little or no evidence base are also areas in which marketing strategies would be applicable (see, e.g., the discussion of reducing the use of general anesthesia in dental practices by Lawther et al., 1997).

As the growing number of governments, businesses and private funding sources focus on these conditions of consumer excess, we see the social marketing paradigm expanding to accommodate this cultural shift to an Age of Demarketing. As defined by Kotler and Levy (1971), demarketing is '... that aspect of marketing that deals with discouraging customers in general or a certain class of customers in particular on a temporary or permanent basis.'

The question becomes: How do we start to incorporate demarketing thinking into our social management approach? We can begin by thinking about the job of social marketing strategy to influence the level, composition and timing of demand to achieve a desired public or social benefit in the marketplace. Thus, the aim may be to raise, stabilize, lower or eliminate demand for certain products such as for condoms, illicit drugs, tobacco products or fast food. The aim may also be to alter the composition of groups that participate in the demand, such as when we attempt to reduce disparities among groups who use certain products or engage in specific unhealthy behaviors. The aim may be to influence the demand to occur sooner or later. We might also choose to reduce the quality or functional appeal of the product, raise the price to use it, make it more difficult to obtain or access it, and reduce or eliminate promotion (e.g., advertising; cf. Kotler and Roberto, 1989, pp. 175–176).

As the examples above suggest, demarketing is another name for demand reduction. It is one aspect of demand management and control, and, as we can see all around us, consumer marketers understand how to stimulate demand. This leads to the question: What situations prompt us to consider reducing demand? There are four such situations:

1. *Managing an existing shortage.* California is short of water and must ration it to competing users. Frequent energy blackouts also require campaigns to discourage unnecessary or wasteful energy consumption.
2. *Avoiding potential shortages.* There is overfishing that must be curtailed in order to maintain the fish supply. Timber land is growing scarce because many timber companies fail to plant new trees.

3. *Minimizing harm to individuals.* Discouraging cigarette smoking, misusing prescription medications, eating too much food high in sugar, salt and fat.
4. *Minimizing harm to nature or unique resources.* Discouraging too many people from visiting ecological preserves, national parks or other over-attended areas.

Another alternative to demarketing is that non-governmental organizations (NGOs) such as environmental and health groups can try to pressure for the 'right' behavior through promotion, litigation and other means. Indeed, we can distinguish between 'downstream demarketing', where the NGO puts pressure on those who would misuse resources, and 'upstream demarketing,' where the NGO tries to convince the government to adopt formal measures such as legislation, regulation, taxation or incentivization. If the latter measures are successful, they will reduce the misuse of resources.

Integrating demarketing and social marketing

Demarketing strategies have played a significant, if unacknowledged, role in the global tobacco war. While many participants would not be familiar with the term, demarketing objectives and strategies are readily apparent. In the tobacco control field, 'countermarketing' has been used to describe promotional efforts such as mass media campaigns (Farrelly et al., 2002). However, other tobacco control efforts aimed at product, price and place restrictions have rarely been conceptualized into a marketing mix framework, with the exception of the ASSIST project as described by Lefebvre (2008).

Recently, Shiu et al. (2009) defined demarketing as having the objective to decrease demand by discouraging consumption or use of products such as alcohol and cigarettes. In the context of the 4Ps, they identified demarketing strategies for tobacco control:

- *Product* – restrict availability of tobacco products; increase availability of tobacco-surrogate products (e.g., nicotine gum); highlight product harm and decrease product attractiveness.
- *Price* – increase taxes and increase pricing.
- *Place* – decrease consumption spaces; decrease distribution spaces; impede purchase of tobacco, with no sales to minors.
- *Promotion* – promote anti-smoking health agenda; decrease advertising space for tobacco companies and have mandatory warning labels.

The investigators then went on to develop and test a model of demarketing using data from the International Tobacco Control Four Country Survey – a nationally representative, longitudinal panel survey of adult smokers in four countries that was designed to evaluate whether and how a number of key government policy initiatives that addressed one or more elements of the marketing mix led to reductions in tobacco consumption. The authors used structural equation modeling to test the hypothesized relationships among policy initiatives aimed at each of the 4Ps and attitudes toward smoking, attitudes toward the tobacco industry and intentions to quit smoking at two points in time.

They found a direct significant effect of each demarketing (policy) element on intention to quit. They also noted that only the promotion and price demarketing elements impacted all three outcome variables: attitude toward the tobacco industry, attitude toward smoking and intention to quit smoking. *Product*, in terms of product replacement and displacement through the promotion of NRT (nicotine replacement therapy) and behavioral support programs, was found to be a less effective means for changing smokers' attitude toward smoking and intention to quit smoking. Smoking restrictions at work and in public places as *Place* demarketing approaches did not influence attitude but had a small direct effect on intention to quit.

Two lessons the researchers draw for social marketers are:

1. Social marketers and policymakers cannot assume individual demarketing measures will be effective in changing the attitudes and behavior of the priority audience. Rather, a comprehensive demarketing mix, aimed at decreasing the attractiveness of tobacco and impeding the availability and consumability of cigarettes, is needed to result in measurable changes.
2. *Ad hoc* and one-off demarketing measures are unlikely to have the desired effect. The results show an effect over time of the 4Ps of demarketing, suggesting that governments should equip anti-smoking campaigns with sufficient and sustained demarketing resources.

The identification and implementation of integrated demarketing strategies by setting objectives for each element of the marketing mix (P) may be quite useful when managing or avoiding shortages of resources or minimizing harm to individuals and natural resources are important. It may also prove to be an important organizing strategy for programs aimed at reducing excessive consumption, such as are needed to combat obesity where the number of people in the world with excess weight surpasses those who are underweight (Caballero, 2007).

It is important to recognize that demarketing strategies can also have unintended effects. These concerns will arise whenever an effort is made to reduce or ban something that is desired by some fraction of the population. First, the anti-consumption campaign might make the product or service more desirable: banning a book or movie often has this effect, as has a national mass media campaign directed toward reducing marijuana use among youth (Hornik et al., 2008). Second, it can create a criminal class that will prosper during the induced scarcity, as in the prohibition era when the United States banned alcohol consumption or the illegal transportation of tobacco products across state and national boundaries to avoid excise taxes. Third, human rights advocates will complain about the government's intrusion into (what they consider to be) citizens' 'right to privacy' decisions.

Deliberate use of demarketing techniques for improving public health and social conditions are at an early stage of exploration and research. We encourage social marketers to consider the use of demarketing where the program objective is to reduce use of specific products and services, reduce engagement in specific behaviors, change organizational or business practices and craft healthier public policies. Turning the usual social marketing approach on its head, we suggest integrated demarketing efforts that focus on:

- Developing segmentation strategies and user research that seeks to understand how to demotivate current practices among 'early or late discontinuers' of behaviors such as tobacco smoking (cf. Redmond, 1996).
- Reducing the number of features; reducing the salience, quality and/or attractiveness of the currently practiced behavior, used product or service.
- Realigning the incentives and costs of the current (discouraged) products, services and behaviors to make them financially, psychologically and/or socially more costly; increase opportunity costs for continuing to engage in behaviors or use current products and services.
- Changing the environment so that current products and services are more difficult to access; current behaviors are more difficult to engage in; and otherwise reduce opportunities and access to them to maintain current usage and/ or practice rates.
- Eliminating or restricting promotional (advertising, sales, public relations, sponsorships) activities that encourage use of products and/ or services or support current practices and behaviors.

- Designing and positioning products, services and messages that align demarketing objectives with personally relevant and valued self-identities and social roles among priority groups.

Demarketing provides another powerful set of tools for social marketers to become even more effective in their social change efforts. In addition, we believe that demarketing will become an important tool among those who are striving to create a more sustainable world and interrupt the cycle of consumerism and resource depletion while also not creating other untoward effects such as increasing unemployment due to lowered demand for certain goods and services.

CONCLUSION

Our discussion of behavioral economics, design thinking and demarketing is intended to provoke thought and discussion about how they may be useful strategies to apply within a social marketing heuristic. We recognize that there is little empirical base from which to implement these approaches to the solution of public health or social problems, and we hope that by highlighting the approaches it will encourage more research and exploration of their utility and feasibility.

In Table 5.2, we summarize where behavioral economics, design thinking and demarketing might be applied in social marketing research and practice. The impact of behavioral economics may be most pronounced in considering the *Price* of adopting or discontinuing specific behaviors. Design thinking may be ideally suited to considering the *Product* – including designing behaviors that fit people's lives as well as for product and service design (cf. Miettinen and Koivisto, 2009; Pilloton, 2009). Demarketing can be viewed as blending all 4Ps of the marketing mix and also aiming for policy changes to nudge and sustain healthier and more socially responsible behavioral choices. Yet, we also believe that including ideas from all three of these perspectives will lead to a deeper understanding of the people we wish to serve, the environments in which they make choices, the market research we conduct and the programs we implement.

Through this presentation we also intend to broaden the scope of social marketing to include wicked problems such as healthcare reform, consumerism and sustainability. And in some of the discussion we hope we have presented alternative ways to think about social marketing problems and solutions, methods of conducting research and framing marketing as being appropriate not

Table 5.2 Where behavioral economics, design thinking and demarketing might be incorporated into social marketing research and practice

Marketing element[a]	Behavioral economics	Design thinking	Demarketing
Situation analysis	√		√
Priority market profile (research)	√	√	
Marketing objectives	√	√	√
Priority market barriers, benefits and competition (research)	√	√	√
Product		√	√
Price	√		√
Place	√	√	√
Promotion			√
Evaluation			

[a] Marketing elements adapted from the social marketing planning primer (Kotler and Lee, 2008, p. 36).

only for individual-level action but also for organizational, policy and cultural shifts.

An open yet critical perspective to what models we use to inform our approach to social puzzles, how we go about generating possible solutions to them and where in the personal–social–ecological context we direct our marketing efforts makes room for the innovation we believe is vital for social marketing to be a force for social change in the years ahead. Likewise, we also believe in an unwavering focus on people and the reality they live in, and the use of the marketing mix as an organizing framework to design approaches that satisfy both individual and societal needs.

KEY WORDS: Abductive reasoning; behavioral economics; consumerism; demand reduction; demarketing; designing thinking; heuristics; market inefficiencies; patient-centered care; policy change; sustainability.

Key insights

- Behavioral economics is a useful model for social marketing to improve people's decision-making in environmental, health and poverty programs.
- Design thinking, with its focus on a people-centered process for practical, creative resolution of problems or issues, can lead to more relevant behavioral offerings, new or improved products and services, new processes or experiences for consumers or users and new social and organizational systems.
- The recognition of the finite resources and negative impacts on our planet are ushering in an 'age of demarketing' in which social marketing can

be used to reduce demand and overconsumption ranging from environmental and natural resource issues to medical procedures and substance abuse.

- Incorporating these perspectives into social marketing research and practice may lead to a deeper understanding of the people we wish to serve, the environments in which they make choices, the market research we conduct and the programs we implement as well as a broadening of our scope to include topics such as healthcare reform, consumerism and sustainability.

REFERENCES

Amir, O., Ariely, D., Cooke, A., et al. (2005) 'Psychology, behavioral economics and public policy', *Marketing Letters*, 16: 443–454.

Andreasen, A.R. (1995) *Marketing Social Change: Changing Behavior to Promote Health, Social Development, and the Environment.* San Francisco, CA: Jossey-Bass.

Ariely, D. (2008) *Predictably Irrational: The Hidden Forces That Shape Our Decisions.* New York: HarperCollins.

Backinger, C., Thornton-Bullock, A., Miner, C., et al. (2010) 'Building consumer demand for tobacco-cessation products and services: The National Tobacco Cessation Collaborative's Consumer Demand Roundtable', *American Journal of Preventive Medicine*, 38: S307–S311.

Berger, W. (2009) *Glimmer: How Design Can Transform Your Life, and Maybe even the World.* New York: The Penguin Press.

Bertrand, M., Mullainathan, S. and Shafir, E. (2006) 'Behavioral economics and marketing in aid of decision making among the poor', *Journal of Public Policy and Marketing*, 25: 8–23.

Berwick, D.M. (2002) 'A user's manual for the IOM 'Quality Chasm' Report', *Health Affairs*, 21: 80–90.

Berwick, D.M. (2009) 'What 'patient-centered' should mean: Confessions of an extremist', *Health Affairs*, 28: w555–w565.

Brown, T. (2008) 'Design thinking', *Harvard Business Review*, June: 84–95.

Brown, T. (2009) *Change by Design: How Design Thinking Transforms Organizations and Inspires Innovation.* New York: HarperCollins.

Brown, T. and Wyatt, J. (2010) 'Design thinking for social innovation', *Stanford Social Innovation Review*, Winter: 30–35.

Caballero, B. (2007) 'The global epidemic of obesity: An overview', *Epidemiologic Reviews*, 29: 1–5.

Dearing, J.W., Maibach, E.W. and Buller, D.B. (2006) 'A convergent diffusion and social marketing approach for disseminating proven approaches to physical activity promotion', *American Journal of Preventive Medicine*, 31: 11–23.

Dolan, P., Hallsworth, M., Halpern, D., King, D. and Vlaev, I. (2010) 'MINDSPACE: Improving behaviour through public policy'. London: Institute for Government. Available at: http://www.instituteforgovernment.org.uk/content/133/mindspace-influencing-behaviour-through-public-policy [accessed 28 December 2010].

Farrelly, M.C., Healton, C.G., Davis, K.C., et al. (2002) 'Getting to the truth: Evaluating national tobacco countermarketing campaigns', *American Journal of Public Health*, 92: 901–907.

Flavin, C. (2010) Preface. *2020 State of the World: Transforming cultures: From consumerism to sustainability.* New York: W.W. Norton and Company.

Hornik, R., Jacobsohn, L., Orwin, R., Piesse, A. and Kalton, G. (2008) 'Effects of the National Youth Anti-Drug Media Campaign on youths', *American Journal of Public Health*, 98: 2229–2236.

Kagel, J.H. and Winkler, R.C. (1972) 'Behavioral economics: Areas of cooperative research between economics and applied behavioral analysis', *Journal of Applied Behavior Analysis*, 5: 335–342.

Kotler, P. and Lee, N.R. (2008) *Social Marketing: Influencing Behaviors for Good* , 3rd edn. Los Angeles, CA: Sage Publications.

Kotler, P. and Levy, S. (1971) 'Do marketing, yes, de-marketing', *Harvard Business Review*, November–December: 74–80.

Kotler, P. and Roberto, E.L. (1989) *Social Marketing: Strategies for Changing Public Behavior.* New York: The Free Press.

Lakoff, G. (2004) *Don't Think of an Elephant! Know your Values and Frame the Debate: An Essential Guide for Progressives.* White River Junction, VT: Chelsea Green Publishing Company.

Laurel, B. (ed.) (2003) *Design Research: Methods and Perspectives.* Cambridge, MA: The MIT Press.

Lawther, S., Hastings, G.B. and Lowry, R. (1997) 'Demarketing: Putting Kotler and Levy's ideas into practice', *Journal of Marketing Management*, 13: 315–325.

Levitt, S.D. and Dubner, S.J. (2005) *Freakonomics: A Rogue Economist Explores the Hidden side of Everything.* New York: HarperCollins.

Lefebvre, R.C. (2007). IDEO's questions for social marketers. On Social Marketing and Social Change [17 April]. Available at: http://socialmarketing.blogs.com/r_craiig_lefebvres_social/2007/04/ideos_questions.html [accessed 24 December 2010].

Lefebvre, R.C. (2008) Social marketing and tobacco control policy. On Social Marketing and Social Change [27 October]. Available at: http://socialmarketing.blogs.com/r_craiig_lefebvres_social/2008/10/social-marketing-for-tobacco-control.html [accessed 27 November 2010].

Lefebvre, R.C. (2009) 'The change we need: New ways of thinking about social issues', *Social Marketing Quarterly*, 15: 142–144.

Lefebvre, R.C. (2010) 'Designing behaviours for health', *Touchpoints*, 2: 58–61.

Lefebvre, R.C., Doner, L., Johnston, C., et al. (1995) 'Use of database marketing and consumer-based health communication in message design: An example from the Office of Cancer Communications' "5 a Day for Better Health" program', in E. Maibach and R. Parrott (eds), *Designing Health Messages: Approaches from Communication Theory and Public Health Practice.* Newbury Park, CA: Sage Publications, pp. 217–246.

Lombardi, V. (2005) 'What is design thinking? Noise between stations'. Available at: http://noisebetweenstations.com/personal/weblogs/?page_id=1688

Martin, R. (2009) *The Design of Business: Why Design Thinking is the Next Competitive Advantage.* Boston, MA: Harvard Business Press.

Miettinen, S. and Koivisto, M. (eds) (2009) *Designing Services with Innovative Methods.* Helsinki: University of Art and Design.

Mintz, S.W. and Du Bois, C.M. (2002) 'The anthropology of food and eating', *Annual Review of Anthropology*, 31: 99–119.

Parker, R. (2001) 'Sexuality, culture, and power in HIV/AIDS research', *Annual Review of Anthropology*, 30: 163–179.

Pilloton, E. (2009) *Design Revolution: 100 Products that Empower People.* New York: Metropolis Books.

Redmond, W.H. (1996) 'Product disadoption: Quitting smoking as a diffusion process', *Journal of Public Policy and Marketing*, 15: 89–97.

Rogers, E. (1995) *Diffusion of Innovations*, 4th edn. New York: The Free Press.

Shiu, E., Hassan, L.M. and Walsh, G. (2009) 'Demarketing tobacco through governmental policies – The 4Ps revisited', *Journal of Business Research*, 62: 269–278.

Smith, B. (2010) 'Behavioral economics and social marketing: New allies in the war on absent behavior', *Social Marketing Quarterly*, 16:137–141.

Stone, D. (1997) *Policy Paradox: The Art of Political Decision-making.* New York: W.W. Norton and Company.

Sutton, S.M., Balch, G.I. and Lefebvre, R.C. (1995) 'Strategic questions for consumer-based health communications', *Public Health Reports*, 110: 725–733.

Thaler, R.H. and Sunstein, C.R. (2009) *Nudge: Improving Decisions about Health, Wealth, and Happiness.* New York: Penguin Books.

The Worldwatch Institute. (2010) *State of the World: Transforming Cultures from Consumerism to Sustainability.* New York: W.W. Norton and Company.

Wallack, L. (1990) 'Media advocacy: Promoting health through mass communication', in K. Glanz, F.M. Lewis and B.K. Rimer (eds), *Health Behavior and Health Education: Theory, Research, and Practice.* San Francisco, CA: Jossey-Bass.

Wansink, B. and Sobal, J. (2007) 'Mindless eating: The 200 daily food decisions we overlook', *Environment and Behavior,* 39: 106–123.

Wansink, B., Just, D.R. and McKendry, J. (2010) 'Lunch room redesign', *New York Times,* October 21.

Available at: http://www.nytimes.com/interactive/2010/10/21/opinion/20101021_Oplunch.html?ref=contributors [accessed 26 November 2010].

Young, S, and Caisey, V. (2010) 'Mind shift, mode shift: A lifestyle approach for reducing car ownership and use based on behavioural economics and social marketing', *Perspectives in Public Health,* 130: 136–142.

Zaltman, G. (2003) *How Customers Think: Essential Insights into the Mind of the Market.* Boston, MA: Harvard Business School Press.

6

Critical Marketing: Theoretical Underpinnings

Michael Saren

INTRODUCTION

Hastings (2007) argues that marketers must pursue a genuinely critical analysis of our discipline. Other marketing authors have also called for a wider critical approach, advocating, 'altering the institutions that form the social system within which the individual operates' (Goldberg, 1994) and addressing flaws, not in 'the loose threads of the individual', but in the 'fabric of society' (Wallack et al., 1993). Critical marketing analysis and concepts have an important role at the theoretical level in problematizing hitherto uncontentious marketing areas to reveal underlying institutional and theoretical dysfunctionalities.

The chapter is structured as follows. The first section explains the role of critique in marketing and its relevance as an underpinning for social marketing. There follows an outline of some of the main topics critical marketing scholars have chosen in their challenge to mainstream, managerial representations of marketing phenomena. These cover the core marketing concept, the role of markets, marketing knowledge and philosophy, critical theory and consumer behavior. These critiques all bring into question mainstream ideas and assumptions, which underpin more managerially oriented marketing and consumption theories. These sections also point out some of the major implications of these criticisms for social marketing.

ROLE OF CRITIQUE IN MARKETING

Arnold and Fisher (1996) describe how the emerging marketing discipline in the 1960s was surrounded, on the one hand, by marketing 'apologists' who wanted to keep marketing clearly defined within the firm, and on the other, by 'reconstructionists' who were pushing for an even broader, macromarketing perspective. They posited three strands to marketing thought:

- *'Apologists'* – taking a traditional view: marketing is good because it helps the economy. Its domain is, and should be limited to, the firm (e.g. Luck).
- *'Social marketers'* – turning the power of marketing to social good, thereby compensating for its deficiencies with better outcomes (e.g. Kotler, Levy, Andreasen).
- *'Reconstructionists'* – critical of marketing concept and process, not just its outcomes.

In some respects critical marketers are the successors of Arnold and Fisher's last grouping, 'reconstructionists'. Critical marketing does share attention with social aspects of marketing, but not only in terms of *outcomes*, good and bad. It goes beyond critique of marketing outcomes, often problematizing the marketing concept itself and its antecedents and contexts. Critical marketing will often focus on the social *context* within which marketing occurs: the social and cultural forces that frame and affect it. Above all, critical marketers question marketing knowledge, ways of knowing, established theories and ideas and methods of research.

From a range of different approaches, critical authors have questioned many aspects of marketing, from its theoretical underpinnings to its practical outcomes, including the following:[1]

1. The ideological premises and underlying assumptions of marketing theory and practice.
2. Specific marketing activities and practices: for example, customer databases, product labeling, advertising and loyalty schemes.
3. The effects of the marketing system: for example, social exclusion, material and social waste, creation of false needs and identities and commodity fetishism.
4. The ethics, morality, 'values' of marketing.
5. Understanding and knowledge of marketing – models and methods of analysis, role of academics, market research, consulting and marketers 'know-how'.
6. Validity of marketing ideas and concepts.

It is obvious from this list that these topics and the subjects which they necessarily involve – power, culture, ideology, ethics – do not fit at all neatly into sub-fields of marketing such as services, B2B, social marketing, consumer behaviour, not-for-profit, etc. Thinking about marketing in terms of conventional categories limits the possibilities and range of critique. To paraphrase Foucault (1980), categories create outcomes. Thus, instead of taking the conventional views of marketing, by definition, critical marketers have viewed it very differently from marketing as exchange or management or relationships or as communication. These managerial or functionalist categories inherently limit the key concepts and issues which are subjected to critique.

Furthermore, the reductionism inherent in more conventional marketing groupings tends to obscure important underlying and holistic phenomena that are important for critical analysis but which are not wholly revealed by looking at partial sub-areas. These phenomena include the underlying socio-economic mechanisms, structures and relations as well as more general concepts such as identity, culture and knowledge. Many conventional studies of marketing in any one industry are split into traditional market categories of consumption, supply, processing and manufacture, main product types, distribution systems and advertising, and each is researched and analyzed separately. For the analysis of the topics discussed in this chapter, this type of structure is completely unsuitable, not least because it renders the

marketing system itself – and of course broad socio-cultural and economic conditions – to a secondary level, which can be only partially revealed and critically studied in each sub-area.

Marketing is still largely perceived by many outside of the discipline as the creator of wants and needs through selling and advertising, and marketing academics have received considerable external criticism that their work fails to address these issues and the assumptions on which they are based. There is an enormous opportunity here for social marketing to address these criticisms directly, not least because many of the behaviors which aim to correct are at least exacerbated, or in some cases even caused, by the activities or effects of the marketing industry. In their examination of the contribution of social marketing to the critical debate, Gordon et al. (2007) argue that a major part of social marketing is to '(i) critically examine the effects of commercial marketing on the health and welfare of society and (ii) apply these same tools and techniques to the resolution of social and health problems' (p. 159). They also provide examples of critical studies of commercial marketing that have informed social policy decision-making by providing guidance regarding (a) specific social marketing campaigns aimed at attitude or behavior change and (b) effective regulatory and legal regimes.

Furthermore, the methodological limitations of much conventional marketing research can result in only partial explanations of important aspects of consumer behavior by ignoring, for example, underlying socio-economic mechanisms, structures and relations. Such underlying phenomena are precisely those which social marketers are interested in and can often provide rich analyses and explanations for social aspects of consumers' behavior. Social marketing can utilize and develop critical research methodologies in order to study such underlying social and behavioral phenomena, often from a more holistic perspective than commercial market research methods permit.

The next sections outline some of the main approaches that critical marketing scholars have taken in their challenge to mainstream, managerial representations of marketing phenomena.

CRITIQUE OF THE MARKETING CONCEPT

Several authors have tackled the apparent contradiction between the espoused free market values of the marketing concept and the powerful control apparatus and technologies of marketing management. Dawson (1972), for example, argued for the 'human concept', which he felt was 'more responsive to human needs in their totality than the marketing concept'. One stream of critique has focused upon the values and ideology underlying these pillars of mainstream marketing thought. Desmond (1998), for instance, traces marketing's ethics from the early 20th century when the first marketing scholars were educated in the tradition of German historicism and the social dynamics of the free market. Desmond shows that this view of marketing, as a practice satisfying human needs through exchange, is anything but value-free; on the contrary, it inherently contains utilitarian values, which, simply put, prescribe the ideal as the greatest happiness for the greatest number. In espousing and enacting its core 'concept', marketing thus engages in the reproduction and naturalization of utilitarian values.

Building on utilitarian ideals, the Marshallian notion of economic competition has dominated Western economic thinking since the 19th century. This view presumes a 'perfect' market, where consumer choice decides which companies survive and which fail and therefore firms are driven to innovate and achieve cost-effective delivery of high-quality goods and services at lower prices for the benefit of all. Free economies are thus structured to encourage competitive behavior through consumer choice, and to discourage the associated practices of anti-competitive behavior (Sirgy and Su, 2000). This model of rational decision-making consumers freely pursuing their choices in the marketplace has been central to the marketing concept, where 'the customer is King', and meeting their needs and wants profitably are deemed to be on the only true route to marketing success.

The implicit assumption of consumer sovereignty and choice, which underpins the marketing concept, is that maximizing consumer choice and therefore more is always 'better'. Thus, marketing doesn't just lead to more choice, it also arguably leads to *abundance and excess* and the necessary provision of more than consumers need or want. Battaille (1988) argues that all human systems lead to excess and waste. Thus, in this respect, marketing values are merely reflecting the human condition, which always creates more than is needed and therefore produces waste. It was Veblen (1899) who first detailed the modern 'conspicuous consumption' behavior of the *nouveau riches*, and the manner in which they employed certain types of goods and services as registers of their new social position. Other critics of US consumer society include Vance Packard's critical analysis of the methods and effects of the advertising industry in *The Hidden Persuaders* (1957) and J.K. Galbraith's economic analysis of the *Affluent Society* (1958). There has also been a strong critical element in some of the anthropological studies of consumer-driven society such as Douglas and Isherwood's *World of Goods* (1978). More recently, Naomi Klein's influential critique of global consumer capitalism and branding, *No Logo* (2001), offers a critical analysis of contemporary global capitalism

The notion of consumer freedom and sovereignty has been subjected to various other critical readings. Hirschman (1993) has studied the language employed in marketing textbooks, which, she argues, are littered with metaphors of war, combat and captivity. Market segments are 'targeted' for 'penetration'. Market share must be 'fought for' and 'won'. Customers must be 'locked-in' lest they 'defect' to the opposition. Thus, consumers are worked upon until they are 'captive', although unaware of this captivity (Du Gay, 2001). If consumers' freedom –'inner and empirical' in Horkheimer's (1967) words – is lost and they exercise their choices in the marketplace only as captives, then the customer is not king, not an autonomous agent, but a royal *subject*.

As Morgan (1992) points out, this state of affairs reflects marketing's dominant technical-rational view of knowledge, from which it follows 'naturally' that consumers are knowable entities with characteristics that can be captured like natural phenomena. Thus, marketing has generated 'technologies of governance', historically predominantly through market research and now through IT and customer relationship management. The discourse of marketing ensures the never-ending need for marketing because of its dual 'dialectical' role in its attempts to know the customer and its attempts to sell to the customer. 'This incessant dialectic is a black hole into which marketing expertise is poured with variable effects' (Morgan, 1992, p. 140).

These critiques of the 'sovereignty' – or even the 'free' will – of the consumer raise some important issues for social marketers. Most fundamental of these is whether and how this dominance of the marketing apparatus and subjugation of the consumer can be countered by social marketing campaigns. One common solution is to utilize the same techniques of persuasion as the commercial marketers, only to turn them to social ends. Another is to campaign for legal or voluntary regulation of specific methods and types of appeal, as in the smoking and drinks industries. Also, social marketers are in a strong position to question, from the critical point of view, whether any of these types of initiatives address the underlying institutional imbalance which exists between business and the consumer – contrary to the espoused values of the marketing concept.

CRITICAL THEORY

Within marketing, Bradshaw and Firat (2007) employ the prefix 'critical' to signal that the perspective subscribes to Frankfurt School critical theory, based on the work of theorists such as Adorno (1991), Marcuse (1964) and Horkheimer (1967). Other writers on critical marketing draw their inspiration from wider philosophical and theoretical sources, including feminist theory (Bristor and Fischer, 1993), postmodernism (Firat and Venkatesh, 1995), poststructuralism (Fournier and Grey, 2000), literary criticism (Stern, 1990), semiotics (Mick, 1986), deconstruction (Stern, 1996) and radical ecology (Kilbourne, 2004). For example, Murray and Ozanne (1991) discussed the relevance and application of the work of the Frankfurt School for marketing, which Hetrick and Lozada (1994) then critiqued and further developed. In the UK and Europe there have been attempts to take a more critical approach to the subject in the 1990s such as a conference and the book *Rethinking Marketing: Towards Critical Marketing Accountings* (Brownlie et al., 1999). However, the philosophies and methodologies comprising the portmanteau label 'critical' in marketing do not necessarily always sit very comfortably together. What these do have in common with the critical theorists of the Frankfurt School is that they all subscribe to emancipatory aspirations in their analysis and critique of marketing theory and practice. Such critical attempts are still however a minority position within the dominant logic of scientific marketing.

Outside the academic marketing discipline, there is a long history of critical analysis of consumer capitalism that has inspired many critical marketing researchers, who have drawn on this work from other disciplines. As Gabriel and Lang note in the second edition of their book *The Unmanageable Consumer*:

> Cultural studies have dissected shopping malls as cathedrals of consumption and students of organization have focussed on the limits of the ethos of customer service. Identity construction has come to be viewed increasingly through the prism of lifestyles. Choice, modelled on the affluent consumer experience, has become the central tenet of many political and ethical discourses. At the same time, there is an increasing awareness among academics of the ecological limits to the consumerist orgy, which are already alarming observers of climate change, raw materials and natural resources such as soil, water and air 2006, p. vii).

There is also much more Marxist-based literature which provides a wide range of critique of marketing. Baran and Sweezy's analysis of *Monopoly Capital* (1964) relegates all marketing activity to the surplus appropriation from labor. In *One-Dimensional Man* (1964), Marcuse discusses the loss of individuality and the rise of conformity as endogenous to advanced industrial society in which the marketing apparatus plays an important role. Another example is Adorno and Horkheimer's *Dialectic of Enlightenment* (1997), in which market research and positioning are likened to the techniques of propaganda (1997, p. 123). The critique of the commodification of culture is further developed by Adorno in the *Culture Industry* (1991) and in the emancipatory thesis of Fromm's *To Have or to Be* (1978).

More recently, aesthetic practices have gained increasing importance in the marketing field. The creation of immaterial, emotional and what may be called aesthetic value has become a prevalent marketing axiom over the past decades that often emphasizes the 'creativity' involved, the closeness to 'art' and the aesthetic component (Schroeder, 2005). Evidence of this trend is manifest in many innovative marketing practices, ranging from printed advertising to the creation of plastic virtual architectures that provide complex, multi-layered experiences for consumers.

Techniques inspired by arts are particularly manifest in consumption atmospheres which offer complex aesthetic experiences for consumers. Despite such developments, aesthetics arts-based approaches to marketing theory are underdeveloped. Biehl (2007) shows that there is enormous potential here in applying the 'new aesthetics' based on Frankfurt Sschool critical theory which draws on aesthetics and performance research. It provides new insights into concepts such as experiences and atmospheres which are increasingly important for the marketing debate. The Frankfurt writers work on the aesthetic dimension of capitalism and modes of representation is linked with the 'new aesthetics' in Böhme's (2003) *Critique of the Aesthetic Economy* which aims at making the broad range of aesthetic reality transparent and available for critical analysis. This theory of perception is concerned with the relation between environmental qualities and human states and emphasizes that the task of aestheticians is no longer to deal with only the fine arts but also to address the full range of aesthetic agency including the realm of marketing.

Some postmodernist writers have placed a strong emphasis on marketing phenomena and consumer society in their analysis of contemporary conditions. An outstanding example, which may have implications for social marketers, is Jean Baudrillard, who, in an attempt to avoid the materialist assumptions of Marxist critical theory, argues for a critical analysis of consumer society that is based on the sign-value of commodities and the creation of hyperreality (Baudrillard, 1988, 1994). Acknowledging the symbolic value of commodities, rather than their use value, Baudrillard opened the way for new themes within critically oriented marketing and consumer research: for example, consumption and identity, possessions and the self, advertising and semiotics.

Such topics are also of central interest to social marketers, who could adopt this semiotic approach to the analysis of social phenomena: for example, by analyzing the symbolic value of consumer behavior such as smoking, as well as its social role, its 'satisfaction', psychological and other bases of its commodity appeal. Thus, the wider role and effects of undesirable consumer behaviors could be analyzed in terms of the relationships between consumption, identity, possessions and the self.

CRITIQUE OF MARKETS

Exchange theory is central to understanding how markets behave. Indeed, Bagozzi sees marketing *as* exchange in his *American Behavioral Scientist* (1978) paper on 'A Theory of Transactions in the Marketplace'. Arguably, the dominant conceptualization of marketing phenomena in the normative marketing management literature is based on the notion of exchange (Bagozzi, 1978). Any marketing ideas or actions involve the *exchange* of products, services, knowledge and money. Thus, in this view, three components must exist as *sine qua non* for an exchange to occur: a seller, a buyer and a product

- Marketing production
- Marketing products
- Consumers and consumption

Whereas traditional marketing management literature sees any exchange occurring within what they call the external or macro environment, critical marketers regard each of these objects above as located within and fundamentally conditioned by a much wider context that includes socio-economic conditions, mediated communications, culture and power relations. To the critical marketer the market exchange is seen as a constitutive and reproductive (rather than reactive and responsive) interaction characterized by politics, ideology and discursive closure.

This raises the issue of what markets are. Araujo et al. (2008) question the ontological status of market forms and practices by studying the various means of 'market-making' by managers. They demonstrate that market boundaries are

not 'definable' from any single position – far less an equilibrium' – but rather they are contested by the actors involved. Wensley (1990) also takes a critical approach by examining the limits to the market exchange analogy. The nature of transactions between provider and user in different exchange contexts is analyzed, revealing two issues in particular: the degree to which the specific market transaction is user or supplier specified and the degree to which the user is regarded as active or passive. Wensley demonstrates that the biggest problem for the market exchange analogy arises with the shift from user to supplier specification, particularly in public sector and professional service contexts.

Kilbourne et al. (1997) consider the broad issues of quality of life and sustainable consumption. They argue that micromarketing cannot examine the relationship between these issues *critically* because the essence of the relationship lies in the dominant social paradigm. Only macromarketing can address this relationship effectively by expanding the domain of inquiry to include technological, political and economic benefits and costs of consumption, thus challenging the dominant social paradigm itself.

Moreover, the marketing process has alienated the consumer from production, resulting in people being estranged from one another as well as from the creation of goods. One way in which marketers achieve this, as suggested by Carù and Cova (2003), is by offering consumers extraordinary experiences, which enable them to engage physically, mentally, emotionally, socially and spiritually in the consumption of the product or service. They also unveil the North American roots of this romantic vision, supporting such an idea of extraordinary experiences, and critically evaluate the impact of this vision on the disappearance of consumers' 'contemplative time'. Following this idea of the 'estrangement' of people from each other and their consumption, social marketers could consider how their campaigns and bases of appeal could try to offer people extraordinary experiences, which enable them to others and their own behavior in a way that is physically, mentally, emotionally, socially and spiritually connected and more engaged.

A contemporary debate concerns the role of marketing in economic development and the applicability of marketing concepts and management activities in the Third World. This raises the role of marketing in post colonialism (Varman and Vikas, 2007), which takes a critical approach to this topic within the broad framework of 'development studies'. The purpose is to ascertain the underlying principles and assumptions in the development of marketing thought and thereby to facilitate the evaluation and critique of the role of marketing in the development process. They assess marketing perspectives in terms of their fundamental assumptions and key features as and when they fall into three schools of thought: modernization, institutional and radical.

One issue arises here for the global reach social marketing and the application in poorer less developed countries of specific techniques which have been successfully applied in the developed world. In addition to obvious cultural differences, the post-colonial condition of many countries might in a sense make them immune from what they might perceive as a form of imposed social imperialism. In any case, social marketers must be aware of the ethnocentric origins and cultural bias of their marketing techniques when applied to developing societies.

CRITIQUE OF CONSUMER BEHAVIOR AND IDENTITY

Many early marketing academics were trained in economics and this was the lens through which they usually regarded marketing theory, so generally the consumer was conceptualized as making 'rational' choices between product offerings (e.g. Alderson, 1957) and depicted in terms of 'rational economic man'. But no act of consumption takes place without some form of stimulation, which may not be at all rational. Later, in the 1960s, a lot of marketing utilized the techniques, tools and language of psychology as it attempted to acquire the means to understand 'customer' behavior, the customer being the espoused central focus of business. Most marketing textbooks nowadays tend to locate the stimulation of needs within the framework of Maslow's hierarchy of needs, which proposes that we satisfy needs at different levels. It is, however, a fairly simplistic analysis of human motivation, and while it offers a basic framework, it has attracted a number of criticisms compared with other models and theories of motivation.

One alternative to Maslow's hierarchy was a figure and research area developed by Ernest Dichter (1960) and other motivation researchers work which was heavily criticized at the time by Packard (1957) and others for its suggestion of messages and images received by the individual below the level of consciousness, which implied the use of subliminal or subconscious manipulation of the consumer. This has received renewed attention and some criticism in recent years of subconscious manipulation through product placements and celebrity endorsements in high-exposure films (Weiner, 1992). The 1970s saw a rise in popularity of behavioral decision theory in consumer research, such as James Bettman's

(1979) book, *An Informational Processing Theory of Consumer Choice*, which draws on insights from cognitive science, alongside the rise of 'scientific' experimentation.

In the last 20 years, however, there has been a particularly strong backlash against quantitative perspectives in consumer behavior, especially the information processing view of the consumer, and the development of numerous innovative, interdisciplinary and often critical perspectives rooted in interpretivist, ethnographic and semiotic methods. While acknowledging that motivation underpins most human behavior, these researchers have looked at a variety of other influences, including perception and the senses, memory and nostalgia and fantasy and fiction, as stimulants of consumer experiences. They adopt more macro, cultural perspectives, and conceptualizing consumers as socially connected beings with a concomitant focus on consuming, rather than buying, and on societal issues rather than a solely managerial focus.

Other critical work followed from those engaged in consumer researches, who, by definition, view marketing very differently from the managers' perspective. In this group are researchers who explore how consumers use products, brands and consumption practices as resources for the construction of identity(ies) (Belk, 1988; Walendorf and Arnould, 1988; Elliott, 1997, 2004; Elliott and Wattanasuwan, 1998). Belk (1988) employs the term 'extended self' to encompass the role of possessions in the consumer's identity. He argues that knowingly or unknowingly we regard our possessions as part of ourselves – in other words, 'we are what we have'. Belk presents three key arguments for this as follows:

1. **The nature of self-perception encompasses possessions**. The subjective existence of an extended identity is highlighted by phenomena such as the investment of psychic or physical energy in the products we make our own, the diminished sense of self when certain possessions are lost and the ritual function of objects which anthropological studies have found in all societies. The ritual role of possessions and the person can be observed most clearly when the objects are associated with birth, matrimony and death; that is, points of the transformation of 'self'.

2. **The relationships between having, doing and being**. Objects in our possession also enable us to do things we otherwise could not: for example, an axe to chop wood, a horse to travel. Beyond a functional role of extending one's capacity for '*doing*', possessions are also used symbolically to demonstrate or reinforce *who* we are. This is most obviously the case with a uniform or a badge, but many other apparently

functional products are nowadays used symbolically to extend the owners identity or *being* in some way: for example, clothes, hairstyles, automobiles, houses, furnishing, etc.

3. **Processes of self-extension incorporating objects.** Building on the relationship between having and being, Belk describes the various ways through which we learn to regard an object as part of self. First, by owning, controlling or mastering objects; secondly, by creating it; and finally by *knowing* them. Belk (1988) argues that consumers are doing more than displaying their status or identity through products, *a la* Veblen. They are creating an 'extended self' by *appropriating and incorporating* the objects and symbols of their consumption, such that they become what they consume.

Others outside marketing have proposed different ways in which consumption is related to self/identity, from various critical standpoints (e.g. Douglas and Isherwood, 1978; Fromm, 1978; Sirgy, 1982; Gergen, 1991). This stream of research assumes that *ads make identities available* to consumers as raw materials for identity construction. Or, in Elliott's words,

> The consumption of symbolic meaning, particularly through the use of advertising as a cultural commodity, provides the individual with the opportunity to construct, maintain, and communicate identity and social meanings (Elliott, 1997, p. 285).

Many of the critical writings on consumer identity stress identity as being partially constituted and *always in process*. This is partly because the individual's identity as a consumer does not exhaust the 'total' subject. We are obviously not only consumers but also citizens, parents, professionals, sisters, brothers, neighbors, thinkers, drivers, travellers, etc. The consumer self is sometimes compared with a *bricolage*: that is, constructed by mixing 'bits and pieces' from commodities and products available in the marketplace. One way of conceiving of the partiality and dynamic of consumers' identity is to recognize that the unfulfilled desire, the essential incompleteness, *is* the consumer identity: that is, that absence or lack which in modern society's restricted economy the human being *tries to fill* through consumption (Saren et al., 2007). This accounts for the role of marketing in stimulating desires and the need for fantasy and fetishism in the commodity form. Furthermore, if it is unfulfilled desire that lies at the heart of the so-called consumer identity, this also accounts for the necessary eventual *dissatisfaction* on the part of the consumer, because of the logic of the market which always must create yet more demand, thus never fully satisfying, contrary to its espoused 'satisfaction of needs' rhetoric.

Another critical concern has centred on whether consumers can and should escape the market or not (Firat and Venkatesh, 1995; Kozinets, 2002; Arnould, 2007), especially under the disciplining and constraining effects of marketing practices, ideology and discourse (Marion, 2004). One problem for authors on either side of this debate is that the question itself forces the authors to adopt a trope of 'inside versus outside' the market which carries with it the implicit idea of an emancipated space that is somehow free from the influence of the capitalist marketplace. These authors emphasize consumers' own attempts to create spaces of autonomy and control in relation to the market through practices of resistance and anti-market activism (Peñaloza and Price, 1993; Fournier, 1998), group action and consumer movements (Herrmann, 1992; Kozinets and Handelman, 2004), consumer complaints and boycotts (Fournier, 1998; Friedman, 1999), promoting fair trade (Strong, 1996; Smith and Cooper-Martin, 1997), so-called 'anti-marketing' campaigns such as Adbusters (Rumbo, 2002), or more mundane everyday resistance to the market (Catterall and Maclaran, 2001).

Another possible site of resistance is examined by Goulding and Follett (2001), in which the consumer's use of their body as a practice of resistance is studied. The relationship between the body, identity and the development of a sense of selfhood is well documented in the literature (Thompson and Hirschman, 1995). This links with the widening context and forms of consumer resistance (Fournier, 1998). Eccles and Hamilton's (1999) have suggested that consumer autonomy can be found in situations that we often interpret as extreme consumerist behavior, such as addictive consumption, which may be, on the contrary, the only activity undertaken by these people where they *do feel in control*.

Critical consumer research about the topics discussed above is of obvious relevance to social marketers even more so than commercial marketing. Not only is extreme or addictive consumer behavior a concern but also, more generally, *almost all* consumer misbehavior which social marketers seek to ameliorate is directly concerned with the body: for example, obesity, smoking, drinking, self-harm, drug taking and violence. Therefore, it appears obvious that such critical studies that have examined consumers' attitudes to and with relationship to their bodies is of direct relevance here. Furthermore, these studies suggest that a broader holistic research focus is required in order to understand such behavior. This requires more research into the relationships between consumption, identity, possessions and the self.

MARKETING ASSUMPTIONS AND KNOWLEDGE

Marketing knowledge is the foundation of the discipline and it underpins all of its theories and practices. However, there is no clear agreement about the nature of marketing knowledge. Many of the earliest examples of critique in academic marketing were concerned with the methodologies and theoretical underpinnings of academic marketing research itself. Under the heading of 'marketing as science versus art', this debate filled the marketing journals up to the mid-1960s (Alderson and Cox, 1948; Bartels, 1951; Buzzell, 1964). What Alderson and Cox mean by the development of marketing theory is the generation of general or abstract principles that enable us to better understand and predict marketing-related phenomena. This focus on prediction and control represents a particularly restrictive view of marketing theory as it applies primarily to managerial issues. It reflects a view that equates marketing with those activities pursued by the individual firm, rather than with a broader, societal – or macromarketing – perspective (Wilkie and Moore, 2006).

Anderson's (1983) paper in the *Journal of Marketing* provided the first formal, critical examination of established marketing research assumptions from an alternative philosophical position. He agreed with the premise that there is a single social and natural reality, but questioned whether this reality could be discovered via a single scientific method. Scientific inquiry, Anderson proposed, was a social and historical exercise, with the resulting knowledge products 'affected as much by sociological factors as by purely "cognitive" or empirical consideration' (Anderson, 1986, p. 156). What this meant for the production of knowledge in marketing was that we should embrace multiple, philosophical positions and each of these will inevitably possess specific advantages and limitations that should be explicitly recognized by the researcher.

Many would regard the first major work from within the marketing discipline that attempted to break totally with the dominant ideology and practice of academic marketing research as *Philosophical and Radical Thought in Marketing*. In this book, Firat et al. (1987) critique the discipline's managerial orientation, its emphasis on empirical research at the expense of theory and its overwhelming 'quantitative bias'. But it was Arndt (1985a) who first set out a framework for defining alternative philosophical orientations in marketing. He argues that by limiting itself to one of these, logical empiricism, marketing has remained essentially one-dimensional. Drawing upon Morgan's (1980) organizational studies framework, Arndt (1985a) analyses and categorizes the different 'paradigms' and associated metaphors in marketing theory, identifying four main paradigms which contain *different assumptions* about the nature of the marketing discipline and the study of marketing phenomena (Arndt, 1985a, p. 15).

Arndt argues that each of these four paradigms contains 'different metatheoretical assumptions about the nature of science, the subjective-objective dimension and the explicitness of long-term conflicts in society. There are also assumptions about the nature of the marketing discipline and the study of marketing phenomena' (Arndt, 1985a, p. 15), Arndt classifies the four paradigms in marketing as (i) logical empiricist, (ii) socio-political, (iii) subjective world and (iv) liberating paradigms:

1. The **logical empiricist paradigm** emphasizes measurability and intersubjective certification of research results. Overall, this paradigm takes a mechanistic approach, assuming that marketing relations have an autonomous existence independent of the observer and a systematic character resulting in regularities in marketing behavior and equilibrium-seeking marketing systems. Neoclassical economics provides the basis for many of its typical metaphors such as *instrumental man* with rational decision-making and the *organism metaphor* for the organized behavior and environmental learning of the marketing system.

2. The **socio-political paradigm** is similarly based on the assumption of a real and measurable world of marketing phenomena and predictable uniformities in marketing behavior. Unlike the value-free and equilibria assumptions of logical empirical theories, however, this paradigm explicitly recognizes conflicts of interests, resources and relations in marketing exchanges and systems. The metaphors of this paradigm constitute *the political markets and economies* and even spaceship *earth,* the global, ecological approach of much of what would nowadays be called green marketing.

3. The **subjective world paradigm** rejects the existence of social reality in any verifiable and objective sense. Reality is conceived of as the product of the subjective experiences and inter-experiences of individuals. Consequently, marketing phenomena cannot be understood from the perspective of an external observer, but must be studied from the viewpoint of the participant. It thus incorporates the interpretivist and social constructionist approaches. The paradigm, moreover, adopts the motivational and psychology-based metaphor *of irrational man*, the pheomenological metaphor of *experiencing man* with an existential

and semiological basis, and the *language and text* metaphor, and tries to build the understanding of the behavior of marketing actors on the basis of stories, myths, rhetoric and discourse.

4. **The liberating paradigm** also takes a social constructionist perspective with respect to the ontological status of reality but focuses on the social, economic and technological processes that constrain and control human beings in the marketing system. The role of theoretical inquiry is to identify and analyze the conflicts and contradictions in the system and point the way to emancipation. critical theory adherents within this paradigm often take *alienation* and *victimization* as metaphors for the oppressed groups in modern mass consumer society.

A strong case was made by Arndt (1985b) that the marketing discipline has been dominated by one of his four paradigms, that is, logical empiricism, and today there remain few reasons to believe otherwise. Arndt argued for pluralism in orientations and paradigms for the development of marketing theory. This is one route for developing critical marketing, one that aims at fulfilling not only the liberating paradigm but also, taking up Arndt's call for pluralism, the socio-political and subjective paradigms (Saren et al., 2007).

Arndt's major contribution to the debate about marketing philosophical approach and knowledge was that he introduced marketing scholars to a number of alternative paradigms from which they could engage in research. Along with the traditional logical empiricist paradigm, he describes the subjective world paradigm, the socio-political paradigm and the liberating paradigm. It is only through the application of all four paradigms, he argues, that marketing can develop. In practice, this might mean including in the agenda of a critical marketing project questions that explicitly involve research into the conflictual and political character of market exchanges, marketing and consumption; the existential and phenomenological aspects of marketing actors (marketers, consumers, distributors, etc.) and their actions; and the disciplining and constraining effects of marketing practices. Good examples of research that takes these broader issues into account are Hackley (2001), who takes a social constructionist view of marketing, and Wooliscroft, who studied how the historical development of theory in marketing was affected by wider socio-political events: 'World War II, the Cold War, the Space Race, the Nuclear Race and the Korean War... which were responsible for changing the direction of marketing education, research and theory'. (Wooliscroft, 2004)

The practical implications of this for research dealing with critical topics are, first, that the underlying paradigmatic underpinning should to be made explicit at the outset. These philosophical assumptions could be defined and identified and lead to some guiding questions, which follow from them. These might include 'scoping' questions such as: What is the nature of reality and how would we recognize it? What would data or research evidence look like? What type of linkages are we looking for between phenomena: for example, causation, systems and interpretation? What form would a good explanation or argument take?

These philosophical questions are of course also critical for social marketing research, which has been based on mechanistic methodological approaches derived from the logical empiricist paradigm that emphasizes measurability and intersubjective certification of research results. Surely, some other approaches are even more appropriate to social marketing research, such as social constructions, historical methods, socio-political analyses, subjective and experiential approaches, discourse analyses and the study of power relations in marketing itself. In an increasingly information-saturated world the adoption of more critical analyses beyond those derived from logical empiricism are even more important for social marketing because its knowledge bases as well as its messages need to be firmly rooted in order to be communicated and understood.

KEY WORDS: Role of critique in marketing; marketing assumptions and knowledge; critical theory; critical methods for social marketing.

Key insights

- Critique of the Marketing Concept
  There is a contradiction between the espoused free market values of the marketing concept and the powerful control apparatus and technologies of marketing management. This raises important issues for social marketers, most fundamentally whether and how this dominance of the marketing apparatus and subjugation of the consumer can be countered by social marketing campaigns.
- Critical Theory
  Outside the academic marketing discipline, there is a long history of critical analysis of consumer capitalism that has inspired many critical marketing researchers. Social marketers can adopt critical analyses of consumer behaviors in terms of the relationships between consumption, identity, possessions and the self: for example, a social phenomenon such as smoking can be studied in terms of its social role, its 'satisfaction' and the

psychological and relational bases of its commodity appeal.

- Critical Marketing Methodologies
  The methodological limitations of much conventional marketing research can produce partial explanations of behavior, ignoring underlying socio-economic mechanisms, structures and relations. Critical marketing goes beyond the critique of marketing outcomes, often using interpretivist, ethnographic, historical, sociopolitical, experiential studies, discourse analyses and semiotic methodologies. Social marketing can utilize and develop such critical research methodologies to study underlying social and behavioral phenomena.

NOTE

1 For an overview of critical marketing topics and methods, see Brownlie et al. (1999) and Saren et al. (2007).

REFERENCES

Adorno, T.W. (1991) *The Culture Industry: Selected Essays on Mass Culture,* London: Routledge.

Adorno, T.W. and Horkheimer, M. (1997) *Dialectic of Enlightenment,* London and New York: Verso.

Alderson, W. (1957) *Marketing Behavior and Executive Action.* Homewood, IL: Richard D. Irwin.

Alderson, W. and Cox, R. (1948) 'Towards a theory of marketing', *Journal of Marketing,* 13(2): 137–152.

Anderson, P.F. (1983) 'Marketing, scientific progress, and the scientific method', *Journal of Marketing,* 47(4): 18–31.

Anderson, P.F. (1986) 'On method in consumer research: A critical relativist perspective', *Journal of Consumer Research,* 13(2): 155–173.

Araujo, L., Kjellberg, H. and Spencer, R. (2008) 'Market practices and forms: Introduction to special issue', *Marketing Theory,* 8: 1–14.

Arndt, J. (1985a) 'On making marketing science more scientific: Role of orientations, paradigms, metaphors, and puzzle solving', *Journal of Marketing,* 49(Summer): 18–23.

Arndt, J. (1985b) 'The tyranny of paradigms: The case for paradigmatic pluralism in marketing', in N. Dholakia and J. Arndt (eds), *Changing the Course of Marketing: Alternative Paradigms for Widening Marketing Theory.* Greenwich, CT: JAI Press, pp. 3–25.

Arnold, M. and Fisher, J. (1996) 'Counterculture, criticisms and crisis: Assessing the effect of the sixties on marketing thought', *Journal of Macromarketing,* 16(Spring): 118–133.

Arnould, E.J. (2007) 'Can consumers escape the market?' in M. Saren, P. Maclaran, C. Goulding, et al. (eds), *Critical Marketing: Defining the Field.* Oxford: Butterworth-Heinemann, pp. 139–155.

Bagozzi, R.P. (1978) 'Marketing as exchange: A theory of transactions in the marketplace', *American Behavioral Scientist,* 21(March/April): 535–556.

Baran, P. and Sweezy, P. (1964) *Monopoly Capital.* London: Penguin.

Bartels, R. (1951) 'Can marketing be a science?' *Journal of Marketing,* 51: 319–328.

Battaille, G. (1988) *The Accursed Share* (R. Hurley, trans.). New York: Zone Books:.

Baudrillard, J. (1988) *Selected Writings.* Stanford, CT: Stanford University Press.

Baudrillard, J. (1994) *Simulacra and Simulation,* Michigan: University of Michigan Press.

Belk, R.W. (1988) 'Possessions and the extended sense of self', *Journal of Consumer Research,* 15: 139–168.

Bettman, J. (1979) *An Informational Processing Theory of Consumer Choice.* Reading, MA: Addison-Wesley.

Biehl, B. (2007) *Business is Showbusiness.* Wie Topmanager sich vor Publikum inszenieren, Frankfurt: Campus.

Böhme, G. (2003) 'Contribution to the critique of the aesthetic economy', *Thesis Eleven,* 73: 71–82.

Bradshaw, A. and Firat, A.F. (2007) 'Rethinking critical marketing', in M. Saren, R. Elliott, P. Maclaran, et al. (eds), *Critical Marketing: Defining the Field.* London: Elsevier.

Bristor, J.M. and Fischer, E. (1993) 'Feminist thought: Implications for consumer research', *Journal of Consumer Research,* 19(4): 518–536.

Brownlie, D and Saren, M. (1995) 'The commodification of marketing knowledge', *Journal of Marketing Management,* 11(7): 619–628.

Brownlie, D., Saren, M., Wensley, R. and Whittington, R. (eds) (1999) *Rethinking Marketing: Towards Critical Marketing Accountings.* London: Sage Publications.

Buzzell, R.D. (1964) 'Is marketing a science?' *Harvard Business Review,* 41: 32–40.

Carù, A. and Cova, B. (2003) 'A critical approach to experiential consumption: Fighting against the disappearance of the contemplative time', 3rd International Critical Management Studies Conference, Lancaster University, July 2003.

Catterall, M. and Maclaran, P. (2001) 'Tactical resistance to the strategies of the market', 2nd International Critical Management Studies Conference, Manchester School of Management, UMIST, July 2001, strategy paradigmsintegrational framework'.

Dichter, E. (1960) *The Strategy of Desire.* New York: Doubleday.

Dawson, L.M. (1972) 'The human concept: A new philosophy for business', in D.G. Kurtz (ed.), *Marketing Concepts, Issues and Viewpoints.* Michigan: D.H. Mark Publication.

Desmond, J. (1998) 'Marketing and moral indifference', in M. Parker (ed.), *Ethics and Organisation* London: Sage Publications.

Douglas, M. and Isherwood, B. (1978) *The World of Goods: Towards an Anthropology of Consumption.* London: Allen Lane.

Du Gay, P. (2001) 'Epilogue: Servicing as cultural economy', in A. Sturdy, I. Grugulis and H. Willmott (eds), *Customer Service: Empowerment and Entrapment*. Basingstoke: Palgrave.

Eccles, S. and Hamilton, E. (1999) 'Voices of control: Researching the lived experiences of addictive consumers', 1st International Critical Management Studies Conference, Manchester School of Management, UMIST, July 1999.

Elliott, R. (1997) 'Existential consumption and irrational desire', *European Journal of Marketing*, 31(¾): 285–296.

Elliott, R. (2004) 'Making up people: Consumption as a symbolic vocabulary or the construction of identity', in K. Ekstrom and H. Brembek (eds), *Elusive Consumption: Tracking New Research Perspectives*. Oxford: Berg.

Elliott, R. and Wattanasuwan, K. (1998) 'Brands as resources for the symbolic construction of identity', *International Journal of Advertising*, 17(2): 131–145.

Firat, F. and Venkatesh, A. (1995) 'Liberatory postmodernism and the reenchantment of consumption', *Journal of Consumer Research*, 22: 239–267.

Firat, N.D. and Bagozzi, R.P. (eds) (1987) *Philosophical and Radical Thought in Marketing*. Lexington: Lexington Books, pp. 97–116.

Foucault, M. (1980) *Power/Knowledge: Selected Interviews and Other Writings* (ed. C. Gordon). New York: Pantheon Books.

Fournier, S. (1998) 'Consumer resistance: Societal motivations, consumer manifestations, and implications in the marketing domain', *Advances in Consumer Research*, 25: 88–90.

Fournier, V. and Grey, C. (2000) 'At the critical moment: Conditions and prospects of critical management studies', *Human Relations*, 53: 7–32.

Friedman, N. (1999) *Consumer Boycotts: Effecting Change through the Marketplace and the Media*. New York: Routledge.

Fromm, E. (1978) *To Have or To Be?* London: Abacus.

Gabriel, Y. and Lang, T. (2006) *The Unmanageable Consumer: Contemporary Consumption and Its Fragmentations*, 2nd edn. London: Sage Publications.

Galbraith, J.K. (1958) *The Affluent Society*. London: Hamish Hamilton.

Gergen, K. (1991) *The Saturated Self: Dilemmas of Identity in Contemporary Life*. New York: Basic Books.

Goldberg, M.R. (1994) 'Social marketing: Are we fiddling while Rome burns'. Presidential Address, Society for Consumer Psychology, 19 February 1994.

Gordon, R., Hastings, G., McDermott, L. and Siquier, P. (2007) 'The Critical role of social marketing', in M. Saren, P. Maclaran, R. Elliott, et al. (eds), *Critical Marketing: Defining the Field*. London: Elsevier.

Goulding, C. and Follett, J. (2001) 'Subcultures, women and tattoos: An exploratory study', *Gender Marketing and Consumption*, Association for Consumer Research, 6: 37–54.

Hackley, C. (2001) *Marketing and Social Construction*. London, Routledge.

Hastings, G. (2007) *Social Marketing: Why Should the Devil Have All the Best Tunes?* Oxford, UK: Elsevier.

Herrmann, R.O. (1992) 'The tactics of consumer resistance: Group action and marketplace exit', *Advances in Consumer Research*, 20: 130–134.

Hetrick, W.P. and Lozada, H.R. (1994) 'Construing the critical imagination: Comments and necessary diversions', *Journal of Consumer Research*, 21: 548–558.

Hirschman, F.C. (1993) 'Ideology in consumer research, 1980 and 1990: A Marxist and feminist critique', *Journal of Consumer Research*, 19: 537–555.

Horkheimer, M. (1967) 'Zur kritik der instrumentellen vernunft. (Towards a critique of instrumental reason)', Europäische Verlagsanstalt, Frankfurt am Main.

Kilbourne, W.E. (2004) 'Sustainable communication and the dominant social paradigm: Can they be integrated?' *Marketing Theory*, 4(3): 187–208.

Kilbourne, W., McDonagh, P., Prothero, A. (1997) 'Sustainable consumption and the quality of life: A macroeconomic challenge to the dominant social paradigm', *Journal of Macromarketing*, 17: 4–24.

Klein, N. (2001) *No Logo*. London: Flamingo.

Kozinets, R. and Handelman, J. (2004) 'Adversaries of consumption: Consumer movements, activism, and ideology', *Journal of Consumer Research*, 31(3): 691–704.

Kozinets, R.V. (2002) 'Can consumers escape the market? Emancipatory illuminations from burning man', *Journal of Consumer Research*, 29: 20–38.

Marcuse, H. (1964) *One-Dimensional Man: Studies in the Ideology of Advanced Industrial Society*. Boston, MA: Beacon Press.

Marion, G. (2004) *L'Idéologie Marketing*. Paris: Eyrolles.

Mick, D.G. (1986) 'Consumer research and semiotics: Exploring the morphology of signs, symbols, and significance', *Journal of Consumer Research*, 13: 196–213.

Morgan, G. (1980) 'Paradigms, metaphors, and puzzle solving in organization theory', *Administrative Science Quarterly*, 25(4): 605–622.

Morgan, G. (1992) 'Marketing discourse and practice: Towards a critical analysis', in M. Alvesson and H. Willmott (eds), *Critical Management Studies*. London: Sage Publications, pp. 136–158.

Murray, J.B. and Ozanne, J.L. (1991) 'The critical imagination: Emancipatory interests in consumer research', *Journal of Consumer Research*, 18(2): 129–144.

Packard, V. (1957) *The Hidden Persuaders*. London: Longmans, Green & Co.

Peñaloza, L. and Price, L.L. (1993) 'Consumer resistance: A conceptual overview', *Advances in Consumer Research*, 20: 123–128.

Rumbo, J.D. (2002) 'Consumer resistance in a world of advertising clutter: The case of Adbusters', *Psychology & Marketing*, 19(2): 127–148.

Saren, M., Maclaran, P., Elliott, R., et al. (eds) (2007) *Critical Marketing: Defining the Field*. London: Elsevier.

Schroeder, J.E. (2005) 'The artist and the brand', *European Journal of Marketing*, 39(11/12): 1291–1305.

Sirgy, M.J. (1982) 'Self-concept in consumer behavior: A critical review', *Journal of Consumer Research*, 9: 287–300.

Sirgy, M.J. and Su, C. (2000) 'The ethics of consumer sovereignty in an age of high tech,' *Journal of Business Ethics*, 28: 1–14.

Smith, N.C. and Cooper-Martin, E. (1997) 'Ethics and target marketing: The role of product harm and consumer vulnerability', *Journal of Marketing*, 61(3): 1–19.

Stern, B. (1990) 'Literary criticism and the history of marketing thought: A new perspective on "reading" marketing theory', *Journal of the Academy of Marketing Science*, 18(4): 329–336.

Stern, B. (1996) 'Deconstructive strategy and consumer research: Concepts and illustrative exemplar,' *Journal of Consumer Research*, 23(September): 136–147.

Strong, C. (1996) 'Features contributing to the growth in ethical consumerism. A preliminary investigation', *Marketing Intelligence & Planning*, 14(5): 5–13.

Thompson, C. and Hirschman, E. (1995) 'Understanding the socialized body: A poststructuralist analysis of consumer's self conceptions, body images and self care practices', *Journal of Consumer Research*, 32: 139–153.

Varman, R. and Vikas, R.M. (2007) 'Freedom and consumption: Toward conceptualising systemic constraints for subaltern consumers in a capitalist society', *Consumption, Markets and Culture*, 10(2): 117–131.

Veblen, T. (1899/1995) *The Theory of the Leisure Class: An Economic Study of Institutions*. London: Penguin.

Walendorf, M. and Arnould, E.J. (1988) 'My favourite things; A cross-cultural inquiry into object attachment, possessiveness and social linkage', *Journal of Consumer Research*, 14: 531–547.

Wallack, L., Dorfman, L., Jernigan, D. and Themba, M. (1993) *Media Advocacy and Public Health: Power for Prevention*. Newbury Park, CA: Sage Publications.

Weiner, B. (1992) *Human Motivation: Metaphors, Theories and Research*. London: Sage Publications.

Wensley, R. (1990) 'The voice of the consumer? Speculations on the limits to the marketing analogy', *European Journal of Marketing*, 24(7): 49–60.

Wilkie, W. and Moore, E. (2006) 'Examining marketing scholarship and the service-dominant logic perspective of marketing', in S. Vargo and R. Lusch (eds), *The Service-Dominant Logic of Marketing*. New York: M.E. Sharpe, pp. 266–278.

Wooliscroft, B. (2004) 'Paradigm dominance and the hegemonic process'. PhD thesis, University of Otago, New Zealand.

7

New Approaches Toward Resistance to Persuasion

Petia K. Petrova and Robert B. Cialdini

The efforts of many social marketing campaigns are focused on protecting consumers from massive advertising that increases risky behaviors such as smoking (Pechmann and Knight, 2002; Pechmann and Shih, 1999), alcohol abuse (Casswell and Zhang, 1998; Grube and Wallack, 1994; Wyllie et al., 1998), unhealthy eating (Brownell and Horgen, 2004; Halford et al., 2004, 2007, 2008; Harris et al., 2009; Hastings et al., 2003; Murray, 2001), ecological deterioration, credit card mismanagement, gambling abuse and drug misuse or abuse (Volkow, 2006). Unfortunately, such efforts are often unsuccessful. Anti-smoking advertising campaigns are often found to be ineffective (Chassin et al., 1990; Pechmann and Reibling, 2000). Disclaimers, disclosures and product warnings have not been proven effective (Andrews, 1995; Argo and Main, 2004; Hankin et al., 1998; Johar and Simmons, 2000; Schwarz et al., 2007; Skurnik et al., 2005). Even corrective advertising often fails to reduce false beliefs (Dyer and Kuehl, 1974; Jacoby et al., 1982; Johar, 1996).

Spurred by the real challenges faced by many organizations, we examine recent behavioral research on the topic of resistance. More specifically, we provide suggestions on (1) how to effectively create resistance to potentially harmful messages and (2) how to reduce resistance to social marketing programs.

WHAT CONSTITUTES AN EFFECTIVE COUNTERARGUMENT?

Research into the process of persuasion reveals that the impact of a persuasive communication depends to a large extent on the personal reactions of the audience to the message (Greenwald, 1968). As a central assertion of the cognitive response model of persuasion this idea has spurred a number of studies demonstrating that counterargumentation is a key element of the persuasion process (Brock, 1967; Greenwald, 1968; Osterhouse and Brock, 1970; Petty and Cacioppo, 1986; Petty et al., 1981). This line of research suggests that an effective way to increase resistance is to encourage people to generate counterarguments or provide them with ready counterarguments (Eagly et al., 2000; Killeya and Johnson, 1998; Osterhouse and Brock, 1970; Petty and Wegener, 1998). Surprisingly, however, although considerable attention has been devoted to the processes through which counterargumentation undermines persuasion, less attention has been devoted to the *content* of the counterarguments that are most likely to create resistance to a message. Yet, recent behavioral research suggests that there are several types of counterarguments that are likely to be particularly powerful in creating resistance. We examine their features in the following sections.

Counterargument alignment

If we wish to create maximal resistance to a message, should we design counterarguments that attack the specific claims in that message or is it more effective to provide competing information that reveals another side of the issue? For example, tobacco products are commonly advertised with images of attractiveness and fun, creating a positive stereotype of smokers (Mazis et al., 1992;

Pechmann and Knight, 2002; Pechmann and Shih, 1999). At the same time, anti-smoking campaigns often provide information about the negative health consequences of smoking without undermining its positive stereotype. As research examining the effectiveness of antismoking advertising reveals, these messages have increased perceptions of risk. However, they have had little impact on the favorable image of smoking promoted in tobacco advertising (Romer and Jamieson, 2001). Thus, it has been noted that a more efficient way of reducing tobacco consumption might be to attack the positive images associated with smoking and associate smoking with negative stereotypes (Blum, 1994; Pechmann and Knight, 2002).

Research in several domains provides evidence in support of this suggestion. From a functional perspective, appeals designed to change a behavior are more likely to be effective when they focus on the function that the behavior serves (Clary et al., 1998; Lavine and Snyder, 2000; Sanderson and Cantor, 1995). This functional alignment effect has been demonstrated across diverse domains, including consumer products (DeBono, 1987; Shavitt, 1990), volunteer work such as long-term work with AIDS victims (Snyder et al., 2000) and adolescent sexual behaviors (Sanderson and Cantor, 1995).

Behavioral research further suggests that aligning the counterarguments with the content of the message they are designed to undermine is an effective strategy for creating resistance. Early research on inoculation, for example, examined two types of strategies for creating resistance to future exposures to a message – refutational defense and supportive defense (McGuire, 1961, 1962, 1964). To create resistance against a message challenging a cultural truism (e.g., 'mental illness is not contagious'), participants in the refutational defense are presented with the truism and two arguments against it. Then, they are asked to either generate or read statements refuting the arguments against the truism. In the supportive defense, participants are presented with two arguments defending the truism and are asked to generate or read statements supporting the arguments. Later, participants are presented with an essay arguing against the truism, after which their beliefs in the truism are assessed.

The results of such experiments have demonstrated that both the refutational and supportive defense resulted in greater beliefs in the truism in comparison with a control condition. Furthermore, although the refutational defense was not more effective than the supportive defense in strengthening the beliefs before the attack, after the attack, participants exposed to the refutational defense retained stronger beliefs in the truism than participants exposed to the supportive defense (McGuire, 1964). Moreover, after refuting the arguments in the initially presented message against the truism, participants showed resistance not only to a subsequent message employing the same arguments, but the effect of the refutational counterarguments transferred to a subsequent message presenting different arguments against the truism (McGuire, 1961).

Research further suggests that persuasive appeals tend to be more effective when the nature of the appeal is aligned with the basis of the attitude. Attitudes based on affect are easier to change with affect-based appeals, while cognition-based attitudes are more susceptible to cognitive appeals (Clarkson et al., 2011; Edwards, 1990; Edwards and von Hippel, 1995; Fabrigar and Petty, 1999). For example, Fabrigar and Petty (1999) asked participants either to taste a new beverage (affective basis) or read information about the taste of the beverage (cognitive basis). Then, they exposed participants either to affect- or cognition-based persuasion. In the affect-based persuasion, participants tasted or smelled the beverage, which this time had a less pleasant taste and smell attributed to the different temperature at which the beverage was served. In the cognition persuasion, participants read a message about how the taste or smell of the beverage becomes less pleasant if it is not served very cold. The results revealed that the affective persuasion had stronger effect on affective than cognitive attitudes. By contrast, cognitive persuasion was more successful against cognitive than affective attitudes. This message alignment effect occurred even when the attribute dimensions of the attitude object (taste vs smell) mismatched and even when both the affect- and cognition-based messages were written, thus controlling for alignment of direct/indirect experiences (Fabrigar and Petty, 1999).

In another domain, research reveals an alignment effect in regard to whether the initial attitude is based on abstract or specific claims. In a study by Pham and Muthukrishnan (2002), participants viewed an ad presenting abstract claims (e.g., 'The best pen money can buy') or specific claims (e.g., 'Omega 3 provides sloped design and optimal balancing'). During a second session, participants saw a *Consumer Reports* article that provided either abstract counterarguments ('There is nothing special about this pen') or specific counterarguments ('The package was too difficult to open'). When the ad contained specific claims, the specific counterarguments resulted in greater revision of brand evaluations. However, when the ad contained abstract claims, the abstract counterarguments were more damaging.

To further examine the question of counterargument alignment, we tested whether aligning the *specific content* of a counterargument with the claims of the persuasive message will result in further increases in resistance (Petrova et al., 2007a). We asked participants to evaluate a series of messages presented in two sessions one week apart. Most of the messages were filler ads unrelated to the study with the exception of (1) an ad promoting a fictitious allergy drug called Levatin (presented during the first session) and (2) a countermessage from *Consumer Reports* warning consumers about the drug (presented during the second session). We tested two versions of the Levatin ad. One of the versions presented evidence from clinical studies demonstrating the effectiveness of Levatin. The other version provided evidence from clinical studies reporting low side effects. Accordingly, the *Consumer Reports* article reported evidence from better-controlled studies demonstrating that either Levatin was ineffective for a large portion of the patients or Levatin caused significant side effects.

The results revealed that when the drug was advertised as highly effective, counterarguments about low effectiveness decreased participants' evaluations of Levatin to a greater extent than counterarguments about possible side effects. On the other hand, when Levatin was advertised as a safe way to relieve allergy symptoms, the same information about low effectiveness was less detrimental than information about possible side effects. Because the specific information about safety and effectiveness was the same across conditions, the superior effect of the aligned counterarguments was not driven by the differential strength of their specific content.

Additional analysis revealed that although the aligned counterarguments had an overall stronger negative effect on the evaluations of Levatin than the non-aligned counterarguments, this difference was significant only among participants who perceived the *Consumer Reports* article as highly credible. This last finding is particularly important, as it suggests that the use of aligned counter information is particularly suitable for organizations that have earned the trust of the public. We conducted a subsequent study to test this possibility by directly manipulating the source of the counter information (Petrova et al., 2011a).

Again, we asked college students to evaluate a set of messages. Among them was an ad for a fictitious energy drink called Delight. The ad promoted the beverage either as a way to maintain a healthy lifestyle or an excellent source of energy. Later, participants viewed a countermessage providing general information either that energy drinks contain unhealthy ingredients or that the energy from such drinks lasts only a few hours, decreasing energy afterward. The counter message came from either the US Department of Health and Human Services or a familiar manufacturer of vegetable juices – V8. When asked about the trustworthiness of the source of the countermessage, participants evaluated the US Department of Health and Human Services as less trustworthy than V8. Subsequently, a different pattern of results emerged, depending on the source of the countermessage. Regardless of whether the drink was promoted as a way to maintain a healthy lifestyle or an excellent source of energy, the aligned counterarguments had a stronger undermining effect than the non-aligned counterarguments. However, this was the case only when the message came from the more trusted source (Petrova et al., 2011a).

These findings suggest that when the source of the countermessage is perceived as credible, counterarguments that are aligned with the persuasive message will be more effective in creating resistance than equally negative information that does not specifically address the message claims. Such a conclusion is consistent with research demonstrating that anti-smoking advertisements reinforcing negative smoking stereotypes (e.g., 'smoking stinks', 'how to spot a nerd') can offset the effects of common tobacco ads depicting images of young, attractive, glamorous and sexy people who are having fun (Pechmann and Knight, 2002).

Yet, the evidence regarding the superiority of aligned counterarguments has a broader set of implications for social marketing campaigns sponsored by organizations trusted by the public. Skin cancer, for example, is the most common form of cancer (Glanz et al., 2002). Yet, despite relatively easy prevention, skin cancer rates are on the rise, which is due in part to increased exposure through the use of tanning beds. Indeed, tanning bed use is a major risk factor for both melanoma and non-melanoma skin cancer (Geller et al., 2002). Regular users of indoor tanning are eight times more likely to have melanomas as compared with non-users (Glanz et al., 2002; Westerdahl et al., 2000). At the same time, to speed the tanning process, suntan bed manufacturers have developed tanning beds that produce higher levels of UVB rays and thus increase the risk of skin cancer to users (World Health Organization, 2003). To protect consumers, the World Health Organization (WHO) warned that there were adverse health effects associated with tanning bed use and suggested that no person under 18 should use a tanning bed (World Health Organization, 2003, 2005). Our findings regarding the effectiveness of aligned counterclaims, however, suggest that a different approach should be considered. To counter the appeals of youth and beauty used by the tanning industry, messages designed to reduce tanning should make consumers aware that tanning can prematurely age and wrinkle skin. When they come from a credible source, such aligned counterclaims may be more effective than the health-focused approaches currently used.

In other domains, messages promoting nutritious eating should undermine the appeals of fun, happiness, and being 'cool' with which unhealthy food products are advertised (Folta et al., 2006; Harrison and Marske, 2005). Messages promoting safe driving should undermine the commercial depictions of joy and excitement of high speed. Similarly, anti-debt campaigns should attack the specific appeals of luxurious lifestyle and freedom used by credit lenders. Coming from organizations that have earned the trust of the consumer, these aligned countermessages are likely to create higher levels of resistance than countermessages unrelated to the reasons for undertaking the undesired behavior.

Revealing evidence for dishonesty and manipulative intent

Examinations of various anti-smoking campaigns reveal that whereas messages depicting the negative health effects of smoking have been generally ineffective, one of the most successful ways to decrease tobacco consumption was to provide evidence for the deceptiveness of tobacco advertising (Goldman and Glantz, 1998). For example, among teens, exposure to the American Legacy Foundation's TRUTH campaign was associated with more negative attitudes toward the tobacco industry and lower intent to begin smoking (Farrelly et al., 2002, 2005; Hershey et al., 2005).

Starting with the Yale approach to attitude change (Hovland and Weiss, 1951; Hovland et al., 1953), the effect of source credibility on persuasion has been subject to extensive research (Eagly et al., 1978; Fein et al., 1997; Mills and Jellison, 1967; Priester and Petty, 1995). Across various domains, research demonstrates that when a persuasive attempt is perceived as dishonest or manipulative, its impact is significantly undermined (Byrne et al., 1974; Campbell, 1995; Drachman et al., 1978; Ellen et al., 2000; Fein et al., 1997; Jones and Wortman, 1973; Lutz, 1985; MacKenzie and Lutz, 1989). For example, pointing out a persuader's undue manipulative intent in a trial setting tends to render the persuader's (otherwise convincing) message ineffective (Fein et al., 1997). Similarly, in a marketing context, researchers have found that persuasive impact is undermined if the influence agent is perceived as using trickery (Campbell, 1995; Ellen et al.,

2000; Lutz, 1985; MacKenzie and Lutz, 1989). Revealed dishonesty can have damaging long-term consequences (Anderson, 1968; Cialdini et al., 2004; Cosmides and Tooby, 1992; Rothbart and Park, 1986; Trafimow, 2001). Once a ruse is recognized, people resist information associated with it and its perpetrator (Eagly et al., 1978).

Importantly, revealing the manipulative attempt of the source of a message can result in resistance to messages presented not only by the same source but also by other sources. For example, in a study by Darke and Ritchie (2007), participants viewed an ad for a dishwasher which contained several misleading claims (e.g., unbeatable performance for less; more features than other leading national brands). Participants then received information that *Consumer Reports* magazine had ranked the dishwasher as one of the worst dishwashers on the market. Subsequently, participants viewed another ad which provided information about another product (an answering machine). The ad compared the product with two competing brands and asserted that the advertised brand was superior to both of the other competing brands. The results revealed that participants who were misled by the dishwasher ad evaluated the answering machine more negatively than participants who did not see the misleading ad. Moreover, this effect was significant, regardless of whether the second ad was from the same advertiser or not.

Subsequent studies further demonstrated that the effects of revealed manipulative attempts persisted when the second ad was presented several days later, when the second ad made claims on a different dimension (e.g., false product claims influenced perceptions of deal value), and regardless of the similarity between the misleading ad and the subsequently presented ad (Darke and Ritchie, 2007; Darke et al., 2008). Once aware of the deception, people became more distrustful of further persuasive claims and applied this bias not only to the original source of deception but also to other sources and other types of claims.

Given these findings, can we teach people to resist misleading appeals that they may encounter in the future by presenting them with examples of other deceptive messages? This possibility was examined by Sagarin and colleagues (2002). Participants viewed examples of magazine ads which used authority figures in a legitimate or illegitimate way (e.g., the authority is an expert or not an expert in the product, such as an actor playing a doctor). Several days later a research assistant posing as a representative from the campus daily newspaper asked participants to evaluate the articles and advertisements in a new newspaper insert. Two of the ads in the newspaper insert were authority based, one legitimate and one illegitimate.

The results revealed that seeing examples of legitimate and illegitimate uses of authorities increased participants' ratings of the ads containing legitimate authorities. However, it did not decrease the ratings of the ads containing illegitimate authorities in comparison with the control condition. Perhaps, although participants differentiated between the legitimate and illegitimate uses of authorities, they did not feel vulnerable to the ads using illegitimate authorities. A subsequent study examined this possibility by testing a manipulation designed to dispel this illusion of invulnerability. Participants examined a deceptive ad and wrote down their evaluations of the ad. Having the responses in front of them, participants were told how the ad had manipulated them. Only after participants' experienced their vulnerability did they become more resistant to deceptive appeals; also, they became more persuaded by legitimate appeals (Sagarin et al., 2002).

CREATING RESISTANCE TO STRONGER OPPONENTS

The evidence regarding the role of counterargumentation in persuasion has a clear implication: should we wish to create resistance to an adversary's persuasive attempt, find a way to make aligned counterarguments or information revealing the deceptiveness of your rival available to audience members when they encounter the opponent's communication. But, this is not easily accomplished. In contrast to the controlled settings of laboratory experiments, outside the lab, communicators face the task of making their claims salient during the presentation of the opponent's message days or weeks later. This goal requires that communicators somehow arrange for the audience to recall their points while focused on an opposing message – a focus that naturally renders the rival's arguments much more salient and accessible.

This general problem of differential salience is compounded when poorly funded public organizations must contend against the massive marketing budgets of corporate entities. When ads are seen repeatedly, the availability of the arguments in the ad is bolstered each time the audience is exposed to it. In addition, the arguments in the ad become more familiar and this familiarity further increases their acceptance (Bacon, 1979; Hasher et al., 1977; Hawkins and Hoch, 1992; Petrova et al., 2011c; Schwarz et al., 2007; Zajonc, 1968, 1980).

In order to neutralize frequently delivered harmful messages, social marketing campaigns must not only create effective counterarguments but also find a way to make them prominent in consciousness at the time audience members receive and process those ads.

The poison parasite defense

Through what mechanism and by what device could we prompt people to recall one set of arguments while experiencing another? In a program of research, along with colleagues, we have examined one particular strategy designed to provide a solution to this problem (Cialdini et al., 2011; Petrova et al., 2006, 2011b). Our examination of the vast literature on memory uncovered a pair of promising candidates: Endel Tulving's (1983) 'encoding specificity' mechanism and the use of retrieval cues as mnemonic devices. According to the encoding specificity principle, retrieval cues operate to increase the probability that a given memory will be recalled; and, the best retrieval cues are those stimuli that were present when the memory was formed (Tulving, 1983; Tulving and Schacter, 1990; Tulving and Thomson, 1973). Thus, reinstating the retrieval cues that were present during encoding greatly facilitates recall (Healy and Bourne, 1995; Keller, 1987, 1991a, b, c).

There seemed to us an intriguing upshot of the foregoing analysis for constructing a defense against an opponent's illegitimate persuasive appeal: after designing an effective countermessage, one should build into the countermessage stimuli that are present in the rival appeal. That would have the consequence of causing one's points to be recalled (by virtue of the common retrieval cues) whenever audience members experienced the opponent's message. Not only should this strategy solve the problem of the differential salience and familiarity of the opponents' arguments that naturally occurs when the opponent's message is presented at a later point but also it should also solve the problem of differential access to the audience's attention when one's adversary can reach the audience more often. That is, if one has arranged for one's own points to be raised to consciousness in audience members' minds each time the competitor raises his or her points, then the playing field of presentation opportunities will have been leveled.

We have labeled this strategy the Poison Parasite Defense because it consists of two elements, one poisonous and one parasitic. The poisonous component is the presence of effective counter information that undercuts the opponent's assertions. The parasitic component is the presence of retrieval cues that bring the counter information to mind whenever recipients are exposed to those assertions.

In an initial test of the Poison Parasite strategy we showed participants series of ads among which was an ad for a political candidate ('Stephen Pickett, The Pro-Education Candidate'). The ad offered several arguments in support for its pro-education contention (e.g., Mr Pickett had been a teacher for 10 years, had served as chairman of the county public school district and had supported a 20% increase in school revenues in one year). After viewing a series of filler ads, participants viewed one of *five* versions of a countermessage.

1. In the *Poison Parasite* condition, the countermessage urged voters not to vote for Mr Pickett and punctured each of his pro-education credentials with countervailing information. To enhance the accessibility of these counterarguments at later presentations of the target ad, we incorporated in the countermessage mnemonic links to the target ad by including an exact replica of the original Pickett ad.
2. In the *Links Plus Mere Derogation* condition, participants viewed the same countermessage as those in the Poison Parasite condition except that instead of revealing the deceptiveness of Pickett's claims, each of Mr Pickett's pro-educational credentials was assigned an 'F' grade in red ink (as if by a teacher's hand) and a dunce cap was superimposed on his photo.
3. In the *Poison Parasite Plus Mere Derogation* condition, participants viewed the same countermessage as those in the Poison Parasite condition except that additional source derogation was injected by assigning 'F' grades to his claims and superimposing a dunce cap on his head.
4. In the *Mere Counterarguments* condition, participants viewed a different countermessage from that of the other experimental conditions. It did not contain any mnemonic links to the original Pickett ad. Instead, it included an image of a ballot box backdrop. The message also provided a set of counterclaims to the candidacy of Stephen Picket that were not based on duplicity (e.g., he lacked experience in city government) and urged voters not to vote for Stephen Pickett.
5. In a *Control* condition, participants viewed an ad for a different political candidate, for a different electoral race.

One week later, participants once again viewed a set of ads including the original Pickett ad and reported their evaluations of the ad and intentions to vote for the candidate. The results revealed that participants who saw the two Poison Parasite countermessages (*Poison Parasite* and *Poison Parasite Plus Mere Derogation*) were less likely to vote for the candidate relative to participants who viewed the non-Poison Parasite countermessages (*Links Plus Mere Derogation* and *Mere Counterarguments*) or the *Control* message promoting another candidate. Further meditational analysis revealed that the resistance-enhancing effect of the Poison Parasite strategy on voting intentions was fully mediated by decrease in the perceived honesty of the Pickett ad.

Could the Poison Parasite Defense remain effective even when after the presentation of the Poison Parasite message the opponent continues to repeatedly deliver his message over an extended period of time? Moreover, if the Poison Parasite Defense increases the salience of the counterarguments with each presentation of the opponent's message, can it create continuously decreasing impact of the opponent's message with each subsequent presentation? We examined this possibility in a subsequent study conducted over a period of five weeks (Petrova et al., 2006, 2011b).

In five consecutive sessions one week apart, participants evaluated a number of ads. During the first session we presented participants with several ads, including a magazine ad promoting the environmental record of a chemical company, Zelotec, which they saw twice during the session. One week later participants saw another series of ads, among which was a countermessage against Zelotec. In the *Poison Parasite* condition the message was sponsored by the Committee for the Primacy of Earth, and stated 'The Zelotec Corporation wants you to believe that they protect the environment. But, what you can't see in this promotional photo is that Zelotec pollutes the groundwater and contaminates the soil around its manufacturing plants, affecting all who live in the area.' To create mnemonic links between the countermessage and the Zelotec ad, we included in the countermessage a reduced image of the original Zelotec ad. In the *Mere Counterarguments* condition, participants viewed a message containing a photo of a high-rise glass and steel building, the caption for which read, 'The Zelotec Corporation wants you to believe that they protect the environment. But, what you can't see in this promotional photo of their corporate headquarters is that Zelotec pollutes the groundwater and contaminates the soil around its manufacturing plants, affecting all who live in the area.' In the *Control* condition, participants viewed an unrelated ad. Then at three separate sessions, one week apart from each other, participants repeatedly viewed the Zelotec ad among other filler ads.

The results revealed that immediately after their presentation, the two countermessages were equally effective in reducing participants' evaluations of Zelotec. However, during the next three weeks when participants repeatedly saw the Zelotec ad, the Poison Parasite countermessage resulted in lower evaluations of Zelotec than the countermessage that did not contain mnemonic links or the control ad. Including mnemonic links in the countermessage had a ruinous effect on the evaluations of Zelotec, even though the countermessage was seen (just once) four full weeks earlier and even though it was seen *five times* less often than the Zelotec ad. More importantly, when the counter information was presented along with mnemonic links, seeing the Zelotec ad repeatedly resulted in a persisting decrease in the ratings of the company (Petrova et al., 2006, 2011b).

These findings suggest an intriguing possibility. Even when an organization does not have access to the audience as often as the corporations promoting various harmful products, it is possible to create lasting and even increasing resistance. To achieve this, social marketing messages should incorporate retrieval cues that increase the saliency of the counterarguments against the ads promoting the products with each presentation of these ads. For example, in implementing this suggestion, anti-tobacco messages not only should present information undermining the claims with which smoking is promoted but also should use elements from these ads in order to create mnemonic links to the tobacco ads.

Indeed, some support for this approach already exists in a set of events that began in the mid- 1960s when the Federal Communications Commission applied its 'fairness doctrine' to the issue of tobacco advertising. According to the 'fairness doctrine,' for every three tobacco ads that appeared on radio or TV, free air time had to be given to one ad espousing opposing views. For the first time, anti-tobacco forces such as the American Cancer Society could afford to air counter ads to the tobacco company messages. They did so via counter ads that disputed the images created in tobacco company commercials, providing counterarguments that tobacco use led to diseased health, damaged attractiveness and slavish dependence. However, the American Cancer Society counter ads also used the image of the Marlboro Man to deliver these counterarguments, which created mnemonic links to the original tobacco ads. For example, one commercial featured a Marlboro Man-like cowboy smoking a cigarette in a saloon. When he encountered a rival cowboy and attempted to draw his weapon, he started wheezing, coughing and gasping for air. During that scene, the narrator concluded, 'Cigarettes – they're killers.'

From their first appearance in 1967, the counter ads began to undercut tobacco sales; after a quarter-century climb, per capita consumption dropped precipitously in that initial year and continued to sink during the three years that these anti-tobacco ads were aired. The majority of the decline has since been traced to the impact of the counter ads;

moreover, when the ads ended, so did the attendant decrease in tobacco consumption (McAlister et al., 1989; Simonich, 1991; Warner, 1981).

OVERCOMING RESISTANCE TO PERSUASION

To be effective in changing behavior, it is essential for social marketing campaigns to overcome individuals' resistance to the advocated change (e.g., health-promoting behaviors, environmentally friendly consumption, safe driving). Research from the social sciences suggests several strategies that social marketing campaigns can implement to overcome resistance. We have organized these strategies in three groups based on three types of resistance that people tend to experience: reactance, skepticism, and inertia (Knowles and Riner, 2007). Reactance refers to the negative reaction to the threat of one's freedom (Brehm, 1966). Skepticism is a form of resistance to the content of the message with which one is presented and involves greater scrutiny. Inertia involves the desire to retain the status quo.

Reducing reactance

Reactance has been shown to have strong effect on behavior (Bushman and Stack, 1996; Heilman, 1976; Worchel et al., 1975). For instance, labels warning individuals of the violent content of an entertainment program increased interest in viewing the program (Bushman and Stack, 1996). Similarly, choice of unhealthy foods increased after reading recommendations for healthier alternative brands (Fitzsimons and Lehman, 2004). Given these findings, it is important for social marketing campaigns to ensure that the recommendations they provide will not be met with reactance.

One way to reduce reactance is to advocate the desired behavior instead of prohibit the opposite behavior (Winter et al., 2000). Another way is to legitimize even a minimal level of compliance. For example, adding the phrase 'even a penny will help' almost doubled compliance with a request for donating to the American Cancer Society without substantially decreasing the donation amounts (Cialdini and Schroeder, 1976).

Social marketers can further reduce reactance by demonstrating how the recommended behavior is consistent with previous choices, existing values, or desirable traits. For example, people who were told that they are generous made on average larger contributions to a charity (Kraut, 1973). Similarly, people labeled by a bogus personality test as kind helped another person significantly more frequently than people labeled as intelligent (Strenta and DeJong, 1981). These findings demonstrate that it is important to bring into awareness the values that people possess that are consistent with the advocated direction.

Paradoxically, one can reduce reactance toward a message by merely acknowledging that the person might be feeling some resistance (Knowles and Linn, 2004; Knowles and Riner, 2007). In one study, participants who were asked 'I know you might not want to, but would you mail this letter for me' agreed at a 100% rate in comparison with a 71% compliance when they were just asked, 'Would you mail this letter for me? ' (Knowles and Riner, 2007). Similarly, acknowledging audience freedom to choose whether to agree with the proposed change (e.g., 'but you are free to accept or refuse,' 'I don't want to oblige you' or 'that's up to you') can paradoxically decrease resistance to the recommended course of action (Guéguen and Pascual, 2000; Guéguen et al., 2011). For example, in one study (Guéguen et al., 2011) the researchers went home to home soliciting help in recording household waste. The researchers asked: *'Would you agree to fill out a sorting book for one month in which the quantity of glass, plastic and paper will be registered? As often as you put waste in the trash, you will have to note the date and the quantity of waste, by weighing your garbage bags or by counting the number of bottles.'* Forty two percent of the participants agreed. In another condition, the researchers made the same request but added at the end: *'Of course you are free to accept or to refuse.'* After adding this phrase at the end of the request, 68% of the participants agreed and took the sorting book to record the quantity of the different types of waste each day. One month later, the researchers went to the participants' homes to take the sorting book back. The results revealed that in the 'but you are free' condition 44% of the sorting books were neatly completed for each single day of the past month. In the control condition, only 14% of the sorting books were completed as requested. Thus, from all participants who were initially contacted, 30% completed the survey for the whole 30 days in the 'but you are free' condition, while only 6% did so in the control condition. Adding the phrase 'but you are free' not only decreased resistance but also created a lasting commitment to carry on the behavior.

Overcoming skepticism

The most straightforward way to reduce skepticism is to provide strong counterarguments that defuse possible objections. As we discussed earlier, when the source of a message is perceived as credible, counterarguments that directly refute the audience objections are likely to be particularly effective (Petrova et al., 2007, 2011a).

Because people use the behavior of others as information about what is the correct action, one can reduce skepticism by also demonstrating that many others are engaging in the recommended behavior. For example, hotels frequently adopt environmental programs by displaying cards in the rooms asking guests to reuse their towels. Informing guests that the majority of people reuse their towels increased towel reuse by 26% in comparison with a message simply emphasizing the importance of protecting the environment (Goldstein et al., 2008).

Skepticism is also substantially reduced when the message is presented in a narrative story. This encourages processing the information in a holistic way rather than counterarguing the specific points in the message (Adaval and Wyer, 1998; Green, 2006; Green and Brock, 2000). For example, in a study by Slater and Rouner (1996), college students read a message about the harmful effects of alcohol consumption. For half of the participants the message presented statistics from government agencies and scientific sources. For the other half, the message included a story about a specific student and the destructive influence of alcohol in his life. When the messages were consistent with the students' values, the statistical evidence was more persuasive. However, when the messages were incongruent with the students' values, the narrative story was more persuasive (Slater and Rouner, 1996).

A related strategy involves directly encouraging the audience to imagine undertaking the desired action (Petrova and Cialdini, 2008). For example, imagining taking a trip, starting a new job, or donating blood increased intentions to engage in these activities (Anderson, 1983; Petrova and Cialdini, 2005). Importantly, when using this strategy, social marketing campaigns must ensure that the audience can easily generate the suggested images. The difficulty imagining the behavior can have a backfiring effect (Petrova and Cialdini, 2005; Mandel et al., 2006).

Skepticism can also be undermined when people are in a situation in which they have to generate arguments in support of the position. As the role-playing research suggests, communicating a message to others can change the communicator's own attitudes (Eagly and Chaiken, 1993; Janis and King, 1954). For example, participants who pretended to be advocates for a position that they normally opposed later showed considerably more acceptance of that position compared with participants who merely heard the message. By engaging in role-playing, participants focused on the arguments in favor of the position and became more open-minded (Greenwald, 1969). Research also shows that communicators tend to modify their message about an issue to be congruent with their listeners' attitude (Higgins and Rholes, 1978). Because people are likely to use their verbal encoding of stimulus information to reconstruct and evaluate the original input (Higgins and Rholes, 1978), over time, speakers' memories and attitudes tend to become consistent with the message they generated rather than the information they originally received (Higgins and Rholes, 1978).

It should be noted, however, that the difficulty of generating arguments in favor of a position can result in more negative attitudes (Schwarz et al., 1991). Moreover, the difficulty of simply articulating information can influence one's attitudes in a negative direction (Petrova, 2006a; Petrova et al., 2011d). Thus, social marketers should ensure that they provide messages that are easy to remember and easy to transmit (Petrova, 2006b). For example, including technical information and scientific language may provide convincing support. However, when it is difficult to communicate this information to others, individuals may become less persuaded by the message.

Overcoming inertia

Inertia is caused by unwillingness to spend energy to contemplate on new ideas. Thus, to overcome inertia, one has to find a way to motivate the audience to consider the issue and undertake the suggested behavior. Scientific research has identified several ways to achieve that, but two stand out as especially relevant for social marketing: (1) simplify the decision-making process and (2) provide self-affirmation.

Even when choices are limited to just two options, they frequently involve difficult tradeoffs such as rewards versus risks and enjoyment versus effort. The difficulty making these tradeoffs can have various unintended consequences (Petrova et al., 2011c; Thompson et al., 2009). It can create decision paralysis and choice deferral and reduce motivation and commitment to implement the choice. For example, the difficulty of choosing between writing an essay about an article that was short and dull versus one that was longer and interesting caused authors to write poorer essays in comparison to those who were assigned one of the alternatives (Thompson et al., 2009). To increase the likelihood that a decision will be implemented, social marketers need to ensure that people are not overwhelmed by the decision.

Often, inertia is based on uncertainty, fear and defensiveness. An effective way to overcome the resulting resistance is to boost individuals' confidence through self-affirmation. This can be achieved by providing a success experience or reminding individuals of something that they are proud of (Jacks and O'Brien, 2004). For example, women who had affirmed an important personal value were more likely to accept threatening health information (Sherman et al., 2000). Similarly, when alcohol drinkers were presented with an article linking alcohol consumption to breast cancer, they shifted their attention away from the threatening information. This bias, however, reversed when the participants first described their most important personal value and wrote a one-page essay about why it was important to them (Klein and Harris, 2009).

CONCLUSION

The topic of resistance to persuasion is particularly relevant to social marketers. We focused on recent research revealing how social marketing campaigns can increase resistance to messages promoting harmful behaviors and reduce resistance to messages promoting beneficial behaviors.

Our analysis of the most effective ways to create resistance revealed a general insight: the information that is most likely to undermine a specific behavior does not need to be the most potent or familiar or instructive aspect of the situation. Rather, it is the one that is most likely to be prominent in consciousness at the time of the decision. Thus, when communicators are perceived as credible, counterarguments aligned with the claims of the message are more effective in creating resistance than equally negative information that does not address the claims. Furthermore, in addition to providing counterarguments that can effectively undermine a message, social marketers must ensure that these counterarguments will be accessible long after their exposure. An effective way to accomplish this goal is to create a mnemonic link between the counterarguments and the message.

Since resistance processes can undermine the effectiveness of social marketing campaigns, we also reviewed strategies that such campaigns can utilize in reducing resistance. We focused on three sources of resistance – reactance, skepticism and inertia.

To reduce reactance, social marketing campaigns can encourage small commitments, remind people how the recommended action is consistent with existing choices, values and qualities that they possess, acknowledge the freedom to choose whether to agree with the proposed course of action and advocate instead of prohibit actions. Skepticism can effectively be reduced with effective counterarguments, consensus information, storytelling, imagery information and encouraging communicating the message. To overcome inertia, social marketing programs should simplify the decision-making process. When people feel inertia based on uncertainty, fear or defensiveness, one can reduce this type of resistance through self-affirmation.

Directions for future research

Despite the recent insights into the process of resistance, there is still more knowledge available about how to create effective persuasive messages than how to create resistance to harmful messages. Further research is needed to redress this imbalance. One possible direction is in investigating novel strategies that would be effective in creating resistance, particularly to messages that provide misleading information.

Another direction is in examining situational variables that are likely to affect resistance. For example, since generating counterarguments requires cognitive resources, we can expect many of the suggested strategies for increasing resistance to have stronger effects among individuals who have the motivation and ability to process the message systematically (Romero et al., 1996). As the extent to which individuals are likely to systematically process a message is greatly influenced by the its personal relevance, future research is needed to examine the effectiveness of the reviewed strategies across messages of high and low personal relevance.

Distraction or cognitive load can also influence type of processing (e.g., Osterhouse and Brock, 1970; Petty et al., 1976). Since messages presented in fast pace (such as TV commercials) are particularly difficult to counterargue, future research is needed to examine the effectiveness of the reviewed strategies with different presentation formats. Even if individuals are free to take unlimited time to read the messages in a non-distracting environment, they may still become more susceptible to persuasion after devoting self-regulatory resources on another task (Fennis et al., 2009; Wheeler et al., 2007). We can also expect self-regulatory resources to be more depleted at the end of the day because of the many independent acts of willpower required during the day (Baumeister and Heatherton, 1996). During this time of the day, it may be particularly difficult to resist persuasive messages. Similarly, individuals whose

daily life poses great self-regulatory demands (e.g., dieting, quitting smoking, fighting an illness) may have lower ability to resist persuasion.

Future research is also needed to examine personality variables related to resistance. For example, individuals high in need for cognition are more likely to have attitudes that are resistant to change, are more likely to engage in effortful cognitive processing of the persuasive message (Haugtvedt and Petty, 1992), and are more likely to generate counterarguments against the message. Research also reveals that individuals with moderate self-esteem are more likely to be persuaded than individuals with high or low self-esteem (Rhodes and Wood, 1992). Several personality scales related to resistance to persuasion have also been developed, including skepticism (Obermiller and Spangenberg, 1998), defensive confidence (Albarracín and Mitchell, 2004), resistance to persuasion (Briñol et al., 2004) and bolstering versus counterarguing (Briñol et al., 2004). Research is needed to build on this work and further examine the effects of individual differences related to resistance.

Finally, growing evidence suggests important differences in the influence processes across cultures (Barrett et al., 2004; Cialdini et al., 1999; Petrova et al., 2007b; Wosinska et al., 2009). Future research examining the processes of resistance across cultures will have important implications for global social marketing and social marketing across different segments.

KEY WORDS: Resistance to persuasion; counterarguments; counterargument alignment; persuasion; communication; influence; social marketing; consumer welfare; public health; anti-smoking advertising; source credibility; deception; inoculation; retrieval cues; reactance; skepticism; inertia.

Key insights

- Organizations holding the public trust can generate resistance to harmful messages by providing counterarguments directly aligned with the claims of those messages.
- Social marketing campaigns can induce resistance to misleading messages by revealing the manipulative attempt of the message source.
- Social marketers must ensure that their counterarguments will be accessible in memory long after their presentation. An effective way to accomplish this is to create a mnemonic link between the counterarguments and the messages they are designed to undermine.

- To reduce reactance, social marketing campaigns should encourage small commitments, remind people how the recommended action is consistent with their choices and values, acknowledge audience freedom to choose whether to accept the recommendation and advocate instead of prohibit actions.
- Skepticism can be reduced with effective counterarguments, consensus information, powerful stories, engaging the audience imagination, and encouraging communicating the message to others.
- To overcome inertia, social marketing programs should simplify the decision-making process or when the inertia is based on uncertainty or fear, boost individuals' confidence.

REFERENCES

Adaval, R. and Wyer, R.S. (1998) 'The role of narratives in consumer information processing', *Journal of Consumer Psychology*, 7(3): 207–245.

Albarracín, D. and Mitchell, A.L. (2004) 'The Role of defensive confidence in preference for proattitudinal information: How believing that one is strong can sometimes be a defensive weakness', *Personality and Social Psychology Bulletin*, 30: 1565–1594.

Anderson, C.A. (1983) 'Imagination and expectation: The effect of imagining behavioral scripts on personal intentions', *Journal of Personality and Social Psychology*, 45(2): 293–305.

Anderson, N.H. (1968) 'Likableness ratings of 555 personality-trait words', *Journal of Personality and Social Psychology*, 9(3): 272–279.

Andrews, J.C. (1995) 'The effectiveness of alcohol warning labels: A review and extension', *American Behavioral Scientist*, 38: 622–632.

Argo, J.J. and Main, K.J. (2004) 'Meta-analyses of the effectiveness of warning labels', *Journal of Public Policy and Marketing*, 23(2): 193–208.

Bacon, F.T. (1979) 'Credibility of repeated testimonials: Memory for trivia', *Journal of Experimental Psychology: Human Learning and Memory*, 5(3), 241–252.

Barrett, D.W., Wosinska, W., Butner, J., et al. (2004) 'Individual differences in the motivation to comply across cultures: The impact of social obligation', *Personality and Individual Differences*, 37: 19–31.

Baumeister, R.F. and Heatherton, T.F. (1996) 'Self-regulation failure: An overview', *Psychological Inquiry*, 7: 1–15.

Blum, A. (1994) 'Paid counter-advertising: Proven strategy to combat tobacco use and promotion', *American Journal of Preventive Medicine*, 10(3): 8–10.

Brehm, J.W. (1966) *A Theory of Psychological Reactance*. New York: Academic Press.

Briñol, P., Rucker, D.D., Tormala, Z.L. and Petty, R.E. (2004) 'Individual differences in resistance to persuasion: The role of beliefs and meta-beliefs', in E.S. Knowles and J.A. Linn (eds), *Resistance and Persuasion*. Mahwah, NJ: Erlbaum, pp. 83–104.

Brownell, K.D. and Horgen, K.B. (2004) *Food Fight: The Inside Story of the Food Industry, America's Obesity Crisis, and What We Can Do about It*. New York: McGraw-Hill.

Brock, T.C. (1967) 'Communication discrepancy and intent to persuade as determinants of counterargument production', *Journal of Experimental Social Psychology*, 3: 296–309.

Bushman, B.J. and Stack, A.D. (1996) 'Forbidden fruit versus tainted fruit: Effects of warning labels on attraction to television violence', *Journal of Experimental Psychology: Applied*, 2: 207–226.

Byrne, D., Rasche, L. and Kelley, K. (1974) 'When "I like you" indicates disagreement', *Journal of Research in Personality*, 8: 207–217.

Campbell, M.C. (1995) 'When attention-getting advertising tactics elicit consumer inferences of manipulative intent: The importance of balancing benefits and investments', *Journal of Consumer Psychology*, 4: 225–254.

Casswell, S. and Zhang, J.F. (1998) 'Impact of liking for advertising and brand allegiance on drinking and alcohol-related aggression: A longitudinal study', *Addiction*, 93: 1209–1217.

Chassin, L., Presson, C.C. and Sherman, S.J. (1990) 'Social psychological contributors to the understanding and preventing of adolescent cigarette smoking', *Personality and Social Psychology Bulletin*, 16: 133–151.

Consumer Affairs (2007) http://www.consumeraffairs.com/news04/2007/01/ftc_weight_loss.html.

Cialdini, R.B. and Schroeder, D. (1976) 'Increasing compliance by legitimizing paltry contributions: When even a penny helps', *Journal of Personality and Social Psychology*, 34: 599–604.

Cialdini, R.B., Wosinska, W., Barrett, D., Butner, J. and Gornik-Durose, M. (1999) 'Compliance with a request in two cultures: The differential influence of social proof and commitment/consistency on collectivists and individualists', *Personality and Social Psychology Bulletin*, 25: 1242–1253.

Cialdini, R.B., Petrova, P.K. and Goldstein, N.J. (2004) 'The hidden costs of organizational dishonesty', *Sloan Management Review*, 45(3): 67–73.

Cialdini, R.B., Petrova, P.K., Demaine, L.J., Barrett, D.W., et al. (2011) 'The Poison Parasite Defense: A strategy for sapping a stronger opponent's persuasive strength', Working paper, available at: http://mba.tuck.dartmouth.edu/pages/faculty/petia.petrova/working_papers.html.

Clarkson, J.J., Tormala, Z.L., and Rucker, D.D. (2011) 'Cognitive and affective matching effects in persuasion: An amplification perspective', *Personality and Social Psychology Bulletin*, in press, published online on July 6, 2011.

Clary, E.G., Snyder, M., Ridge, R.D., et al. (1998) 'Understanding and assessing the motivations of volunteers: A functional approach', *Journal of Personality and Social Psychology*, 74: 1516–1530.

Cosmides, L. and Tooby, J. (1992) 'Cognitive adaptations for social exchange', in J.H. Barkow, L. Cosmides and J. Tooby (eds), *The Adapted Mind: Evolutionary Psychology and the*

Generation of Culture. New York: Oxford University Press, pp.163–228.

Darke, P.R. and Ritchie, R.B. (2007) 'The defensive consumer: Advertising deception, defensive processing, and distrust', *Journal of Marketing Research*, XLIV: 114–127.

Darke, P.R., Ashworth, L.T.A. and Ritchie, R.B. (2008) 'Damage from corrective advertising: Causes and cures', *Journal of Marketing*, 72(6): 81–97.

DeBono, K.G. (1987) 'Investigating the social adjustive and value expressive functions of attitudes: Implications for persuasion processes', *Journal of Personality and Social Psychology*, 52: 279–287.

Drachman, D., deCarufel, A. and Insko, C.A. (1978) 'The extra credit effect in interpersonal attraction', *Journal of Experimental Social Psychology*, 14: 458–467.

Dyer, R.F. and Kuehl, P.G. (1974) 'The corrective advertising remedy of the FTC: An experimental evaluation', *Journal of Marketing*, 48–54.

Eagly, A.H. and Chaiken, S. (1993) *The Psychology of Attitudes*. Fort Worth, TX: Harcourt Brace Jovanovich College Publishers.

Eagly, A.H., Wood, W. and Chaiken, S. (1978) 'Causal inferences about communicators and their effect on oppinion change', *Journal of Personality and Social Psychology*, 36(4): 424–435.

Eagly, A.H., Kulesa, P., Brannon, L.A., Shaw, K. and Hutson-Comeaux, S. (2000) 'Why counterattitudinal messages are as memorable as proattitudinal messages: The importance of active defense against attack', *Personality and Social Psychology Bulletin*, 26: 1392–1408.

Edwards, K. (1990) 'The interplay of affect and cognition in attitude formation and change', *Journal of Personality and Social Psychology*, 59(2): 202–216.

Edwards, K. and von Hippel, W. (1995) 'Hearts and minds: The priority of affective versus cognitive factors in person perception', *Personality and Social Psychology Bulletin*, 21: 996–1011.

Ellen, P.S., Mohr, L.A. and Webb, D.J. (2000) 'Charitable programs and the retailer: Do they mix?' *Journal of Retailing*, 76(3): 393–406.

Fabrigar, L.R. and Petty, R.E. (1999) 'The role of the affective and cognitive bases of attitudes in susceptibility to affectively and cognitively based persuasion', *Personality and Social Psychology Bulletin*, 25(3): 363–381.

Farrelly, M.C., Healton, C.G., Davis, K.C., et al. (2002) 'Getting to the truth: Evaluating national tobacco countermarketing campaigns', *American Journal of Public Health*, 92: 901–907.

Farrelly, M.C., Davis, K.C., Haviland, M.L., Messeri, P. and Healton, C. (2005) 'Evidence of a dose–response relationship between "truth" antismoking ads and youth smoking prevalence', *American Journal of Public Health*, 95: 425–431.

Fein, S., McCloskey, A.L. and Tomlinson, T.M. (1997) 'Can the jury disregard that information? The use of suspicion to reduce the prejudicial effects of pretrial publicity and inadmissible testimony', *Personality and Social Psychology Bulletin*, 23: 1215–1226.

Fennis, B.M., Janssen, L. and Vohs, K.D. (2009) 'Acts of benevolence: A limited-resource account of compliance with charitable requests', *Journal of Consumer Research*, 35: 906–924.

Fitzsimons, G.J. and Lehmann, D.R. (2004) 'Reactance to recommendations: When unsolicited advice yields contrary responses', *Marketing Science*, 23(1): 82–94.

Folta, S.C., Goldberg, J.P., Economos, C., Bell, R. and Meltzer, R. (2006) 'Food advertising targeted at school-age children: A content analysis', *Journal of Nutrition Education and Behavior*, 38: 244–248.

Geller, A.C., Colditz, G., Oliveria, S., et al. (2002) 'Use of sunscreen, sunburning rates, and tanning bed use among more than 10,000 US children and adolescents', *Pediatrics*, 109: 1009–1014.

Glanz, K., Saraiya, M. and Wechsler, H. (2002) 'Guidelines for school programs to prevent skin cancer', *MMWR*, 51(RR04): 1–16.

Goldman, L.K. and Glantz, S.A. (1998) 'Evaluation of antismoking advertising campaigns', *Journal of American Medical Association*, 279: 772–777.

Goldstein, N.J., Cialdini, R.B. and Griskevicius, V. (2008) 'A room with a viewpoint: Using social norms to motivate environmental conservation in hotels', *Journal of Consumer Research*, 35: 472–482.

Green, M.C. (2006) 'Narratives and cancer communication', *Journal of Communication*, 56: 163–183.

Green, M.C. and Brock, T.C. (2000) 'The role of transportation in the persuasiveness of public narratives', *Journal of Personality and Social Psychology*, 79: 701–721.

Greenwald, A.G. (1968) 'Cognitive learning, cognitive response to persuasion, and attitude change', in T.C. Brock, A.G. Greenwald, and T.M. Ostrom (eds), *Psychological Foundations of Attitudes*. San Diego, CA: Academic Press, pp. 147–170.

Greenwald, A.G. (1969) 'The open-mindedness of the counterattitudinal role player', *Journal of Experimental Social Psychology*, 5: 375–388.

Grube, J.W. and Wallack, L. (1994) 'Television beer advertising and drinking knowledge, beliefs, and intentions among school children', *American Journal of Public Health*, 84: 254–259.

Guéguen, N. and Pascual, A. (2000) 'Evocation of freedom and compliance: The "but you are free … " technique', *Current Research in Social Psychology*, 5: 64–270.

Guéguen, N., Joule, R.V., Fischer-Lokou, J., et al. (2011) 'I'm free but I'll comply with your request: Generalization and multidimensional effects of the "but you are free", *Journal of Applied Social Psychology*, in press.

Halford, J.C.G., Gillespie, J., Brown, V., Pontin, E.E. and Dovey, T.M. (2004) 'Effect of television advertisements for foods on food consumption in children', *Appetite*, 42: 221–225.

Halford, J.C.G., Boyland, M.J., Hughes, G., Oliveira, L.P. and Dovey, T.M. (2007) 'Beyond-brand effect of television (TV) food advertisements/commercials on caloric intake and food choice of 5–7-year-old children', *Appetite*, 49: 263–267.

Halford, J.C.G., Boyland, E.J., Hughes, G.M., et al.. (2008) 'Beyond-brand effect of television food advertisements on food choice in children: The effects of weight status', *Public Health Nutrition*, 11: 897–904.

Hankin, J.R., Sloan, J.J. and Sokol, R.J. (1998) 'The modest impact of the alcohol beverage warning label on drinking during pregnancy among a sample of African-American women', *Journal of Public Policy & Marketing*, 17: 61–69.

Harris, J.L., Bargh, J.A. and Brownell, K.D. (2009) 'Priming effects of television food advertising on eating behavior', *Health Psychology*, 28: 404–413.

Harrison, K. and Marske, A.L. (2005) 'Nutritional content of foods advertised during the television programs children watch most', *American Journal of Public Health*, 95: 1568–1574.

Hasher, L., Goldstein, D. and Toppino, T. (1977) 'Frequency and the conference of referential validity', *Journal of Verbal Learning and Verbal Behavior*, 16: 107–112.

Hastings, G., Stead, M., McDermott, L., et al. (2003) 'Review of research on the effects of food promotion to children' children'. Available at: www.foodstandards.gov.uk/multimedia/pdfs/foodpromotiontochildren1.pdf (accessed 20 February 2009).

Haugtvedt, C.P. and Petty, R.E. (1992) 'Personality and persuasion: Need for cognition moderates the persistence and resistance of attitude change', *Journal of Personality and Social Psychology*, 63: 308–319.

Hawkins, S.A. and Hoch, S.J. (1992) 'Low-involvement learning: Memory with evaluation', *Journal of Consumer Research*, 19: 212–225.

Healy, A.F. and Bourne, L.E., Jr (1995) *Acquisition and Retention of Knowledge and Skills*. Thousand Oaks, CA: Sage Publications.

Heilman, M.E. (1976) 'Oppositional behavior as a function of influence attempt intensity and retaliation threat', *Journal of Personality and Social Psychology*, 33: 574–578.

Hershey, J.C., Niederdeppe, J. and Evans, W.D. (2005) 'The theory of "truth": How counterindustry media campaigns affect smoking behavior among teens', *Health Psychology*, 24: 22–31.

Higgins, T.E. and Rholes, W.S. (1978) 'Saying is believing: Effects of message modification on memory and liking for the person described', *Journal of Experimental Social Psychology*, 14(4): 363–378.

Hovland, C.I. and Weiss, W. (1951) 'The influence of source credibility on communication effectiveness', *Public Opinion Quarterly*, 15: 635–650.

Hovland, C.I., Janis, I.L. and Kelley, H.H. (1953) *Communication and Persuasion: Psychological Studies of Opinion Change*. New Haven, CT: Yale University Press.

Jacks, J.Z., and O'Brien, M.E. (2004). 'Decreasing resistance by affirming the self', in E.S. Knowles and J.A. Linn (eds), *Resistance and Persuasion*. Mahwah, NJ: Lawrence Erlbaum Associates, pp. 235–257.

Jacoby, J., Nelson, M.C. and Hoyer, W.D. (1982) 'Corrective advertising and affirmative disclosure statements – their potential for confusing and misleading the consumer', *Journal of Marketing*, 46: 61–72.

Janis, I.L. and King, B.T. (1954) 'The influence of role playing on opinion change', *Journal of Abnormal and Social Psychology*, 49: 211–218.

Johar, G.V. (1996) 'Intended and unintended effects of corrective advertising on beliefs and evaluations: An exploratory analysis', *Journal of Consumer Psychology*, 5(3): 209.

Johar, G.V. and Simmons, C.J. (2000) 'The use of concurrent disclosures to correct invalid inferences', *Journal of Consumer Research*, 26(4): 307–222.

Jones, E.E. and Wortman, C. (1973) *Ingratiation: An Attributional Approach*. Morristown, NJ: General Learning Corp.

Keller, K.L. (1987) 'Memory factors in advertising: The effect of advertising retrieval cues on brand evaluations', *Journal of Consumer Research*, 14(December): 316–333.

Keller, K.L. (1991a) 'Memory factors in advertising: The effect of retrieval cues on brand evaluations', in A.A. Mitchell (ed), *Advertising Exposure, Memory, and Choice*. Mahwah, NJ: Erlbaum, pp. 11–48.

Keller, K.L. (1991b) 'Cue compatibility and framing in advertising', *Journal of Marketing Research*, 28(February), 42–57.

Keller, K.L. (1991c) 'Memory and evaluations in competitive advertising environments', *Journal of Consumer Research*, 17(March), 463–476.

Killeya, L.A. and Johnson, B.T. (1998) 'Experimental induction of biased systematic processing: The directed thought technique', *Personality and Social Psychology Bulletin*, 24: 17–33.

Klein, W.M.P. and Harris, P.R. (2009) 'Self-affirmation enhances attentional bias toward threatening components of a persuasive message', *Psychological Science*, 20(12):1463–1467.

Knowles, E.S. and Linn, J.A. (2004) 'Approach-avoidance model of persuasion: Alpha and omega strategies for change', in E.S. Knowles and J.A. Linn (eds), *Resistance to Persuasion*. London: Lawrence Erlbaum Associates, pp. 117–148.

Knowles, E.S. and Riner, D.D. (2007) 'Omega approaches to persuasion: Overcoming resistance', in A.R. Pratkanis (ed), *The Science of Social Influence*. New York: Psychology Press, pp. 83–114.

Kraut, R.E. (1973) 'Effects of social labeling on giving to charity', *Journal of Experimental Social Psychology*, 9(6): 551–562.

Lavine, H. and Snyder, M. (2000) 'Cognitive processes and the functional matching effect in persuasion: Studies of personality and political behavior', in G.R. Maio and J.M. Olson (eds), *Why we Evaluate: Functions of Attitudes*. Mahwah, NJ: Lawrence Erlbaum Associates, pp. 97–131.

Lutz, R.J. (1985) 'Affective and cognitive antecedents of attitude toward the ad: A conceptual framework', in L. Alwitt and A. Mitchell (eds), *Psychological Processes and Advertising Effects*. Hillsdale, NJ: Lawrence Erlbaum Associates, pp. 45–65.

McAlister, A.L., Ramirez, A.G., Galavotti, C. and Gallion, K.J. (1989) 'The relationship of perceived beer ad and PSA quality to high school students' alcohol-related beliefs and behaviors', in R.E. Rice and C.K. Atkin (eds), *Public Communication Campaigns.* Newbury Park, CA: Sage Publications, pp. 291–307.

McGuire, W.J. (1961) 'The effectiveness of supportive and refutational defenses in immunizing and restoring beliefs against persuasion', *Sociometry*, 24: 184–197.

McGuire, W. J. (1962) 'Persistence of the resistance to persuasion induced by various types of prior beliefs defenses', *Journal of Abnormal and Social Psychology*, 64: 241–248.

McGuire, W.J. (1964) 'Inducing resistance to persuasion: Some contemporary approaches', in L. Berkowitz (ed.), *Advances in Experimental Social Psychology.* San Diego, CA: Academic Press, 1: 191–229.

McGuire, W.J. and Papageorgis, D. (1962) 'Effectiveness of forewarning in developing resistance to persuasion', *Public Opinion Quarterly*, 26: 24–34.

MacKenzie, S.B. and Lutz, R.J. (1989) 'An empirical examination of the structural antecedents of attitude toward the ad in an advertising pretesting context', *Journal of Marketing*, 53: 48–65.

Mandel, N., Petrova, P.K. and Cialdini, R.B. (2006) 'Images of success and the preference for luxury brands', *Journal of Consumer Psychology*, 16: 57–69.

Mazis, M.B., Ringold, D.J., Perry, E.S. and Denman, D.W. (1992) 'Perceived attractiveness of models in cigarette advertisement', *Journal of Marketing*, 56(January): 22–37.

Mills, J. and Jellison, J.M. (1967) 'Effect on opinion change of how desirable the communication is to the audience the communicator addressed', *Journal of Personality and Social Psychology*, 56: 82–92.

Murray, B. (2001) 'Fast-food culture serves up super-size Americans', *American Psychological Association Monitor*, December: 33–34.

Obermiller, C. and Spangenberg, E.R. (1998) 'Development of a scale to measure consumer skepticism toward advertising', *Journal of Consumer Psychology*, 7(2): 159–186.

Osterhouse, R.A. and Brock, T.C. (1970) 'Distraction increases yielding to propaganda by inhibiting counterarguing', *Journal of Personality and Social Psychology*, 15: 344–358.

Pechmann, C. and Knight, S.J. (2002) 'An experimental investigation of the joint effects of advertising and peers on adolescents' beliefs and Intentions about cigarette consumption', *Journal of Consumer Research*, 29(June): 5–19.

Pechmann, C. and Reibling, E.T. (2000) 'Anti-smoking advertising campaigns targeting youth: Case studies from USA and Canada', *Tobacco Control*, 9: 18–31.

Pechmann, C. and Shih, C.F. (1999) 'Smoking scenes in movies and antismoking advertisements before movies: Effects on youth', *Journal of Marketing*, 63: 1–13.

Petrova, P.K. (2006) 'Fluency effects: New domains and consequences for persuasion'. Doctoral dissertation, Arizona State University.

Petrova, P.K. and Cialdini, R.B. (2005) 'Fluency of consumption imagery and the backfire effects of imagery appeals', *Journal of Consumer Research*, 32(December): 442–452.

Petrova, P.K. and Cialdini, R.B. (2008) 'Evoking the imagination as a strategy of influence', in C. Haugtvedt, P. Herr and F. Kardes (eds), *Handbook of Consumer Psychology.* Mahwah, NJ: Lawrence Earlbaum Associates, pp. 505–525

Petrova, P.K., Cialdini, R.B., Barrett, D., Goldstein N. and Maner J. (2006) 'Effective counter persuasion: Creating lasting resistance to a stronger opponent', *Advances in Consumer Research,* 33: 276.

Petrova, P.K., Cialdini, R.B., Goldstein, N.J. and Griskevicius, V. (2007a) 'Protecting consumers from harmful advertising: What constitutes an effective counter claim? Paper presented at the Transformative Consumer Research Conference, Hanover, NH.

Petrova, P.K., Cialdini, R.B. and Sills, S.J. (2007b) 'Consistency-based compliance across cultures', *Journal of Experimental Social Psychology*, 43: 104–111.

Petrova, P.K., Cialdini, R.B., Goldstein, N.J. and Griskevicius, V. (2011a) 'Protecting consumers from harmful advertising'. Manuscript submitted for publication. Available at http://www.linkedin.com/in/petiapetrova

Petrova, P.K., Cialdini, R.B. and Goldstein, N.J. (2011b) 'Creating resistance to persisting persuasive attempts', Working paper. Hanover, NH: Tuck School of Business at Dartmouth.

Petrova, P.K., Schwarz, N. and Song, H. (2011c) 'Fluency and social influence: Lessons from judgment and decision-making', in D. Kenrick, N. Goldstein and S. Braver (eds), *Six Degrees of Social Influence: Science, Application, and the Psychology of Robert Cialdini.* Oxford, NY: Oxford University Press, forthcoming.

Petrova, P.K., Goukens, C. and Cialdini, R.B. (2011d) 'Keep on talking: A dual process theory of fluency', Working paper. Hanover, NH: Tuck School of Business at Dartmouth.

Petty, R.E. and Cacioppo, J.T. (1986*) Communication and Persuasion: Central and Peripheral Routes to Attitude Change.* New York: Springer-Verlag.

Petty, R.E. and Wegener, D.T. (1998) 'Attitude change', in D.T. Gilbert, S.T. Fiske and G. Lindzey (eds), *The Handbook of Social Psychology*, 4th edn. New York: McGraw-Hill, pp. 323–390.

Petty, R.E., Wells, G.L. and Brock, T.C. (1976) 'Distraction can enhance or reduce yielding to propaganda: Thought disruption versus effort justification', *Journal of Personality and Social Psychology*, 34: 874–884.

Petty, R.E., Cacioppo, J.T. and Goldman, R. (1981) 'Personal involvement as a determinant of argument-based persuasion', *Journal of Personality and Social Psychology*, 41: 847–855.

Pham, M.T. and Muthukrishnan, A. (2002) 'Search and alignment in judgment revision: Implications for brand positioning', *Journal of Marketing Research*, 39: 18–30.

Priester, R.J. and Petty, R.E. (1995) 'Source attributions and persuasion: Perceived honesty as a determinant of message scrutiny', *Personality and Social Psychology Bulletin*, 21(6): 637–654.

Rhodes, N. and Wood, W. (1992) 'Self-esteem and intelligence and affect influenceability: The mediating role of message reception', *Psychological Bulletin*, 111: 156–171.

Romer, D. and Jamieson, R. (2001) 'Advertising, smoker imagery, and the diffusion of smoking behavior', in P. Slovic (ed), *Smoking: Risk, Perception and Policy*. Thousand Oaks, CA: Sage Publications, pp. 127–155.

Romero, A.A., Agnew, C.R. and Insko, C.A. (1996) 'The cognitive mediation hypothesis revisited', *Personality and Social Psychology Bulletin*, 22: 651–665.

Rothbart, M. and Park, B. (1986) 'On the confirmatory and disconfirmatory of trait concepts', *Personality and Social Psychology Bulletin*, 50: 13–142.

Sagarin, B.J., Cialdini, R.B., Rice, W.E. and Serna, S.B. (2002) 'Dispelling the illusion of invulnerability: The motivations and mechanisms of resistance to persuasion', *Journal of Personality and Social Psychology*, 83: 526–541.

Sanderson, C.A. and Cantor, N. (1995) 'Social dating goals in late adolescence: Implications for safer sexual activity', *Journal of Personality and Social Psychology*, 68: 1121–1134.

Schwarz, N., Strack, F., Bless, H., et al. (1991) 'Ease of retrieval as information: Another look at the availability heuristic', *Journal of Personality and Social Psychology*, 61: 195–202.

Schwarz, N., Sanna, L., Skurnik, I. and Yoon, C. (2007) 'Metacognitive experiences and the intricacies of setting people straight: Implications for debiasing and public information campaigns', *Advances in Experimental Social Psychology*, 39: 127–161.

Shavitt, S. (1990) 'The role of attitude objects in attitude functions', *Journal of Experimental Social Psychology*, 26: 124–148.

Sherman, D.A.K., Nelson, L.D. and Steele, C.M. (2000) 'Do messages about health risks threaten the self? Increasing the acceptance of threatening health messages via self-affirmation', *Personality and Social Psychology Bulletin*, 26: 1046–1058.

Simonich, W.I. (1991) *Government Antismoking Policies*, New York: Peter Lang.

Slater, M.D. and Rouner, D. (1996) 'Value-affirmative and value-protective processing of alcohol education messages that include statistical evidence or anecdotes', *Communication Research*, 23: 210–235.

Skurnik, I., Yoon, C., Park, D.C. and Schwarz, N. (2005) 'How warnings about false claims become recommendations', *Journal of Consumer Research*, 31: 713–724.

Snyder, M., Clary, E.G. and Stukas, A.A. (2000) 'The functional approach to volunteerism', in G. R. Maio and J.M. Olson (eds), *Why We Evaluate: Functions of Attitudes*. Hillsdale, NJ: Lawrence Erlbaum Associates, pp. 365–394.

Strenta, A. and DeJong, W. (1981) 'The effect of a prosocial label on helping behavior', *Social Psychology Quarterly*, 44(2): 142–147.

Thompson, D.V., Hamilton, R.W. and Petrova, P.K. (2009) 'When mental simulation hinders behavior: The effects of process-oriented thinking on decision difficulty and performance', *Journal of Consumer Research*, 36(December): 562–574.

Trafimow, D. (2001) 'The effects of trait type and situation type on the generalization of trait expectancies across situations', *Personality and Social Psychology Bulletin*, 27: 1463–1468.

Tulving, E. (1983) *Elements of Episodic Memory*. New York: Oxford University Press

Tulving, E. and Schacter, D.L. (1990) 'Priming and human memory systems', *Science*, 247: 301–306.

Tulving, E. and Thompson, D.M. (1973) 'Encoding specificity and retrieval processes in episodic memory', *Psychological Review*, 80: 352–373.

Volkow, N.D. (2006) 'Efforts of the National Institute on Drug Abuse to prevent and treat prescription drug abuse – testimony before the Subcommittee on Criminal Justice, Drug Policy, and Human Resources Committee on Government Reform', *United States House of Representatives*, July 23. Available at: http://www.drugabuse.gov/Testimony/7-26-06Testimony.html [accessed 6 February 2007].

Warner, K.E. (1981) 'Cigarette smoking in the 1970's: The impact of the anti-smoking campaign on consumption', *Science*, 224: 729–731.

Westerdahl, J., Ingvar, C., Masback, A., Jonsson, N. and Olsson, H. (2000) 'Risk of cutaneous malignant melanoma in relation to use of tanning beds: Further evidence for UV-A carcinogenicity', *British Journal of Cancer*, 82: 1593–1599.

Wheeler, S.C., Briñol, P. and Hermann, A.D. (2007) 'Resistance to persuasion as self-regulation: Ego-depletion and its effects on attitude change processes', *Journal of Experimental Social Psychology*, 43: 150–156.

Winter, P.L., Sagarin, B.J., Rhoads, K., Burrett, D.W., and Cialdini, R.B. (2000) 'Persuading to encourage or discourage: Perceived effectiveness of prescriptive proscriptive messages', *Environmental Management*, 26: 589–594.

Worchel, S., Arnold, S.E. and Baker, M. (1975) 'The effect of censorship on attitude change: The influence of censor and communicator characteristics', *Journal of Applied Social Psychology*, 222–239.

World Health Organization (2003) Artificial tanning sunbeds: Risks and guidance. Retrieved 17 October, 2005, from http://www.who.int/uv/publications/sunbedpubl/en.

World Health Organization (2005) The World Health Organization recommends that no person under 18 should use a sunbed. Retrieved 18 July, 2005, from http://www.who.int/mediacentre/news/notes/2005/np97/en/

Wosinska, W., Cialdini, R.B., Petrova, P.K., et al. (2009) 'Resistance to deficient organizational authority: The impact of culture and connectedness at the workplace', *Journal of Applied Social Psychology*, 39(4): 834–851.

Wyllie, A., Zhang, J.F. and Caswell, S. (1998) 'Responses to televised alcohol advertisements associated with drinking behavior of 10–17-year-olds', *Addiction,* 93: 361–71.

Zajonc, R.B. (1968) 'Attitudinal effects of mere exposure', *Journal of Personality and Social Psychology: Monograph Supplement,* 9: 1–27.

Zajonc, R.B. (1980) 'Feeling and thinking: Preferences need no inference', *American Psychologist,* 35: 151–175.

Marketing Planning

8. SEGMENTATION AND TARGETING – L. DONER LOTENBERG, C. SCHECHTER AND J. STRAND

This chapter on audience segmentation reviews the three-step process and methods used: (1) to divide a market into groups based on shared criteria; (2) to select one or more groups to give highest priority in planning and (3) to develop a product positioning and marketing plan for satisfying their needs and wants. The chapter begins with a discussion of the reasons segmentation is an essential component of social marketing and a brief historical overview of the development of segmentation in marketing. Case studies are used to illustrate an overview of segmentation basis variables, methods for identifying segments and criteria for selecting segments to target. The chapter also offers advice for overcoming organizational barriers to segmentation that so often prevent social marketers from allocating ample time and resources to this important element in the social marketing process.

9. COMPETITION AND POSITIONING – G. NOBLE AND D.Z. BASIL

A framework for understanding competition and positioning in social marketing is presented by Noble and Basil. Competitive analysis is an essential step in the development of a successful social marketing intervention; however, the variety of sources and the range of different forms it takes can make competition difficult to identify compared with its identification within commercial marketing. Using a commercial marketing technique of classifying levels of competitive analysis, the authors apply their competition matrix to Andreasen's four levels of competition, and, by way of illustration, apply it to childhood obesity and the anti-drink driving 'Road Crew' intervention. Noble and Basil propose that their matrix would also work with another commercial marketing technique of co-opetition, where social marketers would also consider complementors. Finally, they discuss positioning strategies, a practice social marketers should use to ensure their target audience readily and positively distinguishes their intervention from its competitors.

10. THE SOCIAL MARKETING MIX: A CRITICAL REVIEW– K. PEATTIE AND S. PEATTIE

The success of social marketing is based on the strategy of borrowing and applying commercial marketing techniques and philosophies, the 4Ps marketing mix being a central element. The authors reflect on whether it is wise to adopt a concept that is subject to considerable criticism without a critical re-evaluation. This chapter reviews the commercial and social marketing critiques of the marketing mix and notes that the translation of the concepts from commercial to social marketing has been extremely literal, with time and effort expended to 'force fit' ideas and practices. They propose reformulating the traditional marketing mix to one based around social marketing's particular challenges and one that reflects emerging relationships and service-based marketing concepts.

11. COMMUNICATIONS IN SOCIAL MARKETING – D.L. ALDEN, M.D. BASIL AND S. DESHPANDE

The authors put forward their framework of integrated social marketing communications (ISMC) for social marketers to plan their communications strategy. Its principles are to ensure the focus of the communication is pro-social behavior change and actions, and not to focus on information provision; to keep the brand promise consistent across the communication channels and to integrate the promotion element of the 4Ps marketing mix with the other three elements. The authors review the academic and applied literature for social marketing communications in developed and developing countries and note a number of knowledge gaps and questions for future research.

12. NEW MEDIA IN SOCIAL MARKETING – D. MAYS, J.B. WEAVER III AND J.M. BERNHARDT

The authors describe how new media have changed the manner in which consumers engage with information and communicate with others. They discuss strategies for incorporating new media into social marketing interventions, and speculate about the role new media and technologies can play in future social marketing activities. They warn us that, despite the tremendous potential new media offers social marketers for interacting with consumers, we should proceed cautiously, seeking answers to both strategic and logistical questions about specific segments of consumers' levels of acceptance, trust and mastery.

8

Segmentation and Targeting

Lynne Doner Lotenberg, Carol Schechter
and John Strand

OVERVIEW

Segmentation and targeting are essential components of social marketing; they are the processes
used to identify groups with similar needs or
wants and develop and deliver offerings that provide something members of the group value.
Conducting a segmentation study and then using
the results is a three-step process.

1. Segmentation: dividing a market or audience into
   groups based on one or more criteria.
2. Targeting: determining which of those groups to
   target.
3. Developing product positioning and marketing
   strategies tailored to the specific needs and
   wants of each target group.

This process can be used with any market or
audience – members of the public, professionals,
policymakers or organizations. The goal is to
identify segments whose members are similar to
each other and distinct from other groups in how
they would respond to the social marketing program. Segments might differ in the costs and
benefits they associate with a behavior; their
wants, needs and values; how or where they can
be reached or the communication approaches that
will reach them best.

WHY SEGMENT?

When reflecting on the nature of markets, consumer behavior and competitive activities, it is
obvious that no product or service appeals to all
consumers and even those who purchase the same
product may do so for diverse reasons (Wind and
Bell, 2008: 222).

Similarly, the goal of social marketing is to
develop and deliver offerings that appeal to the
individuals whose behavior we would like to
change. Yet each person has a unique constellation
of beliefs, values, resources and restrictions that
affect what they want, what they need and what
they do. It is not possible to design an offering that
reaches appeals to, and can be accessed by every
person equally.

With few exceptions, organizations do not have
the resources to design a custom offering for each
individual. By using systematic segmentation and
targeting, we can ensure offerings are designed to
reach and appeal to a large group of individuals
willing or able to make the desired behavior
change. In addition, researchers have found
that market segmentation encourages consumer
orientation by keeping organizations closely
in touch with their consumers, 'ensuring more
efficient resource allocation and resulting in

programs which are better attuned to customer needs' (Dibb and Simkin, 2009, p. 1; citing Albert, 2003; Beane and Ennis, 1987; Freytag and Clarke, 2001). Well-done segmentation and targeting strengthens social change efforts by enabling limited resources to achieve the greatest amount of change.

HISTORY

The concept of segmenting markets was first introduced by Smith in 1956, who wrote, 'Market segmentation involves viewing a heterogeneous market as a number of smaller homogeneous markets, in response to differing preferences, attributable to the desires of customers for more precise satisfactions of their varying wants.' Segmentation has been viewed as a key marketing concept since the early 1960s and a significant portion of the marketing research literature focuses on it (Wind and Bell, 2008). Nonetheless, use of segmentation has been far from universal in commercial, non-profit or social marketing practice.

A reader new to the literature could easily conclude that segmentation's primary practical use is to develop advertising and other communications. In a 2006 article, Yankelovich and Meer lamented that 'market segmentation has become narrowly focused on the needs of advertising' and other authors have noted that segmentation is neglected by many companies (see Weinstein, 2004; Wind and Bell, 2008). In the social sector, many of the frameworks and review articles addressing segmentation are specific to health communication (see, e.g., Slater, 1996; Sutton et al., 1995). However, authors in the commercial sector have noted that an increasing number of companies and organizations are employing segmentation approaches (Dibb and Simkin, 2009; Weinstein, 2004; Wind and Bell, 2008). Similarly, a cursory review of the literature shows an increasing number of papers discussing segmentation for social marketing programs – a welcome development, since, historically, government agencies, in particular, were resistant to segmentation and targeting because they believed their mandate was to reach 'everyone.' However, some may be embracing segmentation a bit too much: some programs oversegment or create unnecessary segments by identifying differentiating variables and segmenting on them even though they do not necessarily impact behavior.

An overview of the development of segmentation as a marketing approach is provided by Yankelovich and Meer (2006). They note that the earliest segmentation emphasized grouping individuals on demographic traits, such as age, sex, education levels and income. One common approach was to include in advertising a person whom the target group resembled or wished they did. Another approach was to emphasize emotional rather than functional benefits that the product offered. In 1964, Daniel Yankelovich suggested broadening the use of segmentation, looking at traits such as values, tastes and preferences which were more likely to influence purchases and using segmentation to inform product innovation, pricing and choice of distribution channels in addition to advertising. By the 1970s, social scientists began to use attitudinal indicators for segmentation, and in 1978, the Values and Lifestyle (VALS) program, a commercial research service developed by the Stanford Research Institute, launched the era of psychographic segmentation. VALS classified individuals into one of nine enduring psychological types and was widely used by consumer product companies and advertising agencies.

Wind and Bell (2008) outline a number of recent developments in segmentation, including (1) advances in database marketing and innovative distribution approaches as a result of the revolution in information technology and strategy; (2) an internet-fueled expansion of segmentation methods and the ability to implement market segmentation research more effectively and (3) a subtle shift in the bases of segmentation from a historical emphasis on demographics and other characteristics, preferences, usage rates, etc., to a contemplation of customer lifetime value (CLV) and explicit calculation of CLV. They suggest Gupta and Lehmann (2003) as a source for the latter.

The use of international segmentation has also increased as technological developments have led to increased globalization (Steenkamp and Ter Hofstede, 2002). In the past it was common for international organizations to use *multi-domestic strategies*, in effect treating each country as a separate market by tailoring products for local needs and preferences and developing distinct advertising, pricing and distribution strategies. Segmentation was conducted within each country. Over time, national borders have become less important for many industries, and organizations have moved toward *global* or *pan-regional* strategies. Segmentation can be used to identify individuals in different countries that have more in common with each other than with other people in the same country. In such situations, using similar marketing strategies in multiple countries leads to lower costs for production, promotion and distribution, while still delivering offerings that are responsive to consumer needs and wants. Case study 3 on a multi-country anti-smoking campaign provides an example.

SEGMENTATION

Conducting a segmentation study involves two critical decisions: developing the basis for the segmentation – that is, deciding what variables people will be segmented on – and determining the segmentation method to be used. Once the segmentation has been conducted, resulting segments are then profiled.

Develop basis for segmentation

People or organizations can be grouped in many ways. A good segmentation will:

- Identify conceptually distinct groups that respond in different ways to different elements of the marketing mix.
- Be mutually exclusive so that each unit of analysis – person, household, organization, etc. – will fit into only one segment.
- Be measurable, since certain potential segmentation variables can be difficult to measure as a practical matter.
- Result in segments that can be – and will be – used, as the marketing literature notes that many segmentations fail to be implemented for reasons such as segmentation objectives that were inconsistent with the organization's overall strategy, insufficient operational capabilities to implement the segmentation results, and management discomfort with segments that do not make sense to them (Sausen et al., 2005; Wind, 1978; Yankelovich and Meer, 2006).

Considering a number of factors can help determine which variables will provide the most useful segmentation.

Type of decision(s) to be made using the segmentation results
Segmentation objectives can include identification of new target markets, product-related decisions (e.g., positioning, price, design, communication), retaining customers, increasing customer satisfaction or value, determining appropriate resource allocations, clearer identification of market opportunities and better design of marketing programs (Dibb, 1998; Dibb and Simkin, 2001; Kotler, 2002; Meadows and Dibb, 1998; Sausen et al., 2005; Wind, 1978). The decisions that will be made drive both the type of information needed and the group of people from which it should come (Wind and Bell, 2008; Yankelovich and Meer, 2006). For example, consider the following goals and corresponding information needs:

- New product concepts or introductions: purchase or usage data from individuals who use related products or engage in related behaviors that satisfy similar needs or wants.
- Pricing decisions: price sensitivity (alone or in conjunction with usage patterns).
- Promotion: benefits sought, media usage, psychographic/lifestyle information from those who engage in the behavior of interest.
- Distribution: benefits sought in location; convenience.

Type of behavior to be changed and its importance to the market
Writing about customer purchases, Yankelovich and Meer (2006) recommend varying what the segmentation should try to find out based on the gravity of the decision. For example, for shallow – or low-involvement – decisions, such as choosing relatively inexpensive consumer products (i.e., a brand of soft drink), segmentation can examine factors such as buying and usage behavior, willingness to pay a small premium for higher quality and degree of brand loyalty. For middle-of-the-spectrum decisions, such as visiting a clinic about a medical condition or switching car brands, segmentation should try to identify whether the consumers are do-it-yourself or do-it-for-me types, their needs and their social status, self-image and lifestyle. For deep – or high-involvement – decisions, such as choosing a medical treatment or deciding where to live, segmentation should explore their core values and beliefs relating to the decision.

Segmentation variables
Some common bases of segmentation are now described.

Behavioral. Individuals are divided based on their engagement in or response to a behavior. This is often the best starting point for segmentation (Kotler and Armstrong, 2004). Behavioral segmentations can take a number of forms; one of the simplest is to divide individuals into those who perform the behavior and those who do not. However, in many instances, more groupings are useful. For example, the Texas WIC program (see Case Study 1) divided pregnant mothers into those who had never used WIC, those who had previously used it but did not currently do so and those who currently used it. Many commercial marketers divide users into heavy, medium, light and non-users. At other times, behavioral segmentation is appropriate because different groups need to (or will be willing to) take different actions.

For example, for a campaign to reduce nutrient pollution flowing into the Chesapeake Bay, the largest estuary in the United States, The Chesapeake Bay Program segmented homeowners living in the Washington, DC area into those who do their own yard work (84%) and those who hire a yard service (16%). The former were asked to fertilize their lawns in the fall rather than the spring; the latter, to hire an environmentally responsible lawn service. A survey was conducted to determine the size of the segments and measure attitudes and behaviors related to environmental concern and lawn care (Landers et al., 2006).

Demographics and other personal characteristics. Divisions are by age, sex, education, ethnicity/race, income, marital status, occupation, presence of children, etc. This is a very common approach to segmentation, yet demographic characteristics are often considered poor segmentation variables, if used alone, because in many instances they do not predict behavior (Wind and Bell, 2008; Yankelovich and Meer, 2006). For some social marketing efforts addressing specific health topics, an initial demographic segmentation is appropriate. For the US CDC's (Centers for Disease Control and Prevention's) annual influenza campaign 'the Flu Ends with U,' initial segmentation for 2010–2011 started with four priority groups: mothers of children and adolescents (0–18 years); young adults 19–24 years of age; people 25–49 years of age living with asthma and/or diabetes (representing the most prevalent chronic health conditions among persons with severe H1N1 illness) and adults 65–75 years of age. Extensive formative research was conducted with each of these groups to understand their respective knowledge, attitudes and behaviors regarding vaccines (AED, 2010). Program planners then crafted separate but complementary media, marketing and advertising strategies to inspire action. The result was a suite of creative print, online and broadcast materials tailored to specific audiences and outlets, to encourage vaccination by educating them about CDC's clinical vaccination recommendations and to dispel mistrust and misperceptions. These materials were disseminated through an extensive network of national partners, and media outreach tools include matte articles, educational roundtables, radio media tours and public service announcements.

Psychographics. Divisions are by social status, lifestyle or attitudes. Psychographic segmentations can provide insights into the lifestyles, attitudes, self-image and aspirations of people who use a particular product or engage in a particular behavior; as a result, this type of segmentation is considered useful for developing communication campaigns, brand reinforcement and positioning, but not useful for predicting product purchases, product development or pricing (Yankelovich and Meer, 2006) – or health behaviors (Donovan and Henley, 2003). One challenge is that the cluster analysis used to create psychographic segments results in overlap across segments; as Donovan and Henley note,

> 70 per cent of Cluster A might agree with the statement 'I prefer visiting natural wilderness areas to man-made entertainments such as SeaWorld' versus 35 per cent of Cluster B agreeing with the statement – a statistically significant difference. Nevertheless, 35 per cent of Cluster B do share this characteristic with Cluster A (2003: 214).

An example of a combined psychographic and behavioral segmentation strategy is provided in Case Study 2.

Geographic. Organizations may choose to operate in some locales but not others, or to customize offerings to meet local needs and preferences (e.g., consumer product companies tailor their flavorings to regional tastes) or environmental constraints (Kotler and Armstrong, 2004, provide examples of hotel chains creating smaller properties in less-populated markets and retailers creating smaller footprint stores in urban centers). One example of using geographic segmentation in social marketing is the USAID NetMark project in Ethiopia. To help control malaria, the government of Ethiopia distributed free insecticide-treated nets (ITNs) to households. However, levels of ITN awareness and use were low among free-net beneficiaries, the majority of whom resided in rural and peri-urban settings where mass media was not readily available. The NetMark project segmented the market, choosing to focus on rural and peri-urban settings, and then used communication tactics appropriate to these settings. The project chose specific rural and peri-urban areas and then collaborated with community mobilizers and government health extension workers to work through community-based organizations and carry out door-to-door campaigns in these areas. NetMark also used a media-equipped van to reach community-based organizations with educational films about malaria (USAID/AED, 2007).

Benefits sought. Divisions are based on the benefits people associate with a behavior, good or service. For example, Stead and colleagues (1997) found that four different subgroups associated different benefits with physical activity: competing against an opponent; bettering their own personal best (e.g., in running or swimming); improving their body image and getting out to meet people or maintain friendships. For the Chesapeake Bay Program campaign mentioned above, formative research identified that benefits of environmental improvement were not as salient as immediate personal rewards, and program planners decided to emphasize personal benefit with a humorous approach. The slogan of the multimedia campaign became 'Save the Crabs – then Eat 'Em.' The program included partnerships with local lawn care companies, restaurants and well-known chefs, along with ads and other collateral, including a consumer website. In spite of a small budget, a post-intervention survey showed increased awareness of lawn care behaviors that contribute to Bay pollution, and decreased intent to fertilize in the spring.

Using theories and models

Theories and models of behavior and behavior change can make segmentation more efficient by helping us identify the factors that influence behavior change and systematically think through individuals' processes of behavior change. A review of the many theories and models of value to social marketers is beyond the scope of this chapter; however, the work of Fishbein and colleagues can be used as a starting point. They conducted a thorough review of five theories and models that contain 'almost all of the variables that have been utilized in attempts to understand and change a wide variety of human behaviors' (2001: 4): the health belief model, social cognitive theory, the theory of reasoned action, the theory of self-regulation and self-control and the theory of subjective culture and interpersonal relationships. They identified eight variables that 'appeared to account for most of the variance in any given deliberate behavior' (2001: 4), three of which were shown to be necessary and sufficient to produce any behavior: 'a person must have a strong *positive intention* to perform the behavior in question; the individual must have the *skills necessary* to carry out the behavior and *the environment must provide a context of opportunity, or be free from constraints*, such that the behavior can occur' (Fishbein, et al., 2001:5; *italics* added). Consideration of these variables is a good first step for determining an appropriate segmentation basis; Lotenberg (2010) suggests using them to formulate three questions which we have adapted to reflect their use for segmentation:

1. Does the population of interest divide into groups based on **opportunity** to engage in the desired behavior?

2. Does the population of interest divide into groups based on **motivation** to engage in the desired behavior?
3. Does the population of interest divide into groups based on the **ability** to engage in the desired behavior?

Reflecting on the questions in this order will ensure that opportunity is assessed first. Lotenberg (2010) notes that this is critical because it *must* be present for the behavior to occur yet many social marketing programs do not have the ability to provide opportunity (or managers do not believe that they do) and instead skip to addressing motivation or ability.

If segmenting by motivation appears to be worth pursuing, the remaining five variables identified by Fishbein and colleagues (2001) often influence an individual's intent to perform a behavior: social (normative) pressure; a belief that the advantages of performing the behavior outweigh the disadvantages; the degree to which a behavior is consistent with one's self-image; emotional reactions to the behavior (whether taking the action would feel good or bad) and self-efficacy (belief that one has the capability to take the action). These behavioral determinants can be appropriate segmentation bases. For example, in Case study 2, which describes segmenting parents, self-efficacy was one of the variables on which segments differed. When developing segmentations, it also important to consider that an individual's opportunity, motivation and ability are not always constant; they can vary across situations and internal states. Valid and useful segmentations will therefore divide groups based on the factors that will influence behavior in the desired setting. For example, a person might weigh advantages and disadvantages of specific foods differently when making lunch at home, when ordering at a fast-food drive-thru while on the way to a meeting and when going to a nice restaurant for a special celebration. Similarly, a new mother may have the skills to breastfeed at home, but may need to develop self-advocacy or other skills to successfully transfer this behavior to the workplace (Lotenberg, 2010).

A specific model of behavior often used as a segmentation basis in social marketing is the transtheoretical model of stages of change (Prochaska et al., 2002). It is valuable because it provides a simple, validated list of questions to use to divide people into different stages (precontemplation, contemplation, preparation, action and confirmation/maintenance) and gives guidance on intervention strategies for different stages (e.g., emphasizing benefits in the early stages and costs in the later ones). Hastings (2008) points out that some caution should be exercised in applying the model, in that it has been recognized that individuals do not necessarily move in a linear fashion through each stage and may not consciously move through each phase. Later versions of the model take note of these issues (Andreasen, 1995; Hastings, 2008).

Methods of segmentation

A number of methodologies can be used to conduct segmentation research; using a combination of methods often provides the most useful result. The case studies presented in this chapter highlight some common practices, such as starting with a survey and then augmenting the findings with qualitative research to better explore the benefits and barriers to individuals associated with the desired behavior, as was done for the Texas WIC program. When quantitative data analysis is used, methods can range from simple (creating segments based on one variable, such as smoking status or program participation) to complex multivariate approaches such as the CHAID and cluster analysis approaches discussed in the case studies.

Many social marketing programs start by identifying existing studies that include data on the behaviors of interest, such as large government surveys. These studies often also include demo-

---

Case Study 1   Using Segmentation to Increase Enrollment in a Public Health Program

In the United States, the Special Supplemental Nutrition Program for Women, Infants and Children (WIC) provides nutrition education, supplementary nutritious foods, and referrals to appropriate health and social services. Women who are pregnant, who have had a baby in the past six months or who are breastfeeding an infant less than one year, as well as infants and children less than 5 years old, are eligible for WIC if they live in households with incomes at or below 185% of the US federal poverty level and are at nutritional risk.

The Texas WIC program used segmentation and targeting to develop a social marketing plan to increase WIC enrollment. The process began with a survey of 15,000 pregnant Medicaid (government-provided health insurance for low-income residents) recipients who were automatically income-eligible for WIC. The 28-item mail survey was developed, translated into Spanish, and pretested in urban and rural settings. Of the 2944 respondents, 64.6% were 'current' WIC participants ($n = 1842$), 5.5% were 'previous' participants ($n = 156$) and 28.2% had 'never' enrolled in WIC ($n = 852$).

Survey data were analyzed using frequency distribution, cross tabulations and chi-square automatic interaction detection (CHAID). CHAID analyses were used to compare the relationship between multiple independent variables (sociodemographic characteristics) and the dependent variable of WIC enrollment. CHAID creates a 'tree' that segments the respondents into distinct subgroups and identifies the subgroups with the highest and lowest proportion of respondents exhibiting the dependent variable. CHAID analysis identified the segment with the highest proportion of women not participating in WIC (49.4%): women who were non-Hispanic white, not married, and not receiving food stamps (a government program providing food assistance to low-income families; income criteria are stricter than for WIC). Similarly, CHAID identified a segment with the lowest proportion of currently enrolled WIC participants: women who were non-Hispanic white; married, divorced, separated or widowed and not receiving food stamps.

The survey and follow-up focus groups (5; $n = 38$) and telephone interviews ($n = 81$) with never-enrolled women provided insight into why women did not enroll. Major reasons included confusion about eligibility, reluctance to accept government assistance for fear of stigmatization and embarrassment; valuing self-sufficiency; fearing loss of dignity by accepting free food and expectations of disrespectful treatment by WIC staff and grocery cashiers.

Research findings were used to develop a comprehensive social marketing plan which re-positioned WIC as a temporary nutrition-education and health-referral program in which families can maintain their pride and self-esteem rather than a food-assistance program. Audience segmentation results were used to determine regions within the state and specific media outlets where advertising should be placed; advertisements addressed common misperceptions about WIC eligibility and embarrassment about accepting government assistance. To address service delivery problems, the plan recommended methods to decrease waiting times, customer service training programs for WIC staff and grocery store cashiers, and ongoing collection of program enrollment and satisfaction data, introduction of a peer–buddy system and improved nutrition education materials and activities.

Source: Bryant et al. (2001).

graphic data, but may lack other information useful in designing effective marketing efforts, such as information on respondents' lifestyles, leisure time activities and media habits. In some instances, syndicated commercial marketing databases are more useful to social marketers if they contain information on the behaviors of interest.

Some commercial vendors offer geodemographic segmentation systems that can be useful. These systems include geoSmart in Australia; MOSAIC, available in 20 countries; ACORN in the United Kingdom and PRIZM in the United States. Each system works by assigning households to demographically (and, for some, behaviorally) distinct segments. For example, by merging the US CDC's Behavioral Risk Factor Surveillance System database with the PRIZM database, researchers were able to segment binge drinkers – individuals who self-reported consuming five or more drinks on at least two occasions in the past 30 days. The merged dataset identified the top 10 clusters with the highest concentration of adults engaging in binge drinking and provided estimates of the market areas where they resided (Moss et al., 2009).

Profiling

Once a group has been segmented, developing a profile of each segment provides the information needed to choose which segments to target and then to develop marketing strategies customized to their characteristics. Profiles typically outline the size of each segment and whatever characteristics are helpful for developing strategies to bring about the desired behavior change. For population-based programs, demographic characteristics – age, sex, marital status, education, income, presence of children, etc. – are common. This information is often supplemented with psychographics – attitudes, interests and opinions, lifestyle, etc., – as well as media habits for promotional campaigns.

Targeting: selecting segments

Good segmentations identify the groups most worth pursuing' (Yankelovich and Meer, 2006: 2).

Undifferentiated marketing is the term used to describe targeting the whole market with one offer rather than segmenting; *differentiated marketing* involves designing separate offers for two or more market segments; *concentrated (or niche) marketing* involves focusing limited resources on niches

that may be overlooked by larger competitors and *atomization* or *segment-of-one* marketing involves customizing offers for individual consumers (Weinstein, 2004). Available resources should play a large role in determining which type of marketing to pursue. Common criteria for selecting segments include:

- *Size.* Targets should be big enough to warrant attention and have the potential to make an impact on the problem being tackled (Hastings, 2008).
- *Accessibility.* Useful segments are those that the program has the distribution channels and resources to reach effectively and efficiently.
- *Responsiveness,* or likelihood to change.
- *Actionable.* The sponsoring organization has sufficient resources to develop programs that can serve the segments.
- *Pertinence* to organizational mission.

Donovan and colleagues (1999) and Donovan and Henley (2003) developed the TARPARE model to help understand segments and assess the viability of addressing them with limited resources.

T: Total number of people in the segment; generally, the greater the number, the higher the priority.

AR: Proportion of people At Risk in the segment, based on assessments of proportions classified as low, medium or high risk with respect to the issue; associated risk factors and expected benefits of risk reduction in the segment. In general, the greater proportion at risk, the greater potential return and therefore the category's higher priority.

P: Persuasibility of the target audience; generally, the more feasible it is to change the attitudes or behaviors of the segment, the higher the priority of the segment.

A: Accessibility of the target audience – how easy (and cost-efficient) it is to reach each segment via available channels.

R: Resources required to meet target audience needs – financial, human and structural – and whether the resources are available to reach each segment or would have to be added.

E: Equity – including social justice considerations, such as whether small groups warrant special programs for reasons of equity.

TARPARE was developed as a qualitative assessment, though it can also be represented as a weighted multi-attribute model – see Donovan and Henley (2003) for details.

Case Study 2   Segmenting Parents to Increase Their Involvement with Preteens

Parental involvement with preteens appears to act as a protective factor against the lure of tobacco use, yet a sizeable proportion of parents do not spend a lot of time with their preteens. The US Centers for Disease Control and Prevention (CDC) used segmentation and targeting to identify parents who would be willing to become more involved, and then developed *Got a Minute? Give it to Your Kid,* a campaign kit for state and local tobacco control programs to use to reach them.

Early work included a review of the parenting literature and convening an expert panel. From these emerged seven types of effective parenting interventions, which were ultimately narrowed to two possibilities that were strongly supported in the literature, could be most easily communicated, showed the greatest potential for interesting parents and would not overlap too much with other campaigns aimed at parents: (1) convincing parents less involved with their children to become more involved (e.g., encourage more awareness of their child's life, more activities with their child and better monitoring of where their child is) or (2) attempt to spur parents who were not setting clear rules to set and enforce such rules. CDC also decided to focus on parents of children aged 9–12: the years immediately before children are likely to be offered their first cigarette at age 12.

A mixture of qualitative and quantitative research methods was used to segment audiences. Initial focus groups divided parents into those who were heavily involved with their child's life (doers) and those who were less involved (non-doers) and explored what might get them more involved or setting clear rules. Both groups were eager to connect better with their children but not eager to set or enforce rules about tobacco or other subjects.

In addition to the focus groups, a combination behavioral and psychographic segmentation was used to find clusters of parenting styles. The analysis used data from Healthstyles, a survey of adults containing demographic, psychographic and health and wellness questions. First, 21 items from the Healthstyles survey that measured parenting styles were factor analyzed. Next, k-means cluster analysis of the resulting factors categorized parents into groups with maximum similarity within each group, but maximum distinction between groups. Researchers chose a three-cluster solution:

1. On-target parents, who appeared high in positive involvement, rule setting, enforcement and confident that they could protect their children from behavioral and health risks.
2. Non-enforcers, who were very involved in their child's life and well-being, articulated clear rules but were lax in enforcing them and lacked confidence that they could protect their children.
3. Less-involved parents, who showed the lowest levels of involvement and rule setting, though they were not quite as lax in rule enforcement as the non-enforcers, and who were somewhat lacking confidence that they could protect their children from behavioral risks.

Other questions in the database were then used to develop a profile of each group, including size estimates and media use. CDC chose to target less-involved parents. The profiling revealed that this group was not demographically distinct (i.e., its members could be found in a variety of demographic groups), wanted to spend more time with their children but did not know how, had low self-efficacy on a wide range of behaviors, tended to be overwhelmed and had a great deal of trouble finding time to spend with their children.

The segmentation research was used to develop a campaign that emphasized offering parents simple ways to get more involved with their child. Campaign materials emphasized the parents' desired benefit of better communication with their preteen, offered suggestions that would require little parental time (to overcome that barrier) and modeled the behavior to improve self-efficacy. Equipped with ideas and improved confidence, parents should then be more likely to engage in the behaviors targeted by the campaign, establishing an involved parenting style that is likely to act as a protective factor against tobacco use.

Sources: AED (2002) and Centers for Disease Control and Prevention (n.d.).

IDENTIFYING AND OVERCOMING ORGANIZATIONAL BARRIERS TO SEGMENTATION

Organizations confront a number of barriers to successfully conducting useful segmentation studies, including shortage of data, unsuitable personnel, operational problems and resistance to change (Dibb and Simkin, 2009). Once a segmentation study has been conducted, three common pitfalls that often result in disappointment with the results are excessive interest in consumers'

Case Study 3   Segmentation for a Multi-Country Anti-Smoking Campaign

In 2005, the European Union launched an anti-smoking campaign, 'Help – for a life without tobacco,' across its (at that time) 25 member states. Campaign goals were to encourage a tobacco-free lifestyle, help existing smokers to stop smoking and reduce passive smoking. Television advertisements were the main component of the campaign; they aired in January and September in both 2006 and 2007 on national television channels and three pan-European providers. Three advertisements were developed to address each theme, conveying that tobacco is a problem that takes many forms, including the dangers of people starting smoking, the difficulty but importance of people stopping and the damaging effects of environmental tobacco smoke on non-smokers. All used a persuasive approach and were linked with a unifying slogan and an ironic device (substituting a party whistle for a cigarette).

For the segmentation, researchers used data from a 10-minute telephone survey conducted in 2006 and 2007; total sample sizes (with a goal of 1000 per country) were 24,125 in 2006 and 24,161 in 2007. Segmentation analysis was restricted to current smokers who had seen at least one of the three advertisements ($n = 2474$ for 2006 and $n = 2491$ for 2007). Researchers first used chi-square tests and ANOVA to assess degree of awareness of the advertisements; smokers were more aware of the advertisements than non-smokers or ex-smokers. Next, they used confirmatory factor analysis to assess the reliability and validity of the three main constructs of interest: attitudes toward the campaign, comprehension of main messages and level of responsible thinking (elaboration). At both waves, measurement models revealed adequate fit, so the items used to measure each construct were averaged together in a scale. Finally, they used hierarchical clustering followed by k-means analysis to segment smokers in the 2006 study on the scaled variables ($n = 1767$ after cases with missing data were excluded). The result was three clusters: Message Involved ($n = 759$; 43%), Message Indifferent ($n = 691$; 39%) and Message Distanced ($n = 317$; 18%). For the Message Involved, all three variables – attitude, comprehension and responsible thinking – had greater relevance. In addition, this group had the highest intent to quit smoking and smoked significantly less than the Message Distanced. Attitude, comprehension and responsible thinking had average relevance to the Message Indifferent; this group tended to be younger and to comprehend, but not think responsibly about, the anti-smoking message. Members of the Message Distanced were the least likely to think responsibly about the message and had the lowest intention to quit (71% said they had no intention of doing so). To validate the clusters, researchers replicated the analysis using the 2007 data. They also found no significant differences in the proportion of smokers from each country in each cluster across the two years of data. They concluded that the clusters were stable.

Researchers also examined the proportion of each cluster within each member state, and found that they were not evenly distributed; Austria, Hungary, Lithuania, the Netherlands and Spain had greater proportions of Message Indifferents and fewer Message Involveds than countries including Cyprus, Czech Republic, Finland, Germany, Ireland, Malta, Poland, Portugal, Slovakia, Slovenia and the United Kingdom.

Source: Walsh et al. (2009).

identities, which distracts from the product features that matter most to current and potential customers; too little emphasis on actual consumer behavior and undue absorption in the technical details of segmentation, leading to segments which management doesn't understand or trust (Yankelovich and Meer, 2006).

Dibb and Simkin (2009) developed a series of 'rules' to help bridge the theory/practice divide that often occurs when organizations conduct and attempt to implement segmentation studies; they split guidance into before, during and after segmentation. Advice includes applying appropriate resources, seeking early stakeholder support, encouraging commitment by articulating benefits, managing expectations and producing a detailed

implementation plan so that people, budgets, program and managers' outlooks are aligned with the segments and priorities.

KEY WORDS: Market segmentation; targeting; profiling; segmentation; target market.

Key insights

- Market segmentation and targeting is critical and often under-used in social marketing. Beyond guiding development and delivery of communications, segmentation studies can be used to identify new target markets, develop products and services, inform pricing decisions, inform distribution, increase customer satisfaction or value and determine resource allocations.

- Advances in database marketing and technology have improved our ability to conduct market segmentation research effectively and efficiently, and have made it more feasible to develop pan-regional or global segmentation strategies.
- Strong segmentations identify conceptually distinct groups that respond in different ways to different elements of the marketing mix. Segmentations can be based on geography, behaviors, benefits sought, psychographics, demographics or other personal characteristics. The choice should be based on the type(s) of decisions to be made using the results.
- Targeting decisions should take into account the size of the segment, its accessibility and likely responsiveness to the offering, and whether the organization has the necessary resources to serve the segment(s).
- Since segmentation studies require substantial resources and commitment, it is critical to actively manage their conceptualization, implementation and application.

REFERENCES

AED (2002). *Audience Segmentation Recommendations: Employing Parenting for Prevention of Youth Tobacco Use.* Submitted to the Centers for Disease Control and Prevention/Office of Smoking and Health. Washington, DC: AED.

AED Center for Health Communication (2010). *Communicating about Influenza Vaccination 2010–11: Formative Research with Parents, Young Adults, Older Adults and People with Asthma or Diabetes.* Submitted to CDC National Center for Immunization and Respiratory Diseases. Washington, DC: AED.

Andreasen, A.R. (1995) *Marketing Social Change.* San Francisco, CA: Jossey-Bass.

Bryant, C., Lindenberger, J., Brown, C., et al. (2001) 'A social marketing approach to increasing enrollment in a public health program: A case study of the Texas WIC Program', *Human Organization,* 60(3): 234–246.

Centers for Disease Control and Prevention (n.d.). '*Got a Minute? Give it to Your Kid.* A ready-to-Use Tobacco Control Program Focusing on Parents', Atlanta, GA: CDC.

Dibb, S. (1998) 'Market segmentation: Strategies for success', *Marketing Intelligence and Planning,* 16: 394–406.

Dibb, S. and Simkin, L. (2001) 'Market segmentation: Diagnosing and treating the barriers', *Industrial Marketing Management,* 30: 609–625.

Dibb, S. and Simkin, L. (2009) 'Implementation rules to bridge the theory/practice divide in market segmentation', *Journal of Marketing Management,* 25(3): 375–396.

Donovan, R.J., Egger, G.J. and Francas, M. (1999) 'TARPARE: A method for selecting target audiences for public health interventions', *Australian and New Zealand Journal of Public Health,* 23(3): 280–284.

Donovan, R.J. and Henley, N. (2003) *Social Marketing: Principles and Practice.* Victoria: IP Communications.

Fishbein, M., Triandis, H.C., Kanfer, F.H., et al. (2001) 'Factors influencing behavior and behavior change', in A. Baum, T.A. Revenson and J.E. Singer (eds), *Handbook of Health Psychology.* Mahwah, NJ: Lawrence Erlbaum, pp. 3–17.

Gupta, S. and Lehmann, D.R. (2003) 'Customers as assets', *Journal of Interactive Marketing,* 17: 9–24.

Hastings, G. (2008) *Social Marketing: Why Should the Devil Have All the Best Tunes?* Oxford: Butterworth-Heinemann.

Kotler, P. (2002) *Marketing Management.* Englewood Cliffs, NJ: Prentice-Hall.

Kotler, P. and Armstrong, G. (2004) *Principles of Marketing,* 10th edn. Upper Saddle River, NJ: Prentice-Hall.

Landers, J., Mitchell, P., Smith, B., Lehman, T. and Conner, C. (2006) '"Save the Crabs, then Eat 'Em": A culinary approach to saving the Chesapeake Bay', *Social Marketing Quarterly,* 12: 15–28.

Lotenberg, L.D. (2010) 'Place: Where the action is', *Social Marketing Quarterly,* 16:130–135.

Meadows, M. and Dibb, S. (1998) 'Assessing the implementation of market segmentation in retail financial services', *International Journal of Service Industry management,* 9: 266–285.

Moss, H.B., Kirby, S.D. and Donodeo, F. (2009) 'Characterizing and reaching high-risk drinkers using audience segmentation', *Alcoholism: Clinical and Experimental Research,* 33(8): 1336–1345.

Prochaska, J.O., Redding, C.A. and Evers, K.E. (2002) 'The transtheoretical model and stages of change', in K. Glanz, B.K. Rimer, and F.M. Lewis (eds), *Health Behavior and Health Education: Theory, Research and Practice,* 3rd edn. San Francisco, CA: Jossey-Bass. pp. 99–120.

Sausen, K., Tomczak, T. and Herrmann, A. (2005) 'Development of taxonomy of strategic market segmentation: A framework for bridging the implementation gap between normative segmentation and business practice', *Journal of Strategic Marketing,* 13: 151–173.

Slater, M.D. (1996) 'Theory and method in health audience segmentation', *Journal of Health Communication,* 1: 267–283.

Smith, W. (1956) 'Product differentiation and market segmentation as alternative marketing strategies', *Journal of Marketing,* 21: 3–8.

Stead, M., Wimbush, E., Eadie, D.R. and Teer, P. (1997) 'A qualitative study of older people's perceptions of aging and exercise: The implications for health promotion', *Health Education Journal,* 56: 3–16.

Steenkamp, J-B.E.M. and Ter Hofstede, F. (2002) 'International market segmentation: Issues and perspectives', *International Journal of Research in Marketing,* 19: 185–213.

Sutton, S.M., Balch, G.I. and Lefebvre, R.C. (1995) 'Strategic questions for consumer-based health communications', *Public Health Reports,* 110: 725–733.

USAID/AED. (2007) *NetMark 2008 Strategy and Work Plan.* Washington, DC: USAID/AED.

Walsh, G., Hassan, L.M., Shiu, E., Andrews, J.C. and Hasting, G. (2009) 'Segmentation in social marketing: Insights from the European Union's multi-country, anti-smoking campaign', *European Journal of Marketing*, 44(7/8): 1140–1164.

Weinstein, A. (2004) *Handbook of Market Segmentation: Strategic Targeting for Business and Technology Firms*, 3rd edn. Binghamton, NY: Haworth Press.

Wind, Y. (1978) 'Issues and advances in segmentation research', *Journal of Marketing Research*, 25: 317–337.

Wind, Y. and Bell, D.R. (2008) 'Market segmentation', in M.J. Baker and S. Hart (eds), *The Marketing Book*, 6th edn. Oxford: Elsevier.

Yankelovich, D. and Meer, D. (2006) 'Rediscovering market segmentation', *Harvard Business Review*, 84(6): 141–145.

9

Competition and Positioning

Gary Noble and Debra Z. Basil

INTRODUCTION

Competition is a consequence of free choice. As Henderson (1983) suggests, the basic principles of competitive systems have been with us since the beginning of time. Nature itself is highly competitive, a point Darwin made in his *On the Origin of Species*. In commercial marketing terms, competition has been described as the 'process by which independent sellers vie with each other for customers in a market' (Weitz, 1985: 229). For marketers operating in the commercial world, identifying and analyzing the competition is a critical component in the development of a firm's marketing strategy. Understanding the competition is the basis for a firm's competitive advantage and for decisions in such key areas as segmentation, targeting and positioning (Clark and Montgomery, 1999). Ideally, selecting a suitable market position should be a result of a firm having identified its competition and understanding the relative advantages that similar products and firms have in a target market. Many believe that the success of any marketing strategy depends on the strength and quality of the competitive analysis that underpins it (Henderson, 1983). In the context of social marketing, the same situation exists: recognising and understanding the nature of the competition confronting a social marketing intervention is fundamental to the social marketing planning process and to ensuring the success of an intervention.

In this chapter, we review literature and offer a framework for understanding competition in social marketing. We begin by examining how basic differences between commercial and social marketing call for a variation in approaches to the process of competitor analysis. Based on this discussion we take a consumer viewpoint to competition and propose a framework for social marketers to consider when faced with the task of identifying and understanding the competitive forces likely to impact on a planned intervention. To illustrate the utility of our framework we provide examples of its application. The chapter goes on to advocate cooperation as a counter-force to competition. Finally, we discuss the relationship between competitive analysis and the concept of positioning.

COMPETITION IN THE CONTEXT OF SOCIAL MARKETING

Although social and commercial marketing share a historical bond, there are important differences between them. This results in a need for two distinct approaches to the process of competitive analysis. One of the most fundamental differences relates to the nature of the marketing proposition that each addresses. In the commercial world, the marketing proposition often involves a product that includes both tangible and intangible attributes designed to satisfy a set of consumer needs, wants or desires in a manner that positions the offering more favourably in the target audience's mind when compared with similar market offerings from other firms. The term 'competition' in this environment refers to a rivalry between products or firms attempting to satisfy similar customer needs and wants (Donovan and Henley, 2003; Grier and Bryant, 2005). The production and sale of motor vehicles represents a simple example; car manufacturers manipulate tangible (e.g. shape, colour, size and performance) and intangible (e.g. brand and status) attributes to meet selected customer needs and so position their product more favourably in these customers' minds relative to other cars and brands in the same market. The marketing proposition that most social marketers face usually comprises mainly intangible attributes or calls for a choice between one or more behaviours that may be existing or even habitual (Hastings, 2007). Not only do social marketing offerings involve intangible attributes – such as the adoption of an idea, value, belief or attitude – but also they frequently do not satisfy an immediate demand or desire within the targeted audience. As Hastings (2007) points out, social marketing often involves hard and sustained work by an individual over a long period of time to give deferred and probabilistic rather than immediate short-term benefits and gratification. For example, beating an addiction to nicotine requires personal effort and dedication over a long time period in the hope of lowering the possibility of suffering from a cancer or cardiovascular-related illness sometime in the future. The benefits and attractiveness of this offering can be compared with the low effort and immediate gratification a smoker can gain simply by lighting up a cigarette. Such fundamental differences in the nature of the market proposition require alternative conceptualisations of both the notion of competition and the process of competitive analysis in the context of social marketing.

In keeping with the belief that most social marketing involves a choice between behaviours, Kotler and Lee (2008: 164) suggest social marketing interventions face three forms of competition, namely:

- Behaviours the target audience would prefer over the ones being promoted.
- Behaviours the target audience are entrenched with – existing behaviours.
- Organisations and individuals who project counter or opposing messages to the desired behaviour.

Peattie and Peattie (2003) argue against this conceptualisation of competition which labels the current and preferred behaviour of the target audience as the main competitive forces. They suggest that this conceptualisation can be likened to a commercial marketer believing their main competition is from customers not adopting a product. As a result, they suggest a more abstract conceptualisation of competition, framing it as a 'battle of ideas' (Peattie and Peattie, 2003: 375). They argue that this battle revolves around a process where the adoption of a desired behaviour involves attracting the attention of the target audience and then convincing them to accept the

social marketing proposition being put forward. Within this process, they suggest competition comes in the form of 'competing ideas' (Peattie and Peattie, 2003: 376), which they see as originating from four separate sources:

- *Commercial counter-marketing* – the promotion of behaviours by commercial firms that are in direct opposition to that of the social marketer, for example fast food restaurants. This source of competition appears similar to Kotler and Lee's (2008) third form of competition.
- *Social discouragement* – these ideas include social values or norms that are in opposition to those being promoted by the social marketer such as the discouragement to adopt a behaviour by socially significant others, including peers.
- *Apathy* – the individual's lack of interest or concern for a behaviour change. Peattie and Peattie suggest that apathy may not be a direct competitor but rather an important factor in preventing change or behaviour adoption.
- *Involuntary disinclination* – refers to the reasons, both rational and irrational, that prevent an individual from adopting a behaviour change, for example physical addiction.

Yet a further conceptualisation of competition is provided by Rothschild, who suggests that competition is 'any environmental or perceptual force that impedes an organisation's ability to achieve its goals' (Hastings, 2003: 7). This is an extremely broad conceptualisation of competition that alerts the social marketer to the need to take a global view of what competition is and the different forms it can take. Rothschild's view of competition echoes that of Andreasen and Kotler (2003: 53) who suggest that competition, in its most basic sense, is 'whatever the customer thinks it is'.

These broader conceptualisations of competition alert the social marketer to the idea of direct and indirect forms of competition. For example, in a campaign designed to encourage children to eat more fruit it is most likely that 'junk food' would be regarded as the 'direct' competitor. However, the social marketer would also need to stay alert to the various forms of 'indirect' competition to such a campaign; this would include any foodstuff that could be seen as an alternative purchase choice, including fresh vegetables! These broader conceptualisations of competition also act to focus attention on situations where a number of organisations target the same audience and social or health issue but use different social marketing interventions, in effect creating a competitive environment (Hastings, 2003; Wayman et al., 2007; Weinberg and Ritchie, 1999). It also makes clear the notion that seemingly unrelated efforts can be competitive if they vie for the time and attention of the selected target market. These types of situations can occur where government and non-government organisations independently develop interventions designed to address a similar health or social issue. The impact of unrelated, complementary and competitive interventions need to be considered in any competitive analysis, as they have the potential to confuse a target audience in an already dense communication environment, or in the case of conflicting messages, to even oppose one another. For example, a government agency may promote condom use as a way of addressing the spread of HIV-AIDS, while a non-government group with strong religious views may attempt to address this issue with the same target audience by promoting monogamy. Although both bodies are aiming to address the same issue, they effectively increase the choice for the target audience; with increased choice, there is the potential for market clutter and the risk of confusion among the target audience.

A discussion of the term 'competition' is incomplete without identifying the relationship between the terms 'competition', 'costs' and 'barriers'. Barriers represent elements standing in the way of behaviour adoption and which are not synonymous with what a target audience is currently doing. Barriers can be classed as internal or external (McKenzie-Mohr, n.d.). Barriers relating to an individual's personal skills, knowledge, attitudes or ability are examples of internal barriers. External barriers include structural elements that hinder the behaviour and lie outside the individual. An example of an external barrier to public transport use would be low availability or scheduling which does not match the needs of a target audience. The term 'cost' represents what the target must give up to adopt a desired behaviour. Again this is not always synonymous with what they are currently doing. Kotler et al. (2002) suggest a useful framework to classify costs based on the work of Michael Porter (1998). They suggest that costs be classified as either 'exit' or 'entry' costs. Exit costs are those associated with abandoning a current behaviour, such as the pleasure sensations that will stop if the behaviour is ceased. Entry costs are those associated with adopting a new behaviour, such as the costs associated with buying a bicycle and helmet before embarking on a bicycle riding fitness programme. It should also be recognised that costs can be either monetary or non-monetary. As Kotler et al. (2002) point out, monetary costs are often those associated with purchasing tangible objects and services that accompany a behaviour change such as a bicycle helmet, sunscreen, smoking cessation aids or gym membership fees. They also suggest non-monetary costs relate to:

- Time and effort to adopt a new behaviour (e.g. the time and effort to cook a nutritious meal).
- Psychological risks associated with a new behaviour (e.g. the possibility of finding you have cancer after attending a screening programme).
- Physical discomfort or loss of pleasure associated with a new behaviour (e.g. a mammogram X-ray or craving for a cigarette).

In developing a social marketing intervention it is important to understand all three of these elements (competition, barriers and costs) to maximise the intervention's effectiveness. For the purposes of this chapter we use the term 'competition' as an overarching one that includes the elements of costs and barriers, so providing a complete picture of the competitive environment an intervention may need to consider. Including costs and barriers into the competitive environment follows the broad-natured conceptualisation of competition proposed by both Rothschild (Hastings, 2003) and Andreasen and Kotler (2003).

The foregoing discussion demonstrates that, as Wayman et al. (2007) suggest, there is no consensus on a single definition or even conceptualisation of the term 'competition' among social marketers. However, there does appear to be agreement that the process of competitive analysis is an essential step in the development of a successful social marketing intervention. There is also agreement that the nature of the competition confronting a social marketer is often more complex than that confronting a commercial marketer, and therefore any literal transfer of competitive analysis methods between these two forms of marketing is likely to prove problematic (Peattie and Peattie, 2003). There is further agreement in the literature that, in the context of social marketing, competition can come from a variety of different sources in a range of different forms, and may be quite difficult to identify.

IDENTIFYING COMPETITION

Competition in a social marketing context can be extremely difficult to identify, because it is both 'subtle and varied' as Woodside notes (2008). In social marketing articles, competition is a frequently overlooked factor. Many do not address it at all. Others address it only cursorily. Still others address it in an implicit manner. For example Bryant et al. (2001) identify competition as one of the six key principles that differentiate social marketing from other behaviour change approaches, and define it as 'the behaviour currently practiced'. In their case study of a Texas programme for women, infants and children they do not specifically identify their competitors per se; instead, they thoroughly identify the barriers and costs their target market faces. These are implicitly identified as competitors.

Noble et al. (2007) demonstrate a competitive analysis in their article on the paradoxical food-buying behaviours of parents. Barriers and competition are closely intertwined. Expediency and the desire to avoid conflict are identified as competitors in their study. As with Bryant et al. (2001), barriers and competition are treated synonymously.

Similarly, in a dissertation by Donofrio (2000) addressing tobacco prevention in youth, competition is not explicitly addressed. Perhaps in cases such as this the competition is simply too blatant to mention: a campaign seeking to reduce smoking faces the obvious competition of smoking behaviour. More generally, the competition for extinguishing a behaviour is somewhat different than the competition for encouraging a behaviour. Behaviour adoption interventions compete with myriad other potential behaviours that the target does currently. When seeking to extinguish a behaviour, on the other hand, the most direct form of competition is typically the behaviour you wish to extinguish. A smoking cessation intervention, for example, faces smoking as its primary competitor. However, the focal behaviour is often almost inextricably intertwined with other behaviours which can also be seen and act as competitors. Again using smoking cessation as an example, drinking at a bar with friends may involve smoking. The constellation of these behaviours becomes competition, and not simply the behaviour the social marketer is seeking to extinguish. Commercial marketing has long recognised the importance of consumption constellations, or groupings of symbolically related products which are used together (Solomon and Buchanan, 1991). The concept is equally applicable to social marketing. When seeking to extinguish a behaviour, an entire consumption constellation may be involved. This then presents additional competition for the social marketer.

The many complexities of defining and identifying competition have led some in the literature to attempt to classify forms of social marketing competition on the basis of 'levels of competitive analysis'. The importance of recognizing different levels of analysis in competition is evident in commercial marketing. In a case study of the fast food industry, Subway successfully developed a healthy eating niche market which most fast food providers were very slow to recognise as 'competition'. Only when McDonald's took note (when Subway actually had more US outlets than McDonald's!) did McDonald's begin offering

healthier items, and other fast food restaurants followed suit. By failing to perform a higher-level competitive analysis using the concept of fast food instead of hamburger restaurants, these companies were caught off guard by Subway, a new, and somewhat different, competitive market entrant (Basil et al., 2005). Similarly, a levels of analysis approach has been used by social marketers as well (e.g. Andreasen, 2006). We use this approach in the remainder of this chapter, offering a framework for assessing competition.

LEVELS OF COMPETITION

In commercial marketing, levels of competitive analysis commonly include the generic, form, industry and, finally, the brand level of competition (Hastings, 2003). In social marketing, Andreasen has developed a model (Andreasen, 2006) that has evolved from earlier versions of his work (Andreasen 1995, 2002; Andreasen and Kotler, 2003), resulting in four levels of competition for social marketing: generic competition, enterprise competition, product competition and brand competition (Andreasen, 2006: 155–157). We have adopted these four levels of analysis for the purposes of this chapter. In Andreasen (2006), the levels of analysis are demonstrated by example, but are not explicitly defined. For our purposes we define them as follows:

- *Generic-level competition* – forces that deter attention from your broad topic area. This includes unrelated issues that compete for the target's limited time and attention, issues that compete for funding or government attention and issues that encourage behaviours counter to that which you are advocating. For example, consider the broad topic area of childhood obesity; if the target audience is consumed by worry about the economy, will they pay attention to childhood obesity? Will government funding be available to address childhood obesity, or will funding instead go to adult job training programmes? For a social marketer intending to address childhood obesity through a bicycle riding intervention, at this level competition is broadly anything that keeps the target from addressing childhood obesity.
- *Enterprise-level competition* – within your broad topic area, forces that deter the target from addressing the issue. At this level the focus becomes narrower, though still quite general. For example, in the context of childhood obesity, the two general approaches of increasing physical activity and altering nutritional intake

are evident. For the social marketer intending a bicycle riding intervention, anything that keeps the target from physical activity is competition at this level, which may even include efforts to address childhood nutrition.

- *Product-level competition* – within your issue, forces that deter the target from addressing your specific topic. At this level the focus has narrowed greatly. For example, for an intervention encouraging bicycle riding, anything that deters the target from individual sport is competition. This may even include physical activities such as team sports.
- *Brand-level competition* – within your specific topic area, forces that deter the target from adopting your intervention. This is the most narrow, specific level of analysis. For example, at this level other forms of individual sport besides bicycle riding may be competition for your intervention, even though they may combat childhood obesity.

While the terminology differs somewhat among various writers, there is significant overlap in the levels of analysis proposed and it is clear that social marketers must consider their competition at various levels of analysis. It is also clear that each level represents a successively lower level of abstraction. The value of this approach is that it encourages social marketers to consider their competition at both an abstract level, which enables comprehension of the big picture, and at a very specific level, which facilitates tactical planning. Figure 9.1 shows the relationship between these four levels of analysis and how each level is driven by the target individual's perceptions and needs. Taking a target-centric approach, Figure 9.1 addresses the issue of childhood obesity from the perspective of a parent. In this chapter, we organise our discussion around these various levels of analysis, adopting Andreasen's (2006) terminology of generic, enterprise, product and brand to create a 'competition matrix'.

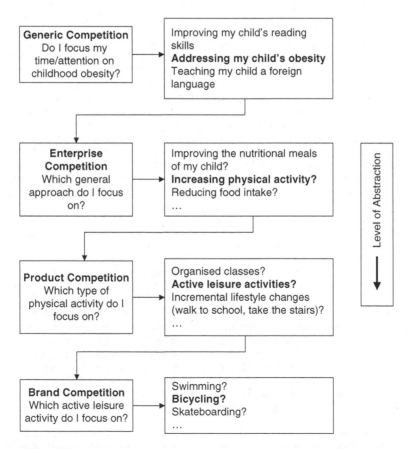

Figure 9.1   Levels of competitive analysis – childhood obesity from a parent's perspective. Adapted from Andreasen and Kotler (2003)

THE COMPETITION MATRIX

Overlaying each of the four proposed levels of analysis are two key competitive dimensions. First is the nature of the competition: Is it organisational (an entity) or not (internal to the individual or part of the general environment)? This is a concept alluded to in our earlier discussion of the term 'barriers' and noted by both Hastings (2003) and Wayman et al. (2007). Hastings (2003: 8) utilises the terms 'purposeful' and 'inertial' competition to make this point. Purposeful competition entails an identifiable entity with purposes at odds to those of the social marketing campaign. Fast food restaurants thus represent purposeful or entity-based competition to healthy eating campaigns. Inertial competition, on the other hand, includes elements that are internal to the individual as well as elements from the general environment that are unrelated to a specific entity. Internal elements often relate to maintaining the status quo. General environmental elements include elements such as peer pressure or lack of a supportive culture. Inertial competition suggests that in the short run individuals prefer to maintain their existing behaviours. These notions were similarly expressed by Wayman et al. (2007), who suggest competition can be either organisational based or behaviour based. They place behaviour-based competition within the context of product competition and, again, see the dominant form of this competition being the entrenched existing behaviour that the social marketer may be trying to change. In discussing organisational-based competition they make the point that this form of competition includes organisations with competing messages as well as organisations that are competing for funds to support their social marketing intervention. That is, they take a very broad view of the impact of this form of competition. In this chapter, we have termed organisational competitors *'entity based'* and all other forms of competition as *'non-entity based'* to underscore the importance of identifying whether or not a specific external entity is involved. At any level of competitive analysis, and with any specific intervention, the social marketer can identify the various entity and non-entity competitive forces at work, as we shall demonstrate later in the chapter.

The second key dimension to consider is whether the entity or non-entity competitive forces are competing or complementary to your intervention. Ritchie and Weinberg (2000) identify three types of competition, which fall along a continuum of collaboration. With collegial competition, entities share a common goal and they often collaborate to solve the problem. Alternative competition represents situations where differences exist regarding how to address the common goal, so collaboration may or may not occur. Finally, combative competition exists when organisations' means of addressing the common goal are diametrically opposed.

Nalebuff and Brandenburger, in their book entitled *Co-opetition* (1996; 15), address the notion of collaborating with competitors as well. They stress the importance of complements (offerings that supplement or benefit your own offering) and coin the phrase 'complementor' to represent those who provide important complements. For example, if your campaign seeks to address childhood obesity by encouraging bicycle riding, skateboarding and swimming may represent complementary behaviours as they address childhood obesity through an alternate means.

Complementarity suggests the existence of another force that is working in a manner that contributes to your own purpose. The related issue of collaboration occurs when a social marketer creates an alliance with another entity. In these cases the social marketer may collaborate with another entity to more effectively execute their intervention. At times an entity that would otherwise be a direct competitor may become a collaborator. These collaborative efforts can provide benefits to the social marketer, providing much needed resources; however, in some cases, they may be quite controversial. For example, a beer company may join forces with a social marketer to provide safe rides home after drinking. Some social marketers believe that it is inappropriate to partner with certain sorts of 'sin' companies, no matter what resources they offer. We make no effort to resolve this dispute here, only to note it.

A competing entity need not be adversarial for the results of their efforts to erode the effectiveness of yours (Ritchie and Weinberg, 2000). For example, a needle exchange programme may erode the effectiveness of a drug use reduction campaign (Kotler and Lee, 2008: 164). Despite a lack of intent, this sort of 'friendly competition' can negatively impact your success. By contrast, 'combative' competition suggests organisations going head to head against one another, seeking to persuade the same target to perform diametrically opposed behaviours, as with the abortion debate (Ritchie and Weinberg, 2000). Sometimes the distinction between competing and complementary forces is a matter of level of analysis. What represents a competing force at a specific, tactical level may become a complementary force at a broader, more abstract level. For example, a campaign designed to encourage a reduction in drinking alcohol may reduce the impact of your social marketing campaign encouraging drinkers to take a taxi home, but at the broader level both efforts may successfully reduce driving while intoxicated.

Emerging from this discussion is a competition matrix where these two dimensions, *entity/non-entity* and *complementary/competing* can be crossed to more clearly explicate the full range of competitive possibilities. Competing behaviours can be either entity based or non-entity based, as can complementary behaviours (see Figure 9.2). Both dimensions occur along a continuum. Entities can compete with your efforts while in some way also providing complementary offerings. McDonald's, for example, may generally serve as a competitor to healthy eating while also offering complementary alternatives such as salads, thus making a dichotomous categorisation inappropriate. The entity/non-entity categorisation will most commonly be represented by a dichotomy; however, there may be cases whereby the entity categorisation is best understood on a continuum as well. Such cases would involve pseudo-entities such as informal clubs that influence behaviour. This framework provides a full picture of the competitive environment an intervention may face and can be applied at any level of competitive analysis.

Next we apply this competition matrix to Andreasen's (2006) four levels of analysis. At each level we use the hypothetical example of childhood obesity and the real-world example of the 'Road Crew' intervention (www.roadcrewonline.org) to demonstrate the applicability of the framework.

'Road Crew' is a social marketing intervention designed to reduce drunk driving. We will apply this case to each level of analysis to demonstrate the applicability of our framework to a real-world situation. Road Crew was initiated in an effort to reduce drunk driving in Dane County, Wisconsin, an area with high rates of drunk driving. The programme offers rides to, from, and between drinking establishments for a low cost, allowing

individuals to drink without driving. The programme is operated by the Wisconsin Department of Transportation, the University of Wisconsin School of Business and the Tavern League of Wisconsin, USA (www.roadcrewonline.org). Research has demonstrated a reduction in alcohol-related accidents since the inception of Road Crew (Rothschild et al., 2006). Our analysis will focus specifically on the role of taverns and the Tavern League. We recognise that this is a controversial example because some social marketers criticise alliances with 'sin' organisations. We use this example simply for its broad applicability to our framework. The fact that controversy exists here is a reminder of the added complexity faced by social marketers.

Generic level of competition

At the generic level of analysis (Figure 9.3), social marketers recognise where their offerings fit within an overall landscape of possible alternatives. Xerox, for example, determined that their scope should be document management rather than simply photocopying. This encourages the social marketer to consider the primary benefits of their intervention. At this level the social marketer considers issues such as whether they are addressing longevity, for example, or quality of life. While this may seem obvious, it is not necessarily so. Consider for example, a situation where a city council has decided to mount a social marketing campaign to encourage bicycle riding on their newly-laid city-wide bicycle path. While a non-specific campaign might increase path use, to maximise intervention effectiveness social marketing requires identifying the needs of a selected target market. At the generic level, the city council must consider why the path was built. Was it to increase the health of the citizenry? Was it to reduce traffic congestion? Or was it simply built to attract prospective businesses? Each of these requires a different approach to the social marketing intervention, or in the case of attracting business perhaps no intervention is needed. Next, we apply the competition matrix to our two examples: childhood obesity and Road Crew, at the generic level.

Using the example of childhood obesity to demonstrate the application of the competition matrix, at the generic level, childhood obesity is the topic area. Anything diverting attention from childhood obesity is a competitor; anything focusing attention on childhood obesity is a complementor. Organisations with which the social marketer forms alliances represent collaborators, a special class of complementor. Each successive level narrows the unit of analysis.

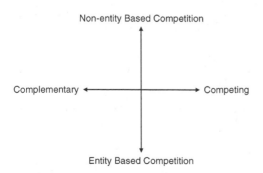

Figure 9.2   Competition matrix

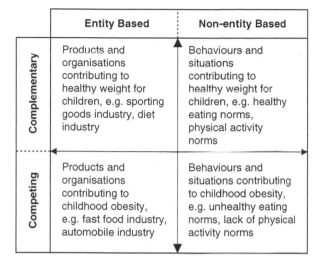

	Entity Based	Non-entity Based
Complementary	Products and organisations contributing to healthy weight for children, e.g. sporting goods industry, diet industry	Behaviours and situations contributing to healthy weight for children, e.g. healthy eating norms, physical activity norms
Competing	Products and organisations contributing to childhood obesity, e.g. fast food industry, automobile industry	Behaviours and situations contributing to childhood obesity, e.g. unhealthy eating norms, lack of physical activity norms

Figure 9.3   Generic-level competition matrix

Figures 9.3–9.6 apply the example of childhood obesity to the competition matrix, but each contains only a few examples of competition due to space constraints. A full competitive analysis would contain an exhaustive list of all potential competitors and complementors at each level of analysis.

Competitors at this level encompass anything contributing to childhood obesity. At this level, broad industry classes are considered. This includes industries that cater to children with unhealthy eating options, such as soda pop, candy and chips. It may also include industries that discourage physical activity such as computer and video games. Complementors may relate to diet, such as diet pills, fad diets and even surgeons. They may also relate to exercise, such as the sporting goods industry. Non-entity based complementary behaviours may encompass various forms of reducing food intake and increasing exercise. Note that complementary behaviours are labelled as such because they encourage the target behaviour; this does not necessarily mean that they are positive behaviours.

Applying a level of analysis approach to Road Crew, at the generic level, those involved with alcohol serve as complementors. This is because they help to focus attention on the general topic of drinking, as does Road Crew. Taverns are involved with alcohol; thus, they serve as entity-based complementors for the Road Crew intervention at this level. Similarly, any social marketing effort relating to alcohol is an entity-based complementor. All other topic areas become competitors as they shift focus from the issue of alcohol.

Enterprise level of competition

The second level of analysis is the enterprise level (Figure 9.4). Here we begin to consider our focus more specifically. We identify the overall industry category within which we compete. Continuing the example of childhood obesity, our focus narrows from childhood obesity in general to more specific means of reducing childhood obesity, choosing between a focus on diet or a focus on physical activity. We focus on physical activity for this example. We begin to consider what specific industries might compete with our goals.

At the enterprise level, competition for the social marketer wishing to address childhood obesity by increasing physical activity is whatever discourages children from being active. This may be various electronic media forms, including television, video games and computer games. All are forms of entity-based competition for us. There are, however, some electronic mediums that serve to encourage complementary behaviour, such as specific video games that encourage physical activity. This differentiation occurs at the next level of analysis, the product level, which provides for these finer distinctions.

Turning to our Road Crew example, we see a shift in classification. At the enterprise level our focus narrows from those related to alcohol in general (representing the generic level of analysis) to those serving alcohol away from home. With the stated goal of reducing drunk driving, all establishments serving alcohol away from home can be viewed as competitors. This includes restaurants with liquor licenses, night clubs and taverns. Thus, while taverns are part of the general

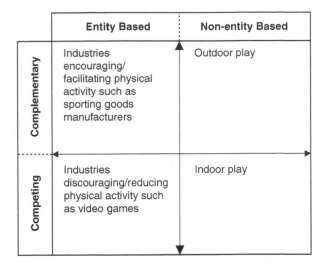

Figure 9.4   Enterprise-level competition matrix

alcohol industry, and thus are categorised as complementors, at the generic level, they serve as
entity-based competitors at the enterprise level.

Product level of competition

At the product level (Figure 9.5), social marketers
further narrow their focus by identifying the type
of behaviour their intervention will promote.
Turning to our childhood obesity example, in the
previous level of analysis we focused on physical
activity. In the case of physical activity, is it an
increase in general activity throughout the day,
encouragement to participate in organised sport,
or promotion of a particular leisure activity? In
our example we focus on promoting active leisure.
The social marketer now determines which specific product types divert attention from active
leisure. The social marketer may determine that
physically inactive video games are competitors,
whereas physically active video games are complementors. Friends may potentially serve as both
competition and complementors.

Again, addressing our Road Crew example,
at the product level of analysis our focus

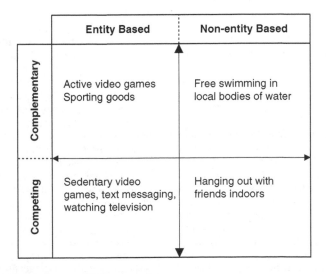

Figure 9.5   Product-level competition matrix

again narrows. We begin to discern between various establishments serving alcohol away from home, and assess each category individually. Taverns are addressed as a unique group. Taverns supply alcohol to individuals away from home, creating a situation where the drinker may have to drive home. Unlike restaurants, taverns primarily focus on serving alcohol. Thus, at the product level taverns are viewed as entity-based competitors.

Brand level of competition

Brand represents the final level of analysis. This stage addresses competition for the choice of specific behaviours. For individual social marketers, at the brand level, competition represents the other behaviours their target may choose over the behaviour they are advocating. Our competition matrix can be applied to this level of competition as well (see Figure 9.6). This is the most concrete level of application. At this level, competitors should be identified as specifically as possible. It is not sufficient to identify 'sedentary video games' as a competitor at this level, for example. Instead, identify which specific video games are gaining the attention of the target market. This level of detail can be helpful in the design of interventions, by potentially allowing for the incorporation of elements that appeal to the target.

Continuing our application of the competition matrix to the issue of childhood obesity, we focus on encouraging bicycle riding as the selected social marketing intervention. At this level, specific competitors should be identified. In this process it may become apparent that all video games are not competitors. For example the Wii fitness game package, which offers several video games incorporating physical exercise, can be an entity-based complementor rather than a competitor because it encourages non-riders to learn to ride or encourages bike riders that bike riding can be fun. The Nintendo DS Mario Kart game, on the other hand, may represent an entity-based competitor when it is used frequently by their target market as an alternative form of entertainment. Figure 9.6 represents an example of our proposed competition matrix applied to a social marketing campaign to encourage bicycle riding to reduce childhood obesity.

A final look at the Road Crew example shows another narrowing of focus. We move from the broad category of taverns to specific entities within the tavern category. At the brand level of analysis the Tavern League is a specific brand within the product category of taverns. Taverns may be viewed as competitors, as we see in the product level analysis above, but the Tavern League has partnered with the Road Crew intervention to reduce drunk driving in a very specific way that maintains or possibly increases their business while successfully combating the problem of drunk driving by removing an obstacle many people face in drinking in bars. Thus, an entity that on the surface may seem to be a competitor can actually be a useful complementor or even collaborator.

The levels of analysis approach applied here provides a useful framework for assessing one's competitive situation. It is important, however, not to become 'bogged down' in the intricacies

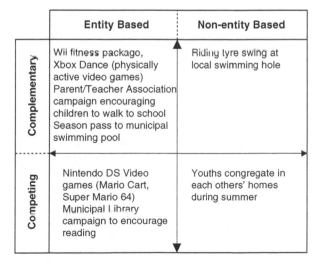

	Entity Based	Non-entity Based
Complementary	Wii fitness package, Xbox Dance (physically active video games) Parent/Teacher Association campaign encouraging children to walk to school Season pass to municipal swimming pool	Riding tyre swing at local swimming hole
Competing	Nintendo DS Video games (Mario Cart, Super Mario 64) Municipal Library campaign to encourage reading	Youths congregate in each others' homes during summer

Figure 9.6 Brand-level competition matrix

of definition. It is possible to argue the placement of many competitor concepts within this framework; similarly, it could be argued that this multi-level approach to competitive analysis has only limited application in situations where there is a single behaviour with a bipolar set of outcomes (whether people exercise their right to vote in an election) but what really matters is thoroughly assessing competition at each of the various levels of abstraction.

CO-OPETITION

Rather than facing the competition head-on, some social marketers find ways to mitigate or eliminate the competition through various means. Ideally, social marketers will turn competitors into complementors (Nalebuff and Brandenburger, 1996) whenever possible, even collaborating with some. This notion has been termed 'co-opetition' (Noorda, cited in Nalebuff and Brandenburger, 1996: 4). More specifically, co-opetition is a game theory based strategy that 'combines competition and cooperation' where seeming competitors can actually provide benefits to each other, often at the larger level of analysis (Nalebuff and Brandenburger, 1996: book cover). The matrix proposed here incorporates this notion through the identification of complementary and competing behaviours.

Co-opetition is based on game theory (von Neumann and Morgenstern, 1944), which has been the topic of research in many fields for decades. It began as an applied military strategy, moving into applied mathematics and further blossoming in economics. Game theory recognises that many interdependent factors are at play, and seeks to identify the best possible strategy in a competitive context (Nalebuff and Brandenburger, 1996). Nash (1951) proposed an equilibrium point exists when every player has made what they believe to be the best strategic choice possible for themselves, *given the strategic choices of the other players*. For social marketers, this stresses the importance of knowing one's competition, and the likely strategy that competition may take. In the face of an economic recession, for example, will McDonald's introduce a 'treat yourself in hard times' campaign, offering comfort food? This form of competition would be highly relevant to a social marketer encouraging healthy eating.

Nalebuff and Brandenburger (1996) have applied this approach to propose five key components (players, added values, rules, tactics and scope) of identifying one's most successful potential strategy. They apply the acronym PARTS to represent these elements.

Players involved: Identify all relevant parties. In commercial marketing, key players include the company itself, customers, suppliers, competitors and complementors (Nalebuff and Brandenburger, 1996). The situation can be modified for social marketing. Social marketing suppliers may include those providing intervention materials, communication materials, the augmented product and even those providing funding. Although the term 'customer' is shunned by some social marketers (Hastings, 2007), the analogous group in social marketing terms may include the target market as well as secondary targets such as support individuals, peers and parents. Co-opetition suggests that it is as important to recognise complementors as it is to recognise competitors.

Added value: Understand the value of the intervention to society. This is determined by assessing the overall cost to society, both financial and non-financial, with and without the intervention. For social marketers it is important to try to recognise all forms of contribution. Will the social marketer's bicycle riding intervention reduce government expenditures on health care? Will it reduce traffic congestion and thus road repair expenses, if parents no longer have to drive their children to various locations? Will it increase demand for bicycles, thus appealing to bicycle manufacturers? Having a thorough understanding of worth to all potential players will help the social marketer develop a maximally beneficial strategy.

Rules: Understand the rules of the game (Nalebuff and Brandenburger, 1996). In commercial marketing, the rules may vary but the focus on profit and customer satisfaction is usually critical. Social marketers, however, usually must balance the needs of many groups, and may be unwilling to take certain paths for ethical reasons. Consider, for example, a social marketing intervention seeking to reduce underage drinking. Is it appropriate for a major liquor producer to supply materials for the intervention? Such a move would shift the liquor manufacturer from competitor to complementor, and specifically a collaborating complementor, but is it ethically justifiable? The social marketer may have to make difficult decisions such as these, often playing by rules much more stringent than a commercial marketer faces.

Tactics: Understand the methods used to mould perceptions. Perception is reality. Success and failure often rely on how different players perceive the situation. Social marketers must be cognizant of the perceptions of all players.

Scope: Understand the scope of the issue. The levels of analysis proposed here can be very helpful in this regard, by encouraging the social marketer to consider the issue at various levels of abstraction. When all levels of analysis are taken into account, other routes to success may become apparent.

Although the concept of co-opetition has not yet been applied to social marketing, we believe its applicability is evident. The value of the co-opetition approach has been recognised in commercial marketing. In some cases co-opetition may encourage consumer adoption of new technologies: for example, high-definition TVs increase the need for high-definition sources such as cable and DVD (Garcia et al., 2007). Co-opetition can enhance financial performance in firms: both cross-departmental cooperation and cross-departmental competition lead to learning, which thus benefit the firm (Xueming et al., 2006). Co-opetition has been applied to the healthcare industry as well (Gee, 2001; LeTourneau, 2004).

The notion of co-opetition blends well with our proposed competition matrix, because it highlights the importance of considering complementors and perhaps turning competitors into complementors. Additionally, the concept of co-opetition encourages us to analyse the full scope of issues by considering the various levels of analysis proposed here. For example, if a social marketer's goal is to reduce accidental handgun shootings, handgun retailers might be seen as competition. They supply the weapons, after all. The picture changes, however, if we view the situation from a different level of analysis. Handgun safety and handgun suppliers represent the product level of analysis. If we shift to the brand level we consider specific forms of safety, for example locking up handguns, and specific forms of competition and complementarity, for example buying specific handgun devices for locking the handgun. In this way handgun retailers can move from competitors to complementors. Specifically, they can offer handgun locking devices for sale, thus encouraging handgun safety while increasing their own sales revenue. Rather than focusing on the potentially lethal effects of having handguns in the home, the intervention can work collaboratively with handgun retailers to encourage the vigilant use of handgun locking devices, as was done in Washington State, USA (Britt, cited in Kotler et al., 2002). Thus, a competitor may become a complementor.

POSITIONING

So far we have proposed that identifying and understanding the competition is important in developing a successful social marketing intervention. This knowledge can be used in various ways: not only does it help you decide if a potential competitor can become complementary to your actions but also it guides the process of positioning your social marketing intervention with the target audience. In simple terms, positioning represents where your offering lies in the minds of consumers, relative to the competition. Although it is a 'managerial' process, it is important to emphasise that positioning is based around how the target audience members perceive any offering. More formally, the process of positioning can be defined as:

> The act of designing the organization's actual and perceived offering in such a way that it lands on and occupies a distinctive place in the mind of the target market – where you want to be (Kotler and Lee, 2008).

In this section of the chapter we briefly examine the concept of positioning within the context of social marketing interventions.

The concept of positioning was introduced and brought to prominence by Al Ries and Jack Trout in their 1970s best-selling book *Positioning: The Battle for Your Mind*. They argued that we live in an over-communicated society and, as a defence to this volume of everyday communication, our minds screen out much of the information offered. To address the issue, Ries and Trout (2001: 24) suggest that marketers 'create a position in the prospect's mind'. As Hastings (2007) notes, successful creation of this position requires you to both know how the consumer sees your offering and how your offering measures up to the competition. Positioning relates to the target market's subjective evaluation of your offering relative to the competition, not to any objective measure of it.

In commercial marketing, positioning is created in the form of a product which is endowed with a set of attributes. For example, an automobile can be designed and built to offer a range of different attributes such as price, safety, comfort, fuel efficiency and so on. The product's position is usually determined relative to certain product attributes deemed most important to the target audience. For example, an automobile manufacturer may determine that reliability and fuel efficiency are the two most important product attributes to their target market. The marketer would determine how their automobile rates on these attributes relative to the competition's ratings and develop a position around these attributes. How different makes and models of automobiles compare on these two attributes can be plotted on what is labelled 'a perceptual map'. This is usually a simple 2 × 2 or perhaps 2 × 3 matrix. These perceptual maps are useful in providing insights into how one product or brand is perceived and positioned against its competitors as well as the number and degree to which competitors have similar ratings on the key attributes and are competing on the same attributes. This level of competition or competitive intensity is determined by assessing distances between brands and is usually determined by measuring Euclidian distance or city block distance (see Ghose, 1994 for further explanation of these forms of measurement). Figure 9.7 represents a simple hypothetical example for automobiles.

Individuals will have a different perceptual map for different product categories such as automobiles, fast food outlets, hotels, etc., and for different behaviours and social or health-related issues such as obesity, exercise, organ donation, road safety, and so on (Kotler and Lee, 2008). Before attempting to identify a suitable position for any behaviour change intervention, social marketers must be clear as to who their target audience is and who (or what) the competition is. Only then can they develop a successful positioning strategy. In other words, the social marketer must consider how the intervention is perceived and currently positioned in the minds of the target audience relative to the competition, regardless of the form that competition takes (entity or non-entity). Is the intervention perceived as an occasional behaviour or something that must be done regularly? Is it viewed as a pleasant, short-term experience or an unpleasant experience that provides only long-term benefits when compared with a current behaviour?

In addition to individuals having different perceptual maps for different products, health and social issues, they have different maps for each level of competition. In the world of commercial marketing, Hooley et al. (2008) argue that the principles of positioning apply to any of three distinct competitive levels: companies, products and brands.

At the companies level, for example, consumers may develop a perceptual map of the names and identities of different supermarkets selling the same basic range of grocery items, at the product level they may map grocery products from different manufactures at similar price points, while at a brand level they may map differences between brands in the same product category such as different hair care brands. A critical point that Hooley et al. (2008) make is that these levels can relate to one another. Virgin is a UK-based company focusing on entertainment, media and travel. Although these products seem unrelated, Virgin believes the value of a 'mega-brand' can be built on consumer perception of Virgin's 'hip' brand identity, perhaps through customer loyalty (http://www.virgin.com/home.aspx). If the position of Virgin at each competitive level can influence the next level, Virgin can secure a niche in the consumer's mind. Andreasen's (1995) comment that social marketers must often develop a strategy for each level of competition supports the argument of Hooley et al. (2008). Social marketers should consider the need and implications of a positioning strategy at each of the four levels of competition we have discussed and consider the relationship between the positioning strategies at each level.

Returning to our childhood obesity example, how social marketers wish to position their intervention at the generic level (the topic area of childhood obesity) is likely to influence the method they might select to reduce childhood obesity, such as through increasing physical

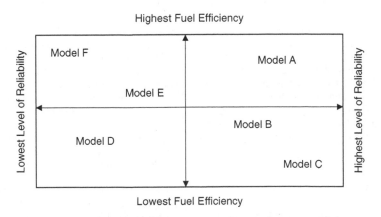

Figure 9.7   **Perceptual map of reliability and fuel efficiency for automobiles**

activity (enterprise level), which influences the form of physical activity such as active play (product level) and, finally, the specific behaviour of bicycle riding (brand level). Social marketers need to carefully consider positioning at each competitive level to ensure consistency in the minds of the target audience, focusing on target perception at all times.

If we consider positioning in the context of our Road Crew example, we must identify where this offering lies in the minds of the target audience. Again, it is important to consider positioning at each level of analysis. The relevant target audience may shift at varying levels of analysis. At a generic level, funding sources may be a primary concern. How are alcohol-related issues prioritised within the context of government funding? This may speak to how Road Crew should position itself within a generic alcohol context. Beyond this, at the enterprise level: What is the current landscape for drunk driving reduction efforts? And what position might be unique and beneficial? Next, at the product level, positioning within the context of partying and/or binge drinking with a group must be considered: How could this effort be more beneficial for the target audience? Finally, at the product level, How is Road Crew positioned relative to other means of getting home safely by vehicle when drinking, such as designated drivers and taking a taxi cab? Is Road Crew seen as an easier/cheaper/more fun alternative by the target market?

The purpose of positioning is to ensure the target audience readily and positively distinguishes your social marketing intervention from the competition. In commercial marketing, differentiation and competitive position are frequently built around a firm, product or service's benefits relative to the competition. More specifically, the aim is to demonstrate to the consumer that the benefits of your firm, product or service are superior to the competition. Kotler (2003) suggests that in identifying how your offering is superior, you should also consider if the differences are, among other factors: important to the target audience; easily communicated and understood by the target audience; affordable by the target audience; superior to the competition and distinctive, not being easily imitated by the competition. Achieving these differentiation goals is often possible by focusing attention on customer benefits and how those benefits are judged and perceived in the minds of the target audience. However, as Kotler and Lee (2008) note, it is not always possible in social marketing to build a strong position around just the benefits of a social marketing intervention. The competitive analysis may also suggest that the promotional goal for an intervention needs to be something other than

drawing attention to the benefits associated with adopting a new behaviour. The goal may be to simply highlight a behaviour change, address barriers to change, mitigate the impact of entity based competitors or reposition an existing behaviour change campaign. As a result Kotler and Lee (2008) suggest five possible positioning strategies, each distinguished by the goal or focus of the intervention. These positioning strategies are:

1. Benefit-focused, in which the benefits of the desired behaviour are the focus of the positioning strategy.
2. Behaviour-focused, where the emphasis is on highlighting a description of the behaviour the social marketer is attempting to promote.
3. Barriers-focused, with an emphasis on highlighting ways and means to overcome or mitigate the target audience's perceptions of the barriers to adopting a new behaviour.
4. Competition-focused, where the emphasis is on highlighting the weaknesses or negative qualities of a competing behaviour or organisation.
5. Repositioning-focused, where a current intervention needs to be relocated in the target audience's mind due to the emergence of a new target audience or perceived image issues with the current intervention.

Kotler and Lee's (2008) list of possible positioning strategies is a useful framework for social marketers to think through both the goal of their intervention and what it is that needs to be concentrated on in the target audience's mind at each competitive level to implement a successful intervention.

Positioning is an important component of developing a social marketing intervention that follows the selection of a target audience and the identification of the competition at each competitive level. Positioning is about occupying a distinctive place inside the target audience member's mind in comparison with the competition. Just as social marketers need to consider competition at different levels, they also need to consider the need for an inter-related positioning strategy that links to each competitive level. Whether building a positioning strategy focused along the lines suggested by Kotler and Lee (2008) or on other aspects of the intervention, the key is to remember that as a marketer 'you don't sell products, you create positions' (Hooley et al., 2008: 209).

CONCLUSION

This chapter has examined the issue of competition and the concept of positioning in the context of social marketing. Although problematic to define the term 'competition', we have adopted a broad conceptualisation in line with Rothschild (Hastings, 2003) and Andreasen and Kotler (2003) to suggest that competition is what the target audience perceives it to be and includes the barriers and costs to adopting a behaviour change. Although there is no consensus among social marketers on what competition is, there is general agreement that it occurs at different competitive levels.

In this chapter we have suggested four levels at which competition occurs – the generic, enterprise, product and brand levels – based primarily on the work of Andreasen (1995, 2002, 2006). We have argued that competition at each of these four levels can be categorised along two continua – competing versus complementary and entity versus non-entity based competition – to create a competition matrix. We have demonstrated a systematic approach to analysing the competition at each of these levels by using our competition matrix. This approach moves the social marketer through several layers of abstraction to create an exhaustive picture of the competition that an intervention faces.

Conceptualising competition at these levels has two significant advantages for social marketers. First, it mitigates the possibility of misreading the competition. As Andreasen (1995: 153) states, 'It is very often the case that marketers have read the competition all wrong'. For example, in trying to address childhood obesity in children of working mothers, social marketers may consider the main issue to be a lack of knowledge of what constitutes a healthy diet. In this case the intervention is set at the enterprise level and may only consider the competition at this level. However, in reality, as Noble et al. (2007) found in their study, the issue may not be one of nutritional knowledge but rather an issue of time: poor working mothers with insufficient time to prepare and cook nutritious meals. In reality, the major competitive issue is at the product level, where the pressure of work is competing with time in the kitchen. In this case, social marketers have misread the competition. By systematically working through each competitive level using the competition matrix, the possibility of making this error is reduced.

The second advantage of the conceptualisation of competition is that it encourages social marketers to identify complementary forces that may on first impression be seen as competing. The notion of co-opetition provides a framework in which to re-evaluate how different entities and non-entities can be viewed within the 'game'. The competition matrix we propose explicitly brings the principles of co-opetition into the process of competitive analysis. Co-opetition is an area that currently receives little attention among social marketers, but may, in the future, be a means for social marketers to gain valuable resources to fund and support their interventions.

In the final part of this chapter we have demonstrated a link between competitive analysis and positioning. Specifically, locating your social marketing intervention in the mind of the target audience members in relation to the competition is positioning. Just as competition occurs at different levels, we also suggest positioning strategies need to be considered in relation to each of the four competitive levels. In some instances, how your intervention is perceived by the target audience at the generic level can impact on the clarity and success of the position at the brand level.

In summary, this chapter highlights the importance and complexity of both the competitive analysis and positioning stages in the process of developing a successful social marketing intervention. It is easy to overlook these stages in the process and focus only on the most evident level of analysis such as developing the promotional message. However, a narrow focus means that a social marketer is likely to overlook an opportunity to understand the issue from the target audience's perspective. Social marketing interventions that ignore the alternatives facing the target audience are unlikely to overcome the competitive environment of fast, convenient and appealing alternatives.

KEY WORDS   Social marketing; competitive analysis; positioning; competition; costs and barriers; levels of competition; competition matrix; co-opetition.

Key insights

- Competition is whatever the target audience perceives it to be, and includes barriers and costs of the advocated behaviour.
- Competition must be examined at various levels of abstraction; a competitor at one level of abstraction may be a complementary force at another level.
- The competition matrix categorises competition along two continua: competing versus complementary and entity versus non-entity. Applying the competition matrix can help to assure all forms of competition are identified and addressed.
- Positioning involves identifying the placement of your offering within the minds of the target audience members, relative to the competition. Positioning must also be considered at various

levels of abstraction. Knowing and managing your position relative to the competition is essential for the success of any campaign.

REFERENCES

Andreasen, A.R. (1995) *Marketing Social Change*. San Francisco, CA: Jossey-Bass.

Andreasen, A.R. (2002) 'Marketing social marketing in the social change marketplace', *Journal of Public Policy and Marketing*, 21: 3–13.

Andreasen, A.R. (2006) *Social Marketing in the 21st Century*. Thousand Oaks, CA: Sage Publications.

Andreasen, A.R. and Kotler, P. (2003) *Strategic Marketing for Nonprofit Organizations*, 6th edn. Upper Saddle River, NJ: Pearson Education.

Basil, M., Deshpande, S., Usher, J. and Basil, D.Z. (2005) 'Fast food business strategies: Responding to nutritional concerns and competition', *ICFAI Journal of Business Strategy*, 2(4): 24–31.

Bryant, C., Lindenberger, J., Brown, C., et al (2001) 'A social marketing approach to increasing participation in a public health program: A case study of the Texas WIC program', *Human Organization*, 60(3): 234–246.

Clark, B.H. and Montgomery, D.B. (1999) 'Managerial identification of competitors', *Journal of Marketing*, 63(July): 67–83.

Donofrio, H.A.H. (2000) 'Tobacco prevention communication campaigns: Profiling the susceptible and receptive adolescent'. PhD dissertation, the Florida State University College of Communication.

Donovan, R. and Henley, N. (2003) *Social Marketing. Principles and Practice*. Melbourne: IP Communications.

Garcia, R., Bardhi, F. and Friedrich, C. (2007) 'Overcoming consumer resistance to innovation', *MIT Sloan Management Review*, 48(4): 82–88.

Gee, E.P. (2001) *Seven Strategies to Improve your Bottom Line*. Chicago, IL: Health Administration Press.

Ghose, S. (1994) 'Visually representing consumer perceptions: Issues and managerial insights', *European Journal of Marketing*, 28 (10): 5–18.

Grier, S. and Bryant, C.A. (2005) 'Social marketing in public health', *Annual Review of Public Health*, 26: 319–339.

Hastings, G. (2003) 'Competition in social marketing', *Social Marketing Quarterly*, 9(3): 6–10.

Hastings, G. (2007) *Social Marketing. Why Should the Devil have all the Fun*. Jordan Hill, Oxford: Elsevier.

Henderson, B.D. (1983) 'The anatomy of competition', *Journal of Marketing*, 47(2): 7–11.

Hooley, G., Piercy, N.F. and Nicoulad, B. (2008) *Marketing Strategy and Competitive Positioning*, 4th edn. Harlow: Pearson Education.

Kotler, P. (2003) *Marketing Management. International Edition*, 11th edn. Upper Saddle River, NJ: Pearson Education.

Kotler, P. and Lee, N.R. (2008) *Social Marketing. Influencing Behaviours for Good*, 3rd edn. Thousand Oaks, CA: Sage Publications.

Kotler, P., Roberto, N. and Lee. N. (2002). *Social Marketing. Influencing the Quality of Life*, 2nd edn. Thousand Oaks, CA: Sage Publications.

LeTourneau, B. (2004). 'Co opetition: An alternative to competition', *Journal of Healthcare Management*, 49(2): 81–83.

McKenzie-Mohr, D. (n.d.). 'Community based social marketing: Quick Reference'. At: http://www.cbsm.com/Reports/CBSM.pdf. [accessed 18 February 2009].

Nalebuff, B.J. and Brandenburger, A.M. (1996) *Co-opetition*. London: HarperCollins Business.

Nash, J. (1951) 'Non-cooperative games', *The Annals of Mathematics*, 54(2): 286–295.

Noble, G., Stead, M., Jones, S.C. McDermott, L. and McVie, D. (2007) 'The paradoxical food buying behaviour of parents; Insights from the UK and Australia', *British Food Journal*. 109(5): 387–398.

Peattie, S. and Peattie, K. (2003) 'Ready to fly solo? Reducing social marketing's dependence on commercial marketing theory', *Marketing Theory*, 3(3): 365–385.

Porter, M. (1998) *Competitive Strategy*. New York: The Free Press.

Ries, A. and Trout, J. (2001) *Positioning: The Battle for Your Mind*. New York: McGraw-Hill.

Ritchie, R.J.B. and Weinberg, C.B. (2000) 'A typology of non-profit competition: Insights for social marketers', *Social Marketing Quarterly*, VI(3): 64–71.

Rothschild, M.L., Mastin, B. and Miller, T.W. (2006) 'Reducing alcohol-impaired driving crashes through the use of social marketing', *Accident Analysis and Prevention*, 38(6): 1218–1230. Doi: 10.1016/j.aap.2006.05.010.

Solomon, M.R. and Buchanan, B. (1991) 'A role-theoretic approach to product symbolism: Mapping a consumption constellation', *Journal of Business Research*, 22(2): 95–109.

von Neumann, J. and Morgenstern, O. (1944) *Theory of Games and Economic Behaviour*. Princeton, NJ: Princeton University Press.

Wayman, J.J.C., Beall, T., Thackeray, R. and McCormack Brown, K.R. (2007) 'Competition: A social marketer's friend or foe', *Health Promotion Practice*, 8(2): 134–139.

Weinberg, C.B. and Ritchie, R.J.B. (1999) 'Cooperation, competition and social marketing', *Social Marketing Quarterly*, 5(3): 117–126.

Weitz, B.A. (1985) 'Introduction to special issue on competition in marketing', *Journal of Marketing Research*, 22(August): 229–236.

Woodside, A. (2008) 'Anti-social behaviour: Profiling the lives behind road rage', *Marketing Intelligence & Planning*, 26(5): 459–480.

Xueming, L., Slotegraaf, R.J. and Pan, X. (2006) Cross-functional 'coopetition': The simultaneous role of cooperation and competition within firms', *Journal of Marketing*, 70(April): 67–80.

10

The Social Marketing Mix – A Critical Review

Ken Peattie and Sue Peattie

INTRODUCTION – CAN I BORROW YOUR TOOLS?

Social marketing's success has been based on the simple but effective strategy of pursuing and promoting behavioral change for social good by 'borrowing' and applying the philosophy, practices and tools of commercial marketing. Although not without potential complications and pitfalls, this appears entirely sensible and mostly goes unchallenged. The discipline of commercial marketing has had a century to evolve into a highly developed and powerful field of knowledge and practice, with an unrivalled ability to influence the daily behaviors of citizens across the globe. The American Marketing Association (AMA) website lists some 114 scholarly marketing journals (of which only a handful address social, health or public sector marketing), and there are many more journals dedicated to business and management, or to specific industries, that also carry marketing-based research. Entering the word 'marketing' into Google Scholar brings up over 2.6 million distinct results. Whether you are searching for courses, conferences, professors or practitioners, it is clear that the world is full of knowledge about how to change peoples' behavior derived from commercial marketing.

Applying this accumulated marketing know-how to pursue social goals is such a simple and efficient idea that it seems like the proverbial 'no-brainer'. This, perhaps, is the root of some of the problems faced by social marketing scholars and practitioners. To equip itself, instead of engaging in 'product development', social marketing has adopted tools and ideas from commerce somewhat uncritically. This chapter aims to provide a critical perspective on a central element of social marketing knowledge directly inherited from commercial marketing – the *marketing mix*. It considers the origins and evolution of the conventional marketing mix before considering its application in social marketing:

- 'Can the conventional mix concept be successfully translated from commerce into social marketing?'.
- 'Can it be used as it is, or does it need to be adapted for use in social contexts?'.
- 'Is it wise to adopt a concept that is subject to considerable criticism, without a critical re-evaluation?'.

These are some of the questions that this chapter seeks to address in search of a distinctive and more effective approach to the social marketing mix.

ORIGINS OF THE MARKETING MIX

Conventionally, the marketing mix represents the interface between a company and its customers, and comprises the variables that marketers control and manipulate to win the custom and loyalty of their target market. The mix elements also represent the foundations of the marketing discipline. As a statement, this may evoke horror among the marketing purists who view the marketing philosophy as the foundation of marketing, and the mix simply as the final outcome of the marketing management process. Nevertheless, it is true, as revealed in Bartels' (1988) *The History of Marketing Thought*. When marketing emerged as a discipline, it was very focused on the practical management of the mix (even if the term had yet to be coined). The first overtly marketing courses were established early in the 20th century under labels such as *The Marketing of Products* at the University of Pennsylvania, and *The Distribution of Products* at the University of Ohio, both in 1905 (Bartels, 1988). As the field developed up to 1920, the focus was also on advertising and salesmanship, and on the distributive trades and the role of 'middlemen', including retailing, wholesaling, distribution, import/export, credit and payment collection. The marketing student then benefited from a combination of insights from the established discipline of economics, with others from the emerging discipline of psychology. In the 1920s, rapid growth in many consumer markets focused attention on new product development, and on applying the relatively new science of market research to understand emerging trends in markets and buying habits (although initially this emphasized geography and the creation of sales territories more than consumer behavior).

Marketing knowledge relating to the management of the mix was therefore established long before the consumer-orientated marketing philosophy emerged to become the keystone of 'modern' marketing. Although the phrase. 'The consumer is king' was coined in the 1912 market report *Department Store Lines* by Charles Parlin (cited in Bartels, 1988), a true consumer orientation in marketing scholarship was only first glimpsed in Charles Phillips' book *Marketing* in 1938. By the beginning of the 1950s, the previously dominant 'functionalist' school of marketing thought, with its emphasis on how to secure the successful development, distribution and sale of products, was rapidly evolving into the 'marketing management' school of thought. This conceived marketing as a managerial process of decision making and problem solving which focused on understanding and satisfying customer needs (at a profit) through the optimal configuration of the mix variables at the marketer's command. Kotler (1972), in the book which became the mainstay of global marketing teaching for several decades, summed it up thus:

> marketing management seeks to determine the settings of the company's **marketing decision variables** that will maximize the company's objective(s) in the light of the expected behaviour of noncontrollable **demand variables**. (1972: 42)

The term 'marketing mix' to describe those decision variables was apparently first coined by Neil Borden during an address as president of the AMA in 1953. During this speech he reflected on an idea expressed earlier by Culliton (1948) that a marketer was someone who combined different ingredients to develop the right response to the market and the demands of consumers. The next step was to create a menu or checklist of those ingredients to aid those searching for the perfect marketing recipe. This process began with Frey's (1956) *The Effective Marketing Mix,* and Borden himself contributed a relatively long list of 12 factors in 1964. However, it was McCarthy's (1964) simpler four 'P' factors of *Product, Price, Place* and *Promotion* that successfully captured the imagination, and lodged in the memory banks, of the marketing community. Although marketing thinking has continued to evolve, the conventional 4Ps mix has proved remarkably enduring. It has been regularly dismissed and attacked over a number of perceived weaknesses, omissions or negative side effects and various alternatives have been proposed. Despite this, it has endured, although cynics might suggest this is simply a testament to the challenge of asking marketing students to hold more than four things in their head at one time, and the recall benefits of naming variables using the same first letter. Not only has the mix concept endured despite the criticisms but also it has been extended beyond the realms of consumer product marketing from which it emerged, into new fields including social marketing.

THE CONVENTIONAL MIX – A CRITICAL PERSPECTIVE

Over the years numerous authors have sought to improve upon the traditional 4P marketing mix without disposing of it. Some have subdivided the classic P factors. Lipson and Darling (1971) extended the common subdivision of promotion into four (personal selling, advertising, sales promotion and public relations) to the other P components, to create 16 variables. Other approaches have sought to extend the list of P factors. 'Packaging' was suggested as worth separating from 'Product' for consideration as a distinct P (Nickels and Jolson, 1976). As services marketing emerged as a distinct subdiscipline, it developed its own extended mix to consider the important roles of 'People', 'Process' and 'Physical Evidence' in service delivery (Booms and Bitner, 1981). Other P factors suggested as supplements to the mix included 'Productivity', 'Processing of information', 'Publications', 'Partnerships', 'Procedures' and 'Planning'. By the time of the 1983 UK Marketing Education Group Conference dedicated to revisiting the 4Ps, the P tally was even pushed as high as 20 (Kent, 1986). Although marketing academics generally agree that the 4Ps are too simplistic, they have also criticized the seven P services mix for being more complicated, or have found other extended P lists too difficult to agree upon (Rafiq and Ahmed, 1995).

Others have been more critical of the basic foundations of the conventional mix (see, e.g., O'Malley and Patterson, 2002; Constantinides, 2006). One recurring criticism is that the mix paints an instrumentalist picture of marketing in which variables are manipulated in order to '*do*' things to the customer. Others have suggested that the mix too readily compartmentalizes marketing efforts and relates them to individual products, when in practice there are frequent strategic inter-dependencies between products and between different marketing campaigns (Kent, 1986). Some critics have suggested a transformational approach is needed to orientate the mix more toward customer relationships or exchange, and some have even managed to find an alternative letter (e.g., Bennett's 1997 Five Vs of Value, Viability, Variety, Volume and Virtue).

There are three other critiques of the conventional mix that are worth considering in relation to its applicability for social marketing:

1. Its original success came from allowing marketers to broaden consideration of purchasing behavior beyond issues of price and the mindset of rationality and microeconomics. At the time this was a genuine step forward, but one with little resonance in social marketing where microeconomics is less dominant and in some cases irrelevant.
2. The conventional mix is primarily producer orientated, and therefore cuts across the consumer orientation that underpins the marketing discipline (Dixon and Blois, 1983; Grönroos, 1994; Shaw and Jones, 2005). The product is what the producer produces. The price is (usually) set by the producer according to the product's cost or what the producer believes the market will bear. The other Ps are dominated by how the product is distributed through the producer's channels, and promoted to consumers.
3. The 4Ps model was never intended by McCarthy to consider a wider range of stakeholders than the end user (Silverman, 1995), and yet for social marketing applications it is often building successful relationships between the target adopter and other stakeholders that is the key to successful behavior change.

Despite such criticisms, the 4Ps have remained a central article of faith for marketers, both commercial and social, which Kent characterized as 'blind faith', noting that:

> The concept of the four Ps is just a classification, a handy mnemonic for remembering some of the key elements of the so-called 'marketing mix'. It does not amount to a 'theory' or even a 'model' in the usual sense of those terms (1986: 149).

Even considered as a handy checklist, the mix is weak. Van Waterschoot and Van den Bulte (1992) analyzed the 4Ps against the criteria for a useful schema and discovered that it has three major flaws:

*   The properties of characteristics that are the basis for classification have not been properly identified.
*   The categories are not mutually exclusive (so that you can have retailer-specific promotional product pricing offers.
*   There is a catch-all subcategory (sales promotion) that is continually growing in importance and into which is placed almost every form of interaction between consumers and producers (or intermediaries) that is not overtly a purchase, an advert or a sales service encounter.

Kent concludes that: 'It is in many ways unfortunate that McCarthy's mnemonic was ever coined, since it has served to undermine serious attempts to research what are the key marketing variables' (1986: 153). Despite all such criticisms (many of which are captured by O'Malley and Patterson, 2002 and Constantinides, 2006), the classic 4Ps mix has endured. Its defenders insist that the critics are missing the point because it is simply one component of the broader Managerial School of Marketing, and that abstracting the mix for analysis is misleading because this disconnects it from its theoretical base and customer orientation (Möller, 2006). Social marketing perhaps risks making the same mistake, abstracting the mix for adoption without considering the need for a different theoretical base for a social marketing mix. Doing so would indeed reduce the social mix to a flawed and limited checklist of commercial marketing variables, inherited from a parent discipline without learning from the parent's mistakes.

TOWARD AN ALTERNATIVE SOCIAL MARKETING MIX

In a paper entitled 'Ready to fly solo? Reducing social marketing's dependence on commercial marketing theory' (Peattie and Peattie, 2003), we argued that perhaps the time had come for social marketers to focus more on developing their own distinctive ideas, or at least to actively reforge the tools they have inherited to better suit their use in the social domain. The paper sought to critically evaluate the role of exchange, the nature of competition, and the use of the 4P mix, and how transferable commercial marketing thinking about them was into social contexts.

We first became intrigued with these issues after following an online discussion thread about the theoretical basis of the discipline, which evolved during autumn 2002 within the Georgetown Social Marketing ListServer. Dozens of leading social marketing practitioners and scholars contributed to this debate, and it high-lighted that:

- There was a debate about whether or not social marketing had its own distinctive theoretical base.
- There were some very different interpretations of particular social marketing concepts (such as the social product).
- Interpretations of the nature and validity of concepts which had been translated from com-mercial marketing varied considerably between social marketers working in different fields.

This debate continued for weeks, with many contributions (and its themes have periodically resurfaced ever since), but the following quota-tions from five of the participants, gives a flavor of the struggle that social marketers seemed to be having with the 4P mix:

Most published works in the field define product (and I'm paraphrasing) as (1) the behavior we want to elicit along with (2) the benefits that will accrue as a result and (3) whatever tangible elements we throw into the mix to encourage the exchange. If we agree, however, that part of the social market-ing strategy development process involves the manipulation/modification of the major Ps in order to elicit a desired behavior, and if one of those Ps **is** the behavior we're trying to elicit, then what we have (it seems) is a tautological planning model where we are modifying the very thing we are trying to bring about.

Until quite recently, I had never seen product equated with behavior. This linkage seems to have appeared in the social marketing literature quite recently, and I'm not sure it appears in the com-mercial marketing literature.... To me, the most basic view of the product is the bundle of benefits that a person gets in return for behaving a certain way (the price is the bundle of costs that a person

must relinquish). A person behaves in a certain way in order to receive the benefit in return for paying the price.... Behavior is not a P. Product is a P, and it tries to provide a benefit to the target in return for the behavior we seek.

I usually include benefits in the PRICE P (net ben-efit and costs). So if you put the package of ben-efits in the PRODUCT P, what do you conceptualize as being in the PRICE P (especially in Social Marketing cases)? Maybe this seems obvious to others but I've often had trouble when I've tried to use the 'benefit package' definition of PRODUCT in a model with discrete definitions for each part of the model (the Ps).

I have to disagree that a commercial product can also become a social product. This even though some commercial products may be necessary to facilitate behavioral change in the social market, such as in the case of condoms for safe sex. However, condoms would be better defined in the social market as a social technology that facilitates the adoption of a social product and would be complementary to a social marketing mix.

While I think that the 4 P's offer some insight into motivating certain behaviors – buy this product, use this product – I no longer turn to the 4Ps when working on social marketing efforts within social change programs. I don't teach the 4Ps to my classes either (unless they actually have some Ps to work with). I think this is an example where social marketing has gotten stuck trying to apply market-ing principles where they don't really help – but we can't let them go.

It was clear from the debate that the process of translating concepts from commercial to social marketing was proving far from straightforward. It also illustrated that social marketing practition-ers had difficulty relating to some key concepts as they were being taught and articulated by social marketing scholars. Ironically, this rather suggests a lack of a customer perspective among social marketing scholars, if the tools and ideas they are providing for their customers are not well under-stood and do not meet their needs. This was con-firmed by the National Social Marketing Centre's study on social marketing and public health (Haffenden et al., 2008: 9), which highlighted among its findings that:

For many respondents, particularly in public health, the terminology and jargon of social marketing was difficult to understand and off-putting. Respondents generally considered that the theory and language of social marketing was complex and it was evident that there was some nervous-ness about 'getting it wrong'. Many people were apprehensive of the considerable theory behind social marketing and found it difficult to understand and apply fully.

Some readers might prefer to interpret this as some form of shortcoming on the part of those working in public health. More likely, however, is that it reflects the shortcomings of conventional social marketing theory and terminology which they find 'jargonistic', difficult to relate to, and which clearly does not meet their needs as customers. If this is how our customers (who are always right) feel, then it appears to be time for social marketers to return to the drawing board to rethink social marketing theory (Peattie and Peattie, 2003). The conventional 4P mix is a prime candidate for such reconsideration.

In commercial marketing, one argument for retaining the traditional mix is that it is popular among practitioners and embedded in how they think and operate, because it reflects their own conventional marketing education (Constantinides, 2006). The same argument does not hold in social marketing, where many of the practitioners that become involved in campaigns are having to learn about the mix as if they were learning a foreign language. This raises questions as to whether it is the right marketing dialect to teach them.

Rethinking the social product

In the online discussion referred to above, it was the concept of 'product' that caused the most disagreement. Whether or not some or all of behaviors, benefits and supporting campaigns tools (such as information or tangible supporting technologies) were part of the product proved contentious. In commercial marketing things are perhaps simpler:[1] the company produces something for consumers, who accrue benefits from consuming it. Adopting a customer orientation encourages commercial marketers to envisage the product as the 'bundle of benefits' that the consumer enjoys. It therefore seems logical for social marketers to assume that since the person who adopts the behavior will (typically) be the one who enjoys the benefits from doing so, then the behavior must be the 'product'.

Working backwards, the logic of this analogy does not hold together very well. The behavior itself is not produced by the social marketer or their organization, it is not owned by them and then transferred to, or consumed by, the recipient. The marketer may facilitate it, but it is the target adopter who ultimately 'produces' the behavior. Similarly, to see the components of the campaign as the product is also misleading, since the benefits to the target adopter largely come from the

behavior, not from the components of the campaign. Before this becomes too circular, it would seem that the problem lies in trying to force fit the concept and label of 'product' into a social marketing context.

At this point the reader might wonder whether this debate about using the word 'product' in social marketing really matters, or whether it just represents a pedantic debate which is academic in the least complimentary meaning of that word. It does matter for two reasons. The first reason is that it is unhelpful to have a situation in which different people operating within a field are using the same borrowed word to mean significantly different things: this risks making the discipline appear confused, as well as confusing, to those working in fields into which we are trying to extend the use of social marketing. The second reason is that it risks importing into social marketing practice unintended consequences and risks associated with the implications of the word 'product'. Imagine for a moment the fun a mischievous newspaper editor could have highlighting the use of the word 'product' in a social marketing campaign seeking to promote child adoption services. The job of publicly explaining that the 'products' involved were not actually the children, but the benefits that would accrue to children and families from successful adoptions, would be an unenviable task for the social marketer involved.

What therefore can be proposed as an alternative to the social product? The following suggestion within the ListServer discussion highlighted one alternative approach (which also stayed with the alliterative Ps):

> I equate product (for both commercial and social marketing) with 'promise'. I think marketing activities are undertaken in order to get consumers to take action to attain a 'promise' which achieves corporate objectives for either profit, a healthier society or a reduced government spending on hospital admissions etc. Commercial marketing encourages consumer to purchase Omo or Tide to attain the promise, not of clean clothes, but of 'whiter than white' whites, of creating a happy family etc. Domestic violence prevention social marketing activities are aimed at encouraging young people to take certain types of behaviours to attain the promise of happy, healthy, safe relationships, a sense of wellbeing and of attachment to their communities. Call me overly simplistic but for my money the product is really the promise.

This view of social product effectively articulates the anticipated value (to individuals or society) of targeted individuals (or groups) engaging in the desired behavior. We, however, would argue for a slightly different P word, since 'promise' has some negative connotations linked to a selling orientation and problems of over-promising. Instead, we would argue that social marketers offer their targets 'Social Propositions' connecting the desired behavior with the benefits that will accrue (to the target adopters or to others). Examples of the types of propositions that social marketers have put to their target market include that exercising to get fit can improve your sex life; that cycling to work instead of driving is economical, healthy and good for the planet or that using your vote helps to build a better society for all of us. Such social propositions are perfectly understandable to the stakeholders that social marketers work with as propositions, without having to explain why the social marketer is insisting on using the special word 'product' and exactly what it means.

Rethinking price

In social marketing, the concept of price superficially appears to create less confusion than product. Social price is reinterpreted as relating to the social cost of behavior change to the target, and is viewed as analogous to the economic cost to consumers represented by price in conventional marketing. These could include monetary costs, opportunity costs, time, energy costs, lifestyle change costs or psychic costs (Kotler and Zaltman, 1971; Fine, 1981). Once again, careful deconstruction of this analogy reveals both its shortcomings and the potential for confusion.

One of the reasons that talking about 'price' can be confusing in social marketing is that adopting the behaviors proposed can involve both monetary benefits for their targets and monetary costs. Some interventions involve tangible elements that need to be purchased (such as condoms for safe sex) or involve the use of services, such as public transport, or the use of a gym, which cost money. Other interventions, for example involving smoking cessation or energy saving, can involve direct and positive economic benefits from adopting the behavior. Others may involve direct financial incentives being offered to the target to adopt the behavior. All of this makes 'price' a rather poor descriptor for this aspect of the social marketing mix.

Again, the logical questions are whether it matters if social marketers mean 'cost' when they talk about 'price' and whether managing social costs is analogous to setting prices when managing the mix. To address the second question first, Bloom and Novelli (1981) noted that 'pricing strategy' poses difficulties for social marketers. They note that while commercial marketers set prices to maximize financial returns for the provider, the social marketer does almost the opposite, by trying to minimize costs for the recipient. They also note that social marketers have difficulty measuring their 'prices'. A monetary price is a universally understood and consistent concept, and a given price means the same to all consumers, even if they vary in how they perceive its value and affordability. The costs of adopting a particular social behavior will vary between individuals. The key social costs of taking more exercise by jogging or cycling would vary not just in scale, but also in nature between potential adopters who were shy, or timid, or obese, or who were time-poor or who had small children to care for. No single currency exists to express, compare or trade-off such costs.

The adopter's perception of the costs involved also appears to vary at different points in the Stage of Change model (Prochaska and DiCelemente, 1983) and although the perceived value of a commercial product might vary between old, new and potential users, prices are usually consistent for all (loyalty discounts or new customer deals notwithstanding). As Bloom and Novelli (1981) explained, the social marketer cannot set and control the costs to customers in the way that commercial marketers can attempt to manage prices. What the marketing mix gave to marketing managers was freedom from the perspective in economics that the market sets prices through the interaction of supply and demand. Manipulation of the commercial mix offered marketers the opportunity to influence prices and to manage customer expectations and experiences, and thereby influence demand. In social marketing, the perceived social costs will be subjective and unique to each target customer and will be determined by them. This reflects Andreasen's (1995) concept of the 'importances' attached by individual targets to the different costs and benefits linked to the social marketing intervention.

Price and cost are clearly different things, and the issues involved in setting and managing commercial product prices are also clearly different to those involved in managing social costs. Therefore, trying to relate to a 'price' for a social behavior, as analogous to the price of a commercial product, seems misguided and potentially confusing to those learning about social marketing. As Sirgy et al. (1985) point out, the absence of price-setting mechanisms, the difficulty in measuring social 'prices' and the subjective nature of social costs combine to badly discredit the private marketplace analogy

More potentially helpful for social marketers is the concept of 'transaction costs', which is commonly used in economics, although less commonly by commercial marketers (often to the bemusement of the economists).[2] In conventional marketing, transaction costing attempts to encompass all forms of cost throughout the consumption process, including monetary, time, effort and other psychic costs. Therefore, for the purchaser of a new car this would include not just the monetary price paid, but also the time and effort to short-list and test models, the costs of insurance and fuel, the effort to clear a space in the garage to house it, the depreciation that sets in as soon as the car is bought and even the worry about whether someone will scratch its shiny new paint.

In practice, and in the absence of a monetary price to worry about, social marketers typically adopt a transaction costs-based approach, but this would be strengthened if its theoretical roots were recognized and exploited. Given the choice, it seems strange that social marketing has imported the relatively weaker and less applicable concept of price instead of the more robust and applicable concept of transaction costs. For social marketing the label 'Social Costs of Involvement' fails miserably when it comes to beginning with a P, but it is a much better expression of the realities of social marketing.

Achieving behavior change therefore involves the social marketer framing a social proposition to the target audience in which the benefits that accrue from the behavior outweigh the perceived social costs of involvement. Social marketers, through manipulation of their marketing mix, can seek to lower those perceived costs for their customers, to achieve the right perceived value balance and contribution to quality of life in order to motivate and hopefully maintain behavioral change.

Rethinking place

The 'place' variables in commercial marketing reflect the roots of marketing in tangible products reaching customers through economic exchange and their physical distribution through intermediaries within a supply chain. The concept of place later evolved to include the management of the environments in which products were sold to consumers or at which services were provided. Since social marketers are asking their customers to adopt a particular behavior, rather than to buy a particular product or service, the degree to which 'place' issues are meaningful in social marketing contexts varies widely. A campaign to promote child health through immunization will involve logistical challenges of delivering vaccines, together with a requirement to get the customer to a place of service encounter, which will closely mirror the place management challenges of both

services and product marketing. Other campaigns will target behaviors that will not depend directly on any service or product deliverables from the social marketer, and where the key behaviors occur in the home: for example, a campaign to reduce domestic water usage would be unlikely to involve any 'place' issues resembling commercial marketing.

There is also a potential for confusion linked to the word 'place' because of the application of social marketing campaigns in non-commercial contexts. Outside of the world of marketing scholarship, the word 'place' has other meanings. In social geography, it relates to a spatial perspective and particularly to an emphasis on communities and the perceived sense of 'place' among their members. Personal experience suggests that many geographers are heavily involved in developing policies and practical solutions for social issues concerning the environment, transport and housing. Any social marketers seeking to work with them to develop solutions will discover that geographers associate very different meanings with the word 'place'. Similarly, community-based social marketing has emerged as an important school of thought and approach within the discipline (McKenzie-Mohr and Smith, 1999), but here the community 'place' aspects operate at the level of marketing strategy development, not at the operational level of managing the mix. The opportunity for community-based social marketing campaigns to be developed in which all the partners involved are using the word 'place', yet all meaning something different, is considerable.

A much more appropriate concept for social marketers to use would be 'accessibility'. Behavior change typically depends on access to something, which could be sources of information, expertise or support, tangible products to support the behaviour, or physical locations involved in either the behavior under consideration (such as a gym) or needed to deliver the intervention (like health clinics). Services marketers have argued that the product-marketing derived concept of place should be superseded by the concept of accessibility in services (Booms and Bitner, 1981), and it also appears better suited to social marketing and the range of social propositions and behavioral contexts it covers.

The concept of accessibility can cover spatial dimensions, and where there are physical product components to a social marketing proposition, the distribution issues will resemble those in commercial marketing. Accessibility can also relate equally well to opportunities, and the ease with which the target audience can gain access to the proposition's benefits, even when there are no tangible or spatial dimensions to the intervention. This reflects the growing importance in consumer behavior research placed on the influence of context and opportunity, particularly on pro-social behaviors (Ölander and Thøgersen, 1995).

One access channel that may have growing implications for social marketing in the future is the internet. Although it has often proved less successful at facilitating commercial exchanges than seemed likely during the dot.com bubble, the internet can be an effective tool for creating interaction and building customer relationships. This is particularly true for the young, who are prime internet users and a key audience in several social marketing arenas (Peattie, 2002). As the internet increasingly frees us from the spatial limitations of the traditional concept of 'place', so the alternative approach of accessibility grows increasingly important.

Promotion

The final P of 'Promotion' is where the commercial marketing analogy appears strongest. For many organizations, social marketing is an approach which evolved from social communication, and this mirrors the origins of commercial marketing and its emergence from the study of advertising and selling. The two sets of marketers frequently use the same communications tools such as advertising, public relations, events, promotional items and websites. Increasingly, the same communications agencies help design and execute campaigns for both, and stylistically social marketing communication often seeks to emulate commercial campaigns (despite greater budget constraints). The demands of planning, testing, developing and implementing promotional campaigns are seen as highly comparable, and commercial marketing communication theories and practices are seen as entirely transferable to social contexts.

Again, however, there is a danger of importing the weaknesses, as well as the strengths, of commercial marketing. Conventional marketing communications theory has suffered from the dominance of physical systems-based communications theories dating back to the 1940s and 1950s. Models representing the encoding and transmission of a message by a sender, to be received and decoded by an audience (with more or less interference), persist in both standard textbooks and commercial marketing campaigns. Such a unidirectional and instrumentalist approach to communication is also often reflected in social campaigns. This may have been exacerbated by the dominance of health applications in social marketing, and the long-standing influence of the *health belief model* in the study of health behaviors and how to change them (Janz and Becker,

1984). As a model it is almost entirely driven by an information-deficit perspective and the need to correct misinformation, provide information about risks and behaviors, spell out the consequences of behaviors, provide supportive 'how to' information and engage in general awareness raising.

Communication theory has long since progressed beyond a focus on information transfer to emphasize communication as a social process that stresses interaction, involvement and shared understanding (Parrott and Maibach, 1995). These are all values that are frequently important within social campaigns. Although more socially constructed models of communication are acknowledged in discussions at the leading edge of marketing theory and practice, they are yet to be widely reflected in the mainstream. Communications theory and sociology represent important additional sources for ideas and practices which can be accessed by social marketers (Parrott and Maibach, 1995). This would allow social marketers to replace the unidirectional and information-based P of 'promotion' with the more reciprocal, interactive and social concept of 'social communication'.

One reason that such a reconceptualization of this element of the mix would help social marketers is that it would better connect them with the realities of modern society and influences on behavior. Social networking services such as Facebook and Twitter are increasingly important as sources of information, interaction and understanding for citizens. They are overshadowing the traditional promotional channels for messages from both commerce and social policy and are even supplanting traditional electronic media like email. During December 2008, Neilsen Online research showed there were 242 million unique visitors globally to social networking communities compared with 236 million to email sites (Burmaster, 2009). Soldiering on, using the terminology of conventional promotion, simply risks social marketers losing touch with the communications realities of modern society.

IN SEARCH OF THE MISSING SOCIAL MIX LINK

The alternative social mix elements we propose of social proposition, social cost, accessibility and social communication is partly an evolution of the thinking of Schultz et al. (1992) in developing a more consumer-orientated mix built around four Cs of Consumer Need, Cost, Convenience and Communication. They sought to escape from the product and production orientation that the 4P mix encouraged, but using consumer need instead of 'product' in social contexts, which often deal with unsought benefits, is also problematic. It also potentially opens marketers up to the charge of artificially creating needs, something which they have generally sought to avoid.

An interesting question arises beyond finding equivalent social alternatives for each of the four Ps, as to whether the social marketing mix contains anything that is not a part of the commercial mix. After some deliberation, the authors would propose that there is an element which commonly exists within the mix for social campaigns, but which is not generally a part of mix management in commerce (although it is a part of marketing strategy in commerce). That missing social mix element is the management of 'stakeholder involvement'.

Effective stakeholder management is clearly an important aspect of commercial marketing. Commercial marketers want good relationships with intermediaries, local communities and the media, but these relationships tends to be at a strategic and organizational level rather than something that is managed as a mix element for a specific campaign. A commercial campaign will communicate with, and through, stakeholders other than the end consumer (e.g. through retailers or through the media for a given trade), but that is more typically part of an ongoing relationship. The success of individual social marketing campaigns is very often dependent on involving specific stakeholders beyond the target audience. Consider one of the most iconic success stories of social marketing, the Road Crew campaign to reduce drink driving (Rothschild and Deshpande, 2003). Its success depended on involving the brewers as sponsoring partners, bars as point-of-sale communicators and bartenders as brand advocates, community organization to set up the social proposition of a limousine-based drive-you-anywhere service, and a network of volunteer drivers to deliver it. It is difficult to conceive of a commercial campaign that would be so dependent for success on the goodwill and involvement of other stakeholders.

Not all social marketing campaigns depend on involving a complex range of stakeholders: some are simple affairs involving just a relationship between the social marketer and their target audience. However, the frequency with which the successful social campaigns documented within the literature seem to depend on the involvement of family members, communities, voluntary organizations, health professionals and others in order to create and maintain the desired behaviour change is remarkable, and appears to be of a completely different order to such instances in commercial marketing. The value of this proposed extension of the social marketing mix will require further

debate and research, but seems a promising avenue to explore in search of a more suitable mix for social marketing applications.

THE VERSATILITY OF THE MIXES: THE SOCIAL MIX IN DIFFERENT CONTEXTS

Since we began arguing for the need to rethink the social marketing mix, the reaction of other social marketers has been interestingly polarized. Some react very strongly against the idea. They see it as bordering on the heretical and as throwing away the strengths that the discipline has developed. They see the need to contort the conventional marketing mix labels in order to fit the realities of social marketing campaigns as a small price to pay to apply the power of proven and well-understood commercial marketing concepts. They also point to the 'sunk cost' of social marketing texts already written using the 4P mix, and the potential disruption and confusion caused by rewriting these and relabelling the mix (although this seems to be an argument in favor of the ossification of the discipline at the expense of its potential development[3]). Others react very strongly in favor of reframing the mix. For them it is liberating to no longer have to force-fit what they do and describe to the labels imported from commercial marketing. For them the benefits of no longer having to provide translations of marketing 'jargon' for partners, users and learners outweighs any costs associated with creating some conceptual distance from commercial marketing. For them it represents the opportunity to take forward steps in custom-made shoes, rather than being made to march on wearing someone else's boots.

Those who argue for and against the retention of the conventional social marketing mix will each tend to bring forward examples to illustrate that either (a) the conventional marketing mix concepts and labels work equally well in social marketing campaigns, or (b) that they don't, respectively. Interestingly, each camp seems to use different types of social marketing campaigns as proof of their argument. This suggested to us that understanding the social marketing mix also requires an understanding of the range of contexts that social campaigns are employed across. Some contexts are very similar to commercial marketing challenges. Marketing the social proposition that 'exercise will make you feel better, look better and stay healthy' is almost indistinguishable from the challenge of marketing a home gymnasium as a commercial product. Marketing the benefits of rejecting domestic violence is a very different type of proposition, even though at a fundamental level, both are promoting the physical well-being of individuals. One of the key reasons that participants in the original ListServer discussion seemed to be having difficulty about agreeing what the concept of social 'product' meant was that it had to stretch across so many different types of campaign context.

A social marketing proposition can be disassembled to consider the attributes of the behavior, the benefits and the relationships between them. Figure 10.1 envisages some key dimensions of social propositions, and how they can vary among different contexts, largely building on ideas put forward by Andreasen (1995) in identifying the characteristics which are unique to social marketing. It focuses on how the perceived benefits and benefit/behavior links vary across different types of intervention context. It does not consider how the behavior might vary in terms of the target audience's predisposition for or against it, or how perceived social costs might vary. These are more difficult to generalize about for a specific campaign context, since they will vary among the target audience.

For any social marketing context, a profile for the social proposition can be drawn up according to:

Principal benefit recipient: in health campaigns the main beneficiary is usually the individual whose behavior is changing, while tackling domestic violence benefits the family unit. Volunteering programs typically bring local community benefits, while donating blood will benefit others across society.

Benefit timescales: the benefits vary in terms of when they become evident. Contributing to a local civic litter-pick produces immediate results. Changing behaviors to combat climate change will produce long-term benefits.

Benefit–behavior link: the community benefits of a litter-pick are mostly obvious as well as immediate (although others like increased civic pride may be less so). The socio-environmental benefits of reduced carbon emissions must effectively be taken on trust by individuals, based on the scientific consensus.

Consensus: some social propositions, such as the benefits of eating fresh fruit or of taking exercise, are widely agreed upon. Other propositions, such as the relative risks and benefits of alcohol consumption or how much sun exposure is or is not healthy, generate less social and expert consensus about costs and benefits and how they link to specific behaviors.

Sensitivity: social issues vary in terms of sensitivity. The proposition that 'eating fresh fruit is good for your health' is unlikely to offend or cause controversy compared with a proposition based on addicts being encouraged to use state-funded and controlled drugs. Since social

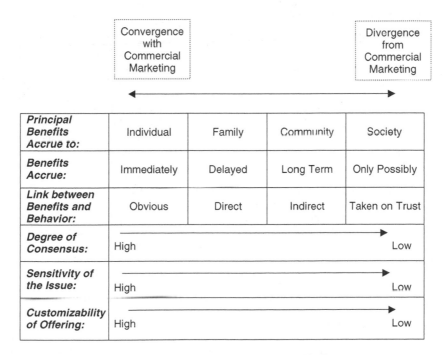

Figure 10.1   Key variations in the context for social marketing propositions

marketing campaigns aim to change the behaviors and lifestyles of the target audience, to meet objectives set by others, they are more likely than commercial campaigns to involve social sensitivities surrounding the determination of social norms and the risk of stigmatizing the campaign targets. In some cases controversy can reflect a lack of consensus; in others it is because social campaigns clash with other strongly held values, beliefs or traditions.

Customizability: some social propositions can be tailored to the individual's needs in delivery, for example through a personalized diet or exercise plan. Other propositions relating to promoting involvement in democracy, or combating racism, offer much less scope for customization.

Social marketing contexts with components tending to the left of the model will typically be closest to conventional commercial marketing challenges. For example, exercise programs can be marketed at individuals, customized to meet their needs, and the well-being benefits are immediately obvious (along with some effort-related costs), and there is a high degree of consensus about the value of the behavior involved. The commonalities between the social marketer of exercise campaigns, and the commercial marketer of gym services, will be considerable. Social marketing contexts tending toward the right-hand side of the model will typically have less in common with most commercial marketing, requiring much more caution in applying commercial concepts. Social marketers seeking to promote involvement in democracy or contributions to environmental protection are dealing with contexts where any tangible benefits (beyond the 'feel-good' factor from involvement) accrue more to society than to the individual. They are also potentially more controversial, and are often difficult to demonstrate or to connect to the desired behavior in practice.

It is important to appreciate that this model is not a dichotomy, with social marketing to the right, and commerce to the left. Specific commercial contexts will share characteristics of the right-hand side of the model. Some commercial products may be socially sensitive (e.g. linked to sex or health issues), products like chocolates or flowers are frequently purchased for consumption by other people, and commercial offerings like books or artworks cannot be customized for individual consumers. Similarly, the perceived positioning of an intervention within the model may vary between individuals who will perceive its benefits differently, or may not be easy to isolate for campaigns which involve a variety of benefits and beneficiaries. Smoking cessation programs will provide short- and long-term health and economy benefits for individuals and families and long-term savings for society.

What the model attempts to illustrate is that there is a range of contexts and context variables that will differ among social marketing campaigns. The conventional 4P social marketing mix will work better for campaigns whose characteristics reflect the left-hand side of the model (and therefore have the greatest synergies with mainstream commercial campaigns). However, as the social context moves more to the right, so the conventional mix labels, and the concepts they represent, become an increasingly poor fit with the realities of the social marketing campaigns. The alternative social marketing mix that we propose has much greater versatility (or perhaps more literally elasticity), in that the labels and concepts work well across all the different types of social marketing contexts.

THE MAROONING OF THE SOCIAL MARKETING MIX?

There is an interesting social phenomenon concerning the transplanting of groups of individuals from their country of origin and home culture into a new country and culture as immigrants. Immigrant communities may absorb some of the values and practices of their new host culture, but they will also typically seek to maintain many cultural practices and values from their home country. In doing so, they will preserve aspects of their home culture as it was, but they will become disconnected from how that home culture then evolves. Over time this creates the paradoxical situation in which, for example, typically 'British' traditions are maintained in former colonies long after they have fallen out of fashion in the UK. Similarly, members of Asian families living in the UK or the USA may return to their ancestral home to find that their cousins in India, China or Pakistan are the ones now holding the less traditional and more Westernized values. The immigrant generation become the guardians of the values and culture of their homelands as they remember it, while the values and culture within that homeland move on.

This situation is also reflected in the evolution of marketing thinking, and how 'old' marketing thinking is being preserved and defended within social marketing, while 'new' marketing thinking is emerging from practice and theory. This evolving new logic of marketing has been captured succinctly and articulated powerfully by a number of scholars in recent years (particularly

Grönroos, 2007). Vargo and Lusch (2004), writing in the *Journal of Marketing*, chart the evolution of marketing thinking. The 'marketing management' school of thought, to which the marketing mix is central, emerged between 1950 and 1980. During the 1960s, the 4P mix had become dominant in commercial marketing, and in 1969 Kotler and Levy proposed the broadening of marketing's use and of the application of the marketing mix into non-profit fields. Two years later the foundations of social marketing were set out by Kotler and Zaltman (1971), based around the translation of the customer perspective, the marketing management process and the marketing mix into social contexts.

Since 1980, marketing thinking has evolved by understanding marketing as a broader social and economic process. This has included the emergence of challenges to the value of the conventional marketing mix, and the breaking free of subdisciplines like the emergence of services marketing for which the dominant logic of marketing derived from product-based marketing was found to be inadequate (Vargo and Lusch, 2004). Constantinides (2006) explores the criticisms of the conventional 4P mix from a number of subdisciplinary perspectives. This analysis reveals that the internal and product orientation of the 4P model and its lack of interactivity make it weakest and least applicable when operating in spheres such as relationship marketing, services marketing and E-marketing. In other words it is the types of marketing most like social marketing where the limitations of the mix have been most clearly visible, yet social marketing theory and education remain wedded to the 4Ps inherited from the commercial marketing of mass-produced goods.

As Vargo and Lusch (2004) explain, in the traditional goods-centred dominant logic of commercial marketing: 'The customer is the recipient of goods. Marketers do things to customers; they segment them, penetrate them, distribute to them and promote to them'; this is in contrast to the emerging service-centred dominant logic where 'The customer is a co-producer of service. Marketing is a process of doing things in interaction with the customer' (2004: 7). This vision of marketing as the interactive co-production of service which delivers value benefits to the customer is central to the new marketing logic they propose, and works so much better to describe and understand the interaction between social marketers and their target audience than an analogy rooted in the production, distribution and consumption of tangible products.

The fondness that many in social marketing have for the conventional social mix is understandable given how much it brought to the field

when it was first proposed in the 1970s. However, there is a danger that as the mainstream of marketing thinking moves on, social marketers will be left marooned, on an island of 1970s thinking and terminology, cut off from the mainland and failing to benefit from the new things that marketing thought and practice has to offer. Schultz and Schultz (1998) argue that 21st-century marketing is typified by the growing power of the consumer, and the control consumers have over technology and their ability to access information and purchase opportunities regardless of time and place. As the power of consumers grows, along with their ability to choose and manage relationships with businesses, so the value of the 4P mix, which reflects an earlier era of manufacturer power, diminishes.

CONCLUSION

Time for a re-mix?

It is interesting to revisit the original paragraph written by Culliton (1948) that provided the inspiration for the idea of the marketing mix by describing a marketer in business as:

> a 'decider', and 'artist' – a 'mixer of ingredients', who sometimes follows a recipe prepared by others, sometimes prepares his own recipe as he goes along, sometimes adapts a recipe to the ingredients immediately available, and sometimes experiments with or invents ingredients no one else has tried (1948: 6).

The early evolution of social marketing thinking has followed a recipe prepared by others, with a little adaptation, in applying the commercial 4Ps mix to social contexts. For a young discipline this made perfect sense, the pre-prepared recipe from product marketing saved time and effort and imported the instant credibility that came with commercially proven ideas. As the field developed, so the differences between social and commercial marketing became more obvious, and became a subject for discussion by leading social marketing academics, including Bloom and Novelli (1981), Andreasen (1995) and Kotler and Lee (2007). However, the tenor of the debate about the differences between the two fields has tended to downplay them and their significance, rather than to confront those differences and explore their implications. Further development of the field may require a greater focus on the distinctive needs of social marketers, and how to develop a marketing recipe of ideas and tools that is customized to suit their needs and tastes.

Prochaska and DiClemente (1983) provide an observation linked to their stage of change model that provides one explanation why the need to question the benefits of the mix may emerge. They argue that early progress toward accepting the need for behavior change is typically more a function of stressing the perceived benefits, whereas further progress was often then made by reducing the perceived costs associated with that change. Perhaps the initial adoption of marketing principles into social contexts depended on highlighting the benefits that would accrue, but future progress will depend on a greater recognition of some of the drawbacks involved if that adoption becomes too unquestioning.

In summary, social marketing's strength and success has been built on adopting commercial marketing processes, philosophies, tools and terminology to achieve behavioral change for social good. However, the process of translating commercial concepts and terms into social marketing has been extremely literal. The result is that time and effort is expended in trying to contort, label and 'force-fit' ideas and practices within social marketing to form exact parallels with mainstream marketing. Ironically, this is a rather product-oriented approach, with a focus on the mainstream marketing principles (the product) rather than the needs of the customer (those within the social marketing discipline). The result is that social marketing practitioners are often left uncertain, or at least unable to agree, about the meaning and/or relevance of some of the most fundamental marketing concepts. It is difficult to escape the conclusion that one of the most important steps forward that social marketing as a field could take for its future would be to finally move beyond the 4Ps, which seem to create far more problems than they solve. Even as moderate a step as to rethink the existing 4Ps, to adapt them better to social contexts, would help by applying a social mix which speaks of:

- Social propositions – instead of products.
- Social cost of involvement – (including any financial costs) instead of price.
- Accessibility – instead of place.
- Social communication – instead of promotion; and adds.
- Stakeholder involvement – to reflect the frequent importance in delivering social campaigns of a mix of stakeholder contributions.

These alternative mix headings, although not a radical change, more comfortably fit the discussion of the social mix within leading texts (such as Kotler and Lee, 2007) than the 4P headings that social marketing scholars continue to wrestle with. In developing its own custom-made and unique theoretical base and vocabulary, social marketing would simply be following the path of other marketing subdisciplines such as services marketing in recognizing and moving beyond the limits of the conventional 4P mix. In leaving the 4Ps behind, social marketers would also create an opportunity to catch up with the contemporary thinking of the marketing academy more generally and what it has to offer them.

KEY WORDS   Marketing mix; 4Ps; marketing management; critical perspective; social marketing contexts.

Key insights

- The 4P 'marketing mix' is a core element of commercial marketing theory adopted by social marketing.
- The differences between the two marketing forms mean that social marketing practitioners and scholars appear to struggle to translate and apply the mix into social contexts accurately and consistently.
- Criticisms of the conventional mix reveal the risks inherent in applying it to social marketing too literally.
- An alternative mix based around the particular challenges of social marketing and reflecting emerging relationship and service-based marketing concepts may be needed to support the future development of the field.

NOTES

1 'Commercial marketing' can cover a great number of things but for simplicity here it relates to the typical conventional marketing exchange involving a tangible product.

2 In certain marketing applications, like online commerce, a transaction costs approach has been explicitly applied.

3 There is also a delicious irony in this. McCarthy's (1960) book *Basic Marketing: A Managerial Approach* was so popular that it swept away all those marketing texts that came before it (Shaw and Jones, 2005). Now the mix model, which once so refreshed the discipline, is dogmatically retained to an extent that is hampering its further development.

REFERENCES

Andreasen, A.R. (1995) *Marketing Social Change*. San Francisco, CA: Jossey-Bass.

Bartels, R. (1988) *The History of Marketing Thought*, 3rd edn. Homewood, IL: Richard D. Irwin (1st edn, 1976.)

Bennett, A.R (1997) 'The five Vs – a buyer's perspective of the marketing mix', *Marketing Intelligence and Planning*, 15(3): 151–156.

Bloom, P.N. and Novelli, W.D. (1981) 'Problems and challenges in social marketing,' *Journal of Marketing*, 45(2): 79–88.

Booms, B.H. and Bitner, M.J. (1981) 'Marketing strategies and organization structures for service firms', in J.H. Donnelly and W.R. George (eds), *Marketing of Services*. Chicago, IL: American Marketing Association, pp. 47–51.

Borden, N.H. (1964) 'The concept of the marketing mix', *Journal of Advertising Research*, 4(2): 2–7.

Burmaster, A. (2009) *Global Places and Networked Faces*. New York: Neilsen. Online.

Constantinides, E. (2006) 'The marketing mix revisited: Towards the 21st century marketing', *Journal of Marketing Management*, 22(3/4): 407–438.

Culliton, J.W. (1948) *The Management of Marketing Costs*. Division of Research, Graduate School of Business Administration. Boston, MA: Harvard University.

Dixon, D.F. and Blois, K.J. (1983) 'Some limitations of the 4 P's as a paradigm for marketing', in M. Christopher, M.H.B. McDonald and A. Rushton (eds), *Back to Basics, Proceedings of the 1983 Marketing Education Group Conference*. Cranfield School of Management, pp. 92–107.

Fine, S.H. (1981) *The Marketing of Ideas and Social Issues*. New York: Praeger.

Frey, A.W. (1956) *The Effective Marketing Mix*. Hanover, NH: Dartmouth College.

Grönroos, C. (1994) 'From marketing mix to relationship marketing towards a paradigm shift in marketing', *Management Decision*, 32(2): 1–19.

Grönroos, C. (2007) *In Search of a New Logic for Marketing*. Chichester: Wiley.

Haffenden, S., Handford, A. and Hunt, M. (2008) *Social Marketing and Public Health: Who's Doing What, How is it Being Done and What Support is Required?* London: National Centre for Social Marketing.

Janz, N.K. and Becker, M.H. (1984) 'The health belief model: A decade later', *Health Education Quarterly*, 11: 1–47.

Kent, R.A. (1986) 'Faith in the four Ps: An alternative', *Journal of Marketing Management*, 2(2): 145–154.

Kotler, P.K. and Levy, S.J. (1969) 'Broadening the concept of marketing', *Journal of Marketing*, 33: 10–15.

Kotler, P.K. and Zaltman, G. (1971) 'Social marketing: An approach to planned social change', *Journal of Marketing*, 35(3): 3–12.

Kotler, P.K. (1972) *Marketing Management: Analysis, Planning and Control*. Englewood Cliffs, NJ: Prentice-Hall.

Kotler, P.K. and Lee, N.R. (2007) *Social Marketing: Improving the Quality of Life*, 3rd edn. Thousand Oaks, CA: Sage Publications (1st edn, 1989).

Lipson, H.A. and Darling, J.R. (1971) *Introduction to Marketing: An Administrative Approach*. London: John Wiley and Sons.

McCarthy, E.J. (1960) *Basic Marketing*. Homewood, IL: Richard D. Irwin.

McKenzie-Mohr, D. and Smith, W.A. (1999) *Fostering Sustainable Behavior: An Introduction to Community-Based Social Marketing*. Garbiola Island, BC: New Society Publishers.

Möller, K. (2006) 'Marketing mix discussion – Is the mix misleading us, or are we misreading the mix?' *Journal of Marketing Management*, 22(3/4): 439–450.

Nickels, W.G. and Jolson, M.A. (1976) 'Packaging – The fifth P in the marketing mix', *Advanced Management Journal*, 41: 13–21.

O'Malley, L. and Patterson, M. (2002) 'Vanishing point: The mix management paradigm re-viewed and retro-introspective', *The Marketing Review*, 3: 39–63.

Parrott, R.L. and Maibach, E. (eds) (1995) *Designing Health Messages: Approaches from Communication Theory and Public Health Practice*. Newbury Park, CA: Sage Publications.

Peattie, S. (2002) 'Using the Internet to communicate the sunsafety message to teenagers', *Health Education*, 102(5): 210–218.

Peattie, S. and Peattie, K. (2003) 'Ready to fly solo? Reducing social marketing's dependence on commercial marketing theory', *Marketing Theory*, 3(3): 365–385

Phillips, C.F. (1938) *Marketing*. Boston, MA: Houghton Mifflin.

Prochaska, J.O. and DiClemente, C.C. (1983) 'Stages and processes of self-change of smoking: Toward an integrative model of change', *Journal of Consulting and Clinical Psychology*, 51: 390–395.

Rafiq, M. and Ahmed, P.K. (1995) 'Using the 7Ps as a generic marketing mix: An exploratory survey of UK and European marketing academics', *Marketing Intelligence and Planning*, 13(9): 4–15.

Rothschild, M.L., Mastin, B. and Miller, T.W. (2006) 'Reducing alcohol-impaired driving crashes through the use of social marketing', *Accident Analysis and Prevention*, 38(6): 1218–1230.

Schultz, D. and Schultz, H. (1998) 'Transforming marketing communication into the twenty-first century', *Journal of Marketing Communications*, 41): 9–26.

Schultz, D.E., Tannenbaum, S.I. and Lauterborn, R.F. (1992) *Integrated Marketing Communications: Putting It Together and Making It Work*. Lincolnwood, IL: NTC Business Books.

Silverman, S.N. (1995) 'An historical review and modern assessment of the marketing mix concept', in K. Rassuli, S.C. Hollander and T.R. Nevett (eds), *Proceedings of the 7th Conference on Historical Research in Marketing*. Fort Wayne, IN:, pp. 25–35.

Sirgy, M.J., Morris, M. and Samli, A.C. (1985) 'The question of value in social marketing: Use of a quality-of-life theory to achieve long-term satisfaction', *American Journal of Economics and Sociology*, 44(2): 215–228.

Van Waterschoot, W. and Van den Bulte, C. (1992) 'The 4P classification of the marketing mix revisited', *Journal of Marketing*, 56(4): 83–93.

Vargo, S.L. and Lusch, R.F. (2004) 'Evolving to a new dominant logic for marketing', *Journal of Marketing*, 68: 1–17.

11

Communications in Social Marketing

Dana L. Alden, Michael D. Basil and Sameer Deshpande[1]

AN OVERVIEW OF INTEGRATED SOCIAL MARKETING COMMUNICATIONS

Marketing communications are a critical component of commercial marketing. They are equally important for social marketing. Our review of best practices concludes that social marketing communications are most effective when three principles are followed. First, the brand promise is promoted *consistently* across the different elements of the communications mix (e.g., advertising, public relations, sales promotion and social media). Second, the promotion 'P' is *integrated* with the 'other' 3Ps of product, price and placement. Third, the focus of the communications is not on providing information but on pro-social behavior change and actions such as trial and maintenance. While commercial marketers generally emphasize the first principle when they refer to integrated marketing communications, we argue that social marketers can significantly enhance the effectiveness of their interventions and ongoing programs by keeping all three in mind as they plan the promotion component of their 4P strategy, an approach we refer to as integrated social marketing communications (ISMC).

Within the ISMC framework, social marketing promotion is an integrated element of the overall social marketing effort (Grier and Bryant, 2005; Maibach, 2002). Although creative campaigns can generate interest on their own, trial and maintenance are more likely when high-quality, reasonably priced and readily available products are offered along with a compelling and relevant

brand promise. With this solid foundation, the brand promise rings true. Without it, social marketing communications may inflate expectations, leading to disappointment and abandonment of the behavior following trial. Thus, ISMC stresses the importance of integrating communications with the other mix elements, making adoption of the behavior as attractive as possible by informing the audience of valued benefits and ease of access as well as motivating trial and reinforcing maintenance (Deshpande et al., 2004; Smith, 2009). Numerous examples from the academic and applied social marketing literatures suggest that social marketers continue to rely too strongly on knowledge and awareness building tactics such as advertising and PR, while other ISMC tools such as sales promotion and personal selling are underused. In the ISMC model, all promotion mix tools (advertising, PR, social media, sales promotion, direct marketing and personal selling) are employed to consistently position the targeted behavior (Shimp, 2006). When employed effectively, ISMC provides not only consistency in the brand promise across the communications mix but also results in synergy, so that the impact of the whole is greater than the sum of the parts.

Consider, for example, how ISMC might be used to help increase adoption of a pro-social behavior such as bike riding. The goals of the campaign could be to facilitate the use of bikes (product) for commuting, exercise and recreation using easily accessible bike paths (place) and their 'ease' of use (low price). First, the ISMC manager would work with others to ensure that each of the three Ps above delivered maximum value to the target market. Second, as opposed to hanging posters and running public service announcements (PSAs) highlighting the benefits of bike riding, the ISMC manager would use promotion strategies that more directly encourage brand trial and maintenance. Thus, the campaign might revolve around community bike days and feature activities such as a celebrity bike race or a bike ride scavenger hunt. There could be opportunities to win T-shirts and new bikes. The event could launch a 'log your miles' sweepstakes for a chance to win prizes that would encourage people to continue riding. Thus, advertising and PR would play important roles in increasing awareness and interest but lesser roles in moving the market to action. Importantly, regardless of the promotion tool employed, the brand promise would be consistently positioned through all channels.

ISMC's coordination with the other 3Ps, behavioral focus and consistent brand promise offer multiple advantages to social marketers. First, the ISMC approach is designed to optimize the quality of the offer for the target market. Second, emphasis on action-oriented promotion elements can enhance motivation, opportunity and ability (Rothschild, 1999). Returning to the bike ride example, motivation to enact a desired behavior is increased through a contest or coupon, opportunity through the availability of trial events and ability through knowledge gained by attending the event, for example, through the use of brand ambassadors salespeople to demonstrate low-cost ways to perform the behavior (Anh et al., 2009). Finally, with ISMC, all elements of the promotion mix – advertising, public relations (PR), sales promotion, direct marketing and personal selling – are considered. Each mix element is designed to deliver the same brand promise. This makes the brand promise easier to understand and remember. Furthermore, as noted, consistency in the ISMC efforts produces synergies across all of the promotional elements (Shimp, 2006).

ISMC IS MORE THAN COMMUNICATION AND EDUCATION

Integrated social marketing communications is more than communication and education. To a large extent, many efforts identified as 'social marketing' have centered on communication campaigns. Most prominently this includes a focus on using the mass communication media to promote health. The focus on communications may be partly due to the fact that social marketing was predated by 'information campaigns' (Hyman and Sheatsley, 1947; Mendelsohn, 1973). This

background may have shaped early conceptualizations of social marketing as the 'promotion of social objectives' (Kotler and Zaltman, 1971). Despite marketers' calls for the use of social marketing, many approaches continue to focus on information campaigns.

An emphasis on education and promotion is evident in many 'social marketing' efforts in the USA, Canada, the UK and Australia. For most of these examples the intervention was primarily or exclusively built around informational messages (Lefebvre, 2011). This reflects the influence of public health and health education (recently labeled as health promotion). This influence has expanded the application of social marketing to a wider variety of contexts, but has also muddied the waters between education and marketing so that communication is seen as the dominant arm of marketing weaponry. Examples of education-based social marketing efforts can be seen in a wide variety of applications, including alcohol use (DeJong et al., 2006; Gomberg et al., 2001), food choice (Bellows et al., 2005; Reger et al., 1998), physical activity (Bauman et al., 2001; Bellows et al., 2008; Berkowitz et al., 2008; Hillsdon et al., 2001; Huhman et al., 2007, 2008), sexually transmitted diseases (STDs; Ahrens et al., 2006; Bull et al., 2008; Darrow and Biersteker, 2008; Futterman et al., 2001; Kennedy et al., 2000; Montoya et al., 2005; Plant et al., 2010) and tobacco (Dietz et al., 2008; Hersey et al., 2003).

Evidence suggests that the informational approach tends to have limited effects, as words alone rarely address the real barriers and motivators for behavior change. Most evaluations find changes in knowledge or awareness (e.g., Dietz et al., 2008; Hersey et al., 2003; Huhman et al., 2008). A few have found behavioral effects such as getting an STD test (Futterman et al., 2001) and switching from high- to low-fat milk (Reger et al., 1998) or even more complex behaviors such as using a condom (Kennedy et al., 2000). In many cases, behavioral effects were more likely in populations reporting greater awareness of the campaign (Huhman et al., 2007, 2008; Montoya et al., 2005; Plant et al., 2010). Similarly, social norms campaigns have reported changes in estimates of how common a behavior is (e.g., DeJong et al., 2006; Gomberg et al, 2001), without altering whether or not people do the behavior (e.g., Bull et al., 2008; Darrow and Biersteker, 2008; Dietz et al., 2008; Hersey et al., 2003; Huhman et al., 2008).

Recent meta-analyses of health communication campaigns have also concluded that communication-only efforts aimed at the public are generally more effective in altering knowledge than in shaping behaviors (Abroms and Maibach, 2008; Keller and Lehmann, 2008; Snyder et al., 2004).

This may be largely due to the education focus of such communication campaigns. Admonitions from the field of social marketing can be seen as early as 1971 (Kotler and Zaltman, 1971). Quotes from recent interviews of social marketing experts conducted in preparation of this chapter reinforce the previous point:

> At fault to a large extent is the tendency of social campaigners to assign advertising the primary, if not exclusive, role in achieving their social objectives. In the standard texts on social marketing, the coverage of communication tends to share the weakness of commercial marketing in that it conceives communication largely as an information transfer process. The over-emphasis on communication as information delivery has been addressed by a number of people in the social marketing field in recent years. (Ken and Sue Peattie, Cardiff University)

> The challenge is that too much of social marketing is just thought of as communications. Not enough thought about product or other Ps. (Bill Smith, Academy for Educational Development)

In the case of developing countries, social marketing communication efforts have been more varied, often with greater focus on behavioral outcomes (Lefebvre, 2011). Of course, there are many programs that have employed educational appeals in the attempt to alter behavior. These include campaigns on reducing inappropriate antibiotic use (Goossens et al., 2006) and increasing multivitamin use (Warnick et al., 2004). Many other social marketing efforts in developing countries, however, have supported the distribution of a tangible product such as mosquito netting (Abdulla et al, 2001; Minja et al., 2001; Schellenberg et al., 2001) or condoms (Eloundou-Enyengue et al., 2005; Foss et al., 2007). There is some evidence that the ISMC approach was first practiced in Asia where tangible product distribution and promotion dominated the field from the start (Harvey, 1999). This continues to be particularly true in South and South-East Asia where contraceptives are used as tools to promote behaviors consistent with behavioral objectives such as fertility management and prevention of HIV/AIDS.

> The world of social marketing is distinctly bifurcated into the industrialized country behavior change communications programs, where most of the academics in the social marketing world are focused. The social marketing of contraceptives, on the other hand, is focused on the advertising and selling of a product. This means that market research is brand oriented and contraceptive social marketers engage advertising agencies much as commercial companies do. Typically, the agency is charged with increasing the sales of a particular brand of contraceptive. (Phil Harvey, President DKT International)

Regardless of emphasis, however, outcomes are more and more often measured in terms of behavior change objectives: for example, product ownership (Minja et al., 2001), product use (Abdulla et al., 2001; Eloundou-Enyengue et al., 2005; Foss et al., 2007; Warnick et al., 2004), or product use effects such as, in the case of mosquito netting, reduced anemia (Abdulla et al., 2001) or lower infant mortality (Schellenberg et al., 2001). Thus, ensuring that meaningful proportions of the ISMC budget are allocated to action-oriented tactics such as personal selling, direct marketing and sales promotion appears critical to success in both developing and developed countries.

THE IMPORTANCE OF INTEGRATING ISMC AND THE MARKETING MIX

There are many examples of the application of other aspects of commercial marketing methods such as consumer analysis, segmenting, targeting, branding and positioning in social marketing. However, two gaps are observed. First, these concepts often serve merely as background investigations for public education campaigns. As a result, use of the tools is often limited to producing messages. Second, while substantial emphasis is placed on these concepts, there is less emphasis on other aspects of the marketing mix (e.g., developing an augmented product to supplement the behavior change product with benefits valued by the target market; Burroughs et al., 2006; Quinn et al., 2006). Often, mass media messages are created without accompanying marketing strategies that increase the likelihood of real behavioral change. For example, a 'social marketing' program may produce an ad encouraging people to eat more fruits and vegetables, perhaps explaining their value, but not produce free recipe books, sponsor promotional events or offer coupon discounts that increase the benefits and reduce the costs of trial. In general, 'calls to action' without additional incentives too often result in little or no behavioral change (Rothschild, 1999).

ISMC recommends use of more effective and comprehensive strategies that are coordinated with and integrated into the other 3Ps of the marketing mix.

Part of the challenge of increasing ISMC application as advocated in this chapter is rooted in the definition of the social problem. For example, binge drinking on college campuses is often seen as a public health challenge that demands public health solutions, that is, primarily focusing on discouraging current behaviors by providing information about risks. However, a marketing approach that includes secondary and possibly primary research on the targeted segment might find that the problem is associated with the lack of alternative ways to socialize on campus. Taking a customer-focused, value-benefit approach, the ISMC manager might work with others in the project to develop attractive alternative substitute products or services such as dance or movie nights and then promote those activities using additional incentives valued by the market to encourage trial and continued attendance.

Commercial marketing draws theory from a whole range of academic disciplines such as economics, sociology, anthropology and psychology (Marketing Staff of the Ohio State University, 1965; Wilkie and Moore, 2003). Social marketing, however, seems to draw disproportionately on psychology, most recently cognitive social psychology. The focus on psychological theories can be seen in the variety of conceptual work that has been carried out in ISMC. Some of the key theories that have been applied include the health belief model (Rosenstock, 1966), protection motivation model (Rogers, 1975), social learning theory (Bandura, 1977), theory of reasoned action (Ajzen and Fishbein, 1980), theory of planned behavior (Ajzen, 1991), extended parallel process model (EPPM; Witte, 1994), stages of change (DiClemente and Prochaska, 1998) and subjective expected utility (SUT; Keller and Lehmann, 2008).

> Most of the theory [is] from the health communi-cation and commercial marketing fields ... so [there is often] no defined theory per se, but lots to draw on. Despite its age, Information Processing Theory still seems to underpin a lot of social mar-keting communication thinking and practice and the Stage of Change Model still seems to have a lot of influence on thinking about targeting, timing and tone. The Theory of Planned Behavior and its siblings still seem very popular amongst researchers. (Ken and Sue Peattie, Cardiff University)

The result of this emphasis on psychological theory is that the social marketing field has more understanding of the reactions to advertising per-suasion than it does to other ISMC tools such as sales promotion or other 3P marketing mix com-ponents. The persuasion model focus has resulted in an understanding of factors such as message

structure (Maibach, 2002) and the relative impact on attitudes of appeals employing message ele-ments such as fear and social normative influence (Hastings et al., 2004). However, greater acknowl-edgement of other disciplines can help broaden our strategies and increase integration of ISMC with other aspects of the marketing mix. For example, economics may help social marketers develop a deeper understanding of cost-related factors including explicit exchange of money or other benefits as in commercial marketing. Most social marketing interventions, for various rea-sons, are aimed at individual change. Sociologists are often critical of these efforts as not sufficiently focused on the structural 'upstream' changes that are the central focus of sociology (e.g., Andreasen, 2006; Dorfman et al., 2005). For example, in a recent case study that involved the application of social franchising and social marketing principles to improve reproductive health care in Vietnam, Ngo et al. (2009) note the importance of develop-ing attitude and behavior change strategies for multiple upstream stakeholders, including policy-makers and staff and service users, rather than focusing only on end-users. Greater consideration of sociological theories could help social market-ers understand and use social forces in support of their efforts.

> We are surprised at the extent to which there isn't that much 'social' in social marketing communications research.... Issues of advocacy, 'upstream' social marketing, social support networks, community based social marketing are just some areas where there are interesting communications issues to research beyond the campaign-target interface. (Ken and Sue Peattie, Cardiff University)

Additional evidence for our assertion that social marketers should use ISMC tools in coordination with other marketing mix elements can be found in a meta-analysis of condom distribution pro-gram effects. This study suggests that increased condom distribution and not awareness led to a growth in condom use (Cohen et al., 1999). Another example is the 'Road Crew' program that provided discounted rides to drinkers and resulted in decreased drinking and driving (Deshpande et al., 2004; Rothschild et al., 2006). Overall, social marketing efforts need to focus on behavior change by being part of an overall social market-ing program that increases product accessibility and provides real value to the target market (Rothschild, 2009; Smith, 2009). In other words, making the behavior easier or augmenting the behavior is usually more effective than simply providing information about the problem and solution (Kotler and Roberto, 1989). For these reasons, we recommend that ISMC managers draw on multiple academic perspectives and coordinate with others in the project to optimize the other 3Ps and effectively integrate promotion.

Future research

Theories that explain or studies that show how ISMC should be integrated with the other 3Ps in social marketing are lacking. The main issues can be divided according to the traditional '4Ps.'

Turning first to products, should ISMC strategies promoting low-investment products such as condoms differ from those promoting high-investment products such as hybrid cars? Should they differ for essential goods such as healthy food versus those that substantial numbers of consumers see as less essential such as bike helmets? Should strategies promoting tangible products differ from those promoting intangible products such as microloans?

Turning to price, questions arise regarding optimal ways to frame messages, for example, offering increased monetary benefits (bonus packs) versus reducing the monetary cost for the desired behavior (through coupon redemption)? How about comparing monetary tactics to those that are non-monetary? Does appeal type matter to pricing tactic? For example, is it effective to use fear appeals to convey increased non-monetary costs of competing behaviors? When are humor appeals appropriate in light of pricing tactics? Similar questions could be asked regarding place management strategies. How do we effectively communicate the enhanced convenience of acquiring or using a product? In a campaign that intends to promote hand hygiene among healthcare professionals, what would be the most effective ISMC mix to increase staff use of hand sanitizing dispensers next to each hospital bed?

In addition to questions about the 4Ps, expansion of social marketing's basket of theories is needed. As noted earlier, multiple academic disciplines are available for use: economics, psychology and sociology as well as anthropology, cultural studies, history and religion. One of the best ways to insure their consideration is to employ multidisciplinary teams. Tapping into these other disciplines can help us better understand relevant issues. For example, by considering drinking as a ritual (Triese et al , 1999), social change managers will be encouraged to think of strategies that differ from ones currently used: that is, fear tactics and normative theory (Deshpande and Rundle-Thiele, inpress).

ISMC SHOULD HAVE A BEHAVIORAL FOCUS

Social marketers should borrow from our commercial brethren to focus more on behavior. The gap between commercial and social marketing in this regard is found in both theoretical and practical work (Jones and Rossiter, 2002). Many social marketing projects assume a high-involvement model in which people follow a sequence of seeking information, changing attitudes and then behaving accordingly (Ray et al., 1973). However, audience members often lack interest in the behavior that campaign managers want to promote. Much of commercial marketing, however, is based more on lower-involvement approaches that attempt to alter behavior directly using free trials, coupons and other methods (Barry, 1987). Since targeted groups in social marketing are often not highly involved with the behavior advocated, it would be wise to emulate low-involvement communication strategies practiced by commercial marketers.

An example of potentially misplaced emphasis on beliefs and attitudes rather than behavior is the field's history of emphasizing fear appeals. Questions about the effectiveness of fear appeals have been raised since the 1950s (Benet et al., 1993; Janis and Feshbach, 1953; Sternthal and Craig, 1974). This approach argues that frightening consumers increases involvement and higher action likelihood. Fear appeals attempt to change beliefs about the costs of a current behavior. In commercial marketing this is typically done when the costs of the desired behavior are reduced or the benefits are enhanced (Kotler and Lee, 2008). Consistent with this notion, research has demonstrated that increasing efficacy and providing alternative behaviors are more effective than fear alone (e.g., Witte, 1994). Furthermore, there is evidence that fear is often de-motivating relative to behaviorally focused incentives such as those used in commercial marketing (Hastings et al., 2004).

While fear, social norms and efficacy are important tools, it is interesting to note how different they are from the most commonly used content tools in commercial marketing – including stories, music, celebrities, humor and sex (Gulas and Weinberger, 2006; Koudelova and Whitelock, 2001; Lin, 1998). Social marketing communication programs have not tried to 'push the envelope' to effect behavior to the degree that commercial marketing has (Reichert et al., 2001). For example, the avoidance of sex appeals for topics such as condoms is unfortunate, given evidence that sex appeals may be more effective (Reichert, et al, 2001; Scott and Johnson, 2006).

Missing in our research is the emotional side other than fear appeals. There is not enough focus on the emotional side of what we're trying to get people to do. (Alan Andreasen, Georgetown University)

Some of the cautiousness in social marketing may be a result of funding and mandates. But the influence of cautious stakeholders on creativity can be very limiting. Nevertheless, social marketing could work within the 'limited creativity' framework and make a greater use of 'big ideas,' as found in commercial marketing (Ogilvy, 1985) such as Mastercard's 'Priceless' and Nike's 'Just Do It' campaigns. Commercial marketing has also exhibited a greater level of creativity in terms of the selection of media, channels and vehicles in order to affect a behavioral response: for example, employment of social media channels (Facebook, Twitter, etc.) as part of the 'just-in-time' concept to promote movie openings.

Another important tool in effecting pro-social behavior change is the community-based approach (Bryant et al., 2007). Due to the historical emphasis on psychology, social marketing campaigns tend to focus on influencing individual consumers, clients or patients. We need to better understand how grassroots social change occurs and contrasts with media-based social marketing campaigns. How does the role of ISMC differ between community-based and media-based approaches? What is the role of advertising and PR in these cases? Is direct marketing the most important ISMC component in such campaigns? How does direct marketing differ from community approaches when applied to upstream segments?

It will also be helpful to understand the nature of tailoring approaches appropriate for community-based campaigns. Often, such customization occurs as a result of one-on-one interactions, such as interactions between prospects and brand ambassadors engaged in personal selling. How will the new technology enable hyper-tailoring of campaigns? Verbal and non-verbal communication plays an important role in face-to-face interaction at the grassroots level. Research is lacking as to what strategies will optimize outcomes. Research is needed to help social marketers more effectively target influential stakeholder and support groups as part of the overall campaign.

We [also] don't know enough about policy communication. If we really want to change health-related and other pro social actions, they are driven by policy approval and funding. But we don't know nearly enough about how to influence that system. (Susan Kirby, Kirby Marketing Solutions)

Future research

It is important to increase understanding of how creative appeals and repetition could be used to optimize the likelihood of inducing the desired behavior. For example, how should ISMC creative content and weight plans differ for campaigns that intend to promote limited-time behaviors (child immunization) versus campaigns that intend to promote sustainable behaviors (daily workouts)? A potential determinant is the stages of change model (DiClemente and Prochaska, 1998). For example, are fear appeals more appropriate at the pre-contemplation stage (to attract attention) but less effective at the preparation stage when the mix weight should shift to more trial behavior incentive tactics? As another example, what is the most relevant creative tactic (e.g., personal testimonials) and delivery channel (e.g., using brand ambassadors) for the contemplation stage?

With regard to the question of behavior, what can we learn from commercial marketing on how to encourage action through sales promotion, direct marketing and personal selling? Loyalty programs are a major sales tool in commercial marketing, yet little is known about the effectiveness of these as behavioral incentives in a social marketing context. One social marketing example was a US program that targeted expecting mothers with chemical dependencies: it offered them a $50 gift card if they visited the clinic for testing and counseling. At the end of that initial appointment, clients were offered an additional gift card if they kept their follow-up appointment in two weeks. Clinic managers reported the program had met with great success as this was an incentive that was highly valued by the target market (Hawaii Public Radio News, April 2009). Although this is a single example, it suggests a potential approach and the need for additional research that evaluates the relative efficacy of different types of sales promotion incentives to inducing trial and maintaining pro-social behaviors, especially with low-motivation groups.

In addition to developing better theory on ISMC and individual consumer behavior, it is important to research more effective ways to influence upstream policymakers and horizontal social group influencers who may otherwise block adoption. Here too, however, ISMC communication should emphasize customized direct marketing and personal selling as opposed to general information provision which should be done in earlier education stages. As social marketing scholars increasingly point out the importance of upstream-focused ISMC (Andreasen, 2006), research is needed on communication strategies that will help achieve behavioral objectives for these groups, such as motivating policymakers to formulate and implement laws regarding provision of 'emergency contraception' through pharmacies. A critical area of inquiry in this regard involves development of theory concerning the likelihood that a combination of upstream and downstream campaigns will be more effective than either one alone. For example, would cooking classes held in local restaurants during closed hours be a good means to encourage use of healthy foods at home in the downstream segment or would it be better to focus on the upstream segment first?

Other questions upstream behavior change include determining which ISMC components make sense in these campaigns? Are personal selling and direct marketing more critical than other components? Does sales promotion have a role to play in upstream campaigns? How do media strategies and tactics apply to upstream campaigns? How can we best utilize interactive technologies to influence upstream players, especially when compared to traditional media? Finally, how do these strategies differ from downstream campaign strategies? Clearly, some of the promotional incentives that are appropriate and effective for downstream segments would not be appropriate for use with policymakers and some other upstream segments.

Finally, ISMC behavior change theories should also develop from practice. Given the applied nature of social marketing, it would be useful for theorists to identify and address key questions with which practitioners grapple. The question of how to 'brand' a social marketing effort is important. Also, when should campaign managers apply social forces such as social norms and other 'third person effects' that invoke others? Practitioners are really interested in the prediction value of a theory. However, it is difficult for them to gauge which theories can be applied most effectively in different contexts. Practitioners would benefit from knowing which theory would work the best to change behavior under specific circumstances.

I think that theories and frameworks are a useful starting point, but practitioners do not have the time to review the academic literature for evidence on appropriate segmentation strategies or the most appropriate behavioral theories for specific target groups and behaviors or the most effective distribution channels – they need clear guidelines to assist them in developing cost-effective, efficacious interventions. (Sandra Jones, University of Wollongong)

INTEGRATING ACROSS ISMC MIX ELEMENTS

ISMC stresses the importance of a considering all possible communication channels and, for those that are selected, ensuring that the brand promise is consistently promoted. Thus, in addition to paid advertising and public service announcements (PSAs), public relations, sales promotion, direct marketing and personal selling should all speak with a single message (Shimp, 2006). To achieve this objective, a high level of coordination is required across the mix elements. In the commercial sector, this has proven difficult because one agency often handles advertising, another sales promotion, a third public relations and so forth. Different approaches to integration have been proposed but, at the end of the day, it is the responsibility of the ISMC brand manager to assure this happens and to get all communication partners on the same brand promise page.

Future research

Research is needed on ways to integrate the brand promise across all elements of the ISMC mix. Commercial marketers have been interested in this issue for some time. However, many of these insights are proprietary. Still, the questions are important for social marketers. For instance, how do we maintain a brand promise and brand image that is consistent with what is communicated via traditional advertising and through a wide potential range of direct marketing channels? The technological revolution has altered the media scene. Internet, wikis, social networking sites, cell phones and PDAs have increased information access and networking opportunities. Similarly, the lines between traditional and new media have evaporated. One can read a story in a newspaper, listen to a radio show or see a program on TV, and then gain more information on the internet. Social marketing campaigns are slowly but steadily embracing these technologies to promote pro-social behaviors. However, research on the effectiveness of such media changes is lacking. The issue of integration across ISMC becomes all the more important in the light of new technologies (see, e.g., the CDC's recent use of Twitter in its response to the threat of a swine flu outbreak in the USA; Blackshaw, 2009).

CONCLUSION

In this chapter, we have argued that the main role of ISMC should be to support pro-social behavior change that is part of a larger social marketing program. As such, we recommend that the first two stages of the AIDA (attention, interest, desire and action) model be de-emphasized by ISMC researchers and practitioners. Instead, we would like to see ISMC projects build on basic public education campaigns that have already increased awareness and knowledge of the targeted behavior. In essence, our argument is that the first two components of the AIDA model are the proper focus of public health, environment and arts education campaigns. Meanwhile, the focus of ISMC in social marketing should be on using the tools of marketing communications that lead to trial and maintenance of some socially desired behavior (such as exercise, recycling or smoking cessation).

How do we focus ISMC on supporting SM behavior change? We propose four critical components:

1. **Theoretical focus:** when planning ISMC, consider theories of behavior change besides those that emphasize knowledge as the only precursor to behavior change. Only when substantial pre-behavior change groundwork is required to change behavior should we focus on education theory (e.g., general health promotion). And, even then, we would like to see theory develop and case studies undertaken regarding effective coordination with public education specialists rather than having social marketers spend significant resources developing their own theory and practice regarding mass education campaigns.

2. **Promotion mix:** when planning ISMC, de-emphasize the general awareness building tactics of the marketing communications mix (e.g., advertising and PR) and emphasize mix tactics that are known to more effectively drive behavior (e.g., direct marketing, personal selling and sales promotion). Advertising and PR may be needed (e.g., to remind the target market of the pro-social brand), but they need to be connected with behavior-inducing incentives valued by the target market, e.g., promoting maintenance using a loyalty program. Whatever tools are used, it is important to assure consistency of the brand promise across all channels.

3. **Other 3Ps:** when planning ISMC, it is important to carefully integrate communication promotions with the other social marketing Ps. Their centrality is critical to achieving behavior change through trial and maintenance. For example, if the brand includes a tangible product (e.g., use of a nicotine patch in a smoking cessation campaign), use a price-based offer to make the benefit of exchange more concrete and motivate the trial. Other message strategies that should

be considered as part of an ISMC include (a) increasing perceptions of product accessibility, (b) providing a concrete demonstration of the ease of product use and (c) promoting ways that the target market can reduce investment costs (financial and time) associated with the pro-social behavior.

4. **Multiple segments:** when planning ISMC, don't only target intended adopters but also upstream policymakers and horizontal social group influencers who may otherwise block adoption. Here too, ISMC communication, in addition to public education, should consider direct marketing (including newer social media) and personal selling for the specific benefits they provide, including the ability to address, in-depth, policymakers' concerns and counter-arguments.

To conclude, ISMC should involve much more than education-based or high-involvement models of behavior change. We believe that focusing on ISMC approaches aimed at generating trial and reinforcing maintenance is an optimal way for the field to make meaningful contributions above and beyond those of education campaigns that emphasize awareness and knowledge. Scholars in the past have differentiated education and marketing on the basis of what each promotes (knowledge vs behavior). We contribute to this understanding by proposing a shift from awareness and knowledge-building communication strategies to those that directly result in actual behavior. In this way, the fields of public education, social marketing and ISMC will find substantial common ground and a synergy for the good of society that is truly greater than the sum of their individual parts.

KEY WORDS   Promotion, integrated social marketing communication; advertising; behavior change communication.

Key insights

- Communication should use a variety of avenues (e.g., advertising, public relations, sales promotion, direct marketing and social media).
- The message should be consistent or reinforcing across these communication components.
- The communication program must be integrated with the overall marketing strategy of product, price and placement.
- The focus should not be on information, but on creating pro-social behavior change and actions through trial and maintenance.

NOTE

1   All authors contributed equally to the chapter. They are listed in the alphabetical order of their last names.

REFERENCES

Abdulla, S., Schellenberger, J.A., Nathan, R., et al. (2001) 'Impact on malaria morbidity of a programme supplying insecticide treated nets in children aged under 2 in Tanzania: Community cross sectional study', *British Medical Journal*, 322: 270–273.

Abroms, L.C. and Maibach, E.W. (2008) 'The effectiveness of mass communication to change public behavior', *Annual Review of Public Health*, 29: 219–234.

Ahrens, K., Kent, C.K., Montoya, J.A., et al. (2006) 'Health Penis: San Francisco's social marketing campaign to increase syphilis testing among gay and bisexual men', *PLOS Medicine*, 3: 2199–2203.

Ajzen, I. (1991) 'The theory of planned behavior', *Organizational Behavior and Human Decision Processes*, 50: 179–211.

Ajzen, I. and Fishbein, M. (1980) *Understanding Attitudes and Predicting Social Behavior*. Englewood Cliffs, NJ: Prentice-Hall.

Andreasen, A.R. (2006) *Social Marketing in the 21st Century*. Newbury Park, CA: Sage Publications.

Anh, D.N., Alden, D.L., Nguyen, H. and Dinh, N. (2009) 'Developing and launching the government social franchise model of reproductive healthcare service delivery in Vietnam', *Social Marketing Quarterly*, 15: 71–89.

Bandura, A. (1977) *Social Learning Theory*. Englewood Cliffs, NJ: Prentice-Hall.

Barry, T.E. (1987) 'The development of the hierarchy of effects: An historical perspective', *Current Issues and Research in Advertising*, 10: 251–295.

Bauman, A.E., Bellew, B., Owen, N. and Vita, P. (2001) 'Impact of an Australian media campaign targeting physical activity in 1998', *American Journal of Preventative Medicine*, 21: 41–47.

Bellows, L., Cole, K. and Gabel, J.A. (2005) 'Family fun with new foods: A parent component to the food friends social marketing campaign', *Journal of Nutrition Education and Behavior*, 38: 123–124.

Bellows, L., Anderson, J., Gould, S.M. and Auld, G. (2008) 'Formative research and strategic development of a physical activity component for obesity prevention in preschoolers', *Journal of Community Health*, 33: 169–178.

Benet, S., Pitts, R.E. and LaTour, M. (1993) 'The appropriateness of fear appeal use for health care marketing to the elderly: Is it OK to scare granny?', *Journal of Business Ethics*, 12: 45–55.

Berkowitz, J.M., Huhman, M., Heitzler, C.D., et al. (2008) 'Overview of formative, process, and outcome evaluation used in the VERB campaign', *American Journal of Preventative Medicine*, 34: S222–S229.

Blackshaw, P. (2009) 'In a time of crisis, sexy and flashy doesn't count: Ten things marketers can learn from the CDC's response to the swine flu epidemic'. Retrieved from the world wide web on 12 May, 2009: http://adage.com/digital/article?article_id=136355. Ad Age Digital.

Bryant, C.A., Brown, M.C., Kelli, R., et al. (2007) 'Community-based prevention marketing: Organizing a community for health behavior intervention', *Health Promotion Practice*, 8: 154–163.

Bull, S.S., Posner, S.F., Ortiz, C., et al. (2008) 'POWER for reproductive health: Results from a social marketing campaign promoting female and male condoms', *Journal of Adolescent Health*, 43: 71–78.

Burroughs, E.L., Peck, L.E., Sharpe, P.A., et al. (2006) 'Using focus groups in the consumer research phase of a social marketing program to promote moderate-intensity physical activity and walking trail use in Sumter Country, South Carolina', *Preventing Chronic Disease: Public Health Research, Practice, and Policy*, 3: 1–13.

Cohen, D.A., Farley, T.A., Bendimo-Etame, J.R., et al. (1999) 'Implementation of condom social marketing in Louisiana, 1993 to 1996', *American Journal of Public Health*, 89: 204–208.

Darrow, W.W. and Biersteker, S. (2008) 'Short-term impact evaluation of a social marketing campaign to prevent syphilis among men who have sex with men', *American Journal of Public Health*, 98: 337–343.

DeJong, W., Schneider, S.K., Towvim, L.G., et al. (2006) 'A multisite randomized trial of social norms marketing campaigns to reduce college drinking', *Journal of Studies of Alcohol*, 67: 868–879.

Deshpande, S. and Rundle-Thiele, S. (inpress) 'Segmenting and targeting American university students to promote responsible alcohol use: A case for applying social marketing principles', *Health Marketing Quarterly*, 28(4).

Deshpande, S., Rothschild, M.L. and Brooks, R. (2004) 'New product development in social marketing', *Social Marketing Quarterly*, 10: 39–49.

DiClemente, C.C. and Prochaska, J.O. (1998) 'Toward a comprehensive, transtheoretical model of change', in W.M. Miller and N. Heather (eds), *Treating Addictive Behaviors*, 2nd edn. New York: Springer, pp. 3–24.

Dietz, N.A., Delva, J., Woolley, M.E. and Russello, L. (2008) 'The reach of a youth-oriented anti-tobacco media campaign on adult smokers', *Drug and Alcohol Dependence*, 93: 180–184.

Dorfman, L., Wallack, L. and Woodruf, K. (2005) 'More than a message: Framing public health advocacy to change corporate practices', *Health Education and Behavior*, 32: 320–336.

Eloundou-Enyengue, P.M., Meekers, D. and Calves, A.E. (2005) 'From awareness to adoption: The effects of AIDS education and condom social marketing on condom use in Tanzania (1993–1996)', *Journal of Biological Sciences*, 37: 257–268.

Foss, A.M., Hossain, M., Vickerman, P.T. and Watts, C.H. (2007) 'A systematic review of published evidence on intervention impact on condom use in sub-Saharan Africa and Asia', *Sexually Transmitted Infections*, 83: 510–516.

Futterman, D.C., Peralta, L., Rudy, B.J., et al. (2001) 'The ACCESS (Adolescents Connected to Care, Evaluation, and Special Services) Project: Social marketing to promote HIV testing to adolescents, methods and first year results from a six city campaign', *Journal of Adolescent Health*, 29: S19–S29.

Gomberg, L., Schneider, S.K. and DeJong, W. (2001) 'Evaluation of a social norms marketing campaign to reduce high-risk drinking at the University of Mississippi', *American Journal of Drug and Alcohol Abuse*, 27: 375–389.

Goossens, H., Guillemot, D., Ferech, M., et al. (2006) 'National campaigns to improve antibiotic use', *European Journal of Clinical Pharmacology*, 62: 373–379.

Grier, S. and Bryant, C.A. (2005) 'Social marketing in public health', *Annual Review of Public Health*, 26: 319–339.

Gulas, C.S. and Weinberger, M.G. (2006) *Humor in Advertising: A Comprehensive Analysis*. Armonk, New York: M.E. Sharpe.

Harvey, P. (1999) *Let Every Child Be Wanted: How Social Marketing is Revolutionizing Contraceptive Use around the World*. Westport, CT: Auburn House.

Hastings, G., Stead, M. and Webb, J. (2004) 'Fear appeals in social marketing: Strategic and ethical reasons for concern', *Psychology and Marketing*, 21: 961–986.

Hersey, J.C., Niederdeppe, J., Evans, W.D., et al. (2003) 'The effects of state counterindustry media campaigns on beliefs, attitudes, and smoking status among teens and young adults', *Preventative Medicine*, 37: 544–552.

Hillsdon, M., Cavill, N., Nanchahal, K., Diamond, A. and White, I.R. (2001) 'National level promotion of physical activity: ACTIVE for LIFE campaign', *Journal of Epidemiology and Community Health*, 55: 755–761.

Huhman, M., Potter, L.D., Duke, J.C., et al. (2007) 'Evaluation of a national physical activity intervention for children: VERB campaign, 2002–2004', *American Journal of Preventative Medicine*, 32: 38–43.

Huhman, M., Bauman, A. and Bowles, H.R. (2008) 'Initial outcomes of the VERB campaign: Tweens' awareness and understanding of campaign messages', *American Journal of Preventative Medicine*, 34: S241–S248.

Hyman, H.H. and Sheatsley, P.B. (1947) 'Some reasons why information campaigns fail', *Public Opinion Quarterly*, 11(3): 412–423.

Janis, I. and Feshbach, S. (1953) 'Effects of fear-arousing communications', *Journal of Abnormal and Social Psychology*, 48: 78–92.

Jones, S.C. and Rossiter, J.R. (2002) 'The applicability of commercial marketing theory to social marketing: Two case studies of current Australian social marketing campaigns', *Social Marketing Quarterly*, 8: 6–18.

Keller, P.A. and Lehmann, D.R. (2008) 'Designing effective health communications: A meta-analysis', *Journal of Public Policy and Marketing*, 27: 117–130.

Kennedy, M.G., Mizuno, Y., Seals, B.F., Myllyluoma, J. and Weeks-Norton, K. (2000) 'Increasing condom use among adolescents with coalition-based social marketing', *AIDS*, 14: 1809–1818.

Kotler, P. and Lee, N.R. (2008) *Social Marketing: Influencing Behaviors for Good*. Newbury Park, CA: Sage Publications.

Kotler, P. and Roberto, N. (1989) *Social Marketing: Strategies for Changing Behavior*. New York: Free Press.

Kotler, P. and Zaltman, G. (1971) 'Social marketing: An approach to planned social change', *Journal of Marketing*, 35: 3–21.

Koudelova, R. and Whitelock, J. (2001) 'A cross-cultural analysis of television advertising in the UK and Czech Republic', *International Marketing Review*, 18: 286–300.

Lefebvre, R.C. (2011) 'An integrative model for social marketing', *Journal of Social Marketing*, 1: 54 – 72.

Lin, C.A. (1998) 'Uses of sex appeals in prime time advertising', *Sex Roles*, 38: 461–475.

Maibach, E.W. (2002) 'Explicating social marketing: What is it and what isn't it?' *Social Marketing Quarterly*, 8(4): 7–13.

Marketing Staff of the Ohio State University (1965) 'A statement of marketing philosophy', *Journal of Marketing*, 29: 43–44.

Mendelsohn, H. (1973) 'Some reasons why information campaigns can succeed', *Public Opinion Quarterly*, 37: 50–61.

Minja, H., Schellenberg, J.A., Mukasa, O. (2001) 'Introducing insecticide-treated nets in the Kilombero Valley, Tanzania: The relevance of local knowledge and practice for an information, education, and communication (IEC) campaign', *Tropical Medicine and International Health*, 6: 614–623.

Montoya, J.A., Kent, C.K., Rotblatt, H., et al. (2005) 'Social marketing campaign significantly associated with increases in syphilis testing among gay and bisexual men in San Francisco', *Sexually Transmitted Diseases*, 32: 395–399.

Ngo, A.D., Alden, D.L., Hang, N. and Dinh, N. (2009) 'Developing and launching the Government Social Franchise Model of reproductive health care service delivery in Vietnam', *Social Marketing Quarterly*, 15: 71–89.

Ogilvy, D. (1985) *Ogilvy on Advertising*. New York: Vintage Books.

Plant, A., Montoya, J.A., Rotblatt, H., et al. (2010). 'Stop the sores: The making and evaluation of a successful social marketing campaign', *Health Promotion Practice*, 11: 23–33.

Quinn, G.P., Hauser, K., Bell-Ellison, B.A., Rodriguez, N.Y. and Frias, J.L. (2006) 'Promoting pre-conceptual use of folic acid to Hispanic women: A social marketing approach', *Maternal and Child Health Journal*, 10: 403–412.

Ray, M.L., Sawyer, A.G., Rothschild, M.L., et al. (1973) 'Marketing communications and the hierarchy of effects', in P. Clarke (ed), *New Models for Mass Communication Research*. Beverly Hills, CA: Sage Publications, pp. 147–176.

Reger, B., Wootan, M.G., Booth-Butterfiled, S. and Smith, H. (1998) '1% or less: A community-based nutrition campaign', *Public Health Reports*, 113: 410–416.

Reichert, T., Heckler, S.E. and Jackson, S. (2001) 'The effects of sexual social marketing appeals on cognitive processing and persuasion', *Journal of Advertising*, 30: 13–27.

Rogers, R.W. (1975) 'A protection motivation theory of fear appeals and attitude change', *Journal of Psychology*, 91: 93–114.

Rosenstock, I.M. (1966) 'Why people use health services', *Milbank Memorial Fund Quarterly*, 44: 94–124.

Rothschild, M.L. (1999) 'Carrots, sticks and promises: A conceptual framework for the management of public health and social issue behaviors', *Journal of Marketing*, 63: 24–37.

Rothschild, M.L. (2009) 'Separating products and behaviors', *Social Marketing Quarterly*, 15: 107–110.

Rothschild, M.R., Mastin, B. and Miller, T.W. (2006) 'Reducing alcohol-impaired driving crashes through the use of social marketing', *Accident Analysis and Prevention*, 38: 1218–1230.

Schellenberg, J.R.M.A., Abdulla, S., Nathan, R., et al. (2001) 'Effect of a large-scale social marketing of insecticide-treated nets on child survival in rural Tanzania', *Lancet*, 357: 1241–1247.

Scott, L.A.J. and Johnson, B.T. (2006) 'Eroticizing creates safer sex: A research synthesis', *The Journal of Primary Prevention*, 27: 619–640.

Shimp, T.A. (2006) *Advertising, Promotion, and Other Aspects of Integrated Marketing Communications*, 7th edn. Florence, KY: Cengage Learning.

Smith, B. (2009) 'The power of the product P, or why toothpaste is so important to behavior change', *Social Marketing Quarterly*, 15: 98–106.

Snyder, L.B., Hamilton, M.A., Mitchell, E.W., et al. (2004) 'A meta-analysis of the effect of mediated health communication campaigns on behavior change in the United States', *Journal of Health Communication*, 71–96.

Sternthal, B. and Craig, C.S. (1974) 'Fear appeals: Revisited and revised', *Journal of Consumer Research*, 1: 22–34.

Triese, D., Wolburg, J.M. and Otnes, C.C. (1999) 'Understanding the "social gifts" of drinking rituals: An alternative framework for PSA developers', *Journal of Advertising*, 28(2): 17–31.

Warnick, E., Dearden, K.A., Slater, S., et al. (2004) 'Social marketing improved the use of multivitamin and mineral supplements among resource-poor women in Bolivia', *Journal of Nutrition Education and Behavior*, 36: 290–297.

Wilkie, W.L. and Moore, E.S. (2003) 'Scholarly research in marketing: Exploring the "4 Eras" of thought development', *Journal of Marketing*, 22: 116–146.

Witte, K. (1994) 'Fear control and danger control: A test of the Extended Parallel Process Model (EPPM)', *Communication Monographs*, 61: 113–134.

12

New Media in Social Marketing

Darren Mays, James B. Weaver III and
Jay M. Bernhardt

INTRODUCTION

For today's social marketing professionals, new communication media are powerful tools for health promotion, disease prevention, and influencing social change. Despite adoption and rapid diffusion of new media in the general population, their use for social marketing activities has been limited (Abroms et al., 2008). Understanding these new media and their potential for content interactivity and constant connectivity with large, diverse populations is critically important for future social marketing sciences and practice. In the emerging new media environment, determining which media among an array of applications are the most useful for social marketing activities is becoming an increasingly complex, but exciting, challenge. Consequently, it is critically important for social marketing professionals to closely examine the use of new media by wide-ranging audience segments and address key practical and strategic concerns when deploying new media in specific social marketing programs.

In this chapter we describe how new media are changing the way that consumers communicate, share information, and interrelate with one another and discuss the implications of these changes for social marketing. This chapter explicitly focuses on health marketing, which applies the strategies and tactics of health communication and social marketing to create, communicate, and deliver health information and interventions using consumer-centered and science-based approaches to protect and promote the health of diverse populations (Bernhardt, 2006). Our discussion of new media, however, has much broader applicability to the field of social marketing.

The chapter is organized into four sections. In the first section, we provide an orientation to several 'new media,' discuss how they are used, describe the prevalence of use, and provide examples of each. In section two, we discuss major trends that have occurred as a result of the adoption of new media, focusing on how new media have changed the manner in which consumers engage information and interact with others. In the third section, we detail some of the potential implications of these trends for social marketing, discuss some strategies for incorporating new media into social marketing interventions and assessing their impact, and describe new media trends that social marketers should be aware of for the future. Finally, we summarize the key ideas presented in this chapter and speculate about the role of new media and technologies in future social marketing activities.

NEW MEDIA AND PREVALENCE OF USE

What are new media?

The notion of 'new' communication media is historically and culturally relative. Telegraphy, telephones, radio, television, and computer technologies have all been, at one point in their development, new technological innovations.

Even today, some of these traditional media (e.g. televisions and computers), which have become commonplace in industrialized nations, are minimally deployed in many regions of the world. For our purposes, it is the convergence of the innovations underlying these earlier technologies (e.g. communication via high-speed wire, wireless, and digital) into powerful, personalized applications that is the hallmark of contemporary new media. Specifically, we use the term 'new media' to refer to the variety of emerging, interactive communication applications, such as participatory media (e.g. 'web 2.0'), personal wireless devices, and other interactive digital content. Throughout this chapter, we also refer to information 'consumers' as those individuals who actively seek and/or obtain information. Table 12.1 presents an overview of new media discussed in this chapter.

The adoption of new media has dramatically changed the way many people seek information and interact with others, resulting in new communicative behaviors that have major implications for social marketing research and practice (Bernhardt et al., 2009; Fox and Bernhardt, in press). Many potential consequences of new communication media were first articulated by communication scholars over a decade ago following the emergence of personal computing and internet technologies (Rogers, 1996). Today, we increasingly recognize that one consequence of contemporary new media is that they allow consumers constant access to information and substantially increase consumer engagement in information exchange (Della et al., 2008; Fox and Bernhardt, in press; Lefebvre, 2007).

The process through which new media are evaluated and adopted by consumers has been extensively described by Rogers (2003) using his diffusion of innovations theory. In short, this theory outlines several factors impacting the rate at which new ideas and technologies spread through societies. Diffusion of innovations also projects the adoption of a new innovation as progressing through several stages – used first by 'innovators,' then 'early adopters,' the 'early majority,' and the 'late majority' – and recognizes that some consumers may never embrace an innovation (i.e. 'laggards'). Currently, many new media (e.g. mobile phones) are experiencing widespread adoption (i.e. late majority stage), while others (e.g. iPhones, Blackberries) are only being utilized by a smaller core of consumers (i.e. early adopters). These differential adoption patterns for the new media discussed in this chapter are illustrated in Figure 12.1.

As can be seen in Figure 12.1, the adoption curve illustrates that the diffusion process typically occurs over time, with the number of users increasing in an S-shaped pattern. In the next section, we outline the adoption progress of several new media with considerable potential for social marketing activities, focusing specifically on web 2.0 applications and wireless mobile devices.

Participatory media

Participatory media, also known as 'web 2.0' applications, are internet-based new media technologies intended to be interactive and consumer-centered. With web 2.0 applications consumers can interact with others, create content, and have extensive control over content that is subsequently shared with others through these channels (O'Reilly, 2005). Several web 2.0 applications – social networking websites, web logs or blogs, wikis, sharing sites, and virtual worlds – are exemplified in Table 12.1. The most broadly diffused among these media are social networking websites, which include popular brands such as MySpace, Facebook, and Bebo, as well as numerous topic-specific internet forums. Using these applications, consumers can create personal profiles, share photos, create blogs, and exchange text messages with others. Many users create a list of 'friends' and join vast interest groups, both formal and informal (e.g. hobbies, parenting, university alumni). Adoption of social networking websites has increased rapidly over the last decade (i.e. early majority stage illustrated in Figure 12.1). Current estimates suggest that the majority of teens (55%) and over a third of adults are using social networking applications (Lenhart, 2009; Lenhart and Madden, 2007). Facebook, for example, recently reported more than 500 million unique participants worldwide (Facebook, 2011).

Web logs or 'blogs' are another web 2.0 application with relatively large user groups. Blogs are websites maintained by an individual or group that provide commentary on news and personal experiences across a range of topical areas. An example of a health-related blog is http://blog.aids.gov, an offshoot of the US Department of Health and Human Services HIV/AIDS website (http://aids.gov), focusing on new media implementations in response to the global HIV/AIDS epidemic. A 'micro-blog' is a recently emerging type of blog that allows for sharing of only very brief snippets of information (usually 140 text characters or fewer). Micro-blogs are supported by applications such as Twitter and Plurk. An example of a health-related micro-blog is maintained by the American Public Health Association (http://twitter.com/PublicHealth), which posts regular updates to subscribers on a variety of public health topics. The adoption of blogs and

Table 12.1 Descriptions, characteristics, and examples of new media

Technology	Description	Characteristics	Example(s)
Social network websites	Interactive websites in which users are able to create a profile, which might contain personal information, photos, blogs, music, messages from other users, and a list of 'friends'	Users interact with their friends by sharing information through public or private messages, posting photos, writing and commenting on personal blogs, and giving gifts	www.myspace.com www.facebook.com www.bebo.com
Personal wireless devices	Portable devices that allow consumers to connect with information and others	Portable wireless devices enable consumers to have voice conversations, send and receive text messages, access email, the internet, and a host of other activities	Cellular/mobile phones 'Smart' phones Personal digital assistants Portable media players
Blogs	Blogs provide commentary on various topics, report on news, relay information, and/or share personal experiences	Bloggers generally write on a particular subject. Blogs typically include hyperlinks to related blogs, news articles, and other online information. Most blogs have a comment section following each blog post in which readers and bloggers can share comments	http://blog.aids.gov http://www.cdc.gov/healthmarketing/blog.htm http://getreadyforflu.blogspot.com/
Wikis	A wiki is an online collaboration tool allowing multiple users to post and edit content about a particular subject	Users can post information about a topic, which can subsequently be added to, changed, or deleted by other users. An effective tool for asynchronous online information sharing	www.wikipedia.com www.healthwikinews.com
Sharing sites	Interactive websites where users can share information with others in many different formats	Users can share web links, news clips, photographs, video, audio, and other content	www.youtube.com www.flickr.com www.digg.com
Virtual worlds	A virtual world is an internet site where users, or residents, interact with one another through avatars. An avatar is a virtual representation of an individual	Avatars act much as people do in the real world, living, working, playing, building structures, attending events, and traveling throughout the Second Life environment. The action is controlled by users	www.secondlife.com www.whyville.com
eGames	Electronic games, or eGames, are interactive games that are played through an electronic application such as the internet, a video game console, or a mobile phone	eGames provide users with opportunities for training on a specific topic, to build new skills and knowledge, and to engage in physical activities	CDC eGames BAM and Choose Respect Dance, Dance Revolution

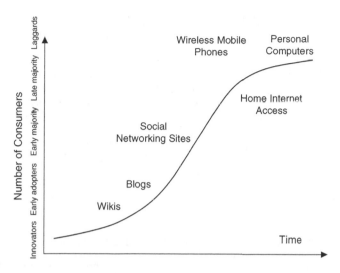

Figure 12.1   Diffusion curve of new media

micro-blogs is still in the earliest diffusion stages (Figure 12.1). Available estimates suggest that about 8% of adult internet users maintain a blog (Lenhart and Fox, 2006) and over 190 million users from around the world subscribe to the micro-blog Twitter (Schonfeld, 2010), which continues to grow rapidly. There is reason to expect that use of blog and micro-blog applications will demonstrate continued growth in years to come.

Other examples of participatory media highlighted in Table 12.1 include sharing sites, such as YouTube, Flickr, and digg, which enable users to share content such as videos and photographs, and 'tag' appealing content such as web links and news stories. Additionally, new media such as wikis, virtual worlds, and eGames are experiencing growing adoption and may be useful for social marketing endeavors as well.

Personal wireless devices

Personal wireless devices (PWDs) have been available to consumers for a number of years, but worldwide their adoption status varies substantially. Specifically, in many developed countries, PWDs are broadly diffused and adoption rates have peaked, while in other regions of the world PWD adoption is rapidly growing. Data from the United States show, for example, that a majority of Americans (93%) own cellular (also called cell or mobile) phones or other PWDs, accounting for approximately 292 million individuals in the United States (CTIA The Wireless Association,

2010). In the developing world, on the other hand, where traditional communications infrastructures are often less developed, the use of mobile phones is increasing rapidly (Cellular-News, 2008a, b, 2010). Recent estimates indicate over 5 billion consumers use mobile phones globally, representing an astounding 71% of the world's population (Cellular-News, 2010). These data also project a 22% annual growth in mobile phone adopters globally, with substantial adoption increases in South America, Africa, India, China, and other parts of Asia (Cellular-News, 2008a, b). Projections suggest an additional half-billion consumers will own PWDs globally by the end of 2012 (Cellular-News, 2008a). The expansive reach of PWDs around the globe highlights their potential as powerful social marketing tools.

Although basic PWDs such as cellular phones are extensively used in many developed countries, there is a recent proliferation of PWDs that enable communication functions beyond basic voice and text messaging services (Horrigan, 2007). Many recently developed PWDs (i.e. Blackberry, iPhone, etc.) combine diverse functionality, yielding what some have called a 'communication Swiss Army knife' (SmartReply, 2006). Advanced PWDs, for example, often provide applications and functions known as 'mobile media,' such as internet and email access, multimedia audio and video capabilities, and global positioning system navigation. Recent trends in ownership of (and demand for) advanced PWDs suggests expansive growth in adoption is anticipated (Cellsigns, 2007; Nielsen Mobile, 2007a, b; Rainie and Keeter, 2006; SmartReply, 2006; Yi et al., 2008).

TRENDS RESULTING FROM NEW MEDIA USE

The participatory consumer

Social marketing scholars have attributed the transformation of consumers from more passive recipients of information (i.e. the 'target audience') to active participants in the information-exchange process as one consequence of the emergence of new media (Lefebvre, 2007). New media users assume increased information seeking, production, manipulation, and creation capabilities, resulting in a more personalized, interactive, and engaging experience for consumers (Lefebvre, 2007). The argument, however, is not that audiences, as traditionally conceived, were simply passive 'receivers' of information. Prior communication theories suggest that the 'audience' has always engaged with information as it was received (Dominick, 2005). Yet, in traditional communication models, the communication process was conceived as 'few-to-many,' where a small number of intermediaries (e.g. print and broadcast media) acquired and prioritized primary information from selected sources and then interpreted and disseminated that information to large, heterogeneous audiences in a controlled manner (Dominick, 2005). This, in essence, is the classic mass communication process where information is 'pushed' through intermediary media organizations to consumers.

By contrast, the emergence of new media has enabled an alternative disintermediated information-seeking environment. Rather than relying on information pushed to them by media organizations, new media consumers can 'pull' personalized information from diverse sources (Lefebvre, 2007; Shapiro, 1999). In this consumer-centered new media milieu, individuals can actively acquire, prioritize, and interpret information when, where, how, and from whom they want it (Fox and Bernhardt, in press). It is not simply the case, however, that new media are emerging and replacing traditional information sources (i.e. mass media) – they have been 'added to the mix' of channels through which consumers can seek information (Bernhardt et al., 2009). One challenge facing social marketing professionals is how to balance the deployment of traditional mass media dissemination strategies with development of innovative ways to engage new media users in order to maximize the reach and impact of their programs (Lefebvre, 2007).

The participatory nature of new media may also enable social marketers to engage with consumers in ways that are consistent with ideas from relationship marketing (see Chapter 3). A central element to relationship marketing is the development of sustained, interactive relationships with networks of consumers. A defining characteristic of communication between marketers and consumers in relationship marketing is that consumer engagement leads to two-way (i.e. dialogues) or multiway interactions. New media offer opportunities to communicate and engage with consumers in an interactive and participatory manner, and many new media (e.g. social networking sites) are built around extensive networks of consumers. Seen from this perspective, new media may help social marketers apply the ideas of relationship marketing to social marketing endeavors by establishing robust relationships with consumers through sustained and interactive communications.

Simultaneous media use

'Media multi-tasking' involves using several communication media (e.g. computer applications, television, telephone) concurrently. Considerable evidence suggests that media multi-tasking is a widespread and frequent behavior for many consumers (Castells et al., 2007; Papper et al., 2004; Roberts et al., 2005). While media multi-tasking appears to be most prominent among youths (Henry J. Kaiser Family Foundation, 2007; Roberts et al., 2005;), the behavior is also prevalent among adults (Papper et al., 2004). Chatting on the phone while watching a television program, for example, is a common media multi-tasking experience. New communication media exponentially expand simultaneous media use combinations (e.g. playing a video game, watching television, talking on the telephone, text messaging, and checking a social network newsfeed...simultaneously). These data bolster the idea that many new media consumers are 'relentlessly connected'(Castells et al., 2007; Della et al., 2008). By immersing themselves in content from multiple channels simultaneously, it appears that many consumers substantially increase overall information exposure (Henry J. Kaiser Family Foundation, 2007; Papper et al., 2004). Unfortunately, the implication of media multi-tasking on information acquisition and knowledge development is unclear. Similarly, effective social marketing strategies to amplify consumers' attention to messages within the competitive media multi-tasking environment are not readily apparent.

IMPLICATIONS FOR SOCIAL MARKETING

Understanding the relevance and importance of new media

The long-term goal of social marketing activities is sustained, population-level impact on targeted health and social outcomes. Prior to applying new media for social marketing, however, an understanding of the relevance and applicability of new media within the population of interest must be developed. As we previously described, many new media are achieving widespread adoption and are at the cutting edge. Social marketers must be cautious, however, not to spontaneously incorporate these media into projects simply because they are 'buzz worthy.' The decision to deploy new media should be informed by a detailed assessment of which applications represent the most relevant and efficient means to create messages and products that can engage intended audiences (Thackeray et al., 2008).

Several strategic and logistical considerations should be addressed within the specific population of interest prior to using new media for social marketing activities. The perceptions about new media evident within a particular population can significantly impact the effectiveness of some applications. Such perceptions may include level of acceptance, level of receptivity, and attitudes and beliefs about the media as a source of information (Thackeray et al., 2008). Recent survey research suggests, for example, that the degree of trust consumers place in new media as information sources appears to be a particularly important factor influencing how such media are used to seek information (Edelman, 2008).

Consistent with existing frameworks for the development of health promotion and disease prevention interventions (Bartholomew et al., 2006), Thackeray and colleagues (2008) detailed specific questions to consider prior to using new media for social marketing endeavors (see Table 12.2). These questions include: Do the media meet a specified need within the population of interest? Can the population of interest be effectively analyzed and segmented based on new media use? Can the impact of the media be evaluated and interpreted? Are the media relevant to and accepted by the target population? Are there social costs, such as the loss of support within the priority population, involved with using or not using the media (Thackeray et al., 2008)?

Other key considerations include those related to media access. It is essential to understand the extent to which access to the new media is a barrier to its use. Similarly, do members of the popu-

Table 12.2 Strategic and practical questions to consider prior to using new technologies for health marketing

Population characteristics	Can the needs of the population of interest be addressed by using new media?
	What are the media use behaviors among those in the population of interest?
	Can the population be broken down and segmented based on their use of new media?
	What members of the population use new media the most? Is it best suited to target a certain segment of the population?
	Is access to the media a barrier to achieving program objectives? If so, what prevents access within the population of interest?
	Do members of the population of interest prefer to use the media and are they comfortable doing so? Do they have the knowledge and skills needed to use the media?
	Is the new media accepted by members of the target population?
	Are there costs that may result from using new media, such as loss of support, trust, or credibility in the population of interest?
Resource issues	Is there substantial monetary cost associated with the use of the media? Are these costs justifiable relative to the potential benefits?
	What proportion of programmatic resources (e.g. time, financial) is needed to invest in this media? Will that divert resources from other important aspects of the program?
	Are key program stakeholders aware of the new media and the relevance within the population of interest?
Program objectives and implementation	Does the medium augment the proposed strategy in some way in order to achieve program objectives?
	Does the application of new media help reduce costs involved for members of the target population to access the social marketing message(s)/product(s)?
	Is it possible to evaluate the impact of the new media on the health and social outcome(s) of interest?

Adapted from Thackeray et al. (2008).

lation of interest have the requisite knowledge and skills to use the media (Jenkins, 2006; Thackeray et al., 2008)? The process of resolving strategic and logistical concerns such as these should be strengthened by involving key program stakeholders (e.g. community leaders) to examine the feasibility and applicability of new media within the population of interest (Hamilton et al., 2008).

Preservation of user-defined networks

Health communication and social marketing scholars have referred to the communication processes occurring via new media as 'horizontal' since, as discussed earlier, consumers are able to create and share information within social networks instead of relying on information from 'experts' (Fox and Bernhardt, in press). Consistent with these observations, evidence increasingly suggests that one of the primary reasons why consumers use new media to seek health information is an elevated sense of confidence in information obtained from sources they perceive as a peer, or a 'person like me'(Edelman, 2008). In other words, in the new media, environment factors such as source credibility, trust, and likeability that have been consistently linked to the persuasiveness and effectiveness of health messages in prior research (O'Keefe, 1990) appear crucial.

Consumers' apparent skepticism of information from unfamiliar sources appears warranted. Prior research suggests that it may be difficult to confirm the veracity of information from sources such as blogs, social networking sites, and other similar sources (Clemmitt, 2006), possibly leading consumers to seek information from those with whom they more closely identify. Consequently, appearing as an outsider within established consumer networks may diminish social marketers' credibility and trust, and negatively impact the effectiveness of their efforts. One viable strategy for overcoming this potential limitation is to target opinion leaders within online consumer networks to facilitate information dissemination. Collaborating with opinion leaders – individuals within a group who are capable of informally influencing the perceptions, attitudes, and behaviors of others – is a well-established strategy for diffusing new ideas and/or innovations (Rogers, 2003). Tapping the influence of opinion leaders may enable social marketers working in new media environments to enhance their perceived relevance, credibility, and trustworthiness and, in turn, their potential impact.

An applied example from the US Centers for Disease Control and Prevention (CDC) illustrates this approach in practice. In 2006 and 2007, the CDC hosted a series of online seminars or 'webinars' to educate prominent bloggers about influenza. The CDC conducted these webinars to raise awareness and increase knowledge of seasonal influenza vaccination among bloggers, encourage bloggers to write about seasonal influenza vaccination, and educate bloggers as to how to develop persuasive messages encouraging vaccination behaviors. The webinar specifically targeted bloggers who write about influenza or health to groups who are high-priority populations for vaccination (e.g. elderly, parents of young children). Following the webinars, the participating bloggers' influenza-related posts and their readers' comments on these entries were monitored. The results of this effort suggest that many of the webinar participants subsequently wrote about seasonal flu vaccination in their blogs. An example of a webinar participant's flu vaccination post, can be found on the American Public Health Association's 'Get Ready for Flu' blog (http://getreadyforflu.blogspot.com/).

Going mobile

Portable wireless devices represent a particularly promising media for social marketing because of the extensive worldwide reach made possible by their expanding global adoption. Equally important, there is growing evidence illustrating the viable application of PWDs in health promotion activities targeting behaviors such as alcohol use (Weitzel et al., 2007), physical activity (Consolvo et al., 2006; Gasser et al., 2006; Hurling et al., 2007), diet (Tsai et al., 2007), smoking (Obermayer et al., 2004; Vidrine et al., 2006), diabetes management (Hee-Seung and Hye-Sun, 2005; Mamykima et al., 2008), outpatient appointment adherence (Downer et al., 2005; Koshy et al., 2008), and sexual health (Levine et al., 2008). A recent systematic review of PWD-based text message behavior change interventions suggests that such interventions can have a positive impact on behavior change outcomes (Fjeldsoe et al., 2009). Although most of these projects were small-scale, convenience-sample, efficacy studies testing individually tailored behavioral interventions (Fjeldsoe et al., 2009; Gasser et al., 2006; Hee-Seung and Hye-Sun, 2005; Hurling et al., 2007; Mamykima et al., 2008; Obermayer et al., 2004; Tsai et al., 2007; Weitzel et al., 2007) their findings are illuminating.

Unfortunately, larger-scale effectiveness studies examining the application of PWDs for social marketing in population-based settings are lacking at this time. Similarly, there is limited evidence regarding the qualities of PWD-based applications, such as user preferences toward mobile-based communications, influencing subsequent health outcomes. Instead, existing studies focus primarily on PWD users' assessments of mobile application design components within specific contexts (Halifax et al., 2007; Mamykima et al., 2008; Pinncock et al., 2007; Tsai et al., 2007). Critical questions for social marketing practice – such as the receptiveness of PWD users toward unsolicited health promotion and disease prevention messaging via their mobile devices – remain unanswered.

Finally, there is only preliminary evidence for the applicability of user-initiated approaches for PWD-based interventions (i.e. messages that are provided in response to an expressed need by the PWD user). Levine and colleagues (2008), for example, developed and tested a text message-based sexual health information and referral service among youths in San Francisco, California. In this program, mobile phone users could send short messages to a five-digit phone number and receive culturally tailored, sexual health information and referrals to local sexual health services via text messages on their PWD (Levine et al., 2008). The results from the SexInfo project are promising, suggesting that users found the service acceptable and that it was accessed frequently during the initial adoption period (Levine et al., 2008). Using a similar strategy, the CDC, in partnership with the Kaiser Family Foundation and others, launched an information resource allowing PWD users to text message 'KnowIt' (566948) and solicit information about local HIV testing centers via a text message response.

Understanding population characteristics, preferences, and media use

Targeting social marketing programs to diverse populations is critical to successfully influencing the outcomes of interest, particularly behavior change (O'Sullivan et al., 2003). The process of understanding audience characteristics, preferences, and media use behaviors allows social marketers to create messages and products that are responsive to the characteristics and preferences of the target population (Kreuter et al., 1999; Rimal and Adkins, 2003; Slater, 1996). The proliferation and adoption of new media presents a number of challenges for social marketers, however, in segmenting diverse populations based on new media use. In particular, few data are available to better inform social marketers about the dynamic nature of user engagement via new media, including multitasking behaviors and aspects of interpersonal engagement.

Several issues contribute to the complex considerations social marketers face when trying to understand and segment populations of new media users. For example, selecting the appropriate channels through which social marketing messages and products are promoted based on the use of new media is becoming more challenging because of multitasking behaviors. In addition, understanding the competing messages to which consumers are exposed is becoming increasingly difficult in light of these behaviors. Consumers may be exposed to competing messages from multiple sources at once, or may be simultaneously or sequentially viewing a promotional message about a health promotion product and competing messages encouraging them to make unhealthy choices.

The new media environment requires careful and critical consideration of these dynamic aspects of media use. A number of additional factors beyond use/non-use of media within a discrete time period should be considered. Consumers' use of new media may, for example, range from simply obtaining information through wikis or blogs, to interacting with others, to creating user-generated content and sharing it with others. In this regard it is vital not only to understand the characteristics of those who are accessing new media but also how often, and in which activities they are engaging. Finally, it is also essential to examine how these aspects of new media use relate to other characteristics that may influence the health and social outcomes of interest – including socio-demographic characteristics and other psychosocial factors.

Multi-channel approaches

Not only are consumers seeking information from multiple media often simultaneously but also evidence shows that health promotion efforts relying on a single channel have limited impact (Snyder and Hamilton, 2002; Snyder et al., 2004). The effectiveness of messages is often moderated by how much consumers are involved with messages and find them to be relevant (Petty and Cacioppo, 1986). Given this evidence, social marketers should consider using multiple, interactive channels in order to increase user engagement and message relevance and improve their chances of successfully influencing health and social outcomes.

Recent events support the notion that consumers are actively engaged through multiple, interactive channels, not relying on a single source. One mainstream example is the 2008 Summer Olympic Games (see Bernhardt et al., 2009). NBC's coverage of this global event included thousands of hours of televised coverage (Heistand, 2008), over 3000 hours of online video content (Voigt, 2009), and interactive online features, including social networking tools that enabled consumers to share with others online. Much of the coverage of the games was also available via PWDs, including text message alerts, mobile web content, and mobile video (NBC Universal, 2008).

An important aspect of NBC's coverage of the 2008 Summer Olympic Games is that it exemplifies how widespread exposure to content was distributed across the multi-channel coverage of the games. Following the games, analysis of television viewership and access to online content show that the 2008 coverage reached previously unsurpassed television audiences (*Sports Business Daily*, 2008) and that web content dedicated to the games resulted in an unprecedented number of users (Stetler, 2008). Post-games analyses of exposure through different channels show that the multi-channel approach increased exposure to the games, with many users accessing content in new ways. In particular, web and mobile coverage showed promising results, and mobile content in particular attracted many consumers who had never viewed such information using PWDs (Kaplan, 2008).

Examples such as the 2008 Summer Olympic Games suggest that new media may offer fresh opportunities for customer engagement when used in combination with traditional channels. From the perspective of social marketing, this event provides an example of the ways in which new media can be combined with traditional channels for a multi-channel approach that increases reach and depth of engagement among consumers (Bernhardt et al., 2009).

Cost and access issues

Despite an apparent reduction in the 'digital divide' in recent years (Horrigan, 2008), there are still important gaps in access to new media, particularly those which are web based. Inequalities in access to these media may stem from the lack of required resources (e.g. prohibitive costs) or they may be a result from a conscientious choice not to use the media as an information resource. Furthermore, as Jenkins (2006) describes, not only are issues of access important but also a perceived participation gap, where many consumers may lack the ability or motivation required to use these media to their full capacity, is of concern. Despite the rapid adoption of many new media, many are also still in their early adoption stages (Figure 12.1; Jenkins, 2006). An understanding of how issues such as new media access and

participation affect consumers of interest for a particular social marketing effort is critical to maximizing the intended impact (Table 12.2).

Evaluating the impact of new media

As others have described in detail in this Handbook, the evaluation of social marketing programs can be very challenging (Chapter 13). While behavior change is frequently the outcome of interest for social marketing endeavors, actually inducing measurable changes in behavior is often difficult to achieve. There are, however, a number of intermediate outcomes specific to new media use that may be valuable indicators of success for those who are evaluating social marketing programs.

General website usage data, such as page visits, views, and content downloads, can be a useful, albeit limited, measure of exposure to social marketing programs that rely on the internet as a platform for communication (Tian et al., 2010). In addition, as Galen Panger of Google has recently pointed out (Panger, 2009), the metrics employed to evaluate the impact of new media should be specific to both the activities and media utilized. A number of examples are useful to clarify this idea. For instance, if it is of interest to assess broad measures of the reach of a social marketing program among target consumers, capturing the number of subscribers to a particular new media channel represents one potentially useful marker of program reach. Outcomes such as 'followers' on Twitter, 'friends' on Facebook, and subscribers to a YouTube channel or blog are general metrics of subscribers that can be useful to gauge the overall reach attained through certain new media channels (Panger, 2009).

Additional metrics provide a more specific idea of consumer engagement attained through new media channels. Capturing the number of 'retweets' on Twitter, for example, will give evaluators an idea as to how many times a particular message was retransmitted by their followers within a given time period (Panger, 2009). Similarly, assessing engagement through metrics such as the number of 'comments' and 'likes' on Facebook, the number of times that content was shared via postings within social network sites, and overall user ratings of videos posted to YouTube and similar channels can provide social marketing program evaluators with an estimate of consumer activity and involvement within these channels.

Unfortunately, most new media metrics cannot be directly linked to the objective outcomes of social marketing programs (e.g. behavior change) in a causal manner. Furthermore, there is no universally agreed upon metrics 'gold standard' pointing to the best methods for evaluating the impact of new media (Huxley, 2009). Nevertheless, carefully choosing new media metrics that correspond closely to the program activities and represent logical intermediate outcomes between program activities and the ultimate outcomes of interest can provide social marketers with an idea of the contribution new media make to progress toward successfully influencing the intended outcomes.

The future: New media forecasting

As described earlier in this chapter, in the past several years there has been rapid growth in the use of new media around the globe. New media such as social networking sites (e.g. Facebook), microblogs (e.g. Twitter), and PWDs have demonstrated expanding market segments and these media are now a part of everyday life for millions of consumers. While these new media increase the number of channels through which social marketers can engage consumers, the rapidly changing media environment can also make it difficult to determine which new media channels are the most efficient for effectively reaching audiences of interest.

The evolving new media environment makes it difficult to predict which specific channels (e.g. Facebook, Twitter, YouTube) will persist and which may no longer exist in the future (Kaplan and Haenlein, 2010). One point that is very clear is that media with the characteristics described above – channels that enable extensive networks of consumers to actively engage one another – are not disappearing any time soon. Furthermore, there appears to be a pattern where many of these channels are converging with one another, which will likely lead to even more extensive opportunities for social marketers to interact and engage with consumers. For example, many popular video game consoles (e.g. Nintendo Wii, Microsoft Xbox) are now capable of accessing the internet, which allows users to interact with one another while playing video games and engage in other activities, such as download videos and movies (Stone, 2010). Other relatively new entertainment technologies, such as Blu-ray disc players, also allow users to connect to the internet and stream movies and music.

The convergence of participatory media described above and the vast reach of PWDs is another important trend for social marketers to keep in mind in the future (Kaplan and Haenlein, 2010). Innovations in mobile web technology delivery, which will make it easier to gain access to the internet through PWDs, and the rapid growth in use of both participatory new media and PWDs, suggest that 'Mobile Web 2.0' may represent one of the most important channels for social marketing programs in the future. Industry estimates suggest that the use of participatory media on PWDs will grow tremendously in the future, indicating that this particular channel may be one of the most important avenues for social marketers to reach populations of interest in the future (Kaplan and Haenlein, 2010). In addition, 'Mobile Web 2.0' is a channel that will have global reach and impact, suggesting that it will be particularly important for social marketers practicing in international contexts (Kaplan and Haenlein, 2010).

CONCLUSION

New communication media – such as participatory media and personal wireless devices – represent interactive, engaging channels through which consumers can be reached. New media also represent opportunities to connect with consumers who may otherwise be difficult to reach, particularly in international contexts, and to connect consumers with each other. Increasingly, many new media are demonstrating widespread adoption among consumers and are becoming an important source of information in consumers' daily lives. When considered in the context of other more traditional communication channels (e.g. television, radio, internet, etc.), new media may provide a critical resource augmenting future social marketing activities.

Many questions remain unanswered regarding the use of new media for social marketing, however, and social marketers should be cautious not to adopt these media simply because they are novel and innovative. Rather, social marketers should carefully consider whether new media will help to achieve the intended impact within the population of interest. This includes seeking answers to both strategic and logistical questions and fully considering the perspectives of consumers. Careful concern of such factors will allow social marketers to incorporate these new media to promote social marketing messages and products, and enhance efforts to promote health, prevent disease, and enhance social outcomes.

KEY WORDS   New media; social media; mobile technology; social marketing; health marketing; behavior change; consumers.

Key insights

- Increasing adoption of new media has drastically changed the ways consumers communicate, share, and seek information, creating new opportunities for social marketing professionals.
- The most widely used new media include participatory media (e.g. social networking websites, blogs, wikis) and personal wireless devices (e.g. cellular phones, smart phones).
- With many new media the consumer assumes greater information production, manipulation, and creation capabilities, which facilitates more active participation in the information exchange process.
- Many consumers are 'relentlessly connected' often simultaneously to multiple information resources.
- Prior to using new media for social marketing endeavors in public health and other disciplines, social marketers must carefully consider a number of practical and logistic questions.

ACKNOWLEDGMENTS

The views expressed in this chapter are those of the authors and do not necessarily represent the views of the US Department of Health and Human Services or the Centers for Disease Control and Prevention. The preparation of this chapter was supported in part by an appointment to the Research Participation Program at the Centers for Disease Control and Prevention administered by the Oak Ridge Institute for Science and Education through an interagency agreement between the US Department of Energy and Centers for Disease Control and Prevention (author D.M.). The authors wish to thank Ms Amanda Hall for her assistance with the literature and data in this chapter.

REFERENCES

Abroms, L.C., Schiavo, R. and Lefebvre, R.C. (2008). 'New media cases in *Cases in Public Health Communication and Marketing*: The promise and potential', *Cases in Public Health Communication and Marketing*, 2: 3–10.

Bartholomew, L.K., Parcel, G.S., Kok, G. and Gottleib, N.H. (2006). *Planning Health Promotion Programs: An Intervention Mapping Approach*. San Francisco, CA: Jossey-Bass.

Bernhardt, J.M. (2006) 'Improving health through health marketing', *Preventing Chronic Disease*, 3(3): 1–3.

Bernhardt, J.M., Mays, D., Eroglu, D. and Daniel, K. L. (2009) 'New communication channels: Changing the nature of customer engagement', *Social Marketing Quarterly*, XV(Suppl): 7–15.

Castells, M., Fernanadez-Ardevol, M. and Sey, A. (2007) *Mobile Communication and Society: A Global Perspective*. Cambridge, MA: MIT Press.

Cellsigns (2007) *Text Message Statistics*. Retrieved 30 June 2008, from http://www.cellsigns.com/industry.shtml

Cellular-News. (2008a) *Global Mobile Phone Users Top 3.3 Billion by end-2007*. Retrieved 28 January 2009, from http://www.cellular-news.com/story/31352.php?source=newsletter

Cellular-News. (2008b) *Mobile Phone Subscribers Pass 4 Billion Mark*. Retrieved 28 January 2009, from http://www.cellular-news.com/story/35298.php

Cellular-News. (2010) *Mobile Phone Subscriber Base Passes the 5 Billion Mark*. Retrieved 10 January 2011, from http://www.cellular-news.com/story/44103.php

Clemmitt, M. (2006) 'Cyber socializing: Are internet sites like MySpace potentially dangerous?' *CQ Researcher*, 16(27): 625–648.

Consolvo, S., Everitt, K., Smith, I. and Landay, J.A. (2006) 'Design requirements for technologies that encourage physical activity', Paper presented at the Computer Human Interactions.

CTIA The Wireless Association (2010) *Wireless Quick Facts: Year End Figures*. Retrieved 10 January 2011, from http://www.ctia.org/media/industry_info/index.cfm/AID/10323

Della, L.J., Eroglu, D., Bernhardt, J.M., Edgerton, E. and Nall, J. (2008) 'Looking to the future of new media in health marketing: Deriving propositions based on traditional theories', *Health Marketing Quarterly*, 25(1/2): 147–174.

Dominick, J.R. (2005) *The Dynamics of Mass Communication: Media in the Digital Age*, 8th edn. New York: McGraw-Hill.

Downer, S.R., Meara, J.G. and Da Costa, A.C. (2005) 'Use of SMS text messaging to improve outpatient attendance', *Medical Journal of Australia*, 183(7): 366–368.

Edelman (2008) *Edelman Trust Barometer: The Ninth Global Opinion Leaders Study*. New York.

Facebook (2011) *Statistics*. Retrieved 10 January 2011, from http://www.facebook.com/press/info.php?statistics

Fjeldsoe, B.S., Marshall, A.L. and Miller, Y.D. (2009) 'Behavior change interventions delivered by mobile telephone short-message service', *American Journal of Preventive Medicine*, 36(2): 165–173.

Fox, S. and Bernhardt, J.M. (in press) 'Health communication 2.0: The promise of peer participation', in L.F. Rutten, B.K. Rimer and B.W. Hesse (eds), *The Future of Health Communication and Informatics: Challenges and Opportunities*. Cresskill, NJ: Hampton Press.

Gasser, R., Brodbeck, D., Degen, M., et al. (2006) 'Persuasiveness of a mobile lifestyle coaching application using social facilitation'. Paper presented at the First International Conference on Persuasive Technology for Human Well-Being.

Halifax, N.V., Cafazzo, J.A., Irvine, M.J., et al. (2007) 'Telemanagement of hypertension: A qualitative assessment of patient and physician preferences', *Canadian Journal of Cardiology*, 23(7): 591–594.

Hamilton, L., Dennings, K. and Abrams, L.C. (2008) 'RE3.org: A case study of using new media to promote recycling in

North Carolina', *Cases in Public Health Communication and Marketing,* 2: 178–189.

Hee-Seung, K. and Hye-Sun, J. (2005) 'A nurse short message service by cellular phone in type-2 diabetic patients for six months', *Journal of Clinical Nursing,* 16: 1082–1087.

Heistand, M. (2008) *NBC Olympics Coverage Will Be Pervasive.* Retrieved 2 September 2008, from http://www.usatoday.com/sports/columnist/hiestand-tv/2008-07-08-olympicstv_N.htm

Horrigan, J.B. (2007) *A Typology of Information and Communication Technology Users.* Pew Washington, DC: Internet and American Life Foundation.

Horrigan, J.B. (2008) *Home Broadband Adoption 2008.* Retrieved 25 August 2008, from http://www.pewinternet.org/PPF/r/257/report_display.asp

Hurling, R., Catt, M., Boni, M., et al. (2007) 'Using internet and mobile phone technology to deliver an automated physical activity program: Randomized controlled trial', *Journal of Medical Internet Research,* 9(2).

Huxley, S. (2009) *New Media Strategies: Measurement Presentation.* Retrieved 31 December 2009, from http://www.adcouncil.org/files/seminar_series/EvaluatingSocialMedia/Huxley.pdf

Jenkins, H. (2006) *Convergence Culture: Where Old and New Media Collide.* New York: New York University Press.

Henry J. Kaiser Family Foundation (2007) *The Digital Opportunity: Using New Media for Public Education Campaigns.* Retrieved 15 July 2008, from http://www.kff.org/entmedia/entmedia01907pkg.cfm

Kaplan, A.M. and Haenlein, M. (2010) 'Users of the world, unite! The challenges and opportunities of Social Media', *Business Horizons,* 53: 59–68.

Kaplan, D. (2008) *NBC Claims Audience Measurement Gold with TAMI; Online Uniques Go from 4.2 Million to 7.8 Million.* Retrieved 10 December 2008, from http://www.paidcontent.org/entry/419-nbc-claims-audience-measurement-gold/

Koshy, E., Car, J. and Majeed, A. (2008) 'Effectiveness of mobile-phone short message service (SMS) reminders for ophthalmology outpatient appointments: Observational study', *BMC Ophthalmology,* 8(9).

Kreuter, M.W., Strecher, V.J. and Glassman, B. (1999) 'One size does not fit all: The case for tailoring print materials', *Annals of Behavioral Medicine,* 21(4): 276–283.

Lefebvre, R.C. (2007) 'New technology: The consumer as participant rather than target audience', *Social Marketing Quarterly,* 13(3): 32–42.

Lenhart, A. (2009) 'Adults and social network websites', *Pew Internet Project Data Memo.* Retrieved 28 January 2009, from http://www.pewinternet.org/PPF/r/272/report_display.asp

Lenhart, A. and Fox, S. (2006) *Bloggers.* Retrieved 12 November 2008, from http://www.pewinternet.org/pdfs/PIP%20Bloggers%20Report%20July%2019%202006.pdf

Lenhart, A. and Madden, M. (2007) *Teens, Privacy and Online Social Networks.* Washington, DC: Pew Internet and American Life Foundation.

Levine, D., McCright, J., Dobkin, L., Woodruff, A.J. and Klausner, J.D. (2008) 'SEXINFO: A sexual health text messaging service for San Francisco youth', *American Journal of Public Health,* 98(3): 393–395.

Mamykima, L., Mynatt, E.D., Davidson, P.R. and Greenblatt, D. (2008) 'MAHI: Investigation of social scaffolding for reflective thinking in diabetes management'. Paper presented at the Conference on Human Factors in Computing Systems, Florence, Italy.

NBC Universal (2008) *NBC Olympics Mobile.* Retrieved 2 September 2008, from http://www.nbcolympics.com/mobile/index.html

Nielsen Mobile (2007a) *Off-Portal Premium SMS Transactions Generated Nearly $215 Million in Download Purchases and $35 Million in Voting/Sweepstakes Revenues During Q1 2007.* Retrieved 30 June 2008, from http://www.nielsenmobile.com/html/PremiumSMSJune2007revised.html

Nielsen Mobile (2007b) *Telephia: Mobile Video Popularity Reaching New Heights with Triple-Digit Growth in Revenues and Subscribers.* From http://www.nielsenmobile.com/html/MobileVideoJune2007.html

Obermayer, J.L., Riley, W.T., Asif, O. and Jean-Mary, J. (2004) 'College smoking-cessation using cell phone text messaging', *American Journal of College Health,* 53(2): 71–78.

O'Keefe, D.J. (1990) *Persuasion: Theory and Research.* Thousand Oaks, CA: Sage Publications.

O'Reilly, T. (2005) *What is Web 2.0? Design Patterns and Business Models for the Next Generation of Software. 2007.* From http://www.oreillynet.com/pub/a/oreilly/tim/news/2005/09/30/what-is-web-20.html

O'Sullivan, G.A., Yonkler, J.A., Morgan, W. and Merritt, A.P. (2003) *A Field Guide to Designing a Health Communication Strategy.* Baltimore, MD: Johns Hopkins University.

Panger, G. (2009) *Social Media Effectiveness.* Retrieved 31 December 2009, from http://www.adcouncil.org/files/seminar_series/EvaluatingSocialMedia/Panger.pdf

Papper, R.A., Holmes, M.E. and Popovich, M.N. (2004) 'Middletown media studies: Media multitasking ... and how much people really use the media', *The International Digital Media and Arts Association Journal,* 1: 5–56.

Petty, R.E. and Cacioppo, J.T. (1986) 'Elaboration likelihood model of persuasion', *Advances in Experimental Social Psychology,* 19: 123–205.

Pinncock, H., Slack, R., Pagliari, C., Price, D. and Sheik, A. (2007) 'Understanding the role of mobile phone-based monitoring on asthma self-management: Qualitative study', *Clinical and Experimental Allergy,* 37: 794–802.

Rainie, L. and Keeter, S. (2006) *Cell Phone Use.* Washington, DC: Pew Internet and American Life Project.

Rimal, R.N. and Adkins, A.D. (2003) 'Using computers to narrowcast health messages: The role of audience segmentation, targeting, and tailoring in health promotion', in T.L. Thompson, A.M. Dorsey, K.I. Miller and R. Parrott (eds), *Handbook of Health Communication.* Mahwah, NJ: Lawrence Erlbaum Associates, pp. 497–535.

Roberts, D., Foehr, U. and Rideout, V. (2005) *Generation M: Media in the Lives of 8–18 Year Olds* (No. 7251). Menlo Park, CA: Kaiser Family Foundation.

Rogers, E.M. (1996) 'Up to date report', *Journal of Health Communication,* 1: 15–24.

Rogers, E.M. (2003) *Diffusion of Innovations,* 5th edn. New York: Simon and Schuster.

Schonfeld, E. (2010, June 8) *Costolo: Twitter Now Has 190 Million Users Tweeting 65 Million Times a Day.* TechCrunch, http://techcrunch.com/2010/06/08/twitter-190-million-users/

Shapiro, A.L. (1999) *The Control Revolution.* New York, NY: Public Affairs.

Slater, M. (1996) 'Theory and method in audience segmentation', *Journal of Health Communication,* 1: 267–283.

SmartReply (2006) *Best Practices: A Blueprint for Building a Retail Mobile Marketing Program.*

Snyder, L.B. and Hamilton, M.A. (2002) 'A meta-analysis of US health campaign effects on behavior: Emphasize enforcement, exposure, and new information and beware the secular trend', in R.C. Hornik (ed), *Public Health Communication: Evidence for Behavior Change.* Mahwah, NJ: Erlbaum.

Snyder, L.B., Hamilton, M.A., Mitchell, E.W., et al. (2004) 'A meta-analysis of the effect of mediated health communication campaigns on behavior change in the United States', *Journal of Health Communication,* 9: 71–96.

Sports Business Daily (2008) *NBC Averaging 16.9 Rating through Wednesday's Olympics Coverage.* Retrieved 3 December 2008, from http://www.sportsbusinessdaily.com/article/123472

Stetler, B. (2008) *Web Audience for Games Soars for NBC and Yahoo.* Retrieved 3 December 2008, from http://www.nytimes.com/2008/08/25/sports/olympics/25online.html?_r=1andhp

Stone, B. (2010) *Nintendo Wii to Add Netflix Service for Streaming Video.* Retrieved 14 January 2010 from http://www.nytimes.com/2010/01/13/technology/companies/13netflix.html

Thackeray, R., Neiger, B.L., Hanson, C.L. and McKenzie, J.F. (2008) 'Enhancing promotional strategies within social Marketing programs: Use of Web 2.0 social media', *Health Promotion Practice,* 9(4): 338–343.

Tian, H., Brimmer, D.J., Lin, J.S., Tumpey, A.J. and Reeves, W.C. (2010) 'Web usage data as a means of evaluating public health messaging and outreach', *Journal of Medical Internet Research,* 4: e52.

Tsai, C.C., Lee, G., Raab, F., et al. (2007) 'Usability and feasibility of PmEb: A mobile phone application for monitoring real time caloric balance', *Mobile Network Applications,* 12: 173–184.

Twitterfacts.com (2008) *Twitter Facts: Facts and Opinions on Twitter and the Twittosphere.* Retrieved 23 February 2009, from http://www.twitterfacts.blogspot.com/

Vidrine, D.J., Arduino, R.C., Lazev, A.B. and Gritz, E.R. (2006) 'A randomized trial of a proactive cellular telephone intervention for smokers living with HIV/AIDS', *AIDS,* 20(2): 253–260.

Voigt, K. (2009) *Olympics Enter the '2.0' Era.* Retrieved 3 December 2008, from http://www.cnn.com/2008/TECH/07/09/oly.media.index.html

Weitzel, J.A., Bernhardt, J.M., Usdan, S., Mays, D. and Glanz, K. (2007) 'Using wireless handheld computers to reduce the negative consequences of drinking alcohol', *Journal of Studies on Alcohol and Drugs,* 68: 534–537.

Yi, J., Maghoul, F. and Pedersen, J. (2008) 'Deciphering mobile search patterns: A study of Yahoo! mobile search queries'. Paper presented at the International World Wide Web Conference.

Research – Its Roles and Techniques

13. EVALUATION IN SOCIAL MARKETING – M. STEAD AND R.J. MCDERMOTT

This chapter addresses three major questions: Why evaluate? What should be measured? How should it be measured? While examining both process and impact evaluation issues, Stead and McDermott discuss the selection of indicators for intervention uptake and change at the individual and community levels. They also compare qualitative, quantitative and mixed methods approaches used in evaluation, examine budgetary and reporting issues, and address the challenges that accompany evaluation of social marketing interventions.

14. QUALITATIVE RESEARCH METHODS IN SOCIAL MARKETING – S. PETTIGREW AND M. ROBERTS

The authors describe the role qualitative research methods can play in social marketing programme design and evaluation. They begin with an overview of the major research methodological approaches – ethnography, grounded theory and case studies – and then explore data collection techniques, including individual interviews, observations, focus groups, project techniques and internet research. In addition to providing examples of how these techniques have been used in social marketing, the authors discuss the strengths and limitations of qualitative research in formative research and evaluation phases. Their comparison of the various quantitative methods available and extensive reference list will help social marketers select the methods best suited to specific project demands.

15. MEASUREMENT IN QUANTITATIVE METHODS – F.J. HARRIS

In this chapter on quantitative research methods, Harris guides the reader through an overview of the design of social marketing research or evaluation using quantitative methods to maximum effect. Noting that it is essential to consider the entire research process at a project's outset, particularly the nature of responses that will be elicited from participants and how these will be analysed, the evaluation methods described are: research design and data collection methods, sampling, question design and measurement, timing issues, ethical issues and finally, data analysis and interpretation. The author highlights the vital role quantitative methods play in building an evidence base to guide social marketing interventions and to help bring about policy changes.

13

Evaluation in Social Marketing

Martine Stead and Robert J. McDermott

INTRODUCTION

The term 'evaluation' comes from the Latin *valere* meaning 'to be strong' or 'to have worth' (Verduin and Clark, 1991). This origin is indicative that values are important in evaluation. According to Balch and Sutton: 'The root purpose of evaluating is to see what, if anything, can be done better than what is being done or was done' (1997: 61). Evaluation in social marketing assesses whether a programme has been implemented according to plan and the degree to which it has met its goals and objectives. As with most other interventions that foster voluntary behaviour change, social marketers are increasingly required to demonstrate that their interventions or campaigns 'work.' Social marketing initiatives are especially relevant to the point of evaluation, because they often represent departures from traditional or more conventional behaviour change strategies (McDermott, 2004). Whereas funders who are asked to invest in social marketing programmes want to know that their money is being spent wisely, persons involved in the design and delivery of social marketing endeavours need to know whether or not they are succeeding. Evaluation is, therefore, a critical component of any social marketing initiative.

Evaluation takes place before, during and after a programme. It helps shape programme content and quality. It examines the delivery process, the immediate outcomes and subsequent long-term impact on priority audiences. It assesses whether the programme has changed audience behaviour or altered the environment to make

healthy behaviour easier. In short, it tells one whether the programme has made a difference. It also may provide insight as to *why* a programme has (or has not) succeeded, as well as how it can be improved.

Effective evaluations have certain important characteristics or standards (Figure 13.1). According to the US Centers for Disease Control and Prevention (2004), evaluations should have the following properties:

- **Utility**: including *stakeholder identification, evaluator credibility, information scope and selection* (i.e. information is pertinent to the programme needs of stakeholders), *values identification* (i.e. perspectives, procedures and rationale used to interpret findings are described, thereby making the basis for value judgments clear), *report clarity* (i.e. programme context, purpose, methods and findings), *report timeliness* and *evaluation impact* (i.e. follow-up action by stakeholders is fostered, so that the relevance and utility of the evaluation is increased).
- **Feasibility**: including *practical procedures* that minimise disruptions to consumer audiences, *political viability* to take into account different perspectives or points of view and minimise the potential for bias or misapplication of results and *cost-effectiveness* that produces data of meaningful value that justify the expenditure of resources.
- **Propriety**: including a *service orientation* that assists organisations and other stakeholders in having their needs met, *formal agreements* in writing so that parties are obligated to adhere

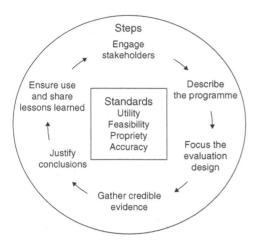

Figure 13.1   A framework for conducting programme evaluation. Source: US Centers for Disease Control and Prevention (2004). Available at: http://www.cdc.gov/eval/framework.htm

to all conditions pertinent to the evaluation, *rights of human subjects* that are respected and protected, *human interactions* that occur with dignity and without harm or feeling of being threatened, a *complete and fair assessment* of the programme under examination, *disclosure of findings* that is thorough, without prejudice, and that is made accessible to all persons with legal rights to see and examine these findings, potential *conflicts of interest* that are revealed so as not to compromise findings and subsequent application of findings, and *fiscal responsibility* that is reflected and accounted for ethically.

- **Accuracy**: including *programme documentation*, a clear description of the programme, *context analysis*, an examination and identification of the likely influences on a programme's operation and functioning, *purposes and procedures* of the evaluation, *defensible information sources*, *valid information*, *reliable information*, *systematic information* that is reviewed for error, *analysis of quantitative information*, *analysis of qualitative information*, *justified conclusions* so that stakeholders can assess their usefulness for decision making, *impartial reporting* that protects against bias, prejudice, or distortion, and *meta-evaluation*, that is, review and assessment of the evaluation process and procedures themselves to determine their strengths and weaknesses.

This chapter examines the tasks most pertinent to evaluating social marketing programmes. We discuss evaluation in four sections:

- Why evaluate?
- What should be measured?
- How should it be measured?
- Particular evaluation challenges in social marketing.

WHY EVALUATE?

Some authorities have suggested that if the purpose of 'research' is 'to prove,' then the purpose of 'evaluation' is 'to *im*prove' (Patton, 1997). The answer to 'Why evaluate?' sets the evaluation design in motion (McDermott and Sarvela, 1999). Social marketing interventions have numerous stakeholders including the organisation or firm initiating the campaign, the funding agency, the consumers towards whom the campaign is directed, the professional evaluation community and other individuals and groups. The list below identifies some additional *Why*s for evaluating social marketing initiatives:

- To improve a programme's credibility for consumers and the persons or agencies funding it.
- To determine if a programme is being implemented as planned (i.e. evidence of programme fidelity).
- To track programme progress to make mid-course revisions, if necessary.
- To determine the appropriateness of the 'match' between 'outcomes' (voluntary changes in behaviour) and programme objectives.
- To determine whether programmes are meeting their stated objectives (quality assurance).
- To see whether programmes not only are meeting their objectives but also are doing so 'efficiently' (i.e. cost-effectively).
- To assist decisions about whether one aspect of the marketing mix is more productive than another aspect (e.g. the 'right' product but the wrong promotion).
- To compare all the actual effects of a programme (good and bad, intended and unintended 'side effects') with the wants and needs of the priority audience so as to improve the programme (i.e. the offer) and community relations.
- To have a programme judged by 'critics' (programme experts) who can meet the public's demand for accountability.
- To interpret and explain the context in which programmes operate so as to have insight about improving them, or establishing them in new or different venues.
- To assess the potential relationship between behaviour and policy.
- To select wisely from an array of programme alternatives.

- To use findings to identify new problems or new audiences around which future interventions can be planned.

Being clear about *why* one is evaluating helps with subsequent decisions about the appropriate type and scale of evaluation. For instance, if the main purpose is to assess whether the programme is delivered as planned, an appropriate evaluation will be one concerned with the feasibility of implementation (process evaluation). However, if one must demonstrate impact on behaviour, the evaluation must be one capable of measuring whether behaviour has changed over a given period of time (summative evaluation).

Balch and Sutton (1997) aptly point out that programme stakeholders do not always agree on what the specific objectives of a social marketing intervention are. Thus, a type of pre-evaluation, also known as an evaluability assessment, needs to be undertaken whereby consensus about what a programme is supposed to accomplish is established. Smith describes evaluability assessment as:

> ... a diagnostic and prescriptive tool for improving programs and making evaluations more useful. It is a systematic process for describing the structure of a program (i.e. the objectives, logic, activities, and indicators of successful performance); and for analysing the plausibility and feasibility for achieving objectives, their suitability for in-depth evaluation, and their acceptability to program managers, policymakers, and program operators' (1989: 1).

McDermott and Sarvela indicate that evaluability assessment should build consensus about a programme's descriptive elements – its size and scope, duration, clarity and specificity, complexity and time frame. 'Evaluation is of limited value if a program has no clear objectives, when they are ill-defined, or when the program boundaries are obscured' (1999: 13). Finally, Smith (1989) argues that evaluability assessment can be a *summative tool* to determine if a programme has sufficient description to be evaluable, a *formative tool* to guide changes in the programme's current form that will increase the likelihood of it being effective, and a *planning tool* to clarify programme objectives and the required resources to achieve quality.

Assessing behaviour change – for example, whether a social marketing programme has improved immunisation rates, or increased the proportion of eligible women who receive baseline mammograms – can be difficult. Measuring behaviour change requires a complex evaluation design with baseline measures, a comparison group that did not participate in the intervention, samples selected appropriately and large enough for adequate power and statistical conclusion validity, and so on. When a social marketing programme is being implemented on a large scale, with high stakeholder expectations of impact, this kind of evaluation is essential to assess whether continued investment is appropriate. For smaller programmes, the resources needed for assessment of behaviour change would be proportionate to the scale of the project.

A full-scale evaluation of behavioural outcomes may not always be appropriate. If a programme employs a particularly innovative, untested approach, or addresses a behavioural issue not previously tackled, it may be more prudent to focus evaluation on 'getting the intervention right' before moving to a complex, labour-intensive and costly summative (outcome) evaluation. Alternative foci for the evaluation instead might be whether the intervention is credible and engaging for the priority audience, and whether it is practical to implement and the various intervention components complement each other. This is discussed further below under 'Process evaluation.' Moreover, if the problem behaviour undertaken is one that truly has defied change in the past, for demonstration purposes, evaluation might consist simply of assessing the extent to which members of the priority audience have moved along a continuum of change – for example from *pre-contemplation* to *contemplation* (Prochaska et al., 1992).

WHAT SHOULD BE MEASURED?

Considerations for selecting the indicators of intervention uptake and change

Choosing the most appropriate measures of change is challenging but important to get right. The measures should be directly relevant to the objectives of the programme – for example if the aim is to increase consumption of fruits and vegetables, then accurate 'before and after' measures are needed. The more precisely specified the objectives are, the easier it should be to identify appropriate measures of change.

A conventional and easily understood method for establishing objectives is the *SMART* way (Ambler, 2006). This acronym refers to the characteristics of well-written objectives – that is, objectives that are *S*pecific (are concrete, detailed and well-defined), *M*easureable (are quantifiable and allow for comparison), *A*chievable (are feasible and potentially responsive to action), *R*ealistic (take resources and sustainability into account) and *T*ime-bound (have a timeline for attainment). Objectives should consist of strong, action-oriented words, some examples of which can be found in Bloom's taxonomy (Bloom, 1956; Harrow, 1972; Krathwohl et al., 1973).

The temptation of some evaluators is to be too ambitious in their approach, such as focusing on outcomes that are beyond the capability of the intervention to influence, that are too difficult to measure given the available resources, or unlikely to effect a change within the timescale of the study. For example, in the *Believe in All Your Possibilities Social Marketing Campaign*, designed to prevent and control smoking and alcohol consumption among middle school students, evaluation focused on the fidelity of implementing six intervention components: (1) tobacco and alcohol citations given to youths observed by law enforcement officials; (2) follow-up tobacco education for youths who receive tobacco citations; (3) 100% smoke-free schools; (4) utility of a locally produced parent-oriented video that assists parents in communicating with youths and teaching about controlling access to tobacco and alcohol; (5) using state-mandated achievement tests to introduce relevant tobacco and alcohol information to teachers and youths and (6) theatre-as-education live performances carried out by older youths that illustrate refusal skills and enhance youth competency for putting them into action (Bryant et al., 2007). Had initial evaluation examined rates of new uptake or declines in the use of these substances, the campaign may have appeared to be a failure because: (1) the campaign 'dose' at the community level was small in the beginning; (2) the evaluation could neither control nor measure all of the environmental or local cultural factors influencing use of these products and (3) in the absence of a 'matched' community, evaluation could not address the milieu of other elements (e.g. secular trend, youth/family migration in and out of the community), thereby adding layers of complexity to the measurement task. Ironically, policymakers and other local decision-makers often want evaluations to deliver hard behavioural outcome statistics, sometimes just months after programme launch. These statistics, even if they are collected, often have little meaning and their adoption can lead to erroneous conclusions and subsequent policy recommendations.

Reporting change at the level of the individual

According to Smith (1999), a social marketer seeks measurable change in the elements that make the desired behaviour *easier* to do (than

previously perceived by consumers), *more fun* to do (than behaviours that compete with it for the consumer's attention) and *more popular* to do (i.e. provides a better perceived 'return on investment' than other behaviour options). The evidence of change is referred to by some social marketers as having made 'the needle move' (McDermott, 2004). Such evidence of movement can be determined through measuring changes in:

- Actual behaviour, behavioural intention, or stage of readiness to adopt the behaviour.
- Knowledge and beliefs.
- Awareness of the problem and of the campaign.
- Participation or utilisation rates with respect to some service.
- Consumer (or customer) satisfaction.

Reporting change does not have to be especially cryptic. Hence, behaviour can be reported as directly as:

1. Percentage change in the priority audience segment (e.g. high school students reporting alcohol use in the past 30 days decreased from 49% to 31%).
2. Percentage increase or decrease (e.g. alcohol use during the previous 30 days among high school students decreased by 18%).
3. Measures focusing on secondary audiences (e.g. there was a 14% increase in the proportion of parents who said they monitored the whereabouts of their high school-aged children).
4. Odds ratios (e.g. whereas boys aged 9–13 years old participating in the *VERB Summer Scorecard* programme were 1.30 times more likely to be active 6–7 days/week than their non-participant peers, girls in this same age group were 1.46 more likely to be active 6–7 days/week).
5. Programme 'side effects,' that is, unintended outcomes that could be positive or negative (e.g. *VERB Summer Scorecard* had a significantly greater proportion of participants among *emerging tweens, youths* 9–11 years old, than among *transitioning tweens, youths* 12–13 years old).

One also may see change measured as behavioural intention rather than behaviour itself. Although actual behaviour change provides a more dramatic indicator of having 'moved the needle,' behavioural intention provides an acceptable alternative when either of two conditions is met – whenever exposure time to the social marketing campaign is minimal (e.g. the programme is new), or whenever the objective is to move people along the continuum of change (e.g. pre-contemplation → contemplation) as described by the transtheoretical model (Prochaska et al., 1992). As level of participation in the *VERB Summer Scorecard* physical activity promotion programme increased, a dose–response effect was found in terms of future intention to participate again, with odds ratios ranging from 4.42 (at least part of one scorecard completed) to 7.50 (more than one scorecard completed).

Whereas social marketers measure the success of their endeavours by behaviour change, sometimes they also want to know how much the campaign has altered consumer knowledge and beliefs. In the early stages of a programme or right after its conclusion, knowledge and belief assessment can help to gauge the potential for movement in the direction of desired behaviour change. The results of such an evaluation can provide conclusions about knowledge change as shown here:

- The priority audience's ability to recall facts promoted in a campaign (e.g. *among women, breast cancer is the most commonly diagnosed cancer after non-melanoma skin cancer, and is the second leading cause of cancer deaths after lung cancer*).
- The priority audience's ability to provide specific information from authoritative sources (e.g. *according to the National Cancer Institute, current oral contraceptive users have a relative risk of developing breast cancer that is 24% higher than non-users*).
- The priority audience's ability to recite recommendations from authoritative sources (e.g. *mammography screening every 12–33 months significantly reduces mortality from breast cancer, especially among women aged 50–69*).

In addition to changes in knowledge, some measures can attempt to capture beliefs as indicators of campaign response. Beliefs can be reflected in *attitude* change (e.g. *breastfeeding is good for my baby*) or *opinion* change (e.g. *breastfeeding is easy to do*) following a breastfeeding promotion intervention. Sometimes measures can assess *value* change, such as after an intervention about the health risks of sun exposure and artificial tanning devices (e.g. *maintaining a year-round tan is not worth my risking skin cancer*).

Reporting change at the level of community

Changes to the physical environment, modifications in the community infrastructure or the development and implementation of policies that facilitate change in the priority behaviour are further measures that signal the success of social marketing interventions. Social marketing success is probably more strategic and sustaining when it influences management of a community's economic, social and physical environments (Hastings et al., 2000).

Although nearly every developed country makes its people aware of the value of physical activity, a frequent barrier to greater participation is the absence of safe and accessible places to be physically active. Creating a demand that results at a later time in improvement of the so-called 'built environment' enables people to overcome this barrier. Therefore, establishing parks or improving their aesthetics, building community swimming pools, designing bike trails, providing lighted pathways, fixing cracked or uneven sidewalks, making recreational areas safe and resistant to crime and crafting new walkways all increase physical activity opportunities within communities. Evaluation personnel can count or otherwise track modifications to a community's infrastructure, and then, use 'before and after' observations to determine the impact which those modifications have on behaviour.

In the youth-centric *VERB Summer Scorecard* physical activity programme, a factor that initially limited youth participation was the lack of cheap and available transportation. Subsequently, a partnership was established with the community's public transportation system, allowing the 'scorecard' with which youths monitored their physical activity also to serve as a bus pass on the days when community-sponsored events occurred. This infrastructural or policy change impacted youth participation significantly (Bryant et al., 2010).

Interventions which involve policy change can foster adoption of the product (i.e. the behaviour) often faster and more efficiently than interventions directed at the individual level. Fully or fairly comprehensive indoor smoking bans have been enacted in several countries such as France, Ireland, Israel, Italy, Norway and the UK (Depondt, 2009), and their impact on smoking prevalence, cessation and norms is being rigorously evaluated (e.g. Brown et al., 2009; Fong et al., 2006a; McKee et al., 2009). Stringent compulsory nutritional standards for all food and drink sold in schools have been imposed in the UK in an attempt to curb rising levels of childhood obesity and to improve children's diet (Department for Education and Skills, 2006; Department of Health, 2004). Similar measures are enacted in some parts of the USA; in California, such action was, in part, a result of a social marketing intervention targeting key leaders in education (McDermott R.J., et al., 2005).

Attributing behaviour change to specific policies is challenging for evaluators: policy measures are often implemented in conjunction with other measures, or occur as part of wider societal shifts in values and norms, making it difficult to isolate the exact impact of the policy measure; studies often lack comparison groups; it may be many years before changes take effect; and so on. An example of how these challenges can be overcome is provided by the International Tobacco Control (ITC) Policy Evaluation Study, a longitudinal multi-country evaluation of the impact of the World Health Organization Framework Convention on Tobacco Control policies. As policies are introduced at different stages, countries unaffected by policies serve as comparators for implementing countries (Fong et al., 2006b).

Other indicators of change at the community level

Campaign *awareness* is a measurable outcome of social marketing interventions. Although it is a low-level evaluation indicator because it is not a true measure of success, it nevertheless provides data concerning the extent to which the campaign was recalled by the priority or intended audience.

Suppose one was interested in assessing audience awareness of Baltimore, Maryland's *Believe Campaign* to reduce the amount of drug use in the city (Linder and Associates, Inc., 2002). There are at least three ways in which an evaluator could determine campaign awareness (Kotler et al., 2002). First, one could assess what is called *unaided awareness*, where people are surveyed but not prompted about the event of interest. For instance, community members might be asked: 'What have you seen or heard lately about drug use in Baltimore?' Secondly, a technique examining *aided awareness* could be used to offer community members one or more prompts. For example: 'What have you seen or heard lately about the campaign against drug use called *Baltimore's Believe Campaign*?' Finally, a technique known as *proven awareness* could be employed. Community members might be asked: 'Where did you actually read or hear about *Baltimore's Believe Campaign*?'

Whereas awareness may be viewed as a programme outcome, it also may be a vital indicator during the beginning stages of a campaign. For example, if it becomes clear that a significant proportion of the intended audience segment is unaware of the *product*, it is possible that previous data regarding *price*, *promotion* or *place* may have been incorrect or that the campaign somehow wandered off strategy during the implementation phase. Evaluators may be required to carry out new formative research or conduct another examination of previously assembled data to determine whether re-focusing campaign efforts is necessary. Most good social marketers know that product awareness follows a type of diffusion-dissemination process. Thus, early judgements about lack of success may be premature. Marketers also know that evidence of product awareness does not necessarily translate into the desired action of behavioural change. One must be cautious about thinking that audience *awareness* equates with audience *penetration*.

The effect of a programme on behaviour also can be determined by measuring at least two additional constructs – *consumer participation* and *consumer satisfaction*. For the former construct, rates of participation in the behaviour of interest (the product) based on estimates of eligible persons in the audience segment provide some measure of audience penetration. The use of rates in this instance, as in epidemiological investigations, facilitates comparisons across time and audiences. For the latter construct, evaluation ratings of consumer satisfaction with a particular service using Likert-type scales, numeric rating scales and similar methods can provide evidence of change (i.e. improvement) as a result of the intervention.

How much change can I expect to see?

As a rule, public health officials have high expectations and often think they will see more change in a short period of time than is realistic. It may be beneficial to remember that even modest changes in behaviour can affect health status, influence morbidity and mortality rates, and impact on healthcare costs. Therefore, some things that appear to undergo negligible change may have a profound effect on important health variables. In commercial marketing, a movement of just a few percentage points in market share between competitors can have a large effect on revenue. In social marketing, as in other behavioural intervention strategies, expectations must be realistic. It may be wise to compare observed change in one's programme to historic rates and rates of change due to previous interventions.

Evaluating costs

Cost analysis seeks an accurate accounting of programme costs so that, among other things, marketers can determine how much it cost to achieve a particular level of change. Whereas a comprehensive discussion of cost analysis is beyond the scope of this chapter, some fundamental points are identified. At a minimum, evaluators should identify the costs associated with programme implementation. Levin (1988) offers a three-part method for cost determination:

- Identify the ingredients of the programme.
- Estimate the cost of each ingredient as well as the total cost of programme.
- Analyse costs using a standard approach.

Programme ingredients have to include both full-time and part-time personnel as well as volunteers, plus all costs associated with facilities, equipment and materials. When ingredients have been identified, a value must be placed on them. One needs to estimate the costs of volunteer labour or donated materials as if the sponsoring organisation actually paid for these goods or services. When large programmes are considered, unit costs (e.g. costs per audience segment) may be relevant to measure and report. Therefore, the cost of a social marketing programme may even be assessed by measuring and reporting the per person cost of getting the behaviour adopted.

Process evaluation

Interest in process evaluation – the study of programme implementation – has grown in the last couple of decades. Several factors have contributed to this growth (Linnan and Steckler, 2002).

First, evaluators and policymakers have recognised the need to understand why programmes sometimes 'fail.' The rise of evidence-based practice and policymaking has thrown a spotlight on how relatively few interventions succeed in changing behaviour and on the need to understand why this is the case. Process evaluation can help us to understand whether a programme's lack of impact is due to a failure of programme *theory* (it was the wrong sort of programme) or a failure of *implementation* (it was potentially the right sort of programme but it was badly or inadequately implemented).

Secondly, there is growing interest in the replicability and sustainability of programmes: What factors are important for successful implementation in other settings? What needs to be improved for the programme to be able to be sustained beyond the life of the evaluation?

Thirdly, behaviour change interventions are becoming more complex. With this increasing complexity comes a need to understand how the different elements of programme work – or not – together to produce effects. Where programmes are complex, consisting of multiple strands, approaches and implementers, it is even less safe to assume that implementation is as intended or consistent across all elements of the programme

than it is with 'simple' interventions – underlining further the need for process evaluation.

Finally, there has been a growth in intervention approaches which do not lend themselves easily to more traditional experimental models of evaluation, such as multi-faceted community programmes, media advocacy and community development. Such approaches are often unpredictable and difficult to control, making evaluation particularly challenging. Here, one of the key tasks for the evaluator is to record, describe and analyse the processes of engagement and change within the intervention so as to help make sense of outcome results and to help others learn from the intervention's experience (Nutbeam 1998).

Process evaluation measures, explores and analyses six aspects of programme implementation: dose and reach; quality; fidelity; engagement; deliverability and intervention logic.

'**Dose**' and '**reach**' concern the *amount* of programme activity and the number of people involved. Measuring dosage involves monitoring, for example, the number of brief advice sessions given by a general practitioner, the number of smoking cessation groups held, referrals to a service, leaflets distributed, task force meetings convened and so on. Measuring reach involves counting the people reached by these activities and analysing their characteristics. Usually, the actual dosage and reach would be compared with the desired dosage and reach to assess the extent to which the programme generated the intended amount of activity and reached the people it was meant to. When considering dosage and reach, it is important to consider dose 'received' as well as dose 'given' – in other words, while 62% of the intended target group may have received the leaflet, how many actually read it or kept it?

Examining implementation '**quality**' moves beyond dosage to ask, 'Was the programme delivered *well*?' This is particularly relevant where programmes involve face-to-face interaction, where factors such as good communication skills, empathy, rapport and ability to motivate may be critical to achieving results.

Related to 'quality' is the concept of implementation '**fidelity**.' This concerns the extent to which activities were delivered exactly as intended and consistently across all sites and implementers. It is often examined in school-based substance use prevention programmes, where it is assumed that a certain level of implementation must be achieved in order for effects to occur (Dusenbury et al., 2003). Typical questions explored in an assessment of fidelity include: Did the implementers cover all the content when delivering the programme? Did they keep to programme timings? Did they use the recommended teaching and learning methods? (Dane and Schneider, 1998; Stead et al., 2007a).

'**Engagement**' concerns the target group's immediate response to the programme. If the target group does not like, trust or feel inspired by a programme, then regardless of how theoretically logical or well implemented it is, it is unlikely to work. Assessing engagement therefore involves exploring and measuring issues such as target group identification with the programme (Do they feel it is speaking to them?), comprehension of the programme message, perceptions of the programme source or brand, how the programme makes people feel, perceptions of the programme's cultural relevance and so on. These kinds of measures may also be examined in evaluations of programme outcomes: for example, evaluations of communications campaigns often include measures of identification with the campaign, understanding of the message and perceived relevance alongside measures of impact on behaviour (e.g. Stead et al., 2005).

One of the most useful aspects of process evaluation is examination of programme '**deliverability**' – how easy or difficult a programme is to implement, and the factors which help and hinder its implementation. As noted above, understanding this is crucial if programmes are to be improved and transferred to other settings or continued after the lifetime of the study. Programme delivery may be affected positively or negatively by a wide range of factors, including the skill of the implementer, the ease or difficulty of the programme itself (e.g. whether it needs a lot of preparation), the type of target group, the amount of management support, and so on. Figure 13.2 illustrates the kinds of factors that might be identified.

Finally, process evaluation can help understand, unpack and critique the **logic model** underpinning an intervention. If the programme is trying to increase skills or change attitudes, do the components actually target those variables? If it is a multi-component programme, do the different strands complement and interact with each other, or are they implemented and experienced in isolation?

HOW SHOULD IT BE MEASURED?

Quantitative, qualitative and mixed methods approaches

The 'How' in programme evaluation considers the specific designs and measures that are used to acquire the kind of feedback that allows judgement

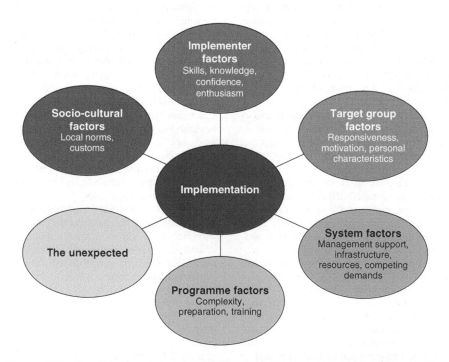

Figure 13.2   Possible typology of factors influencing programme implementation

about the worth or value of the intervention. Only a conceptual overview of these approaches is presented in this chapter because the following two chapters go into more detail, and 'methods' textbooks are readily available. Evaluators do, in fact, have many tools at their disposal and can choose from quantitative designs, qualitative designs, or mixed methods designs to answer the pertinent evaluation questions.

Quantitative methods and designs (e.g. quasi-experimental or experimental designs with control groups) are pertinent to certain types of questions and inform the evaluator about what has changed and the extent to which it has changed. In short, how effective was the social marketing intervention compared with a control situation? Or, how well did the social marketing intervention perform compared with other interventions that have been tried in the past? Was the programme that was delivered actually responsible for the results that were recorded? If successful, would this same intervention also work in other settings, at other times, and with other audiences? Evaluators must be aware of threats to internal validity (Campbell and Stanley, 1966; Cook and Campbell, 1979) and should try both to control for them and measure them. Some of these confounding threats may be beyond the evaluator's control (McDermott, 2004). Overall, social marketers want to know what was the success of the product, how much change took place and to what extent did the priority audience adopt the desired behaviour?

Quantitative designs enable the evaluator to describe 'What happened' or 'How much' happened. However, only *qualitative* methods and designs provide the type of rich data that inform social marketers about 'Why' something worked (or did not work) and 'How' it did (or did not). Why did the social marketing programme fail to produce the desired or expected behaviour change? If the social marketing campaign *did* produce the desired outcomes, what were the key elements, events or contextual inputs to the campaign that fostered its success?

Patton (1987) identifies several circumstances for which qualitative methods are useful for conducting evaluations. Some applicable circumstances to social marketing include when:

- Marketers want to understand the dynamics of how a programme works.
- In-depth information is sought about particular audience segments, contexts or programme venues.
- The programme being attempted has unique qualities about it.
- There is interest in determining how consumers view or experience the programme under evaluation.

- Quantitative measures are inadequate for answering specific evaluation questions.
- Evaluation is still exploratory, perhaps because the intervention is attempting to address a behaviour change problem that has defied other interventions in the past.
- There is a desire to add depth and richness to statistical data garnered from quantitative methods.

Some authorities argue about whether quantitative methods are superior to qualitative methods or vice versa. Hopefully, it is evident that such an argument is akin to debating the question of which tool is better, a hammer or a chain-saw? If one wants to drive a nail into a board, a hammer is the better option. On the other hand, if one needs to cut down an oak tree, use the chain-saw instead. In evaluating social marketing programmes, the choice of methods is a matter of the evaluator's needs and the answers being sought to specific stakeholder questions.

Because both quantitative and qualitative methods are powerful tools, contemporary evaluators increasingly see the advantages of using *mixed method designs*, thereby taking advantage of the strengths of both approaches and minimising the weaknesses of either. The triangulation of measurement optimises the potential that the results are accurate and will be applicable to stakeholder needs. Therefore, the evaluation of a given social marketing undertaking may include multiple quantitative strategies (e.g. surveys employing mail, telephone or internet options) or qualitative strategies (e.g. in-depth face-to-face interviews, information collected through informal interviews, recorded anecdotal remarks and observational data).

In a typical case scenario, qualitative methods such as in-depth interviews may help evaluators apply age-appropriate language or culturally relevant concepts as they design a quantitative survey for a specific audience. After the quantitative survey has been administered, qualitative methods may be useful for gaining better understanding of how to interpret survey findings.

In assessing the effects of a social marketing programme that promotes the selection of healthful food options, observing buying behaviour in a grocery store or the purchasing of lunch items in a school cafeteria can confirm or refute responses that consumers provide to a quantitative survey. Data acquired through focus group interviews may identify which campaign elements were least useful or most compelling with respect to purchasing considerations and decisions. Moreover, the examination of various records (e.g. requests for nutrition materials, cash register receipts at grocery stores or restaurants, registrations in nutrition classes, etc.) may combine quantitative and qualitative measures that provide feedback about the reach, intended effects and side effects of a programme.

The importance of timing

The issue of 'When to evaluate' is also an important evaluation consideration. Social marketing campaigns lend themselves to multiple temporal points:

- *Prior* to a campaign to obtain a baseline measure of current behaviour.
- *During* a campaign's implementation phase to monitor fidelity so that mid-course corrections can occur, if necessary.
- *After* the campaign to seek evidence that the consumer has adopted the product, that is the behaviour of interest.
- *Long after* the campaign has been completed to collect evidence of intervention decay or recidivism, thereby suggesting a need for a programme 'booster.'

Consequently, deciding *when* to evaluate has implications for selecting the evaluation design, choosing what to measure, making budgeting decisions and considering other resource allocations. In a thorough end-to-end evaluation, monitoring fidelity of implementation, making mid-course corrections to such things as placement or promotion and determining immediate and long-term effects of the campaign will use all of the time points identified above. Mid-course corrections are vital evaluation considerations. As Andreasen puts it: 'If necessary mid-course corrections are not made, all a final, formal evaluation at the end of the project will tell you is: (a) you screwed up and (b) it is too late to fix it' (1995: 94).

Assigning budget to evaluation

Even experienced evaluators may underestimate the budget required to carry out a thorough and comprehensive programme evaluation. Moreover, evaluators often find themselves in competition for funds with persons who plan and deliver the social marketing programme, so there may be arguments surrounding these monetary elements. This potential for competition among key players underscores the need for evaluation teams to work closely with programme planning teams so that each group understands the other's needs. It is vital that marketers see the benefit that thorough evaluation can provide. Strong evaluation can help

to 'market' social marketing, to popularise it and to interest others in using this approach for undertaking challenging behaviour change in resistant audience segments. No one can say for sure what the magnitude of an evaluation budget ought to be. The unique features of individual programmes play a role in estimating every evaluation budget. However, thorough evaluation can be done only rarely with a monetary figure that is less than 20% of the overall programme budget. In fact, a larger figure may be necessary if one is to carry out baseline measures, monitor programme implementation in its early stages and then perform post-programme follow-up and assess priority audiences at a later date for evidence of intervention retention and decay.

Internal versus external evaluation

The question of who is the better choice for conducting programme evaluation, an *internal evaluator* or an *external evaluator*, is discussed at length by McDermott and Sarvela (1999). An internal or 'in-house' evaluator who is directly associated with the social marketing campaign no doubt has superior understanding of the programme and its goals. The person or team of individuals to whom evaluation is assigned may have been involved in the formative research that gave rise to the marketing mix. Furthermore, internal staff members are likely to possess a more thorough knowledge of the programme's contextual elements and the 'culture' in which it exists.

An external evaluator who has never been involved with the programme, its formative research, concept development or marketing mix brings impartiality to the assignment. External evaluation that is perceived to be impartial or dispassionate may lend credibility to favourable programme outcomes. In consideration of costs and the respective strengths of internal versus external evaluators, a 'hybrid vigour' compromise may be reached where internal evaluation is conducted during the formative stages of the social marketing campaign, and external evaluation becomes operational during the summative (outcome) stage.

Reporting results

The last step in evaluation is reporting the results, as well as interpreting those results, using a format that is utilisation-focused and easily understood. A good evaluation report facilitates decision making by stakeholders. Because of the scientific content of some evaluations, written reports can read at a complex or technical level.

However, they should never be unnecessarily esoteric. Consumers of evaluation reports are usually less intrigued by the sophistication of the sampling procedures and the statistical analyses than they are by the meaning of the results that describe the performance of the programme. Even having a well-written evaluation report may not guarantee that it is understood and enjoyed by all stakeholders. However, having clearly stated aims of the evaluation, and working closely with stakeholders on the front end of an evaluation, will assist the process of producing a report that is utilisation-focused and reader-friendly.

What should an evaluation report include? 'Skeletally speaking' it should contain a front cover, a title page, acknowledgements, a table of contents, lists of figures, graphs, tables, exhibits and other relevant displays, an executive summary, a background description of the programme that was evaluated, including programme aims and other details, a description of the aims and methods relevant to the evaluation, the results, a discussion of the results, conclusions and recommendations about the programme and appendices. In addition, the report may include an examination of the costs associated with the programme.

Results are findings presented in factual, descriptive terms. Evaluators consider both *hard data* (primarily quantitative) and *soft data* (primarily qualitative). The former includes results that have the properties of reliability and validity. The latter consists of commentaries, testimonials, casual observations and anecdotal evidence that tell evaluators about some of the characteristics of the programme that may not have been measured intentionally. Whereas some stakeholders might be inclined to focus *only* on hard data, soft data should not be discarded. Albert Einstein is attributed as having said: 'Not everything that can be counted counts, and not everything that counts can be counted.' Thus, qualitative or soft data, as pointed out earlier in this chapter, may have extraordinary value in providing insights about programme strengths and weaknesses, including what to evaluate in the next cycle of the programme's operation.

How data are organised and presented may be critical to reader comprehension. For rapid perusal, survey results can be summarised on a facsimile of the questionnaire itself. Whereas results can be presented clearly in a narrative format, a narration often is tedious to read, and does not easily allow timely identification of a particular point of interest. Thus, a visual display of data is useful and offers many options: tables, figures, bar graphs, line graphs and pie charts (also known as circle charts or sector charts).

Evaluators can pilot test data displays with potential stakeholders to determine the approach that is most helpful. Perhaps, the question for the report creator to remember is: 'How can I best display my data to assist readers in interpreting them, and drawing relevant conclusions that will be helpful in programme planning, future decision making and other important tasks?'

Is there a best way to offer interpretation of results or provide discussion, conclusions and recommendations? The keys to a well-written discussion of results are *balance, clarity* and *objectivity* (McDermott and Sarvela, 1999). Although it might go without saying, the report writer must remember the importance of presenting the results honestly, and avoiding temptation to disseminate only 'good news.' All evaluations yield learning, and sometimes, what is learned from accounts of intervention failures contributes as much to understanding as success stories do. Evaluators also must be sensitive so as to avoid drawing conclusions that exceed what the data actually reveal. Whereas it is invaluable for evaluators and programme managers to work closely together, there may be some tendency for the evaluator to report results or identify conclusions that are pleasing regardless of their actual validity. There may be some pressure applied by key programme players to report only selected findings, or to 'weigh' some findings more heavily than others. Such subtle pressures or biases speak to the value of having external evaluators.

A social marketing programme rarely achieves all of its objectives, and few if any programmes are without flaws. Andreasen offers the reminder: 'Campaigns never turn out as planned' (2006: 98). Therefore, a good evaluation is a balanced report that cites all identified programme strengths and weaknesses. If available data fail to lead to an indisputable conclusion about the programme's value, that fact should be pointed out as well.

Clarity is a characteristic of a report that is especially noteworthy where conclusions or recommendations are concerned. What qualities of a recommendation enhance its 'user friendliness,' and improve its utility? Some suggestions adapted from Hendricks and Papagiannis (1990) are listed below for their possible relevance to social marketing programmes:

- Consider all *pertinent* issues to be 'fair game,' not only the preordained ones but also ones that arise while conducting the evaluation.
- Think about recommendations throughout the course of the evaluation, not just at its conclusion. Potential recommendations can be noted as soon as impressions are formed, and reviewed for applicability at the end.

- Draw recommendations from a variety of sources, including ones from other studies that attempted to change the same behaviour or other social marketing interventions that may have application to *this* programme.
- Work closely with programme personnel in all stages of the evaluation process so that stakeholders do not feel 'ambushed' or surprised by recommendations with which they become confronted. As recommendations begin to 'crystallise,' the evaluation team and key decision-makers should build acceptance together.
- Keeping in mind the programme's political, social and organisational context, *realistic* recommendations should be offered with the caveat that ethics and objectivity also guide the designation of recommendations.
- Suggest possible future implications for various stakeholder groups if the recommendations are acted upon (or not acted upon).
- Accompany recommendations with implementation strategies that consider existing resources only as well as future or anticipated resources.
- Organise recommendations that facilitate understanding (e.g. high priority vs lower priority, short term vs long term, major vs minor, structural vs cosmetic and so on).

PARTICULAR EVALUATION CHALLENGES IN SOCIAL MARKETING

All evaluation is challenging. The nature of the problems addressed by social marketing and the context in which social marketing evaluators work bring particular challenges (Stead and Gordon, 2010):

1. The behaviours addressed in social marketing programmes are often complex, deep-rooted and challenging. Multiple measures may be needed to capture the different dimensions of a changed behaviour (consider, e.g., how many different processes and changes may be involved in 'eating more healthily'). Change may take a long time to occur, requiring evaluation over many years. The sensitive nature or stigma surrounding some behaviours may pose particular challenges to evaluators in terms of research participants' anxiety or discomfort in talking about them, fear of the consequences of disclosure and so on.
2. Whereas in some fields of evaluation, methods can be replicated in subsequent studies, the nature of social marketing means that 'one size fits all' approaches to evaluation may not be appropriate. Social marketing puts the consumer at the centre of every intervention and initiative, and this means

that messages, services, products and activities should be designed with the needs of the particular target consumer group in mind. Whereas the *principles* behind a social marketing programme may be transferable, programmes should always be adapted for local needs and contexts. This makes evaluation particularly challenging, because it too will need to adapt to each unique programme.
3. Social marketing initiatives typically involve multiple actions and channels: products, promotional materials, services, publicity and so on. Such complex interventions do not lend themselves to a precise statement of independent variables whose effects can be measured and easily replicated. Complex interventions require more complex and flexible evaluation approaches than the randomised controlled trial (RCT), which is best suited to the assessment of relatively simple interventions (Fawcett et al., 1997; McQueen, 2001).
4. Social marketing programmes are, by their nature, designed to reflect, and be implemented in, real-world conditions: in schools, in neighbourhoods, in people's homes and in workplaces. This means that it is very difficult to control the context in which an intervention is implemented. As Livingstone (2005) points out, it is difficult in naturalistic settings to eliminate possible confounding variables. In social science, the 'perfect study' often simply cannot exist, for technical, ethical or other reasons.
5. Social marketing programmes are not always predictable. 'Fuzzy' interventions are ones which do not remain 'stable,' that evolve and alter in response to changing contexts (Øvretveit, 1998). A social marketing programme may evolve flexibly in response to changing needs and circumstances, or in response to research findings suggesting that a certain strategy needs modifying. The problems are intensified when the intervention is one which seeks not to impact on individual knowledge, attitudes and behaviour but to tackle social and environmental determinants of health by impacting on communities, structures and policies (Jackson and Waters, 2005; McKinlay, 1993). Evaluation designs need to be correspondingly flexible and pragmatic (Stead et al., 2002).

Every evaluation of a social marketing initiative provides an opportunity to advance learning about social marketing – to improve social marketers' understanding of how behaviour is influenced and to increase the repertoire of possible intervention strategies. This means that every evaluation should also include an element reflecting on the 'social marketingness' of the intervention: What principles or features of social marketing were

Table 13.1 Andreasen's benchmark criteria for social marketing

Benchmark		Explanation
1	Behaviour change	Intervention seeks to change behaviour and has specific measurable behavioural objectives
2	Consumer research	Intervention is based on an understanding of consumer experiences, values and needs Formative research is conducted to identify these Intervention elements are pre-tested with the target group
3	Segmentation and targeting	Different segmentation variables are considered when selecting the intervention target group Intervention strategy is tailored for the selected segment/s
4	Marketing mix	Intervention considers the best strategic application of the 'marketing mix.' This consists of the four Ps of *product, price, place* and *promotion*. Other *P*s might include *policy change* or *people* (e.g. training is provided to intervention delivery agents). Interventions which only use the promotion *P* are social advertising, not social marketing
5	Exchange	Intervention considers what will motivate people to engage voluntarily with the intervention and offers them something beneficial in return. The offered benefit may be intangible (e.g. personal satisfaction) or tangible (e.g. rewards for participating in the programme and making behavioural changes)
6	Competition	Competing forces to the behaviour change are analysed. Intervention considers the appeal of competing behaviours (including current behaviour) and uses strategies that seek to remove or minimise this competition

Source: Andreasen (2002).

particularly of interest in this intervention? Was the intervention a 'good' example of social marketing?

A useful approach here may be to apply the Andreasen (2002) six benchmarks of social marketing as a guide to whether an intervention is a proper application of social marketing principles (Table 13.1). Applying this framework to each evaluated social marketing intervention – asking whether and how it meets each of the six criteria – provides a useful test of the intervention's 'social marketingness' and also yields valuable learning about, say, the different ways in which competition can be addressed and the different types of mutually beneficial exchange that can be formulated. This is also a helpful approach when conducting systematic reviews and literature reviews of the effectiveness of social marketing (e.g. Stead et al., 2007b). The six benchmarks can be used as a checklist to ascertain whether an intervention should be included in the review as an example of social marketing. This is more reliable than judging solely on the basis of how an intervention is labelled by its developers and implementers, which can result in some interventions which are *not* social marketing being included in the evidence base, and others which may not use the label social marketing but which actually follow social marketing principles being excluded (McDermott L. et al., 2005).

KEY WORDS: Social marketing; evaluation; research; objectives; outcomes and indicators; measurement/measures; methods: quantitative, qualitative and mixed methods; process evaluation; evaluation challenges; feasibility; acceptability; engagement; learning.

Key insights

- Evaluation is an essential component of any social marketing programme. It tells us what impacts a programme has on behaviour – and, just as importantly, why it has or has not succeeded and how it can be improved.
- Social marketing evaluators are interested in changes not only in behaviour but also in awareness, attitudes, norms, community infrastructure, organisational behaviour and policy.
- The evaluation design must be appropriate to the intervention objectives and the type of intervention. It may be appropriate in some contexts to focus on feasibility and acceptability before attempting to measure behaviour change outcomes.
- Process evaluation – the study of how interventions are implemented – yields valuable information about how programmes succeed or fail in different contexts and how they can be better supported in real-world settings.

- Evaluation is challenging because social marketing interventions tend to be heterogeneous, complex and multi-faceted, and do not lend themselves readily to traditional experimental designs.
- Every social marketing evaluation can contribute to learning not only about that particular intervention or issue but also about social marketing in general.

REFERENCES

Ambler, G. (2006) *Setting SMART Objectives*. Accessed 8 September 2009 from http://www.thepracticeofleadership.net/2006/03/11/setting-smart-objectives/.

Andreasen, A.R. (1995) *Marketing Social Change*. San Francisco, CA: Jossey-Bass.

Andreasen, A.R. (2002) 'Marketing social marketing in the social change marketplace', *Journal of Public Policy and Marketing*, 21: 3–13.

Andreasen, A.R. (2006) *Social Marketing in the 21st Century*. Thousand Oaks, CA: Sage Publications.

Balch, G.I. and Sutton, S.M. (1997) 'Keep me posted: A plea for practical evaluation', in M.E. Goldberg, M. Fishbein and S.E. Middlestadt (eds), *Social Marketing – Theoretical and Practical Perspectives*. Mahwah, NJ: Lawrence Erlbaum Associates.

Bloom, B.S. (1956) *Taxonomy of Educational Objectives, Handbook I: The Cognitive Domain*. New York: David McKay Co., Inc.

Brown, A., Moodie, C. and Hastings, G.B. (2009) 'A longitudinal study of policy effect (smoke-free legislation) on smoking norms: ITC Scotland/UK', *Nicotine & Tobacco Research*, 11(8): 924–933.

Bryant, C.A., McCormack Brown, K.R., McDermott, R.J., et al. (2007) 'Community-based prevention marketing: Organizing a community for health behavior intervention', *Health Promotion Practice*, 8(2): 154–163.

Bryant, C.A., Courtney, A.H., McDermott, R.J., et al. (2010) 'Promoting physical activity among youth through community-based prevention marketing', *Journal of School Health*, 80(5): 214–224.

Campbell, D.T. and Stanley, J.C. (1966) *Experimental and Quasi-Experimental Designs for Research*. Boston, MA: Houghton Mifflin.

Cook, T.D. and Campbell, D.T. (1979) *Quasi-Experimentation*. Boston, MA: Houghton Mifflin.

Dane, A.V. and Schneider, B.H. (1998) 'Program integrity in primary and early secondary intervention: Are implementation effects out of control?' *Clinical Psychology Review*, 18: 23–45.

Department for Education and Skills (2006) *Nutritional Standards for School Lunches and Other School Food*. www.teachernet.gov.uk/wholeschool/healthyliving.

Department of Health (2004) *Choosing Health: Making Healthier Choices Easier*. Public Health White Paper: Crown.

Depondt, F. (2009) 'Commentary: Indoor smoking bans', *Emagazine.com*. Retrieved 15 September 2009 from http://www.emagazine.com/view/?3530.

Dusenbury, L., Brannigan, R., Falco, M. and Hansen, W.B. (2003) 'A review of research on fidelity of implementation: Implications for drug abuse prevention in school settings', *Health Education Research*, 18(2): 237–256.

Fawcett, S.B., Lewis, R.K., Paine-Andrews, A., et al. (1997) 'Evaluating community coalitions for prevention of substance abuse: The case of Project Freedom', *Health Education and Behavior*, 24(6): 812–828.

Fong, G.T., Cummings, K.M., Borland, R., et al. (2006b) 'The conceptual framework of the International Tobacco Control (ITC) Policy Evaluation Project', *Tobacco Control*, 15(Suppl 3): iii3–iii11.

Fong, G.T., Hyland, A., Borland, R., et al. (2006a) 'Reductions in tobacco smoke pollution and increases in support for smoke-free public places following the implementation of comprehensive smoke-free workplace legislation in the Republic of Ireland: Findings from the ITC Ireland/UK Survey', *Tobacco Control*, 15(Suppl 3): iii51–iii58.

Harrow, A. (1972) *A Taxonomy of the Psychomotor Domain: A Guide for Developing Behavioral Objectives*. New York: David McKay Co., Inc.

Hastings, G., MacFadyen, L. and Anderson, S. (2000) 'Whose behaviour is it anyway? The broader potential of social marketing', *Social Marketing Quarterly*, VI(2), June: 46–58.

Hendricks, M. and Papagiannis, M. (1990) 'Do's and don'ts for offering effective recommendations', *Evaluation Practice*, 11(2): 121–125.

Jackson, N. and Waters, E. (2005) 'Criteria for the systematic review of health promotion and public health interventions', *Health Promotion International*, 20(4): 367–374.

Kotler, P., Roberto, N. and Lee, N.R. (2002) *Social Marketing: Improving the Quality of Life*. Thousand Oaks, CA: Sage Publications.

Krathwohl, D.R., Bloom, B.S. and Masia, B.B. (1973) *Taxonomy of Educational Objectives, the Classification of Educational Goals. Handbook II: Affective Domain*. New York: David McKay Co., Inc.

Levin, H.M. (1988) 'Cost-effectiveness and educational policy', *Educational Evaluation and Policy Analysis*, 10, 51–69.

Linder and Associates, Inc. (2002). *Baltimore Believe – Progress Report. Phase I*. Retrieved 15 September 2009 from http://www.rebuildingmadison.info/BelieveReport.pdf.

Linnan, L. and Steckler, A. (eds) (2002) *Process Evaluation for Public Health Interventions and Research*. San Francisco, CA: Jossey-Bass.

Livingstone, S. (2005) 'Assessing the research base for the policy debate over the effects of food advertising to children', *The International Journal of Advertising*, 24(3): 273–296.

McDermott, R.J. (2004) 'Essentials of evaluating social marketing campaigns for health behavior change', *The Health Education Monograph Series*, 21: 13–20.

McDermott, R.J. and Sarvela, P.D. (1999) *Health Education Evaluation and Measurement: A Practitioner's Perspective*, 2nd edn. Madison, WI: WCB/McGraw-Hill.

McDermott, L., Stead, M. and Hastings, G. (2005) 'What is and what is not social marketing: The challenge of reviewing the evidence', *Journal of Marketing Management*, 21(5–6): 545–553.

McDermott, R.J., Berends, V., Brown, K.R.M., et al. (2005) 'Impact of the California Project LEAN school board member social marketing campaign', *Social Marketing Quarterly*, 11(2): 18–40.

McKee, S.A., Higbee, C., O'Malley, S., et al. (2009) 'Longitudinal evaluation of smoke-free Scotland on pub and home drinking behaviour: Findings from the International Tobacco Control (ITC) Policy Evaluation Project', *Nicotine and Tobacco Research*, 11(6): 619–626.

McKinlay, J.B. (1993) 'The promotion of health through panned socio-political change – challenges for research and policy', *Social Science and Medicine*, 36(2): 109–117.

McQueen, D.V. (2001) 'Strengthening the evidence base for health promotion', *Health Promotion International*, 16(3): 261–268.

Nutbeam, D. (1998). Evaluating health promotion – progress, problems and solutions *Health Promotion International*, 13(1): 27–44.

Øvretveit, J. (1998) *Evaluating Health Interventions*. Milton Keynes: Open University Press.

Patton, M.Q. (1987) *How to Use Qualitative Methods in Evaluation*. Newbury Park, CA: Sage Publications.

Patton, M.Q. (1997) *Utilization-Focused Evaluation*. Thousand Oaks, CA: Sage Publications.

Prochaska, J.O., DiClemente, C.C. and Norcross, J.C. (1992) 'In search of how people change. Applications to addictive behaviors', *American Psychologist*, 47(9): 1102–1114.

Smith, M.F. (1989) *Evaluability Assessment: A Practical Approach*. Boston, MA: Kluwer Academic Publishers.

Smith, W.A. (1999) *Social Marketing Lite*. Retrieved 9 September 2009 from http://www.nsfc.wvu.edu/smart/training/toolkit/page3/social_marketing/Social_MarketingLite.pdf. Washington, DC: Academy for Educational Development.

Stead, M. and Gordon, R. (2010) 'Providing evidence for social marketing's effectiveness', in J. French, C. Blair-Stevens, D. McVey and R. Merritt (eds), *Social Marketing and Public Health*. Oxford: Oxford University Press.

Stead, M., Hastings, G. and Eadie, D. (2002) 'The challenge of evaluating complex interventions: A framework for evaluating media advocacy', *Health Education Research Theory and Practice*, 17(3): 351–364.

Stead, M., Tagg, S., MacKintosh, A.M. and Eadie, D.R. (2005) 'Development and evaluation of a mass media theory of planned behaviour intervention to reduce speeding', *Health Education Research*, 20: 36–50.

Stead, M., Gordon, R., Angus, K. and McDermott, L. (2007b) 'A systematic review of social marketing effectiveness', *Health Education*, 107(2): 126–140.

Stead, M., Stradling, R., MacNeil, M., MacKintosh, A.M. and Minty, S. (2007a) 'Implementation evaluation of the Blueprint multi-component drug education prevention programme: Fidelity of school component delivery', *Drug and Alcohol Review*, 26(6): 659–664.

US Centers for Disease Control and Prevention (2004). *Standards for Effective Program Evaluation*. Retrieved 15 September 2009 from http://www.cdc.gov/eval/standard.htm#utility.

Verduin, J.R. Jr and Clark, T.A. (1991) *Distance Education: The Foundation for Effective Practice*. San Francisco, CA: Jossey-Bass.

14

Qualitative Research Methods in Social Marketing

Simone Pettigrew and Michele Roberts

INTRODUCTION

This chapter discusses the current and potential role of qualitative research methods in social marketing. The major methodological approaches and the specific data collection and analysis methods that can be used to achieve social marketing objectives are outlined and examples are provided of diverse research projects that have used these methods to improve social welfare. Of note is that many of these studies are not explicitly described in the literature as social marketing projects – they originate primarily from the fields of health, marketing and management. However, in many cases they provide examples of the effective use of those forms of qualitative research that have yet to be used extensively in our field, but have considerable potential for future application.

Qualitative methods are difficult to define because they are broad in scope and used across multiple disciplines that view them in somewhat different ways. As a result, they are typically defined by what they are not, rather than what they are. For example, Calder (1977: 353) described qualitative research as being characterized by 'the absence of numerical measurement and statistical analysis.' Similarly, Glaser (1992: 11) defined qualitative analysis as 'any kind of analysis that produces findings or concepts and hypotheses… that are not arrived at by statistical methods.' In general, qualitative methods are recognized as those forms of data collection and analysis that generate words, rather than numbers, to describe phenomena.

Qualitative approaches are considered most appropriate where the operationalization of concepts is problematic and it is therefore difficult to use statistical methods of measuring the phenomenon of interest (Barnes, 1996). They are especially useful for explicating the competing views that can coexist in relation to the same issue (Jones and Hunter, 1995; Mitchell and Branigan, 2000). Quantitative approaches, by comparison, are better suited to research tasks that involve the concrete operationalization of concepts and statistical analysis of causal relationships (Denzin and Lincoln, 1994). Quantitative methods are argued to provide greater objectivity, but by necessity generate less 'thick description' of the phenomenon of interest (Belk, 1990; Marcus, 1986).

When using a qualitative approach, the intention of the researcher is to explore all possible issues or variables relating to the phenomenon rather than to test pre-identified concepts (Harper, 1994). Even in medical research, where the gold standard has long been the randomized controlled trial (RCT), there is a growing appreciation of the need for detailed, exploratory data and the benefits of qualitative methods in providing access to such data (Malterud, 2001; Mays and Pope, 2000; Pope and Mays, 2009). The ability of qualitative research to explicate the effects of both macro- and micro-level forces makes it especially useful at the formative stage of social marketing campaigns where it is necessary to explore the meanings assigned to diverse phenomena, including behaviors, messages, materials, events and circumstances (Lefebvre and Flora, 1988;

Sofaer, 1999). While less common, a qualitative approach can also be appropriate for process evaluation research where the target group's responses to various elements of an intervention are assessed (Grier and Bryant, 2005; Speller et al., 1997). However, quantitative methods are usually preferred for outcome evaluations because of the need to report uptake rates (Douglas, 2008).

The sections to follow outline many of the major methodological approaches and the specific data collection and analysis methods that are used in qualitative research. This is followed by a discussion of the relative strengths and weaknesses of qualitative methods and how these can be minimized to enhance social marketing outcomes.

METHODOLOGICAL APPROACHES

Much qualitative research is undertaken without reference to an overarching methodological framework. In such cases, researchers select one or more of the available qualitative data collection methods and use them to generate information relating to the topic of interest. This approach reflects a general exploratory orientation to the research task and can be useful in providing insight into a particular issue, either in isolation or in conjunction with other data collection methods. There are, however, several methodological frameworks that can provide a more structured approach to knowledge creation. Of particular relevance to social marketing are ethnography, grounded theory and case studies.

Ethnography

For some research topics, self-report data provide an inadequate understanding of the underlying factors contributing to the phenomenon of interest. This is especially the case where macro-environmental forces are particularly influential and individuals are unable to appreciate or articulate the nature of this influence. Given the importance of environmental factors to the successful implementation of social marketing campaigns, ethnographic approaches that seek to explicitly document these factors can be very useful in the formative research stage of intervention design (Meyer and Dearing, 1996).

Originating from anthropology, ethnography is a naturalistic research method that has a specific interest in the role of cultural forces on individuals' behavior (Geertz, 1975; Sarantakos, 1993). The two primary aims of ethnography are to appreciate individuals' worlds through their own eyes and to document and understand their social interactions (Arnould and Wallendorf, 1994; Barnes, 1996). These outcomes are achieved through a process of participant observation that requires the researcher to actively participate in the social processes under investigation. Interviews and observations usually accompany participant observation to give the researcher deep insight into how group members think, feel and act (Sarantakos, 1993). Owing to its naturalistic form, ethnographic research requires the researcher to forego most of the control associated with other forms of data collection. While initial locations and types of informants may be specified in advance, the *in situ* nature of data collection obliges the researcher to 'go with the flow' and adapt to circumstances as they unfold (Lincoln and Guba, 1985). This requires sampling to be emergent, meaning that it is dependent upon insights gleaned from previous data collection activities and hence necessitates concurrent data collection and analysis (Belk et al., 1988).

An ethnographic approach allows researchers to obtain first-hand experience of the issues facing the population of interest and therefore to better understand their world view. It is especially useful for accessing groups that are marginalized from society and are less well understood by policy-makers. Ethnography has thus been a popular method among researchers investigating issues such as illicit drug use (Hopson et al., 2001; Myers and Stolberg, 2003), alcohol consumption among indigenous peoples (Brady, 1992, 1993; Rowse, 1993) and the experience of homelessness (Hill, 1991, 2001). It has also been used effectively with specific occupational groups such as mine workers (Cullen et al., 2008) and fire-fighters (Staley, 2009).

A distinct disadvantage of ethnographic research is the time and often emotional commitment that must be invested in the project. It can take months or years to fully engage with a community or group at a level appropriate for a detailed understanding to occur. Hill (1991) invested months of volunteer time at a homeless women's shelter to develop familiarity and rapport with residents prior to engaging them in interviews to discuss their coping strategies. Herman and Musolf's (1998) work with discharged psychiatric patients involved many years of repeat interviews, attendance at self-help group meetings and interactions with friends, families and co-workers to perform a comprehensive analysis of the difficulties experienced by ex-patients during their reintegration into society.

Ethnographic approaches can also be used to evaluate interventions. Hopson et al. (2001) assessed the effectiveness of an HIV/AIDS outreach programme in an inner city area in the USA by recruiting 'peer leaders' with the same ethnic background as the target group. These peer leaders were trained in how to deliver outreach programs and how to assess their effectiveness. They then spent time in the community assisting in the delivery of programs and reporting on how they could be improved. Similarly, Monaghan et al. (2008) placed researchers in the field to document the take-up rate of safety glasses among fruit harvester crews to assess the success of a programme that provided the glasses and promoted their use.

Ethnographic research can be conducted in an overt or covert fashion. An overt approach involves informing research subjects of the nature of the study and the role of the researcher. While this may alter people's behavior, it is argued that prolonged immersion in the field can result in a level of habituation to the presence of the researcher that causes behavior to revert to normal (Celsi et al., 1993). A covert approach may be warranted where the research topic relates to behaviors that would be unlikely to revert, such as those that are illegal or otherwise socially unsanctioned. For example, Winlow et al. (2001) used a covert ethnographic approach to study the violence experienced and enacted by bouncers (doormen). In this instance, a covert approach was deemed appropriate because alerting the bouncers to the presence of a researcher would be likely to substantially alter their behavior. However, there are obvious ethical issues associated with covert data collection and these need to be closely considered prior to undertaking this approach to ethnographic research (Punch, 1986).

Grounded theory

Grounded theory initially emerged as an alternative approach to research in sociology in the 1960s. Glaser and Strauss (1967) argued that the discipline was becoming stale due to an overemphasis on developing grand, or meta, theories. They proposed that researchers should instead focus on specific social issues and develop substantive theories to explain them. In order to achieve this, they advocated a departure from deductive theory development in preference for inductive theory generation that relies on data collection and analysis prior to consulting existing knowledge on the topic of interest.

By going directly into the field, rather than commencing with existing theoretical constructs, the objective is to minimize contamination from the preconceptions that can develop from exposure to other researchers' interpretations of the same or related phenomena (Locke, 1996). Rigor

is maintained through the use of formalized procedures such as theoretical or purposive sampling, extensive coding and the constant comparative method of data analysis. The objective is to explicitly acknowledge the similarities and differences that exist in the dataset, which are then used to derive theoretical categories that explicate the phenomenon under investigation (Glaser, 1992; Glaser and Strauss, 1967). The literature is accessed after an interpretation starts to emerge and is used to consolidate and extend the interpretation (Strauss and Corbin, 1990).

With the emphasis on theory building in grounded theory, negative case analysis is an important element that can enhance the robustness of the interpretation and therefore its explanatory power. Negative case analysis involves actively seeking contradictions to the emerging interpretation in order to test its veracity (Glaser and Strauss, 1967). By attempting to identify exceptions to the rule, the researcher identifies the boundaries and limitations of the substantive theory that is being developed.

With its focus on social problems, grounded theory aims to move beyond the provision of explanations to the production of information of value to the social actors under study (Annells, 1996). An explicit objective of grounded theory is thus to suggest strategies that may resolve the problem by empowering affected individuals and groups (Glaser, 1992). For example, Lawn et al. (2002) used grounded theory to understand the role of smoking in the lives of those suffering from mental illness. Their analysis found that smoking not only provides a distraction and form of self-medication to alleviate symptoms but also it can constitute a symbol of control for those who feel that they lack autonomy in other aspects of their lives. Some sufferers also regarded cigarettes as reliable, non-judgemental friends, illustrating that encouraging smoking cessation among members of this group may need to address the psychosocial benefits derived from smoking as well as the physical aspects of addiction. In addition, the findings point to the possible need to prioritize harm reduction over abstinence for those with mental illnesses in recognition of the complex interaction between smoking and symptom management.

In its pure form, grounded theory involves the identification of at least one core category that accounts for the social processes causing the phenomenon of interest plus the properties or dimensions of the category (Glaser, 1992; Glaser and Strauss, 1967). Together, the core category(s) and its associated properties constitute a substantive theory of the phenomenon. However, it has been noted that in many cases researchers may engage in data collection and analysis prior to conducting a literature search, but then choose to produce a thematic or descriptive account of the phenomenon without drilling down to a specific core category and its associated properties (Pettigrew, 2000). This is recognized as a grounded approach rather than grounded theory, and is increasingly being accepted as a legitimate research approach in its own right (e.g. Andronikidis and Lambrianidou, 2010; Bush et al., 2003; Roddy et al., 2006).

Grounded theory can be useful to social marketers on several fronts. In the first instance, its objective of explicating social phenomena makes it ideally suited to exploring topics of interest to social marketers. For example, grounded theory has been used to study diverse social issues such as domestic violence (Kearney, 2001; Tilley and Brackley, 2005), the experience of obesity (Sarlio-Lahteenkorva, 1998), attitudes to water consumption (DeLorme et al., 2003), alcohol consumption (Pettigrew, 2002a) and the influence of cocaine use on parenting behaviors (Kearney et al., 1994). Second, its capacity to generate theoretical rather than merely descriptive accounts of behavior makes grounded theory useful for those attempting to understand complex relationships between multiple variables (Barnes, 1996; Kools et al., 1996; Wuest, 1995). For example, Wuest et al. (2002) used the grounded theory method to examine the broad area of the social determinants of women's health. As social marketers typically deal with multi-factorial problems, a method that has the potential to provide detailed and analytical accounts of the problem under investigation can ensure that as many relevant factors as possible are considered in any resulting recommendations or campaigns.

Grounded theory has also been found useful for evaluating interventions. In their assessment of a school-based alcohol and drug prevention project, MacDonald and Green (2001) used grounded theory to explore prevention workers' experiences when implementing the program. They identified a core category that they titled Reconciling Concept and Context. This category related to the difficulties faced by the prevention workers when attempting to integrate an external system featuring a specified set of values and goals that were not completely aligned with the values and goals of the school contexts in which implementation was supposed to occur. MacDonald and Green developed a model of the processes involved in project implementation and a typology of prevention worker roles to provide guidance for future program refinement. A further example is Potter and Carpenter's (2008) evaluation of a UK-based parenting-support program for fathers. Their grounded thematic analysis demonstrated the effectiveness of the social marketing approach that had been adopted in the development of the program.

Case studies

Also originating from sociology and often used in organizational research, the case study method provides a further methodological framework for social marketers. Yin's (2009: 18) detailed definition of the case study method is as follows:

> A case study is an empirical inquiry that investigates a contemporary phenomenon in depth and within its real-life context, especially when the boundaries between phenomenon and context are not clearly evident....The case study inquiry copes with the technically distinctive situation in which there will be many more variables of interest than data points, and as one result relies on multiple sources of evidence, with data needing to converge in a triangulating fashion, and as another result benefits from the prior development of theoretical propositions to guide data collection and analysis.

According to this definition, most studies that are ostensibly published as case studies are merely descriptive accounts of a particular situation or phenomenon, rather than representing rigorous, theory-focused case study research as intended by those who have developed and refined the method.

Similar to ethnography and grounded theory, a case study approach typically commences with a problem or issue that the researcher wishes to investigate. The focus is thus on the social or organizational issue of interest rather than predefined variables (Yin, 1981). One of the primary triggering mechanisms for using a case study approach is where the number of variables that could impact the phenomenon of interest is too great to be catered for in experimental or survey research (Keen and Packwood, 1995).

The case study method involves an in-depth analysis of a small number of sample units. The unit of analysis can be an event, a site, a group of informants or a type of experience (Sofaer, 1999). Cases are selected according to their ability to demonstrate explanatory power and there is no intention to generalize the findings outside of the case, except in the most propositional way (Smith, 1990).

Case studies are usually, although not always, qualitative in approach. The types of qualitative data utilized by case study researchers include interviews, observations and documents (Sofaer, 1999). Using multiple data sources provides a form of triangulation within the project that can enhance its credibility (Yin, 2009). Overlapping data collection and analysis is an important aspect of the case study method as it allows constant refinement of data collection to ensure emergent issues are incorporated into subsequent data collection activities (Eisenhardt, 1989). The researcher examines the various data points, actively seeking both correspondences and disjunctures, the latter being particularly useful for identifying central areas of conflict that require resolution (Perren and Ram, 2004).

While the case study method is occasionally used for formative or scoping research – for example, Goodman et al.'s (2007) assessment of the adequacy of existing physical activity services for seniors – it is more commonly employed in process evaluations. The ability of the method to explicate the multiple factors impacting intervention implementation makes it useful for obtaining a detailed understanding of how individuals or groups respond to new policies or programs, either longitudinally or, more commonly, at specific points in time (Yin, 2009). Given that process evaluation research tends to be less frequently undertaken than formative research, the adoption of the case study method in social marketing and related areas is correspondingly low.

Where a case study approach has been employed, it has been demonstrated to be efficacious across a wide variety of subject areas. Examples include explorations of employees' reactions to organizations' alcohol policies (Ames et al., 1992), attitudes of stakeholders to a school-based health promotion program (Leurs et al., 2008), the strengths and weaknesses of an HIV/AIDS prevention campaign (Lombardo and Leger, 2007), the use of new information by medical practitioners when enacting their roles (Gabbay, 2003) and the potential of nutrition-related health promotion programs among specific ethnic groups (Mundel and Chapman, 2010).

DATA COLLECTION METHODS

The range of data collection methods classified as qualitative includes interviewing (e.g. individual depth interviews, paired interviews, small group interviews and focus groups), observations, projective techniques and internet research. These data collection methods are discussed below in terms of their current and potential application in social marketing.

Interviews

By far the most commonly used qualitative method in social marketing research is interviewing.

In particular, individual depth interviews and focus groups are often used by researchers engaging in the formative and process evaluation phases of social marketing projects. Individual interviews are especially useful for giving interviewees the time and space to discuss the beliefs and values that motivate their behavior (Arnould and Wallendorf, 1994), while focus groups allow the interviewer to observe the interaction and negotiation that can occur between individuals in relation to particular issues (Fontana and Frey, 1994).

Interviews allow the researcher to communicate directly with members of the target group, facilitating the development and refinement of programs that specifically address their needs (Merritt et al., 2009; Thackeray, 2003). The use of interviews has been common in the development of anti-smoking campaigns. Given the higher rates of smoking among the less affluent (Whitlock et al., 1997), there has been a focus on disadvantaged smokers and the barriers, motivators and facilitators relevant to their cessation behaviors (MacAskill et al., 2002; Paul et al., 2010; Roddy et al., 2006; Stead et al., 2001). Interviewing is an especially effective method of obtaining data from this group because of their lower literacy levels and the resulting challenges they experience when participating in surveys (Hahn et al., 2004). In aggregate, these studies found that many disadvantaged smokers want to quit but face significant hurdles in the form of peer group norms, a lack of other recreation options, fear of failure, ongoing exposure to tobacco promotion, the expense of cessation products and a lack of knowledge of available services. Other interview research in this area has explored smokers' attitudes toward smoke-free legislation (Heim et al., 2009), smokers' perceptions of the ability of communication materials to attract attention and motivate behavioral change (Gallopel-Morvan et al., 2009) and the potential of medical practitioners to encourage quitting from both smokers' (Butler et al., 1998) and practitioners' viewpoints (Coleman et al., 2004).

Interviews have been used to explore numerous other social issues for the purpose of informing program development. Examples include attitudes relating to child vaccination (Gardner et al., 2010), recycling (Prestin and Pearce, 2010), condom use (Bull et al., 2002), mental illness (Secker et al., 1999), HIV/AIDS (Morin et al., 2003), obesity prevention (Bellows et al., 2008), physical activity (Burroughs et al., 2006), nutrition (Hampson et al., 2009), soft drink consumption (Hattersley et al., 2009) and worksite food supply (Devine et al., 2007).

In terms of program evaluation, interviews can be conducted with program implementers or members of the intervention recipient group to investigate their experiences and their suggestions for program enhancement (Farquhar et al., 2006). This approach has been found to be useful in exploring the barriers faced by the target audience in participating in the intervention (Bryant, 2001), and the difficulties encountered by practitioners in implementing interventions as intended by the designers (Jones and Hunter, 1995; Sofaer, 1999). These benefits can assist program developers to understand, document and address the often steep learning curves experienced during new program implementation (Bradley et al., 1999).

Observation

Given the tendency for considerable variation to exist between people's accounts of their behaviors and their actual behaviors, it has been suggested that researchers should avoid relying solely on self-report data (Barnes, 1996; Huberman and Miles, 1994; Wallendorf and Belk, 1989). Observation data can provide an alternative or supplementary source of information relating to the topic of interest. This can be especially useful where social desirability bias is likely to influence self-report data (Guinn et al., 2010). As noted by Adler and Adler (1994: 389), observation is 'freed from subjects' whimsical shifts in opinion, self-evaluation, self-deception, manipulation of self-presentation, embarrassment and outright dishonesty.'

As well as overcoming intentional or unintentional misrepresentation, covert observation has the potential to offer a different perspective because there is less likelihood of the data collection process contaminating the behaviors of social actors. In addition, observation can provide insight into motivations of which individuals may be unaware (Dichter, 1964; Rust, 1993). Macro factors such as cultural and social forces can encourage conformity in behavior, yet prevent individuals from recognizing their actions as anything other than autonomous (Kluckhohn, 1967). By allowing conformity to become apparent, observation can assist researchers to appreciate the degree of influence of higher-level forces, especially when used in conjunction with other data collection methods (Piirto, 1991).

There are various logistical issues that need to be addressed when planning observation episodes. These include determining whether observation will be overt or covert (and if covert, how this is to be achieved); selecting appropriate locations and time periods for observations and managing the training, safety and debriefing of observers (Petticrew et al., 2007). Decisions relating to these issues will be based on the social marketing objectives of the particular program. For example, when evaluating the effectiveness of a police intervention to reduce the sale of alcohol to minors,

researchers recruited 13- to 16-year-old children to act as buyers (Willner et al., 2000). This covert study required careful recruitment and training of the children to ensure their involvement was approved by their parents, their preparation for the task was appropriate (e.g. girls were instructed to avoid wearing make-up to prevent them looking older) and they were aware of the behaviors expected of them during their attempted purchases. Other observational studies have investigated children's fruit and vegetable consumption (Ross, 1995), the effectiveness of a family intervention targeting physical activity and diet (Patterson, 1988) and the availability of condoms in prostitution areas (Piot et al., 2010).

Projective techniques

While not commonly used outside of psychology, the ability of projective techniques to generate alternative forms of data makes them of potential use to social marketers (Merritt et al., 2009). Projective exercises require research subjects to creatively respond to ambiguous stimuli, thereby projecting their own thoughts and feelings into their responses. The argument is that this approach provides access to subconscious motivations and attitudes and can elicit responses that subjects would choose not to disclose if asked directly (McGrath et al., 1993; Rogers and Beal, 1958; Rook, 1988). In this way, projective techniques can be useful to researchers seeking deep insight into human motivations.

The wide range of projective techniques includes word associations, sentence completion activities, thematic apperception tests, picture response activities, picture drawing, collage construction, dialogue bubbles, photo-elicitation, card sorting, choice ordering and mental scenarios (Donoghue, 2000; Rook, 1988). However, there are almost no limits to the kinds of projective activities that can be conceptualized to tap into subjects' 'inner selves' (Levy, 1985). More unusual examples include asking subjects to paint their feelings or to tell their favourite jokes (Richman, 1996).

In the field of marketing, one of the earliest and best-known applications of projective techniques was Haire's (1950) exploration of housewives' perceptions of two shopping lists that varied on only one item – one list included Nescafé instant coffee and the other Maxwell House drip grind coffee. The study identified biases in favour of the drip grind coffee resulting from the assumption that the fictional owner of the shopping list was a better homekeeper because of her willingness to spend more time making coffee. The innovative nature of this study led to numerous replications and critiques over the years (e.g. Anderson, 1978; Fram and Cibotti, 1991). Since the Haire study, projective techniques have been used to study attitudes to a wide range of consumption-related topics, including milk (Steele, 1964), alcohol (Aaker and Stayman, 1992; Ackoff and Emshoff, 1975; Pettigrew, 2002b; Pettigrew and Charters, 2008) and gift giving (Mick et al., 1992; Sherry et al., 1993).

In areas related to social marketing, projective techniques have been used most frequently with children. The weaker cognitive, written and verbal abilities of children make it more difficult to use standard interviewing or survey techniques (Irwin and Johnson, 2005). This results in the need to employ data collection methods that can access complex data with less reliance on reading, writing and verbal skills (John, 1997). Projective techniques have been found to be effective in eliciting children's thoughts and feelings across a range of social issues, including general health (Backett and Alexander, 1991), the relationship between food and health (Sijtsema et al., 2007), food choices (Ells, 2001), the attributes of a healthy school (MacGregor et al., 1998), smoking (MacFadyen et al., 2003), mental health (Miraudo and Pettigrew, 2002), road safety (Collins, 1995) and attitudes toward people living with AIDS (Gonzalez-Rivera and Bauermeister, 2007).

Projective techniques have also been used in the development and testing of communications materials. Leathar (1980) used an anthropomorphizing approach by asking low-income smokers to describe the kind of person different anti-smoking messages would be if they were human. Standard interviewing had been unable to ascertain why one message was preferred over another by the target audience, but the projective exercise found that the smokers described one message as being 'a middle-class person' and the other 'a working-class person,' and that they viewed the latter as being more relevant to themselves. Wiehagen (2007) asked African-American men and women in gender-segmented focus groups to design materials that would encourage colorectal cancer screening. By projecting their beliefs about what they felt other people would best respond to, the participants provided important insights into the most salient issues relating to screening behaviors.

Other researchers have effectively used photovoice activities (also known as photo-elicitation) in advocacy efforts to sensitize policymakers to the plight of certain groups in society (Wang and Burris, 1997). Newman et al. (2009) used photographs taken by those suffering from spinal cord injuries to develop brochures and create a YouTube video clip to increase community awareness of the difficulties faced by those who are wheelchair-bound. Similarly, Necheles et al. (2007) had adolescents from low-income neighborhoods take photographs of the aspects of their environments that they felt affected their health. The results were used to develop materials targeting their peers and school administrators to encourage healthier environments and behaviors. The use of images in this way involves subjects projecting their feelings about an issue into their photographic outputs, which can then be used to communicate the most important aspects of the issue to other stakeholders.

Social marketers wishing to use projective techniques need to be cognizant of the criticisms these methods can attract. The highly subjective nature of their design and implementation can engender discomfort in those seeking assurance regarding validity and reliability. The very ambiguity that gives projective techniques their value is also the source of most concern for detractors, some of whom have argued that meaningful conclusions can only be drawn by those with training in clinical psychology (Yoell and Largen, 1974). Even advocates acknowledge that the substantial degree of interpretation required during analysis can make projective techniques more challenging than other data collection methods (Donoghue, 2000; Hussey and Duncombe, 1999; Richman, 1996). It has been suggested that researchers should consciously decide whether a literal interpretation of the responses will be made or whether a deeper meaning will be sought that requires a greater degree of interpretation (Levy, 1985).

There can also be implementation difficulties with projective techniques. Decisions must be made as to whether subjects will be given limited or unlimited time to complete the tasks, whether they should respond verbally or in writing and the degree of direction that should be provided in any instructions accompanying the stimuli. Some difficulties are group- or technique-specific, such as the need to prevent conferral among children when they are completing projective tasks in a group environment (MacGregor et al., 1998), or the need to provide training for more complex and autonomous tasks such as photovoice activities (Newman et al., 2009).

Proponents of projective techniques argue that the potential benefits outweigh subjectivity problems. They point to the ability of these techniques to mine beneath the superficial rationalizations that are often offered up by interviewees (Rook, 1988; Williams, 1958), especially where there are status or sensitivity issues that can result in strong social desirability biases (Haire, 1950; Pettigrew and Charters, 2008). They can also overcome common problems of interviewees either not holding well-formed beliefs about the topic of interest or lacking the ability to clearly articulate their beliefs (Belk et al., 2003; Day, 1989; Hussey and Duncombe, 1999). This can make projective techniques especially useful when interacting with children because of their less-developed reasoning skills (John, 1999). Projective techniques are also very flexible in application as they can be administered either on their own or as ice-breakers or discussion tools during interviews and focus groups (Day, 1989; Donoghue, 2000). Further benefits are that they can be enjoyable for those responding to them (Belk et al., 2003; Rook, 1988; Zober, 1955), and can thus provide an effective antidote to respondent fatigue (Will et al., 1996).

Internet research

The advent of the internet in 1991 has brought unforeseen changes to the way people communicate (Maignan and Lukas, 1997). Today, almost 1.7 billion people around the world are estimated to have access to the internet and its massive array of information and entertainment (International Telecommunications Union, 2010). The extensive penetration of this technology makes it of great interest to social marketers wanting to relate to people on levels that cannot be achieved with other media (see Chapter 12). Perhaps the strongest indicator of the value and reach of this channel is the level of investment of commercial marketers in internet-based promotion to inform and persuade current and potential customers (Catterall and Maclaran, 2002). Global spending on internet advertising is estimated to exceed US$72 billion in 2011, constituting approximately 15% of the global advertising spend across all mediums (ZenithOptimedia, 2010).

The rapid increase in spending on internet advertising signals the potential to reach groups that are well represented on the internet. Young people, for example, are especially heavy users and are more inclined than other age groups to provide extensive information about their beliefs and behaviors online (Huffaker, 2006). While initially there were pronounced differences in the way young men and young women used the internet (with an emphasis on playing games vs chatting and shopping, respectively), communication with peers has now become a primary function for both groups (Gross, 2004; McKay et al., 2005).

The internet can be of use to social marketers in various ways. In the first instance, it is a ready source of primary and secondary data that can be used to inform campaigns and interventions. In terms of primary data, web panels provide rapid and cost-effective access to many segments of the population (Birnbaum, 2004; Kraut et al., 2004). Web panel members provide their personal details and subsequently receive questionnaires targeting samples fitting specific profiles (Farrell and Petersen, 2010). In return for their participation, panel members typically receive money or credits that they can redeem for a range of goods and services (e.g. Brigham et al., 2009).

In terms of secondary data, chat rooms, bulletin boards and social networking sites contain massive quantities of information across almost limitless topics. These data can be valuable in exposing researchers to the array of variables associated with the phenomenon of interest and the colloquial terms used by the target segment to refer to these variables (Merchant, 2001). Interactions between online actors can demonstrate meaning in the making, allowing analysis of the nature of the interactions and how consensus is, or is not, achieved (Sandlin, 2007). Such interactions can be a valuable source of data relating to issues that are inappropriate to raise directly with certain populations. For example, discussing recreational drug use or sexual activity with young teens in a research context may unintentionally normalize this behavior (Williams et al., 2006). Accessing existing data relating to these issues on the internet can circumvent this problem. In addition, the anonymity of the internet provides encouragement for individuals to share information that they may withhold in more traditional data collection contexts (Hogg et al., 2004). It may also reduce some of the social desirability bias that confounds research in many areas of interest to social marketers (Brener et al., 2003). This ability to delve beneath people's usual defences introduces an ethical consideration that has yet to be satisfactorily addressed: Should online data be considered fair game for researchers seeking to obtain information that individuals may not realize is being used for such a purpose? In particular, the internet can provide access to information uploaded by those who may be considered vulnerable research subjects, such as children and the mentally unwell.

In an effort to enhance the legitimacy and integrity of internet research, Kozinets (2002) developed the method of netnography to guide researchers. Netnography is a blend of ethnography, content analysis and discourse analysis that is used to access and analyse individuals' opinions and reported behaviors as described online. Kozinets outlined several stages that he argued are essential to the ethical and effective practice of netnography. These include nominating a specific research objective; selecting internet forums that can provide access to discussions on the topic of interest; obtaining informed consent from forum users wherever possible; downloading data from the selected sites; analyzing the downloaded data, being careful to consider the contextual aspects of particular segments of text; developing an interpretation of the phenomenon under investigation as it is represented online and engaging in member checking with members of the target group. Others have since argued that informed consent is not a necessary step when the information is publicly available and not shared on password-protected sites, and as a result that member checking is also not always appropriate or possible (Langer and Beckman, 2005).

Some social marketing studies have employed netnography principles to good effect in the formative research phase. For example, Pettigrew et al. (2009) examined Australian teenagers' comments about alcohol consumption on numerous blog sites to explore the dominant motivators, facilitators and barriers to binge drinking. Their findings demonstrated the salience of vomiting in teenagers' decisions relating to alcohol consumption versus other forms of recreational drug taking. This outcome sensitizes policymakers to the possible unintended consequences of associating alcohol consumption with vomiting and thereby inadvertently encouraging migration to illicit drugs that are less likely to have this effect on users.

As is the case for other qualitative methods, internet research can be useful for providing insight and clarity into issues identified quantitatively. For example, a Canadian study of adolescents' participation in sport involved multiple national surveys to identify usage patterns. The researchers then accessed relevant websites where teens discussed their exercise behaviors to obtain an explanation of the trends observed in the quantitative data (Berger et al., 2008). The internet data yielded detailed examples of the family conflict that can prevent adolescents from being as active as they would like.

In addition to the internet being an important source of qualitative data, it has benefits in terms of program implementation. Standard websites, file-sharing sites (such as YouTube, Flickr and Slideshare) and social networking sites can be repositories of campaign materials and information resources that can be accessed by members of the target audience. Such approaches have been found to be useful for quit smoking (Hoek and Watkins, 2009) and adolescent sexual health campaigns (Evans et al., 2010). Such sites can also constitute a feedback mechanism whereby people comment on current and past campaigns. Overall, the potential of the internet for program implementation and evaluation is vast and largely untapped.

DATA ANALYSIS

Qualitative data analysis processes are markedly different from those used in quantitative data analysis. While software is available to assist with data management, these programs merely facilitate the coding process and cannot perform any of the conceptual analysis required to produce meaningful outcomes (Bringer et al., 2006). The researcher remains the primary data analysis tool; hence, a greater degree of subjectivity in analysis and outputs is expected and tolerated relative to quantitative data analysis (Denzin and Lincoln, 1994). To make meaning of data inputs, the qualitative researcher engages in the processes of coding and constant comparison, as described below. These tasks may be undertaken manually or, increasingly, with the assistance of software programs.

Coding is essentially a process of data reduction whereby larger quantities of text come to be represented by smaller amounts of text that in some way describe the observed phenomenon. The word labels attached to chunks of text can reflect existing theoretical concepts or new concepts emerging from the data (Strauss and Corbin, 1990). The chunks of text assigned to the label can be as small as one word or as large as an entire interview transcript.

Through the coding process, the larger data set is dismantled and then reconstructed into a hierarchy of codes that has explanatory power (Goulding, 1998). The coding hierarchy that is developed should be capable of encompassing both convergent and outlying data points to produce a robust interpretation (Arnould and Wallendorf, 1994). It is often considered that coding adds legitimacy to the qualitative data analysis process because it offers an explanation for the resultant theory and assists others in their efforts to assess or replicate the research (Fontana and Frey, 1994; Glaser and Strauss, 1967).

During coding, the researcher engages in constant comparison of the data. The constant comparative method of data analysis was initially articulated as part of the grounded theory method, but has since become used more broadly within qualitative research. Constant comparison involves the researcher continually making comparisons between different incidents appearing in the data and between specific incidents and any emerging theoretical interpretation (Barnes, 1996). By following this process, the researcher aims to identify underlying themes that explicate the behavior or issue of interest. Reflecting the complexity of human behavior, these themes should incorporate both convergences and contradictions within the data (Wells, 1995). Ideally, analysis occurs prior to the completion of the data collection phase of the study, allowing the emerging interpretation to be tested and strengthened via further purposive sampling (Locke, 1996).

Various data management software programs are currently available for qualitative researchers. These include NVivo, ATLAS.ti, Ethnograph, MAXQDA, HyperRESEARCH and Kwalitan. These programs facilitate analysis by allowing the researcher to code and then retrieve chunks of text, with hyperlinks transporting the user back and forward between coded text and the raw data. Codes can be renamed, merged, moved or deleted with ease, allowing much greater flexibility relative to manual coding. Increasingly sophisticated search functions can also allow researchers to investigate possible relationships between coded concepts (Bringer et al., 2006).

Criticisms of qualitative data analysis software include user frustration during familiarization with the system and the possibility of becoming too removed from the raw data (Kelle, 1997; Lu and Shulman, 2008; Peters and Wester, 2007). Since their emergence in the early 1990s, the software interfaces have become increasingly user-friendly to accommodate novice users, thereby reducing the problems experienced during adoption. Concerns relating to the mechanization of analysis at the expense of informed insight are more difficult to resolve, but it has been suggested that researchers can avoid this outcome by ensuring the coding and analysis processes are guided by the data and theory, rather than being rushed attempts to achieve a result (Richards, 1999).

STRENGTHS AND WEAKNESSES

While qualitative methods are highly valued for the conceptual insights they can provide, the relatively small sample sizes that are typical of qualitative work preclude generalization to broader populations (Calder, 1997). Qualitative techniques are also acknowledged to involve a greater degree of researcher subjectivity (Atkinson, 1992; Johnson, 1990), but this is considered to be outweighed by their ability to provide detailed insights into individuals' motivations and the macro-level variables that affect their behaviors (Manning, 1987). Other recognized challenges of using qualitative methods include their time-consuming nature and the difficulties that can be encountered when reconciling contradictory findings (Farquhar et al., 2006). Thematic analyses in particular can be criticized for being superficial, for taking people's statements at face value and for failing to provide adequate explanations of the phenomenon under investigation (Pope and Mays, 2009).

While the limitations of qualitative methods as generators of objective and generalizable data are commonly acknowledged, the benefits obtained via their use can only be achieved by accepting the imperfections inherent in any methodology relying on human observation and interpretation (Adler and Adler, 1994). Some note that quantitative research is also subjective in that someone determines the issue that is to be the focus of the study and how it is to be examined, illustrating that all research represents someone's value system and hence has a subjective element (Holbrook, 1995; Hudson and Ozanne, 1988). The combination of qualitative and quantitative methods has been proposed as a means of overcoming some of the limitations inherent in each approach, thereby enhancing the quality and usability of research outputs (Hudson and Ozanne, 1988; Strauss and Corbin, 1990; Wallendorf and Belk, 1989). In the context of social marketing, it has been noted that the combination of qualitative and quantitative approaches within a single project can offer a form of methodological triangulation (Black et al., 2001). However, it is important for researchers to appreciate the potential for qualitative research to offer different, not just supporting, insights to those generated by other methods (Pope and Mays, 2009).

CONCLUSION

Qualitative methods have a vital role to play in social marketing. They have limitations but also important contributions to make in our efforts to design and implement effective programs. This chapter has described several qualitative research methodologies and methods that have yet to be used extensively in social marketing but have considerable potential to provide additional insight into social problems and their possible solutions. Along with knowledge of the various quantitative methods available, a thorough understanding of the qualitative repertoire allows social marketers to select the research methods that are best suited to particular tasks. This should enhance the effectiveness of our endeavors, thereby benefiting society and fostering confidence among the policymakers and research funders who determine our ability to make an impact.

KEY WORDS: Qualitative research; interviews; focus groups; projective techniques; ethnography; grounded theory; case study method; observations; internet research; coding; formative research; intervention evaluation.

Key insights

- Qualitative research methods can play an important role in social marketing. They have unique benefits that are of value in program design and implementation.
- Qualitative methodological options include ethnography, grounded theory and case studies. Qualitative data collection methods include interviews, observations, projective techniques and internet research.
- Some of these methodologies and methods are infrequently used in social marketing, indicating the potential to broaden our research repertoire.
- This chapter provides numerous examples of how qualitative approaches have been used in the formative research and process evaluation stages of intervention projects.

REFERENCES

Aaker, D.A. and Stayman, D.M. (1992) 'Implementing the concept of transformational advertising', *Psychology & Marketing*, 9(3): 237–253.

Ackoff, R.L. and Emshoff, J.R. (1975) 'Advertising research at Anheuser-Busch, Inc. (1968–74)', *Sloan Management Review*, Spring: 1–15.

Adler, P.A. and Adler, P. (1994) 'Observational techniques', in N. Denzin and Y. Lincoln (eds), *Handbook of Qualitative Research*. Thousand Oaks: CA: Sage Publications.

Ames, G., Delaney, W. and Janes, C. (1992) 'Obstacles to effective alcohol policy in the workplace: A case study', *Addiction*, 87(7): 1055–1069.

Anderson, J.C. (1978) 'The validity of Haire's shopping list projective technique', *Journal of Marketing Research*, 15: 644–649.

Andronikidis, A. and Lambrianidou, M. (2010) 'Children's understanding of television advertising: A grounded theory approach', *Psychology & Marketing*, 27(4): 299–322.

Annells, M. (1996) 'Grounded theory method: Philosophical perspectives, paradigms of inquiry, and postmodernism', *Qualitative Health Research*, 6(3): 379–393.

Arnould, E.J. and Wallendorf, M. (1994) 'Market-oriented ethnography: Interpretation building and marketing strategy formulation', *Journal of Marketing Research*, XXXI: 484–504.

Atkinson, P. (1992) *Understanding Ethnographic Texts*. Newbury Park, CA: Sage Publications.

Backett, K. and Alexander, H. (1991) 'Talking to young children about health: Methods and findings', *Health Education Journal*, 50: 34–38.

Barnes, D.M. (1996) 'An analysis of the grounded theory method and the concept of culture', *Qualitative Health Research*, 6(3): 429–441.

Belk, R.W. (1990). 'Book review of "Participant observation: A methodology for human studies" by D.L. Jorgensen and "Interpretive interactionism" by N.K. Denzin', *Journal of Marketing Research*, 27(3): 368–370.

Belk, R.W., Sherry, J.F. and Wallendorf, M. (1988) 'A naturalistic inquiry into buyer and seller behavior at a swap meet', *Journal of Consumer Research*, 14(4): 449–470.

Belk, R.W., Ger, G. and Askergaard, S. (2003) 'The fire of desire: A multisited inquiry into consumer passion', *Journal of Consumer Research*, 30(3): 326–351.

Bellows, L., Anderson, J., Gould, S. and Auld, G. (2008) 'Formative research and strategic development of a physical activity component to a social marketing campaign for obesity prevention in preschoolers', *Journal of Community Health*, 33(3): 169–178.

Berger, I.E., O'Reilly, N., Parent, M.M., Séguin, B. and Hernandez, T. (2008) 'Determinants of sport participation among Canadian adolescents', *Sport Management Review*, 11(3): 277–307.

Birnbaum, M. (2004) 'Human research and data collection via the Internet', *Annual Review of Psychology*, 55: 803–832.

Black, D., Blue, C. and Coster, D. (2001) 'Using social marketing to develop and test tailored health messages', *American Journal of Health Behavior*, 25(3): 260–271.

Bradley, F., Wiles, R., Kinmonth, A., Mant, D. and Gantley, M. (1999) 'Development and evaluation of complex interventions in health services research: Case study of the Southampton Heart Integrated Care Project (SHIP)', *British Medical Journal*, 318(7185): 711–715.

Brady, M. (1992) 'Ethnography and understandings of Aboriginal drinking', *Journal of Drug Issues*, 22(3): 699–712.

Brady, M. (1993) 'Giving away the grog: An ethnography of Aboriginal drinkers who quit without help', *Drug and Alcohol Review*, 12(4): 401–411.

Brener, N.D., Billy, J.O., and Grady, W.R. (2003) 'Assessment of factors affecting the validity of self-reported health-risk behavior among adolescents: Evidence from the scientific literature', *Journal of Adolescent Health*, 33: 436–457.

Brigham, J., Lessov-Schlaggar, C.N., Javitz, H.S., et al. (2009) 'Test–retest reliability of web-based retrospective self-report of tobacco exposure and risk', *Journal of Medical Internet Research*, 11(3): e35.

Bringer, J.D., Johnston, L.H. and Brackenridge, C.H. (2006) 'Using computer-assisted qualitative data analysis software to develop a grounded theory project', *Field Methods*, 18(3): 245–266.

Bryant, C. (2001), 'A social marketing approach to increasing enrollment in a public health program: A case study of the Texas WIC program', *Human Organization*, 60(3): 234–246.

Bull, S.S., Cohen, J., Ortiz, C. and Evans, T. (2002) 'The POWER campaign for promotion of female and male condoms: Audience research and campaign development', *Health Communication*, 14(4): 475–491.

Burroughs, E.L., Peck, L.E., Sharpe, P.A., et al. (2006) 'Using focus groups in the consumer research phase of a social marketing program to promote moderate-intensity physical activity and walking trail use in Sumter County, South Carolina', *Preventing Chronic Disease*, 5: 1–13.

Bush, J., White, M., Kai, J., Rankin, J. and Bhopal, R. (2003) 'Understanding influences on smoking in Bangladeshi and

Pakistani adults: Community based, qualitative study', *British Medical Journal,* 326(7396): 962–965.

Butler, C., Pill, R. and Stott, N. (1998) 'Qualitative study of patients' perceptions of doctors'advice to quit smoking: Implications for opportunistic health promotion', *British Medical Journal,* 316(7148): 1878–1883.

Calder, B.J. (1997) 'Focus groups and the nature of qualitative marketing research', *Journal of Marketing Research,* 14: 353–364.

Catterall, M. and Maclaran, P. (2002) 'Researching consumers in virtual worlds: A cyberspace odyssey', *Journal of Consumer Behaviour,* 1(3): 228–237.

Celsi, R.L., Rose, R.L. and Leigh, T.W. (1993) 'An exploration of high-risk leisure consumption through skydiving', *Journal of Consumer Research,* 20: 1–23.

Coleman, T., Cheater, F. and Murphy, E. (2004) 'Qualitative study investigating the process of giving anti-smoking advice in general practice', *Patient Education and Counseling,* 52(2): 159–163.

Collins, M. (1995) 'Putting road safety in the picture', *Health Education,* 95(6): 12.

Cullen, E.T., Matthews, L.N.H. and Teske, T.D. (2008) 'Use of occupational ethnography and social marketing strategies to develop a safety awareness campaign for coal miners', *Social Marketing Quarterly,* 14(4): 2–21.

Day, E. (1989) 'Share of heart: What is it and how can it be measured?' *Journal of Consumer Marketing,* 6: 5–12.

DeLorme, D., Hagen, S. and Stout, I. (2003) 'Consumers' perspectives on water issues: Directions for educational campaigns', *The Journal of Environmental Education,* 34(2): 28–35.

Denzin, N.K. and Lincoln, Y.S. (1994) 'Entering the field of qualitative research', in N.K. Denzin and Y.S. Lincoln (eds), *Handbook of Qualitative Research,* Thousand Oaks, CA: Sage Publications.

Devine, C., Nelson, J., Chin, N., Dozier, A. and Fernandez, I. (2007) '"Pizza is cheaper than salad": Assessing workers' views for an environmental food intervention', *Obesity,* 15: 57S–68S.

Dichter, E. (1964) *Handbook of Consumer Motivations: The Psychology of the World of Objects.* New York: McGraw-Hill Book Company.

Donoghue, S. (2000) 'Projective techniques in consumer research', *Journal of Family Ecology and Consumer Sciences,* 28: 47–53.

Douglas, H. (2008) 'Creating knowledge: A review of research methods in three societal change approaches', *Journal of Nonprofit & Public Sector Marketing,* 20(2): 141.

Eisenhardt, K.M. (1989) 'Building theories from case study research', *The Academy of Management Review,* 14(4): 532–550.

Ells, H. (2001) 'Talking pictures in working school lunches', *British Food Journal,* 103(6): 374–382.

Evans, W., Davis, K. and Zhang, Y. (2010) 'Health communication and marketing research with new media: Case study of the parents speak up national campaign evaluation'. Available at: www.casesjournal.org/Volume2.

Farrell, D. and Petersen, J.C. (2010) 'The growth of Internet research methods and the reluctant sociologist', *Sociological Inquiry,* 80: 114–125.

Farquhar, S.A., Parker, E.A., Schultz, A.J. and Israel, B.A. (2006) 'Application of qualitative methods in program planning for health promotion interventions', *Health Promotion Practice,* 7(2): 234 242.

Fontana, A. and Frey, J.H. (1994) 'Interviewing', in N.K. Denzin and Y.S. Lincoln (eds), *Handbook of Qualitative Research.* Thousand Oaks, CA: Sage Publications.

Fram, E.H. and Cibotti, E. (1991) 'The shopping list studies and projective techniques: A 40-year view', *Marketing Research,* 3(4): 14–22.

Gabbay, J. (2003) 'A case study of knowledge management in multiagency consumer-informed communities of practice: Implications for evidence-based policy development in health and social services', *Health,* 7(3): 283–310.

Gallopel-Morvan, K., Gabriel, P., Le Gall-Fly, M., Rieunier, S. and Urien, B. (2009) 'The use of visual warnings in social marketing: The case of tobacco', *Journal of Business Research,* 64(2011): 7–11.

Gardner, B., Davies, A., McAteer, J. and Michie, S. (2010) 'Beliefs underlying UK parents' views towards MMR promotion interventions: A qualitative study', *Psychology, Health & Medicine,* 15(2): 220–230.

Geertz, C. (1975) *The Interpretation of Cultures.* London: Hutchinson & Co.

Glaser, B. (1992) *Emergence vs Forcing: Basics of Grounded Theory Analysis.* Mill Valley, CA: Sociology Press.

Glaser, B. and Strauss, A. (1967) *The Discovery of Grounded Theory.* Chicago, IL: Aldine.

Glaser, B.G. (1992) *Emergence vs Forcing: Basics of Grounded Theory Analysis.* Mill Valley, CA: Sociology Press.

Gonzalez-Rivera, M. and Bauermeister, J.A. (2007) 'Children's attitudes toward people with AIDS in Puerto Rico: Exploring stigma through drawings and stories', *Qualitative Health Research,* 17(2): 250–263.

Goodman, C., Davies, S., Tai, S., Dinan, S. and Iliffe, S. (2007) 'Promoting older peoples' participation in activity, whose responsibility? A case study of the response of health, local government and voluntary organizations', *Journal of Interprofessional Care,* 21(5): 515–528.

Goulding, C. (1998) 'Grounded theory: The missing methodology on the interpretivist agenda', *Qualitative Market Research,* 1: 50–57.

Grier, S. and Bryant, C. (2005) 'Social marketing in public health', *Annual Review of Public Health,* 26: 319–339.

Gross, E.F. (2004) 'Adolescent Internet use: What we expect, what teens report', *Applied Developmental Psychology,* 25: 633–649.

Guinn, C.H., Baxter, S.D., Royer, J.A., et al. (2010) 'Fourth-grade children's dietary recall accuracy for energy intake at school meals differs by social desirability and body mass index percentile in a study concerning retention interval', *Journal of Health Psychology,* 15(4): 505–514.

Hahn, E., Cella, D., Dobrez, D., et al. (2004) 'The talking touchscreen: A new approach to outcomes assessment in low literacy', *Psycho-oncology,* 13(2): 86–95.

Haire, M. (1950) 'Projective techniques in marketing research', *Journal of Marketing,* 14: 649–656.

Hampson, S.E., Martin, J., Jorgensen, J. and Barker, M. (2009) 'A social marketing approach to improving the nutrition of low-income women and children: An initial focus group study', *Public Health Nutrition,* 12(9): 1563–1568.

Harper, D. (1994) 'On the authority of the Image', in N. Denzin and Y. Lincoln (eds), *Handbook of Qualitative Research.* Thousand Oaks, CA: Sage Publications.

Hattersley, L., Irwin, M., King, L. and Allman-Farinelli, M. (2009) 'Determinants and patterns of soft drink consumption in young adults: A qualitative analysis', *Public Health Nutrition,* 12(10): 1816–1822.

Heim, D., Ross, A., Eadie, D., et al. (2009) 'Public health or social impacts? A qualitative analysis of attitudes toward the smoke-free legislation in Scotland', *Nicotine and Tobacco Research,* 11(12): 1424–1430.

Herman, N.J. and Musolf, G.R. (1998) 'Resistance among ex-psychiatric patients: Expressive and instrumental rituals', *Journal of Contemporary Ethnography,* 26(4): 426–449.

Hill, R.P. (1991) 'Homeless women, special possessions, and the meaning of "home": An ethnographic case study', *Journal of Consumer Research,* 18(3): 298–310.

Hill, R.P. (2001) 'Surviving in a material world: Evidence from ethnographic consumer research on people in poverty', *Journal of Contemporary Ethnography,* 30(4): 364–391.

Hoek, J. and Watkins, L. (2009) 'Social support and smoking cessation: How do quitters assist each other?' Australian and New Zealand Marketing Academy Conference, Melbourne, 2009.

Hogg, G., Laing, A. and Newholm, T. (2004) 'Talking together: Consumer communities in healthcare', in B.E. Kahn and M.F. Luce (eds), *Advances in Consumer Research,* 31(1): 67–73. Valdosta: Association for Consumer Research.

Holbrook, M.B. (1995) *Consumer Research.* Thousand Oaks, CA: Sage Publications.

Hopson, R.K., Peterson, J.A. and Lucas, K.J. (2001) 'Tales from the "hood": Framing HIV/AIDS prevention through intervention ethnography in the inner city', *Addiction Research & Theory,* 9(4): 339–363.

Huberman, A.M. and Miles, M.B. (1994) 'Data management and analysis methods', in N.K. Denzin and Y.S. Lincoln (eds), *Handbook of Qualitative Research.* Thousand Oaks, CA: Sage Publications.

Hudson, L.A. and Ozanne, J.L. (1988) 'Alternative ways of seeking knowledge in consumer research', *Journal of Consumer Research,* 14(4): 508–522.

Huffaker, D. (2006) 'Teen blogs exposed: The private lives of teens made public', *American Association for the Advancement of Science (AAAS):* 16–19.

Hussey, M. and Duncombe, N. (1999) 'Projecting the right image: Using projective techniques to measure brand image', *Qualitative Market Research,* 2: 22–30.

International Telecommunications Union (2010) *Measuring the Information Society.* Geneva: International Telecommunications Union. Available at: http://www.itu.int/newsroom/press_releases/2010/pdf/PR08_ExecSum.pdf

Irwin, L.G. and Johnson, J. (2005) 'Interviewing young children: Explicating our practices and dilemmas', *Qualitative Health Research,* 15(6): 821–831.

John, D.R. (1997) 'Presidential address out of the mouths of babes: What children can tell us', in M. Brucks and D. MacInnis (eds), *Advances in Consumer Research,* 25:1–6. Provo, UT: Association for Consumer Research.

John, D.R. (1999) 'Consumer socialization of children: A retrospective look at twenty-five years of research', *Journal of Consumer Research,* 26: 183–213.

Johnson, L.C. (1990) *Selecting Ethnographic Informants.* Newbury Park, CA: Sage Publications.

Jones, J. and Hunter, D. (1995) 'Qualitative research: Consensus methods for medical and health services research', *British Medical Journal,* 311(7001): 376–380.

Kearney, M. (2001) 'Enduring love: A grounded formal theory of women's experience of domestic violence', *Research in Nursing & Health,* 24(4): 270–282.

Kearney, M.H., Murphy, S. and Rosenbaum, M. (1994) 'Mothering on crack cocaine: A grounded theory analysis', *Social Science & Medicine,* 38(2): 351–361.

Keen, J. and Packwood, T. (1995) 'Qualitative research: Case study evaluation', *BMJ,* 311(7002): 444–446.

Kelle, U. (1997) 'Theory building in qualitative research and computer programs for the management of textual data', *Sociological Research Online,* 2(2): 1–14.

Kluckhohn, C. (1967) 'Values and value-orientations in the theory of action: An exploration in definition and classification', in T. Parsons and E.A. Shils (eds), *Toward a General Theory of Action.* Boston, MA: Harvard University Press, pp. 388–433.

Kools, S., McCarthy, M, Durham, R. and Robrecht, L. (1996) 'Dimensional analysis: Broadening the conception of grounded theory', *Qualitative Health Research,* 6(3): 312–331.

Kozinets, R.V. (2002) 'The field behind the screen: Using netnography for marketing research in online communities', *Journal of Marketing Research,* 39(2): 61–72.

Kraut, R., Olson, J., Banaji, M., et al. (2004) 'Psychological research online', *American Psychologist,* 59(2): 105–117.

Langer, R. and Beckman, S.C. (2005) 'Sensitive research topics: Netnography revisited', *Qualitative Market Research,* 8(2): 189–203.

Lawn, S., Pols, R. and Barber, J. (2002) 'Smoking and quitting: A qualitative study with community-living psychiatric clients', *Social Science & Medicine,* 54: 93–104.

Leathar, D. (1980) 'Images in health education advertising', *Health Education Journal,* 39(4): 123.

Lefebvre, R.C. and Flora, J.A. (1988) 'Social marketing and public health intervention', *Health Education Quarterly,* 15(3): 299–315.

Leurs, M., Mur-Veeman, I., Van Der Sar, R., Schaalma, H. and De Vries, N. (2008) 'Diagnosis of sustainable collaboration in health promotion: A case study', *BMC Public Health,* 8: 382–397.

Levy, S.J. (1985) 'Dreams, fairy tales, animals, and cars', *Psychology & Marketing,* 2(2): 67–81.

Lincoln, Y.S. and Guba, E.G. (1985) *Naturalistic Inquiry.* Beverly Hills, CA: Sage Publications.

Locke, K. (1996) 'Rewriting the discovery of grounded theory after 25 years?' *Journal of Management Inquiry,* 5(3): 239–245.

Lombardo, A.P. and Leger, Y.A. (2007) 'Thinking about "Think Again" in Canada: Assessing a social marketing HIV/AIDS prevention campaign', *Journal of Health Communication,* 12(4): 377–397.

Lu, C. and Shulman, S. (2008) 'Rigor and flexibility in computer-based qualitative research: Introducing the Coding Analysis Toolkit', *International Journal of Multiple Research Approaches,* 2: 105–117.

MacAskill, S., Stead, M., MacKintosh, A. and Hastings, G. (2002) '"You cannae just take cigarettes away from somebody and no' gie them something back". Can social marketing help solve the problem of low-income smoking?' *Social Marketing Quarterly,* 8: 19–34.

MacDonald, M. and Green, L. (2001) 'Reconciling concept and context: The dilemma of implementation in school-based health promotion', *Health Education & Behavior,* 28(6): 749–768.

MacFadyen, L., Amos, A., Hastings, G. and Parkes, E. (2003) 'They look like my kind of people: Perceptions of smoking images in youth magazines', *Social Science & Medicine,* 56(3): 491–499.

McGrath, M.A., Sherry, J.F. and Levy, S.J. (1993) 'Giving voice to the gift: The use of projective techniques to recover lost meanings', *Journal of Consumer Psychology,* 2(2): 171–191.

MacGregor, A., Currie, C. and Wetton, N. (1998) 'Eliciting the views of children about health in schools through the use of the draw and write technique', *Health Promotion International,* 13(4): 307–318.

McKay, S., Thurlow, C. and Zimmerman, H.T. (2005) 'Wired whizzes or techno-slaves? Young people and their emergent communication technologies', in A. Williams and C. Thurlow (eds), *Talking Adolescence: Perspectives on Communication in the Teenage Years.* New York: Peter Lang, pp. 185–203.

Maignan, I. and Lukas, B.A. (1997) 'The nature and social uses of the Internet: A qualitative investigation', *The Journal of Consumer Affairs,* 31(2): 346–371.

Malterud, K. (2001) 'Qualitative research: Standards, challenges, and guidelines', *Lancet,* 358(9280): 483–488.

Manning, P.K. (1987). *Semiotics and Fieldwork.* Newbury Park, CA: Sage Publications.

Marcus, G.E. (1986) 'Contemporary problems of ethnography in the modern world system', in J. Clifford and G. Marcus (eds), *Writing Culture: The Poetics of Ethnography.* Berkeley, CA: California Press, pp. 165–193.

Mays, N. and Pope, C. (2000) 'Qualitative research in health care: Assessing quality in qualitative research', *British Medical Journal,* 320(7226): 50–52.

Merchant, G. (2001) 'Teenagers in cyberspace: An investigation of language use and language change in Internet chatrooms', *Journal of Research in Reading,* 24(3): 293–306.

Merritt, R., Christopoulos, A. and Thorpe, A. (2009) 'Where are all the products? Are we really doing social marketing or are we doing social sales?' *Social Marketing Quarterly,* 15(2): 5–13.

Meyer, G. and Dearing, J. (1996) 'Respecifying the social marketing model for unique populations', *Social Marketing Quarterly,* 3: 44–52.

Mick, D.G., Demoss, M. and Faber, R.J. (1992) 'A projective study of motivations and meanings of self-gifts: Implications for retail management', *Journal of Retailing,* 68(2): 122–144.

Miraudo, A. and Pettigrew, S. (2002) 'Helping adolescents achieve positive mental health: Implications for social marketing', *Journal of Research for Consumers,* 4. Available at: www.jrconsumers.com.

Mitchell, K. and Branigan, P. (2000) 'Using focus groups to evaluate health promotion interventions', *Health Education,* 100(6): 261–268.

Monaghan, P.F., Bryant, C.A., Baldwin, J.A., et al. (2008) 'Using community-based prevention marketing to improve farm worker safety', *Social Marketing Quarterly,* 14(4): 71–87.

Morin, S., Vernon, K., Harcourt, J., et al. (2003) 'Why HIV infections have increased among men who have sex with men and what to do about it: Findings from California focus groups', *AIDS and Behavior,* 7(4): 353–362.

Mundel, E. and Chapman, G. (2010) 'A decolonizing approach to health promotion in Canada: The case of the Urban Aboriginal Community Kitchen Garden Project', *Health Promotion International,* 25(2): 166–173.

Myers, P.L. and Stolberg, V.B. (2003) 'Ethnographic lessons on substance use and substance abusers', *Journal of Ethnicity in Substance Abuse,* 2(2): 67–88.

Necheles, J., Chung, E., Hawes-Dawson, J., et al. (2007) 'The teen photovoice project: A pilot study to promote health through advocacy', *Progress in Community Health Partnerships: Research, Education, and Action,* 1(3): 221–229.

Newman, S., Maurer, D., Jackson, A., et al. (2009) 'Gathering the evidence: Photovoice as a tool for disability advocacy', *Progress in Community Health Partnerships: Research, Education, and Action,* 3(2): 139–144.

Patterson, T.L. (1988) 'Direct observation of physical activity and dietary behaviors in a structured environment: Effects of a family-based health promotion program', *Journal of Behavioral Medicine,* 11(5): 447–458.

Paul, C., Ross, S., Bryant, J., et al. (2010) 'The social context of smoking: A qualitative study comparing smokers of high versus low socioeconomic position', *BMC Public Health,* 10(1): 211–218.

Perren, L. and Ram, M. (2004) 'Case-study method in small business and entrepreneurial research: Mapping boundaries and perspectives', *International Small Business Journal,* 22: 83–101.

Peters, V. and Wester, F. (2007) 'How qualitative data analysis software may support the qualitative process', *Quality & Quantity,* 41: 635–659.

Petticrew, M., Semple, S., Hilton, S., et al. (2007) 'Covert observation in practice: Lessons from the evaluation of the prohibition of smoking in public places in Scotland', *BMC Public Health,* 7: 204–211.

Pettigrew, S. (2000) 'Ethnography and grounded theory: A happy marriage?' in S.J. Hoch and R.J. Meyer (eds),

Advances in Consumer Research, 27: 256–260. Provo, UT: Association for Consumer Research.

Pettigrew, S. (2002a) 'A grounded theory of beer consumption in Australia', *Qualitative Market Research*, 5(2): 112–122.

Pettigrew, S. (2002b), 'Consuming alcohol,' in S. Miles, A. Anderson and K. Meethan (eds), *The Changing Consumer: Markets and Meanings*. London: Routledge.

Pettigrew, S. and Charters, S. (2008) 'Tasting as a projective technique', *Qualitative Market Research*, 11(3): 331–343.

Pettigrew, S., Pescud, M., Jarvis, W. and Webb, D. (2009) 'The salience of vomiting in teenagers' binge drinking intentions', Australian and New Zealand Marketing Academy Conference, Melbourne, 2009.

Piirto, R. (1991) 'Socks, ties and videotape', *American Demographics*, 13(9): 6.

Piot, B., Mukherjee, A., Navin, D., et al. (2010) 'Lot quality assurance sampling for monitoring coverage and quality of a targeted condom social marketing programme in traditional and non-traditional outlets in India', *Sexually Transmitted Infections*, 86: 56–61.

Pope, C. and Mays, N. (2009) 'Critical reflections on the rise of qualitative research', *British Medical Journal*, 339: 737–739.

Potter, C. and Carpenter, J. (2008) 'Something in it for dads: Getting fathers involved with Sure Start', *Early Child Development and Care*, 178(7): 761–772.

Prestin, A. and Pearce, K. (2010) 'We care a lot: Formative research for a social marketing campaign to promote school-based recycling', *Resources, Conservation and Recycling*, 54(11): 1017–1026.

Punch, M. (1986). *The Politics and Ethics of Fieldwork*. Beverly Hills, CA: Sage Publications.

Richards, L. (1999) 'Data alive! The thinking behind NVivo', *Qualitative Health Research*, 9(3): 412–428.

Richman, J. (1996) 'Jokes as a projective technique: The humor of psychiatric patients', *American Journal of Psychotherapy*, 50(3): 336–346.

Roddy, E., Antoniak, M., Britton, J., Molyneux, A. and Lewis, S. (2006) 'Barriers and motivators to gaining access to smoking cessation services amongst deprived smokers: A qualitative study', *BMC Health Services Research*, 6: 147–154.

Rogers, E.M. and Beal, G.M. (1958) 'Projective techniques in interviewing farmers', *Journal of Marketing*, 23: 177–179.

Rook, D.W. (1988) 'Researching consumer fantasy', *Research in Consumer Behavior*, 3: 247–270.

Ross, S. (1995) '"Do I really have to eat that?": A qualitative study of schoolchildren's food choices and preferences', *Health Education Journal*, 54: 312–321.

Rowse, T. (1993) 'The relevance of ethnographic understanding to Aboriginal anti-grog initiatives', *Drug and Alcohol Review*, 12(4): 393–399.

Rust, L. (1993) 'Observations: Parents and children shopping together: A new approach to the qualitative analysis of observational data', *Journal of Advertising Research*, 33(4): 65–70.

Sandlin, J.A. (2007) 'Netnography as a consumer education research tool', *International Journal of Consumer Studies*, 31(3): 288–294.

Sarantakos, S. (1993). *Social Research*. South Melbourne: MacMillan.

Sarlio-Lahteenkorva, S. (1998) 'Relapse stories in obesity', *European Journal of Public Health*, 8(3): 203–209.

Secker, J., Armstrong, C. and Hill, M. (1999) 'Young people's understanding of mental illness', *Health Education Research*, 14(6): 729–739.

Sherry, J.F., McGrath, M.A. and Levy, S.J. (1993) 'The dark side of the gift', *Journal of Business Research*, 28: 225–244.

Sijtsema, S., Linnemann, A., Backus, G., et al. (2007) 'Exploration of projective techniques to unravel health perception', *British Food Journal*, 109(6): 443–456.

Smith, N.C. (1990) 'The case study: A useful research method for information management', *Journal of Information Technology*, 5: 123–133.

Sofaer, S. (1999) 'Qualitative methods: What are they and why use them?' *Health Services Research*, 34(5): 1101–1118.

Speller, V., Alyson, L. and Harrison, D. (1997) 'The search for evidence of effective health promotion', *British Medical Journal*, 315(7104): 361–363.

Staley, J.A. (2009) 'Get firefighters moving: Marketing a physical fitness intervention to reduce sudden cardiac death risk in full-time firefighters', *Social Marketing Quarterly*, 15(3): 85–99.

Stead, M., MacAskill, S., MacKintosh, A., Reece, J. and Eadie, D. (2001) '"It's as if you're locked in": Qualitative explanations for area effects on smoking in disadvantaged communities', *Health and Place*, 7(4): 333–343.

Steele, H.L. (1964) 'On the validity of projective questions', *Journal of Marketing Research*, 1(3): 46–49.

Strauss, A. and Corbin, J. (1990) *Basics of Qualitative Research*. Newbury Park, CA: Sage Publications.

Thackeray, R. (2003) 'Use of social marketing to develop culturally innovative diabetes interventions', *Diabetes Spectrum*, 16: 15–20.

Tilley, D.S. and Brackley, M. (2005) 'Men who batter intimate partners: A grounded theory study of the development of male violence in intimate partner relationships', *Issues in Mental Health Nursing*, 26(3): 281–297.

Wallendorf, M. and Belk, R.W. (1989) 'Assessing trustworthiness in naturalistic consumer research', in E. Hirschman (ed), *Interpretive Consumer Research*. Provo, UT: Association for Consumer Research, pp. 69–84.

Wang, C. and Burris, M.A. (1997) 'Photovoice: Concept, methodology, and use for participatory needs assessment', *Health Education & Behavior*, 24: 369–387.

Wells, K. (1995), 'The strategy of grounded theory: Possibilities and problems', *Social Work Research*, 19: 33–37.

Whitlock, G., MacMahon, S., Vander Hoorn, S., et al. (1997) 'Socioeconomic distribution of smoking in a population of 10,529 New Zealanders', *New Zealand Medical Journal*, 110(1051): 327–330.

Wiehagen, T. (2007) 'Applying projective techniques to formative research in health communication development', *Health Promotion Practice*, 8(2): 164–172.

Will, V., Eadie, D. and MacAskill, S. (1996) 'Projective and enabling techniques explored', *Marketing Intelligence & Planning*, 14(6): 38–43.

Williams, M. (1958) 'Farmers' decisions in the use of fertilizer', *American Journal of Agricultural Economics*, 40(5): 1407–1415.

Williams, P., Block, L. and Fitzsimons, G. (2006) 'Simply asking questions about health behaviors increases both healthy and unhealthy behaviors', *Social Influence*, 1(2): 117–127.

Willner, P., Hart, K., Binmore, J., Cavendish, M. and Dunphy, E. (2000) 'Alcohol sales to underage adolescents: An unobtrusive observational field study and evaluation of a police intervention', *Addiction*, 95(9): 1373–1388.

Winlow, S., Hobbs, D., Lister, S. and Hadfield, P. (2001) 'Get ready to duck: Bouncers and the realities of ethnographic research on violent groups', *British Journal of Criminology*, 41(3): 536–548.

Wuest, J. (1995) 'Feminist grounded theory: An exploration of the congruency and tensions between two traditions in knowledge discovery', *Qualitative Health Research*, 5: 125–137.

Wuest, J., Merritt-Gray, M., Berman, H. and Ford-Gilboe, M. (2002) 'Illuminating social determinants of women's health using grounded theory', *Health Care for Women International*, 23(8): 794–808.

Yin, R. (1981) 'The case study crisis: Some answers', *Administrative Science Quarterly*, 26: 58–65.

Yin, R. (2009) *Case Study Research: Design and Methods*, 4th edn. Applied Social Research Methods Series. Thousand Oaks, CA: Sage Publications.

Yoell, W.A. and Largen, R.G. (1974) 'The fallacy of projective techniques', *Journal of Advertising*, 3: 33–46.

ZenithOptimedia (2010) 'Global advertising downturn slows despite disappointing Q1'. Press release ZenithOptimedia. Available at: http://www.zenithoptimedia.com/gff/pdf/Adspend%20forecasts%20July%202009.pdf

Zober, M. (1955) 'Some projective techniques applied to marketing research', *Journal of Marketing*, 20: 262–268.

15

Measurement in Quantitative Methods

Fiona J. Harris

INTRODUCTION

Quantitative methods play a crucial role in building an evidence base to guide social marketing interventions and to help bring about policy changes. This chapter discusses the rationale for using quantitative methods and considers their use in social marketing. Key measurement issues are identified and explored in the research process and the interrelatedness of decisions at each stage is highlighted. The chapter opens by considering the role of quantitative methods in social marketing and discussing their contribution in relation to qualitative methods. Measurement issues are then examined at each stage of the research process, starting with research design and data collection methods, followed by sampling issues, question design and measurement, timing issues in research design, ethical considerations and finally data analysis and interpretation.

THE ROLE OF QUANTITATIVE METHODS IN SOCIAL MARKETING

Qualitative and quantitative methods are often perceived as opposing sides, each with their loyal supporters who treat each other's preferred methods with suspicion and trepidation. However, both types of methods have their uses and limitations and both have valuable contributions to make in the pursuit of knowledge and understanding.

Qualitative methods allow a rich, in-depth exploration of an area about which knowledge and understanding may be lacking (see Chapter 14 for a discussion of qualitative methods). Quantitative methods allow the large-scale testing of hypotheses developed from exploratory qualitative findings using numerical analysis. They enable statistical tests to be used to 'compare obtained results with chance expectation' and help make inferences (Kerlinger, 1992: 174). In general, quantitative methods enable greater control to be exercised over the data that are collected and analyzed and attempt to increase measurement accuracy, objectivity and generalizability.

Thus, to some extent, qualitative and quantitative approaches may appear to be polar opposites, which probably explains the tendency for researchers to align themselves with one or other of them. Oppenheim (1992: 155) described the division as 'a bitter and difficult choice between too much oversimplification for the sake of "good measurement" and a subtler, more flexible approach which may not yield valid, replicable results'. However, qualitative and quantitative methods may be more constructively viewed as complementary methods, rather than mutually exclusive ones. With quantitative methods you can only get answers to the questions you ask and qualitative research plays a vital role in informing quantitative research by helping to identify the relevant questions to ask and to guide appropriate measures.

Quantitative methods have been used in a wide variety of social marketing research, including randomized controlled trials (RCTs) to evaluate interventions designed to increase walking, cross-sectional and longitudinal surveys to assess the impact of the marketing of harmful products such as tobacco, alcohol and fatty foods on behavior and experimental pretesting of public health campaigns. Whittingham et al. (2008) advocated the complementary use of both qualitative and experimental pretesting of public health campaigns to determine the effectiveness of campaign materials to optimize decision making in a campaign's development. For many social marketing programs, whether at the development or evaluation stage, mixed methods are best. Research is used throughout the process to inform decision making and generate learning for future initiatives (see Chapter 13 for a discussion of evaluation in social marketing). For example, in a social marketing project to improve agricultural workers' health a wide range of methods were employed: participant observation provided direct experience of working conditions and behavior; focus groups were used to understand workers' attitudes and behavior toward pesticide use and to develop a questionnaire; interviews were conducted with healthcare providers to gain an appreciation of their knowledge of pesticide-related illnesses and barriers that prevented workers obtaining suitable health care; interviews with employers and supervisors shed light on the structural problems connected with occupational exposure to pesticides and safety practices; a questionnaire was developed, based on the focus group data, to examine identified predictors of two behaviors aimed at reducing pesticide exposure (handwashing and compliance with entry interval regulations) and, finally, an evaluation activity among the research team was carried out (Flocks et al., 2001).

THE RESEARCH PROCESS AND MEASUREMENT CONSIDERATIONS

To be able to get answers to identified questions, it is essential to consider the entire research process at the outset, particularly the nature of responses that will be elicited from participants and how these will be analyzed. The importance of advanced planning cannot be overstated; only by ensuring that the right data are collected in the appropriate format will hypotheses be able to be tested using suitable statistical techniques. Measurement mistakes can rarely be rectified at the analysis stage.

Designing a piece of research or project involves deciding *who* (sampling) will be asked to do *what* (question design and measurement), *how* (research design and data collection methods), *when* (timing issues in research design) and finally the '*so what*?' (data analysis and interpretation), as illustrated in Figure 15.1.

These decisions are interrelated and need to be considered with regard to each other, because each has implications for measurement in quantitative methods. This is illustrated in the Youth Tobacco Policy Study (YTPS), a long-term, cross-sectional three-wave study of the impact of the UK's Tobacco Advertising and Promotion Act on young people's (11–16 year olds') awareness of tobacco marketing (Grant et al., 2008; Moodie et al., 2008). Qualitative research (focus groups and individual interviews) conducted in the development of the questionnaire indicated that the questionnaire needed to be administered by an interviewer in respondents' homes to enable probing, the question order to be controlled and visual prompts to be used to provide adequate privacy to encourage honesty in responses. In addition, a short self-completion questionnaire was used after

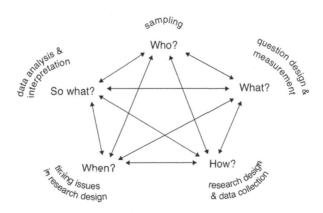

Figure 15.1   The interrelatedness of the research process

the interviewer-administered questionnaire had been completed. The 'how' of research design and data collection methods (including 'where') had to be determined in conjunction with decisions relating to 'what' (the questionnaire), the 'who' data were being collected from, 'when' and how they would be analyzed and interpreted afterward (the 'so what?').

The following sections consider the decisions involved in designing research in the context of social marketing. The first to be considered is the 'how', because although it is dependent upon the broad level of 'what' has to be measured, the specifics and detail of the measurements depend upon and are tailored to the data collection methods. This is followed by the 'who', which also has implications for what is measured, before the 'what', 'when' and ethical considerations are examined. Finally, data analysis and interpretation issues – the 'so what?' – are explored.

RESEARCH DESIGN AND DATA COLLECTION METHODS (THE 'HOW?')

There are two fundamental types of research: experimental and non-experimental. Kerlinger (1992: 315) described true experimentation as follows:

> The true experiment requires the manipulation of at least one independent variable, the random assignment of subjects to groups, and the random assignment of treatments to groups.

Experimental or quasi-experimental designs are suitable in some situations, but not in others. Randomized controlled trials utilize experimental design to test the impact of interventions in public health, employing random allocation of participants to experimental and control groups and statistically testing the effects of a treatment under controlled conditions. However, RCTs do not lend themselves to investigating complex health promotion interventions (Stead et al., 2002). In social marketing, researchers are often unable to manipulate independent variables. For example, participants cannot be randomly allocated as smokers, non-smokers or former smokers; such variables are outside of researchers' control. The fact that participants come to the research with certain characteristics or attitudes that cannot be manipulated within the research design means that their selection cannot be randomized. In such circumstances, an alternative design must be sought. Indeed Kerlinger acknowledged that it was often necessary to use compromise designs. However, quasi-experimental designs are

possible. The International Tobacco Control (ITC) Four Country Survey is an example of a quasi-experimental design; its international samples and longitudinal design allow tobacco control policy changes in a country to be compared before and after implementation and against control samples in other countries (Thompson et al., 2006).

Kerlinger (1992) noted that neither experimental nor non-experimental research is necessarily better or worse, but like qualitative and quantitative methods, each has its strengths and limitations. Experiments allow greater control to be exercised over variables and hence allow more confident interpretation (but not generalization) of the results, but may be artificial and many social marketing problems do not lend themselves to experimental inquiry. Non-experimental research may be more natural and realistic, but allows less control over independent variables and randomization and the results are more susceptible to erroneous interpretation. For example, it is difficult to establish causality between variables because the cause may lie with some other, non-examined variable.

Another approach is econometric studies, which use mathematical and statistical techniques to model social marketing problems through the discipline of economics. Econometric studies tend to examine data at the aggregated population level: for example, using countries as the unit of analysis or modeling fluctuations in advertising expenditure and consumption within a country. Such studies involve complex equations that may not reflect sufficiently the sophistication of the social phenomena they attempt to model (Hastings et al., 2005). Access to and completeness of data, such as advertising expenditure, can also be problematic. Furthermore, econometric studies do not lend themselves to examination of subgroups within a population and thus do not provide the necessary insight into the behavior of certain groups whose behavior social marketing seeks to change: see Hastings et al. (2005) for a fuller discussion of the limitations of econometric studies and MacKintosh et al. (2008) for a discussion of econometric studies in the context of tobacco control.

Regardless of the approach used, efficient research design will '*maximise systematic variance* [the variance in the variables specified in the research hypotheses], *control extraneous systematic variance* [the variance in the variables that may affect the research outcomes] *and minimise error variance* [the error or random variance such as that resulting from measurement errors]' (Kerlinger, 1992: 284). Consideration needs to be given to the collection methods as well as the measures employed, because both can be used to maximize the research variance and minimize the error variance. Various techniques can be used to reduce or eliminate potential error; these are discussed in relation to the different data collection methods that follow.

There are a variety of ways in which data may be collected. Measurement may be made directly by researchers, respondents or automatic recording equipment. For example, researchers may calculate the number of alcoholic units consumed by a respondent based on the number and types of drinks consumed, respondents may estimate the number of alcoholic units they consumed or a Breathalyser may be used to measure a respondent's blood alcohol level. Which method is used will depend upon the research question and hypotheses, the behavior or attitudes of interest, the feasibility of various methods in relation to these and of course financial resources.

Questionnaires are a commonly used method of collecting data in social marketing, but a decision still has to be made about whether they are interview-administered in person or by telephone, self-completed in the presence of a researcher or in private, on paper or electronically. The advantages of interview-administered questionnaires are that the interviewer can explain anything respondents may not understand and can check that respondents do not miss out any questions. The disadvantages are that respondents may be uncomfortable answering questions in front of a researcher, particularly on sensitive topics, and may be inhibited from giving accurate responses and might be more likely to give socially acceptable answers, reducing confidence in the data. This can be counteracted by providing greater privacy, for example, through using show-cards and/or shuffle cards in face-to-face interviews. Such techniques remove the need for interviewers and respondents to voice potentially sensitive response options, by instead using alphabetic or numeric references to the cards. Show-cards have been used successfully in research looking at adolescents' alcohol behavior and attitudes, when parental presence could also be inhibiting (see, e.g., Gordon et al., 2011).

Self-completion questionnaires may elicit more truthful responses by preserving respondents' privacy, particularly if questionnaires are returned anonymously (albeit, this is more difficult with longitudinal designs). However, this has to be weighed against the potential for non-responses to some questions or errors resulting from misunderstandings in the absence of an interviewer, because respondents may be less likely to go to the trouble of contacting researchers to clarify anything that might be unclear in the questions, answer options or instructions. Prior qualitative research can help to ensure that questions are designed appropriately for intended respondents and enable questionnaires to be pretested to identify potential problems.

Telephone data collection can strike a balance between providing a certain amount of perceived privacy in that respondents are invisible to researchers but can still ask for clarification if they need to. However, unless prearranged, the timing of telephone-administered surveys can be intrusive and deter respondents from participating. It may also be difficult for respondents to hold a range of response options in their heads or visualize a scale without having it physically in front of them. So the question formats employed need to take this into account.

It may not be possible to use the same collection methods to collect data in different countries owing to variations in the availability or reliability of postal or telephone services. In such cases, collection methods need to be tailored to the participating countries. For example, in a comparison of reported awareness of tobacco advertising and promotion in China with Thailand, Australia and the USA, questionnaires were administered by telephone in Australia and the USA and by door-to-door interviews in China and Thailand (Li et al., 2009).

SAMPLING ISSUES (THE 'WHO?')

Quantitative methods typically enable standard data to be collected from larger samples of people and patterns and relationships in the data to be tested. A variety of sampling strategies may be employed to try to ensure that the data are representative of a particular population. These fall into two broad categories: probability and non-probability sampling. '*Probability sampling*' involves some form of random sampling at some stage of sample selection, whereas '*non-probability sampling*' does not, using instead non-random sample selection (Kerlinger, 1992). Key texts on sampling theory include Kish (1995), Churchill (1995) and Lynn and Lievesley (1992). Probability sampling is the preferred approach, because statistical inference is based upon the assumption of probability sampling.

Random sampling within a population attempts to minimize bias by giving everyone the same chance of being selected, thereby making it more likely that the sample has similar characteristics to those of the wider population and is thus more representative of that population. Larger samples are preferred because they allow random sampling a better chance of yielding a more representative sample from a population. '*Simple random sampling*' is where the sample is completely randomly selected from a population. This does not mean arbitrary selection, as Oppenheim pointed out; instead 'it is a statistically defined procedure that requires a table or set of random numbers which can be generated by a computer, or can be found at the back of most statistics textbooks' (Oppenheim, 1992: 40). An example of the use of simple random sampling in research is a Danish national health interview survey, in which simple random samples were drawn from the adult Danish population using the Danish Civil Registration System (every person in Denmark has a unique personal registration number) (Ekholm et al., 2009). However, simple random sampling is rarely used in behavioral research owing to the impracticalities of administering this approach. It is usually too difficult and expensive to select a truly random sample directly from a whole population, so that every member of that population has the same probability of being selected. More typically, 'probability sampling strategies' use random sampling at some stage(s) of sample selection, which makes the process more manageable and cost-effective. 'Stratified sampling' involves selecting random samples from predetermined strata within a population such as gender or geographic location. 'Cluster sampling' entails selecting random samples at successive levels, based on a structuring of a population, for example, within regions, towns, local areas, roads and households. With 'systematic sampling' the first person or element is randomly selected from a list within a range of numbers, and people or elements are subsequently selected at intervals of that value working through the list. Care is needed to avoid 'periodicity effects'. For example, if households from an estate of apartment blocks with two-bedroom apartments sandwiching a one-bedroom apartment on each floor were sampled by selecting every third number, either only two-bedroom apartments or only one-bedroom apartments would be selected, which might bias the sample with regard to, for example, age, income and family circumstances.

An example of multistage probability sampling is the approach taken in the ITC Four Country Survey, which is an annual survey that evaluates the psychosocial and behavioral effects of national-level tobacco control policies in the USA, Canada, the UK and Australia. *Stratified sampling* is used to divide the population within each country into several geographic regions, from which the appropriate numbers of respondents are drawn from the strata to achieve proportional representation according to regional population size. *Random sampling* of households using random-digit dialling (RDD) methods is used to fill the stratum quotas, and *systematic sampling* is used to select individual respondents from households in which there is more than one

eligible smoker, according to who has the next birthday (Thompson et al., 2006).

Random sampling, while the most rigorous theoretically and meeting the assumptions for statistical inference, is not always possible in practice. Non-random sampling, referred to as 'non-probability sampling', does not use random sampling, but there is often no realistic alternative in practice. Non-probability sampling includes 'quota sampling', in which people are selected on the basis of certain characteristics such as age, gender and geographical location, and 'accidental sampling' or 'convenience sampling', in which people are selected based merely on their availability. The scientific limitations of non-probability sampling can be offset to some degree through employing knowledge, skill and care when selecting samples and replicating research with other samples (Kerlinger, 1992).

In practice, a combination of probability and non-probability sampling is often used to meet the challenges of the research, while employing as much rigour as possible. For example, the YTPS used a combination of probability and non-probability sampling (see Grant et al., 2008). It attempted to keep selection as controlled as far as possible by drawing participants from a random selection of electoral wards, stratified by Government Office Region and the demographic and lifestyle characteristics of geographical areas (the ACORN geo-demographic classification). However, the final sample was ultimately non-probability, because quota sampling was used to achieve a balance across gender and age groups within each selected electoral ward. In this way, the study maximized the rigor of the initial sampling by using random (i.e. probability) sampling to select the electoral wards, but then used quota (i.e. non-probability) sampling by gender and age to enable these characteristics to be controlled in the subsequent statistical data analysis.

One of the challenges of conducting research in social marketing is the need for access to 'sampling frames'. A sampling frame is a pool or list of members of a particular population of interest. For example, in the Ekholm et al. (2009) Danish national health interview survey cited earlier, the Danish Civil Registration System served as the sampling frame from which the sample was drawn. In longitudinal research, confidence is needed that access to such sampling frames will be possible throughout the duration of the study.

Another challenge is that social marketing research often involves potentially vulnerable populations, because it is typically trying to understand and discover how to change behavior that is harmful to individuals, their family or society, such as smoking, drinking, the consumption of unhealthy food and dangerous driving. People may be considered vulnerable in various ways: for example, physically, cognitively, emotionally and socially. A further challenge is that it may be difficult to reach or recruit participants from particular populations or they may be reluctant to discuss their behavior, given the sensitivity of much social marketing research. For example, in an evaluation of a campaign to increase prescriptions for sugar-free medicines, Evans et al. (1999) noted that it was impossible to make sure that the anonymous pre- and post-intervention questionnaires were completed by the same person or that they reflected the views of all general practitioners in a practice or all pharmacists in a pharmacy. Both challenges have implications for sampling strategies and research design, because whether or not suitable participants can be recruited affects the ability of quantitative methods to test desired hypotheses and draw appropriate conclusions.

Weighting is sometimes used to adjust for disproportionate selection and under-coverage of population subgroups. For example, the ITC Four Country Survey uses weights calculated for each respondent (see Thompson et al., 2006, for details about how these weights are calculated). Bootstrapping techniques (based on a large number of subsamples, rather than relying on statistical assumptions about the population) may also be used to obtain weights (see Efron and Tibshirani, 1993; Lohr, 1999).

Replenishment samples may be used in longitudinal research designs such as the ITC Four Country Survey to replace respondents lost to attrition in order to maintain participant numbers over time. Data from replenishment samples can be compared against data from continuing samples to assess whether the findings are affected by the length of time respondents have participated in the research (Thompson et al., 2006).

QUESTION DESIGN AND MEASUREMENT (THE 'WHAT?')

The value of quantitative analysis relies very much on the quality of the data that are collected; the saying 'garbage in, garbage out' has become a cliché for good reason. Getting the 'what' that is collected right is imperative. By its very nature, much of what data are collected in social marketing research will relate to behavior and attitudes. In many cases, it is not possible, practical or acceptable to observe or measure behavior directly, and attitudes cannot be accessed independently of people. Hence, often research is reliant on asking questions and on participants'

self-reports or inferring something based on participants' behavior. A wealth of quantitative methods and measures are available for collecting social marketing data that might not be able to be accessed in any other way and which can be tailored to the specific needs of the research. In the subsections that follow, the various types of data are considered first, followed by a discussion about deciding on the data to collect and, finally, the measurement criteria that need to be taken into account are explained.

Types of data

Careful attention should be given to the measurement levels of the data that are collected, because the levels needs to be appropriate for what is being measured and they determine to some extent the types of statistical analysis that can later be used to test the research hypotheses. Data may be 'nominal' (categorical), 'ordinal' (ranked in order), 'interval' (measurable units of equal intervals) or 'ratio' (a measurement that has a meaningful absolute zero so that a property assigned the numerical value of 10 may be deemed to represent twice the property assigned a 5) (Kerlinger, 1992).

Nominal data are non-numerical categories such as gender, ethnicity, religion and smoking status. Nominal data require the use of non-parametric methods. A parameter 'is a population value' (e.g. a mean) and non-parametric tests require fewer assumptions to be made about, for example, the research sample population's characteristics or form of distribution and tend to be based on testing some property of the data against chance expectation (Kerlinger, 1973: 286).

Ordinal data provide information about each category's position in relation to other categories, although they do not indicate the size of the intervals between the rankings. Socio-economic status is an example of ordinal data that is often used in social marketing research, in which the classes (A, B, C1, C2, D and E) provide ranking information but the distances between classes are more obscure.

By contrast, the distances or intervals between interval data are the same, so their values can be legitimately added and subtracted. Examples include temperature measured in centigrade or Fahrenheit.

Ratio data, in addition to having equal intervals, also have an absolute and meaningful zero point at which an object has none of the characteristics being measured. Ratio data not only can be added and subtracted but also can be multiplied and divided. Blood alcohol level measured in milligram per cent (mg of alcohol per 100 ml of blood) or measurements in metres and centimetres are examples of ratio data.

In general, finer-level measurements (e.g. exact age rather than age bands such as 20–29, 30–39, 40–49, etc.) are preferred, because there is a greater number of (and more powerful) statistical techniques available that can be used with them. Furthermore, bands can always be constructed from actual measurements if so desired, but precise measurements cannot subsequently be derived if data are collected in bands.

However, the most important consideration in making decisions about measurement levels is ensuring that the levels are appropriate for what is being measured and choosing suitable techniques for later analyzing the resulting data. For example, although nominal-level data have a much narrower and less powerful range of statistical tests available for them, nominal data would be entirely appropriate for measuring smoking status in a study about smoking, for example, using categories of 'smoker', 'non-smoker' and 'former smoker'. Potential techniques for analyzing nominal-level data include logistic regression and multinomial logistic regression. Even where finer-level measures might be available, they may not always be suitable in practice. For example, respondents may be unwilling to reveal their exact age or income. A trade-off may also need to be made between granularity and accuracy, because respondents may not be able to recall time or quantities accurately, and asking for estimates can introduce errors into the data. For example, respondents may not know precisely how frequently they engage in a particular activity or how many advertisements for a product category they have seen, but may be able to indicate more comfortably and confidently into which of a range of frequency bands they would fall.

Technically, scales may be considered ordinal data because equal intervals between scale points cannot necessarily be assumed either within a scale or between scales and people differ in their perceptions. For example, the intervals of a scale intended to measure pain might vary because people have different pain thresholds and their responses to an identical stimulus can differ. However, in practice, scales are very often treated as interval data, and as long as scales are carefully constructed and researchers are mindful of potential distortion from unequal intervals, the treatment of scales as interval data is considered acceptable and indeed necessary to answer important questions in social research.

A variety of scales is used in social marketing. '*Rating scales*' ask respondents to provide a numerical assessment of something. They can take various forms, as illustrated in the following examples taken from research assessing the cumulative impact of alcohol marketing on adolescent drinking (Gordon et al., 2011). Rating scales may be in the form of a graphic scale represented as a line with verbal descriptors marked along it or a scale with categories and/or numbers (e.g. 'How often do you USUALLY have an alcoholic drink?' 'Every day or almost every day (1) – About twice a week (2) – About once a week (3) – About once a fortnight (4) – About once a month (5) – Only a few times a year (6) – I never drink alcohol now (7)'). *Likert scales* are one of the most popular types of scale, with numbers of 1–5 (although seven-point scales are also sometimes used) assigned levels of agreement/disagreement to represent an attitude (e.g. 'Under-age drinking is morally wrong' – '5-strongly agree', '4-agree', '3-uncertain', '2-disagree' and '1-strongly disagree'). '*Semantic differential scales*' consist of a five- or seven-point rating scale with the two extreme ends defined by bipolar opposites (e.g. 'Alcohol Brand X:' 'looks boring – 1 – 2 – 3 – 4 – 5 – looks fun'). '*Inventories*' and '*checklists*' may also used (e.g. 'In the last six months have you noticed cigarettes or tobacco products being advertised on television?' 'Yes (coded 1) – No (coded 0) – I don't know (coded 3 or 0)' (from the ITC Four Countries Study in Harris et al., 2006). See Oppenheim (1992) for advice on constructing various types of scales.

Open-ended questions, although more time consuming to collect and code, can allow more precise data to be collected and can provide a means of collecting data that may be difficult for respondents to summate or rate. For example, respondents may be unable to recall or calculate exactly how many units of alcohol they consumed the last time they had a drink, but may be able to indicate what type(s) of drink and how many of each they last drank, enabling the researcher to calculate later the units of alcohol consumed (see Gordon et al., 2011). However, care does need to be given to the response options offered to participants and the coding schemes used to minimize the potential for ambiguous responses that can result in the miscoding or discarding of data.

Deciding on the data to collect

In order to collect suitable data for testing research hypotheses, decisions need to be made about how each behavior, characteristic or concept will be operationalized in terms of the questions and sets of items that respondents will be asked. Kerlinger (1992: 26–27) distinguished between a 'concept' and a 'construct'. He defined a '*concept*' as expressing 'an abstraction formed by generalization from particulars' and as 'an abstraction formed from observation', such as 'intelligence', 'aggressiveness' or 'achievement'. Kerlinger defined a '*construct*' as 'a concept … [that] has the added meaning, however, of having been deliberately and consciously invented or adopted for a special scientific purpose'. A construct is a concept that is used by scientists consciously and systematically in theories and in observations and measurement. Kerlinger (1992: 27) defined a 'variable' as 'a property that takes on different values' and as the name given to the constructs or properties that scientists study. In order to study a concept empirically, it must first be operationally defined. In other words, which measurable properties or observable behavior will be used as variables to represent a construct must be determined.

Qualitative research can play a vital role in helping to develop and test appropriate questions to ensure that questions are written from the respondents' perspective. It is also invaluable in pretesting questionnaires. For example, in studies looking at alcohol and adolescents (see Gordon et al., 2011; Hughs et al., 1997), initial qualitative research provided an understanding of how adolescents recall and think about their alcohol consumption and enabled questions to be framed around their ways of thinking rather than being based on the researchers' ways of thinking.

Scales or items are often used to measure behavior and attitudes in social marketing. A research instrument consisting of a list of questions or items may need to be developed. This involves a rigorous development process, including the scoping of a concept based on qualitative research and construction of scalar items to reflect the scope, followed by iterative piloting and refinement of the list of items using statistical techniques such as factor analysis (FA), principal components analysis (PCA) and confirmatory factor analysis (CFA) and tests of item reliability and validity: see Oppenheim (1992) for a detailed discussion of instrument development.

Using existing reliable and valid instruments for measuring a concept may be possible and facilitates comparisons with other research, but often an instrument may not be completely appropriate for use in a different context or with a different population or culture. It may be necessary to adapt an instrument, such as by amending the wording or omitting items that do not apply in another context. Alternatively, items may need to be added to adapt an instrument for another culture or context. For example, in a randomized trial of a web-based program to improve fruit and vegetable consumption in a multicultural rural community, Buller et al. (2008) used a validated food frequency assessment but added a question that assessed consumption of red chilli, green chilli and salsa, because these featured widely in the regional diet of the participants in their study. Amended instruments require re-piloting and reassessing in terms of their dimensionality, reliability and validity. In other cases, instruments may not have been published in sufficient detail to enable their use by other researchers or an instrument might be copyrighted. Translation into another language can subtly change the meaning or connotation of scale items and requires reanalysis of an instrument's dimensions.

Researchers need to be alert to potential error in the accuracy of measurements obtained through questioning, both in the wording and way a question and response options are posed and in respondents' ability to access what they perceive to be the required information. Responses can be susceptible to inaccuracy and distortion, because, for example, respondents may misinterpret the question or response options or they may not be able to recall events accurately, they may not have full insight into the reasons for their behavior or they may feel obliged to give socially acceptable answers. All of these can increase the amount of error in the data. Given the sensitive nature of much social marketing research, the way questions are phrased needs to be carefully considered to minimize the potential for respondents to given socially desirable responses. It is important that the choice of words and phrasing be non-judgemental. Oppenheim (1992) provides excellent guidance on designing attitude scale statements and construction of attitude scales.

Behavioral data are also potentially subject to error for a number of reasons. For example, people may behave differently when they know they are being observed and errors may occur in drawing inferences from people's behavior. Owing to the difficulty in observing certain behaviors or asking respondents to report them, 'proxy' or 'surrogate' measures are sometimes used. For example, Ellickson et al. (2005) measured exposure to television beer advertising by asking adolescents how often 'since school started this fall' they had watched televised professional football and basketball and each of four late-night television shows (which frequently showed beer advertisements and had been identified in prior focus group research as favorite programs) using the following response options: 'never or almost never', 'some of the times it's on', 'half of the times it's on', 'most of the times it's on' and 'almost all of the times it's on'. Each of the program items was multiplied by the relevant Nielsen Monitor-Plus data of the number of beer advertisements shown during the programs over the seven-month research period. The six-item scores were then summed to produce a single measure and the square root used in the data analysis to improve its distribution. Thus, an estimate of likely exposure to television beer advertising was used as a surrogate measure of actual exposure, owing to the impracticality of measuring exposure to the advertisements directly. Opportunity-based measures of potential exposure to televised alcohol advertisements were also used in a longitudinal study by Stacy et al. (2004), who recognized that construct validity was difficult to establish with exposure assessments as well as posing potential confounding effects, because such measures may measure something else instead of (or as well as) exposure. If surrogate measures are used, they need to be chosen with care and analyses based on them interpreted with caution.

Thought should also be given to the form and ordering of response options and their impact on subsequent data analysis. Unprompted questions should precede prompted ones to avoid influencing respondents' responses or narrowing their answers. It might seem obvious in retrospect, but ensuring that 'more of something' in response options progresses logically (e.g. from left to right or from top to bottom in Western cultures) will facilitate later analysis and interpretation of the data collected and minimize the amount of recoding and potential for errors to creep into the analysis and findings. Varying the direction of responses (using a mix of positive and negative wording) is often advocated as good practice to prevent response bias developing across multiple items in a questionnaire. Response sets (the tendency to respond in set ways to scale items) include the propensity to agree and to give socially desirable responses. However, there is a danger that respondents may not notice the reverse wording of some items and mistakenly check the wrong response option. Furthermore, positively and negatively worded attitude items may yield responses of different intensity (Falthzik and Jolson, 1974). Having a mixture of positive and reverse-worded items can be particularly problematic for subcultural groups such as ethnic and racial minorities and when used in cross-cultural contexts (Wong et al., 2003). Rephrasing item statements as questions can improve cross-cultural applicability of scales with mixed items (Wong et al., 2003).

Data need to be collected that not only relate to the focus of the research but also represent potential confounding variables. For example, in examining the impact of alcohol marketing on adolescent drinking, data not only need to be collected about adolescents' awareness of alcohol marketing and their drinking behavior and attitudes but also should include a range of control variables such as gender, socio-economic group,

ethnicity, religion, parents', siblings' and peers' drinking behavior and attitudes (see Gordon et al., 2011). Lister et al. (2008: 53) noted that 'achieving and sustaining positive behaviors are the result of complex interactions among individuals, families, peer groups and society'.

Consideration also needs to be given to the type of variables data will represent: whether they are proximal variables (conceptually close), distal variables (conceptually distant) or moderator variables (variables that affect the relationship between the dependent and an independent variable). For example, the ITC conceptual model represents the effects of tobacco control policy as a path leading to activities in the tobacco industry, leading to proximal variables (including consumer awareness of each marketing channel), leading to distal variables (e.g. brand awareness and familiarity), and finally leading to tobacco use behaviors (such as smoking or quitting), while also recognizing moderator variables (e.g. gender, age and education) (MacKintosh et al., 2008).

Measurement criteria

Measures need to meet various criteria, as will now be briefly reviewed:

Validity – ensuring that what is measured actually represents what is intended – is a key issue in quantitative research. Without it, there can be no confidence in the research findings. There are various types of validity.

Internal validity refers to whether an experimental manipulation really had an effect. In other words, did A cause B? This is largely a function of the research design used.

External validity refers to whether relationships found in an experiment can be generalized to other populations. For example, if an experiment found that 13-year-old Welsh children's attitudes toward alcohol were influenced by alcohol marketing, external validity is whether the results could be generalized to 13-year-old English children.

Concurrent or predictive validity are similar and refer to the success with which a measure diagnoses (concurrent validity) or predicts (predictive validity) some outcome of interest. The difference between them is the time interval involved in relating a measure to an outcome or criterion variable. An alternative term that is sometimes used is criterion-related validity, because it assesses a measure in relation to a criterion or dependent variable.

Face validity is the plausibility of a measure: whether it looks as though it does what it says on the label. It is important for harmonious researcher–participant relations that research participants perceive that the data they are asked to provide appear relevant to the purpose of the research (Anastasi and Urbina, 1997).

Construct validity is an assessment of the theoretical underpinnings of a construct. It is the extent to which a measure actually measures a theoretical construct. Factor analysis is a powerful technique for examining construct validity, because it enables the underlying dimensions and groups of items to be identified. Confirmatory factor analysis allows hypothesized dimensions of a construct to be tested. Construct validity may be demonstrated by convergent and discriminant validation. *Convergent validity* is an assessment of a measure's correlation with other measures with which, theoretically, it should correlate. *Discriminant validity* is an assessment of a measure's ability to discriminate a construct from other constructs with which, theoretically, it should not correlate.

Content validity is the extent to which an instrument measures the properties of a concept or construct. It is the adequacy of the coverage of a concept or construct. Content validity is judged through consideration of the items used to measure a concept or construct by a panel of experts.

Reliability refers to the consistency or stability of data. It is the likelihood of getting the same answer(s) if you asked the same question(s) again. It may also be considered the precision of a measure: the extent to which errors in measurement are absent (Kerlinger, 1992). Where factual information is sought, reliability may be increased by asking the same thing in different ways. However, where attitudes are sought, differences in wording can change the question, so as well as trying to ensure that questions are unambiguous, a larger number of questions or sets of items are preferred to even out any bias from the ways in which individual questions or items are worded. It is for this reason that single items should not be used to assess attitudes (Oppenheim, 1992).

TIMING ISSUES IN RESEARCH DESIGN (THE 'WHEN?')

Consideration should also be given to when data would be best collected, in the light of the research questions. If the research is an experiment or an evaluation of a social marketing campaign, then pre- and post-intervention measures may need to be taken. Data from control samples may also need to be collected. For a detailed discussion of experimental designs, see Kerlinger (1992: 302–318).

However, practical limitations, such as the cost, time and pragmatic issues (e.g. re-contacting respondents) may deter the use of repeated measures and longitudinal designs. Hence, cross-sectional designs are more commonly used than longitudinal ones in social marketing research, despite the superior ability of longitudinal studies to establish cause and effect rather than just associations between variables. An example of a cross-sectional design is a questionnaire study that compared young adults' attitudes toward healthy eating, based on whether they lived independently or at home (Piggford et al., 2008). An example of a longitudinal design is a study of exposure to televised alcohol advertisements and subsequent adolescent alcohol use (Stacy et al., 2004). Cross-sectional designs instead often ask about respondents' intentions regarding their future behavior and try to predict factors that might influence this. However, no matter how sincere people's intentions might be, they can be poor predictors of their actual future behavior. Furthermore, the long-term effects of behavioral choices on health may not be apparent until years after a social marketing intervention (Lister et al., 2008).

The timing of research can be crucial. The evaluation of an intervention or social marketing campaign needs to be timed appropriately to minimize the effects of memory deterioration and contamination by other factors such as maturation, while at the same time providing sufficient time for any intervention to take effect. Potential seasonal variation should also be taken into account. For example, alcohol consumption is likely to be higher during the Christmas holiday season than at some other times of year. The variation and typicality of behavior at different temporal points needs to be taken into account when scheduling data collection. Care should also be taken to ensure that if data are collected from different samples, they are comparable in terms of when the data are collected, otherwise differences in the data may be affected by temporal variation. Similarly, if questions are re-administered at different points in time, altering the questions in any way between administrations may affect their validity for statistical comparison.

ETHICAL CONSIDERATIONS

Researchers should collect only data for which they have sound reasons for examining and known uses to which they will be put. For ethical, data protection and pragmatic reasons, unnecessary and unjustified questions should not be asked of participants; questions should not intrude needlessly, nor involve the collection and storage of gratuitous personal information nor waste respondents' time. All of the aforementioned factors will deter individuals from participating and agreeing to take part in any follow-up or subsequent waves of research.

DATA ANALYSIS AND INTERPRETATION (THE 'SO WHAT?')

All of the above decisions about the quantitative research will affect the types of analyses that can be performed on the data and the conclusions that can be drawn. This is why it is vital that the decisions are made in conjunction with the planned analyses at the outset. Prior to analysis, data coding and inputting need to be checked thoroughly to ensure that the data have been recorded correctly and to avoid generating spurious findings during analysis.

There are three broad categories of data analysis that can be performed: *univariate* (on one variable), *bivariate* (on two variables) and *multivariate* (on many variables). Owing to the complexity of most social marketing research, multivariate is likely to be of most use in testing hypotheses while controlling for a variety of other variables. However, univariate and bivariate analyses can help to inform multivariate analysis through preliminary analysis of basic relationships within and between variables. Quantitative methods frequently elicit anxiety in people. Help is at hand though, as there are a number of excellent textbooks designed to take

the fear out of statistical techniques (see, e.g., Field, 2009; Hair et al., 2007; and for univariate and bivariate analyses, see Diamantopoulos and Schlegelmilch, 1997).

The choice of statistical tests will depend on the number and nature of the dependent variable(s) (the variable being looked at to see how it changes or differs between groups of respondents) and independent variables (the variables that affect the change or difference in the dependent variable) and on the sample size (if there are too few cases or observations for a category or level of a variable to be able to include it in an analysis). Table 15.1 provides a categorization of bivariate analyses that may be performed and Table 15.2 shows some of the multivariate analyses available. Please note, however, that the latter is not an exhaustive list.

Social marketing research typically employs a range of statistical techniques, as the following examples from the field of tobacco control policy evaluation show. The effects of the 2003 advertising/promotion ban in the UK on awareness of tobacco marketing (based on data from the ITC Four Country Survey) were examined using a mixture of bivariate and multivariate techniques (see Harris et al., 2006). The general linear model (GLM) repeated measures procedure (for repeated measures MANOVA in SPSS) was used to test whether there were any significant differences between countries before and after the advertising/promotion ban in the number of channels through which respondents noticed tobacco marketing. The McNemar non-parametric test of paired samples was used to test whether post-ban

Table 15.1 Types of bivariate data analysis

Focus of comparison	Number of groups/measures	Type of data	Statistical analysis
Independent groups	2 groups	Nominal	Two-sample chi-square test
		Ordinal	Mann–Whitney U test
		Interval or ratio	Two-sample t test
	3+ measures	Nominal	k-Sample chi-square test
		Ordinal	Kruskal–Wallis one-way ANOVA
		Interval or ratio	One-way analysis of variance (ANOVA)
Repeated measures	2 measures	Nominal	McNemar test
		Ordinal	Paired-samples sign test
		Interval or ratio	Paired-samples t test
	3+ measures	Nominal	Cochran's Q test
		Ordinal	Friedman's two-way ANOVA
		Interval or ratio	t_r-test for all pairs

Adapted from Diamantopoulos and Schlegelmilch (1997, p. 174), with permission from Cengage Learning EMEA Ltd.

Table 15.2 Types of multivariate data analysis

Number of dependent variables (DVs)	Type of DV(s)	Type of independent variable(s) (IVs)	Cluster?	Analysis
	No DVs/IVs		Cases	Cluster analysis
			Variables	Factor analysis (FA)/principal components analysis (PCA)
1 DV	Nominal or ordinal	Nominal or ordinal	–	Log linear analysis
		Nominal, ordinal, interval or ratio	–	Logistic regression
		Interval or ratio		Discriminant function analysis (DFA)
	Interval or ratio	Nominal, ordinal, interval or ratio	–	Multiple regression
Multiple DVs	Interval or ratio	Nominal or ordinal	–	Multivariate analysis of variance (MANOVA)
		Interval or ratio	–	Canonical correlation
Multiple relationships between dependent and independent variables			–	Structural equation modeling (SEM)

awareness of specific channels differed significantly from pre-ban awareness of the channels. Logistic regression was used to test whether the change in awareness of the banned tobacco marketing channels after the ban (coded dichotomously as 'decreased awareness' or 'no change in awareness/increased awareness from not aware to being aware') varied by country, controlling for a range of potentially confounding variables (sex, age, education, ethnicity, income, number of cigarettes smoked per day and whether participants had ever tried quitting). In the latter analysis, a contrast was used to test the change in awareness in the UK against the average of the other three countries. The findings indicated that, after the UK ban, there was a significant decline in tobacco promotion awareness, greater declines in awareness in the newly banned channels and a greater change in awareness in the UK compared with the other three countries.

An example of the use of structural equation modeling (SEM) to test multiple relationships between independent and dependent variables is provided by the Youth Tobacco Policy Study (Brown and Moodie, 2009). SEM was used to test the direct and indirect effects of tobacco advertising and promotion on adolescents' smoking intentions at each of three waves of cross-sectional data, with the indirect effects mediated through normative influences (perceived prevalence, perceived approval, perceived benefit and perceived prevalence by benefit). Waves of data from prior to the UK's Tobacco Advertising and Promotion Act, mid-ban and post-ban were used to examine nor-

mative pathways between adolescents' awareness of tobacco marketing and their smoking intentions. The findings indicated that adolescents' smoking intentions could be significantly decreased by policy measures such as the UK ban on tobacco advertising and promotion, by reducing the normative influence and social acceptability of smoking.

CONCLUSION

This chapter has outlined some of the issues in measurement in social marketing and provides a starting point for thinking about suitable measures in quantitative methods. A broad approach was adopted to enable measurement issues to be related to a wide array of social marketing application areas. Other sources may be consulted for detailed consideration of measures in specific areas (see, e.g., MacKintosh et al., 2008, on measures to assess the effectiveness of restrictions on tobacco marketing communications). However, addressing the important points highlighted in this chapter during the design of social marketing research or evaluation will help quantitative methods to be used to maximum effect.

KEY WORDS: Quantitative methods; measurement issues; research design; types of data; validity; data collection; sampling; question design; data analysis; ethical issues.

Key insights

- Quantitative methods offer valuable means of building an evidence base to guide social marketing interventions and to help bring about policy changes.
- Measurement issues need to be considered at all stages of the research or evaluation process and their interrelatedness acknowledged.
- Careful attention should be given to the measurement levels of the data that are collected to ensure that the levels are appropriate for what is being measured and to enable appropriate statistical techniques to be used later to analyze the resulting data.
- Thought should also be given to the type of variables data will represent within a conceptual model.
- As with any approach, quantitative methods have their strengths and weaknesses.
- Likewise, the limitations on data imposed by the nature of much social marketing need to be recognized.

REFERENCES

Anastasi, A. and Urbina, S. (1997) *Psychological Testing*, 7th edn. Upper Saddle River, NJ: Prentice-Hall.

Brown, A. and Moodie, C. (2009) 'The influence of tobacco marketing on adolescent smoking intentions via normative beliefs', *Health Education Research*, 24(4): 721–733.

Buller, D.B., Woodall, W.G., Zimmerman, D.E., et al. (2008) 'Randomized trial on the 5 a Day, the Rio Grande Way website, a web-based program to improve fruit and vegetable consumption in rural communities', *Journal of Health Consumption*, 13(3): 230–249.

Churchill, G.A. (1995) *Marketing Research: Methodological Foundations*, 6th edn. Fort Worth, TX: Dryden Press.

Diamantopoulos, A. and Schlegelmilch, B.B. (1997) *Taking the Fear out of Data Analysis. A Step-by-Step Approach.* London: Dryden Press.

Efron, B. and Tibshirani, R.J. (1993) *An Introduction to the Bootstrap.* New York: Chapman and Hall.

Ekholm, O., Hesse, U., Davidsen, M. and Kjøller, M. (2009) 'The study design and characteristics of the Danish national health interview survey', *Scandinavian Journal of Public Health*, 37(7): 758–765.

Ellickson, P.L., Collins, R.L., Hambarsoomians, K. and McCaffrey, D.F. (2005) 'Does alcohol advertising promote adolescent drinking? Results from a longitudinal assessment', *Addiction*, 100: 235–256.

Evans, D.J., Howe, D., Maguire, A. and Rugg-Gunn, A.J. (1999) 'Development and evaluation of a sugar-free medicines campaign in North East England: analysis of findings from questionnaires', *Community Dental Health*, 16: 131–137.

Falthzik, A.M. and Jolson, M.A. (1974) 'Statement polarity in attitude statements', *Journal of Marketing Research*, 11(February): 102–105.

Field, A. (2009) *Discovering Statistics Using SPSS*, 3rd edn. London: Sage Publications.

Flocks, J., Clarke, L., Albrecht, S., Bryant, C., Monaghan, P. and Baker, H. (2001) 'Implementing a community-based social marketing project to improve agricultural worker health', *Environmental Health Perspectives*, 109(Suppl 3), June: 461–468.

Gordon, R., Harris, F.J., MacKintosh, A.M. and Moodie, C. (2011) 'Assessing the cumulative impact of alcohol marketing on young people's drinking: cross sectional data findings', *Addiction Research and Theory*, 19(1): 66–75.

Grant, I.C., Hassan, L.M., Hastings, G.B., MacKintosh, A.M. and Eadie, D. (2008) 'The influence of branding on adolescent smoking behaviour: Exploring the mediating role of image and attitudes', *International Journal of Nonprofit and Voluntary Sector Marketing*, 13(3): 275–285.

Hair, J.F., Black, B., Babin, B., Anderson, R.E. and Tatham, R.L. (2007) *Multivariate Data Analysis*, 6th edn. Upper Saddle River, NJ: Prentice-Hall.

Harris, F.J., MacKintosh, A.M., Anderson, S., et al. (2006) 'Effects of the 2003 advertising/promotion ban in the United Kingdom on awareness of tobacco marketing: Findings from the International Tobacco Control (ITC) Four Country Survey', *Tobacco Control*, 15(Suppl III): iii26–iii33.

Hastings, G., Anderson, S., Cooke, E. and Gordon, R. (2005) 'Alcohol marketing and young people's drinking: A review of the research', *Journal of Public Health Policy*, 26(3): 296–311.

Hughs, K., MacKintosh, A.M., Hastings, G., Wheeler, C. and Watson, J. (1997) 'Young people, alcohol, and designer drinks: Quantitative and qualitative study', *British Medical Journal*, 314 (7078) (8 February): 414–418.

Kerlinger, F.N. (1973) *Foundations of Behavioral Research*, 2nd edn. Tokyo: Holt, Rhinehart and Winston.

Kerlinger, F.N. (1992) *Foundations of Behavioral Research*, 3rd edn. Fort Worth, TX: Harcourt Brace College Publishers.

Kish, L. (1995) *Survey Sampling* (Wiley Classics Library). New York: Wiley.

Li, L., Yong, H.-H., Borland, R., et al. (2009) 'Reported awareness of tobacco advertising and promotion in China compared to Thailand, Australia and the USA', *Tobacco Control*, 18: 222–227.

Lister, G., McVey, D., French, J., Blair Stevens, C. and Merritt, R. (2008) 'Measuring the societal impact of behaviour choices', *Social Marketing Quarterly*, 14: 51–62.

Lohr, S.L. (1999) *Sampling: Design and Analysis.* Pacific Grove, CA: Duxbury Press.

Lynn, P. and Lievesley, D. (1992) *Drawing General Population Samples in Great Britain.* National Centre for Social Research.

MacKintosh, A.M., Harris, F.J. and Hastings, G. (2008) 'Measuring the effectiveness of tobacco marketing restrictions', in R. Borland, M. Cummings and C. Dresler (eds), *IARC Handbook on Tobacco Control* (second) (12th handbook in the IARC Handbooks of Cancer Prevention series).

Moodie, C., MacKintosh, A.M., Brown, A. and Hastings, G.B. (2008) 'Tobacco marketing awareness on youth smoking susceptibility and perceived prevalence before and after an advertising ban', *European Journal of Public Health*, 18(5): 484–490.

Oppenheim, A.N. (1992) *Questionnaire Design, Interviewing and Attitude Measurement*. London: Continuum.

Piggford, S., Raciti, M., Harker, D. and Harker, M. (2008) 'The influence of residence on young adult attitudes toward healthy eating', *Social Marketing Quarterly*, 14(2): 33–49.

Stacy A.W., Zogg, J.B., Unger, J.B. and Dent, C.W. (2004) 'Exposure to televised alcohol ads and subsequent adolescent alcohol use', *American Journal of Health Behaviour*, 28(6): 498–509.

Stead, M., Hastings, G.B. and Eadie, D. (2002) 'The challenge of evaluating complex interventions: A framework for evaluating media advocacy', *Health Education Research Theory and Practice*, 17(3): 351–364.

Thompson, M.E., Fong, G.T., Hammond, D., et al. (2006) 'Methods of the International Tobacco Control (ITC) Four Country Survey', *Tobacco Control*, 15(Suppl III): iii12–iii18.

Whittingham, J., Ruiter, R.A.C., Zimbile, F. and Kok, G. (2008) 'Experimental pretesting of public health campaign: A case study', *Journal of Health Communication*, 13(3): 216–229.

Wong, N.Y., Rindfleisch, A. and Burroughs, J.E. (2003) 'Do reverse-worded items confound measures in cross-cultural research? The case of the Material Values Scale', *Journal of Consumer Research*, 30: 72–91.

Dancing with the Devil

16. CRITICAL MARKETING: APPLICATIONS – J. HOEK

The author applies critical marketing theory to an analysis of the commercial marketing of tobacco, alcohol and energy-dense, nutritionally poor foods; all sectors with '*business interests that prosper when public health deteriorates*'. She highlights the importance of upstream social marketing to support downstream initiatives. In other words, the importance of assessing what factors are interfering with social marketing communications and how to create an environment within which social marketing and education initiatives will flourish. Hoek describes factors such as those tactics employed by these three commercial marketing sectors, including creating industry and interest groups, promoting self-regulation of their industry, using industry-funded 'experts', lobbying politicians and applying economic pressures, infiltrating policy groups and castigating academics and research findings that are contrary to their interests. All are factors that would interfere with individuals' attitudes and behavior changes.

17. SOCIAL MARKETING'S RESPONSE TO THE ALCOHOL PROBLEM: WHO'S CONDUCTING THE ORCHESTRA? – S.C. JONES

Using the analogy of an orchestra, Jones demonstrates the potential role the three social marketing 'instruments' of downstream social marketing,

critical marketing and up-stream social marketing, when harmonized together, can have on decreasing the health and social burdens excessive alcohol consumption has on our society. She evaluates their individual strengths and weaknesses using real-world examples and discusses the need to combine the three instruments. The debate over whether social marketers should work with the alcohol industry is summarized and Jones presents her recommendations for social marketers to focus on, highlighting, for example, that public support for the most effective strategies to reduce alcohol-related harm is decreasing across many countries at the same time as alcohol-related harms are increasing.

18. FROM SOCIAL MARKETING TO CORPORATE SOCIAL MARKETING – CHANGING CONSUMPTION HABITS AS THE NEW FRONTIER OF CORPORATE SOCIAL RESPONSIBILITY– G. PALAZZO

Palazzo's essay asserts that advocates of social marketing and advocates of corporate social responsibility (CSR) '*can no longer afford to ignore each other*' within the current global climate. He introduces the reader to the concept of 'corporate social marketing', a 'treaty' that acknowledges the shared interests and common goals that have developed independently. The author acknowledges that, for legitimate reasons, social marketers have traditionally viewed corporations and their marketing activities as part of the problem rather than as part of the solution. As the consumer has become a vital element of CSR, and effective CSR activities will depend on a corporation's ability to get consumers' support, Palazzo explores the potential of social marketing to deliver the foundation for this broader understanding of CSR.

19. ETHICAL CHALLENGES IN COMMERCIAL SOCIAL MARKETING – T.B. ANKER AND K. KAPPEL

In their chapter, Anker and Kappel discuss the relatively new and controversial subject of 'commercial social marketing'. Commercial social marketing refers to programmes sponsored by for-profit corporations that meet six essential social marketing criteria: socially beneficial behavior change objectives; use of marketing research to gain insights to consumers' wants, needs, experiences and values; segmentation and targeting; employment of the full marketing mix based on the 4Ps; exchange of benefits for behavior change and use of strategies to outsmart competing sources. They offer two distinctive case studies to reinforce their argument: the 'Dove Campaign for Real Beauty', which attempts to redefine societal definitions of female beauty; and Novo Nordisk's workplace health program for its own employees. Whether or not you accept the position that commercial campaigns qualify as social marketing, their analysis of the ethical challenges associated with social marketing is thought-provoking and relevant for social marketers working in the public or private sector.

20. INTERNAL SOCIAL MARKETING: LESSONS FROM THE FIELD OF SERVICES MARKETING – A.M. SMITH

Anne M. Smith's chapter introduces social marketers to the concept and merits of internal marketing (IM), a services marketing approach which is used to achieve attitudinal and behavioral change within organisations. She demonstrates its particular relevance to social marketing programs that rely on services (especially health services) as co-producers of behavioral change. The quality of the service and the actions of the service's employees (internal customers) has an impact on the service's consumers' (external customers') behavior. Without addressing the activities, relationships and satisfaction of the internal customers, gaps in an organisation's processes can ultimately result in poor service, customer dissatisfaction and, finally, negative behaviors from the external customers. Smith describes the IM prerequisites for providing high-quality internal and external services, and the significant research agenda made available by the concept.

16

Critical Marketing: Applications

Janet Hoek

INTRODUCTION

Marvin Goldberg (1995) asked whether social marketers were 'fiddling while Rome burned' and argued that researchers who focused on individual behaviour change risked overlooking structural and environmental factors that facilitate and promote risk behaviours, and militate against social marketing messages. Goldberg's challenge behoves us to consider more closely the context in which social and health behaviours occurs, the voices to which consumers may attend and the relative influence these may exert on their behaviour.

Lazer and Kelley (1973) had earlier noted the need to critically evaluate commercial marketing when they argued: 'Social marketing is ... also concerned with analysis of the social consequence of marketing policies, decisions and activities' (1973: ix). Hastings and Saren (2003) extended this reasoning and proposed that: 'Social marketing... can not only help define problems by examining marketing dispassionately and realistically, but, crucially, map out solutions' (2003: 307). Put simply, social marketers' role includes analysing the substance, style and effects of commercial marketing, and critically evaluating how these contribute to wider societal problems.

For more than three decades, critical social marketing researchers have taken up these challenges and explored how commercial marketing shapes and reinforces consumers' behaviour, and complicates communication of social marketing messages. For example, promotions encouraging consumers to eat foods high in fat, salt and sugar,

and to do so more frequently, and to 'upsize' when offered the opportunity, all run counter to 'healthy eating' messages. Programmes promoting greater consumption of fruit and vegetables, for example, aim to shift consumption away from energy-dense and nutrient-poor (EDNP) foods, but may not resonate with consumers, who are offered discounts and other incentives to continue purchasing EDNP products. For social marketers, commercial marketers represent competition, since commercial marketing often runs directly counter to social marketers' objectives. The ongoing tension between social and commercial marketing complicates health and social initiatives, particularly where the relationship between commercial marketing and adverse health outcomes is unambiguous. Weis and Arnesen (2007: 81) described this relationship as '*the unhealthy propinquity between industry and infirmity*', and called for greater analysis of business interests that prosper when public health deteriorates.

This chapter responds to Weis and Arnesen; it critically evaluates the commercial marketing of tobacco, alcohol and EDNP foods, and explores the '*potentially malevolent side*' of marketing to which Hastings and Saren (2003: 314) referred. Such an analysis is necessarily historical, since evaluating the past provides insights into problems of the present and, critically, how these might be addressed. Because commercial marketing is particularly successful when it creates environments conducive to behaviour change, this chapter explores upstream social marketing in detail, with special attention to how policy may modify environments and promote behaviour change. Tobacco and alcohol marketing provide salient examples of the harms that may result from commercial marketing and illustrate why upstream social marketing may be necessary to support downstream initiatives. Food marketing, provocatively described as a modern-day tobacco, provides a current focus for considering further the role and timing of upstream activities (Chopra and Darnton-Hill, 2004).

Whereas this chapter examines upstream interventions, such as policy and regulation, that change consumers' and marketers' environments, these changes will only promote behaviour change if they elicit public support and cooperation. There is, therefore, a symbiotic relationship between upstream and downstream social marketing that means neither will function as effectively alone. Exploring marketing's more malevolent side thus provides a backdrop against which both upstream and downstream relationships can be examined.

TOBACCO MARKETING – CREATING THE DREAM

Tobacco marketing illustrates the movement from a largely uncritical and unfettered environment to one where upstream and downstream activities now work jointly to achieve tobacco-free objectives (Smokefree Coalition, 2009). From the time they first emerged, tobacco advertisements have used aspirational imagery to promote smoking as a glamorous activity that confers social and psychological benefits on tobacco users. Through a process of respondent conditioning, cigarette brands came to possess psychological and emotional attributes and evolved into what Pollay (1990: 10) described as a 'badge' products. He suggested these functioned in two ways:

[1] When a user displays a badge product, this is witnessed by others, providing a living testimonial endorsement of the user on behalf of that brand and product. [2] The use of a badge product associates the user with the brand image, giving the user some of the identity and personality of the brand image.

This reflexivity highlights the powerful emotional attachment smokers have to *their* brand and provides insights into the complex relationships created when products are both defined by and defining of their users.

Tobacco's status as a badge product suggests smokers use cigarette brands to help them move from their actual self to their desired self (Hastings and MacFadyen, 1998). Others expanded on this theme by suggesting that the self-definition and expression facilitated by cigarette brands was apparent in 'fundamental differences in the ways in which different smokers approach and choose between cigarette brands' (Carter, 2003: iii84). These differences reflected associations between brands and imagery that appeal to consumers' '*developmental needs*' and '*individual personalities*' (Arnett and Terhanian, 1998: 133). The relationship between the images evoked by tobacco brands and the emotional benefits consumers seek is now sufficiently well-documented and consistent to support a causal link between tobacco marketing and nicotine addiction. Pierce et al. (1991: 3158) summed up this work when they concluded: 'Our results suggest that tobacco advertising is causally related to young people becoming addicted to cigarettes...'.

Tobacco marketing has heightened brands' salience, provided multiple stimuli that prompted and rewarded purchase and simplified consumers' ability to locate brands by pairing them with distinctive colours and images. Associating tobacco brands with images that appeared incompatible with fatal diseases has reassured smokers and militated against cessation. The ubiquity of tobacco marketing, compounded by the systematic questioning of emerging medical evidence, has transformed cigarettes into what Pollay (2007: 274) described as a '*cultural commonplace*'.

TOBACCO MARKETING – CREATING THE CONTROVERSY

Since the mid-20th century, the health consequences of smoking have become more widely understood among medical communities, though the public's understanding of tobacco-related harms is more debatable. The tobacco litigation of the 1990s gave researchers unprecedented access to industry documents and enabled them to explore how tobacco companies created uncertainty over the risks posed by smoking. For example, comparison of assertions made in the 'Frank Statement' with research evidence reveals stark differences between what industry members knew and what they disclosed. Statements such as: '*We believe the products we make are not injurious to health*' stand in striking contradiction to tobacco executives' knowledge of the causal association between smoking and lung cancer (Doll and Hill, 1950).

Daynard (1991) analysed other disputed areas, including the effects of second-hand smoke and the addictiveness of nicotine, and concluded that, even by the 1990s, tobacco companies still argued there was a lack of causal evidence linking smoking with adverse health outcomes. The tobacco industry's practice of questioning medical evidence created considerable confusion among the public, and helped maintain smokers' behaviour. Michaels and Monforton (2005) described the industry's behaviour as 'manufactured uncertainty', which they suggested was a deliberate strategy to obfuscate the compelling medical evidence linking smoking to fatal diseases. They argued this strategy stalled regulatory action and allowed the tobacco industry to continue marketing its products to a public that, ironically, looked to them for information and reassurance. As Mahood (2003) noted:

> ..., for a smoker who is physiologically unable to refrain from smoking his or her next cigarette, there is a strong tendency to discount information about health risks – and to fall for pseudo-arguments typically provided by the tobacco industry. ('It hasn't been proven that smoking causes cancer' and 'Tobacco is addictive in the sense that drinking soda pop is addictive, etc.').

Smokers confronted with reassurance from tobacco manufacturers, on the one hand, and glamorous and aspirational imagery, on the other, had no reason to doubt either. Given that peer-reviewed medical evidence was questioned and publically described as 'junk science', smokers had little reason to worry about the long-term effects of their addiction. Industry-funded 'experts' were taken to hostile jurisdictions where they undermined scientific evidence, questioned health education and social marketing initiatives, and directly challenged regulatory proposals. These strategies created doubt among policymakers and the public, detracted from cessation campaigns, reduced support for public health interventions and maintained liberal operating environments (Parascandola, 2004).

Industry documents also reveal that, while the industry was reassuring existing smokers, it was attempting to attract new recruits, particularly young people, who offer the greatest profit potential. These actions ran counter to claims that tobacco advertising promoted brand switching among adult smokers, which its proponents argued was its only role in a mature market (Hastings and Aitken, 1995). Instead, the tobacco market was clearly partitioned; specific sub-markets included young people, women and indigenous groups, all of which represented considerable growth potential and were the targets of carefully planned marketing campaigns (Albright et al., 1988; Basil et al., 1991; King et al., 1998; Cummings et al., 2002). For example, efforts to stimulate experimentation among young people included introducing youth-oriented brands, such as KOOL and Camel No. 9, which have been promoted via

music events, in fashion magazines and using social media that have high reach among young people (Freeman and Chapman, 2009).

Nor was marketing aimed simply at age groups likely to experiment; the high recall of tobacco cartoon characters among very young children led Fischer et al. (1991: 3148) to conclude: 'R J Reynolds Tobacco Company is as effective as The Disney Channel in reaching 6 year-old children'. Cartoon characters such as 'Joe Camel', which DiFranza et al. (1991) suggested was modelled on James Bond, created a 'smooth' persona who rode motorcycles and attracted desirable women, and who epitomised the industry's strategy of establishing brands as conduits to desirable attributes.

TOBACCO MARKETING – CREATING THE OVERSEERS

On the one hand, the tobacco industry questioned well-designed and independent scientific research and developed sophisticated campaigns to appeal to groups it claimed not to target; on the other hand, it pre-empted criticisms by establishing self-regulatory groups to oversee marketing practices, a move that protected the status quo and enabled tobacco marketing to continue in largely unrestricted environments. Unless governments had senior members with a particular interest in tobacco control, or had reached bipartisan political agreements, self-regulatory arrangements were left undisturbed (Cunningham, 1996).

Difficulties in containing the *'malevolent'* effects of tobacco marketing were compounded by the powerful economic pressures the tobacco industry brought to bear on governments. Warner (2000: 78) analysed economic myths advanced by the tobacco industry, including claims that:

> Without the cultivation of tobacco, manufacture of tobacco products, and distribution and sale of products, a country's economy will suffer devastating economic consequences. Jobs will be lost, incomes will fall, tax revenues will plummet, and trade surpluses will veer dangerously in the direction of deficits.

Warner's systematic deconstruction of economic arguments highlights how the tobacco industry successfully reframed a public health argument as an economic debate that politicians were more likely to view sympathetically.

The net effect of these carefully organised strategies meant it was not until the latter part of the 20th century that progressive governments began rejecting self-regulatory arrangements and using upstream approaches to restrict tobacco marketing. Initial measures typically limited advertising and promotion activities, and, in some cases, restricted supply (e.g. by stipulating that tobacco products could not be sold to individuals below a specific age) (Thomson and Wilson, 2003).

However, countries proposing or introducing these restrictions faced concerted opposition from the tobacco industry, which established interest groups that complemented the work their industry associations did to oppose regulation, lobby politicians and weaken tobacco control efforts. Evoking the 'legal to sell, legal to promote' claim, the industry employed 'slippery slope' arguments to suggest that restrictions on the sale or marketing of tobacco would be an undesirable extension of government's powers and a precursor to interventions in other areas. The industry claimed circumscribing commercial speech would inevitably reduce self-autonomy and freedom, including individuals' ability to make choices for themselves (Chapman, 1996; Saloojee and Dagli, 2000; Connolly, 2002).

The difficult path upstream social marketers faced has been well-documented (Pollay, 2004). Yet despite legal challenges, vociferous opposition from industry groups and high-level lobbying, policy measures have now successfully restricted tobacco marketing in many jurisdictions. These have brought about environmental change that has directly stimulated reductions in smoking prevalence (Wyckham, 1997; Saffer and Chaloupka, 2000), and created conditions where downstream initiatives may elicit stronger responses.

TOBACCO MARKETING – LOCATING RESPONSIBILITY

Before downstream campaigns to promote cessation and deter initiation could take effect, smokers suffered the harmful consequences of their addiction. Because the tobacco industry had impeded efforts to increase awareness of the serious and widespread risks smokers faced, many who may have quit smoking continued, and subsequently contracted serious and often fatal diseases. Imbalances between what tobacco companies knew and disclosed gave rise to product liability litigation, where smokers attempted to hold the tobacco industry accountable for the damage its products had caused. Plaintiffs argued the industry had not provided unambiguous warnings about the risks of smoking (Borland, 1997; Wakefield et al., 2003), and claimed its marketing made smoking appear glamorous, and created brand imagery

that overwhelmed any risk information that might have been available (Pollay and Dewhirst, 2002). The tobacco industry responded by arguing that as smoking's risks were widely known, smokers could have quit, had they wished to avoid these (British American Tobacco, 2006).

Judges have accepted arguments that individuals were, or ought to have been, aware of the dangers inherent in smoking and have largely discounted the effects of widespread tobacco marketing and manufactured uncertainty. However, the release of internal industry documents made available as part of the US Master Settlements, revealed the industry's detailed knowledge of smoking's adverse effects and its duplicity in continuing to market these products and oppose policy initiatives (Carter and Chapman, 2003; Chapman and Carter, 2003). This discrepancy between the industry's public stance and private knowledge has led to further litigation that has focused on the plaintiff's ability to make informed choices when material information was obfuscated or hidden (Parmet and Daynard, 2000).

Legal argument thus shifted from causality to informed consent and associated concepts, such as 'adequate information'. Chapman and Liberman suggested:

> Relevant questions [to be considered when assessing whether adequate information has been provided] include whether warnings bring clearly and emphatically to the mind of a consumer the risks associated with use; whether they refer to specific risks; and whether they are sufficiently clear or explicit' (2005: 11).

Putting to one side the effect ongoing tobacco marketing and public relations had on smokers' propensity to accept and act on medical warnings, on-pack warnings failed to satisfy these criteria. First, they were unlikely to have attracted smokers' attention, as they were printed in small font on the sides of packages; the warnings thus had neither high salience nor strong impact. Second, they were conditional and non-specific, which limited their likely influence to reinforcing impressions that the risks posed by smoking were uncertain or unknown.

Chapman and Liberman (2005) argued that the greater the risk faced by consumers, and the higher the probability this would eventuate, the greater the responsibility to ensure consumers knew the potential consequences of their actions. These arguments imply that tobacco companies had a moral and legal responsibility to ensure smokers were aware of the risks they faced. However, judgements from the UK (McTear) and New Zealand (Pou) either overlooked or failed to understand the concept of 'adequate information'

(Eames, 2002; Smith, 2005; Lang, 2006) and instead accepted the 'individual responsibility' myth without understanding how nicotine addiction compromised smokers' ability to act freely (Chapman, 2002).

TOBACCO MARKETING – TURNING THE TIDE?

Given the difficulty of constraining the tobacco industry's marketing activities and holding companies accountable for the effects of their actions, current strategies include three approaches: widespread use of social marketing campaigns to support, promote and maintain smokefree behaviours; continuation of demand-side regulation and the development of a new supply-side model.

Social marketing campaigns have recognised that tobacco industry's own strategies could promote smokefree behaviour and have employed media now used by tobacco companies, but to convey health messages (Mahood, 1999; Hoek, 2004). For example, packaging has become a medium that provides health information, reduces the attractiveness of brand imagery and supports campaigns promoting cessation. Although not unchallenged by tobacco companies, which argued that graphic health warnings trespassed on their intellectual property (Carter and Chapman, 2003; Chapman and Carter, 2003), these measures illustrate how social marketers have used the industry's own tools to promote positive behaviour (Hammond et al., 2006) and reclaim what Hastings (2007) described as 'the best tunes'.

Specifically, social marketers have used the more supportive regulatory environment to promote smokefree behaviours as desirable and appropriate, develop new social norms that are not compatible with smoking and create a climate that is more receptive to additional regulatory proposals (Chapman and Liberman, 2005; Chapman and Freeman, 2008). Campaigns range from those making functional offers, such as subsidised nicotine replacement treatments, to more complex exchanges that pair aspirational values with smokefree norms (Newcombe et al. 2009). The visibility of smokefree campaigns reflects the environment created by upstream measures.

The second approach continues the systematic regulatory programme already underway to reduce demand for tobacco products by promoting cessation and deterring initiation. New initiatives have included bans on tobacco retail displays in several jurisdictions (Dewhirst, 2004; Harper, 2006), and increasing momentum for plain packaging, which would remove brand imagery and replace this

with larger graphic health warnings (Freeman et al., 2008). The final approach promotes a more radical solution and focuses less on reducing demand than it does on altering and controlling supply. New 'end-game' initiatives would put in place a public health agency to manage all aspects of tobacco supply; retailers would require licences, tobacco would become a controlled drug and the overriding commercial motive that fuels the tobacco industry's search for new recruits would be removed (Edwards, 2009).

That such 'radical' steps are being taken to reduce smoking prevalence highlights the extraordinary effectiveness of the tobacco industry's marketing strategies. From their members' development and use of profoundly evocative and aspirational imagery, to their ability to harness and exploit emerging media, the tobacco industry demonstrates the power of marketing to sell toxic products in the pursuit of profit.

Although the tobacco industry's behaviour has been unmasked through the availability of their internal documents, they have maintained solid intransigence in the face of new regulatory initiatives (Hurt et al., 2009). Other industries parallel this approach, particularly if their marketing strategies and products put consumers at risk. Thus, the food and alcohol industries have quickly asserted that they are free to promote their legally available products, and called on consumers to take greater responsibility for their actions (Hawkes, 2007; Hurt et al., 2009).

ALCOHOL MARKETING

Debate over the effectiveness of measures to moderate alcohol consumption has many parallels with tobacco control. Hastings et al. (2010) noted the profound effects alcohol advertising has on young people's drinking behaviours and the failings in self-regulatory systems that oversee this advertising. Casswell and Maxwell attributed the fundamental differences between what they described as 'industry friendly policies' (2005: 119) and polices that reduce the visibility of alcohol products and alter consumers' access to these to political pressures.

For example, their review of school-based education programmes concluded that these: 'have generally not been found to have any lasting effects on drinking behaviour' (2005: 133). Despite the strength of evidence supporting this conclusion, and the high cost of these programmes, they concluded that education strategies received strong support 'probably in large part because [they] do not affect any vested interest group' (2005: 133), despite their high cost and the evidence questioning their effectiveness. Caswell and Maxwell also queried the results mass media public information (social advertising) campaigns produced and suggested these had little effect when used in isolation, though could be useful when used to promote awareness of policy change (see also Anderson et al., 2009).

Evaluation of alcohol moderation campaigns highlights the conflict between industry and public health, and the importance of policy that actively supports voluntary behaviour change. The evidence that Caswell and Maxwell (2005) and Anderson et al. (2009) presented suggests education alone is a very weak tool and its continuing popularity as an intervention reflects the political strength of its proponents. Given this, it is not altogether surprising to see the same debate occurring over interventions that would reduce obesity prevalence.

FOOD MARKETING – DÉJÀ VU?

It is undeniable that food, alcohol and tobacco are different products – food is necessary for survival; alcohol consumption, although not crucial to survival, may enhance it; while tobacco is antithetical to survival. Yet, despite these fundamental differences, food has the potential to harm health and well-being, and consumption of foods high in fat, salt and sugar has been linked to many diseases, including cardiovascular disease and cancer (WHO, 2002). Because food poses risks as well as delivering benefits, it has also attracted regulators' and social marketers' attention, many of whom have been concerned to observe tobacco control arguments revisited in a new context (Chopra and Darnton-Hill, 2004). From the establishment of industry and interest groups, the promotion of self-regulation, the use of industry-funded 'experts', lobbying of politicians, infiltration of policy groups and castigation of academics and research findings contrary to their interests, the tactics employed by the food industry have striking parallels to those formerly employed by their tobacco colleagues (Yach et al., 2005; Hoek and Gendall, 2006).

The development of foods that are not nutritious and do not enhance consumers' long-term well-being is also rooted in economic interests. Just as tobacco farmers receive subsidies to support their enterprise, so manufacturers of crops such as corn (the primary ingredient in high-fructose corn syrup) also receive funding that reduces their costs, making them more attractive than more nutritious, but more expensive, ingredients (Tillotson, 2003; Morrill and Chinn, 2004; Schwartz and Brownell, 2007; Story et al., 2008).

The mere availability of inexpensive raw materials provides incentives to develop processed foods, since processing 'adds value' and enhances profitability, supports larger marketing budgets to create and promote demand and thus contributes to the rapid increase in obesity prevalence that has occurred over recent decades (Ogden et al., 2004).

FOOD MARKETING – REACHING THE VULNERABLE

The proliferation of food brands and retail networks means high fat, salt and sugar (HFSS) foods are widely available, particularly in high-deprivation neighbourhoods (Pearce et al., 2007). They are also heavily promoted, especially to children (Seiders and Petty, 2006); Kotz and Story (1994) reported that around half of the advertisements screened during children's television hours featured food products. Furthermore, the proportion of advertisements promoting food has increased; recent estimates suggest American children are exposed to more than 40,000 food advertisements a year (Zuppa et al., 2003). According to Kotz and Story, these advertisements typically promote foods with low nutritional value to children, leading them to conclude: '[t]he diet presented on Saturday morning television is the antithesis of what is recommended for healthful eating for children'.

Furthermore, this advertising affects children's snacking behaviour (Coon et al., 2001). Advertising's influence has raised concerns about the techniques used, such as animation, fantasy and cartoon characters – Joe Camel's close colleagues include Tony the Tiger and the Honey Monster. Child-oriented promotions draw heavily on emotional rather than factual appeals, and so engage children at an imaginative rather than cognitive level. Like tobacco products, HFSS foods are promoted using aspirational imagery, and offer benefits that go well beyond physical satiation. Even if they were capable of critically appraising advertising, children are unlikely to be rationally evaluating the nutritional properties of food promoted to them; nor are they likely to be reviewing the rate at which these foods should be consumed, or contemplating the consequences of excessive consumption.

FOOD MARKETING – CREATING UNCERTAINTY

Although children's vulnerability to advertising claims creates a strong case for regulatory intervention, the food industry, like the tobacco industry, has challenged evidence linking food marketing to obesity (Ambler, 2004; Calfee, 2004). Industry spokespeople have argued that a causal relationship between food advertising and obesity should be clearly established before regulators consider intervening. While longitudinal research programmes could produce this evidence, these require long-term data collection and, in the absence of these data, policymakers often defer acting. An insistence on evidence that will only be available in the longer term thus avoids debate over what could be done, given our knowledge of advertising's effects on behaviour (Swinburn and Egger, 2004).

Food marketers' arguments parallel those advanced by the tobacco industry. Cigarette manufacturers fought a rearguard action to stave off advertising restrictions by arguing that their promotions had no effect on non-smokers and sought only to change brand preferences among existing smokers. Like fast-food manufacturers, tobacco companies claimed that new recruits were attracted to smoking not by advertising, but by the behavior of their peers and other social groups (Smith, 1990), and they continue to dispute the role their marketing plays in smoking initiation. Evidence relating to food advertising, however, suggests it affects primary demand. Hastings et al.'s comprehensive and systematic review of research examining food advertising found only weak evidence of brand switching, but much stronger evidence of category switching (Hastings et al., 2003).

FOOD MARKETING – CREATING THE OVERSEERS

Findings of a product category effect, confirmed by subsequent reviews, create a strong basis for upstream intervention. However, the food industry has pre-empted regulation, again by translating tobacco industry strategies. Specifically, they have created self-regulatory groups that have impeded comprehensive, and arguably more effective, upstream intervention. Industry advertising codes are often reactive and have arguably had little effect on establishing, promoting and maintaining standards, leading a US observer to describe self-regulation of children's advertising thus: '[Children's Advertising Review Unit] says it is a watchdog, but it is empowered to do things so small you need a scanning electron microscope to see it' (Mayer, 2005).

Self-regulation supports education and public information campaigns that provide consumers with technical nutrition information and promote

'informed choice'. For example, voluntary food labelling initiatives pre-empted consideration of alternative formats and use highly numeric formats that consumers find difficult to understand (Grunert and Wills, 2007; Feunekesa et al., 2008). Not surprisingly, hiding information in plain view takes little cognizance of consumers' preferences, has had little or no effect on their ability to differentiate between products' nutrition profiles and has done little to bring about behaviour change (Maubach and Hoek, 2008). These initiatives rely on the same 'individual responsibility' philosophy that the tobacco industry used successfully to delay upstream initiatives and defend suits taken against it.

Litigation taken against fast-food manufacturers has already attempted to hold manufacturers accountable for the risky products they produce and market. Plaintiffs argued that food producers deceived consumers by failing to advise them of the risks they faced if they regularly consumed HFSS foods (McFat-Pelman v McDonald's, 2003). These cases have advanced two key arguments: that companies acted irresponsibly in selling foods that contributed to health problems; and that their marketing activities led consumers to believe the foods sold were not inconsistent with a healthy diet and could be safely consumed, even up to four or five times a week. The defendants rejected claims their foods posed inherent health risks and argued that reasonable consumers would (and should) have known that frequent and extensive consumption of their offerings would lead to obesity, and increased risk of many serious chronic diseases.

These arguments parallel those heard in tobacco cases and raise important questions about the ambit of companies' responsibilities to consumers. Decisions in tobacco cases suggest consumers are expected to accept responsibility for accessing risk information, even when the status and veracity of this has been deliberately undermined. Evidence that tobacco companies failed to make available known risk information was insufficient to support early claims for damages by smokers. In the same way, it appears unlikely that individuals suffering from obesity-induced complications will be able to hold food marketers to account.

The argument that obesity is simply a matter of individual responsibility may seem plausible on one level, as people decide what, when and how much to eat. Furthermore, as the tobacco industry has successfully argued, the risks of obesity (like the risks of smoking) are now well established, although the extent to which consumers make informed choices remains a moot point. Locating responsibility for obesity with individuals overlooks the influence environmental factors have on behaviour and the evidence that the rapid rise in obesity prevalence has not occurred because of deliberate personal choice (Story et al., 2008).

CONCLUSION

If social marketers are to address Goldberg's challenge and demonstrate they are not merely fiddling while Rome burns, they must eliminate or at least ameliorate the harmful effects of commercial marketing. Reviewing the environmental determinants of risk behaviour clarifies the upstream interventions required to create a context in which social marketing and education initiatives will flourish.

Jochelson had earlier exhorted public health researchers to look first to upstream approaches as the most rapid and effective way of promoting behaviour change. She argued that: 'Legislation brings about change that individuals on their own cannot, and sets new standards for the public good' (Jochelson, 2006: 1149). Her reasoning implies interventions that change consumers' environments should not be regarded as constraints, but rather as prerequisites that must be met before consumers can exercise full and free choices. However, as Adshead and Thorpe noted, while legislation can create a context for behaviour change, social marketing and education are required to consolidate and reinforce the changes achieved (Adshead and Thorpe, 2007: 838). Thus, social marketers must consider how initiatives along the intervention continuum can be integrated and future research could explore the characteristics, timing, integration and delivery of effective intervention programmes.

Representatives of marketing's 'malevolent' side appear to believe that environments redolent with commercial imagery, yet tempered by 'information' or 'education', will promote individual responsibility. Yet, these environments have failed to reduce smoking prevalence or risky alcohol consumption and, given this, appear equally unlikely to reduce other risk behaviours (Nestle, 2006). Beliefs that promulgating nutrition information will fill 'knowledge gaps' and promote more healthful behaviours overlook the fact that obesity does not arise, as Swinburn (2006) argued, because of a 'knowledge deficit problem'. Overall, there is ample evidence that education on its own does not change behaviour for the vast majority of the population (Egger and Swinburn, 1997; Kersh and Marone, 2002).

Furthermore, promoting individual responsibility via education programmes implies that knowledge and self-efficacy are sufficiently powerful to overcome the stimuli present in commercial environments, that public health

discourses can be as persuasive and effective as commercial communications, and that the former will be as well-resourced as the latter.

Social marketing supports individual responsibility but recognises that individuals cannot be free to make decisions if they are located in environments that promote unhealthy choices, and it has a stronger record of success than education in introducing new behaviours. However, the most successful tobacco control measures have undoubtedly been increases in taxation, restrictions on marketing (including promotion, distribution, product formulation and pricing), and supply constraints, all of which have reduced the visibility, salience and accessibility of tobacco products. Increasingly, researchers have recognised that upstream measures must complement downstream social marketing to promote sustainable behaviour change and create contexts that support subsequent, more targeted, interventions (Schwartz and Brownell, 2007). This implies that regulators need to reverse the logic on which they currently rely and recognise first, that policy change is needed to create environments that support healthy behaviours, and second, that there is no logical or empirical basis to believe that individual behaviour change initiatives will create healthier macro-environments.

Yet despite the documented success of regulation and the logical basis underpinning regulatory initiatives, they remain measures of last resort. In some cases, this is due to governments' philosophical opposition to regulation, but even progressive governments have been slow to act, and acutely sensitive to 'nanny state' allegations and suggestions they are trying to assume decision-making roles that belong with individuals. Jochelson (2006: 1151) recognised and warned against accepting these assertions, which she argued are the antithesis of reasoned debate: 'Dismissing government intervention as nanny-statist limits debate about the possible benefits of state intervention'. Preference for education initiatives rather than social marketing or regulation reflects weak political will power. Ironically, public support for intervention is often high, yet remains unheard. Further research is thus also required to estimate support for alternative interventions so a disinterested evidence base can be developed and used to inform decisions.

Policy is critically important to bring about rapid change. As Hayne et al. (2004: 392) noted, regulation 'can transform the entire environment in one moment', whereas Rigby et al. (2004: 429) argued: 'the "personal responsibility", approach has been tested over many decades and as a public health policy has clearly failed'. If social marketers' voices are to resonate effectively with consumers and be heard above the prevailing commercial cacophony, attention must first turn to changing the context within which behaviour occurs.

KEY WORDS: Social marketing; education; regulation; self-regulation; alcohol; tobacco; obesity; food marketing; informed choice; individual responsibility.

Key insights

- Greater attention should be paid to consumers' choice environments, particularly where these support and encourage risk behaviours.
- Social marketing risks being a minority voice in environments where rampant and residual marketing continues; until regulators constrain commercial voices, social marketing's full potential effectiveness will not be realised.
- Supportive policy frameworks will enhance the effectiveness of social marketing campaigns and, where environments promote risk behaviours, 'upstream' efforts should precede 'downstream' interventions.
- Policy interventions are not 'nanny statist' but logical and evidence-based measures that promote informed choice.

REFERENCES

A Frank Statement to Cigarette Smokers. Available at: http://www.tobacco.neu.edu/litigation/cases/supportdocs/frank_ad.htm

Adshead, F. and Thorpe, A. (2007) 'The role of the Government in public health: A national perspective', *Public Health*, 121: 835–839.

Albright, C., Altman, D., Slater, M., and Maccoby, N. (1988) 'Cigarette advertisements in magazines: Evidence for a differential focus on women's and youth magazines', *Health Education Quarterly*, 15: 225–233.

Ambler, T. (2004) 'Do we really want to be ruled by fatheads?' *International Journal of Advertising and Marketing to Children*, 5(2): 25–28.

Anderson, P., Chisholm, D. and Fuhr, D. (2009) 'Effectiveness and cost-effectiveness of policies and programmes to reduce the harm caused by alcohol', *Lancet*, 373: 2234–2246.

Arnett, J. and Terhanian, G. (1998) 'Adolescents' responses to cigarette advertisements: Links between exposure, liking, and the appeal of smoking', *Tobacco Control*, 7: 133.

Basil, M., Schooler, C., Altman, D., et al. (1991) 'How cigarettes are advertised in magazines: Special messages for special markets', *Health Communication*, 5: 75–91.

Borland, R. (1997) 'What do people's estimates of smoking risk mean?' *Psychology and Health*, 12: 513–521.

British American Tobacco (2006) Available at: http://www.bat.co.nz/OneWeb/sites/BAT_5LPJ9K.nsf/vwPagesWebLive/80256D0B004C1BC780256ABE00347802?opendocument&SID=&DTC=

Calfee, J. (2004) 'Can advertising make you fat?' American Enterprise Institute Presentation, 20 June.

Carter, S. (2003) 'The Australian cigarette brand as product, person and symbol', *Tobacco Control*, 12: iii79–iii86.

Carter, S. and Chapman, S. (2003) 'Smoking, disease and obdurate denial: The Australian tobacco industry in the 1980s', *Tobacco Control*, 12 (Suppl III): iii23–iii30.

Casswell, S. and Maxwell, A. (2005) 'What works to reduce alcohol-related harm, and why aren't the polices more popular?' *Social Policy Journal of New Zealand*, 25: 118–141.

Chapman, S. (1996) 'The ethics of tobacco advertising and advertising bans', *British Medical Bulletin*, 52: 121–131.

Chapman, S. (2002) 'Blaming tobacco's victims', *Tobacco Control*, 11: 167–168.

Chapman, S. and Carter, S. (2003) '"Avoid health warnings on all tobacco products for just as long as we can": A history of Australian tobacco industry efforts to avoid, delay and dilute health warnings on cigarettes', *Tobacco Control*, 12: 13–22.

Chapman, S. and Freeman, B. (2008) 'Markers of the denormalisation of smoking and the tobacco industry', *Tobacco Control*, 17: 25–31.

Chapman, S. and Liberman, J. (2005) 'Ensuring smokers are adequately informed: Reflections on consumer rights, manufacturer responsibility, and policy implications', *Tobacco Control*, 14: 8–13.

Chopra, M. and Darnton-Hill, I. (2004) 'Tobacco and obesity epidemics: Not so different after all?' *British Medical Journal*, 328: 1558–1560.

Connolly, J. (2002) 'The politics of tobacco advertising', *Thorax*, 57: ii64–ii68.

Coon, K., Goldberg, J., Rogers, B. and Tucker, K. (2001) 'Relationships between use of television during meals and children's food consumption patterns', *Paediatrics*, 107: e1–e9.

Cummings, K., Morley, C., Horan, J., Steger, C. and Leavell, N. (2002) 'Marketing to America's youth: Evidence from corporate documents', *Tobacco Control*, Suppl 1: 15–17.

Cunningham, R. (1996) Chapter 12: 'Plain packaging'. *Smoke and Mirrors*. Available at: http://www.bvsde.paho.org/bvsacd/cd53/plain.pdf

Daynard, R. (1991) 'Recent developments in tobacco litigation', *Tobacco Control*, 1: 37–45.

Dewhirst, T. (2004) 'POP goes the power wall? Taking aim at tobacco promotional strategies utilized at retail', *Tobacco Control*, 13: 209–210.

DiFranza, J.R., Richards, J.W., Paulman, P.M., et al. (1991) 'R.J.R. Nabisco's cartoon camel promotes Camel cigarettes to children', *Journal of the American Medical Association*, 266(22): 3149–3153.

Doll, R. and Hill, A.B. (1950) 'Smoking and carcinoma of the lung. Preliminary report', *British Medical Journal*, 221(ii): 739–748.

Eames, J. (2002) British American Tobacco Australia Services Limited v Cowell (as representing the estate of Rolah Ann McCabe, deceased).

Edwards, R. (2009) 'Daring to dream: The endgame for tobacco supply in New Zealand'. Paper presented at the Public Health Association Conference, 1–0 September, Dunedin, New Zealand. Abstract available at: http://www. pha.org.nz/conference/2009confprogramme.pdf

Egger, G. and Swinburn, B. (1997) 'An "ecological" approach to the obesity pandemic', *British Medical Journal*, 315: 477–480.

Feunekesa, G., Gortemakera, I., Willemsa, A., Liona, R. and van den Kommerb, M. (2008) 'Front-of-pack nutrition labelling: Testing effectiveness of different nutrition labelling formats front-of-pack in four European countries', *Appetite*, 50: 57–70.

Fischer, P., Schwartz, M., Richards, J. Jr, Goldstein, A. and Rojas, T. (1991) 'Brand recognition by children aged 3 to 6 years', *Journal of the American Medical Association*, 266: 3145–3148.

Freeman, B. and Chapman, S. (2009) 'Open source marketing: Camel cigarette brand marketing in the "Web 2.0" world', *Tobacco Control*, 18: 212–217.

Freeman, B., Chapman, S. and Rimmer, M. (2008) 'The case for the plain packaging of tobacco products', *Addiction*, 103(4): 580–590.

Goldberg, M. (1995) 'Social marketing: Are we fiddling while Rome burns?', *Journal of Consumer Psychology*, 4(4): 347–372.

Grunert, K. and Wills, J. (2007) 'A review of European research on consumer response to nutrition information on food labels', *Journal of Public Health*, 15: 385–399.

Hammond, D., Fong, G., McNeill, A., Borland, R. and Cummings, K. (2006) 'Effectiveness of cigarette warning labels in informing smokers about the risks of smoking: Findings from the International Tobacco Control (ITC) Four Country Survey', *Tobacco Control*, 15(Suppl III): iii19–iii25.

Harper, T. (2006) 'Why the tobacco industry fears point of sale display bans', *Tobacco Control*, 15: 270–271.

Hastings, G. (2007) *Social Marketing: Why Should the Devil Have All the Best Tunes?* Oxford: Butterworth-Heinemann.

Hastings, G. and Aitken, P. (1995) 'Tobacco advertising and children's smoking: A review of the evidence', *European Journal of Marketing*, 29(11): 6–17.

Hastings, G. and MacFadyen, L. (1998) 'Editorial', *Tobacco Control*, 7: 107–108.

Hastings, G. and Saren, M. (2003) 'The critical contribution of social marketing: theory and application', *Marketing Theory*, 3(3): 305–322.

Hastings, G., Stead, M., McDermott, L. (2003) 'A review of research on the effects of food promotion to children'. Report prepared for the Food Standards Authority by the Centre for Social Marketing, Strathclyde University. Available at: http://www.ism.stir.ac.uk/pdf_docs/final_report_19_9.pdf

Hastings, G., Brooks, O., Stead, M., et al. (2010) 'Alcohol advertising: The last chance saloon', *British Medical Journal*, 23 January: 184–186.

Hawkes, C. (2007) 'Regulating and litigating in the public interest: Regulating food marketing to young people worldwide: Trends and policy drivers', *American Journal of Public Health*, 97(11): 1962–1973.

Hayne, C., Moran, P. and Ford. M. (2004) 'Regulating environments to reduce obesity', *Journal of Public Health Policy*, 25(3–4): 391–407.

Hoek, J. (2004) 'Tobacco promotion restrictions: Ironies and unintended consequences', *Journal of Business Research*, 57(11): 1250–1257.

Hoek, J. and Gendall, P. (2006) 'Advertising and obesity: A behavioral perspective', *Journal of Health Communication*, 11: 409–423.

Hurt, R., Ebbert, J., Muggli, M., Lockhart, N. and Robertson, C. (2009) 'Open doorway to truth: Legacy of the Minnesota tobacco trial', *Mayo Clinic Proceedings*, 84: 446–456.

Jochelson, K. (2006) 'Nanny or steward? The role of government in public health', *Public Health*, 120: 1149–1155.

Kersh, R. and Marone, J. (2002) 'The politics of obesity: Seven steps to government action', *Health Affairs*, 21(6): 142–153.

King, C. III, Siegel, M., Celebucki, C. and Connolly, G. (1998) 'Adolescent exposure to cigarette advertising in magazines: An evaluation of brand-specific advertising in relation to youth readership', *Journal of the American Medical Association*, 279: 516–520.

Kotz, K. and Story, M. (1994) 'Food advertisements during children's Saturday morning television programming: Are they consistent with dietary recommendations?' *Journal of the American Dietetic Association*, 94: 1296–1300.

Lang, J. (2006) Brandon Pou and Kasey Pou vs British American Tobacco (New Zealand) Limited and W D & H O Wills (New Zealand) Limited. CIV-2002-404-1729.

Lazer, W. and Kelley, E.J. (1973) *Social Marketing: Perspectives and Viewpoints*. Holmewood, IL: Richard D. Irwin.

Lord Nimmo Smith, McTear vs Imperial Tobacco. Available at: http://www.scotcourts.gov.uk/opinions/a2126_01. html

McFat Litigation I – Pelman v. McDonald's Corp., 237 F. Supp.2d 512 (S.D.N.Y. Jan 22, 2003). Available at: http://biotech.law.lsu.edu/cases/food/pelman01.htm.

Mahood, G. (1999) 'Warnings that tell the truth: Breaking new ground in Canada', *Tobacco Control*, 8: 356–361.

Mahood, G. (2003) 'Canada's tobacco package label or warning system: "Telling the truth" about tobacco product risks'. Available at: http://www.who.int/tobacco/training/success_stories/en/best_practices_canada_package.pdf

Maubach, N. and Hoek, J. (2008) 'The effect of alternative nutrition information formats on consumers' evaluations of a children's breakfast cereal'. Paper presented at the International Non-Profit and Social Marketing Conference, Wollongong, July 15–16.

Mayer, C. (2005) 'Minding Nemo; Pitches to kids feed debate about a watchdog', *Washington Post*, 27 February. Available at: http://www.commercialalert.org/issues-article.php?article_id=338&subcategor y_id=69&category =1 (quoting Gary Ruskin, Executive Director of Commercial Alert).

Michaels, D. and Monforton, C. (2005) 'Manufacturing uncertainty. Contested science and the protection of the public's health and environment', *American Journal of Public Health*, 95(S1): S39–S48.

Morrill, A. and Chinn, C. (2004) 'The obesity epidemic in the United States', *Journal of Public Health Policy*, 25(3/4): 353–366.

Nestle, M. (2006) 'Preventing childhood diabetes: The need for public health intervention', *American Journal of Public Health*, 95(9):1497–1499.

Newcombe, R., Hoek, J. and Walker, S. (2009) 'Sustainability and smokefree behaviour: An evaluation of a social norms campaign'. Paper presented at International Non-Profit and Social Marketing Conference. Melbourne, Australia. 14–15 July. Available at: http://www.insmconference.vu.edu.au/documents/papers/Hoek_Newcombe_Walker.pdf

Ogden, C., Carroll, M., Curtin, L., et al. (2004) 'Prevalence of overweight and obesity in the United States, 1999–2004', *Journal of the American Medical Association*, 295: 1549–1555.

Parascandola, M. (2004) 'Skepticism, statistical methods, and the cigarette: A historical analysis of a methodological debate', *Perspectives in Biology and Medicine*, 47(42): 244–261.

Parmet, W. and Daynard, D. (2000) 'The new public health litigation', *Annual Review of Public Health*, 21: 437–454.

Pearce, J., Blakely, T., Witten, K. and Bartie, P. (2007) 'Neighbourhood deprivation and access to fast-food retailing: A national study. *American Journal of Preventive Medicine*, 32(5): 375–382.

Pelman v McDonald's Corp. United States District Court, Southern District of New York. 02 Civ. 7821 (RWS).

Pierce, J.P., Gilpin, E., Burns, D.M., et al. (1991) 'Does tobacco advertising target young people to start smoking? Evidence from California', *Journal of the American Medical Association*, 266: 3154–3158.

Pollay, R. (1990) 'How cigarette advertising works: Rich imagery and poor information', 20 October, History of Advertising Archives. Available at: http://www.smoke-free. ca/defacto/D057-Pollay-HowCigaretteAdvertisingWorks. pdf (accessed 14 September 2005).

Pollay, R. (2004) 'Considering the evidence, no wonder the court endorses Canada's restrictions on cigarette advertising', *Journal of Public Policy and Marketing*, 23: 80–88.

Pollay, R. (2007) 'More than meets the eye: On the importance of retail cigarette merchandising', *Tobacco Control*, 16: 270–274.

Pollay, R.W. and Dewhirst, T. (2002) 'The dark side of marketing seemingly "light" cigarettes: Successful images and failed fact', *Tobacco Control*, 11(Suppl 1): i18–i31.

Rigby, N., Kumanyika, S. and James, P. (2004) 'Confronting the epidemic: The need for global solutions', *Journal of Public Health Policy*, 25(3/4): 418–434.

Saffer, H. and Chaloupka, F. (2000) 'The effect of tobacco advertising bans on tobacco consumption', *Journal of Health Economics*, 19: 1117–1137.

Saloojee, Y. and Dagli, E. (2000) 'Tobacco industry tactics for resisting public policy on health', *Bulletin of the World Health Organisation*, 78(7): 902–910.

Schwartz, M. and Brownell, K. (2007) 'Actions necessary to prevent childhood obesity: Creating the climate for change', *The Journal of Law, Medicine & Ethics*, 35: 78–89.

Seiders, K. and Petty, R. (2004) 'Obesity and the role of food marketing: A policy analysis of issues and remedies', *Journal of Public Policy and Marketing*, 23(2): 153–169.

Smith, G. (1990) 'The effect of advertising on juvenile smoking behavior', *International Journal of Advertising*, 9: 57–80.

Smokefree Coalition. (2009) 'Tupeka kore/Tobacco Free Aotearoa/New Zealand by 2020', Smokefree Coalition. Wellington. Available at: www.sfc.org.nz/pdfs/TheVision2020.pdf (accessed 7 January 2010).

Story, M., Kaphingst, K., Robinson-O'Brien, R. and Glanz, K. (2008) 'Creating healthy food and eating environments: Policy and environmental approaches', *Annual Review of Public Health*, 29: 253–272.

Swinburn, B. (2006) 'Submission to the Health Select Committee Inquiry into Obesity and Type 2 Diabetes. Cited in White, J. The Health Select Committee Inquiry into Obesity and Type 2 Diabetes in New Zealand: An initial analysis of submissions'. Available at: http://www.foe.org.nz/arcives/HSCAnalysis.pdf

Swinburn, B. and Egger, G. (2004) 'The runaway weight gain train: Too many accelerators, not enough brakes', *British Medical Journal*, 329: 736–739.

Thomson, G. and Wilson, N. (2003) 'The tobacco industry in New Zealand: A case study of the behaviour of multinational companies', eScholarship Repository, University of California. Available at: http://repositories. cdlib.org/tc/reports/NZ

Tillotson, J. (2003) 'Pandemic obesity: Agriculture's cheap food policy is a bad bargain', *Nutrition Today*, 38(5): 186–190.

Wakefield, M., McLeod, K. and Clegg-Smith, K. (2003) 'Individual versus corporate responsibility for smoking-related illness: Australian press coverage of the Rolah McCabe trial', *Health Promotion International*, 18(4): 297–305.

Warner, K. (2000) 'The economics of tobacco: Myths and realities', *Tobacco Control*, 9: 78–89.

Weis, W. and Arnesen, D. (2007) 'When the forces of industry conflict with the public health: A free market malignancy', *AHCMJ*, 3(2): 81–94.

WHO (2002) 'Diet, nutrition and the prevention of chronic diseases'. Report of a joint WHO/FAO expert consultation, Geneva. WHO technical report series; 916. Available at: http://whqlibdoc.who.int/trs/WHO_trs_916.pdf

Wyckham, R. (1997) 'Regulating the marketing of tobacco products and controlling smoking in Canada', *Canadian Journal of Administrative Sciences*, 14(2): 141–165.

Yach, D., McKee, M., Lopez, A.D. and Novotny, T. (2005) 'Improving diet and physical activity: 12 lessons from controlling tobacco smoking', *British Medical Journal*, 330: 898–900.

Zuppa, J., Morton, H. and Mehta, K. (2003) 'Television food advertising: Counter-productive to children's health? A content analysis using the Australian guide to healthy eating', *Nutrition and Dietetics*, 60(2): 78–84.

17

Social Marketing's Response to the Alcohol Problem: Who's Conducting the Orchestra?

Sandra C. Jones

In Chapter 16 of this Handbook, Janet Hoek reminds us of Goldberg's caution to social marketers to ensure that we are not 'fiddling while Rome burns'. Taking the analogy one step further, I would argue that we need to make sure we are all playing the same tune. Social marketing can be very effective in bringing about behaviour change; critical marketing can be very effective in drawing attention to commercial activities that damage public health; and up-stream social marketing can be very effective in bringing about supportive policy change. When we combine these three approaches, we can bring about powerful changes that improve society's health and well-being, but when each is playing a different tune all we achieve is noise.

This chapter focuses on social marketing's response to concerns regarding excessive alcohol consumption and increasing alcohol-related harms, commencing with an overview of the nature and scope of the 'alcohol problem' and the evidence on the effectiveness of different interventions. The chapter next focuses on each of the three social marketing 'instruments' in turn, outlining the (potential) role of: downstream social marketing, critical marketing, and upstream social marketing. It then discusses the need to bring these three instruments into harmony, canvasses the issue of working with the alcohol industry, draws some conclusions and offers recommendations to social marketers who are endeavouring to address this complex social issue.

WHY SHOULD WE WORRY ABOUT ALCOHOL?

Unlike tobacco, which is harmful when consumed as intended by the manufacturer, alcohol is a product which is associated with both harms[1] and benefits – making for heated debates about the need to address the alcohol problem. However, systematic reviews of the evidence on the health effects of alcohol consumption conclusively demonstrate that the net effect to society is detrimental (Rehm et al., 2009). In 2004, 4.6% of the global burden of disease and 3.8% of deaths around the world were attributable to alcohol (Rehm et al., 2009). It is also important to note, although much harder to quantify, the social harms associated with alcohol consumption – such as domestic violence, reduced productivity, physical and verbal assault, property damage, and damage to personal relationships. In the UK, the costs associated with alcohol consumption are estimated at between £20 billion and £55.1 billion (House of Commons Health Committee, 2010).

While alcohol-attributable morbidity and mortality is more than three times as common in males as in females, the age distribution of this harm is more evenly spread. Much of the public concern, and political will, in relation to excessive alcohol consumption has focused on under-age drinkers (defined as less than 21 years in the USA, and less than 18 years in Australia and the UK). However, worldwide, approximately one-third

(33.6%) of the alcohol-attributable burden of disease in 2004 is among people aged 15–29, closely followed by people aged 30–44 years (31.3%), but remains substantial among people aged 45–59 years (22.0%) (Rehm et al., 2009). Thus, while it may be politically 'popular' – and certainly newsworthy – to talk about the alcohol problem as a problem of youth, the reality is that harmful drinking needs to be addressed across society as a whole. Focusing on small groups will only bring about small changes in overall consumption, and continue to engender a culture in which 'our' drinking is acceptable and 'their' drinking is problematic. Furthermore, it is only when we address alcohol consumption at a population level that we will be able to provide an environment for young people which does not model (excessive) drinking as a normative social behaviour.

It is also interesting to note that a common theme in media and public discussions is that the drinking problem is nothing new, and that people (particularly in countries such as the UK and Australia) have always drunk at high levels. However, the evidence shows that in the UK, for example, alcohol consumption declined steadily throughout the 19th century (other than a brief spike in the early 1920s); consumption began to increase in the 1960s, with the majority of the increase in stronger drinks such as wine and spirits (House of Commons Health Committee, 2010). These changes in consumption – including a doubling of consumption among 11–15 year olds between 1990 and 2006 – have been attributed to the affordability and availability of alcohol, marketing and changes in culture (House of Commons Health Committee, 2010), although many would argue that marketing, along with the proliferation of pro-alcohol messages in the media, has been a key driver of these cultural changes.

WHAT DOES THE EVIDENCE TELL US?

There have been several comprehensive reviews of the effectiveness and cost-effectiveness of interventions to reduce alcohol-related harms. The most recent of these, consistent with previous reviews, concluded that the most effective strategies are: increasing the price and reducing the availability of alcohol; banning alcohol advertising; drink-driving interventions (such as random breath testing and low or zero blood alcohol concentration restrictions for inexperienced drivers); and individual interventions with at-risk drinkers (Anderson et al., 2009; Babor et al., 2010).[2]

In Australia, the National Preventative Health Taskforce reported that, based on a study of the cost-effectiveness of interventions, governments could achieve more than 10 times the health gain by reallocating (without increasing) their current investments in programmes to reduce alcohol-related harms (Doran et al., 2010). The interventions identified as comprising the optimal packaged approach (in order of cost-effectiveness) were volumetric taxation, advertising bans, increasing the minimum drinking age to 21 years, brief interventions in primary care, licensing controls, drink-driving mass media campaigns and random breath testing (Doran et al., 2010).

To adequately address this complex problem, we need to call on all of the instruments available to social marketers, to ensure that each is properly tuned, and that they are all playing the same song. The following three sections review each of these instruments in turn.

THE FIRST INSTRUMENT: (DOWNSTREAM) SOCIAL MARKETING

The first instrument – and the one that immediately comes to mind when we think of social marketing for alcohol harm reduction – is traditional (or downstream) social marketing. Evidence reviews of the effectiveness of alcohol harm reduction interventions consistently conclude that school-based education does not reduce drinking levels or drinking-related harms (Anderson et al., 2009; Jones et al., 2007), that 'public education campaigns' are ineffective (Babor et al., 2010), and that industry-funded educational programmes actually result in positive views about alcohol and the alcohol industry (Smith et al., 2006).[3]

Social marketing campaigns *can* produce positive changes in drinking behaviours, with a recent review noting that several studies showed significant short-term effects and two showed some effect over two years (Stead et al., 2007). However, these successful interventions were, generally speaking, those that incorporated all the elements of social marketing rather than unidimensional 'education' or 'communication' campaigns.

There are a range of 'checklists' and frameworks for defining the components of effective social marketing programmes; while they may differ on the number of steps, or the exact wording of the elements, they generally agree on the underlying principles. As a discussion of the various frameworks is beyond the scope of this chapter, the UK National Social Marketing Centre's (NSMC) benchmark criteria is used as an exemplar. This checklist reminds us that effective social marketing programmes incorporate: customer orientation; a clear focus on behaviour;

the use of theory to inform and guide development; deep understanding and insight into consumer motivation; clear analysis of the full cost to the consumer and the exchange; an analysis of internal and external competition; a developed segmentation approach; and an appropriate methods mix (National Social Marketing Centre, 2006).

However, the evidence suggests that the effectiveness of social marketing programmes that are restricted to communication campaigns – or communication and enforcement – may (in the current climate) be limited to specific behaviours such as drink driving – and that for many other behaviours they can be ineffective (or even counterproductive), as the following case study shows. Many (government) 'social marketing' campaigns follow the same approach as the school-based programmes – 'educate them about the harms and they will change'. Thus, it is not surprising that in the main they fail to bring about behaviour change.[4]

When we are assessing the effectiveness of campaigns such as the one described above, it is important to consider the context in which these messages are conveyed. It is perhaps not surprising that a government campaign warning young people of the harms associated with alcohol use falls on deaf ears when it is delivered in a pro-alcohol, advertising-saturated media environment (which reinforces the belief that alcohol is harmless, socially normative and essential to having a good time). As the UK Health Select Committee pointed out, the £17.6 million the UK government spent on alcohol information and education campaigns in 2009/10 pales into insignificance against the £600–800 million the industry spends each year promoting alcohol.

Conversely, there is evidence for the effectiveness of social marketing in addressing driving under the influence of alcohol. As pointed out by Grube and Stewart (2004), the success of policy approaches such as penalties for driving under the influence require the policy to be implemented and enforced and to be communicated to the target audience. They conclude their review of strategies to prevent impaired driving with the statement that 'Alcohol policies are most effective when they are adequately implemented and vigorously enforced and when there is awareness of both the policy and the enforcement efforts on the part of the intended targets' (p. 205).

In summary, it is unlikely that even the most carefully designed and implemented social marketing intervention (e.g. one which follows the NSMC criteria) will bring about individual-level behaviour change when the behaviour we are targeting is one that is accepted, and even encouraged, by the social and commercial environment in which the behaviour occurs. This is where our other instruments need to be working in unison.

THE SECOND INSTRUMENT: CRITICAL MARKETING

As Hastings reminds us (e.g. Hastings and Saren, 2003), social marketers should also engage in critical marketing, as our knowledge of marketing

---

The Australian Government National Alcohol Campaign 2000–2002 (Drinking Choices)

The main focus of the campaign was on drinking, intoxication, and harm among Australian teenagers; and the target audiences were teenagers and parents.

The evaluation of the programme in late 2002 found high levels of recall in both target groups (King et al., 2003). More than two-thirds (78%) of the parents surveyed reported seeing advertising about teenage drinking directed towards parents or teens, 38% correctly recalled that the advertising message was about 'consequences of drinking', and 51% reported talking to their teenagers about alcohol in the last three months. Almost as many of the young people surveyed (70%) reported that they had 'seen, read or heard advertising about teenagers and drinking alcohol in the previous month' and 26% reported talking to their parents in the last three months about alcohol.[5] However, this awareness did not result in changes in drinking behaviours. The evaluation found no change in the proportion of teenagers reporting that they had consumed more than 10 alcoholic drinks in their life (54% at baseline and evaluation) and no significant change in reported drinking in the last two weeks or last seven days, although the proportion who reported that they had drunk alcohol on more than two occasions in the past two weeks declined (from 30% to 25%). Among males, there was no significant change in the proportion reporting that they consumed five or more standard drinks on the last drinking occasion (baseline 57%, evaluation 62%) or seven or more standard drinks (baseline 43%, evaluation 49%). However, among females, there was a significant increase in proportion reporting that they consumed five or more standard drinks on the last drinking occasion (from 42% to 55%) and seven or more standard drinks (from 27% to 37%).

principles positions us to be able to critically assess the effects of marketing on the health and well-being of society. Given the almost ubiquitous nature of alcohol marketing, we cannot bring about any real change without first critically engaging with messages and tactics the industry is using to promote the use (and often the excessive use) of its products.

The alcohol industry spends vast sums of money in promoting its products around the globe. For example, in the USA alone, the industry spent over $547 million on advertising in 2007, with the bulk of this expenditure being print advertising ($410 million), followed by television advertising ($118 million) (Center for Science in the Public Interest, 2008a). It is interesting to note that, despite a growth rate of 3,947% in television expenditure between 1999 and 2006, there was a slight reduction in television advertising between 2006 and 2007 and a concurrent increase of almost $100 million in print advertising. It has been suggested that the academic and public interest in the effects of television alcohol advertising, along with changes in media usage patterns, may be encouraging the industry to seek out less-visible media for promoting its products.[6] It is also important to note, as pointed out by the Center for Science in the Public Interest (2008a), that this massive expenditure of $547 million is only the tip of the iceberg, as it includes only measured media: that is, it does not include point-of-purchase displays, sponsorships, festivals, internet, or other unmeasured expenditures. In the UK, it is estimated that the alcohol industry spends £200 million on advertising (television, radio, press, outdoor, and cinema), with a total 'marketing communications' spend of between £600 million and £800 million (House of Commons Health Committee, 2010).

While a comprehensive review of alcohol marketing is beyond the scope of this chapter, the following subsections highlight some recent critical analyses of alcohol marketing – organised by the 4Ps – demonstrating the need for social marketers to focus their efforts on identifying questionable marketing tactics, and bring these to the attention of both the policy makers and the community at large.

Product

Perhaps the most widely discussed alcohol product category at the current time is the 'alco-pop' or 'ready-to-drink (RTD)' – beverages made with a spirit or wine base and a non-alcoholic mixer such as juice or soft drink, served in a premixed package (Gates et al., 2007). They were first introduced in Australia in the mid-1990s, then later into Europe, the UK, and the USA (Jernigan,

2007). These products have been criticised due to their sweet taste, attractive design and packaging, and low price – and thus their evident appeal to young people (Mosher and Johnson, 2005). In Australia, the 2007 National Drug Strategy Household Survey (Australian Institute of Health and Welfare, 2008) found that the three most common drinks reported by females aged 17 and under were bottled RTDs, canned RTDs, and bottled spirits: almost four times as many as selected bottled wine, and more than five times as many as selected regular-strength beer, low-alcohol beer, and cask wine. Among boys of the same age, RTDs, bottled spirits, and regular-strength beer were the most common, and selected by three to four times as many respondents as bottled and cask wine. Preference for RTDs is lower in older age groups, with bottled RTDs a 'usual drink' for 47.3% of females and 26.4% of males aged 20–29; and canned RTDs for 37.1% of females and 47.6% of males aged 20–29; with both types down to less than 11% of males and females aged 40+.

However, what is particularly interesting – and under-researched – is the increasing range of products in this category. While these products were initially positioned as predominantly brightly coloured, sweet-tasting drinks targeted at female drinkers, and are often still described in the literature as 'highly-sweetened' drinks that are fruit-flavoured or fruit or milk based, the market in Australia is dominated by bourbon and whisky-based RTD products, with many containing more than two standard drinks per serve (Jones and Barrie, 2010). Following the introduction of the 'alcopop tax' in Australia in 2008, a strategy to address high levels of drinking among young people, media outlets quoted 'industry sources' as stating that 'they were expecting high-alcohol content "wino-pops" to hit the shelves within weeks' (*Daily Telegraph*, June 17). This was effectively a new product category designed solely to get around the increased taxation on spirit-based RTDs, and thus enable the continuing production of a high-potency low-cost product that is predominantly consumed by younger drinkers.[7]

A product category that has received far less attention in academic research – and surprisingly little interest from policymakers – is the alcohol energy drink (AED). Energy drinks first hit the market in the late 1990s, and have rapidly become a major segment of the soft drink market, particularly among 12–24 year olds (Simmon and Mosher, 2007). Within two years of their introduction, energy drinks also became a popular mixer for spirits (especially vodka), followed in 2000 with the introduction of pre-mixed alcohol energy drinks (which are packaged and marketed in a very similar style to non-alcoholic energy drinks).

Alcohol energy drinks are also often at the upper end of the alcohol strength continuum, containing a higher quantity of pure alcohol than same-sized RTDs. These products are particularly concerning, as the combination of the stimulant (energy drink) and a depressant (alcohol) can mask the perceived effects of alcohol, resulting in increased consumption and lack of awareness of the amount of alcohol consumed. There is a small, but growing, body of evidence from health researchers that consumption of these products is associated with higher levels of total alcohol consumption and increased alcohol-related harms (O'Brien et al., 2008). There are also newspaper reports of associations between AED consumption and increased aggression (MacDonald, 2007), blackouts, and non-consensual sex (Gallagher, 2006; Weideman, 2006). For example, when researchers surveyed 802 patrons exiting seven drinking establishments in a college bar district in Florida (Thombs et al., 2009b), they found that consuming energy drinks mixed with alcohol was associated with a three-fold increase in the odds of leaving a bar intoxicated (breath alcohol content ≥ 0.08 g/210 l), and a four fold increase in the odds of intending to drive from the bar district (after adjusting for potential confounders).

As well as the health implications of the consumption of large quantities of stimulants such as caffeine and guarana, in combination with alcohol, one of the concerns that has been raised in relation to these products is that they are packaged in a way that often makes them difficult to distinguish from soft drinks (Andrews, 2007; Simmon and Mosher, 2007). It is also concerning that alcohol-energy drinks are often sold for approximately the same price as non-alcoholic energy drinks. For example, a price comparison in California (Simmon and Mosher, 2007) found that three alcoholic brands (Rockstar 21, Sparks, and Tilt) could be purchased in convenience stores for 25% less than three non-alcoholic brands (Rockstar Juiced, Lost Energy, and SoBe Adrenalin Rush). Similarly, our price comparison in New South Wales (NSW), Australia, found that a range of alcoholic and non-alcoholic energy drinks could be purchased for approximately three dollars each (although, unlike the USA, these were not sold in the same store but in a bottle shop and a service station in the same street). This is a marketing issue – yet, to date, social marketers have been absent in the debate on the appropriateness of the marketing (and perhaps even the existence) of this product category.

Price

There is considerable evidence from studies conducted across three decades that there is an inverse relationship between the price of alcohol and the level of consumption (Coate and Grossman, 1988; Levy and Sheflin, 1983; Osterberg, 1995), and that this effect is even more pronounced among young people (Chaloupka and Weschler, 1996; Kenkel, 1993; Grossman et al., 1994; Sutton and Godfrey, 1995). For example, as early as the 1970s, an experimental study in the USA found that alcohol consumption more than doubled during simulated 'happy hours' among both heavy and light drinkers (Babor et al., 1978).

It is thus not surprising – although concerning – that recent studies have found that price-based promotions remain common, and that they continue to result in excessive consumption of alcohol. This effect has been shown in relation to both on-premise and off-premise alcohol pricing. In relation to on-premise promotions, a study of 291 patrons exiting bars in a campus community found that participating in a drink special (such as '2-for-1' or 'ladies drink free') was associated with a four fold increase in the risk of a blood alcohol concentration (BAC) ≥ 80 mg/dl (Thombs et al., 2008); a subsequent study of 383 patrons exiting college bars found that 'all-you-can-drink' specials were significantly associated with higher exiting blood alcohol content (Thombs et al., 2009a). Conversely, in a subsequent study of 804 patrons exiting college bars, these researchers found that a 10-cent increase in the cost per gram of ethanol was associated with a 30% reduction in the risk of exiting patrons being intoxicated (O'Mara et al., 2009).

In relation to off-premise purchases, the literature is limited, but that which does exist demonstrates a similar effect. In a study of the correlates of the in-store promotions for beer, based on analysis of supermarket scanner data from 64 market areas across the USA, Bray et al. (2007) found that large-volume units are more likely to be promoted than smaller package sizes. Based on evidence from previous market research that has shown in-store merchandising and promotions can substantially increase beer sales and that purchasing large package sizes may increase total consumption, they concluded that the prevalence of sales promotions for large-volume beer packages may result in increased beer consumption. They conducted a subsequent study (Bray et al., 2009), designed to determine whether these promotions resulted in brand-switching rather than increased purchase per se (which is often the industry argument – that is, that alcohol advertising does not create or increase demand, it simply causes people to choose a different brand). This study demonstrated that consumers were more likely to purchase a higher-volume package of their usual brand than to switch brands, and the authors concluded that 'volume-based price discounting induces people to buy larger-volume packages of beer and may lead to an increased overall beer consumption' (p. 607).

Place

While countries differ in the range of outlets permitted to sell alcohol for on-premise and off-premise consumption (e.g. the USA allows sales of alcohol from supermarkets and convenience stores), what is consistent across countries is the evidence that the greater the number of outlets (and the longer the trading hours) the greater the alcohol-related harm, as confirmed in a recent systematic review of 44 studies on alcohol outlet density and 15 studies on trading hours (Popova et al., 2009). This is particularly the case with on-premise consumption, with substantial evidence that extended trading hours are associated with higher rates of intoxication and subsequent harms. These findings are not unique to a particular country. Stockwell and Chikritzhs (2009) concluded from a review of controlled studies in the UK, the USA, Australia and New Zealand that 'the balance of reliable evidence from the available international literature suggests that extended late-night trading hours lead to increased consumption and related harms' (p. 153). A study of the effects of a July 2002 ban on alcohol sales after 11.00 p.m. in Diadema, Brazil – which analysed homicide data from 1995 to 2005 – found that the new restriction led to a decrease of nine murders per month (Duailibi et al., 2007).

The critical analysis of the distribution (or 'place') of alcohol should also include consideration of the distribution of messages *about* alcohol, as well as the promotional strategies that occur within, and bring drinkers, to 'places'. In the USA, Pasch et al. (2009) found that billboard alcohol advertisements were common near schools, particularly in disadvantaged neighbourhoods. When researchers in NSW (Australia) reported their finding that alcohol was the most advertised product on billboards within a 250 metre radius of primary schools, with up to 25 advertisements per square kilometre, the Outdoor Media Association 'hit back', saying that they had recently introduced a policy (to take effect the following March) which would 'require outdoor media operators to limit the advertising of alcohol products on fixed inventory located within a 150 metre sight line of a school' (Lister, 2008).[8]

Music and event sponsorships in Australia and New Zealand include Jim Beam concert tours and campus band competitions; Jack Daniels music industry awards and summer rock festivals; and

Lion Nathan Sydney and Adelaide Festivals, Fashion Week and Big Day Out (SHORE, 2006). In 2007, Smirnoff spent $1.5 million on an 'exclusive' music event designed solely to persuade 1500 'trendsetters' to trial its RTD products (Sinclair, 2007). Some of the more bizarre alcohol promotions, which demonstrate the ability of the industry to engage in truly appalling marketing, while staying within the scope of the law, include: a 'Bikini Party' at a Melbourne nightclub in 2006 (unlimited free alcohol for women wearing a bikini); 'a bare-chested and top-hatted dwarf walking the length of a bar pouring free booze down the throats of patrons' (news.com.au, 2008); and Oldham (UK) nightclub's 'January Sale' with 'all you can drink' on Friday nights for £5.99 (Chapman, 2009).

Promotion

There is increasing evidence from countries around the globe of associations between:

- Advertisement liking and under-age drinking (Austin and Nach-Ferguson, 1995).
- Exposure and alcohol expectancies (e.g. Grube, 1995; Lipsitz et al., 1993).
- Exposure and drinking intentions (e.g. Austin and Meili, 1994; Grube and Wallack, 1994; Kelly and Edwards, 1998).
- Exposure and current or future drinking (Atkin, 1990; Atkin et al., 1983, 1984; Casswell and Zhang, 1998; Connolly et al., 1994; Wyllie et al., 1998).

While many of these findings have been debated by the industry, due to their largely cross-sectional nature, more recently several longitudinal studies have demonstrated clearly that exposure to alcohol advertising *does* increase adolescent drinking. For example, Snyder et al. (2006) found that for each additional advertisement a young person saw (over the monthly youth average of 23), they drank 1% more; and for each additional dollar per capita spent on alcohol advertising in a local market, young people drank 4% more. Stacy et al. (2004) found that children who viewed more alcohol ads in seventh grade were more likely to drink alcohol in the eighth grade; Ellickson et al. (2005) found that exposure to magazine alcohol advertising in seventh grade predicted frequency of drinking in ninth grade.

Numerous studies from the USA, the UK, and Australia have demonstrated that young people are exposed to high levels of alcohol advertising. For example, a recent analysis of alcohol advertising on the US national cable television found that each one-percentage point increase in adolescent viewership was associated with 7% more ads for beer, 15% more for spirits, and 22% more for alcopops (Chung et al., 2010). In Australia, King et al. (2005) found that exposure to alcohol advertising via metropolitan free-to-air TV in Sydney and Melbourne (the two largest cities) among 13–17 year olds is only slightly less than among 18–29 year olds. Similarly, a recent analysis of alcohol advertising in the US magazines found that those products most consumed by under-age drinkers (beer, vodka, rum, and alcopops) were significantly more frequently placed in magazines with a high youth readership (King et al., 2009).

Debates about the amount of exposure to alcohol advertising often overlook the importance of the *content* of the advertising. In relation to young people, key features that have been shown to increase advertisement awareness, recall and liking are music, cartoon characters, animals, stories and humour (e.g. Chen et al., 2005).[9] However, the impact of alcohol advertising goes beyond these direct associations between exposure and drinking behaviours – other concerns include the effect of alcohol advertising on young people's (and, I would argue, adults') perceptions of drinking as a normative behaviour (e.g. Casswell, 1995; Lieberman and Orlandi, 1987) and the reinforcement of gender and racial stereotypes (e.g. Alaniz and Wilkes, 1998).

Alcohol advertising and promotion encourages positive associations with alcohol and links drinking alcohol with attractive symbols and role models. For example, beer advertisements often suggest that the product can help the drinker to be more relaxed, happy and successful; and advertisements for spirits, wine and 'alcopops' (alcoholic lemonades) often link consumption of the product with social, sexual, and business success (Jones et al., 2009).

Many countries, including the UK and Australia, have a self-regulatory system for alcohol advertising in which the advertisers determine the clauses of the code and monitor advertiser compliance. Thus, a key challenge is to ensure that alcohol advertisers comply with the rules that they themselves established (but, in many cases, appear unwilling or unable to follow). Numerous studies of the self-regulation of (alcohol) advertising have concluded that these systems are ineffective and lacking in rigour; concerns include their reactive nature, which requires a consumer to complain before action is taken, low levels of community awareness of the complaint system and the absence of punitive measures for advertisers found to breach the rules. (See the following section on the role of, and need for, government regulation.) The following case study illustrates the ability of the industry to circumvent its self-imposed codes of practice.

Alcohol advertising self-regulation in the UK

The UK Committee of Advertising Practice states on its website that 'Admired around the world for its creativity, the UK advertising industry sets the standard in successful self-regulation' and describes the self-regulatory codes of practice as 'designed to protect consumers'. In 2009, Gerard Hastings conducted a review of alcohol industry documents as part of the House of Commons Select Committee Review (Hastings, 2009). The following is a summary of a few of Hastings' findings in the context of three of the clauses of the code.

18.1 *Marketing communications must be socially responsible and must contain nothing that is likely to lead people to adopt styles of drinking that are unwise. For example, they should not encourage excessive drinking…*

The brand positioning documents for Sidekick refer to shots being 'Used to crank up the evening, accelerate the process of getting drunk with less volume of liquid'; and Smirnoff's documents that 'potency can be communicated in a number of ways by Smirnoff…for the consumer both result in increased purity and therefore increased strength'.

18.2 *Marketing communications must not claim or imply that alcohol can enhance confidence or popularity (and)*

18.3 *Marketing communications must not imply that drinking alcohol is a key component of the success of a personal relationship or social event.*

Hastings cites numerous examples from creative briefs and planning documents that certainly appear to 'imply' exactly that. Lambrini is described as a 'social lubricant' that 'can make you and the girls forget your dull working week and transform you into the glamour pusses you know you should be'; and Peñka vodka 'releases my Super Me…. Because when I drink it, I feel I am in the know and part of an elite group'.

To really understand the workings of the industry, and for a great example of the type of critical marketing we *should* be doing, I recommend you read Hastings' report in full (and particularly the discussion of Carling's use of advertising creativity to skirt around the edges of the CAP Code).

THE THIRD INSTRUMENT: GOING UPSTREAM

As stated above, the evidence on which are the most effective interventions to reduce alcohol-related harms is clear. However, these strategies – such as reducing access, increasing price and regulating or banning advertising and sponsorship – are rarely implemented by government.

The Australian government response to the evidence

The Alcohol and Public Policy Group report that countries with greater restrictions on advertising have fewer alcohol-related problems. Furthermore, they conclude that industry self-regulation tends to be largely ineffective, and that an effective system requires an independent body with the power to veto advertisements, rule on complaints and impose sanctions (International Centre for Alcohol Policies, 2001).[10]

Despite repeated reviews of the self-regulatory system, which have consistently found that it is ineffective in preventing (young) people from being exposed to inappropriate messages about alcohol (Jones and Donovan, 2002; Jones et al., 2008, 2009), the government has declined to take action on the regulation of alcohol advertising. In 2008, Senator Fielding (an Independent MP) introduced the 'Alcohol Toll Reduction Bill', calling for the government to: require health information labels on all alcohol products; restrict TV and radio alcohol advertising to after 9 p.m. and before 5 a.m.; require all alcohol ads to be pre-approved by a government body comprising an expert from the medical profession, alcohol and drug support sector, accident trauma support sector and the alcohol industry; and ban alcohol ads which are aimed at children or which link drinking to personal, business, social, sporting, sexual, or other success.

After months of written submissions, days of Hearings, and predictions in the media of radical changes to the regulation of alcohol marketing, the Senate Committee concluded (Senate Standing Committee on Community Affairs, 2008):

- In relation to alcohol labelling: *The appropriate pathway for any proposed change to the labelling of alcoholic products is through assessment by Food Standards Australia New Zealand (FSANZ).*
- In relation to the regulation of alcohol advertising: *The inquiry highlighted some deficiencies with the current ABAC Scheme for pre-vetting alcohol advertisements and adjudicating complaints.*

However, the Committee also notes the relatively low number of public complaints recorded concerning alcohol advertising in recent years. The Committee does not agree that there is a compelling case for a dual system on industry quasi-regulation and government regulation of alcohol advertising....

- In relation to alcohol advertising during sport: *The Committee recommends that the Ministerial Council on Drugs Strategy, the Monitoring of Alcohol Advertising Committee, and the ABAC Scheme Management Committee consider additional safeguards to ensure that alcohol advertising during sport coverage, if it continues, does not adversely influence children and young people.*

The UK government response to the evidence

In late 2009, the House of Commons Health Select Committee (HSC) reported to government on the harms associated with alcohol consumption in the UK, and the most effective (evidence-based) strategies to address this spiralling problem. The Committee was particularly scathing in pointing out the prior failure of government to respond to the evidence:

> Faced by a mounting problem, the response of successive Governments has ranged from the non-existent to the ineffectual. In 2004 an Alcohol Strategy was published following an excellent study of the costs of alcohol by the Strategy Unit. Unfortunately, the Strategy failed to take account of the evidence which had been gathered. (p. 5)

The primary criticism (as with the Australian government) was that the strategy emphasised the policies which the evidence showed were ineffective and de-emphasised, or ignored, those for which there was strong evidence.

In all, the 2009 HSC made 45 recommendations to government: 13 of these related to NHS services, and are outside the scope of this chapter; three related to 'education and information policies'; 13 to 'marketing and the drinks industry'; five to 'licensing, binge-drinking, and crime and disorder'; three to 'supermarkets and off-licence sales'; and eight to 'prices: taxes and minimum prices'. The government agreed with the recommendation to 'educate' the public and was nominally supportive of unit labelling of drinks (but only as a voluntary industry initiative). However, they did not agree to a ban on advertising, independent regulation of alcohol promotions, the involvement of young people in the process of regulation,[11] extension of codes to better cover alcohol sponsorship, mandatory restrictions on billboard advertising near schools,[12] a 9.00 p.m. watershed for alcohol advertising, restricting cinema advertising to films classified as age 18+, restrictions on advertising in media or at events where more than 10% of the audience are under 18, or a ban on alcohol advertising on social networking sites. They also did not agree to strategies that would increase the price or reduce the availability of alcohol.

What is particularly interesting about these decisions is not just the acceptance of strategies with the least evidence of effect and refusal of those with the strongest evidence, but the rationale given for these decisions. The government response focused on the few studies that questioned the effectiveness of these strategies, and discounted other evidence with parenthetical comments such as 'this related to mainly US based studies' (p. 26). However, their reasons for not supporting these strategies, while stated as facts, were devoid of any evidence base. For example:

a 9pm watershed ban or a ban on alcohol advertising would most likely have a significant impact on the creative industries (p. 27)

the proposed restriction would have a significant impact on the cinema industry…leading to a significant reduction in the diversity of films for UK audiences, job losses, a reduction in revenue … and ticket price rises for cinema goers (p. 28)

Such sweeping conclusions draw an interesting division between public health considerations, for which decades of evidence from carefully controlled studies are not sufficient to persuade government, and industry considerations which appear to need neither evidence nor even a named source.[13] In the rare event that governments can be encouraged to take evidence-based actions, the results can be substantial – as the following case study demonstrates.

THE NEED TO AGREE ON THE TUNE

One of the key reasons that the alcohol industry (and its related industries) have been so successful in opposing the introduction of effective measures is that they have succeeded in singing from the same songsheet. When we advocate for the banning of alcohol advertising, the voices of the alcohol industry – the advertising (creative) industry, the media planners and buyers and the media industry – raise their voices in harmony to argue that this will be ineffective in reducing alcohol-related harms, but will be the death of the industry and the loss of livelihoods (which we have seen above is nicely echoed in the tunes played by our governments). In the words of Clemenger Executive Chairman, Robert Morgan:

Above all, we need to unite. We need to focus on the central issue, to generate trust by government and the community. We need to consider industry-wide voluntary action to control the agenda and, of course, to continue to provide evidence on the ineffectiveness of ad bans (Addington, 2009).

The industry also demonstrates a consistent ability to bring on board other 'stakeholder' groups, and engage them in parallel protests to support the industry's objectives. For example, in Australia, sporting associations have been powerful spokespeople in the industry's campaign to maintain alcohol sponsorship of sport (Jones, 2010). The Director of the West Australian Football League, for example, argued that Foster's (a beer brand) 'have a responsible drinking policy…' and that the dependence on sponsorship money should be the primary consideration:

Let's say someone has research that says for the sake of our community it should be banned…. Before they bring it out, they need to do a quick check – what community clubs are getting money and who's going to fund them…. Don't do

---

A good news story

In April 2008, the Australian Government introduced an 'alcopops tax' – increasing the excise tax on spirit-based RTDs to a similar rate to that of other spirit-based alcohol products (at the time, an increase from $39.36 to $66.67 per litre of pure alcohol). The industry argued strongly that this would serve only to encourage young people (the main target of the intervention) to switch from alcopops to 'more harmful' products. However, an analysis of sales data for the period May–July 2008 (compared with the same period in the previous year) showed that alcopop sales decreased by 91 million standard drinks but spirit sales increased by only 35 million standard drinks; after incorporating concurrent changes in beer and wine consumption, the net effect was a reduction in overall alcohol consumption of 64 million standard drinks over a three-month period (Chikritzhs et al., 2009).

anything until you can answer that question (*Midland Reporter*, 2009).

It is, in part, our failure as social marketers (and public health advocates) to achieve the same harmony that minimises our potential to bring about meaningful change. Due to the complex nature of the alcohol problem, and the role of alcohol in our society, we often find ourselves working almost in opposition to each other – much to the delight of the industry, who are then able to argue that 'even the experts don't agree' and thus there is no need for greater regulation of the marketing of alcohol. The following two examples, which are in no way unique, demonstrate the way that strategies which may serve to reduce harm among one group can serve to increase harm among another; or that reduce one alcohol-related problem have the potential to increase another.

Standard drink labelling in Australia

Research in the early 1990s demonstrated that standard drink labels (often referred to as 'unit labelling') significantly reduce the mean error in adults' estimations of alcohol content, concluding that standard drink labelling would assist drinkers who *wished to drink within low risk drinking guidelines* (Stockwell et al., 1991). Thus, in Australia, the Ministerial Council on Drug Strategy recommended the introduction of a policy requiring the inclusion of standard drink information on all alcohol beverages (Stockwell, 1993).

In response to increasing concerns about excessive alcohol consumption, particularly by young people, researchers argued that the problem was lack of awareness of the amount of alcohol in a usual serving size and advocated for clearer labelling and expenditure on public communication campaigns. Thus, in 2006 the Australian alcohol industry voluntarily introduced new standard drink logos, which were three times the size of the existing standard drink statements – reflecting a view that providing people with clear information about standard drinks will enable them to drink safely.

We conducted a qualitative study with undergraduate university students to assess awareness, and use, of standard drink labelling (Jones and Gregory, 2009). Participants were generally in agreement that they noticed standard drink labels, and took these into account when choosing what to purchase (and consume). However, this was predominantly to help them choose stronger drinks (to reduce the amount of liquid consumed; reduce the time taken to get drunk; and, among males, to engage in competitive behaviour). The predominant reason for using standard drink labelling was value for money – to choose the most 'cost effective' way of getting drunk. Thus, we found that contrary to the industry position that introducing more visible labelling will assist people to make more responsible drinking choices, we found that it assisted young people to make more irresponsible choices. Further, it appeared that a primary outcome of the introduction of these more visible labels has been to divert attention from the more important questions. This is not to suggest that standard drink labelling is not a valuable tool for those who want to drink responsibly. Rather, it demonstrates that any such intervention needs to be combined with other evidence-based policies (less popular with industry) that address the price, availability, and marketing of alcohol.

Road Crew

Perhaps one of the best-known social marketing interventions from the US is 'Road Crew':

> ... the innovative approach to reducing drunk driving. Pioneered in several rural Wisconsin counties, Road Crew has proven itself to be a popular and easy way for drinkers to get around without their vehicles, while keeping communities safe from drivers who have had too much to drink (http://www.roadcrewonline.org/about).

This novel social marketing intervention was developed to address the problem of drink-driving in rural communities, based on formative research which showed that young people living in these communities were driving home intoxicated due to perceived lack of alternatives to driving home after a night out.

An evaluation of the first two years of the programme concluded that 19,757 rides were taken (over half by the target group of 21–34 year olds), alcohol consumption did not change significantly, and 15 crashes were avoided

(Continued)

(*Continued*)

(Rothschild et al., 2006). The programme has subsequently expanded to include six counties serving 36 communities (http://www.roadcrewonline.org/about).

So what's the problem?

While the Road Crew project appears to have reduced drink-driving rates, and the number of crashes, it raises important questions about who decides the 'good' in a social marketing intervention. The programme could well be commended for, rather than taking an 'education' approach of simply telling young people that drink-driving is bad, instead taking a 'social marketing' approach and developing an exchange that is of value to the target audience. On the other hand, it could be argued that programmes such as Road Crew serve to reinforce the perception that excessive drinking is both normative and unavoidable.[14] Research with young college women suggests that driving to a social event is the *most effective strategy* for young people who want to refrain from drinking but still remain within the group (Wiese and Jones 2008). This is seen as the only 'acceptable' reason for not drinking, significantly reducing the peer pressure on the non-drinker, and a strategy that is regularly used by young people who want to socialise without consuming alcohol (and without having to tell their peers that they don't want to drink). Similarly, a quick Google search on the phrase 'excuses for not drinking' confirms that 'tell them you're driving' is the primary coping strategy offered to young people as a way of avoiding drinking.

This perception that alcohol consumption is both normative and unavoidable is pervasive even in public health messages and social marketing campaigns. Many organisations conduct an annual event in which people pledge to refrain from drinking for a month (and they usually elect for February as the shortest month). This potentially powerful message – that it *is* possible to abstain from alcohol for 28 days – is undermined by the ability to 'buy' a day off (as many times as you 'need' to during the month). For example, in the Australian FebFast 'You don't have to miss out on a special event! You can purchase a $25 date stamped Time Out Certificate to have a guilt-free day off from your FebFast. Alternatively, if a friend wants to buy a Time Out for you, they can purchase one here' (http://www.febfast.com.au/). Similarly, 'Dry July' allows you to buy a 'Golden Ticket' so 'you can enjoy some drinks on any given day without feeling too guilty' (http://www.dryjuly.com/). In the USA, they have the 'Alcohol Free Weekend' on the first weekend in April; perhaps a concession to the evident impossibility of surviving a whole four weeks without alcohol?

SHOULD WE SLEEP WITH THE ENEMY?

Perhaps we should first ask: 'Do we know when we are sleeping with the enemy'? The 'competition' to the promotion of responsible drinking comes not only from the industry itself (see section on critical marketing and comments below) but also from the social norm of (excessive) drinking and the pervasive pro-alcohol messages in our media discourse. This is perhaps most obvious in the examples given above regarding organisations who seek to raise awareness (or funds) but convey a subtle message that refraining from drinking is not socially feasible. Similarly, we often see partnerships between health organisations and commercial entities that promote a 'health' message while also promoting alcohol consumption – such as the sponsorship of 2006 'Movember' campaign (a men's health campaign designed to increase awareness of prostate cancer, male depression, and testicular cancer, and to raise funds by having men grow a moustache sponsored by friends' donations) by Foster's VB. The 'Pool Room' page on the Movember website showed a group of men in a room filled with VB paraphernalia and all drinking the beer, and included a video entitled 'A Mo Bro never lets someone drink alone', which showed an unhappy man who cheers up when one of his friends buys him a drink (Munro, 2006).

Industry organisations, and individual companies, expend considerable energy (and money) persuading governments, and communities, that they are good social citizens and that they are committed to ensuring that people consume their products in a safe and responsible manner (while at the same time arguing vehemently against any restrictions on the marketing and advertising of their products – even when their marketing tactics are shown to be directly harmful).[15]

Anheuser-Busch spent $19.9 million on 'responsibility' advertising on television between 2001 and 2005, and in 2007 claimed on its website to be 'the global industry leader in promoting responsibility'.[16] However, as noted by the Center for Science in the Public Interest (2008b), this $19.9 million is a tiny drop in a very large ocean; in the same period Anheuser-Busch spent $1.6 billion on television product advertising, $52 million on other television advertising and accounted for 43% of all measured media expenditure by the US beer industry. Perhaps an even more startling comparison: Anheuser-Busch's media budget in 2006 was $607 million, whereas the total 2008 budget of the National Institute on Alcohol Abuse and Alcoholism was only $436 million (Center for Science in the Public Interest, 2008b). However, as Casswell and Thamarangsi (2009) remind us, research suggests that responsible drinking messages are strategically ambiguous. They appear to have both public relations and sales benefits, whereas industry argues that they are designed to improve health (although the lack of evidence of effectiveness of education intervention suggests this is unlikely to be the case).

Charity activities conducted by alcohol companies not only position them as socially responsible but also enable them to encourage consumption of the product; for example, Lion Nathan's XXXX beer conducted a fundraising campaign for cyclone relief that included a 'Beach to Brewery Walk' and a 10c donation for every beer sold at sporting events (SHORE, 2006). This raises the question – for governments, communities, and even researchers – Should we join hands with them (especially when they reach into their deep pockets to fund research, education campaigns, and community resources)?

The last decade has seen the rise of 'independent' organisations – with a mission to change our drinking behaviours – funded by the alcohol industry, such as Drinkaware in the UK and DrinkWise in Australia. In Australia, DrinkWise was established in 2005 by the alcohol industry, receiving $5 million over four years from the Australian government. Since late 2009, DrinkWise has been 'entirely supported by voluntary contributions from across the Australian alcohol industry' (http://www.drinkwise.com.au), and governed by a board of six community and six industry representatives. From its inception, DrinkWise (and the government's decision to hand over $5 million to those least likely to benefit from a reduction in drinking) has been criticised by public health advocates. One of the concerns is DrinkWise's focus on young drinkers – as Robin Room stated on the ABC: 'a message that says well our drink is for adults, is a double-edged message to be giving to a teenager' (does this seem reminiscent of Philip Morris's spectacularly unsuccessful 'just say no' anti-smoking education programmes? see Landman et al., 2002) The almost sole focus on 'education'

campaigns across these organisations (i.e. the strategy shown to be the least effective) also brings into question the industry's commitment to reduce the alcohol toll – Why don't they instead focus on redressing packaging and pricing strategies that provide incentives for excessive consumption?

In 2009, more than 50 senior Australian scientists and health experts were signatories to a letter to the *Medical Journal of Australia* stating that they would not seek or accept funding from DrinkWise, and calling on other researchers and community agencies to consider their positions (Miller et al., 2009). The debate about whether to accept alcohol industry funding is not a new one – with many alcohol companies having a long history of providing grants for alcohol-related research. Many of these organisations also provide grants and resources for community groups. This decision (not) to accept funding from industry organisations is perhaps harder for community-based organisations at a time when other funding is not often available. This is an area of heated debate among researchers and advocates – with some arguing that we must work with the industry to bring about change, and others that by working with the industry we are opening ourselves up to the possibility of a (real or perceived) conflict of interest. It is for this reason that many academic journals now require submitting authors to declare any funding from the alcohol industry.[17]

SO, WHAT IS THE ROLE OF SOCIAL MARKETING?

> ... while public information and education programs are largely ineffective in reducing harmful alcohol consumption [i.e., bringing about individual behaviour change], there is evidence that these programs (and thus, if done well, social marketing) can serve to raise public and political awareness of the need to address alcohol-related harm (Anderson et al., 2009).

Thus, I would argue, the role of social marketing is to work consistently and cohesively to bring about the necessary changes in our communities to address the current, and increasing, levels of alcohol-related harm. To do so will require a combination of customer-focused (downstream) social marketing, critical marketing and strategies to bring about environmental and policy change (or upstream social marketing).

The agenda-setting role of social marketing is of particular importance, given the evidence of existing public opinion regarding interventions to reduce alcohol-related harms. It appears, in the countries for which data are available, that the policies with the widest community support are those that the evidence suggests are ineffective. For example, a survey of over 4000 people in four districts in Finland (Holmila et al., 2009) found that 88% fully support educating the young on dangers related to drinking and 75% fully support providing information on alcohol-related harms (both of which the evidence suggests are ineffective or even counterproductive). However, in relation to those interventions for which there is strong evidence, public support is lacking: increasing the price of alcohol (26% fully support); decreasing alcohol store hours (21%); and banning alcohol advertising (20%).[18] Similarly, in Australia, the 2007 National Drug Strategy Household Survey found that 13% strongly support increasing the price of alcohol; 20% reducing trading hours for pubs and clubs; 26% increasing the legal drinking age; and 40% limiting alcohol advertising on television until after 9.30 p.m. (AIHW, 2008).

What is even more concerning is the evidence of shifts in public opinion over time, with declining support for the majority of evidence-based strategies. Table 17.1 sets out data on levels of

agreement from population surveys in Canada, the USA, and Australia (note that the table shows only the most recent figures for each country – interested readers are referred to the original papers for full data).

As shown in Table 17.1, public support for the most effective strategies to reduce alcohol-related harm is decreasing across many countries at the same time as alcohol-related harms are increasing. A key role for social marketing, therefore, must be a concerted effort – both downstream and upstream – to raise awareness of the effectiveness of strategies such as restrictions on advertising and sponsorship, reductions in availability and increases in price.[19]

CONCLUSION

If, as social marketers, we are to make a contribution to addressing alcohol-related harms in our communities, we need to move the conversation away from 'problem' drinkers (such as young people) and instead talk about our drinking cultures; we need to move away from ineffective (but popular) victim-blaming, high-fear social

Table 17.1 Levels of support for alcohol control policies (proportion of respondents supporting or strongly supporting)

	Most recent figure (year and comparison year in parentheses) and directional change[a]		
	Canada[b] (1994/1989)	USA[c] (2000/1989)	Australia[d] (2004/1993)
Promotion			
Ban on TV advertising	40.2[e] ↓	56.1	≅[f]
Government counter advertising	**50.7 ↓**	**53.0 ↓**	–
Ban sports sponsorship	–	40.1	↑
Access			
Liquor store hours decreased	17.1 ↓	31.5 ↓	↓
No alcohol in corner stores	69.0 ↓	61.8 ↓	↓[g]
Warning labels	**71.6 ↓**	**93.9 ↑**	
Increase alcohol taxes	–	35.3 ↓	↓[h]
Raise minimum drinking age	–	25.8 ↓	↓

NOTE: **Bolded** items are those with no, or limited, evidence of effectiveness.
[a] Shift greater than 5 percentage points (not a 5% change) considered significant.
[b] Giesbrecht et al. (2007).
[c] Greenfield et al. (2007).
[d] Wilkinson et al. (2009) (note % agreement not given; analysis based on mean scores).
[e] 2004.
[f] In Australia, the question was not a 'ban' but a restriction to after 9.30 p.m.
[g] In Australia, where alcohol is not sold in corner stores, the question was 'reduce number of outlets'.
[h] In Australia, the question was phrased as 'increase price' rather than 'increase tax'.

advertising campaigns; and we need to shine an enquiring light on the tactics of commercial marketers. Most importantly, we need to shift the conversation – with the community and with governments – to the strategies that are effective: reducing the availability of alcohol, increasing the price of alcohol, and banning or adequately regulating the advertising and promotion of alcohol (e.g. Anderson et al., 2009).

In order to achieve this, we need to use all of the instruments in our orchestra (downstream, upstream, and critical marketing) and we need to all play the same tune. We need to – as the industry has done – develop a shared purpose and agree on the most effective strategies to bring about these changes; and these strategies need to be informed by the extensive evidence base on the effectiveness of different interventions. This means, for many of us, accepting that traditional (downstream) social marketing, or social advertising, should not be the focus at the present time. It is clear from the reviews of the evidence that in order to bring about widespread change we need to focus on the supply of alcohol: its price, availability, and promotion. Thus, we first need to engage more actively in critical marketing, identifying the inappropriate tactics utilised by the industry to sell ever-greater quantities of alcohol, and holding them to account for the effects of these actions. We then need to increase awareness among both policymakers (upstream) and the general public (downstream) of the role of these factors in accelerating rates of alcohol consumption and alcohol-related harm and work to reduce the ubiquitous promotion of alcohol. It is only when we have achieved this that we will be able to begin to bring about changes in the societal norm of (excessive) alcohol consumption.

KEY WORDS: Alcohol; alcohol marketing; alcohol advertising; regulation; policy; industry; drinking cultures; social norms.

Key insights

- This chapter focuses on social marketing's response to concerns regarding excessive alcohol consumption and increasing alcohol-related harms.
- While it may be politically 'popular' to talk about the alcohol problem as a problem of youth, the reality is that harmful drinking needs to be addressed across society as a whole. We need to move the conversation away from 'problem' drinkers (such as young people), and instead talk about our drinking cultures.

- The most effective strategies to reduce alcohol-related harm are: increasing the price and reducing the availability of alcohol; banning alcohol advertising; drink-driving interventions; and individual interventions for at-risk drinkers. However, governments are consistently reluctant to regulate the alcohol industry.
- It is unlikely that even the most carefully designed and implemented social marketing intervention will bring about individual-level behaviour change without concurrent changes in our social and commercial environment.
- The role of social marketing is to work consistently and cohesively to bring about the necessary changes in our communities to address current and increasing levels of alcohol-related harm. To do so will require a combination of customer-focused (downstream) social marketing, critical marketing, and strategies to bring about environmental and policy change (upstream social marketing).

NOTES

1   For example, alcohol has been categorised as a Group One carcinogen (i.e. carcinogenic to humans) by the World Health Organization, US Department of Health and Human Services, American Cancer Society, and numerous other organisations around the world (putting it in the same category as asbestos, formaldehyde, and mustard gas).

2   Doug Sellman refers to these collectively as the 5+ Solution: 1. Increase the price of alcohol. 2. Increase the purchase age of alcohol. 3. Decrease accessibility of alcohol. 4. Decrease marketing and advertising of alcohol. 5. Increase drink-driving measures. PLUS: Increase treatment opportunities for heavy drinkers (http://www.adanz.org.nz/adanz/subnav/submissions/alcohol%20action%20new%20zealand).

3   Many readers will see parallels with tobacco – see subsequent section on responses to industry campaigns.

4   To paraphrase obesity expert Boyd Swinburn: harmful alcohol consumptions 'is NOT a knowledge-deficit problem' (http://www.scoop.co.nz/stories/GE0703/S00111.htm).

5   It is interesting to note that this is approximately half of the number of parents who recalled having the same conversation, perhaps suggesting either some social desirability bias in the parents' responses, or differences in parents' and teenagers' perceptions of 'talking about alcohol' with one another.

6   Again, there are clear parallels with tobacco – with the bans on advertising resulting in the diversion of marketing budgets to (potentially even more influential) sporting and cultural sponsorships.

7   The need for this strategy may have been exaggerated, given the many other 'tools' at the industry's disposal. For example, a recent study concluded that the multi-pack pricing of RTDs in Australia keeps these products within the budget of most young people and actually provides incentives for increased consumption by effectively making it cheaper to buy, for example, six than five units (Jones and Barrie, 2010).

8   It is interesting to note that they elected to 'limit' rather than ban alcohol advertising near schools; that the policy applies only to 'fixed inventory' (i.e. not movable or mobile signage); and that they chose only a 150 metre radius.

9   Again, note the parallels with tobacco marketing.

10   A similar conclusion has been reached in relation to other product categories – for example, repeated studies of food advertising targeting children have found that these systems have failed to protect consumers or to regulate industry practices (e.g. Dixon, 2007; Kunkel et al., 2009; Wilde, 2009).

11   The self-regulatory system in the UK, as in many countries, is based on an undertaking that certain messages will not be conveyed in advertisements. Thus, the involvement of young people in the assessment of the messages in alcohol advertising is critical to both our understanding of how these messages are interpreted by children and adolescents, and our ability to demonstrate to industry and government that the Codes are being breached (i.e. the yardstick should be the message *received* by audiences).

12   Similar to the situation in Australia, described above, the UK Outdoor Advertising Association (OAA) has a charter which states:

In the interests of responsible advertising to protect minors from undue exposure to alcohol advertising, OAA members *shall consider (as a voluntary and unilateral measure)* not displaying alcohol advertising on their panels located within a 100 metre radius of any school entrance' (OAA, 2008).

13   The industry's strategy of 'manufacturing uncertainty' is most identified with tobacco, but also used other industries which produce hazardous products (see Michaels and Monforton, 2005).

14   Similar criticisms have been levelled at 'designated driver' road safety campaigns that could be interpreted to mean that as long as there is a sober driver it is fine for everyone else to drink excessively.

15   Donna Doane argues that there are a number of 'myths of CSR', including the assertion that codes and management systems change corporate behaviour and that the free market will provide incentives for businesses to engage in sustainable practices (Doane, 2005; also see Rabet, 2009)

16   Not unlike British American Tobacco, which describes itself as 'the world's most international tobacco group, with quality brands sold in more than 180 markets and a *responsible approach to doing business from crop to consumer*' (http://www.bat.com/).

17   As they do for funding from the tobacco, gaming, and pharmaceutical industries.

18   It is likely that this is, in large part, because people are unaware of the role of alcohol advertising in encouraging under-age and excessive drinking (thus, the need for social marketing campaigns to raise awareness of advertising effects) – given high levels of support for banning of fast-food advertising to children, the harms of which have been communicated to, and accepted by, the general population.

19   One potential strategy would be to raise young people's awareness of the strategies utilised by the industry to manipulate their perceptions, attitudes, and behaviours. This could take the form of media literacy training, or a more active approach, such as that effectively used in the case of tobacco by the Florida (and then national) 'Truth' Campaign (Sly et al., 2001).

REFERENCES

Addington T (2009) Morgan calls for regulation united front. *B&T Today*, March 16, 2.

Alaniz ML and Wilkes C (1998) Pro-drinking messages and message environments for young adults. *Journal of Public Health Policy*, 19, 447–471.

Anderson P, Chisholm D and Fuhr DC (2009) Effectiveness and cost-effectiveness of policies and programmes to reduce the harm caused by alcohol. *Lancet*, 373, 2234–2246.

Andrews N (2007) Teens get alcohol in energy drinks. *Daily Herald*.

Atkin CK (1990) Effects of televised alcohol messages on teenage drinking patterns. *Journal of Adolescent Health Care*, 11, 10–24.

Atkin CK, Neuendorf K and McDermott S (1983) The role of alcohol advertising in excessive and hazardous drinking. *Journal of Drug Education*, 13(4), 313–325.

Atkin CK, Hocking J and Block M (1984) Teenage drinking: Does advertising make a difference? *Journal of Communication*, 34(2), 157–167.

Austin EW and Meili HK (1994) Effects of interpretations of televised alcohol portrayals on children's alcohol beliefs. *Journal of Broadcasting and Electronic Media*, 38, 417–435.

Austin EW and Nach-Ferguson B (1995) Sources and influences of young school-age children's knowledge about alcohol. *Health Communication*, 7, 1–20.

Australian Institute of Health and Welfare (2008) 2007 National Drug Strategy Household Survey: Detailed Findings. Drug Statistics Series No. 22. Cat. No. PHE 107. Canberra: AIHW.

Babor TF, Mendelson JH, Greenberg I and Kuehnle J (1978) Experimental analysis of the 'happy hour': Effects of purchase price on alcohol consumption. *Psychopharmacology*, 58, 35–41.

Babor TF, Caetano R, Casswell S, et al. (2010) *Alcohol: No Ordinary Commodity. Research and Public Policy*. Oxford: Oxford University Press.

Bray J, Loomis WB and Engelen M (2007) Correlates of in-store promotions for beer: Differential effects of market and product characteristics. *Journal of Studies on Alcohol and Drugs*, 68(2), 220.

Bray J, Loomis WB and Engelen M (2009) You save money when you buy in bulk. Does volume-based pricing cause people to buy more beer? *Health Economics*, 18, 607–618.

Casswell S (1995) Public discourse on alcohol: Implications for public policy, in H. Holder and G. Edwards (eds), *Alcohol and the Public: Evidence and Issues*. Oxford: Oxford University Press, pp. 190–211.

Casswell S and Thamarangsi T (2009) Reducing harm from alcohol: Call to action. *Lancet*, 373, 2247–2257.

Casswell S and Zhang JF (1998) Impact of liking for advertising and brand allegiance on drinking and alcohol-related aggression: A longitudinal study. *Addiction*, 93, 1209–1217.

Center for Science in the Public Interest (2008a) Fact Sheet: Alcoholic-beverage advertising expenditures. Center for Science in the Public Interest.

Center for Science in the Public Interest (2008b) Fact Sheet: Anheuser-Busch's consumer responsibility campaign into perspective. Center for Science in the Public Interest.

Chaloupka FJ and Weschler H (1996) Binge drinking in college: The impact of price, availability, and alcohol control policies. *Contemporary Economic Policy*, 14(4), 112–124.

Chapman T (2009) Club's £5.99 Booze Deal Slammed. Sky News, 28 January. Available at: http://news.sky.com/skynews/Home/UK-News/Tokyo-Club-In-Oldham-599-Booze-Deal-Slammed-By-Alcohol-Concern-And-MP-Phil-Woolas/Article/200901415211778.

Chen MJ, Grube JW, Bersamin M, Waiters E and Keefe DB (2005) Alcohol advertising: What makes it attractive to youth? *Journal of Health Communication*, 10, 553–565.

Chikritzhs TN, Dietze PM, Allsop SJ, et al. (2009) The 'alcopops' tax: Heading in the right direction. *Medical Journal of Australia*, 190(6), 294–295.

Chung PJ, Garfield CF, Elliott MN, et al. (2010) Association between adolescent viewership and alcohol advertising on cable television. *American Journal of Public Health*, 100(3), 555–562.

Coate D and Grossman M (1988) Effects of alcoholic beverage prices and legal drinking ages on youth alcohol use. *Journal of Law and Economics*, 31, 145–171.

Connolly G, Casswell S, Zhang JF and Silva PA (1994) Alcohol in the mass media and drinking by adolescents: A longitudinal study. *Addiction*, 89, 1255–1263.

Dixon P (2007) *The Network Advertising Initiative: Failing at Consumer Protection and at Self-Regulation*. World Privacy Forum.

Doane D (2005) Beyond corporate social responsibility: Minnows, mammoths and markets. *Futures*, 37(2–3), 215–229.

Doran CM, Hall WD, Shakeshaft AP, Vos T and Cobiac LJ (2010) Alcohol policy reform in Australia: What can we learn from the evidence? *Medical Journal of Australia*, 192, 468–470.

Duailibi S, Ponicki W, Grube J, et al. (2007) The effect of restricting opening hours on alcohol-related violence. *American Journal of Public Health*, 97(12), 2276–2280.

Ellickson PL, Collins RL, Hambarsoomians K and McCaffrey DF (2005) Does alcohol advertising promote adolescent drinking? Results from a longitudinal assessment. *Addiction*, 100(2), 235–246.

Gallagher C (2006) 'On a date? Watch your cocktail,' in *Pretoria News Weekend*, 1 edn. Vol. 25 November. Tshwane.

Gates P, Copeland J, Stevenson RJ, Dillon P (2007) The influence of product packaging on young people's palatability rating for RTDs and other alcoholic beverages. *Alcohol and Alcoholism*, 42(2), 138–142.

Giesbrecht NA, Ialomiteanu A, Anglin L and Adlaf E (2007) Alcohol marketing and retailing: Public opinion and recent policy developments in Canada. *Journal of Substance Use*, 12(6), 389–404.

Greenfield TK, Ye Y and Giesbrecht NA (2007) Views of alcohol control policies in the 2000 National Alcohol Survey: What news for alcohol policy development in the US and its States? *Journal of Substance Use*, 12(6), 429–445.

Grossman M, Chaloupka FJ, Saffer H, Laixuthai A (1994) Effects of alcohol price policy on youth: A summary of economic research. *Journal of Research on Adolescence*, 4(2), 347–364.

Grube J (1995) Television alcohol portrayals, alcohol advertising, and alcohol expectancies among children and adolescents, in SE Martin and P Mail (eds), *Effects of the Mass Media on the Use and Abuse of Alcohol*. NIAAA Research Monograph No. 28. Bethesda, MD: National Institute on Alcohol Abuse and Alcoholism, pp. 105–121.

Grube JW and Stewart K (2004) Preventing impaired driving using alcohol policy. *Traffic Injury Prevention*, 5(3), 199–207.

Grube J and Wallack L (1994) Television beer advertising and drinking knowledge, beliefs, and intentions among schoolchildren. *American Journal of Public Health*, 84(2), 254–260.

Hastings G (2009) *'They'll Drink Bucket Loads of the Stuff', An Analysis of Internal Alcohol Industry Advertising Documents*. Institute for Social Marketing.

Hastings GB and Saren M (2003) The critical contribution of social marketing: Theory and application. *Marketing Theory*, 3(3), 305–322.

Holmila M, Mustonen H, Österberg E and Raitasalo K (2009) Public opinion and community-based prevention of alcohol-related harms. *Addiction Research and Theory*, 17(4), 360–371.

House of Commons Health Committee (2010) *Alcohol: First Report of Session 2009–10*. London: The Stationery Office Limited.

International Centre for Alcohol Policies (2001) Self-regulation of beverage alcohol advertising. ICAP Reports. Washington, DC: ICAP.

Jernigan D (2007) The need for restraint. *Addiction*, 102(11), 1747–1748.

Jones L, James M, Jefferson T, et al. (2007) A review of the effectiveness and cost-effectiveness of interventions delivered in primary and secondary schools to prevent and/or reduce alcohol use by young people under 18 years old. Alcohol and schools: Review of effectiveness and cost-effectiveness. NICE: main report (PHIAC 14.3a), 2007. Available at: http://www.nice.org.uk/nicemedia/pdf/AlcoholSchools ConsReview.pdf.

Jones SC (2010) When does alcohol sponsorship of sport become sport sponsorship of alcohol? A case study of developments in sport in Australia. *International Journal of Sports Marketing & Sponsorship*, 11(3), 250–259.

Jones SC and Barrie L (2010) RTDs in Australia: Expensive designer drinks or cheap rocket fuel? *Drug and Alcohol Review* (online ahead of print).

Jones SC and Donovan RJ (2002) Self-regulation of alcohol advertising: Is it working for Australia? *Journal of Public Affairs*, 2/3, 153–165.

Jones SC and Gregory P (2009) The impact of more visible standard drink labelling on youth alcohol consumption: Helping young people drink (ir)responsibly? *Drug and Alcohol Review*, 28, 230–234.

Jones SC, Hall DV and Munro G (2008) How effective is the revised regulatory code for alcohol advertising in Australia? *Drug and Alcohol Review*, 27, 29–38.

Jones SC, Gregory P and Munro G (2009) Adolescent and young adult perceptions of Australian alcohol advertisements. *Journal of Substance Use*, 14(6), 335–352.

Kelly KJ and Edwards RW (1998) Image advertisements for alcohol products: Is their appeal associated with adolescents' intention to consume alcohol? *Adolescence*, 33, 47–59.

Kenkel DS (1993) Drinking, driving, and deterrence: The effectiveness and social costs of alternative policies. *Journal of Law and Economics*, 36(2), 877–913.

King C III, Siegel M, Jernigan DH, et al. (2009) Adolescent exposure to alcohol advertising in magazines: An evaluation of advertising placement in relation to underage youth readership. *Journal of Adolescent Health*, 45(6), 626–633.

King E, Barbir N, Ball J, Carroll T and Sutton G (2003) *Evaluation of the Third Phase of the National Alcohol Campaign: June–September 2002*. Sydney: Department of Health and Ageing.

King E, Taylor J and Carroll T (2005) *Consumer Perceptions of Alcohol Advertising and the Revised Alcohol Beverages Advertising Code*. Department of Health and Ageing, Sydney, Australia.

Kunkel D, McKinley C and Wright P (2009) *The Impact of Industry Self-Regulation on the Nutritional Quality of Foods Advertised on Television to Children*. Arizona: Children Now.

Landman A, Ling PM and Glantz SA (2002) Tobacco industry youth smoking prevention programs: Protecting the industry and hurting tobacco control. *American Journal of Public Health*, 92(6), 917–930.

Levy D and Sheflin N (1983) New evidence on controlling alcohol use through price. *Journal of Studies on Alcohol*, 44, 929–937.

Lieberman LR and Orlandi MA (1987) Alcohol advertising and adolescent drinking. *Alcohol Health and Research World*, 12, 30–33.

Lipsitz A, Brake G, Vincent EJ and Winters M (1993) Another round for the brewers: Television ads and children's alcohol expectancies. *Journal of Applied Social Psychology*, 23, 439–450.

Lister L (2008) OMA hits back over alcohol ads. *B&T Today*, 11 December, p. 1.

MacDonald B (2007) Red Bull, alcohol and drugs 'can spark violence'. *Irish Independent*, 21 February. Dublin.

Michaels D and Monforton C (2005) Manufacturing Uncertainty: Contested Science and the Protection of the Public's Health and Environment. American Journal Public Health, 95(S1), S39–S58.

Midland Reporter (2009) Division on sport sponsorship. Posted 7 April 2009. Available at: http://midland.inmy community.com.au/news-and-views/local-news/Division-on-sport-sponsorship/7522590/ (accessed 20 April 2009)

Miller PG, Kypri K, Chikritzhs TN, Skov SJ and Rubin G (2009) Health experts reject industry-backed funding for alcohol research. *Medical Journal of Australia*, 190(12), 713–714.

Mosher JF and Johnsson D. (2005) Flavored alcoholic beverages: An international marketing campaign that targets youth. *Journal of Public Health Policy*, 26(3), 326–342.

Munro G (2006) VB subverts men's health campaign. *GrogWatch*, 13 November.

National Social Marketing Centre (2006) *Social Marketing National Benchmark Criteria*. Available at: http://www. nsmcentre.org.uk/component/remository/Tools-and-Guides/Social-Marketing-Benchmark Criteria tool/

News.com.au (2008) Protests over pub's topless 'spirit dwarf'. 3 June. Available at: http://www.news.com.au/protests-over-pubs-topless-spirit-dwarf/story-e6frfkp9-111111 6524637

OAA (2008) *OAA Charter – Standard of Best Practice*. Outdoor Advertising Association of Great Britain Limited. Available at: http://www.oaa.org.uk/images/OAA%20 Charter%20-%20Standard%20of%20Best%20Practice% 20Nov%202008.pdf

O'Brien MC, McCoy TP, Rhodes SD, Wagoner A and Wolfson M (2008) Caffeinated cocktails: Energy drink consumption, high-risk drinking, and alcohol-related consequences among college students. *Academic Emergency Medicine*, 15(5), 453–460.

O'Mara RJ, Thombs DL, Wagenaar AC, et al. (2009) Alcohol price and intoxication in college bars. *Alcoholism-Clinical Experimental Research*, 33(11), 1973–1980.

Osterberg E (1995) Do alcohol prices affect consumption and related problems? In H Holder and G Edwards (eds), *Alcohol and Public Policy; Evidence and Issues.* Oxford: Oxford University Press, pp. 145–163.

Pasch KE, Komro KA, Perry CL, Hearst MO and Farbakhsh K (2009) Does outdoor alcohol advertising around elementary schools vary by the ethnicity of students in the school? *Ethnicity and Health,* 14(2), 225–236.

Popova S, Giesbrecht N, Bekmuradov D and Patra J (2009) Hours and days of sale and density of alcohol outlets: Impacts on alcohol consumption and damage: A systematic review. *Alcohol and Alcoholism,* 44(5), 500–516.

Rabet D (2009) Human rights and globalization: The myth of corporate social responsibility? *Journal of Alternative Perspectives in the Social Sciences,* 1(2), 463–475.

Rehm J, Mathers C, Popova S, et al. (2009) Global burden of disease and injury and economic cost attributable to alcohol use and alcohol-use disorders. *Lancet,* 373, 2223–2233.

Rothschild ML, Mastin B and Miller TW (2006) Reducing alcohol-impaired driving crashes through the use of social marketing. *Accident Analysis and Prevention,* 38(6), 1218–1230.

Senate Standing Committee on Community Affairs (2008) *Report: Alcohol Toll Reduction Bill 2007* [2008], Canberra: Commonwealth of Australia. Available at: http://www.aph. gov.au/senate/committee/clac_ctte/alcohol_reduction/ report/index.htm

SHORE (2006) *Alcohol Marketing in the Western Pacific Region,* Wellington, New Zealand: SHORE.

Simmon M and Mosher J (2007) *Alcohol, Energy Drinks, and Youth: A Dangerous Mix.* Marin Institute.

Sinclair L (2007) Experiential marketers get hands-on with customers through events. *The Australian,* 27 August, 34.

Sly DF, Hopkins RS, Trapido E and Ray S (2001) Influence of a counter-advertising media campaign on initiation of smoking: The Florida 'Truth' campaign. *American Journal of Public Health,* 91, 233–238.

Smith SW, Atkin CK and Roznowski J (2006) Are 'drink responsibly' alcohol campaigns strategically ambiguous? *Health Communication,* 20, 1–11.

Snyder LB, Milici FF, Slater M, Sun H and Strizhakova Y (2006) Effects of alcohol advertising exposure on drinking among youth. *Archives of Pediatrics and Adolescent Medicine,* 160, 18–24.

Stacy AW, Zogg JB, Unger JB and Dent CW (2004) Exposure to televised alcohol ads and subsequent adolescent alcohol use. *American Journal of Health Behavior,* 28(6), 498–509.

Stead M, Gordon R, Angus K and Mc Dermott L (2007) A systematic review of social marketing effectiveness. *Health Education,* 107, 126–191.

Stockwell T (1993) Influencing labelling of alcoholic beverage containers. *Addiction,* 88, 53S–60S.

Stockwell T and Chikritzhs T (2009) Do relaxed trading hours for bars and clubs mean more relaxed drinking? A review of international research on the impacts of changes to permitted hours of drinking. *Crime Prevention and Community Safety,* 11(3), 153–171.

Stockwell T, Blaze-Temple D and Walker C (1991) A test of the proposal to label containers of alcoholic drink with alcohol content in Standard Drinks. *Health Promotion International,* 6, 207–215.

Sutton M and Godfrey C (1995) A grouped data regression approach to estimating economic and social influences on individual drinking behaviour. *Health Economics,* 4, 237–247.

Thombs DL, Dodd V, Pokorny SB, et al. (2008) Drink specials and the intoxication levels of patrons exiting college bars. *American Journal of Health Behavior,* 32(4), 411–419.

Thombs DL, O'Mara RJ, Dodd V, et al. (2009a) A field study of bar-sponsored drink specials and their associations with patron intoxication. *Journal of Studies on Alcohol and Drugs,* 70(2), 206–214.

Thombs DL, O'Mara RJ, Tsukamoto M, et al. (2009b) Event-level analyses of energy drink consumption and alcohol intoxication in bar patrons, *Addictive Behaviors,* 35(4), 325–330.

UK Government (2010) *The Government response to the Health Select Committee Report on Alcohol.* London: The Stationery Office Limited.

Weideman P (2006) Doctor warns about energy-booze rape mix. *The Independent on Saturday,* 3 edn. 25 November. KwaZulu-Natal.

Wiese E and Jones SC (2008) The role of avoidance and protective behavioural strategies in the university drinking environment. Paper presented at the World Social Marketing Conference, London.

Wilde P (2009) Self-regulation and the response to concerns about food and beverage marketing to children in the United States. *Nutrition Reviews,* 67(3), 155–166.

Wilkinson C, Room R and Livingston M (2009) Mapping Australian public opinion on alcohol policies in the new millennium. *Drug and Alcohol Review,* 28, 263–274.

Wyllie A, Zhang JF and Casswell S (1998) Responses to televised alcohol advertisements associated with drinking behaviour of 10 to 17 year olds. *Addiction,* 93, 361–371.

18

From Social Marketing to Corporate Social Marketing – Changing Consumption Habits as the New Frontier of Corporate Social Responsibility

Guido Palazzo

INTRODUCTION

This chapter will examine the relation between two discourses that have until recently been considered to be unrelated or even antagonistic: the discourse on corporate social responsibility (CSR) and the discourse on social marketing. This relation can be explained by how the two discourses developed historically. The chapter will explain the paradigmatic shift that is currently taking place in CSR and will argue that social marketing will become a key issue in the CSR discourse in the future.

First, I will show how globalization challenges the traditional division of labor between corporations and governments. Under the post-national constellation, private actors such as corporations have been politicized and become important players in the production and protection of public goods. While this change seems to open new opportunities for a fusion of the debates on CSR and social marketing, there are good reasons for the rather hostile view of social marketers toward corporations in general and CSR in particular. I will describe the reasons behind the tensions between the two concepts and explain why social marketing and CSR share the same interest in a transformation of consumption habits under the new constellation of globalized value chains. Advocates of social marketing and of CSR can no longer afford to ignore each other. On the contrary, effective CSR activities will depend on the corporate ability to get consumers on board. Social marketing might deliver the foundation for such a broader understanding of CSR. The chapter thus concludes by the introduction of a new concept, which I label *corporate social marketing*.

CORPORATE RESPONSIBILITY IN THE 20TH CENTURY AND THE TECTONIC SHIFT OF THE 21ST CENTURY

What is the role and responsibility of corporations in a free society? During the 20th century, the answer to that question was dominated by neoliberal theory (Friedman, 1970). According to this ideology, corporations are *private actors* who have to maximize profits, while governments are *public actors* who are responsible for guaranteeing that citizens have the freedom to pursue their own interests. Corporations contribute to the public good through their basic economic operations. Beyond the indirect positive effects of their self-interested activities, corporations have no responsibility for the production and protection of public goods. Governments, not corporations, have to take care of the externalities of business operations (Sundaram and Inkpen, 2004).

Globalization is challenging this taken-for-granted division of labor between private corporate activities and public political activities. The regulatory power of governments over corporations is eroding (Habermas, 2001; Kobrin, 2001; Scherer and Palazzo, 2007). While corporations globally expand their activities, regulation mainly remains a national political activity. The assumption that *national* governments can create a regulatory regime that tames *global* corporations becomes doubtful.

Two consequences emerge from this global misbalance of economic and political forces (Scherer and Palazzo, 2008). First, globalization opens a regulatory vacuum. Some of the most pressing social and environmental challenges which are related to private production and consumption have a transnational logic (such as global warming, overfishing of oceans, loss of biodiversity or corruption). These issues *sui generis* cannot be handled within isolated national containers. Second, with their globally expanded value chains, multinational corporations operate in weak or corrupt states such as Bangladesh, Nigeria or Columbia, in failed states such as Sudan or Burma, or in strong, but undemocratic and potentially repressive regimes such as China. In those contexts, a stable and well-functioning regulatory framework does not exist and corporations are exposed to a high risk of violating human rights or becoming accomplices of human rights violations. In public discourse, discussions on such social and environmental atrocities in global value chains are mushrooming and the perception of multinationally networked corporations is strongly affected. They are accused of being one of the main sources of various societal issues such as global warming (Le Menestrel et al., 2002),

ecological dilemmas in general (Shrivastava, 1995), corruption (Nesbit, 1998), poverty (Jenkins, 2005), human rights violations (Banerjee, 2007), cooperation with repressive regimes (Taylor, 2004) and health concerns (Adams, 2005; Palazzo and Richter, 2005). In summary, globalizing business activities threatens the production and integrity of public goods of national societies.

PUBLIC GOODS AND CORPORATE RESPONSIBILITY: THE POLITICIZATION OF THE CORPORATION

As a reaction to the growing power of corporations and the tendency of many to take advantage or even abuse the global regulatory vacuum, there is growing pressure from civil society actors who make harmful corporate behavior transparent (Beck, 2000). Non-governmental organizations (NGOs) have a growing influence over decision-making processes both in governmental and in business organizations and they have started to target corporations instead of governments (Dryzek, 1999; Teegen et al., 2004). Being exposed to increased public scrutiny and pressure by NGOs, investors, mass media and customers, some corporations have started to broaden the understanding of their responsibility in society. Under the post-national constellation, CSR is no longer a concept of legal and moral rule compliance. It rather refers to the obligation to reduce the social and environmental harm to which corporations contribute or from which they benefit.

While the old paradigm of corporate responsibility was more or less built on a liability logic, which 'derives from legal reasoning to find guilt or fault for a harm' (Young, 2008: 194), the new logic, which started in the late 1980s with a critique of the working conditions in factories producing for Nike and Levis (Zadek, 2004), is a logic of social connectedness (Young, 2008). Corporations are held responsible for what their suppliers have done and they engage in programs to improve and control the working conditions within their supply chain (Zadek, 2004). Corporations that have globally expanded their operations or are embedded in globally expanded supply chains have to face a new complexity of social and environmental challenges, which they have to manage.

Some corporations have understood that a selective engineering of social and environmental issues is not sufficient and have started to look at the issues to which they are connected through a much broader lens. They have become political actors (Scherer and Palazzo, 2007) and are engaged in public health, education or social security and the protection of human rights (Kinley and Tadaki, 2004; Matten and Crane, 2005). They are involved in the fight against AIDS, malnutrition, illiteracy and poverty (Margolis and Walsh, 2003). They are engaged in multi-stakeholder initiatives such as the *Forest Stewardship Council* or the *Fair Labor Association* in order to define and enforce behavioral standards along their supply chains or for their industries. And they are perceived as representatives of democracy, promoting peace and stability and fighting against corruption as institutional entrepreneurs (Fort and Schipani, 2004; Misangyi et al., 2008). As the critical discussion on corporate responsibility in a globalizing world demonstrates, there is a growing awareness of the fact that governments cannot solve all the issues linked to the externalities of production. The regulation of production externalities through (national) laws and policies has its limits because corporations are expanding globally while regulators remain nationally bound. The production and protection of public goods – at least as far as it is linked to their supply chain operations – has become a core element of the CSR discourse in theory and practice (Bies et al., 2007; Matten and Crane, 2005). Since this new focus of CSR corresponds to that of social marketing, it seems to be worth examining the potential consequences of this shared interest.

THE ANTI-CORPORATE SPIRIT OF SOCIAL MARKETING

While the debate on corporate social responsibility has thus far mainly dealt with the side effects of *production*, social marketing is mainly about the societal side effects of *consumption*. In post-industrial societies, consumption is replacing production as the main activity and the main point of reference for individual and social identity projects (Gabriel and Lang, 1995; Schor, 1991). The shopping mall has substituted the factory as the defining institution of the post-industrial society (Ritzer, 1999). Whereas important societal challenges in the 20th century were industrial production-related issues and could be (more or less) managed through governmental interventions (e.g. questions of social justice and fair distribution), many current issues are emerging from the externalities of a highly individualized consumption society. Many concerns in today's world are linked to consumption (Domegan, 2008) (such as obesity, smoking, alcohol misuse, AIDS and global warming) and have more to do with the

decisions of individual consumers and less with the decisions of organized actors. For example, 30–40% of environmental degradation is caused by the consumption of private households (Grinstein and Nisan, 2009). The most sensitive fields of consumption that provoke externalities are food and drink consumption, transportation and housing (Peattie and Peattie, 2009).

In order to minimize harm to the consumers themselves and their various societal contexts, social marketing uses commercial marketing principles '...to influence a target audience to voluntarily accept, reject, modify, or abandon a behaviour for the benefit of individuals, groups, or society as a whole' (Kotler et al., 2002: 394; see also Andreasen, 1995; Domegan, 2008). Generally, social marketing does not focus on a specific product, but rather aims at promoting particular propositions for a *behavioral change* such as 'smoking is bad for your health' (Peattie and Peattie, 2009). Its guiding objective is to advance the well-being within post-industrial societies which are profoundly shaped by consumption. Citizens, mainly in their role as consumers, should be influenced in a way that they agree and are motivated to change their deeply engrained consumer or behavioral habits. 'So just as commercial marketers communicate to encourage the trial, adoption, identification with and regular purchase of their products, social marketers communicate to encourage the acceptance, adoption and maintenance of a particular social proposition or behaviour' (Peattie and Peattie, 2009: 264). Such a concept can be applied to a variety of social issues related with the behavior of individuals in general and their consumption behavior in particular. However, social marketing is mainly related to personal health (Peattie and Peattie, 2009), primarily covering the health challenges linked to the consumption of tobacco, alcohol and fast food. In this context, social marketing (mainly) is made manifest in campaigns that intend to reduce the consumption of harmful products. This form of social marketing has also been labeled *de-marketing* (e.g. Grinstein and Nisan, 2009; Peattie and Peattie, 2009; Shiu et al., 2009). By contrast, commercial marketing has to be understood as a process, in which 'individuals and groups obtain what they need and want through creating and exchanging products and values with others' (Kotler, 1988: 3). Corporations use marketing techniques to sell products, brands and lifestyles. Basically, the motivation is to *increase* the consumption of the corporations' products and services. To achieve this objective, commercial marketing aims at shaping brand and product loyalty as early as possible (Bird and Tapp, 2008), because 'keeping existing customers is cheaper and more profitable than winning new ones' (Hastings, 2006: 6–7).

It is obvious, that social marketing runs counter to the intentions of corporations and their attempts to market their products (Piacentini and Banister, 2009). Social marketing, especially in relation to tobacco, alcohol and fastfood consumption, has often been motivated by the desire to analyze, criticize and counteract commercial marketing, with the corporate marketer being the antagonist, if not the enemy (Hastings and Saren, 2003; Peattie and Peattie, 2009). Social marketing aims at discouraging specific customer decisions, particularly in the form of de-marketing (Kotler and Levy, 1971). While social marketers might intend to reduce alcohol and tobacco consumption, especially that of young consumers, the alcohol industry and the tobacco industry, in recent decades, have successfully positioned their products as an important element of a 'cool' lifestyle, focusing on the same audience of young consumers. These industries have widened their range of products and engaged in aggressive price promotion and communication campaigns (Piacentini and Banister, 2009). To counteract such commercial marketing efforts, understanding the 'coolness' of the commercial marketing messages (Bird and Tapp, 2008), uncooling the cool (Lasn, 1999) and destroying the credibility and reputation of the corporate brands (Palazzo and Basu, 2007) has become a key motivation of social marketers. Of course, the discipline of social marketing has a multifaceted nature and cannot be reduced to the above-described aims of (1) reducing harm related to the products of corporations and (2) counteracting commercial marketing. However, the aim of this chapter is not to give a comprehensive overview of the discipline as such but to show the tensions that, so far, have existed between social marketing and commercial marketing.

The current debate on obesity illustrates the antagonistic interests and activities of social marketers and corporate marketers very well. Obesity seems to be one of the most pressing global health concerns in the years to come (WHO, 2004): 40% of all the US American citizens are obese, and even in developing countries obesity has become an issue (WHO, 2007). Consequences that have been linked to obesity range from negative health effects such as type 2 diabetes (Komaroff, 2003) to psychological problems such as stigmatization (Allison and Saunders, 2000). Society has to bear higher medical costs for the prevention, diagnosis and treatment of obesity (CDC, 2004). If the development continues, 'the youth of today may, on average, live less healthy and possibly even shorter lives than their parents' (Olshansky et al., 2005: 1143). Obesity is driven by an interplay of various factors such as genetic predisposition, environmental and socio-cultural factors as well as behavioral aspects (Malik et al., 2006; Nielsen and Popkin, 2003; Thorpe et al., 2003). However, one of the key elements that explains the explosion of obesity in recent years can be found in the lifestyle of individuals and the food choices they make (CDC, 2003). Nutritionists speak of a 'toxic food environment' (Crenson, 2002: A–17). Corporations that produce and promote unhealthy food and beverages certainly contribute to the creation of such a toxic environment. The link between fast food and obesity (Bowman et al., 2004; French et al., 2001; Stender et al., 2007), between marketing and obesity (Seiders and Petty, 2004; Wansink and Huckabee, 2005), as well as the particular vulnerability of children toward advertising in general, and food advertising in particular, has been examined extensively (e.g. Vakratsas and Ambler, 1999; Zuppa et al., 2003). It can hardly be denied that corporations contribute to obesity through their products and their commercial marketing activities. Fast food companies are particularly criticized, because they make use of '...marketing strategies, including statements of nutrition experts to encourage people to buy more of their products – whether or not those products are likely to promote health' (Nestle, 2002: ix). Fast food companies 'promote the sale of food high in sugar, fat and sodium content, unfairly target vulnerable consumers, encourage overconsumption, fail to provide patrons with the information needed to make informed decisions at the point and time of purchase and ultimately shift or externalize the costs associated with consumption of FF to the public' (Adams, 2005: 313). Given its contribution to obesity, the fast food industry has even been described as the *next tobacco* (Parloff, 2003; Wansink and Huckabee, 2005). To this critique, fast food companies are reacting as defensively as the tobacco industry has in the past 40 years. They proceed by making insignificant changes in their products, but put most effort into emphasizing the responsibility of the customers themselves to make informed and reasonable decisions. Much like the tobacco industry, fast food companies frame obesity as the result of individual and autonomous consumption decisions of informed customers, they question the risks related to their products and they present balanced food choices and physical activities as the solution to the issue.

It comes as no surprise that social marketing scholars perceive corporations and their marketing activities rather as part of the problem than as a part of the solution. In the above described context of obesity, this negative perception of corporate actors and activities is, for instance, illustrated by the fact that social marketing is understood as the attempt to 'put effective controls on those who put their commercial interests before your good health' (Hastings, 2006: 8).

CSR AND SOCIAL MARKETING: STRANGE BEDFELLOWS

As I have argued, in the light of globally networked business operations, CSR can be understood as those corporate activities that aim at tackling the negative social and environmental impact of production and products along value chains. In principle, one could argue that CSR and social marketing together cover the two dimensions of externalities – those of production and those of consumption – and thus should be natural allies. However, as described above, social marketing is basically anti-corporate in spirit. It can be interpreted as a public attack on the private commercial marketing activities and intentions of corporations in industries that have a negative impact on individuals and societies. What would the result be if those corporations were to attempt to reduce the social and environmental externalities of their products as they take on a political role in the sense of producing and protecting public goods? Being under public pressure for the externalities that are created through the consumption of their products, corporations in the fast food, tobacco and alcohol industries have started to invest in programs to reduce their externalities. These activities are packaged as a key element of their CSR engagement.

It is obvious that consumer-oriented CSR exposes corporations from those sensitive industries to a real double bind. While their marketing department invests in programs that should increase the consumption of their products, those CSR activities, if successful, will have the contrary effect. Can we assume that corporations in sensitive markets under the pressure of their investors and the expectations of financial markets are ready and able to give priority to the public interest over their profit motive? Anecdotic evidence shows that the economic pressures and mindset within corporations is often too strong and the profit motive probably prevails over the motive to contribute to the common good. Two examples might illustrate the failure of CSR activities in industries that are under the fire of social marketers. As a reaction to the pressure concerning the quality of their food and their marketing activities, McDonald's has started to make information about the ingredients of their products available to the customer. The information can be found on the backside of the

trial tablet. However, instead of being informed, the customer is submerged by myriads of nutritional details and the result of this customer communication is amazing: instead of triggering a deliberation on the health risks of fast food, the simple fact that there is nutritional information is perceived as proof of the quality of the food (Wansink and Huckabee, 2005). It would be naive to believe that this effect is only known to researchers and not to McDonald's marketers.

The same counterproductive effect can be found in the youth prevention programs of the tobacco industry. With the Master Settlement Agreement between 46 US states and the tobacco industry (National Association of Attorneys General, 1998), the responsibility for the health effects of tobacco consumption was shifted from the consumer to the corporate world. Philip Morris, British American Tobacco and other players in the industry are under the legal and moral pressure to invest in youth prevention campaigns. Successful prevention programs could lead to the industry loosing potential customers or having to invest much more money to get new (adult) customers. Ideally, smoking has to be started at an early age if it is to become a stable and lasting habit. Tobacco companies would undermine their own business interest through successful youth prevention. Youth prevention programs initiated and designed by the tobacco industry and their associations focus on two messages: smoking is a risk and smoking is a decision for adults. It has been shown that such a campaign does not reduce smoking but only improves the image of the tobacco companies. To live a risky life and to take adult behavior as a role model is exactly what teenagers want to do – and the industry knows this only too well (Hicks, 2001). As Hastings et al. (1997: 439) have argued, teenagers 'smoke to belong, to rebel, to express their individuality, to take risks to appear more grown up, to be more cool'. Campaigns that are not designed by the tobacco industry, such as the truth campaign in Florida, are much more effective. In this case, the effective message was built around the manipulative and greedy business decisions of irresponsible tobacco managers seeking to maximize their own profits and those of their shareholders (Hicks, 2001). And, again, it would be naive to believe that tobacco managers who design prevention programs do not know that their activities promote the company's image rather than keeping teenagers from smoking.

It would seem that CSR activities in tobacco and fast food companies promote corporate commercial interest rather than the well-being of society at large. It might not even be a necessary precondition that the managers within these industries have unscrupulous characters. They simply might perceive their industry as normal and use the same business frame as in other industries. Being socialized in the economic language game and being under the pressure of financial analysts, their task is to simply increase their markets and market shares and provide their shareholders with a decent profit. However, in their case, the normal business logic has devastating societal side effects. As in the case of the tobacco industry, fast food and alcohol companies are probably unreliable partners for social marketers. Rather than promoting their objectives, social marketers might discredit themselves if they connect their activities to the CSR engagement of companies from those industries. However, while experience with targeted industries shows the difficulties of integrating the externalities of consumption in the CSR universe, there is good reason to believe that social marketing will become a key dimension of CSR in the future.

As I will argue in the next paragraph, the consumer has become a critical element of CSR. While historically, the critique of corporate harm-doing started upstreaming the supply chain (toward suppliers), it is currently also downstreaming the supply chain (toward consumers). There are two main reasons for this development. First, corporations are confronted with questions about their responsibility for the impact of their products on consumers and the impact of the consumption of their products on society: Cars contribute to global warming, computers that are not recycled might be burned in Third World countries, thus producing dioxin, and all kind of products potentially include human rights violations. Second, corporations that engage in CSR depend on the customer to perceive that engagement as an added value and a criterion of their consumption decisions. The future of the CSR movement will probably depend on shared efforts to encourage consumers to join the bandwagon. Without a deeper impact on mainstream consumption, the CSR engagement of corporations might not be sustainable.

CHANGING CONSUMPTION HABITS (1) – FROM UTILITY FUNCTIONS TO SYMBOLIC INTERVENTIONS

While consumers might understand the high risks for themselves and for others linked to specific products, forms of consumption or a specific lifestyle, it seems that this understanding hardly suffices to change detrimental habits. As illustrated by campaigns against tobacco, fast food or binge drinking, building social marketing campaigns on negative health effects is not sufficient to create behavioral change. Such a cognitive approach ignores the social and cultural forces that pertain to the respective behavior (Piacentini and Banister, 2009). Rose et al. (2008: 74) provide criticism, stating that, 'many programs and projects remain essentially information driven'. Social marketing has too often been misconstrued as 'simply social advertising' (Stead et al., 2007: 128).

Advocates of CSR share the misunderstanding and the same disappointment about consumers who receive the right information but continue with the wrong behavior. On a regular base, consumer surveys come to the conclusion that an overwhelming majority of consumers express the willingness to include ethical aspects (e.g. concerning child labor or decent working conditions) in their decision-making. In a recent European survey, for instance, 75% of consumers signaled their respective motivation (Vogel, 2005). However, this does not correspond by far to the real purchasing behavior of those consumers: the same survey found that only 3% of the interviewed citizens had actually included ethical criteria in their consumption decisions. As Vogel (2005: 52) concludes: 'relatively few consumers appear to be willing to change their purchasing habits in response to corporate practices that do not affect them directly'. CSR in the above-described political sense of managing harm along supply chain activities often requires substantial investments on the part of corporations: they have to build up teams in order to analyze their problems, create standards, audit hundreds and thousands of supply chain partners, train their employees and publish CSR-related information in a report. As long as social and environmental criteria do not sufficiently affect the decisions of the average customer, CSR investments hardly affect the bottom line. On the contrary, in many cases, a highly visible CSR engagement – regardless of whether it is serious or just window dressing – might not result in less, but in more public pressure. The more a corporation exposes itself to public scrutiny through its engagement and the related communication, the more unsolved problems might be found, the more distrust might be provoked. It would thus be naive to believe that CSR would automatically have an impact on profits. It does not. One of the main reasons for the difficulty in finding CSR business cases is the relative indifference of customers who continue to use price and quality (including brand reputation) as the key criteria for buying sneakers, T-shirts, flowers, gold, diamonds or cars.

Why is it so difficult to motivate consumers to internalize environmental and social criteria in their decision-making? The main driving force is certainly the spatial-temporal distance between the consumption decision and its positive and negative effects (Osterhus, 1997). Due to the abstractness of that causality, actors can easily disengage from the bad consequences and switch off the normal cognitive and motivational processes that guide behavior (Bandura, 2002). Furthermore, in contexts of dispersed responsibility, action can be replaced by fingerpointing, because there are always others to be found who are, or at least seem to be, more responsible and should act first (Young, 2004). Finally, perceiving the consumer as a rational actor who attempts to maximize his or her utility, and who therefore should be open to rational utility-based arguments, is an inappropriate conceptualization of consumption behavior (see, critically, Caruana and Crane, 2008). The assumption of the rational consumer provokes a misunderstanding about the market potential for responsible consumption, because it 'leads to the widespread assumption that there is a discrete market segment of responsible consumers "out there", waiting to be identified and acted upon by corporations' (Caruana and Crane, 2008: 1497).

Both the social marketer and the CSR manager in corporations want consumers to show a more responsible consumption behavior. They both may happen to overlook the fact that consumption is a symbol-laden cultural practice and that this cultural context of the harmful (consumption) decision at stake has to be changed as well. Change has to happen on both the individual and the societal level (Hastings et al., 2000). This change is rarely triggered through appeals to rationality. Challenging deeply rooted consumption behaviors such as excessive drinking (Piacentini and Banister, 2009) or unsustainable traveling practices (Caruana and Crane, 2008) requires a cultural change, because they are socially habitualized and legitimized practices that are deeply rooted in the individual identity projects of the consumers. As a consequence, the responsible consumer is not first *discovered* and then served; he or she has to be *co-created* through narrations of responsibility that offer meaningful alternative social identities to consumers (Caruana and Crane, 2008). Consumption is a way to express one's individual and group identity. Products and brands thus often dispose of a symbolic value, which consumers use to construct their identity and their social worlds (Belk, 1988; Gabriel and Lang, 1995; Palazzo and Basu, 2007; Reed, 2004). Social marketing campaigns and CSR policies have to take these symbolic values of consumption habits into account in order to be effective (Pavis et al., 1997; Piacentini and Banister, 2009).

CHANGING CONSUMPTION HABITS (2) – FROM GOVERNMENTS TO NETWORKS

Social marketing is currently perceived as a mainly governmental responsibility (Grinstein and Nisan, 2009; Shiu et al., 2009). Given the previous analysis of the eroding power of governments to take care of key societal challenges and the already described emerging political engagement of corporations, private actors might have to play an important role in the development and implementation of social marketing campaigns as well. It can be assumed that the private compensation for the eroding regulatory power over production activities will be mirrored in increasing private efforts to compensate for the inability of governments to gain sufficient control over the negative impact of consumption activities.

Since the problematic behavior unfolds in complex social networks and strong consumer cultures, the solutions also have to be achieved in 'a system of deep collaboration' (Domegan, 2008: 137) between actors from various institutions and organizations. Peattie and Peattie (2009; also Lewis, 2007b) have argued that social marketing campaigns can link the activities of various actors such as political authorities, NGOs, the media and corporations.

Long et al. (2008) have recently described a successful social marketing campaign to increase female awareness of heart disease. According to these authors, one of the key elements of such a successful campaign can be found in the broad coalition of partners that cooperate among other corporations from various industries. However, as the same example illustrates, corporations are mainly included in social marketing campaigns on the basis of pure philanthropy. Consequently, from the perspective of most corporations, social marketing is perceived as an instrument for their own cause-related marketing activities. Cause-related marketing is 'a marketing program that strives to achieve two objectives – improve corporate performance and help worthy causes – by linking fund raising for the benefit of a cause to the purchase of the firm's products and/or services' (Varadarajan and Menon, 1988: 59). Those corporations hope for a positive reputational effect that often results from corporate donations to good causes. In this sense, commercial marketing and social marketing overlap, simply because companies donate money to social marketing campaigns. However, these engagements can be criticized as greenwashing (Crane, 2000), because companies try to wash their image through good deeds while disconnecting their engagement from the serious social and environmental problems to which they are causally linked along their supply chains. It comes as no surprise that such a use of the idea of social marketing by companies has a backlash: it has been shown, for instance, that these mere tactical campaigns create credibility problems for the corporation (Van den Brink et al., 2006), because consumers might doubt the authentic interest of the company in the common good (Forehand and Grier, 2003) or perceive a negative congruence between a cause and a corporation (Menon and Kahn, 2003). Sen and Bhattacharya (2001) have demonstrated that negative CSR information can have an impact on consumers who start to perceive a company as socially irresponsible. Donating money to kindergartens does not compensate for a lack of engagement in the fight against child labor in the corporation's supply chain. Insofar as the social engagement of the company is disconnected from the (potential) harm done by the company in its own business operations, NGOs might build their counter-campaigns on these obvious contradictions and threaten the reputation of the corporate brand (Palazzo and Basu, 2007). These campaigns might result in a 'doppelgänger brand image', defined as a 'family of disparaging images and stories about a brand that are circulating in popular culture by a loosely organized network of consumers, anti-brand activists, bloggers, and opinion leaders in the news and entertainment media' (Thompson et al., 2006: 50).

Cause-related marketing is a misperception by the marketer of the increasing relevance of CSR. If the assumption is true that corporate responsibility is now shifting toward the systematic management of social and environmental issues along supply chains, the future interface between social marketing and CSR will look different: corporations that are under pressure to invest in child-labor-free production are interested in consumers who develop a preference for child-labor-free consumption. A social marketing campaign that aims at a respective behavioral change will link upstreaming CSR activities (to suppliers) to corresponding downstreaming changes in consumer behavior. Such a campaign will require a much more intensive collaboration between social marketers and corporations than the simple philanthropy that giving requires, because it affects the core operations of companies and because it requires a cultural transformation of consumption habits.

CORPORATE SOCIAL MARKETING

This cultural transformation of consumption habits will become one of the most important frontiers of the CSR movement in the future and CSR advocates will have to become social marketers. Following Kotler et al.'s (2002) definition of social marketing, I propose to define *corporate social marketing* as the attempt to influence a target audience to voluntarily accept, reject, modify or abandon behavior that is related to the social and environmental issues co-created by the corporation along its supply chains. As argued above, it is important not to confuse this concept with traditional cause-related marketing spirited forms of engagement. Donations and social activities that are disconnected from the social and environmental challenges corporations face in their business operations might fire back on the corporate reputation and will not be perceived as a real contribution to the common good.

Corporate social marketing activities, as understood here, thus intend to sensitize consumers for the side effects of production and products and to integrate social and environmental criteria in their decision-making processes. In contrast to traditional social marketing, corporate social marketing is less about the harm done to the consumers themselves and their immediate context and more about the harm their consumption decisions do to others distant in space and time. It is less about the immediate side effects of consumption and more about the side effects of production to which the consumer is connected and which he or she can influence. However, as in the case of traditional social marketing, corporate social marketing is about the behavioral change of consumers. A transformation of unacceptable externalities upstreaming the supply chain is difficult to achieve if there is no behavioral change downstreaming the supply chain. If customers at Walmart are only motivated to buy cheap, it is difficult to take the pressure from the suppliers to deliver at ever lower prices, with an increasing risk of human rights violations. In this sense, the harm is not directly created by consumption, but it is socially connected to consumption (Young, 2004).

Building on the understanding of corporate social marketing and extending the Lewis (2007a) concept, I propose the following typology for social marketing policies: consumption is socially connected to various forms of harm-doing:

1. To the consumer him or herself (e.g. binge drinking, fast food).
2. To specific others within the immediate context of the consumer (e.g. second-hand smoking).
3. To the broader community of the consumer (e.g. car accidents provoked by alcohol abuse).
4. To a specific distant context of others (e.g. slave labor, child labor).
5. To the world in general and future others (e.g. global warming effect due to CO_2 emissions).

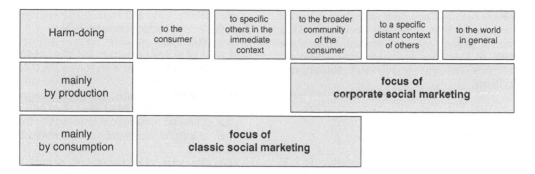

Figure 18.1   From social marketing to corporate social marketing

While the forms of harm-doing 1–3 represent classic social marketing concerns, a broader perspective that includes corporate social marketing would tend to focus on the latter two forms of harm-doing, 4 and 5. Harm-doing in the classic sense is, as argued, a domain in which the cooperation with companies is not only dangerous to the advocated cause but also to the reputation of the social marketer. By contrast, the field of corporate social marketing, which I propose here, offers a broad variety of opportunities to fight for good causes in collaboration with companies.

In recent years, the CSR activities of corporations have transcended the immediate borders of the corporation, its stakeholders and its own challenges. As argued, corporations start to engage in multistakeholder initiatives in order to contribute to overall societal solutions of problems, to which they are connected. Corporate social marketing initiatives will have to follow a similar logic: changing the habits of consumers is a challenge that goes beyond the transformation of the customers of a specific corporation, brand or product. It rather corresponds to the promotion of a new institutional logic. Corporate social marketing campaigns will have problems of effectiveness and legitimacy if they are designed as the initiative of one single corporation and with the mindset of 'just another marketing campaign'. A recent example might illustrate the risks (see box)

As institutional entrepreneurs, companies have to cooperate within and across industries, with governments and civil society activists in order to have the transformational power over deeply embedded habits of the heart. Effective and legitimate corporate social marketing efforts have a broader mission than just the promotion of the sustainable products of one company. They intend to transform the consumer and not to showcase the CSR efforts of a company (independent from the quality of these efforts). They build on broad collaboration. They are focused on issues (e.g. child labor in cotton production, plastic in the ocean), not on specific corporations or

Since the early 1990, Chiquita has started to collaborate with NGOs in order to improve the social and environmental conditions on their banana plantation. Together with Social Accountability and the Rainforest Alliance they started to implement highly demanding external standards and had their operations monitored and certified through independent third-party audits. In 2005, together with the Rainforest Alliance, they started to communicate their CSR efforts to banana consumers in selected European countries such as Sweden, Switzerland and Germany. The Chiquita logo on the bananas is fused with the logo of the Rainforest Alliance, and a huge marketing campaign communicated the company's efforts to the customer. The aim was to create preferences for the Chiquita brand in a market – the banana market – where customers normally take the price as a main reference for their decisions. As a result of their CSR-related marketing campaign, Chiquita faces numerous attacks: In Sweden, environmental activists argued that the Chiquita banana is not green enough; in Switzerland, the fair trade community attacked the corporation, arguing that their banana is not fair enough; and in Germany, they were criticized for their cooperation with a PR agency. While the Chiquita campaign certainly relates to core business operations and built on many years of serious engagement, it cannot yet count as a corporate social marketing campaign as conceptualized in this chapter. The message of this campaign – as in many other cases – was not to transform consumer habits: its aim was to demonstrate how responsible the company was. It aimed at communicating CSR efforts; it did not aim at a moralization of the consumer him- or herself.

specific brands. They gives consumer a broader frame to look at their own decisions, adding options, giving sense and proposing alternative ways to construct individual and communal identities through (responsible) consumption decisions.

CONCLUSION

As advocates of CSR, social marketers seek to advance responsible consumer behavior. Given this shared interest, CSR could be perceived as an ally not an enemy by social marketers. However, given the focus on problematic industries such as tobacco or alcohol, it is very difficult for social marketers to see the potentially bright side of CSR. Furthermore, since it is a core assumption of social marketing that campaigns should aim at improving the welfare of the individual (consumer) and that of society, the assumption that corporations might benefit from a potential cooperation is difficult to digest for social marketers. It would appear to be common sense among social marketers that the motivation behind a social marketing engagement should not be to benefit the organizations that develop and launch the campaign, because in that case, there would be no difference between social and commercial marketing (MacFadyen et al., 2003; Stead et al., 2007). Collaborating with corporations in social marketing campaigns will only be possible, if this (probably too) strict separation of public versus private benefits is put into perspective and corporations are perceived as potential partners. If corporate social marketing helps to reduce the harm done in global value chains by embedding ethical considerations into the decision-making of consumers, there may be good reasons to intensify research and to launch social marketing projects that include corporations as key actors.

KEY WORDS: Corporate social responsibility, globalization, corporate social marketing, multinational corporations, responsible supply chain management, cause-related marketing, transformation of consumption habits.

Key insights

* Social marketing scholars perceive corporations and their marketing activities rather as part of the problem than as a part of the solution. However, in the context of harmful production practices – from child labor to water waste – corporations that are active in corporate social

responsibility (CSR) and social marketers share an interest in changing consumer habits.
* Corporations that are under pressure to invest in child-labor-free production are interested in consumers who develop a preference for child-labor-free consumption.
* The responsible consumer is not first discovered and then served; he or she has to be co-created through narrations of responsibility that offer meaningful alternative social identities to consumers.
* Corporate social marketing is the attempt to influence a target audience to voluntarily accept, reject, modify or abandon behavior that is related to the social and environmental issues co-created by the corporation along its supply chains.
* Corporate social marketing activities, as understood here, thus intend to sensitize consumers for the side effects of production and products and to integrate social and environmental criteria in their decision-making processes.

REFERENCES

Adams, R. (2005) 'Fast food, obesity, and tort reform: An examination of industry responsibility for public health', *Business and Society Review,* 110(3): 297–320.

Allison, D.B. and Saunders, S.E. (2000) 'Obesity in North America. An overview', *Medical Clinics of North America,* March: 305–325.

Andreasen, A. (1995) *Marketing Social Change: Changing Behavior to Promote Health, Social Development, and the Environment.* San Francisco, CA: Jossey-Bass.

Bandura, A. (2002) 'Selective moral disengagement in the exercise of moral agency', *Journal of Moral Education,* 31: 101–119.

Banerjee, S.B. (2007) *Corporate Social Responsibility: The Good, the Bad and the Ugly.* Cheltenham: Edward Elgar.

Beck, U. (2000) *What is Globalization?* Cambridge, UK: Polity Press.

Belk, R.W. (1988) 'Possession and the extended self', *Journal of Consumer Research,* 15: 139–168.

Bies, R.J., Bartunek, J.M., Fort, T.L. and Zald, M.N. (2007) 'Corporations as social change agents : Individual, interpersonal, institutional, and environmental dynamics', *Academy of Management Review,* 32: 788–793.

Bird, S. and Tapp, A. (2008) 'Social marketing and the meaning of cool', *Social Marketing Quarterly,* 1: 18–29.

Bowman, S.A., Gortmaker, S.L., Ebbeling, C.B., Pereira, M.A. and Ludwig, D.S. (2004) 'Effects of fast-food consumption on energy intake and diet quality among children in a national household survey', *Pediatrics,* 113: 112–118.

Caruana, R. and Crane, A. (2008) 'Constructing consumer responsibility: Exploring the role of corporate communications', *Organization Studies,* 29: 1495–1519.

CDC (2003) *Overweight and Obesity: An Overview.* Centers for Disease Control and Prevention.

CDC (2004) *Overweight and Obesity: Economic Consequences.* Centers for Disease Control and Prevention.

Crane, A. (2000) 'Acing the backlash: Green marketing and strategic reorientation in the 1990s', *Journal of Strategic Marketing*, 8: 277–296.

Crenson, M. (2002) 'A toxic fast-food environment afflicts U.S., Crusader says', *Los Angeles Times*, December, 1: A–17.

Domegan, C.T. (2008) 'Social marketing: Implications for contemporary marketing practices classification schemes', *Journal of Business and Industrial Marketing*, 23: 135–141.

Dryzek, J.S. (1999) 'Transnational democracy', *Journal of Political Philosophy*, 7: 30–51.

Forehand, M.R. and Grier, S. (2003) 'When is honesty the best policy? The effect of stated company intent on consumer skepticism', *Journal of Consumer Psychology*, 13: 349–356.

Fort, T.L. and Schipani, C.A. (2004) *The Role of Business in Fostering Peaceful Societies.* Cambridge, UK: Cambridge University Press.

French, S.A., Story, M., Neumark-Sztainer, D., et al. (2001) 'Fast food restaurant use among adolescents: Associations with nutrient intake, food choices and behavioral and psychosocial variables', *International Journal of Obesity*, 25: 1823–1833.

Friedman, M. (1970) 'The social responsibility of business is to increase its profit'. *The New York Times Magazine*, 13 September, reprint in Donaldson, T. and Werhane, P.H. (eds), *Ethical Issues in Business: A Philosophical Approach.* Englewood Cliffs, NJ: Prentice-Hall, pp. 217–223.

Gabriel, Y. and Lang, T. (1995) *The Unmanageable Consumer. Contemporary Consumption and its Fragmentation.* London: Sage Publications.

Grinstein, A. and Nisan, U. (2009) 'Demarketing, minorities, and national attachment', *Journal of Marketing*, 73: 105–122.

Habermas, J. (2001) *The Postnational Constellation.* Cambridge, MA: MIT Press.

Hastings, G. (2006) 'Ten promises to Terry: Towards a social marketing manifesto', *Health Education*, 106: 5–8.

Hastings, G. and Saren, M. (2003) 'The critical contribution of social marketing: Theory and application', *Marketing Theory*, 3: 305–322.

Hastings, G., MacFadyen, L. and Stead, M. (1997) 'Tobacco marketing: Shackling the pied piper', *British Medical Journal*, 315: 439–440.

Hastings, G., MacFadyen, L. and Anderson, S. (2000) 'Whose behaviour is it anyway? The broader potential of social marketing', *Social Marketing Quarterly*, 6: 46–58.

Hicks, J.J. (2001) 'The strategy behind Florida's Truth campaign', *Social Marketing Quarterly*, 10: 3–5.

Jenkins, R. (2005) *Globalization, Production and Poverty.* United Nations University: World Institute for Development Economics Research. Research Paper No. 2005/40.

Kinley, D. and Tadaki, J. (2004) 'From talk to walk: The emergence of human rights responsibilities for corporations at international law', *Virginia Journal of International Law*, 44: 931–1022.

Kobrin, S.J. (2001) 'Sovereignty@bay: Globalization, multinational enterprise, and the international political system', in A.M. Rugman and T.L. Brewer (eds), *The Oxford Handbook of International Business.* New York: Oxford University Press, pp.181–205.

Komaroff, A.L. (2003) 'An update on the obesity problem', *Journal Watch General Medicine*, March 7.

Kotler, P. (1988) *Marketing Management*, 6th edn. Englewood Cliffs, NJ: Prentice-Hall.

Kotler, P. and Levy, S. (1971) 'Demarketing, yes, demarketing', *Harvard Business Review*, 49: 74–80.

Kotler, P., Roberto, N. and Lee, N.R. (2002) *Social Marketing. Improving the Quality of Life*, 2nd edn. London: Sage Publications.

Lasn, K. (1999) *Culture Jam. How to Reverse America's Suicidal Consumer Binge – And Why We Must.* New York: HarperCollins.

Le Menestrel, M., van den Hove, S. and de Bettignies, H.-C. (2002) 'Processes and consequences in business ethical dilemmas: The oil industry and climate change', *Journal of Business Ethics*, 41(3): 251–266.

Lewis, M. (2007a) *States of Reason: Freedom, Responsibility and the Governing of Behaviour Change.* London: Institute for Public Policy Research.

Lewis, M. (2007b) 'Behaviour change and public policy', *Consumer Policy Review*, 17: 247–250.

Long, T., Taubenheim, A.M., Wayman, J., Temple, S. and Ruoff, B.A. (2008) 'The heart truth: Using the power of branding and social marketing to increase awareness of heart disease in women', *Social Marketing Quarterly*, 14: 3–29.

MacFadyen, L., Stead, M. and Hastings, G. (2003) 'Social marketing', in M.J. Baker (ed), *The Marketing Book*, 5th edn. Oxford: Butterworth-Heinemann.

Malik, V.S., Schulze, M.B. and Hu, F.B. (2006) 'Intake of sugar-sweetened beverages and weight gain: A systematic review', *American Journal of Clinical Nutrition*, 84(2): 274–288.

Margolis, J.D. and Walsh, J.P. (2003) 'Misery loves companies: Rethinking social initiatives by business', *Administrative Science Quarterly*, 48: 268–305.

Matten, D. and Crane, A. (2005) 'Corporate citizenship: Towards an extended theoretical conceptualization', *Academy of Management Review*, 30: 166–179.

Menon, S. and Kahn, B.E. (2003) 'Corporate sponsorship of philanthropic activities: When do they impact perception of sponsor brand?', *Journal of Consumer Psychology*, 13: 316–327.

Misangyi, V.F., Weaver III, G.R. and Elms, H. (2008) 'Ending corruption: The interplay among institutional logics, resources, and institutional entrepreneurs', *Academy of Management Review*, 33: 750–770.

National Association of Attorneys General (1998) *Tobacco Master Settlement Agreement.* Available at: http://ag.ca.gov/tobacco/pdf/1msa.pdf.

Nesbit, J.B. (1998) 'Transnational bribery of foreign officials: A new threat for the future of democracy', *Vanderbilt Journal of Transnational Law*, 31: 1273.

Nestle, M. (2002) *Food Politics*. Berkeley, CA: University of California Press.

Nielsen, S.J. and Popkin, B.M. (2003) 'Patterns and trends in food portion sizes, 1977–1998', *JAMA*, 289(4): 450–453.

Olshansky, S.J., Passaro, D.J., Hershow, R.C., et al. (2005) 'A potential decline in life expectancy in the United States in the 21st century', *New England Journal of Medicine*, 352(11): 1138–1145.

Osterhus, T. (1997) 'Prosocial consumer influence strategies: When and how do they work?', *Journal of Marketing*, 61: 1–18.

Palazzo, G. and Basu, K. (2007) 'The ethical backlash of corporate branding', *Journal of Business Ethics*, 73(4): 333–346.

Palazzo, G. and Scherer, A.G. (2006) Corporate legitimacy as deliberation. A communicative framework. *Journal of Business Ethics*, 66: 71–88.

Palazzo, G. and Richter, U. (2005) 'CSR business as usual? The case of the tobacco industry', *Journal of Business Ethics*, 61(4): 387–401.

Palazzo, G. and Scherer, A.G. (2006) 'Corporate legitimacy as deliberation. A communicative framework', *Journal of Business Ethics*, 66: 71–88.

Parloff, R. (2003) 'Is fat the next tobacco?', *Fortune*, 147: 52.

Pavis, S., Cunningham-Burley, S. and Amos, A. (1997) 'Alcohol consumption and young people', *Health Education Research*, 12: 311–322.

Peattie, K. and Peattie, S. (2009) 'Social marketing: A pathway to consumption reduction?' *Journal of Business Research*, 62: 260–268.

Piacentini, M.G. and Banister, E.N. (2009) 'Managing anti-consumption in an excessive drinking culture', *Journal of Business Research*, 62(2): 279–288.

Reed, A. (2004) 'Activating the self-importance of consumer selves: Exploring identity salience effects on judgements', *Journal of Consumer Research*, 31: 286–295.

Ritzer, G. (1999) *Enchanting a Disenchanted World: Revolutionizing the Means of Consumption*. Thousand Oaks, CA: Pine Forge Press.

Rose, C., Dade, P. and Scott, J. (2008) 'Climate change: Motivating consumers', *Consumer Policy Review*, 18: 74–78.

Scherer, A.G. and Palazzo, G. (2007) 'Toward a political conception of corporate responsibility: Business and society seen from a Habermasian perspective', *Academy of Management Review* 32(4): 1096–1120.

Scherer, A.G. and Palazzo, G. (2008) 'Globalization and corporate social responsibility', in A. Crane, A. McWilliams, D. Matten, J. Moon and D. Siegel (eds), *The Oxford Handbook of Corporate Social Responsibility*. Oxford: Oxford University Press, pp. 413–431.

Schor, J. (1991) *The Overworked American: The Unexpected Decline of Leisure*. New York: Basic Books.

Seiders, K. and Petty, R.D. (2004) 'Obesity and the role of food marketing: A policy analysis of issues and remedies', *Journal of Public Policy and Marketing* 23(2): 153–169.

Sen, S. and Bhattacharya, C.B. (2001) 'Does doing good always lead to doing better? Consumer reactions to corporate social responsibility', *Journal of Marketing Research*, 2: 225–243.

Shiu, E., Hassan, L.M. and Walsh, G. (2009) 'Demarketing tobacco through governmental policies – the 4 Ps revisited', *Journal of Business Research*, 62: 269–278.

Shrivastava, P. (1995) 'The role of corporations in achieving ecological sustainability', *Academy of Management Review*, 20: 936–960.

Stead, M., Hastings, G. and McDermott, L. (2007) 'The meaning, effectiveness and future of social marketing', Obesity Reviews, vol. 8, no. 1, pp. 189–193.

Stender, S., Dyerberg, J. and Astrup, A. (2007) 'Fast food: Unfriendly and unhealthy', *International Journal of Obesity*, 31: 887–890.

Sundaram, A.K. and Inkpen, A.C. (2004) 'The corporate objective revisited', *Organization Science*, 15: 350–363.

Taylor, K.M. (2004) 'Thicker than blood: Holding Exxon Mobil liable for human rights violations committed abroad', *Syracuse Journal of International Law and Commerce*, 31(2): 274–297.

Teegen, H., Doh, J.P. and Vachani, S. (2004) 'The importance of nongovernmental organization (NGOs) in global governance and value creation: An international business research agenda', *International Business Studies*, 35(6): 463–483.

Thompson, C.J., Rindfleisch, A. and Arsel, Z. (2006) 'Emotional branding and the strategic value of the doppelgänger brand image', *Journal of Marketing*, 70: 50–64.

Thorpe, L.E., MacKenzie, K., Perl, S., et al. (2003) 'One in 6 New York City adults is obese', *NYC Vital Signs*, 2(7): 1–4.

van den Brink, D., Odekerken-Schröder, G. and Pauwels, P. (2006) 'The effect of strategic and tactical cause-related marketing on consumers' brand loyalty', *Journal of Consumer Marketing*, 23: 15–25.

Vakratsas, D. and Ambler, T. (1999) 'How advertising works: What do we really know', *Journal of Marketing*, 63: 26–43.

Varadarajan, P.R. and Menon, A. (1988) 'Cause-related marketing: A coalignment of marketing strategy and corporate philanthropy', *Journal of Marketing*, 52: 58–74.

Vogel, D. (2005) *The Market for Virtue*. Washington, DC: Brookings Institution Press.

Wansink, B. and Huckabee, M. (2005) 'De-marketing obesity', *California Management Review* 47(4): 6–18.

WHO (2004) *Obesity: Preventing and Managing the Global Epidemic*. Geneva: World Health Organization.

WHO (2007) *WHO Global InfoBase Online*. World Health Organization.

Wolf, K.D. (2008) 'Emerging patters of global governance: The new interplay between the state, business and civil society', in A.G. Scherer and G. Palazzo (eds), *Handbook of Research on Global Corporate Citizenship*. Cheltenham: Edward Elgar, pp. 225–248.

Young, I.M. (2004) 'Responsibility and global labor justice', *Journal of Political Philosophy* 12(4): 365–388.

Young, I.M. (2006) 'Responsibility and global justice: A social connection model', *Social Philosophy and Policy*, 23: 102–130.

Young, I.M. (2008) 'Responsibility and global justice: A social connection model', in Scherer, A. G. and Palazzo, G. (eds), *Handbook of Research on Global Corporate Citizenship*. Cheltenham: Edward Elgar, pp. 137–165.

Zadek, S. (2004) 'The path to corporate responsibility', *Harvard Business Review*, 82: 125–132.

Zuppa, J.A., Morton, H. and Mehta, K. (2003) 'Television food advertising: Counterproductive to children's health? A content analysis using the Australian guide to healthy eating', *Nutrition and Dietetics,* 60(2): 78–84.

19

Ethical Challenges in Commercial Social Marketing

Thomas Boysen Anker and
Klemens Kappel

INTRODUCTION

Academics often assert a clear distinction between commercial marketing and social marketing (e.g. Blitstein et al., 2008: 35–38; Donovan and Henley, 2003: 32–35; McCormack et al., 2008: 272–276; McDermott et al., 2005: 546). Basically, commercial marketing aims at establishing a market exchange (products or services for money), whereas the purpose of social marketing is a welfare exchange (social behavioural change for intangible benefits such as personal well-being) (Brenkert, 2002: 17). In effect, some researchers argue that commercial marketing cannot be characterised as social marketing, due to its inherent motive to raise profits (Fry, cited in Davidson and Novelli, 2001: 71).

However, social marketing increasingly inspires commercial marketing, and a new marketing hybrid – commercial social marketing (CSM) – has arrived. The common theme across most social marketing definitions is that social marketing is the application of marketing techniques to encourage behavioural or attitudinal change in a target group in order to achieve a social goal (e.g. Andreasen, 1995; Dann, 2010; French and Blair-Stevens, 2010; Kotler and Lee, 2008). Along the same lines, we define CSM as the application of marketing techniques to encourage behavioural or attitudinal change in a target group in order to achieve a social goal *that is conducive to a more fundamental corporate goal.*

Two examples illustrate CSM as a growing trend. First, is a quote from Baroness Peta Buscombe, CEO of the Advertising Association, representing the advertising industry in the UK, showing that marketing professionals argue in favour of a link between commercial and social marketing:

> I think of advertising in two ways. One as a commercial conduit. But also it has a powerful role in terms of social marketing. And I think the power of advertising can make such an incredible difference in terms of influencing young people whether it be knife crimes, whether it be binge drinking, whether it be encouraging people to have healthier lifestyles.
>
> (...) What we do [at the Advertising Association], is to encourage the industry to act responsibly, absolutely critical, because we have such a powerful role to play, which is positive ... we are having a very positive role in terms of shifting behavior, encouraging behavioral change in a positive way (Brand Republic, 2008).

Moreover, in a recent report, 'Less smoke, more fire: The benefits and impacts of social marketing', the Chartered Institute of Marketing (CIM) also argues in favour of a link between commercial and social marketing (CIM, 2009).

Second, a number of contemporary commercial marketing campaigns aim at behaviour change in order to achieve a social goal. To mention just a few examples, Pampers' 'Back to sleep' campaign aims at encouraging parents to place babies on their backs to sleep instead of on their tummies in order to prevent sudden infant death syndrome; Dole's '5 A Day' campaign encourages children and parents to eat five servings of fruit and vegetables each day in order to promote public health (Kotler and Lee, 2005: 114–143). And Dove's 'Campaign for real beauty' aims at dismantling dysfunctional, stereotyped ideals of beauty in order to improve the basis of women's self-esteem (Kotler et al., 2008: 73–76).

Thus, whether or not the marketers behind socially oriented commercial campaigns label them 'social marketing', the campaigns nonetheless aim at improving social issues through marketing methods and – given the prevalent understanding of what social marketing is – thereby intuitively qualify as social marketing. Yet, the concept of CSM is rather new and sparks a great deal of controversy; some social marketers are hard pressed to believe that there genuinely is such a thing as CSM. The explanation often lies in the fact that the driving corporate motive in CSM is supporting brand positioning, strengthening brand image and, ultimately, raising profits: the social goal has to be conducive to a corporate one! Given the controversy surrounding the CSM concept, we start by demonstrating that commercial campaigns can deliver on the most crucial social marketing criteria and, thus, should be conceived of as social marketing carried out in a commercial context. Then we go on to analyse and discuss the most important ethical challenges in CSM.

The chapter at a glance

In the section 'Two cases of commercial social marketing', we outline six criteria that full-scale social marketing campaigns and interventions should satisfy. The criteria are (1) behavioural change, (2) consumer research, (3) segmentation and targeting, (4) the marketing mix (4Ps), (5) exchange and (6) social competition. We show – through brief case studies – how two for-profit corporations employ social marketing principles in consumer-oriented campaigns as well as workplace interventions.

In the section 'Ethics in commercial social marketing', we analyse a number of pertinent ethical challenges in CSM, each of which relates to one of the social marketing criteria. The analysis focuses on the following main issues: paternalism, privacy, disproportionate allocation of resources, negative identification, stereotyping, power imbalances and the problem of gaining ownership of social problems.

TWO CASES OF COMMERCIAL SOCIAL MARKETING

In the seminal paper 'Social marketing: An approach to planned social change', Kotler and Zaltman (1971: 5) launched the following definition: '*Social marketing is the design, implementation and control of programs calculated to influence the acceptability of social ideas and involving considerations of product planning, pricing, communication, distribution and marketing research*'. However influential this definition has been, it omits direct reference to behavioural change as a key objective of social marketing. As a corrective measure, Andreasen (1995: 7) proposed what has become a very dominant definition: '*Social marketing is the application of commercial marketing technologies to the analysis, planning, execution and evaluation of programmes designed to influence the voluntary behaviour of target audiences in order to improve their personal welfare and that of society*'.

Though Andreasen's definition provides a useful corrective, it still misses out on the insights of contemporary relationship marketing (Hastings, 2003; Wood, 2008). We are still in need of a powerful, generic social marketing definition that incorporates the consumer as a co-creator of the mutual exchange that lies at the heart of contemporary marketing (Grönroos, 1990, 2006). Andreasen (2002) is very well aware of this problem and has suggested downplaying the importance of generic definitions and instead focusing more on elaborate criteria. We follow this approach, because it allows for a more detailed understanding of CSM and thereby facilitates a more careful ethical analysis. The following six criteria are key to full-blown social marketing campaigns. Andreasen introduced the criteria in the seminal paper 'Marketing social marketing in the social change marketplace' (2002) and the criteria have been adopted by the National Social Marketing Centre, UK, as foundational principles for their social marketing initiatives (French and Blair-Stevens, 2007). On the assumption that the criteria enjoy support from influential academics as well as practitioners, we hold a campaign – whether carried out in a commercial or non-commercial context – to be an instance of social marketing if it meets the criteria in order to achieve a social goal.

1. *Behavioural change.* The aim of social marketing is to obtain (Andreasen, 1995) or improve the prerequisites for (Wood, 2008) behavioural change in order to achieve a social goal.
2. *Consumer research.* Consumers' world views (needs, values, wants and experiences) are revealed through mainly qualitative studies (focus

groups, personal interviews, field observations, persona methods) (Hastings, 2007: 46–49).

3. *Segmentation and targeting.* The target group is narrowed down to specific social groups that share a set of core beliefs, values and desires (Hastings, 2007: 61–68).
4. *Marketing mix.* Strategic use of the 4Ps of the marketing mix: product, place, price and promotion.
5. *Exchange.* In exchange for behavioural or attitudinal change, social marketers offer tangible or intangible benefits (Deshpande et al., 2004).
6. *Competition.* Competing forces to the desired behavioural or attitudinal change are identified and the campaign uses strategies to outsmart this competition.

As Stead and Angus (2007: 24) suggest, the criteria are not rigid determinants, but flexible indicators of a campaign's 'social marketing-ness'. However, we think of criterion 1 as a necessary condition of social marketing, because the very aim of social marketing is to obtain behavioural or attitudinal change. Moreover, note that a genuine CSM campaign needs to draw on a substantial mix of the criteria *in order to achieve a social goal.* Accordingly, a CSM campaign with a commercial and a social goal that does employ all criteria, but only does so to obtain the commercial goal, will fail the test of social marketing-ness. Thus, if a CSM campaign is not fundamentally designed to deliver on the social goal, then it does not qualify as social marketing. And here we need to highlight the fact that social marketing cannot be identified with social advertising (Stead and Hastings, 1997): the amalgamation of product, price, place and promotion (better known as the 4Ps) needs to be conducive – in all its parts – to the promised social goal in order for the CSM campaign to genuinely qualify as social marketing.

CSM is easily confused with cause-related marketing and corporate social marketing. Let us briefly outline the core differences. Cause-related marketing usually builds on an alliance between a for-profit and a non-profit organisation (Varadarajan and Menon, 1988) and involves 'an offer from a firm to contribute a specified amount to a designated cause when customers engage in revenue-providing exchanges' (Carringer, 1994: 16). More recently, cause-related marketing has come to describe a broader range of marketing activities that address social issues to reach corporate objectives (Lafferty et al., 2004; Liu and Liston-Heyes, 2010), which easily leads to a conflation between cause-related marketing and CSM. However, CSM is clearly distinguished from cause-related marketing on one dimension: that is,

by its focus on behavioural and attitudinal change.

CSM and corporate social marketing are essentially the same – they encourage behavioural change to achieve a social goal that is conducive to a corporate one – but corporate social marketing is, as the term suggests, limited to social marketing in relation to a corporate brand (Kotler and Lee, 2005). CSM is sometimes disconnected from corporate brands and linked to specific product brands, as in the case of Dove's 'Campaign for real beauty' (Anker and Stead, 2009), which does not tie into the brand owner's (Unilever) corporate brand values. Therefore, CSM is the generic concept under which corporate social marketing falls.

Before we present the brief CSM case studies, it should be noted that we take commercial consumer campaigns and workplace interventions to be examples of CSM to the extent that a proper analysis reveals that they employ social marketing principles. Thus, a commercial campaign that substantially draws on the social marketing criteria is a CSM campaign regardless of whether it is formally identified or labelled as such.

Prototypical cases of CSM

Corporations have employed social marketing techniques to promote social objectives in the workplace (Stead and Angus, 2007) as well as in the marketplace (Davidson and Novelli, 2001). In what follows, we will introduce a case of employee-oriented as well as consumer-oriented CSM. Then we go on to analyse key ethical problems associated with both kinds of CSM.

Consumer-oriented CSM

In 2004, Unilever launched the 'Dove campaign for real beauty', which aims at redefining the way society views beauty in order to make more women feel beautiful (Kotler et al., 2008: 73–76). The core of the campaign consists of ads on huge billboards, TV and magazines that attractively depict a variety of women all having an attribute (e.g. being curvy or wrinkled), which would normally be considered inappropriate for top models representing the beauty industry's vision of beauty. Dove's 'real beauty' campaign provides a prototypical example of consumer-oriented CSM, because the campaign draws extensively on all of the six criteria in order to reach a social goal.

Dove states that the campaign is a global effort intended to serve as a starting point for societal change (Dove, 2011a). The social goal Dove is aiming at is to dismantle dysfunctional ideals of beauty that make women feel bad about their bodies and introduce new inclusive ideals of beauty in order to change women's perception of beauty and thereby reinforce feelings of self-esteem (criterion 1).

To get a detailed picture of the target group's conception of various issues relating to ideals of beauty and feelings of self-esteem, Dove commissioned a 10-country consumer research study (criterion 2). Thus, the global report 'The real truth about beauty: A global report' (Dove, 2011b) surveyed 3300 girls and women between the ages of 15 and 64. The findings were discussed and interpreted with help from professional scholars (Dove, 2011c).

The campaign employs all of the 4Ps (product, place, price and promotion) (criterion 4). Interestingly, monetary cost is not part of the marketing plan, but social price or costs are. In TV ads like 'Onslaught' and 'Talk to your child before the beauty industry does', the campaign highlights the psychological price or cost women have to pay for being subjects to suppressive social ideals of beauty. Dove offers a tangible, commercial product (cosmetics) as well as a sophisticatedly defined social product (new ideals of beauty). The channels by which the product/social change is promoted include various media, interpersonal channels (SMS-interaction) and the creation of a fund, the 'Dove self-esteem fund'. The means by which the product/social change is promoted include advertising, internet games, expert articles and reports, media advocacy and even sleepover events.

The main campaign target is ordinary women who want to feel beautiful and are unsatisfied with the contemporary ideals of beauty. However, different campaign activities work with much narrower segments and targets (criterion 3). To take just one example, Dove has developed guidelines to help their consumers run workshops in order to develop self-esteem among young girls. These guidelines are made in different versions, which quite clearly target different groups: (a) teachers, (b) mothers and daughters and (c) girl guides or leaders (Dove, 2011d).

In exchange for behavioural or attitudinal change, the campaign offers a real social benefit: self-esteem (criterion 5). The campaign aims at an epistemological exchange with its target: increasing knowledge and awareness of stereotypes that impact negatively on self-esteem. And it aims at an emotional exchange: increasing individual consumers' feelings of worth and self-esteem.

With striking creativity, a series of videos identify and attempt to outsmart competing forces against the desired behavioural and attitudinal change (criterion 6). The video 'Evolution'

identifies as a competing factor the use of modern imaging technology to manipulate images of models in order to make them match stereotyped ideals of beauty. And the video 'Onslaught' depicts the beauty industry (advertising, cosmetic surgery, beauty stereotypes) as a competing force against improving the basis of self-esteem and warns the consumer to 'talk to your daughter before the beauty industry does' (Dove, 2011e).

Dove quite obviously draws on all of the social marketing criteria. What is more, they do so to promote a behavioural or social goal: dismantling dysfunctional ideals of beauty and introducing new inclusive ones in order to support the basis of self-esteem. Accordingly, the 'Campaign for real beauty' is a full-scale social marketing campaign carried out in a commercial context.

One might object that although the programme may qualify as CSM, according to the criteria, it still begs the question: How does this benefit society and the individual? The campaign tries to bring about real social benefits along two dimensions.

First, the campaign aims at alleviating harm caused by dysfunctional stereotypes. Ample research demonstrates that being subject to dysfunctional stereotypes impacts negatively on such diverse things as cognitive processing (Arbuthno, 2009), motivation to adopt a healthy lifestyle (Seacat and Mickelson, 2009) and overall feelings of self-esteem (Dove, 2011b). Thus, it is not surprising that fighting stereotype threats is a key goal in various contemporary non-profit social marketing programmes (e.g. the 'Time to change' campaign run by mental health charities Mind and Rethink (UK), which aims at dismantling negative stereotypes attributed to people suffering from schizophrenia; (Time to change, 2011)). Insofar as the 'Campaign for real beauty' succeeds in dismantling a dysfunctional stereotype that most women are subject to, the campaign actually alleviates social harm caused by commercial marketing.

Second, the campaign aims at promoting good by launching new inclusive ideals of beauty and encouraging the target group to identify with those ideals. On the campaign's basic assumption, justified through comprehensive consumer research, that for the target group self-esteem is partly conditional on perceiving oneself as beautiful, it does provide a real benefit to influence the targeted women to perceive themselves as beautiful: improved self-esteem.

Workplace CSM

In January 2008, Novo Nordisk, a pharmaceutical company, turned its Danish employee health programme into a global, company-wide (31.300 employees in 74 countries) initiative dubbed NovoHealth (Novo Nordisk, 2011). As we shall see, the health scheme provides a key example of workplace social marketing, because it draws on all six social marketing criteria. The overall purpose of NovoHealth is to promote healthy lifestyles among employees: in particular, to increase physical exercise, improve dietary choices and support smoking cessation (criterion 1).

The NovoHealth scheme draws on at least two different streams of consumer research: first, to inform the overall design of the health scheme, a cross-functional working group gathered knowledge about target groups (specifically, variations in food culture); second, NovoHealth representatives continuously collect examples of best practices and share their knowledge with colleagues and the cross-functional working group in order to constantly improve the scheme (criterion 2).

Though there is one unified aim across the company (improving employees' physical health), the scheme draws extensively on geographical segmentation and targeting in that it offers different target groups different health products (criterion 3). As an example, the scheme offers employees in Brazil health classes and daily 15-minute breaks with physical trainers, whereas an online Health Risk Assessment tool has been developed and targeted to employees in the USA.

NovoHealth employs at least three of the 4Ps (product, promotion and place) (criterion 4). The scheme offers a series of products: for example, healthy food adapted to cultural variations; access to exercise; a health check every second year; health education and smoking cessation programmes. The company promotes the scheme through the corporate newsletter (direct marketing), a network of NovoHealth representatives (viral marketing), health fairs and annual 5K runs (events).

In exchange (criterion 5) for participating in the health scheme, the company offers tangible and intangible benefits. In general, the key benefit is intangible and consists in increased individual confidence, social recognition and improved health and well-being. However, local interventions operate with tangible benefits: for example, a $250 bonus to employees in the USA if they take the online health risk assessment.

It is not clear to what extent a thorough competitive analysis (criterion 6) has been carried out to identify the key behavioural barriers confronting the health scheme. However, local initiatives such as the aforementioned health risk assessment for US employees and health education for employees in Brazil are likely to raise individual awareness of specific barriers to personal behavioural change.

On corporate reasons to do good

A common objection to CSM is that the true reason why corporations get involved in promoting social aims is the expected return on investment. As mentioned in the Introduction, the corporate goal is always the primary one because a corporation will not get involved in social causes if they are considered to be detrimental to key corporate objectives. Some social marketers take this to indicate quite clearly that CSM is not genuinely social marketing and that it does not benefit society. In what follows, we provide two short arguments that demonstrate that although CSM is driven by corporate motivation, this does not necessarily compromise the value of CSM.

First, the outcome of a social marketing campaign – commercial or non-profit – is logically independent from the reasons and motivations that explain why the marketers got involved with the campaign. The outcome of a campaign is conditional on the design and execution of the campaign, not on the motivation for doing it.

Second, corporations that choose to address social issues through their commercial marketing activities certainly could have chosen not to do so. The point is that whenever a corporation decides to run a marketing campaign it can choose between (a) doing a conventional campaign that only aims at achieving a corporate goal, or (b) doing a CSM campaign that in addition aims at addressing a social issue. Consequently, if improving social goals is high on one's agenda (as we assume is the case for social marketers), it is irrational *en bloc* to criticise corporations involved in CSM for having the wrong kind of motive, because the alternative (a conventional commercial campaign) is far less likely to be conducive to one's social agenda.

However, it is crucial to be aware that CSM in some cases can have adverse effects. There is evidence that tobacco industry funded anti-smoking campaigns are generally less effective than publicly funded ones; in some cases, industry anti-smoking campaigns have even been found to subtly promote smoking to young people (Landman et al., 2002). The underlying principle, which can decide if running a CSM campaign is ethically justified, can be formulated like this: if a business has a vested interest in promoting the behaviour or attitude which their CSM activities aim at preventing, then the underlying rationale for promoting the social cause is not to be trusted and the business should keep away from CSM in this particular domain.

ETHICS IN COMMERCIAL SOCIAL MARKETING

The aim of commercial marketing is to establish a market exchange (money for products or services). By contrast, social marketing aims at establishing a much more complex and ethically controversial welfare exchange (behavioural change for tangible or intangible benefits; Brenkert 2002: 17; McDermott et al., 2005). As illustration of its normative nature, social marketing has been applied to controversial issues such as: (a) influencing judges to reduce the use of imprisonment as punishment (Hastings, 2007: 229–235); (b) encouraging educated parents to have more children (Donovan and Henley, 2003: 173); (c) motivating people to sign up as organ donors (Jeffreys, 2008); and (d) recruiting young men for the army. Compared to commercial marketing, social marketing interferes more seriously with our lives, because it tries to encourage the target to make behavioural decisions that might impact radically on his or her life in terms of, for example, (a) professional practice (sentencing criminals to social rehabilitation instead of prison); (b) having a baby; (c) imposing emotional distress on close relatives (becoming organ donor); or even (d) jeopardising one's life (becoming a professional soldier).

Accordingly, social marketing is quite often an ethically controversial branch of modern marketing. Though social marketing ethics, as such, is still nascent, the field is evolving rapidly (notable contributions by: Andreasen, 2001; Brenkert, 2002; Callahan et al., 1999; Eagle, 2009; Guttman and Salmon, 2004; Hastings et al., 2004; Laczniak et al., 1979). However, for-profit social marketing is by and large ignored. Apart from Davidson and Novelli (2001), this chapter is a pioneering exploration into the key ethical issues specific to CSM.

Paternalism and behavioural change (criterion 1)

In essence, a person, organisation or state acts paternalistically to the extent that it interferes with an individual's life in order to make him or her better off or prevent him or her from harm even if this is against that individual's own will (Buchanan, 2008; Dworkin, 2010). The problem with paternalism is that it runs counter to the value of personal autonomy that lies at the heart of Western liberal democracy (Kymlicka, 2002).

Social marketing is often prone to paternalism because the key goal of the discipline is to encourage certain actions and ways of living that are defined as good for the target consumer, regardless of whether or not he or she endorses that line of action or way of living (Brenkert, 2002: 22–23; Donovan and Henley, 2003: 170–172).

As an example, social marketers might encourage pregnant smokers to kick the habit, regardless of whether or not the target group endorses a non-smoking lifestyle. Or social marketers might try to influence commuters to feel miserable about driving their cars to work, when public transportation is at hand, even though the target group is quite happy with the freedom and convenience provided by cars and has no desire not to commute by car.

However, some might argue that social marketing after all is not a paternalistic enterprise because the core aim is a welfare exchange between two equally powerful parties: (a) a social marketer who offers a given benefit (e.g. better health) in return for behavioural change (e.g. kicking smoking or drinking) and (b) a consumer who is free to accept or decline the offered welfare exchange.

To clarify matters, we need to distinguish between hard and soft paternalism. It is true that social marketing is not paternalistic in the hard sense: that is, social marketing cannot and does not want to force the consumer to change behaviour. But social marketing is often paternalistic in the soft sense: that is, social marketing encourages and influences the consumer – regardless of whether he or she wants to be targeted or not – to engage in a welfare transaction (e.g. adopt behavioural change for a personal benefit), the existence of which would not have been the case had the social marketer not decided to interfere with the consumer's life.

Tailoring social marketing to the target group's world view

One can reasonably argue that, for any given society, what counts as a 'social goal' and 'social problem' is conditional – not on what those involved in the social problem subjectively define as a problem – but on what the media, policymakers, academics and the general public conceive of as a social problem (Brenkert, 2002). With this understanding, one can go on to argue that CSM can justify imposing social norms and values on its target group if the associated purpose is evidently recognised as worthy and significant by society. But we have to realise that this solution does not make the marketing intervention less paternalistic: it simply distributes the problem to a public and governmental level.

Our suggestion for a truly non-paternalistic solution – which applies to CSM as well as standard non-profit social marketing – is to only induce motivations to behavioural changes and impose social values which the target group desires. On the one hand, a target group can be said to desire a given value or social aim in a direct or conscious way when it is possible to obtain overt statements from the group that it identifies positively with the value or social aim in question. This can be done through the application of ethnographic marketing research methods like focus groups and personal in-depth interviews. On the other hand, a target group can be said to desire a given value or social aim indirectly or tacitly, if ethnographic research methods like participant observation and interdisciplinary culture analysis provide reasonable evidence for the assumption that the group identifies positively with the value or social aim in question. Carefully applied, both methods provide a non-paternalistic starting point for a CSM campaign. But, of course, methods that obtain direct statements of identification with values and social aims provide the strongest ethical justification for employing these values in a CSM campaign.

Dove provides a good example of the stronger form of non-paternalistic CSM; their consumer research revealed, on a transnational scale, direct statements from members of the target group that they viewed contemporary ideals of beauty as a real problem and that they wished for more inclusive ideals of beauty. As such, Dove escaped being paternalistic by tailoring their campaign to the world view of their target.

Paternalism and social contracts

With respect to workplace social marketing, the problem of paternalism takes on special importance. Let us for a moment examine contractarianism, which offers an alternative and rather promising line of arguments to be used with employers who want to defend the claim that, generally, it is not paternalistic to impose values on employees.

Contractarianism is the view that human societies are structured around tacit social contracts that set the rules governing human interaction. Donaldson (1982, 1989), Donaldson and Dunfee (1994, 1995) and Dunfee et al. (1999) have developed a comprehensive social contract approach to business ethics ('Integrative social contracts theory'). They distinguish between two kinds of social contracts: (a) hypothetical macro-social contracts and (b) actual micro-social contracts. Hypothetical macro-social contracts specify the tacit framework that structures human actions through unwritten conventions, requirements and expectations. Actual micro-social contracts elaborate and specify the particular rules that should govern human interaction in actual social contexts (e.g. in communities and workplaces).

When an employer offers an employee a job, a job contract has to be signed (an actual micro-social contract). A common element in such contracts is the requirement of the employee to support the corporate values. With reference to this micro-social contract, the employer can argue that it is not paternalistic to impose values on the employees insofar as the values are congruent with the corporate values, which the employees have promised to support by voluntarily signing the contract.

Although intuitively appealing, this contractarian argument is flawed in our view: on the one hand, it is correct that an employee signs a job contract voluntarily; on the other hand, one must acknowledge the fact that while the particular choice to sign a specific job contract often is rather unconstrained, the choice not to sign any job contract at all is highly constrained. In liberal, capitalist societies, virtually all individuals are subject to the necessity of signing a job contract, because – for most of us – having a decent life is pretty much conditional on doing so.

The point is that although employees can choose relatively unconstrained whether or not to sign a specific job contract, they have to sign a contract with one or another employer in order to lead decent lives. Thus, employees are not free to choose *not* to be subject to this specific type of micro-social contracts, dubbed 'job contracts'. Consequently, the fact that an employee could have chosen not to sign a specific job contract does not guarantee that imposing values on the employee is non-paternalistic. As a consequence, the optimal way to non-paternalistic workplace social marketing interventions is, as outlined above, to make sure that the target group overtly endorses the imposed values. As noted, this could be done by means of qualitative ethnographic methods such as personal interviews or focus groups.

Privacy and consumer research (criterion 2)

All major marketing organisations working in the field of consumer research have codes of conduct that set down the principal moral rules that should govern consumer research. One key ethical principle in consumer research is that of privacy or data integrity. As an example, the Marketing Research Association's (MRA, 2007: 11, 32) 'Code of marketing research standards' acknowledges consumers' right to privacy along two dimensions: control over unwanted information (no unsolicited emails, phone calls, etc.) as well as control over personal information (safeguarding anonymity and not giving or trading personal information to third parties without written consent).

Consumer research into employees' needs and preferences is critical to the design of successful workplace social marketing interventions. While the MRA code of conduct provides good guidelines for consumer research in relation to consumer-oriented CSM, employee-oriented CSM may lead to unanticipated ethical conflicts with privacy. Consider the hypothetical case of an organisation that puts together a health team consisting of employees from different departments. The team is assigned the task to carry out a social marketing health campaign in its workplace. The campaign includes extensive health checks and, in order to inform the process of designing the campaign, the health team interviews a number of employees about personal health status, health beliefs and motivation to live healthily.

As a rule, the information gathered through such a process is very personal and sensitive. And when it is an in-house team of people that gathers the information, it might turn out to be rather difficult to safeguard anonymity and respect control over information. Just imagine a senior manager who requires access to information about an employee's health status and health motivation. In this case, it might be very difficult for the employee in the health team to protect the right to privacy, because the manager does have power to influence his or her working conditions. It takes a strong-willed employee to refuse to pass information about a colleague on to a manager who requests access to this information.

One way of solving this problem is to make sure that everyone in the organisation understands the need to protect anonymity and privacy. This approach can be considerably supported through behavioural sanctions (losing bonuses, denying promotions, dismissal from jobs). Another way would be to hire an external agency to do the consumer research. This would both relieve potential managerial pressure to release the information from the employees, who would otherwise have done the consumer research, and increase the integrity of the employees participating in the consumer research.

Segmentation, cool social problems and negative identification (criterion 3)

Cool social problems

Segmentation and targeting give rise to a number of ethical problems in social marketing (Andreasen, 1995; Bloom and Novelli, 1981; Brenkert, 2002). Most notably, social marketers may choose not to spend resources on some social groups – even though their members are among the worst-off in society – because their situation is too desperate or difficult to resolve (Brenkert, 2002: 21). This problem of 'de-targeting' segments in need of social support certainly does apply to CSM as well, but it takes on a special emphasis.

CSM may choose not to target a segment even though (a) its members are among the worst-off *and* (b) a CSM intervention is *very likely* to resolve the problems. The reason for this is that commercial marketers always have a monetary bottom line. If a social problem does not fit into a corporation's desired image, it is unlikely it will run a CSM campaign aimed at that particular problem. As Donovan and Henley (2003: 174) point out, breast cancer might provide a great fit with corporate image because all women can relate to it, whereas obesity could trigger an undesirable link to bullying, low self-esteem and lack of self-control. Corporations will only fight 'cool' social problems or, at least, social problems that can be approached in a 'cool' manner. As a consequence, CSM can be a source of social inequality in the sense that a disproportionate amount of resources might be allocated to specific social issues that are associated with desirable attributes. And to be sure, disproportionate allocation of resources to fight social and health problems is not just a theoretical possibility: dementia, which costs the UK five times more than cancer, receives 10 times less in research funding than cancer research does (Luengo-Fernandez et al., 2010). The last thing we need is for CSM to broaden such gaps by allocating even more resources to those 'cool' social problems that are already 'over-funded' and, thereby, fuel the problem of social inequality.

Nonetheless, the situation could be turned upside down and used proactively to fight the problem of de-targeting the worst-off. If CSM proves to be more than a temporary trend and becomes an integrated part of social marketing efforts, the most obvious solution to the problem would be to suggest a division of labour, where non-profit social marketing primarily concentrates on controversial problems with which corporations are not interested in being identified. Such a division of labour could possibly free public resources to target social groups which otherwise would have been neglected and, consequently, contribute positively to a more proportionate allocation of resources to run social marketing campaigns.

Negative identification

Negative identification is an attempt to form one's identity in opposition to values one associates with specific persons, social groups or ideals. A very basic problem with targeting is that some segments might identify themselves negatively with other segments. Thus, if marketers promote a social cause, say specific health ideals, to a given segment, S(1), and another segment, S(2), identifies negatively with S(1), then there is a real chance that S(2) would take a negative stance towards the health ideals promoted to S(1). Interim findings from a series of focus group interviews on teenagers' attitudes to food branding and health (ISM, 2009) suggest that 'health' as a social value is sometimes considered 'upper-class' and 'snobbish'. This might indicate that some teenagers associate themselves negatively with healthy living.

The problem of negative identification applies to both non-profit and for-profit social marketing. However, there is a potential difference that calls for addressing the problem in this chapter. Non-profit social marketers do not have any particular interest in trying to influence some segments to identify negatively with, say, the social values that they try to reinforce in a given target group. But for-profit social marketers might have a reason to de-market certain segments. Consider the hypothetical case of a commercial marketing campaign that aims at creating a luxury health brand that appeals exclusively to high-end, affluent consumers. In order to establish the brand as 'exclusive' and 'discerning' in the mind of the target group, it might be tempting (because it is deemed effective) to brand the health values associated with the product as strictly upper-class values. To this end, 'undesirable' segments might be actively discouraged to identify themselves with the health values.

As a rule, discouragement of undesirable segments is a form of discrimination and should therefore not be intentionally applied in marketing campaigns. However, unintentional discouragement can be hard to avoid insofar as some social groups – independently of the marketer's influence – tend to identify negatively with other social groups. Since consumer-oriented CSM might have a commercial interest in discouraging undesirable segments, and they are dealing with issues of great societal importance, they are under a particularly strong requirement to assess the risk of negative identification.

Promotion and stereotypes (criterion 4)

Full-scale social marketing campaigns usually draw on all of the four Ps in the marketing mix (product, place, price and promotion). In relation to CSM, promotion in particular may cause problems. In this section, we show why stereotyping poses a special problem in CSM.

A stereotype is a one-sided representation, prevalent in one or more social groups, of a material (e.g. persons, social groups) or immaterial (e.g. ideals, diseases) entity. In relation to marketing, a predominant stereotype is the one-sided representation of female beauty as being slim, tall, young and White. Along the same lines, the recent strong focus on healthy living has led to a frequent one-sided representation of health as slimness. Consider, for example, Kellogg's breakfast cereal brand Special K, which through frequent explicit and implicit links between the product and health establishes itself as a health brand. Interestingly, the core symbolic value associated with health is slimness and, thereby, the health brand echoes the well-known stereotype from beauty marketing.

Stereotypes can be functional or dysfunctional (De Mooij, 2005: 40). Functional stereotypes work like regulative ideals that guide human actions for the better. If, for example, Nike's 'Just do it' campaign, which stereotypically depicts people who engage in sports as extremely self-confident and cool, motivates people to become more physically active, then we have an instance of a functional stereotype. By contrast, if Special K – which as mentioned above associates being healthy with being very, very slim – influences consumers to feel unhealthy, because they cannot meet the stereotyped and distorted picture of health, then we have an instance of a dysfunctional stereotype.

Stereotype threat is a well-known problem for social marketers and many campaigns try to dismantle dysfunctional stereotypes (e.g. dismantling gender stereotypes that prevent girls from playing soccer/football or men from seeing their GPs).

Yet it is crucial to be aware of the fact that marketing, commercial as well as social, will always be a source of stereotyping. The reason for this is that marketing activities like branding and advertising are designed to 'attract attention and create instant recognition' (De Mooij, 2005: 40–41) and usually try to trigger positive associations between the offering (product, service, behavioural exchange) and attractive ideals (beauty, performance, empowerment, health, etc.). Since advertising is by nature a simplified depiction of reality, it has to rely on the use of stereotypes.

But there is an important difference between standard social marketing and CSM. Whereas CSM certainly does not have a reason to create dysfunctional stereotypes and, due to its social commitment, would be genuinely concerned *not* to do so, CSM still might be less inclined to thoroughly assess the risk of creating dysfunctional stereotypes than its non-profit counterpart. The reason is this: given our foundational assumption that in CSM social goals have to be conducive to corporate ones, it is of secondary importance if a stereotype is socially dysfunctional (e.g. if it distorts consumers' health concept) provided that the stereotype is commercially viable (e.g. strengthens brand image, creates product desire, etc.). To put it differently, CSM can obtain its primary goal even though, as an unintended side effect, it happens to create a dysfunctional social stereotype. In contrast, creating dysfunctional social stereotypes would be undermining to the core purpose of non-profit social marketing, because positive social change is its intrinsic goal.

Asymmetric power relations and exchange (criterion 5)

In relation to the concept of 'exchange', the problem of power imbalances appears. In fact, power relations are sometimes underscored as the key ethical problem in social marketing (Donovan and Henley, 2003: 173–174; Laczniak et al., 1979). It is argued that power imbalances in CSM are likely to be even more problematic and asymmetric due to greater financial resources in the private sector (Davidson and Novelli, 2001: 89–90). Indeed, the problem of power is crucial, but more complex than described by Davidson and Novelli. Compared with standard social marketing, the power imbalances are likely to be less serious in consumer-oriented CSM, but more serious in employee-oriented CSM. Or so we will argue.

Power relations in consumer-oriented CSM

To demonstrate why the power imbalances are likely not to be very significant in consumer-oriented CSM, we need to take a closer look at the concept of power and consumer attitudes towards cause-related marketing.

Inspired by Cunningham's (2003) interpretation of Arendt's (1986) application of the distinction between hard and soft power, we hold an agent A to be in possession of hard power over B to the extent that A can force B to perform a given action X. By contrast, A has soft power over B to the extent that A can influence B's willingness to perform X. In the current context, the major difference between hard and soft power is that soft power always leaves the subject of power with the option to pursue a course of action other than the one the person in power tries to encourage. In terms of marketing studies, the concept of soft power is very significant, because the power of the marketer is that of a 'desire catalyst': marketers'

true power is to intensify existing desires in the target group in order to increase their willingness to engage in a market exchange. Although marketers certainly can be said to try to create new desires, it would be rather controversial to hold that they have the power to push people against their will. But certainly, marketers do have and do capitalise on their soft power to create new and trigger existing desires and intensify willingness to act in their favour.

The next building block for arguing our point is to provide a quick description of consumers' attitudes to non-profit and for-profit marketers that act in favour of a societal cause. Marketing research demonstrates widespread consumer scepticism as to whether companies engaged in corporate social responsibility are in it for the money only (Vanhamme and Grobben, 2008). Of particular interest, Webb and Mohr (1998: 230) reveal that consumers are more sceptical about for-profit cause-related marketing than is the case with non-profit cause-related marketing. A vast majority think that non-profit organisations, which pursue societal aims, genuinely intend to help others. Likewise, a vast majority think that for-profit organisations pursuing societal aims do *not* genuinely intend to help others.

Now the question is how 'scepticism towards an agent's motives' relates to 'soft power'. On the assumption that most people under normal circumstances would be less willing to be influenced by an agent whose motivations they doubt or distrust, it is reasonable to expect most consumers to be less willing to be influenced by CSM than by non-profit social marketing, because of the predominant skepticism towards corporate motives to do good. According to this analysis, non-profit social marketers are likely to have more soft power over their target groups than would for-profit commercial social marketers. Thus, the power imbalances are likely to be less asymmetric in consumer-oriented CSM than is the case with standard non-profit social marketing. However, the argument needs empirical testing.

Power relations in workplace CSM

By contrast, power imbalances are likely to be *more* severe in workplace CSM than in standard social marketing. Why is that?

As a consumer, there are no obvious negative consequences associated with not engaging in a CSM campaign (apart from not getting the benefits the campaign could otherwise have yielded). But as an employee, being critical of a social marketing campaign in one's workplace might damage social recognition from peers and managers, future career opportunities in the firm and, eventually, trigger fear of being fired.

To safeguard personal integrity and weaken the influence of soft power in workplace social marketing campaigns, CSM should always be based on voluntary participation. However, the employer should always be aware of the fact that even though voluntary participation is the principle, employees might very well feel social pressure to get involved with the CSM campaign, because it will be obvious to most employees that participation, of course, is to be viewed as a positive asset from a managerial perspective. Thus, the danger – which is inherent and structurally insoluble – is that workplace CSM campaigns based on voluntary participation are in effect not voluntary due to the tacit social pressure to join them.

Although far from implying that workplace CSM is undesirable as such, the above observation should lead to a greater awareness of the fact that some social marketing initiatives might be unsuitable for workplace use. There is no general golden rule that in advance can discern appropriate from inappropriate elements in workplace social marketing, because 'appropriateness' is relative to workplace culture and the actual values of employees. In case of doubt, the best way to test a social marketing initiative for appropriateness would be to carry out an anonymous survey in which employees rate the appropriateness of the proposed campaign initiative.

Commercial and social competition (criterion 6)

In social marketing, the concept of competition usually refers to the social marketer's attempt to identify and outsmart the key set of behavioural determinants that obstructs the intended behavioural change (Andreasen, 2002; Hastings, 2007: 160–177). In relation to this concept, we will argue that CSM has a potentially harmful reason to try to outsmart other social forces that address the very same social problems.

Gaining ownership of social problems to increase competitive strength

A corporation that tries to solve a social problem through social marketing does have an interest in outsmarting other forces that aim at solving the very same social problem.

As an example, Dove has an interest (perceived or not) in gaining exclusive ownership of its social cause (ideals of beauty linked to self-esteem) insofar as corporations normally will use social marketing as a tool to create a strong corporate brand and increase product brand equity. The rationale underlying this argument is the observation that 'uniqueness' or 'differentiation'

is indicative of brand strength (Aaker, 2002; Keller, 2008). Thus, corporations running CSM campaigns are likely to try to outsmart other forces that address the same problem, because ownership of the problem facilitates brand uniqueness.

The ethical issue is that gaining competitive ownership of social problems might be counterproductive from a societal point of view. Consider the case in which a corporation chooses to fight breast cancer. Given the tremendous size and serious implications of the illness, it would be highly inappropriate to try to gain exclusive ownership of the problem and outsmart other forces that are addressing the same problem; all efforts are greatly needed and therefore it would be unethical to try to impede any such efforts for the sake of increasing brand equity and corporate competitiveness.

Note that having a reason to perform an action does not necessarily imply that one acts on that reason. Although CSM campaigners do have a reason to gain exclusive ownership of the social cause they address, it is not necessarily the case that they decide to act on that reason. The likelihood might be very low, but still it is important to get a clear picture of why corporations get involved in CSM.

The problem of gaining ownership of social problems is very hard to get around, because competitive strength – which is the source of the problem – is a survival benchmark and, as such, corporations do not necessarily have a strong interest in resolving it. The main interest is to be associated with trying to solve social problems, not necessarily to actually solve them. The corporate pay-off of CSM is likely to emerge from the fact that consumers and stakeholders perceive of the corporations as acting socially responsible. In other words, the corporate pay-off is likely to emerge from the *perception* of the corporation as an active socially responsible agent: that is, to emerge independently of whether the problem is perceived to be actually solved or not. Again, consider Dove; they surely have not solved the problem of distorted beauty ideals in contemporary Western society, but they are *perceived* as addressing the problem and, indeed, they have gotten their corporate pay-off. The campaign is reported to have led to a 700% increase in product sales, and increased Dove's share of firming lotions in the UK from 1% to 6% (CIM, 2009: 10).

CONCLUSION

Contemporary commercial marketing gets inspiration from social marketing. This inspiration has led to a new form of marketing – commercial social marketing (CSM). In fact, two different forms of CSM have emerged: consumer-oriented social marketing as well as workplace social marketing. This chapter has shown that CSM – despite its great potential for improving social goals – is subject to a number of ethical challenges that arise due to the fact that, in CSM, social goals have to be conducive to corporate ones. Yet, when carefully assessed for risk, commercial social marketing is a powerful tool to push the social agenda in the right direction.

KEY WORDS: Commercial social marketing; ethics, paternalism, privacy, stereotyping, power imbalances, social competition.

Key insights

- This chapter defines and illustrates commercial social marketing and explains important distinctions.
- We provide an in-depth analysis of core ethical problems in commercial social marketing.
- We show that ethical problems are usually not insoluble and, therefore, that commercial social marketing offers a genuine strategic resource in the fight to address social problems.

REFERENCES

Aaker, D.A. (2002) *Building Strong Brands.* London: Simon and Schuster.

Andreasen, A.R. (1995) *Marketing Social Change: Changing Behavior to Promote Health, Social Development, and the Environment.* San Francisco, CA: Jossey-Bass.

Andreasen, A.R. (ed.) (2001) *Ethics in Social Marketing.* Washington, DC: Georgetown University Press.

Andreasen, A.R. (2002) 'Marketing social marketing in the social change marketplace', *Journal of Public Policy and Marketing,* 21: 3–13.

Andreasen, A.R. (2006) *Social Marketing in the 21st Century.* London: Sage Publications.

Anker, T.B. and Stead, M. (2009) 'What is commercial social marketing? And is it a force for good or bad?' *Proceedings of International Social Marketing and Non-profit Conference,* Melbourne, Australia.

Arbuthno, K. (2009) 'The effects of stereotype threat on standardized mathematics test performance and cognitive processing', *Harvard Educational Review,* 79(3): 448–473.

Arendt, H. (1986) 'Communicative power', in S. Lukes (ed), *Power.* New York: New York University Press, pp. 59–74.

BBC (2010) 'City tram turned into padded cell', available at: http://news.bbc.co.uk/1/hi/england/south_yorkshire/785 0629.stm, accessed 18 March 2009.

Blitstein, J.L., Evans, W.D. and Driscoll, D.L. (2008) 'What is a public health brand?' in W.D. Evans and G. Hastings (eds), *Public Health Branding.* Oxford: Oxford University Press, pp. 25–41.

Bloom, P. and Novelli, W.D. (1981) 'Problems and challenges in social marketing', *Journal of Marketing,* 45(2): 79–88.

Brand Republic (2008) 'Can the government and the advertising industry work together?' (TV interview with Baroness Peta Buscombe, CEO of the Advertising Association, UK). Available at: http://www.youtube.com/watch?v=ELDVNim vQzs (accessed 19 July 2011).

Brenkert, G. (2001) 'The ethics of international social marketing', in A.R. Andreasen (ed), *Ethics in Social Marketing.* Washington, DC: Georgetown University Press, pp. 39–69.

Brenkert, G. (2002) 'Ethical challenges of social marketing', *Journal of Public Policy and Marketing,* 21: 14–25.

Buchanan, D.R. (2008) 'Autonomy, paternalism, and justice: Ethical priorities in public health', *American Journal of Public Health,* 98: 15–21.

Callahan, D., Koenig, B. and Minkler, M. (1999) 'Promoting health and preventing disease: Ethical demands and social challenges', *International Quarterly of Community Health Education,* 18(2): 163–180.

Carringer, P.T. (1994) 'Not just a worthy cause: Cause-related marketing delivers the goods and the good', *American Advertising,* 10: 16–19.

CIM – Chartered Institute of Marketing (2009) 'Less smoke, more fire: The benefits and impacts of social marketing', *Shape the Agenda,* 15.

Cunningham, A. (2003) 'Autonomous consumption: Buying into the ideology of capitalism', *Journal of Business Ethics,* 48(3): 229–236.

Dann, S. (2010) 'Redefining social marketing with contemporary commercial marketing definitions', *Journal of Business Research,* 63(2): 147–153, DOI: 10.1016/j.jbusres.2009. 02.013.

Davidson, D.K. and Novelli, W.D. (2001) 'Social marketing as business strategy: The ethical dimension', in A.R. Andreasen (ed), *Ethics in Social Marketing.* Washington, DC: Georgetown University Press, pp. 70–94.

De Mooij, M. (2005) *Global Marketing and Advertising: Understanding Cultural Paradoxes,* 2nd edn. London: Sage Publications.

Deshpande, S., Rothschild, M.L. and Brooks, R.S. (2004) 'New product development in social marketing', *Social Marketing Quarterly,* 10(3–4): 39–49.

Donaldson, T. (1982) *Corporations and Morality.* Englewood Cliffs, NJ: Prentice-Hall.

Donaldson, T. (1989) *The Ethics of International Business.* New York: Oxford University Press.

Donaldson, T. and Dunfee, T.W. (1994) 'Towards a unified conception of business ethics: Integrative social contracts theory', *Academy of Management Review,* 19(2): 252–284.

Donaldson, T. and Dunfee, T.W. (1995) 'Integrative social contracts theory: A communitarian conception of economic ethics', *Economics and Philosophy,* 11: 85–112.

Donovan, R. and Henley, N. (2003) *Social Marketing: Principles and Practice.* Melbourne: IP Communications.

Dove (2011a) ''Campaign for real beauty mission', available at: http://www.dove.ca/en/#/cfrb/mission_statement.aspx (accessed 19 July 2011).

Dove (2011b) 'The real truth about beauty: A global report', available at: http://www.dove.ca/en/#/expertise/articles/realtruth.aspx (accessed 19 July 2011).

Dove (2011c) 'Meet our experts', available at: http://www.dove.ca/en/#/cfrb/experts/ (accessed 19 July 2011).

Dove (2011d) 'Workshops: Get everything you need to arrange and host a workshop, and give girls the tools they need to feel beautiful', available at: http://www.dove.ca/en/#/CFRB/gallery/workshopsguides_gallery.aspx (accessed 19 July 2011).

Dove (2011e) 'Videos: Thought-provoking films about real beauty and self-esteem', available at: http://www.dove.ca/en/#/features/videos/videogallery.aspx and http://www.youtube.com/watch?v=Ei6JvK0W60I (accessed 19 July 2011).

Dunfee, T.W., Smith, C. and Ross, W.T. (1999) 'Social contracts and marketing ethics', *Journal of Marketing*, 63(3): 14–32.

Dworkin, G. (2010) 'Paternalism', in E.N. Zalta (ed), *Stanford Encyclopedia of Philosophy*. Available at: http://plato.stanford.edu/entries/paternalism/ (accessed 19 July 2011).

Eagle, L. (2009) 'Social marketing ethics: Report prepared for the National Social Marketing Centre'. National Social Marketing Centre (UK).

French, J. and Blair-Stevens, C. (2007) *Big Pocket Guide: Social Marketing*, London: National Social Marketing Centre.

French, J. and Blair-Stevens, C. (2010) 'Key concepts and principles of social marketing', in J. French, C. Blair-Stevens, D. McVey and R. Merritt (eds), *Social Marketing and Public Health*. Oxford: Oxford University Press, pp. 29–43.

Grönroos, C. (1990) 'Relationship approach to marketing in service contexts: The marketing and organizational behavior interface', *Journal of Business Research*, 20: 3–11.

Grönroos, C. (2006) 'On defining marketing: Finding a new roadmap for marketing', *Marketing Theory*, 6(4): 395–417.

Guttman, N. and Salmon, C.T. (2004) 'Guilt, fear, stigma and knowledge gaps: Ethical issues in public health communication interventions', *Bioethics*, 18(6): 531–552.

Hastings, G. (2003) 'Relational paradigms in social marketing', *Journal of Macromarketing*, 23: 6–15.

Hastings, G. (2007) *Social Marketing: Why Should the Devil Have All the Best Tunes?* Oxford: Butterworth-Heinemann.

Hastings, G., Stead, M. and Webb, J. (2004) 'Fear appeals in social marketing: Strategic and ethical reasons for concern', *Psychology and Marketing*, 21(11): 961–986.

ISM – Institute for Social Marketing (2009) 'Food Branding Survey'. A qualitative and quantitative survey of teenagers' attitudes to food branding and health carried out by M. Stead and A. MacKintosh. Reference to the study in this paper is based on the authors' access to interim findings.

Jeffreys, B. (2008) 'Ad prompts surge in organ donors', *BBC Online*. Available at: http://news.bbc.co.uk/1/hi/health/7598278.stm (accessed 19 July 2011).

Keller, K.L. (2008) *Strategic Brand Management*, 3rd edn. Upper Saddle River, NJ: Prentice-Hall.

Kotler, P. and Lee, N.R. (2008) *Social Marketing – Influencing Behaviors for Good*. Thousand Oaks, CA: Sage Publications.

Kotler, P. and Lee, N.R. (2005) *Corporate Social Responsibility: Doing the Most Good for Your Company and Your Cause*. Hoboken, New Jersey: John Wiley & Sons.

Kotler, P. and Zaltman. G. (1971) 'Social marketing: An approach to planned social change', *Journal of Marketing*, 35: 3–12.

Kotler, P., Armstrong, G., Wong, V. and Saunders, J. (2008) *Principles of Marketing – Fifth European Edition*. London: Prentice-Hall.

Kymlicka, W. (2002) *Contemporary Political Philosophy*. Oxford: Oxford University Press.

Laczniak, G.R., Lusch, R.F. and Murphy, P. (1979) 'Social marketing: Its ethical dimensions', *Journal of Marketing*, 43: 29–36.

Lafferty, B.A., Goldsmith, R.E. and Hult, G.T. (2004) 'The impact of the alliance on the partners: A look at cause-brand alliances', *Psychology of Marketing*, 21: 509–531.

Landman, A., Ling, P.M. and Glantz, S.A. (2002) 'Tobacco industry youth smoking prevention programs: Protecting the industry and hurting tobacco control', *American Journal of Public Health*, 92(6): 917–930.

Liu, G. and Liston-Heyes, C. (2010) 'Cause-related marketing in the retail and finance sectors', *Nonprofit and Voluntary Sector Quarterly*, 39(1): 77-101, DOI:10.1177/0899764008326680.

Luengo-Fernandez, R., Leal, J. and Gray, A. (2010) 'Dementia 2010 – The economic burden of dementia and associated research funding in the United Kingdom'. Alzheimer's Research Trust.

McCormack, L.A., Lewis, M.A. and Driscoll, D. (2008) 'Challenges and limitations of applying branding in social marketing', in W.D. Evans and G. Hastings (eds), *Public Health Branding*. Oxford, UK: Oxford University Press, pp. 271–286.

McDermott, L., Stead, M. and Hastings, G. (2005) 'What is and what is not social marketing: The challenge of reviewing the evidence', *Journal of Marketing Management*, 21(5–6): 545–553.

MRA – Marketing Research Association (2007) *The Code of Marketing Research Standards*. Available at: http://www.mra-net.org/ (accessed 19 July 2011).

Novo Nordisk (2011) 'NovoHealth - healthy employees equal a healthy company'. Available at: http://www.novonordisk.com/sustainability/People/NovoHealth.asp (accessed 19 July 2011).

Seacat, J.D. and Mickelson, K.D. (2009) 'Stereotype threat and the exercise/dietary health intentions of overweight women', *Journal of Health Psychology*, 14(4): 556–567, DOI: 10.1177/1359105309103575.

Stead, M. and Angus, K. (2007) 'Review of the applicability and effectiveness of social marketing as an approach to workplace health and wellbeing'. Institute for Social Marketing, University of Stirling, UK.

Stead, M. and Hastings, G. (1997) 'Advertising in the social marketing mix: Getting the balance right', in M.E. Goldberg, M.S. Fishbein and S.E. Middelstadt (eds), *Social Marketing: Theoretical and Practical Perspectives*. Mahwah, NJ: Lawrence Erlbaum Associates.

Time to change (2011) Campaign website available at: http://www.time-to-change.org.uk/ (accessed 19 July 2011).

Vanhamme, J. and Grobben, B. (2008) 'Too good to be true! The effectiveness of CSR history in countering negative publicity', *Journal of Business Ethics* (online first edition: volume, issue and page range not indicated).

Varadarajan, P.R. and Menon, A. (1988) 'Cause-related marketing: A co-alignment of marketing strategy and corporate philanthropy', *Journal of Marketing*, 52(3): 58–74.

Webb, D.J. and Mohr, L.A. (1998) 'A typology of consumer responses to cause-related marketing: From skeptics to socially concerned', *Journal of Public Policy and Marketing*, 17(2): 226–238.

Wood, M. (2008) 'Applying commercial marketing theory to social marketing: A tale of 4Ps (and a B)', *Social Marketing Quarterly*, 14: 76–85.

20

Internal Social Marketing: Lessons from the Field of Services Marketing

Anne M. Smith

INTRODUCTION

Services are often a key element of social marketing programmes aiming to both initiate and sustain behavioural change among consumers. Consequently, the quality of service, as perceived by consumers, will be fundamental to achieving behavioural goals. The impact of service experiences and evaluation on future behaviour has been widely examined in the marketing literature. The factors which consumers evaluate have been explored and relationships have been established between internal customer (employee) and external customer (consumer) satisfaction. When employees are satisfied with the service they receive, they are more likely to show care and concern for customers and 'to go the extra mile' to be helpful and responsive to their needs (Yi and Gong, 2008). A 'chain' has therefore been established (Heskett et al., 1997) between the final consumer's behaviour and the 'service' provided to employees by the organisations in which they work.

In the 1970s, marketing theorists began to focus on 'internal marketing' (IM) as an approach to achieving attitudinal and behavioural change within organisations. Originally developed within the context of services marketing, IM has been described as a philosophy for managing the organisation's human resources based on a marketing perspective (George, 1990) and has now become accepted terminology in all types of organisations (Gummesson, 2002). IM focuses on creating and delivering 'quality services' to both internal and external customers, thus achieving end-user behaviours such as repeat business and positive word-of-mouth communication. Fisk et al. (1993) state that two basic ideas underlie the IM concept: first, everyone in the organisation has a customer; and, second, that internal customers must be sold on the service and happy in their jobs before they can effectively serve the final customer.

There is a vast literature with respect to consumers' service evaluation available to social marketers to aid in understanding how consumers evaluate services and how this impacts on their behaviour. Conversely, IM has been described as ambiguous and 'under-researched' (Pitt and Foreman, 1999; Wieseke et al., 2009). This chapter aims to examine how the adoption of an IM approach can achieve behavioural change among both internal (employee) and external customers so as to achieve social goals, particularly those related to health. The main themes are summarised in Figure 20.1. The chapter begins with an examination of the literature relating to the external customer's behaviour and how this may be determined by their service experiences and consequent evaluations. Then the focus turns to the internal customer (or employee) and examines how their behaviours (as outcomes of their own internal service experience) can impact on the final customer. Finally, the role of IM in

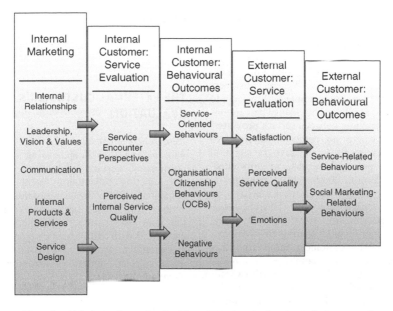

Figure 20.1 **The role of internal marketing in achieving behavioural change: chapter overview**

improving internal services is examined together with conclusions and suggestions for further research.

BEHAVIOURAL OUTCOMES AND THE EXTERNAL CUSTOMER: THE ROLE OF SERVICES

Behavioural change is the ultimate goal for social marketing (Andreasen, 1995; Hastings, 2007). Desired behavioural responses may include changing 'negative' behaviours such as smoking; adopting 'positive' behaviours such as increased physical activity; or sustaining 'positive' behaviours such as good dietary habits. In addition, this may include influencing, positively or negatively, the behaviour of others through word of mouth; advocacy, etc. The central role of services to effective social marketing has been illustrated in a number of studies. Phillipson et al. (2009), for example, emphasise the importance of service location and the role of the general practitioner (GP) in encouraging young people to engage with mental health issues James and Skinner (2009) highlight the importance of the 'servicescape' (physical environment) and service employees in changing the behaviour of homeless street drinkers. Lowry et al. (2004) describe the impact of

services, in particular the attitudes and behaviour of healthcare professionals, on smoking cessation among pregnant women.

Services such as health care play a major role in communicating and engaging with target audiences, providing the means of distribution and creating the environment for co-production between service employees and customers. Dagger and Sweeney (2006) highlight services related to health care, fitness and weight loss; they argue that the impact of marketing on social outcomes is particularly relevant in the service context, where the interactive nature of the exchange process is also likely to influence the quality of life an individual experiences. Additionally, the service-dominant logic (S-D L) of marketing has been described as potentially foundational to social marketing (Desai, 2009; Vargo and Lusch, 2008). Three elements of S-D L – that is, service is the fundamental basis of exchange, service is exchanged for service and that the customer is always a co-creator of value – are described as especially compatible with a social marketing approach (Vargo and Lusch, 2008).

Studies in the commercial sector have shown how customer satisfaction and service quality perceptions are directly related both to behaviours such as word-of-mouth recommendation, customer retention and complaining (Fornell, 1992; Gremler and Brown, 1999; Zahorik and Rust, 1992) and shareholder value (Anderson et al.,

2004; Gruca and Rego, 2005). Positive relationships between customer satisfaction with health services and future health-related behaviour such as compliance with medical advice have been established (Hudak and Wright, 2000; Laing et al., 2002; Woodside et al, 1989). Where consumers perceive alternatives, for example with respect to family planning services, low-quality perceptions can result in switching between service providers. Alternatively, where no perceived alternatives exist, this may result in negative behavioural change and a potential increase in 'unwanted' pregnancies (Smith, 2000). Other behavioural responses to service experiences have been described as 'citizenship' and 'dysfunctional' behaviours (Bettencourt, 1997; Yi and Gong, 2008). The former includes sharing positive experiences with other customers, assisting other customers, treating service employees in a pleasant manner, or making suggestions for the improvement of service. The latter includes critical word of mouth, disruption or uncooperative behaviour.

One problem with relating consumers' service evaluations to behavioural outcomes is the reliance on 'behavioural intentions' (rather than actual behaviour) in many studies. Consumers' behavioral intentions, as outcomes of service evaluation, are often described as a set of multiple (behavioural and non-behavioural) responses and significant attempts have been made to identify the factors which determine such intentions (Cronin et al., 2000; Jang and Namkung, 2009; Singh, 1990; Zeithaml et al., 1996) including within a healthcare context (Choi et al., 2004; Dagger and Sweeney, 2006, 2007; Han et al., 2008). The relationship between evaluations, intended and actual behaviour, however, is complex and tenuous (Chandon et al., 2005; Morvitz, 1997). Explanatory factors may include those attributable to the research process: for example, the respondent's wish to please the researcher, express rational views or avoid complex explanations. Many of the measurement approaches used are subject to method bias, which can distort relationships between constructs (Wirtz and Bateson, 1995). Additionally, intended behaviours are subject to future developments such as environmental change, availability of alternatives and changes in motivation of the respondent. The lack of importance accredited to situational factors in behavioural prediction is considered to be one of the factors explaining the lack of correspondence between behavioural intentions and actual behaviour (Costarelli and Colloca, 2004; Eagly and Chaiken, 1993). However, despite these limitations, researchers focus on determining how best to assess consumers' service evaluations so as to strengthen the observed relationship between evaluation and intention, thus establishing theoretical and measurement validity. The main approaches are discussed in the next section.

THE EXTERNAL CUSTOMER'S SERVICE EVALUATION

Researchers have examined a variety of approaches with respect to conceptualising and measuring consumers' service evaluation with the aim of predicting behavioural intentions (or actual behaviour), including a substantial number of studies within a healthcare context. In particular, the role of customer satisfaction has been contrasted with that of service quality evaluation. Additionally, the role of consumer emotion in service encounters is receiving increasing attention.

Customer satisfaction and service quality evaluation

Marketing authors have emphasised the important relationship between customer satisfaction and customer loyalty, resulting in the behaviours discussed in the previous section (Hallowell, 1996; Han et al., 2008; Heskett et al., 1997; Oliver et al., 1997). However, the problems in defining 'satisfaction/dissatisfaction' have also been highlighted (Oliver, 1981). Early definitions (Anderson, 1973; Engel and Blackwell, 1982) focused on cognitive evaluations similar to those later adopted by service quality researchers. Additionally, early conceptualisations of patient satisfaction in the medical/healthcare literature generally did not distinguish between satisfaction and attitude (Hulka et al., 1970; Roberts and Tugwell, 1987). However, Oliver (1981) argues that:

> Attitude is the consumer's relatively enduring affective orientation ... while satisfaction is the emotional reaction following a disconfirmation experience which acts on the base attitude level and is consumption specific. Attitude is measured in terms more general to product or store and is less situationally oriented (p. 42).

The emphasis on the affective nature of satisfaction was later to constitute a key differentiating factor between customer satisfaction and service quality evaluation. Additionally, authors began to emphasise that satisfaction alone was not enough to generate customer loyalty. Instead, organisations should aim for high levels of satisfaction (Heskett et al., 1994) or to 'delight their customers' (Oliver et al., 1997).

During the 1980s, research on consumers' service evaluation began to focus on service quality. Conceptualised as a 'gap', researchers emphasised cognitive appraisals where consumers compare their expectations with their perceptions (Grönroos, 1984; Lewis and Booms, 1983; Parasuraman et al., 1988). A particular emphasis has been on identifying the dimensions, traits or factors which consumers evaluate. Two distinct dimensions, that is, technical quality (service outcome) and functional quality (service process), are generally agreed (Dagger and Sweeney, 2006, 2007; Grönroos, 1984). Additionally, the five-dimensional classification proposed by the SERVQUAL authors (Parasuraman et al., 1985, 1988, 1991, 1994) is often quoted: that is, tangibles (physical facilities, equipment and appearance of personnel); reliability (ability to perform the promised service dependably and accurately); responsiveness (willingness to help customers and provide prompt service); assurance (knowledge and courtesy of employees and their ability to inspire trust and confidence and empathy (caring, individualised attention the firm provides its customers). Health-related service quality studies have, however, produced equivocal findings that suggest fewer, or more, factors (Babakus and Boller, 1992; Babakus and Mangold, 1992; Bowers et al., 1994; Brady, 2001; Carman, 1990; Dagger and Sweeney, 2006, 2007; Headley and Miller, 1993; Peyrot et al., 1993; Reidenbach and Sandifer-Smallwood, 1990; Smith, 2000; Soliman, 1992; Sower et al., 2001; Vandamme and Leunis, 1993; Walbridge and Delene, 1993). Additionally, evidence from the patient satisfaction literature supports the likelihood of few meaningful factors underlying consumer evaluations of GP services (Hall and Dornan, 1988; Hulka and Zyzanski, 1982; Hulka et al., 1970; Pascoe, 1983; Ware and Hays, 1988; Ware et al., 1978, 1983; Zyzanski et al., 1974). These include, primarily, professional or technical competence, interpersonal qualities or convenience or accessibility of the service.

Other authors emphasise the importance of relationship quality (Crosby et al., 1990) and the role of trust and commitment in enhancing customer satisfaction and consequent behaviour (Aurier and N'Goala, 2009; Bansal et al., 2004; Jones et al., 2010; Morgan and Hunt, 1994). Services may be classified as discrete or continuous (Lovelock, 1983). The former involves consumers in a 'one-off' service experience, whereas the latter involves multiple service experiences and greater potential for developing relational benefits over time (Han et al., 2008). This is particularly relevant where behavioural change requires repeat attendance: for example, GP and clinic services as well as commercial services

such as gyms. Avis et al. (1997) have described how experience of power, control and autonomy are essential in the professional–patient relationship and patients' perceptions of these will influence subsequent evaluation. Additionally, the role of 'continuity of care' has been emphasised (Smith, 2000; Ware et al., 1983; Woolley et al., 1978) and one particular aspect of 'interpersonal qualities' highlighted in many studies is that of doctor–patient communication or 'collaboration' (Barry et al., 2001; Jun et al., 1998; Woolley et al., 1978) (for a full discussion of relationship marketing, see Chapter 3 in this Handbook).

A substantial amount of work has focused on differentiating the constructs of 'consumer perceived service quality' and 'service satisfaction' in terms of patterns of antecedence, causality and nature of determinants. One debate has focused on whether perceived service quality is an antecedent of satisfaction or whether the converse is true. Early conceptualisations built on Oliver's (1981) distinction between 'satisfaction' and 'attitude' highlighted above. Parasuraman et al. (1985, 1988) argued that service quality was 'a global view' similar to attitude while satisfaction was transaction specific. Later work, however, described satisfaction as super-ordinate to service quality in the formation of consumers' intentions (Oliver, 1993; Taylor and Baker, 1994). A second stream of research has focused on the role of perceived value in explaining relationships between satisfaction and quality (Bolton and Drew, 1991; Choi et al., 2004; Cronin et al., 2000; Han et al., 2008). While yet a third approach has been to contrast the cognitive nature of service quality with the more affective nature of satisfaction (Liljander and Strandvik, 1997; Mano and Oliver, 1993; Oliver, 1993). Additionally, while some studies focus on consumers' overall evaluation of a service (Cronin and Taylor, 1992, 1994; Parasuraman et al., 1994) there is an increasing emphasis on the 'service encounter' or 'moment of truth' in determining service-related behaviours (Bettencourt and Gwinner, 1996; Yi and Gong, 2008).

The service encounter and consumer emotion

Shostack (1985) describes any service encounter as having a potential impact on consumer behaviour: for example, those involving telephone or non-personal media such as postal and electronic interactions. Solomon et al. (1985: 100), however, define service encounters as:

> face-to-face interactions between a buyer and a seller in a service setting.

Service encounters involve social interaction between actors (usually the consumer and the service employee) and are based on learned behaviours, or scripts (Abelson, 1981). The root cause of many provider–client interface problems is therefore attributed to the failure of participants to read from a common script (Solomon et al., 1985). Researchers (Bell et al., 2004; Bettencourt and Gwinner, 1996; Bitner et al., 1990; Verhoef et al., 2004) emphasise the dyadic nature of service interactions and the central element of role performances. Service encounter satisfaction (or dissatisfaction) is therefore conceptualised as:

> a function of the congruence between perceived behaviour expected by role players (Solomon et al., 1985: 104).

Figure 20.2 adopts a service blueprinting approach (Fließ and Kleinaltenkamp, 2004; Shostack, 1985) to illustrate the nature of the service encounter involved in a visit to a specialist family planning clinic.

The 'line of interaction' separates the customer from the supplier action area representing the direct interactions between customer and supplier. Those interactions above the 'line of visibility' are those which the customer can identify and

ultimately directly evaluate. Identifiable processes include arrival (which may also include aspects of travel such as receiving directions and advice about transport and car parking); booking in through an encounter with administrative staff; waiting before being called to the appointment; participating in the consultation and any related clinical procedure; being provided with follow-up information or onward referral information and obtaining prescribed contraceptive supplies.

There are a number of potential fail points. Unhelpful reception staff and an unwelcoming environment may deter new customers from continuing with their visit. Inadequate staffing or overdemand for the service may result in long waiting times. There is an inherent paradox with this type of service, as customers may prefer a specialist clinic because of the time spent with them in explaining alternatives and answering questions. Consequently, waiting times may increase. Since the clinic will not have access to the customer's medical records, apart from those specifically relevant to their clinic visits, and the consultation may not have elicited the necessary information, incorrect recommendations may be made. A visit may include consultation with both a nurse and a doctor and lack of coordination and/or availability will further increase waiting times

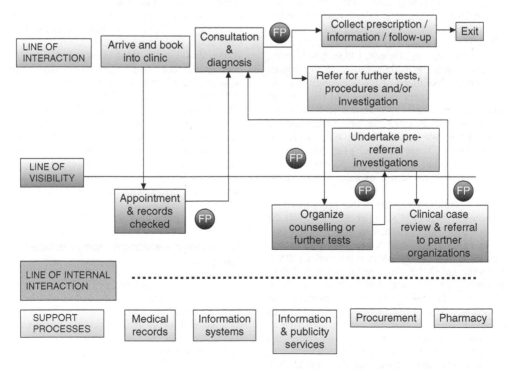

Figure 20.2 A service design blueprint for a specialist family planning clinic. Developed from Fließ and Kleinaltenkamp (2004)

at each stage of the process. Recommended products may not be available from the pharmacy. This may be a particular problem if, subsequently, embarrassment prevents the customer from obtaining these elsewhere. (The 'line of internal interaction' refers to the service received by internal customers and will be discussed later.)

A focus on service encounters has led many researchers to adopt a critical incident methodology (Gremler, 2004) where consumers are required to recount stories of favourable (or unfavourable) encounters and the critical incidents (or significant occurrences) which made them so. Clinic visitors will have expectations relating to the service process: employee knowledge and behaviour; the nature of the 'servicescape' (physical environment); convenience of location and waiting times and outcome, such as availability of relevant contraceptive products and prevention of unwanted pregnancy (Smith, 2000). Critical incidents may involve unhelpful responses to customers' requests or even rude behaviour from clinic staff. Such incidents are likely to impact on service quality and satisfaction evaluations but, in addition, consumers may experience a range of negative, and/or positive, encounter-specific emotions. These may include interest, enjoyment, surprise, distress (sadness), anger, disgust, contempt, fear, shame/shyness and guilt: that is, those which Izard (1977) describes as fundamental and universal. Alternative schemas such as Richins' (1997) consumption-specific emotions also include discontent and worry.

The nature of consumers' emotional responses to service encounters and the subsequent impact on behavioural intentions and behaviour is receiving increasing attention (Allen et al., 1992; Arnould and Price, 1993; De Ruyter and Bloemer, 1999; Dubé and Menon, 2000; Dubé et al., 2003; Grace, 2007; Jang and Namkung, 2009; Liljander and Strandvik, 1997; Mattila and Enz, 2002; Menon and Dubé, 2000; Perugini and Bagozzi, 2001; Price et al., 1995; Smith, 2006). Indeed, Bagozzi et al. (1999) argue that:

> the implications of emotional reactions in purchase situations on complaint behaviours, word-of-mouth communication, repurchase and related actions may differ from various positive and negative emotions and be of more relevance than reactions to satisfaction or dissatisfaction, per se (p. 201).

Appraisal theorists argue that emotions are responses to environmental demands, circumstances and events and how these impact on the individual's prevailing goals and desires (Russell, 1991; Shaver et al., 1987; Smith and Ellsworth, 1985). .A focus on emotional reactions seems particularly appropriate to an evaluation of service encounters within a social marketing context. Service encounters are purposive, task- and goal-oriented acting as social mechanisms for delivering desired outcomes (Bitner et al., 1990). Desired outcomes, or goals, include those which may substantially change the individual's quality of life, and which may include fighting addiction, as in the case of smoking cessation. Definitions which focus on negative valence highlight emotions as being 'unconscious responses to goals which are thwarted/unrealised' (Shaver et al., 1987) and highlight that the salience of goals will further generate negative emotions such as anger or sadness (Watson and Spence, 2007). Encounters may also provoke embarrassment resulting from employee criticism and perceived violations of privacy resulting in anger and humiliation for the consumer (Grace, 2007).

A mediating factor impacting on consumers' encounter-specific emotions and subsequent behaviour is that of attribution (or agency): that is, whether the negative (or positive) experience is attributed to self, other or the situation (Weiner, 1985, 2000). The role of attribution has been examined extensively in the marketing literature as a determinant of consumer-perceived service quality and service satisfaction evaluation (Bitner et al., 1990; Smith and Bolton, 1999). Anger, for example, is an emotion attributed to some 'other' responsibility and control, whereas guilt is associated with high levels of self-responsibility/control (Smith and Ellsworth, 1985). Both self and 'other' attributions are relevant for emotions of embarrassment (Crozier and Metts, 1994; Verbeke and Bagozzi, 2003).

The potential for employee behaviour to differ from that expected by the consumer is considerable and will impact negatively (or positively) on service evaluation. The next section considers the service encounter from the perspective of the internal customer or (employee).

THE INTERNAL CUSTOMER: EMPLOYEE BEHAVIOUR AND SERVICE EVALUATION

In comparison to the substantial literature examining the external customer's evaluation of services, relatively few marketing studies focus on the internal customer or employee. However, a number of authors have assessed the impact of employee behaviour on consumers' service evaluation (Kelley and Hoffman, 1997; Menon and Dubé, 2000; Yi and Gong, 2008); compared employees' and consumers' evaluations of service encounters

(Bitner et al., 1994; Chung-Herrera et al., 2004; Mattila and Enz, 2002) and examined the main requirements of service employees relating to internal service quality (Hui et al., 2004; San Martín, 2008; Singh, 2000). The main elements are illustrated in the second and third columns of Figure 20.1 and are discussed below.

Employee service behaviours

Consumers may encounter a wide range of organisational employees as they attempt to adopt/maintain pro-social behaviours (as illustrated in Figure 20.2). These may include administrative staff, health professionals and others. Employees' service-oriented role and script behaviours are often dictated by external agencies such as professional standards and organisational rules and procedures. These typically form the basis of formal training programmes. In addition, the importance of organisational citizenship behaviour (OCB) has been emphasised: that is, behaviour that is beneficial for an organisation but falls outside formal role requirements (Podsakoff et al., 2000). Bettencourt et al. (2001) describe service-oriented OCBs as citizenship behaviours typically performed by customer contact employees and directed at the customer. These often involve providing help or assistance above and beyond the normal role behaviours expected of employees. Rafaeli et al. (2008), for example, describe such behaviours as including anticipating customer requests, offering explanations/justifications, educating customers, providing emotional support and offering personalised information.

Direct links have been established between service-oriented OCBs and customer satisfaction/service quality evaluation (Kelley and Hoffman, 1997; Morrison, 1996; Rafaeli et al., 2008) and behaviours such as word of mouth and repurchase (Netemeyer and Maxham III, 2007; Payne and Webber, 2006; Schneider et al., 2005; Yi and Gong, 2008), although some studies have failed to find direct effects (Castro et al., 2004). A tension exists, however, between those who emphasise the need to standardise and reward (at least some) role-prescribed behaviour adhering to role scripts and carrying out management's specifications (Van Dolen et al., 2004; Zeithaml et al., 1988) and those who advocate the need to respond to consumers' demands for adaptability requiring employee judgement and flexibility (Bettencourt and Gwinner, 1996; Kiely, 2005). Bitner et al. (1990), for example, identified three types of employee behaviour which would leave the consumer with a memorable, dissatisfying (or satisfying) service encounter: responses to service delivery failure; responses to customer needs and requests and unprompted and unsolicited actions.

A second tension exists between those authors who highlight the positive aspects of 'authenticity' in staff behaviour (Price et al., 1995; Winsted, 2000) and those who emphasise the problems, for example, when employees engage in 'mimetic' rather than 'complementary' behaviour, such as when responding to customer anger (Menon and Dubé, 2000). Yi and Gong (2008) have examined the impact of 'employee dysfunctional behaviours' (EDBs), that is, behaviours that harm organisations and/or their members. Such behaviours, including employees purposefully working slowly or being nasty or rude, were directly related to customer dissatisfaction and customer deviant behaviours (CDBs). Even where service employees intend to provide good service this may not be interpreted as such by the final consumer. Guiry (1992) describes how overzealous service employees may adopt roles of 'dominance' where their attempts to be friendly or helpful may be considered intrusive and inappropriate by consumers. Such behaviour may be due to personality traits, lack of specific role awareness or training and/or lack of understanding of customers.

The internal customer: service evaluation

Service employees potentially have an important role in providing insight into customers' service requirements as well as adapting the service to meet those requirements. However, while some studies have found a high level of congruence between customer and employee perceptions of service (Chung and Schneider, 2002; Schneider and Bowen, 1985), others have found substantial differences (Bitner et al., 1994; Mohr and Bitner, 1991), including between health professionals and their patients (Brown and Schwartz, 1989). Employees' evaluations of their own performance can differ markedly from those of customers (Mattila and Enz, 2002), and supervisor, rather than employee, ratings of service encounters have been shown to be more predictive of consequent customer behaviour (Netemeyer and Maxham III, 2007). Bitner et al. (1994) describe how role and script theory, combined with the routine nature of many service encounters, suggests that customers and employees are likely to share a common perspective. However, when roles are less defined and participants are unfamiliar with expected behaviours, such as a young person's first visit to a smoking cessation or sexual health clinic, possibly combined with inexperienced staff, the potential for negative service encounters is enhanced. There are also differences with respect to attribution. Employees have attributed their inability to satisfy customers to the constraints of the service delivery process, organisational policy and procedures, and sometimes to the misbehaviour of the customers themselves. Conversely, satisfactory encounters are attributed to the employee's own ability and willingness to adjust. Customers are, however, more likely to blame employees (Bitner et al., 1994; Chung-Herrera et al., 2004).

Prior research has established a positive relationship between employee satisfaction and customer satisfaction with services (Crosby et al., 1990; Heskett et al., 1994, 1997; Homburg and Stock, 2004, 2005; Hui et al., 2004; Payne and Webber, 2006). A face-to-face working environment is demanding for contact personnel whose main reward may be professional satisfaction, which has to be maintained at a high level to keep them motivated (Chandon et al., 1997). Front-line staff rely on the quality of service they receive from others and the competencies of co-workers to deliver high-quality service. Solomon et al. (1985) highlight how role and script theory suggest a 'dramaturgical metaphor' involving 'front-stage' and 'back-stage' employees. In Figure 20.2 the 'line of internal interaction' distinguishes between front-stage and back-stage activities required to provide high quality clinic services. This is the separation between the consultation and related processes and support activities. Internal customer relationship requirements comprise administrative functions such as organising appointments and providing accurate customer information including medical records and results of recent tests; accurate and timely laboratory processing services and procurement services, for example, information leaflets and contraceptive supplies. Poor internal service quality will result in dissatisfaction, poor perceptions of quality and negative emotions, which may lead to negative attitudes and behaviours towards external customers (Bettencourt and Brown, 2003) as well as impacting on staff retention. A number of key factors have been found to impact on employee trust, commitment and cooperation, directly resulting in a widening of the service performance gap (Chenet et al., 1999). These factors are role conflict and ambiguity; self-efficacy and perceived control.

Role conflict and role ambiguity

Front-line service employees fulfil a boundary-spanning role between consumers and the organisation (Bitner et al., 1994; Chung and Schneider, 2002; Chung-Herrera et al., 2004). Consequently, employees may experience role conflict (an incongruity within the expectations associated with a role and which can include role overload; Singh, 2000). The problems experienced by employees, who are required to adhere to company policies, rules and regulations while simultaneously providing high standards of customer service, are well documented (Babin and Boles, 1998; Bitner et al., 1990, 1994; Chung and Schneider, 2002, Hartline and Ferrell, 1996; Hartline et al., 2000; Hui et al., 2004). Schneider and Bowen (1985), for example, found that employees experienced role stress, job dissatisfaction and frustration over being unable to give good service because of differences between their own and managements' perceptions of how services should be delivered. They also expressed intentions to change jobs. In addition, role ambiguity (the degree to which information is lacking about role expectations and effective performance of a role) may result from poor communication and performance measurement systems. Role ambiguity maintains a negative relationship with employee job (and life) satisfaction (Babin and Boles, 1998; Hui et al., 2004; Schneider et al., 1980) and is exacerbated by role conflict. Conversely, positive relationships have been identified between employee role clarity and internal customer perceived service quality, perceived external service quality and job satisfaction (Mukherjee and Malhotra, 2006).

Self-efficacy

Central to the social cognitive theory of human behaviour are beliefs of self-efficacy, that is:

> beliefs in one's capabilities to organize and execute the courses of action required to produce given attainments (Bandura, 1997: 3).

Relevant at the individual and collective (team and organisational) level, efficacy beliefs influence choices and courses of action (Hostager et al., 1998). Service quality studies have identified factors which impact on employees' self-efficacy beliefs. Role ambiguity maintains a negative relationship with self-efficacy. However, role conflict can have a positive effect as people search for, and find, successful ways to cope (Bandura, 1986; Hartline and Ferrell, 1996). Research supports the view that self-efficacy beliefs mediate the effect of skills or other self-beliefs on subsequent performance (Pajares, 1997).

Perceived control

Efficacy beliefs are closely related to perceived control and autonomy (Bell and Menguc, 2002). Singh (2000) describes task control, which is 'the perception of latitude and authority in dealing with job-related tasks and control over decisions that affect those tasks' (20), as a powerful resource to aid front-line service employees to cope with role tension. Service employees consider that their lack of knowledge with respect to systems and constraints and lack of authority to do anything can result in a failure to provide a satisfactory service to customers (Bitner et al., 1994). The relationship between employee empowerment (an often contentious concept) and improved customer service has been highlighted by a number of authors (Bell and Menguc, 2002; Hartline et al., 2000; Morrison, 1996). The level of perceived control also has important direct effects on perceived role conflict and increases organisational commitment (Hartline et al., 2000; Singh, 2000).

There is evidence therefore as to the requirements of internal customers if they are to provide quality services to external customers. Furthermore, a growing amount of research has begun to establish relationships between internal and external service-related behaviours. The next section addresses the ways in which organisations can influence employee behaviour through the adoption of an IM approach. The main points are illustrated in the first column of Figure 20.1.

THE ROLE OF INTERNAL MARKETING

Internal marketing was first introduced into the services marketing literature in the 1970s (Berry et al., 1976), yet few studies have directly related the concept to the external customer's service satisfaction/perceived service quality (for exceptions, see Bell et al., 2004; Mukherjee and Malhotra, 2006). More surprising is the relatively sparse attention given to the impact of IM on employees/internal customers (here exceptions include Ahmed et al., 2003; Bell et al., 2004; Mukherjee and Malhotra, 2006; San Martín, 2008). A few case studies have highlighted the potential for an IM approach within a healthcare context: for example, in improving collaboration between internal medical professionals so as to improve services for external customers (Gombeski et al., 1992); providing the basis for internal coordination and communication prior to developing an external marketing campaign for geriatric services (Thomas et al., 1991); and Lee et al. (1991) describe an IM programme aimed at encouraging health service employees to communicate with external customers with the aim of increasing take-up of services.

At one level, IM involves combining marketing and human resource management approaches and techniques (George, 1990; Grönroos, 1990), including learning and competence building

(Chaston, 2000). Dunne and Barnes (2000) describe how an IM programme should create four highly related ingredients: employee motivation; job satisfaction; job involvement and organisational commitment. Morrison (1996) links human resource management to improved service quality, highlighting that an IM approach focuses on the importance of interactions not only between front-line employees and customers but also between employees themselves through improved OCBs. A major aim of IM is to develop an internal customer service orientation within the organisation. Consequently, the concept of 'internal customers' and the development of internal relationships are central.

Internal customer relationships

The relational element of IM has been emphasised (Ballantyne et al., 1995; Bell et al., 2004; Gilmore and Carson, 1995; San Martín, 2008). Gummesson (2002: 189) states:

> the notion of the internal customer brings customer–supplier relationships into the company It requires employees to see other employees as customers who receive deliveries of products, services, documents, messages and decisions...

Internal relationship quality has a positive effect on worker motivation (Bell et al., 2004). Organisations that value teamwork, cohesion and employee involvement achieve higher levels of patient satisfaction (Gregory et al., 2009). Zeithaml et al. (1988) emphasise the role of teamwork in closing the service performance gap. Specific variables include the extent to which: employees view other employees as customers; contact personnel feel upper-level managers genuinely care for them; contact personnel feel they are cooperating (rather than competing) with others in the organisation and employees feel personally involved and committed. Team support provides help with difficult service encounters and is an important means of providing training. Cooperation and support from co-workers leads to role clarity, which in turn influences job satisfaction and organisational commitment (Mukherjee and Malhotra, 2006).

Trust is a key element of relationship marketing approaches, whether these are focused on external or internal relationships. Authors have emphasised the role of trust in internal relationship building (Bowen and Lawler, 1992), as an important antecedent of employee cooperation and commitment (Chenet et al., 1999) and as a determinant of the propensity to engage in OCBs (Morrison, 1996). The role of OCBs, such as 'informal helping', in building internal relationships and enhancing external service quality was discussed earlier. A wide range of vertical and horizontal relationships may be established between teams, co-workers and managers. Additionally, many health services are provided by networks, or partnerships, of cooperating agencies. Fang et al. (2008) describe how managing and building trust at multiple levels is critical to the success of inter-organisational marketing collaborations.

The role of leadership: vision and values

The crucial role of leadership in building trust relationships and developing an organisational culture and climate reflecting a commitment to high levels of service quality is well recognised (Berry, 1995; Berry and Parasuraman, 1992; Berry et al., 1976; George, 1990; Grönroos, 1990; Schneider et al., 2005). Organisational values play a central role in internal marketing theory (Ahmed and Rafiq, 2002; Gummesson, 1987; Varey and Lewis, 1999) and practice (Foreman and Money, 1995) and are the basis of culture (Schein, 1985). Organisational culture and climate are critical determinants of an organisation's ability to deliver superior service and quality to customers (Gregory et al., 2009; Payne and Webber, 2006; Schneider et al., 1998, 2005).

Wieseke et al. (2009) argue that it is the role of leaders, especially middle managers, in building organisational identification (OI) that lays the foundation for internal marketing. OI can involve customers as well as employees and refers to a sense of belonging to an organisation based on positive feelings and a shared vision and values. Organisational support and OI are key factors in encouraging customer-oriented behaviours that fall outside formal role requirements (Bell and Menguc, 2002). Important roles for leaders also include providing clarity of direction and thus lowering role conflict and ambiguity; increasing employee self-efficacy beliefs through providing training and performance feedback and increasing employee- perceived control through enhanced job autonomy (Bowen and Lawler, 1992; Hartline et al., 2000; Morrison, 1996; Wieseke et al., 2009) with the overall objective of improving both internal and external customers' perceptions of service quality.

Communication

Effective service leadership continually communicates a commitment to high levels of service quality. Information gathering, communication and responding to employee feedback have been highlighted as key elements of an IM approach (Lings and Greenley, 2005). Communication and feedback are essential in clarifying goals, expectations and levels of performance required and achieved (Mukherjee and Malhotra, 2006; Zeithaml et al., 1988). Lack of communication was highlighted earlier as a source of employee dissatisfaction directly linked to poor service delivery (Bitner et al., 2004). In addition to requiring relevant information to pass on to customers, communication plays a vital role in building trust relationships with both employees (Rothenberg, 2003) and customers (Crosby et al., 1990; Morgan and Hunt, 1994).

Internal products and services

Central to IM is the development and delivery of 'internal products and services', including practices, plans, structure, vision, mission and values (Thomson, 1990), new performance measures, new ways of working, services and training courses and the job itself (Rafiq and Ahmed, 1993).

A number of these 'products' have already been discussed. Others which are highlighted in relation to service quality are rewards, performance measures and training.

A service climate signals to employees that service quality behaviours are rewarded (Schneider et al., 1998) and the role of rewards in encouraging service-related behaviours and reducing role conflict has been established (Chung and Schneider, 2002; Morrison, 1996). An appreciation of exchange theory and equity theory are fundamental to an understanding of the service–performance gap and the relationships between employee trust, commitment and cooperation (Chenet et al., 1999). Rewards may include a range of intrinsic and extrinsic factors which can motivate employees. Varey and Lewis (1999) describe how IM's focus on social values provides for a richer range of exchanges, both economic and non-economic. However, a rewards system relies on establishing clear performance standards/indicators for subsequent review. Such a system should be seen as fair and equitable as well as providing role clarification (Singh, 2000). One challenge, however, which has been highlighted previously, is that of how to encourage OCBs that are outside formal roles such that it is difficult to formally specify or reward them (Morrison, 1996; Yi and Gong, 2008).

Training, development and other forms of knowledge creation and sharing have a crucial role in reducing role ambiguity, increasing self-efficacy, building relationships and reducing perceived barriers to new behaviours (Schneider and Bowen, 1985).

Training (including development and education) performs a number of essential functions in the delivery of high-quality services and is typically a core element of an IM approach (Berry and Parasuraman, 1992; Foreman and Money, 1995; Grönroos, 1990). First, the need for employees to understand customers has been highlighted (Bitner et al., 2004; Mattila and Enz, 2002). Lowry et al. (2004) provide an illustration of how involvement in training through role play helped health professionals to understand the feelings of pregnant women smokers. These related to both their negative service experiences, where they felt health professionals 'nagged' and 'preached' rather than offered support, and the meaning of the smoking behaviour itself in the lives of the target audience. This approach was evaluated highly by participants and proved to be effective in the intervention. Second, training is required to develop the requisite skills, or competencies, for providing excellent service (Ahmed et al., 2003; Bell and Menguc, 2002; Bettencourt and Gwinner, 1996; Payne and Webber, 2006). Mattila and Enz (2002), for example, emphasise the need for staff training in recognising appropriate behavioural responses to consumer emotions, including anger management and emotional control techniques. Third, customer-oriented training helps to develop supportive internal relationships (Bell et al., 2004) and will enhance the level of social interaction between leaders and followers (Wieseke et al., 2009). Finally, continual training and development will play a part in establishing a social exchange relationship and, hence, a basis for future OCBs (Morrison, 1996). The final section considers the role of service design in providing the 'prerequisites' for both internal and external service quality.

Service design

Employees blame poorly designed procedures and systems for causing negative service encounters that lead to both internal and external customer dissatisfaction (Bell et al., 2004; Bitner et al., 1994). The quality of the service encounter has been described as a function of the quality of the service design (Shostack, 1984; Zeithaml et al., 2006). The service design literature offers additional tools, techniques and insights which are rarely addressed in discussions of IM. The design process creates the environment where internal (front- stage and back-stage) and external customers interact to co-produce the service.

A number of service design models focus on the service encounter. These include service blueprinting (Fließ and Kleinaltenkamp, 2004;

Shostack, 1984), a design approach illustrated in Figure 20.2. Other micro models include quality function deployment (QFD) (Chan and Wu, 2002; Stuart and Tax, 1996), which has been applied within a range of public sector services including health (Dijkstra and van der Bij, 2002; Katz, 2004; Lim and Tang, 2000). QFD establishes relationships between resource allocation decisions, customer satisfaction and competitive position and is driven by the 'voice of the customer' at all stages of the process. Such models can play an important role in facilitating coordination and communication, highlighting interrelationships and creating a common quality focus. The visual display of a substantial amount of information can aid in understanding between teams and functions and illustrates how the various organisational activities link so as to provide a customer (internal and external) focused service.

Edvardsson and Olsson (1996) describe the need to establish essential prerequisites, including customer insight and effective design of customer interfaces; staff needs, skills and knowledge, including training and development requirements; physical facilities, technology and location and systems, structures and processes, including those for communications, rewards and performance measurement. Here there are clear parallels with IM. Additionally, the need for effective leadership at all levels and between organisational functions and teams is emphasised (Johne and Harbone, 2003). Involving service employees in the design and development of services can ensure a higher level of job satisfaction and commitment (Zeithaml et al., 2006); however, this is often not the case. Research indicates a limited role for either external or internal customers (Martin and Horne, 1995; Smith and Fischbacher, 2002, 2005), and a lack of formal, systematic and structured processes in many service organisations (Kelly and Storey, 2000; Sundbo, 1997). Instead, the way in which services often emerge from a process characterised by the conflicting interests and expectations of a variety of stakeholders has been highlighted (Smith and Fischbacher, 2002, 2005) and this can be particularly true of services such as health care. Consequently, service design has been included in the first column of Figure 20.1 as having a vital role to play in improving the quality of service experienced by both internal and external customers and, in doing so, helping to achieve behavioural change.

CONCLUSION

An IM approach offers opportunities to focus marketing concepts and techniques on internal organisational audiences. This is particularly relevant for social marketing programmes – for example, smoking cessation, family planning/ sexual health, alcohol reduction and early cancer screening – that rely on services, and particularly healthcare services, as co-producers of behavioural change. Research shows how the behaviour of service employees (internal customers) can have a significant impact on the behaviour of consumers (external customers). The service encounter provides the stage for role players to enact performances which will impact on their service satisfaction and quality evaluations as well as emotional reactions. Service roles differ dramatically in what is required of the people who perform them (Parish et al., 2008), and customer expectations differ across service contexts (Berry and Bendapudi, 2007). Employee behaviour may differ from that expected by customers as a result of many factors, including lack of understanding of customer requirements, role ambiguity/conflict, low self-efficacy and low levels of perceived control. Alternatively, employees may 'delight' customers through engaging in OCBs that exceed customers' expectations.

Internal marketing emphasises internal customers and their service requirements. The service quality literature highlights 'gaps' (Chenet et al., 1999; Zeithaml et al., 1988) in organisational processes, which can ultimately result in poor service, customer dissatisfaction and consequent 'negative' behaviours. The nature of the relationships between 'front-stage' and 'back-stage' employees and the wider range of horizontal and vertical organisational relationships will determine the level of service experienced by boundary-spanning employees. Other factors include the ability of leaders to create shared values and the vision necessary for a service climate; effective communication; the development of internal products such as customer service-focused rewards and training programmes and a holistic approach to service design. Together, these will provide an environment which generates the behaviours that will match both external and internal customer requirements.

Future directions and suggestions for research

Few social marketing studies address the issues involved in service delivery or focus on employees as target audiences. Similarly, many discussions of IM are conceptual in approach. A significant research agenda exists, which can be summarised into four main themes.

1. The literature suggests a sequential process whereby the adoption of an IM approach can ultimately result in external customers changing their behaviour (as illustrated in Figure 20.1). Studies within a number of service contexts have focused on specific relationships (Chung and Schneider, 2002; Rafaeli et al., 2008) or adopted a more holistic approach and simultaneously examined a number of causal relationships along the chain (Bell and Menguc, 2002; Payne and Webber, 2006). In addition, reciprocal relationships have been examined. Bell et al. (2004), for example, have assessed the impact of external customer behaviour on internal customer relationships. Research is needed at all three levels within a social marketing context to examine the nature of relationships, identify direct and indirect causal and reciprocal effects and to develop further insights into the role of services in achieving behavioural change.

2. Further work is needed to understand the customers' evaluation of services within a social marketing context. Berry and Bendapudi (2007) describe how much of the services literature focuses on 'want services', whereas consumers may not want but need many of the services which social marketers offer. They highlight how service customers may be unwilling to perform the co-producer role: for example, when advised to make lifestyle changes such as stopping smoking. Oliver et al. (1997) state that attempts to 'delight' the customer may not be relevant in all service contexts. There is, therefore, a need for research to understand the nature of customer satisfaction and perceived service quality within these contexts. In addition, researchers are increasingly emphasising the role of subjective affective responses (i.e. feelings and emotions), as opposed to cognition in service evaluation. Several models involving consumers' emotional responses have been developed and tested (Jang and Namkung, 2009; Oliver et al., 1997; Perugini and Bagozzi, 2001). These can be compared with alternative models such as the theory of planned behaviour (Ajzen, 1985), as predictors of behavioural change.

3. Additional contextual research is required to understand the service encounter from both the external and internal customer's perspective. Role and script theory have been adopted by service researchers to explain how consumer (and employee) dissatisfaction results from 'failure to read from a common script' (Solomon et al., 1985) and how expected role behaviours differ between actors in a service setting (Bitner et al., 1994). Ways in which service providers can identify and create common scripts and role congruence between external and internal target audiences should be explored. In particular, the ways in which an appropriate mix of formality and

adaptability can be scripted to help in responding to different target audiences would benefit many social marketing programmes.

4. Research is required which focuses on internal customers and the service which they need and receive from the organisation and wider network. Multiple boundary-spanning roles may be involved in delivering a quality service to the final customer: for example, including a range of health professionals and administrative staff. Service roles vary in emotional and or physical intensity as well as knowledge and skill requirements (Parish et al., 2008). Internal market (employee) segmentation and targeting is considered to be central to IM (Rafiq and Ahmed, 1993; Varey and Lewis, 1999), yet is rarely addressed in studies. There is a need for research to identify the nature of an IM approach, including customised 'internal products and services', which will influence the behaviour of internal target audiences. In particular, the ways in which IM can encourage organisational citizenship behaviours (OCBs), directed at both internal and external customers, should be explored.

KEY WORDS: Service quality; satisfaction; emotions; service encounter; employee behaviour; organisational citizenship behaviours; internal marketing; service design.

Key insights

- Social marketing programmes often rely on services and service employees to communicate with target audiences, distribute the 'social marketing product' and provide the prerequisites for co-creation of value. Consequently, the quality of service will impact on consumers' behaviour and this is particularly true of health-related behaviours.
- The services marketing literature highlights the importance of the service encounter, or 'moment of truth', in consumers' service evaluations. Here, role players (the consumer and employee) enact a 'script' and it is the failure to read from a common script which creates the potential for behavioural discord. The behaviour of service employees can have a significant impact (negatively or positively) on the behaviour of consumers through a process of service evaluation, which is also likely to include emotional reactions.
- Role and script theory suggest a dramaturgical metaphor where 'front-stage' staff fulfil a boundary-spanning role interacting with consumers (external customers). Front-stage (or customer-facing) employees, however, are reliant on

'back-stage' employees within the organisation to provide a level of internal service quality which will enable them to serve the external customer.
- Internal marketing aims to provide the prerequisites for high levels of both internal and external service quality. An IM approach includes: the development of effective internal relationships; creation of a service climate and culture through effective leadership, shared vision and values; a focus on communication; the development of internal products and services such as rewards and training programmes and a systematic approach to service design.
- A chain of direct causal (and reciprocal) effects has been established, linking the behaviour of consumers (external customers) to the IM activities of the organisation.

REFERENCES

Abelson, R.P. (1981) 'Psychological status of the script concept', *American Psychologist*, 36: 715–729.

Ahmed, P.K. and Rafiq, M. (2002) *Internal Marketing: Tools and Concepts for Customer-Focused Management*. Oxford: Butterworth-Heinemann.

Ahmed, P.K., Rafiq, M. and Saad, N.M. (2003) 'Internal marketing and the mediating role of organisational competencies,' *European Journal of Marketing*, 37(9): 1221–1241.

Ajzen, I. (1985) 'From intentions to actions: A theory of planned behavior', in J. Kuhl and J. Beckmann (eds), *Action Control: From Cognition to Behavior*. Heidelberg: Springer, pp. 11–39.

Allen, C.T., Machleit, K.A. and Schultz Kleine, S. (1992) 'A comparison of attitudes and emotions as predictors of behaviour at diverse levels of behavioural experience', *Journal of Consumer Research*, 18(March): 493–504.

Anderson, R.E. (1973) 'Consumer dissatisfaction: The effect of disconfirmed expectancy on perceived product performance', *Journal of Marketing Research*, 10: 38–44.

Anderson, E.W., Fornell, C. and Mazvancheryl, S.K. (2004) 'Customer satisfaction and shareholder value', *Journal of Marketing*, 68(4): 172–185.

Andreasen, A. (1995) *Marketing Social Change – Changing Behaviour to Promote Health , Social Development and the Environment*. San Francisco, CA: Jossey-Bass.

Arnould, E.J. and Price, L.L. (1993) 'River magic: Extraordinary experience and the extended service encounter', *Journal of Consumer Research*, 20: 24–45.

Aurier, P. and N'Goala, G. (2009) 'The differing and mediating roles of trust and relationship commitment in service relationship maintenance and development', *Journal of the Academy of Marketing Science*, 38(3): 303–325.

Avis, M., Bond, M. and Arthur, A. (1997) 'Questioning patient satisfaction: An empirical investigation in two outpatient clinics', *Social Science Medical*, 44: 85–92.

Babakus, E. and Boller, G.W. (1992) 'An empirical assessment of the SERVQUAL scale', *Journal of Business Research*, 24: 253–268.

Babakus, E. and Mangold, W.G. (1992) 'Adapting the SERVQUAL scale to hospital services: An empirical investigation', *Health Services Research*, 26(6): 767–786.

Babin, B.J. and Boles, J.S. (1998) 'Employee behaviour in a service environment: A model and test of potential differences between men and women', *Journal of Marketing*, 62(2): 77–92.

Bagozzi, R.P., Gopinath, M. and Nyer, P.U. (1999) 'The role of emotions in marketing', *Journal of the Academy of Marketing Science*, 27(2): 184–206.

Ballantyne, D.M., Christopher, M. and Payne, A. (1995) 'Improving the quality of services marketing: Service (re) design is the critical link', *Journal of Marketing Management*, 11: 7–24.

Bandura, A. (1986) *Social Foundations of Thought and Action: A Social Cognitive Approach*. Englewood Cliffs, NJ: Prentice-Hall.

Bandura, A. (1997) *Self-Efficacy: The Exercise of Control*. New York, W.H. Freeman and Company.

Bansal, H.S., Irving, P.G. and Taylor, S.F. (2004) 'A three component model of customer commitment to service providers', *Journal of the Academy of Marketing Science*, 32(2): 234–250

Barry, C.A. Stevenson, F.A., Britten, N., Barber, N. and Bradley, C.P. (2001) 'Giving voice to the lifeworld. More humane, more effective medical care? A qualitative study of doctor–patient communication in general practice', *Social Science and Medicine*, 53(4): 487–505.

Bell, S.J. and Menguc, B. (2002) 'The employee–organization relationship, organizational citizenship behaviors, and superior quality', *Journal of Retailing*, 78(2): 131–146.

Bell, S.J., Menguc, B. and Stefani, S.L. (2004) 'When customers disappoint: A model of relational internal marketing and customer complaints', *Journal of the Academy of Marketing Science*, 32(2): 112–126.

Berry, L.L. (1995) 'Relationship marketing of services: Growing interests, emerging perspectives', *Journal of the Academy of Marketing Science*, 23(4), 236–245.

Berry, L.L. and Bendapudi, N. (2007) 'Health care: A fertile field for service research', *Journal of Service Research*, 10(2): 111–122.

Berry, L.L. and Parasuraman, A. (1992) 'Services marketing starts from within', *Marketing Management*, 1: 24–34.

Berry, L.L., Hensel, J.S. and Burke, M.C. (1976) 'Improving retailer capability for effective consumerism response', *Journal of Retailing*, 52(3): 3–14.

Bettencourt, L.A. (1997) 'Customer voluntary performance: Customers as partners in service delivery', *Journal of Retailing*, 73: 383–406.

Bettencourt, L.A. and Brown, S.W. (2003), 'Role stressor and customer-oriented boundary spanning behaviors in service organizations', *Journal of the Academy of Marketing Science*, 31, 394–408.

Bettencourt, L.A. and Gwinner, K. (1996) 'Customisation of the service experience: The role of the frontline employee', *International Journal of Service Industry Management*, 7(2): 3–20.

Bettencourt, L.A., Gwinner, K.P. and Meuter, M.L. (2001) 'A comparison of attitude, personality, and knowledge predictors of service-oriented organizational citizenship behaviors', *Journal of Applied Psychology*, 86(February): 29–41.

Bitner, M.J., Booms, B.H. and Tetreault, M.S. (1990) 'The service encounter: Diagnosing favourable and unfavourable incidents', *Journal of Marketing*, 54: 71–84.

Bitner, M.J., Booms, B.H. and Mohr, L.A. (1994) 'Critical service encounters: The employee's viewpoint', *Journal of Marketing*, 58: 95–106.

Bolton, R.N. and Drew, J.H. (1991) 'A multistage model of customers' assessments of service quality and value', *Journal of Consumer Research*, March, 17(4): 375–384.

Bowen, D.E. and Lawler, E.E. (1992) 'The empowerment of service workers: What, why, how and when', *Sloan Management Review*, 33: 31–39.

Bowers, M.R., Swan, J.E. and Koehler, W.F. (1994) 'What attributes determine quality and satisfaction with health care delivery?' *Health Care Management Review*, 19(4): 49–55.

Brady, M.K. (2001) 'Some new thoughts on conceptualising perceived service quality: A hierarchical approach', *Journal of Marketing*, 65(3): 34–39.

Brown, S.W. and Schwartz, T.A. (1989) 'A gap analysis of professional service quality', *Journal of Marketing*, 53(2): 92–98.

Carman, J.M. (1990) 'Consumer perceptions of service quality: An assessment of the SERVQUAL dimensions', *Journal of Retailing*, 66: 33–55.

Castro, C.B., Armario, E.M. and Ruiz, D.M. (2004) 'The influence of employee organizational citizenship behavior on customer loyalty', *International Journal of Service Industry Management*, 15: 27–53.

Chan, L.-K. and Wu, M.-L. (2002) 'Quality function deployment: A literature review', *European Journal of Operational Research*, 143: 463–497.

Chandon, J-L., Leo, P-Y. and Philippe, J. (1997) 'Service encounter dimensions – A dyadic perspective', *International Journal of Service Industry Management*, 8: 65–86.

Chandon, P., Morwitz, V.G. and Reinartz, W.J. (2005) 'Do intentions really predict behaviour? Self-generated validity effects in survey research,' *Journal of Marketing*, 69(2): 1–14.

Chaston, I. (2000) 'Internal marketing in small manufacturing firms: Extending the concept to encompass organisational learning', in R.J. Varey and B.R. Lewis (eds), *Internal Marketing: Directions for Management*. London: Routledge, pp. 93–108.

Chenet, P., Tynan, C. and Money, A. (1999) 'Service performance gap: Re-evaluation and re-development', *Journal of Business Research*, 46(2): 133–147.

Choi K.S., Cho, W-H., Lee S., Lee, H. and Kim, C. (2004) 'The relationships among quality, value, satisfaction and behavioural intention in health care provider choice', *Journal of Business Research*, 57(8): 913–921.

Chung, B.G. and Schneider, B. (2002) 'Serving multiple masters: Role conflict experienced by service employees', *Journal of Services Marketing*, 16: 70–87.

Chung-Herrera B.G., Goldschmidt, N. and Hoffman, K.D. (2004) 'Customer and employee views of critical service incidents', *Journal of Services Marketing*, 18(4): 241–254.

Costarelli, S. and Colloca, P. (2004) 'The effects of attitudinal ambivalence on pro-environmental behavioural intentions', *Journal of Environmental Psychology*, 24: 279–288.

Cronin, J. Jr, Brady, M.K., Hult, G. and Tomas, M. (2000) 'Assessing the effects of quality, value and consumer satisfaction on consumer behavioural intentions in service environments', *Journal of Retailing*, 76(2): 193–216.

Crosby, L.A., Evans, K.R. and Cowles, D. (1990) 'Relationship quality in services selling: An interpersonal influence perspective', *Journal of Marketing*, 54(3): 68–81.

Crozier, R.W. and Metts, S. (1994) *Facework*. Newbury Park, CA: Sage Publications.

Dagger, T.S and Sweeney, J.C. (2006) 'The effect of service evaluations on behavioral intentions and quality of life,' *Journal of Service Research*, 9: 3.

Dagger, T.S. and Sweeney, J.C. (2007) 'A hierarchical model of health service quality: Scale development and investigation of an integrated model', *Journal of Service Research*, 10(2): 123–142.

Desai, D. (2009) 'Role of relationship management and value co-creation in social marketing', *Social Marketing Quarterly*, 15(4): 112–125.

De Ruyter, K. and Bloemer, J. (1999) 'Customer loyalty in extended service settings: The interaction between satisfaction, value attainment and positive mood', *International Journal of Service Industry Management*, 10(3): 320–336.

Dijkstra, L. and van der Bij, H. (2002) 'Quality function deployment in healthcare: Methods for meeting customer requirements in redesign and renewal', *International Journal of Quality and Reliability Management*, 19: 67–89.

Dubé, L. and Menon, K. (2000) 'Multiple roles of consumption emotions in post-purchase satisfaction with extended service transactions', *International Journal of Service Industry Management*, 11(3): 287–304.

Dubé, L., Cervellon, M.C. and Jingyuan, H. (2003) 'Should consumer attitudes be reduced to their affective and cognitive bases? Validation of a hierarchical model', *International Journal of Research in Marketing*, 20(3): 259–272.

Dunne, P.A. and Barnes, J.G. (2000) 'Internal marketing: A relationship and value creation view', in R.J. Varey and B.R. Lewis (eds), *Internal Marketing: Directions for Management*, London: Routledge, pp. 192–220.

Eagly, A.H. and Chaiken, S. (1993) *The Psychology of Attitudes*. Fort Worth, TX: Harcourt Brace Jovanovich.

Edvardsson, B. and Olsson, J. (1996) 'Key concepts for new service development', *The Service Industries Journal*, 16(2): 140–164.

Engel, J.F. and Blackwell, R.D. (1982) *Consumer Behaviour*, 4th edn. New York: Dryden Press.

Fang, E., Palmatier, R.W., Scheer, L.K. and Li, N. (2008) 'Trust at different organizational levels', *Journal of Marketing*, 72: 80–98.

Fisk, R.P., Brown, S.W. and Bitner, M.J. (1993) 'Tracking the evolution of the services marketing literature', *Journal of Retailing*, 69: 61–103.

Fließ, S. and Kleinaltenkamp, M. (2004) 'Blueprinting the service company: Managing service processes efficiently', *Journal of Business Research*, 57(4): 392–404.

Foreman, S.K. and Money, A.H. (1995) 'Internal marketing: Concepts, measurement and application', *Journal of Marketing Management*, 11(8): 755–768.

Fornell, C. (1992) 'A national customer satisfaction barometer: The Swedish experience', *Journal of Marketing*, 56(January): 6–21.

George, W.R. (1990) 'Internal marketing and organisational behaviour: A partnership in developing customer-conscious employees at every level', *Journal of Business Research*, 20: 63–70.

Gilmore, A. and Carson, D. (1995) 'Managing and marketing to internal customers', in W.J. Glynn and J.G. Barnes (eds), *Understanding Services Management*. Chichester: Wiley, pp. 295–321.

Gombeski, W.R. Jr, Day, J.R., Fay, G.W. and Lowery, M.C. (1992) 'Physician peer review surveys: A management tool for improving quality of patient care', *Journal of Health Care Marketing*, 12(2): 52–59.

Grace, D. (2007) 'How embarrassing! An exploratory study of critical incidents including affective reactions', *Journal of Service Research*, 9(3): 271–284.

Gregory, B.T., Harris, S.G., Armenakis, A.A. and Shook, C.L. (2009) 'Organisational culture and effectiveness: A study of values, attitudes and organisational outcomes', *Journal of Business Research*, 62: 673–679.

Gremler, D.D. (2004) 'The critical incident technique in service research', *Journal of Service Research*, 7: 65–89.

Gremler, D.D. and Brown, S.W. (1999) 'The loyalty ripple effect – Appreciating the full-value of customers', *International Journal of Service Industry Management*, 10(3): 271–291.

Grönroos, C. (1984) 'A service quality model and its marketing implications', *European Journal of Marketing*, 18(4) 36–44.

Grönroos, C. (1990) 'Relationship approach to marketing in service contexts: The marketing and organisational behaviour interface', *Journal of Business Research*, 20: 3–11.

Gruca, T.S. and Rego, L.L. (2005) 'Customer satisfaction, cash flow and shareholder value', *Journal of Marketing*, 69(3): 115–130.

Guiry, M. (1992) 'Consumer and employee roles in service encounters', *Advances in Consumer Research*, 19: 666–672.

Gummesson, E. (1987) 'Using internal marketing to develop a new culture: The case of Ericsson quality,' *Journal of Business and Industrial Marketing*, 2(3): 23–28.

Gummesson, E. (2002) *Total Relationship Marketing*, 2nd edn. Oxford, Butterworth-Heinemann (1st edn, 1999).

Hall, J. and Dornan, M. (1988) 'What patients like about their medical care and how often they are asked', *Social Science Medical*, 21: 935–939.

Hallowell, R. (1996) 'The relationships of customer satisfaction customer loyalty, and profitability: An empirical study', *International Journal of Service Industry Management,* 7(4): 27–42.

Han, X., Kwortnik, R.J. and Wang, C. (2008) 'Service loyalty: An integrative model and examination across service contexts', *Journal of Service Research,* 11: 2242.

Hartline, M.D. and Ferrell, O.C. (1996) 'The management of customer contact employees: An empirical investigation', *Journal of Marketing,* 60(4): 52–70.

Hartline, M.D., Maxham, J.G. and McKee, D.O. (2000) 'Corridors of influence in the dissemination of customer-oriented strategy to consumer contact service employees', *Journal of Marketing,* 64(2): 35–50.

Hastings, G. (2007) *Social Marketing: Why Should the Devil Have All the Best Tunes?* Oxford: Butterworth-Heinemann.

Headley, D.E. and Miller, S. J. (1993) 'Measuring service quality and its relationship to future consumer behaviour', *Journal of Health Care Marketing,* 12(4): 32–41.

Heskett, J.L., Jones, T.O., Loveman, G.W., Sasser, W.E. Jr and Schlesinger, L.A. (1994) 'Putting the service–profit chain to work', *Harvard Business Review,* March/April: 164–170.

Heskett, J.L., Sasser, W.E. and Schlesinger, L.A. (1997) *The Service Profit Chain.* New York: Free Press.

Homburg, C. and Stock, R. (2004) 'The link between sales people's job satisfaction and customer satisfaction in a business-to-business context: A dyadic analysis', *Journal of the Academy of Marketing Science,* 3: 144–158.

Homburg, C. and Stock, R.M. (2005) 'Exploring the conditions under which salesperson work satisfaction can lead to customer satisfaction', *Psychology and Marketing,* 22(5): 393–420.

Hostager, T.J., Neil, T.C., Decker, R.L. and Lorentz, R.D. (1998) 'Seeing environmental opportunities: Effects of intrapreneurial ability, efficacy, motivation and desirability', *Journal of Organisational Change Management,* 11: 11–25.

Hudak, P.L. and Wright, J.G. (2000) 'The characteristics of patient satisfaction measures', *Spine,* 25(24): 3167–3177.

Hui, M.K., Au, K. and Fock, H. (2004) 'Reactions of service employees to organisation–customer conflict: A cross-cultural comparison', *International Journal of Research in Marketing,* 21(2): 107–121.

Hulka, B.S. and Zysanski, S.J. (1982) 'Validation of a patient satisfaction scale: Theory, methods and practice', *Medical Care,* XX(6): 649–653.

Hulka, B.S., Zyzanski, S.J., Cassel, J.C. and Thompson, W.J. (1970) 'Scale for the measurement of attitudes towards physicians and primary health care', *Medical Care,* 8: 429.

Izard, C.E. (1977) *Human Emotions.* New York: Plenum Press.

James, S. and Skinner, H. (2009) 'The Shoreline Project for street drinkers: Designing and running a supported housing project for the "unhousable"', *Social Marketing Quarterly,* 15(3): 49–66.

Jang, S. and Namkung, Y. (2009) 'Perceived quality, emotions and behavioural intentions: Application of an extended Mehrabian–Russell model to restaurants', *Journal of Business Research,* 62: 451–460.

Johne, A. and Harbone, P. (2003) 'One leader is not enough for major new service development: Results of a consumer banking study', *Service Industries Journal,* 23(3): 22–39.

Jones, T., Fox, G.L., Taylor, S.F. and Fabrigar, L.R. (2010) 'Service customer commitment and response', *Journal of Services Marketing,* 24: 16–28.

Jun, M., Peterson, R.T. and Zsidisin, G.A. (1998) 'The identification and measurement of quality dimensions in health care: Focus group interview results', *Health Care Management Review,* 23(4): 81–96.

Katz, G.M. (2004) 'Practitioner note: A response to Pullman's (2002) comparison of quality function deployment versus conjoint analysis', *Journal of Product Innovation Management,* 21: 61–63.

Kiely, J.A. (2005) 'Emotions in business-to-business service relationships', *The Service Industries Journal,* 25(3): 373–390.

Kelley, S.W. and Hoffman, K.D. (1997) 'An investigation of positive affect, prosocial behaviors and service quality', *Journal of Retailing, 73(3),* 407–427.

Kelly, D. and Storey, C. (2000) 'New service development: Initiation strategies', *International Journal of Service Industry Management,* 11: 45–63.

Laing, A., Fischbacher, M., Hogg, G. and Smith, A. (2002) *Managing and Marketing Health Services.* London: Thomson.

Lee, P., Gombaski, W.R. Jr, and Doremus, H. (1991) 'Effective internal marketing: The challenge of the 1990s', *Journal of Health Care Marketing,* 11(2): 58–62.

Lewis, R.C. and Booms, B.H. (1983) 'The marketing aspects of service quality', in L.L. Berry, G.L. Shostack and G. Upah (eds), *Emerging Perspectives on Services Marketing.* Chicago, IL: AMA, pp. 99–104.

Liljander, U. and Strandvik, T. (1997) 'Emotions in service satisfaction', *International Journal of Service Industry Management,* 8(2): 148–169.

Lim, P.C. and Tang, N.K.H. (2000) 'The development of a model for total quality healthcare', *Managing Service Quality,* 10(2): 103–111.

Lings, I.N. and Greenley, G.E. (2005) 'Measuring internal marketing orientation', *Journal of Service Research,* 7(3): 290–305.

Lowry, R.J., Hardy, S., Jordan, C. and Wayman, G. (2004) 'Using social marketing to increase recruitment of pregnant smokers to smoking cessation service: A success story', *Public Health,* 118: 239–243

Lovelock, C.H. (1983) 'Classifying services to gain strategic marketing insights', *Journal of Marketing,* 47(3): 9–20.

Mano, H. and Oliver, R.L. (1993) 'Assessing the dimensionality and structure of consumption experience: Evaluation, feeling and satisfaction', *Journal of Consumer Research,* 20: 451–466.

Martin, C.R. Jr. and Horne, D.A. (1995) 'Level of success inputs for service innovations in the same firm', *International Journal of Service Industry Management,* 6(4): 40–56.

Mattila, A.S. and Enz, C.A. (2002) 'The role of emotions in service encounters', *Journal of Service Research,* 4(4): 268–277.

Menon, K. and Dubé, L. (2000) 'Ensuring greater satisfaction by engineering salesperson response to customer emotions', *Journal of Retailing*, 76(3): 285–302.

Mohr, L.A. and Bitner, M.J. (1991) 'Mutual understanding between customers and employees in service ecounters', *Advances in Consumer Research*, 18: 611–617.

Morgan, R.M. and Hunt, S.D. (1994) 'The commitment–trust theory of relationship marketing', *The Journal of Marketing*, 58(3): 20–38.

Morrison, E.W. (1996) 'Organizational citizenship behavior as a critical link between HRM practices and service quality', *Human Resource Management*, 3(4): 493–512.

Morvitz, V.G. (1997) 'Why consumers don't always accurately predict their own future behaviour', *Marketing Letters*, 8: 57–70.

Mukherjee, A. and Malhotra, N. (2006) 'Does role clarity explain employee-perceived service quality?', *International Journal of Service Industry Management*, 17(5): 444–473.

Netemeyer, R.G. and Maxham III, J.G. (2007) 'Employee versus supervisor ratings of performance in the retail customer service sector: Differences in predictive validity for customer outcomes', *Journal of Retailing*, 83: 131–145.

Oliver, R.L. (1981) 'Measurement and evaluation of satisfaction processes in retail settings', *Journal of Retailing*, 57(3): 25–48.

Oliver, R.L. (1993) 'A conceptual model of service quality and service satisfaction: Compatible goals, different concepts', in T.A. Swartz, D.E. Bowen and S.W. Brown (eds), *Advances in Services Marketing and Management*, Vol. 2, Greenwich, CT: JAI Press, pp. 65–85.

Oliver, R.L., Rust, R.T. and Varki, S. (1997) 'Customer delight: Foundations, findings and managerial insight', *Journal of Retailing*, 73(3): 311–336.

Pajares, F. (1997) 'Current directions in self-efficacy research', in M. Maehr and P.R. Pintrich (eds), *Advances in Motivation and Achievement*, Vol. 10. Greenwich, CT: JAI Press, pp. 1–49.

Parasuraman, A., Zeithaml, V.A. and Berry, L.L. (1985) 'A conceptual model of service quality and its implications for future research', *Journal of Marketing*, 49(4): 41–50.

Parasuraman, A., Zeithaml, V.A. and Berry, L.L. (1988) 'SERVQUAL: A multiple-item scale for measuring consumer perceptions of service quality', *Journal of Retailing*, 64: 14–40.

Parasuraman, A., Berry, L.L. and Zeithaml, V.A. (1991) 'Refinement and reassessment of the SERVQUAL scale', *Journal of Retailing*, 67(4): 420–450.

Parasuraman, A., Zeithaml, V.A. and Berry, L.L. (1994) 'Alternative scales for measuring service quality: A comparative assessment based on psychometric and diagnostic criteria', *Journal of Retailing*, 70(3): 201–230.

Parish, J.T., Berry, L.L. and Lam, S.Y. (2008) 'The effect of the servicescape on service workers', *Journal of Service Research*, 10(3): 220–238.

Pascoe, G. (1983) 'Patient satisfaction in primary health care: A literature review and analysis', *Evaluation and Program Planning*, 6: 185–210.

Payne, S.C. and Webber, S.S. (2006) 'Effects of service provider attitudes and employment status on ctizenship behaviors and customers' attitudes and loyalty behavior', *Journal of Applied Psychology*, 91(2): 365–378.

Perugini, M. and Bagozzi, R.P. (2001) 'The role of desires and anticipated emotions in goal-directed behaviours: Broadening and deepening the theory of planned behaviour', *British Journal of Social Psychology*, 40: 79–98.

Peyrot, H., Cooper, P.D. and Schnapf, D. (1993) 'Consumer satisfaction and perceived quality of outpatient health services', *Journal of Health Care Marketing*, 13(Winter): 24–33.

Phillipson, L., Jones, S.C. and Wiese, E. (2009) 'Effective communication only part of the strategy needed to promote help-seeking of young people with mental health problems', *Social Marketing Quarterly*, 15(2): 50–62.

Pitt, L.F. and Foreman, S.K. (1999) 'Internal marketing's role in organizations: A transaction cost perspective', *Journal of Business Research*, 44: 15–36.

Podsakoff, P.M., MacKenzie, S.B., Paine, J.B. and Bachrach, D.G. (2000) 'Organizational citizenship behaviors: A critical review of the theoretical and empirical literature and suggestions for future research', *Journal of Management*, 26: 513–563.

Price, L.L., Arnould, E.J. and Deibler, S.L. (1995) 'Consumers' emotional responses to service encounters: The influence of the service provider', *International Journal of the Service Industry Management*, 6(3): 34–63.

Rafaeli, A., Ziklik, L. and Doucet, L. (2008) 'The impact of call center employees' customer orientation behaviors on service quality', *Journal of Service Research*, 10(3): 239–255.

Rafiq, M. and Ahmed, P.K. (1993) 'The scope of internal marketing: Defining the boundary between marketing and human resource management', *Journal of Marketing Management*, 9(3): 219–232

Reidenbach, R.E. and Sandifer-Smallwood, B. (1990) 'Exploring perceptions of hospital operations by a modified SERVQUAL approach', *Journal of Health Care Marketing*, 10(4): 47–55.

Richins, M.L. (1997) 'Measuring emotions in the consumption experience', *Journal of Consumer Research*, 24(September): 11–20.

Roberts, J.G. and Tugwell, P. (1987) 'Comparison of questionnaires determining patient satisfaction with medical care', *Health Services Research*, 22: 637–654.

Rothenberg, S. (2003) 'Knowledge content and worker participation in environmental management at NUMMI', *Journal of Management Studies* 40(7): 1783–1802.

Russell, J.A. (1991) 'Culture and the categorisation of emotions', *Psychological Bulletin*, 100(3): 426–450.

San Martín, S. (2008) 'Relational and economic antecedents of organisational commitment', *Personnel Review*, 37(6): 589–608.

Schein, E.H. (1985) *Organisational Culture and Leadership*. San Francisco, CA: Jossey-Bass.

Schneider, B. and Bowen, D.E. (1985) 'Employee and customer perceptions of service in banks: Replication and extension', *Journal of Applied Psychology*, 70: 423–433.

Schneider, B., Parkington, J.J. and Buxton, V.M. (1980) 'Employee and customer perceptions of service in banks', *Administrative Science Quarterly*, 25: 252–267.

Schneider, B., White, S. and Paul, M. (1998) 'Linking service climate and customer perceptions of service quality: Test of a causal model', *Journal of Applied Psychology*, 83: 150–163.

Schneider, B., Ehrhart, M G., Mayer, D.M. and Saltz, J.L. (2005) 'Understanding organisation–customer links in service settings', *Academy of Management Journal*, 48(6): 1017–1032.

Shaver, P., Schwartz, J., Kirson, D. and O'Connor, C. (1987) 'Emotion knowledge: Further exploration of a prototype approach', *Journal of Personality and Social Psychology*, 52(6): 1061–1086.

Shostack, G.L. (1984) 'Designing services that deliver', *Harvard Business Review*, 62: 133–139.

Shostack, G.L. (1985) 'Planning the service encounter', in J.A. Czepiel, M.R. Solomon and C.F. Surprenant (eds), *The Service Encounter*. Lexington, MA: Lexington Books, pp. 243–253.

Singh, J. (2000) 'Performance productivity and quality of frontline employees in service organisations', *Journal of Marketing*, 64(2): 15–34.

Smith, A.K. and Bolton, R.N. (1999) 'A model of customer satisfaction with service encounters involving failure and recovery', *Journal of Marketing*, 36(3): 356–372

Smith, A.M. (2000) 'The dimensions of service quality: Lessons from the healthcare literature and some methodological effects', *The Service Industries Journal*, 20(3): 167–190.

Smith, A.M. (2006) 'A cross-cultural perspective on the role of emotion in negative service encounters', *The Service Industries Journal*, 26(7): 709–726.

Smith, A.M. and Fischbacher, M. (2002) 'Service design in the NHS: Collaboration or conflict?', *Journal of Marketing Management*, 18: 923–951.

Smith, A.M. and Fischbacher, M. (2005) 'New service development: A stakeholder perspective', *European Journal of Marketing*, 39(9/10): 1025–1048.

Smith, C. and Ellsworth, P. (1985) 'Patterns of cognitive appraisal in emotions', *Journal of Personality and Social Psychology*, 48: 813–838.

Soliman, A.A. (1992) 'Assessing the quality of health care: A consumerist approach', *Health Marketing Quarterly*, 10(1/2):121–141.

Solomon, M.R., Surprenant, C., Czepiel, J.A. and Gutman, E.G. (1985) 'A role theory perspective on dyadic interactions: The service encounter', *Journal of Marketing*, 49: 99–111.

Sower, V., Duffy, J., Kilbourne, W., Kohers, G. and Jones, P. (2001) 'The dimensions of service quality for hospitals: Development and use of the KQCAH scale', *Health Care Management Review*, 26(2): 47–59.

Stuart, F.I. and Tax, S.S. (1996) 'Planning for service quality: An integrative approach', *International Journal of Service Industry Management*, 7(4): 58–77.

Sundbo, J. (1997) 'Management of innovation in services', *The Service Industries Journal*, 17(3): 432–455.

Taylor, S.A. and Baker, T.L. (1994) 'An assessment of the relationship between service quality and customer satisfaction in the formation of consumers' purchase intentions', *Journal of Retailing*, 70(2): 163–178.

Thomas, R.K., Farmer, E. and Wallace, B. (1991) 'The importance of internal marketing: The case of geriatric services', *Journal of Health Care Marketing*, 11: 55–58.

Thomson (1990) in Varey and Lewis (1999) op. cit. 'A broadened conception of internal marketing', *European Journal of Marketing*, 33(9/10): 926–944.

Vandamme, R. and Leunis, J. (1993) 'Development of a multiple-item scale for measuring hospital service quality', *International Journal of Service Industry Management*, 4(3): 30–49.

Van Dolen, W., de Ruyter, K. and Lemmink, J. (2004) 'An empirical assessment of the influence of customer emotions and contact employee performance on encounter and relationship satisfaction', *Journal of Business Research*, 57(4): 437–444.

Varey, R.J. and Lewis, B.R. (1999) 'A broadened conception of internal marketing', *European Journal of Marketing*, 33(9/10): 926–944.

Vargo, S.L. and Lusch, R.F. (2008) 'Service dominant logic: Continuing the evolution', *Journal of the Academy of Marketing Science*, 36: 1–10.

Verbeke, W. and Bagozzi, R.P. (2003) 'Exploring the role of self- and customer-provoked embarrassment in personal selling', *International Journal of Research in Marketing*, 20(3): 233–258.

Verhoef, P.C., Antonides, G. and de Hoog, A.N. (2004) 'Service encounters as a sequence of events: The importance of peak experiences', *Journal of Service Research*, 7: 53–64.

Walbridge, S.W. and Delene, L.W. (1993) 'Measuring physician attitudes of service quality', *Journal of Health Care Marketing*, 13(Winter): 6–15.

Ware, J.E. Jr, Davies-Avery, A. and Stewart, A.L. (1978) 'The measurement and meaning of patient satisfaction: A review of the recent literature', *Health and Medical Care Services Review*, 1: 1–15.

Ware, J.E., Snyder, M.K., Wright, W.R. and Davies, A.R. (1983) 'Defining and measuring patient satisfaction with medical care', *Evaluation and Program Planning*, 6: 247–263.

Ware, J.E. and Hays, R.D. (1988) 'Methods for measuring patient satisfaction with specific medical encounters', *Medical Care*, 26: 393–402.

Watson, L. and Spence, M.T. (2007) 'Causes and consequences of emotions on consumer behaviour: A review and integrative cognitive appraisal theory', *European Journal of Marketing*, 41(5/6): 487–511.

Weiner, B. (1985) 'An attributional theory of achievement motivation and emotion', *Psychological Review*, 92(October): 548–573.

Weiner, R (2000) 'Attributional thoughts about consumer behaviour', *Journal of Consumer Research*, 27(December): 382–387.

Wieseke, J., Ahearne, M., Lam, S.K. and van Dick, R. (2009) 'The role of leaders in internal marketing', *Journal of Marketing*, 73(March): 23–145.

Winsted, K.F. (2000) 'Service behaviours that lead to satisfied customers', *European Journal of Marketing*, 34(3/4): 399–417.

Wirtz, J. and Bateson, J.E.G. (1995) 'An experimental investigation of halo effects in satisfaction measures of service attributes', *International Journal of Service Industry Management*, 6(3): 84–102.

Woodside, A.G., Frey, L.L. and Daly, R.T. (1989) 'Linking service quality, customer satisfaction, and behavioural intention', *Journal of Health Care Marketing*, 9: 5–17.

Woolley, F., Kane, R., Hughes, C. and Wright, D. (1978) 'The effects of doctor–patient communication on satisfaction and outcome of care', *Social Science and Medicine*, 12: 123–128.

Yi, Y. and Gong, T. (2008) 'If employees "go the extra mile," do customers reciprocate with similar behavior?' *Psychology and Marketing*, 25(10): 961–986.

Zahorik, A.J. and Rust, R.T. (1992) 'Modelling the impact of service quality on profitability: A review', in T.A. Swartz, D.E. Bowen and S.W. Brown (eds), *Advances in Services Marketing and Management*, Vol 1. Greenwich, CT: JAI Press, pp. 247–276.

Zeithaml, V.A., Berry, L.L. and Parasuraman, A. (1988) 'Communication and control processes in the delivery of service quality', *Journal of Marketing*, 52(2): 35–48.

Zeithaml, V.A., Berry, L.L. and Parasuraman, A. (1996) 'The behavioural consequences of service quality', *Journal of Marketing*, 60(2): 31–46.

Zeithaml, V.A., Bitner, M.J. and Gremler, D.D. (2006) *Services Marketing: Integrating Customer Focus Across the Firm*, 4th edn. New York: McGraw-Hill International Edition (1st edn, 1996).

Zyzanski, S.J., Hulka, B.S. and Cassel, J.C. (1974) 'Scale for the measurement of "satisfaction" with medical care: Modifications in content, format and scoring', *Medical Care*, 12(7): 611–620.

Upstream and Social Change

21. IMPOVERISHED CONSUMERS AND SOCIAL MARKETING – R.P. HILL

The author uses ethnographic data to create composites of five impoverished consumer subpopulations in the Western world: impoverished by homelessness, a reduction in work status, child- or parental-caring responsibilities, criminality, a childhood on welfare, or a lack of local medical care. The social marketing implications of impoverished consumers' experiences of and behaviour in the material world are examined. Hill indicates that any gaps between the goals of funders of social initiatives to promote healthful living and the goals and behaviours of their target impoverished consumers must be acknowledged and closed.

22. SOCIAL MARKETING AND INTERNATIONAL DEVELOPMENT – G. CAIRNS, B. MACKAY AND L. MACDONALD

Social marketing in the economies of the developing world contributes to pro-poor programmes and interventions, and thinking. The authors describe how the focus and the nature of social marketing activities in lower-income countries and developed industrialized countries have progressed and developed in parallel but with some distinct differences in delivery and strategic goals. For example, social marketing practice in the developing world most often relates to the promotion of, and improved access to, products and services rather than ideas and lifestyle changes. The authors argue that both the developing and developed world should share more learning and practical experience to reduce this asymmetry in social marketing research and discourse.

23. SOCIAL MARKETING FOR A SUSTAINABLE ENVIRONMENT – K. PEATTIE

In this chapter, the author clarifies how social marketing will play an important role in promoting a more sustainable economy and society and changing our relationship with the physical environment to prevent overexploitation of the planet's resources. A strength of social marketing is that it can be used to go beyond simply modifying awareness and intentions to effect actual behaviour changes and partnership building. However, Peattie notes that pro-environmental behaviours frequently lack the obvious direct and personal benefits that most health-related social marketing campaigns can use as motivators; thus social marketers have been creative to make environmental campaigns appeal to people. The author also demonstrates a method for segmenting the market for pro-environmental behaviours and describes partnership working between commercial and social partners for the good of the environment.

24. BUSINESS AS UNUSUAL: THE CONTRIBUTION OF SOCIAL MARKETING TO GOVERNMENT POLICY AND STRATEGY DEVELOPMENT – J. FRENCH

In his chapter, French demonstrates the contribution social marketing can make to government policy making and strategy development. He highlights how, historically, marketing has been underused and misinterpreted for behaviour change by governments then covers why social marketing should be adopted. The contribution of social marketing to policy development processes and the formation of strategies are described, followed by examples of tools and techniques social marketers can adopt to promote the uptake of social marketing in government. French advises that politicians and public officials who seek to serve the public should learn how to make positive life choices the easy and natural choices for people, and this means embracing social marketing principles as a core approach to policy and strategy development, as well as a powerful tool for developing specific interventions.

21

Impoverished Consumers and Social Marketing

Ronald Paul Hill

INTRODUCTION

The material lives of impoverished consumers became a legitimate topic for marketing scholars following publication of *The Poor Pay More* by Caplovitz (1963). He describes the difficult circumstances of urban poor as consumers of durable goods that are purchased on credit. Caplovitz found that the poor preferred new versus used and expensive versus economical goods that appeared at first glance to be more appropriate for their socioeconomic class. These counterintuitive preferences led him to conclude that impoverished consumers use compensatory consumption as a way to make up for their inability to advance social status in a manner open to middle-income citizens.

Others viewed this situation differently. Irelan and Besner (1966) believe the poor value the same material possessions and share the same goals for accumulation as affluent consumers; thus, they are not compensating but seeking an equitable portion of societal largesse. Holloway and Cardozo (1969: 5) note 'the poor ... lack [an] adequate income which makes it difficult or impossible to provide themselves with proper housing, education, medical services, and other necessities of life.' Negative emotional reactions are a consequence, including powerlessness to affect future consumer lives, alienation from the primary consumer culture, and apathy due to exploitation (Sturdivant, 1969).

Yet resulting coping strategies reveal a surprising resourcefulness. While authors such as Caplovitz (1963) see irrationality in their purchasing habits, Richards (1966) suggests these strategies have an inherent logic when examined through their lived experiences with the marketing systems in their communities. Holloway and Cardozo (1969: 55) go so far as to state that the poor 'have developed shopping strategies to obtain the best assortment of products they can within budgets limited in size and flexibility.' Andreasen (1975: 40) found even excessive debt is 'a result of careful calculations of the consequences of their actions' seeking to maximize material gain.

Recent studies have expanded this developing paradigm. For example, Hill and Stephens (1997) posit a three-dimensional model of impoverished consumer behavior based on their research with welfare mothers. Their model chronicles the characteristics of marketing practice in poverty communities, the negative emotional consequences for poor consumers, and subsequent coping strategies. Underlying this perspective is the belief that the poor advance their quality of life through a wide range of emotional and behavioral processes. Rather than passively accepting their circumstances as a 'fruitless struggle' (Sturdivant, 1969: 20), they exert control within their consumer worlds.

Lee et al. (1999) build from this framework with research involving the rural poor. Their investigation of healthcare delivery in Appalachia found that the impoverished have many resource strengths (e.g., social capital or community) as well as profound resource deficits (e.g., economic and cultural capital) that require unique roles in exchange relationships with providers. The authors recommend public policymakers interested in improving the consumer lives of the poor pass legislation that is resource sensitive, recognizing benefits of enhancing strengths rather than compensating for weaknesses (see Hill, 2002b).

WORLDWIDE CIRCUMSTANCES

How widespread is impoverishment? Interestingly, consumption opportunities worldwide have advanced over the last 100 years. By the new millennium, total expenditures for goods and services were almost $25 trillion, double the level of 1975 and about six times more than 1950 (UNDP, 2001). Consider also that real consumption in 1900 was only $1.5 trillion – a figure that is dwarfed by the end-of-the-century total expenditures by a factor of 16. Consumer quality of life has improved substantially as a consequence, and the UN notes: 'Living standards have risen to enable hundreds of millions to enjoy housing with hot water and cold, warmth and electricity, transport to and from work – with time for leisure and sports, vacations and other activities beyond anything imagined at the start of this century' (UNDP, 1998: 1).

Of consequence, these advances have not been evenly distributed, with real North/South and East/West inequities (see Adrangi et al., 2004). Information gathered and summarized by the United Nations Development Programme (UNDP) show the 20% of citizens who have the good fortune to reside in the wealthiest nations consume more than 85% of private goods and services, yet their 20% counterpart at the bottom of the economic pyramid receive about 1% of this affluence. Also, consider the following contrasts:

1. Top one-fifth eats 45% of meat and fish; poorest one-fifth, 5%.
2. Top one-fifth uses 58% of all energy; poorest one-fifth, less than 4%.
3. Top one-fifth has 74% of telephone lines; poorest one-fifth, 1.5%.
4. Top one-fifth consumes 84% of paper; poorest one-fifth, 1.5%.
5. Top one-fifth owns 87% of vehicles; poorest one-fifth, less than 1%.

The Human Development Index (HDI), which measures the quality of life of citizenry across countries on three consumption dimensions – longevity, knowledge, and standard of living – shows just one-third of global consumers (or nearly two billion people) live under conditions of low human development, with the most dire conditions in Sub-Saharan Africa and South Asia (Hill and Adrangi, 1999). The UNDP also finds:

1. More than one billion people live on less than $1 a day.
2. One billion people lack literacy.
3. More than one billion people consume unsafe drinking water.
4. Over 800 million people go hungry daily.
5. Nearly 100 million people are homeless.
6. Almost 800 million people are unable to receive health services.

Such statistics expose the deep chasm between postmodern Western societies with resources and an infrastructure to sustain their citizenry and much of the rest of the world that is mired in poverty. These inequities are summarized by a few more telling numbers: ratio of per capita income between the wealthiest 5% of people globally to their poorest 5% counterpart is 165 to 1 (Milanovic, 2007). In total, the rich would earn as much as the poor in just 48 hours of labor judged as an annual wage. Using a different comparison set, the top one-tenth of US citizens have combined income that surpasses the total resources of the bottom two billion inhabitants of the earth. Recent trends suggest that the overall situation is improving, but advances are modest as well as uneven at best (Dollar, 2005).

Any understanding of global impoverishment requires a look at its causes. A unique approach suggests impoverished nations and their citizens suffer from a variety of 'gaps' that prohibit gaining economic ground (Dollar, 2005). Deficits include an *object gap* characterized by a shortfall of resources, commodities, and support such as factories, roads, and raw materials. The other primary category is an *idea gap* when persons lack access to the knowledge base upon which the information and service-focused advanced societies depend for advantage. While detection is important, it fails to give a nuanced perspective of how they come together and combine with other factors to disrupt the lives of various consumers or support their movement out of poverty across impacted nations.

Consider the very different circumstances of Africa and China/India. Widespread famine has devastated the population of the African continent from the dry savannahs to the tropical heartlands (Chossudovsky, 1998). As a result, 23 million have died or were at great risk of dying, while an additional 130 million in 10 countries remained at risk. On the other hand, China and India have seen enormous growth in productivity, boasting an annual rate of about 5% over the previous 20 years compared with 1.6% for the industrialized Western nations. Gains during the 1990s have reduced the World Bank's estimate of acute poverty by 4 percentage points. However, if their successes are removed, poverty rates would have risen among the remaining developing economies, and the recent economic crisis has exacerbated such problems.

THE CONSUMER CULTURE OF POVERTY

Several investigations by the author support the development of a complete look at impoverished consumers' navigation of material culture in the Western world. This work was originally designed to examine beliefs, attitudes, emotions, and survival strategies of such groups as the homeless, welfare mothers, impoverished juvenile delinquents, and the rural poor. To summarize results, composites of five impoverished subpopulations were completed using short stories based on ethnographic data that draw upon such methods as interviews, field notes, participant observation, and non participant observation (Hill, 2001). Findings from this research stream were employed to mold the focal characters, and every example of their interactions with the consumer culture is data-driven.

The first story is based on Hill and Stamey (1990) and presents the trials and tribulations of Jack, a man who recently became homeless. He spends his first homeless night in a municipal shelter but finds the experience threatening and demoralizing. He moves outside, living under a bridge and then into a homeless community that resembles the shantytowns of the Great Depression. His final residence is an abandoned building shared discreetly with two other homeless men. The second short story is grounded in Hill (1991) and focuses attention on Zoë and her family's experience of homelessness. After a difficult childhood, Zoë becomes pregnant with her second child and moves in with the father of this offspring. Unfortunately, his employer reduces his work status to part-time, and the drop in income leads them to leave their modest home. After a series of stays with relatives, Zoë and her children are forced to live in shelters where many of their original possessions are lost and new ones obtained.

Hill (1992) and Ozanne et al. (1998) inform the third story, which profiles Fast Eddie, a late teen living in a poor community. Over time, his relationship with material possessions goes from joyful anticipation, to apathy, to anger at his relative poverty. Eddie falls in with a 'fast crowd' and commits property crimes to gain access to the material world. The consumer lives of Anita and her children in the fourth story are based primarily on Hill and Stephens (1997) and reveal Anita's struggle as a welfare child who vows not to live that life. Unfortunately, her husband is laid off and

the only option for a new job is out of town. He takes the position and works diligently, but is fired after a physical confrontation with his boss, leaving Anita without income. She eventually joins the welfare rolls only to find that the level of support is too low. Lee et al. (1999) inform the rural poverty fifth story, which centers on Tammy and her mother and their lives in a former coal-mining town. Tammy's mother takes ill and they struggle to get medical attention within a reasonable distance from home. The situation deteriorates until they gain access to an alternative delivery system that values social over economic capital. Emergent themes follow (see Hill and Gaines, 2007).

Loss/lack of familial/friendship love

The impact of loss/lack of intimate as well as other-centered love on consumption adequacy is striking. In some situations, it is exacerbated by other-centered disdain or hostility. Quality of life of these people, their families, and their community members are significantly reduced as a consequence, resulting in a variety of negative emotional reactions and behaviors that often fail to improve their circumstances in the face of this adversity. The best example comes from the story of Zoë. Her earliest experiences of family life are quite positive and consistent with the middle-class vision of parental love. However, this situation deteriorates over time to the point where both father and mother trade loving responses for neglect of their children. Consider these excerpts from Zoë's story:

> Her earliest memories were of the good times she had with her parents prior to the birth of her siblings. They did lots of things as a family in those days – picnics, walks in a neighborhood park, and special dinners on holidays. Zoë even remembered when she received her first Barbie doll, and how pleased her parents seemed with her excitement. Unfortunately, their lives changed for the worse over the next several years.
>
> Family problems reached a critical point over a decade ago when she was just 10 years old. Her parents had been fighting more often than usual, and Zoë's father stayed home less and less. One day, during a particularly violent argument between her parents, her father began hitting her mother. All three of the children were reduced to tears at this sight, and they begged their father to stop. After a few more minutes passed, neighbors began banging on the door and threatened to call the police. Her father stopped abruptly and left, and Zoë hadn't seen him since. In fact, he never even returned for his clothing.

The absence of her father transformed their family from a cohesive unit to an assortment of people who went their separate ways. Zoë's mother started staying out late at night with her friends, and she occasionally would allow strange men to sleep in her bedroom. This erratic and irresponsible behavior made Zoë furious at first, but she learned to keep her feelings to herself. As long as she had her bedroom door locked and her siblings inside, she felt some degree of comfort and safety from her mother's escapades.

Zoë and her siblings are removed from their mother's care as a result of this neglect and placed in several foster homes over the years. During this period her initial anxieties mature into anger and depression, and she fails to heed her mother's warnings after they are reunited. Zoë falls in with a fast crowd at school, experimenting with drugs and sex to ease her pain. She becomes pregnant, and this experience is the wakeup call to straighten up her life. Zoë meets and falls in love with a man soon after her baby is born, but their financial circumstances deteriorate. Unfortunately, no one in her extended family can provide more than a short-term material fix for this dilemma. Consider the following passages involving interactions with her man's mother, and her grandmother (consecutively):

When Zoë arrived at his mother's home, she felt an immediate chill in the air. Zoë had met her on a few occasions, and she always felt the woman disapproved of her. She adored her son, as many mothers do, and she felt Zoë wasn't good enough for him. While she did seem to appreciate her only granddaughter from a distance, she was not very interested in caring for her.

When they arrived at her grandmother's doorstep, the woman was just finishing her morning coffee. She was a rather distant person who had battled her own demons all of her life. None of her family had ever come to her for long-term support in the past, including when her own daughter (Zoë's mother) was institutionalized. To Zoë's relief, she listened to her troubles and agreed to let her stay the night. However, Zoë and the girls would have to leave the next morning. The place was just too small to accommodate four people.

Helplessly falling into greater poverty

Their descent into poverty is experienced as beyond their control. While they hold themselves partially responsible for their situations, they are caught up in web of circumstances originating earlier that led to increasing poverty and the loss of cherished possessions. One of the best

examples of this downward spiral involves the process of becoming homeless (Wasson and Hill, 1998). Typically, the person or persons move from a self-sufficient dwelling such as an apartment, because they can no longer afford to pay the bills, to doubling up with friends or relatives. However, after awhile, they 'overstay their welcome', and they are forced to move to government-controlled housing, public or private homeless shelters, or the streets. Once this transition occurs, they find it difficult to shape their living conditions or control their destinies. The experiences of Jack and Zoë are very telling in this regard. For example, the story of Jack opens one morning after a series of interpersonal conflicts leave him living in his car.

Jack woke up in the back seat of his 1981 Ford Mustang, which was parked at the end of the street next to a neighborhood park. His memory of the events of the previous evening was kind of fuzzy. He was living, temporarily, with a friend he had known since high school. He lost his apartment last year, and his parents tired of his 'behavior problems' after about 10 months and kicked him out. His friend Tim was his last hope.

Jack remembered seeing Tim's wife come out of the bathroom after her shower yesterday afternoon. He was lying on their couch, finishing the last few bottles of a 12-pack of beer he purchased earlier that day. Jack said something to her that he thought was kind of clever, but she reacted by turning back around and locking herself in the bathroom. When Tim came home a few minutes later, he told Jack it was time for him to leave.

The scene that followed was typical of his three-week stay with his old friend. They screamed and yelled at each other for about 30 minutes, and Jack said some things about his wife that he now regretted. However, unlike previous fights where they made up in the end and decided to give living together one more try, Tim insisted that he go immediately.

Jack realizes he cannot live in a car much longer without attracting unwanted attention, but he is unable to develop an acceptable alternative. Tim was the only friend willing to let him stay for awhile, and his older brother and parents have a restraining order against him that forbids contact. His only other sibling, a sister, moved to another state some time ago without giving him her new address or phone number. Jack recalls the last time he was with his family, and his mother tearfully handed him a piece of paper with the name and address of a public shelter for homeless men. At the time Jack was insulted by the gesture, but he begins to realize this facility may be his only housing option and reluctantly accedes to give it a try.

Zoë also becomes homeless gradually, though the path she and her family take has its own nuances. The story picks up at the start of her spiral:

Six months later, Zoë discovered she was pregnant again. She told her mother immediately, expecting her mother to be excited about the birth of a true love child. However, her mother reacted angrily, telling Zoë in no uncertain terms that there was no room in their overcrowded apartment for another baby. Besides, she could no longer afford to pay for the extra food and clothing as well as the diapers and other baby products Zoë's children would need.

At first Zoë was disheartened by this response, but her new man greeted her news with an all-together different reaction. He was excited about the birth of the child, and he invited Zoë and her daughter to move in with him while they waited for the baby to be born. His place was even smaller than her mother's was, so they decided to turn his mini living room into a nursery. Their home would be cramped for awhile, but they planned to move to larger accommodations after he received his next raise and promotion to supervisor.

Sadly, things did not go as planned. Her man never received the promotion; instead, he was reduced to part-time status due to a slowdown of activity at the factory. He now earned about two-thirds of his previous income, and they barely were able to pay their bills. A few months later the landlord informed them that the building had been sold to developers who planned to renovate the units and sell them as condominiums. They would have three months within which they must either purchase their home or vacate the premises. Given their current financial situation, they were forced to leave.

Zoë and her husband are compelled to split up since they are unable to find an affordable alternative or a relative or friend willing to house them. At first Zoë and her children move to the home of her man's mother. However, after an alcoholic uncle tries to rape her, she relocates to her own grandmother's house. As noted earlier, they are only allowed to stay one night, and Zoë takes her children and meager belongings to a public shelter for homeless families. This facility lacks privacy and most of their possessions are stolen almost as soon as they arrive. They move again, this time to a private shelter with a more secure environment, but they are asked to leave before they are able to afford more permanent housing. Zoë becomes frightened that they will end up living on the streets.

Consumption restrictions and meager possessions

Impoverished consumers face restricted consumption options that limit their ability to fulfill even the most basic needs. As a consequence, these individuals consume goods and services that are unacceptable to middle-class citizens under ordinary conditions. The term 'secondary consumers' is used to describe their material lives (Hill and Stamey, 1990), and it suggests a lengthy list of scavenging and recycling to acquire discarded goods. Jack's experience of material restriction is telling. After leaving the municipal shelter where he encounters poor treatment, Jack decides to sell his car and move his few possessions under a bridge in a secluded area. He goes into hibernation there, and he experiences new hardships associated with lack of lighting, heating, and cooking. After nearly freezing from the falling night temperatures and running low on supplies, Jack eventually resurfaces only to face significant consumption restrictions that threaten his survival.

In the end, he decided he had no other option but to leave temporarily in search of food. He calmed himself by noting that no one had bothered him so far. Jack checked his wallet and discovered he had exactly $28.33. He put the money back in his wallet and placed it securely in his front pocket. Then he climbed up the ladder, waited for traffic to clear, and jumped up onto the highway.

He decided to go back to the supermarket he patronized during his last shopping trip. Jack made a mental note of what he needed this time. He still had enough toilet paper and toothpaste for the only hygiene activities available to him now. The peanut butter and jelly worked out okay, but the bread had gotten a bit hard over time. Drinks were cold enough – maybe too cold. A hot cup of coffee or soup would be nice but impossible.

Jack entered the market at a brisk pace and grabbed a handheld basket rather than a shopping cart. If he couldn't carry his items in the store, there was no way he would be able to transport them home. He concentrated on foods that were wrapped in single-serving portions. While they were probably more expensive, such foodstuffs were less likely to go stale over time. The cashier charged him $23.50 for the load, and Jack made a mental note that he had $4.83 left, about the same amount he started with before he sold his car.

One result of material restrictions is that individuals are limited to a few utilitarian items that they are able to find safe storage for or keep with them at all times. While the lack of income is always an issue, institutional or logistical constraints also make accumulation of items problematical (see Hill, 1991). This is particularly true over time as the individual or family must move from one location to another as they seek accommodation. Zoë provides a vivid example. She grows up under dire circumstances after the breakup of her parents, and her material world takes a turn for the worse. The situation improves somewhat during early adulthood until the father of her daughter has his wages reduced due to cutbacks by his employer. Zoë moves into a municipal shelter for women and children and their resulting circumstances are quite severe.

> Zoë was assigned living area No. 45, and she was handed sheets and blankets for two beds, three pillows, and some towels, a small tube of toothpaste, and a toothbrush for personal hygiene. The woman told her that the facility was not responsible for the loss of her possessions, and that Zoë was advised to keep them with her at all times. Her mind wandered to a scene where she was bathing her children in a shower stall with their suitcase somehow in attendance. How could that possibly work?
>
> When the woman finished her instructions, Zoë asked if there were any food at the facility for her daughters. The woman told her that food and drink were prohibited in the living quarters, but that there was a large group of fast food restaurants surrounding the facility that accepted city meal coupons. She then passed Zoë $12.00 in script – $5.00 for herself and $3.50 for each of her daughters.
>
> With her family and cargo in tow, Zoë walked down the hallway to the living quarters in search of No. 45. As she entered the room, its size and the level of commotion caught her by surprise. There were 10 rows of enclosed areas that were at least five deep. It took Zoë several minutes to locate her dwelling, since the ordering of the living areas was not readily apparent. She noted immediately that all four shelters surrounding her abode were occupied, and she began to feel claustrophobic. Zoë quickly made the two beds using the sheets and blankets provided. Both were lumpy and worn, and the sheets themselves were threadbare in several places. When this task was completed, she changed the clothing of both daughters and removed the money and identification papers from her suitcase.

Role of the media

The media play a role in communicating the standards for acceptable quantities of goods and services within a society. Impoverished children learn what is available for consumers, and they develop a great sense of need or desire for many products. Over time they establish a baseline standard of living against which they measure their options. Clearly, they come up short, with little indication that the future offers improvement in middle-class consumption opportunities. Eddie's struggle to rise above the culture of poverty provides a powerful example of material benchmarking against cultural norms. Following incarceration, he finally has time to stop and reflect upon the circumstances that led to his arrest. Eddie's thoughts turn to daydreams about various events in his life, especially the best of times when he could buy anything he wanted and was considered a success by his peers. The following excerpt of a memory from his youth demonstrates the role of the media in the formation of his material desires.

> After school Eddie often would go home and sit in front of the television set with his siblings to watch their favorite programs. They enjoyed a variety of cartoon shows as well as situation comedies that portrayed family life. He particularly liked sitcoms such as the *Cosby Show* and *Family Ties*, and his favorite episodes involved holiday events and birthdays. Meals were lovingly prepared and there was always an abundance of his most wanted foods. Families exchanged gifts and Santa Claus visited each year, bringing special presents for everyone.
>
> Eddie liked the advertisements as much as the shows themselves, especially during the time period between Thanksgiving and Christmas. While the programs portrayed the importance of family during the holidays, the commercials demonstrated that the real meaning was in material goods. An endless parade of toys, games, clothes, videos, and other items too numerous to mention danced before his eyes, and he looked at them in eager anticipation. He was fully aware that they were available to good girls and boys, and Eddie felt entitled to his fair share.
>
> Unfortunately, Eddie never experienced holidays like the TV families did. Church groups from more affluent communities donated most of the foodstuffs that they consumed at these meals, and they consisted of a variety of canned and packaged meats, vegetables, and starches. The food wasn't bad, but it certainly did not live up to his fantasies of an old-fashioned holiday feast. Gift giving at Christmas was even more disappointing. Eddie would make lengthy lists of desired items that he

had seen on television, and he would send them to Santa Claus for delivery. During the best of times he would receive one of the smaller toys he had requested, or some piece of clothing that his mother felt he needed such as socks or shoes.

Once on welfare and with an adult sense of the resulting consumer restrictions, Anita blunts her children's emerging interest in material possessions. For example, she ends regular trips to a local shopping mall, one of the few enjoyable distractions from their otherwise grueling lives, because of their insistence that Anita buy them products she cannot afford. Of course, she does not succeed in stemming their demands because images of the joys from this abundance are so widespread, lending credibility/authenticity to their requests. The excerpt below captures the dilemma as Anita attempts to cut short fantasies without damaging their evolving sense of self:

To make matters worse, her children were reaching the age when they begin expressing desires for the myriad products available within our society. Almost daily Anita would hear from one of the older boys that he wanted a particular toy he saw on television, to go to the latest Disney movie, or to have dinner at McDonald's and get a Happy Meal. She briefly considered getting rid of their television set all together in order to stunt their urges, but she decided against it when she realized it was their primary form of entertainment.

Holidays and birthdays during their first year on welfare were particularly traumatic for them. For months prior to [Christmas], the television paraded an endless series of programs and commercials before her children's eyes that showed Santa Claus and loving families enjoying the holiday season. These scenes typically contained beautifully adorned trees, brightly colored seasonal decorations, and individually selected gifts that demonstrated either their love for one another or the fact that they had been good all year long. Anita's children anxiously asked for her reassurance that they had behaved properly during the year so that Santa would come to their house with his bag full of toys. They also were concerned that the small tree and meager decorations in their home didn't display the proper Christmas spirit. Anita told them they were all good boys and that Santa Claus came without regard for the quality of the decor in a home.

Inevitably the day was a disappointment for everybody. All three children rose early, with her eldest son leading the charge. As they looked at the meager number of gifts under the tree, Anita could sense the drop in their enthusiasm level. The children had two items each for them to open, but neither gift was very exciting or desirable. The holiday meal was similarly uninspiring, with few additions beyond their ordinary evening meals. As Anita expected, her eldest son asked what happened and why Santa Claus had ignored the Christmas list he had so carefully prepared and mailed to the North Pole. She responded that Santa wasn't able to make it to their apartment this year, but he promised to bring them extra gifts next time around. This reply satisfied his curiosity for the moment, but Anita wondered what she would tell him if things failed to improve by the following holiday season.

Tenuous present/uncertain future

Even if the poor marshal the full power of resources within their communities, their ability to prosper materially is suspect. The fact is resources are severely limited, suggesting that creative utilization and development would still leave poor community members with unmet essential needs. As a result, efforts fall short, demonstrating the ability of the poor to survive, much less thrive, materially is unlikely. With the tenuous nature of their present consumer lives, opportunities to vision a more positive future is constrained. At best, the prospect of living a life similar to more affluent counterparts is unclear; at worst, their future is restricted like their past and they feel they may fall back into self-defeating behaviors. The following sections of stories involving Tammy and Fast Eddie provide a glimpse into the tenuous nature of material lives of the poor from a long-term perspective. At one extreme, Tammy, whose community social capital is well developed, visualizes continued strength even in the face of an uncertain future.

As Tammy sat alongside the bed holding her mother's hand, she reflected on what things would be like without this woman's presence as a family member and a community advocate. Her mother was the matriarch of the clan – the person who brought everyone together for Sunday dinners, the holidays, and other special occasions. Even during the difficult financial period that followed the closing of the mines, she was able to marshal the resources of the collective group to make sure that no one went without food, clothing, shelter, or transportation. Sharing was a given among them, and this reciprocity helped them truly appreciate one another. Her mother made sure that they learned this important lesson well.

Tammy realized that her life wasn't much different from her mother's. While her husband remained in good health, the loss of his job and their precarious financial situation meant that Tammy was required to work at menial jobs for the foreseeable future in order to survive. Her daughter was experiencing difficulties with a second pregnancy, and Tammy planned to spend as much time as possible assisting her child once her own mother passed. Her younger son had returned home after several years in the big city, and Tammy and her husband were helping him establish a new personal and professional life in their small town.

As Tammy looked down into the face of her mother, she couldn't help but smile. The torch had passed from mother to daughter and the exchange had been seamless. Tammy imagined that in a few years time she would have the same reputation as her mother within their community. The situation in their town may never improve, but her family, friends, and neighbors were here to stay and they were going to do everything in their power to improve their lives. When it came to helping others, Tammy had an excellent teacher in her mother. She hoped that her own daughter would be a willing pupil and exercise a leadership role in their town when her time came.

Tammy's awareness of current and future circumstances is the result of a long-term struggle with her mother's illness. In the end, the failure of the formal medical system gives rise to an alternative treatment and delivery system that is community-based. The strengths of herself, her mother, and the larger community are revealed through this crisis, and Tammy grows to appreciate the social fabric and its meaning to the citizens' material lives. On the other hand, Fast Eddie lives under severe restriction that does not support his growing material needs. After his incarceration, Eddie initially experiences great difficulty adapting to life within the reform program. Strict regimen and loss of personal freedoms are very disconcerting to him. He rebels but eventually follows the rules to avoid dismissal and transfer to a more rigid detention facility. As Eddie increasingly engages this insular community, he begins to experience successes that bolster his sense of self and perception of his potential within the larger society after release. Unfortunately, the resources within his community are inadequate, and Eddie is drawn back to a life of crime.

As the days passed, the initial euphoria about his future prospects evaporated and was replaced with a dark resignation. Most of the schools he hoped to attend were beyond his financial reach, and his ability to secure a loan to cover tuition and expenses was severely constrained because of his felony conviction. The managers of the clothing stores in the mall almost laughed at his equivalency diploma, treating him like an educational second-class citizen. The few that were desperate enough to give him an application withdrew their offers when his background check identified him as a convicted car thief.

Eddie felt that he was at one of the lowest points in his life. After all of his work at Saint Peter's [reform school] he was no better off than he was before he left the neighborhood. Eddie was unable to move forward – none of the options he fantasized about during the latter part of his detention were viable alternatives. He also was uncomfortable going backward – living his previous life would most likely result in real jail time that would make his prior incarceration look like a picnic.

After living in this limbo state for awhile, Eddie drifted back to the streets, seeking comfort by reestablishing relationships with the friends he had recently abandoned. Without money he was seriously constrained in what he could do, and he was dependent upon the successful criminals in his neighborhood, who had taken his place while he was away, for their benevolence. He hoped he could avoid returning to a life of crime, but what else could he do? There was nowhere left to turn.

SOCIAL MARKETING IMPLICATIONS

Much social marketing directed at poor consumers attempts to provide them with information or options that they might not otherwise have or discern. This strategy is appropriate under certain circumstances, but it often fails to recognize the lenses through which poor citizens experience the material world. For example, providing mothers with extensive advice on nutrition and labeling only facilitates better diets for their families if affordable shopping exists within their communities. Also, consider promotions that ask mothers to make sure that they vaccinate their children against avoidable diseases without easing access to medical services for more immediate concerns. Consistent with media portrayals about family life and the lived reality of the poor, social marketing may serve to exacerbate feelings of inadequacy and other negative emotions as described in this chapter.

One possible shift that has occurred occasionally is to concentrate on the strengths of impoverished communities rather than on their weaknesses (see Lee et al., 1999). With this perspective in mind, social marketers abandon the vulnerability context in which they often view the poor and exchange it for one that emphasizes social capital that helps their neighborhoods survive or even thrive under various conditions. Ideas and behaviors are never imposed on lower socioeconomic communities but instead are negotiated in ways that allow the voices of the people living under such dire circumstances to be heard and followed. Thus, any resulting informational remedies for social problems seek to inform impoverished consumers of new ways to utilize inherent advantages. Changes also seek communal action rather than individual efforts alone, since therein lies their true power.

Of course, a focus on strengths such as social capital does not preclude the need for additional resources to augment whatever is currently available. Clearly, the abilities and capabilities that exist within impoverished communities are limited and insufficient to meet all physical, mental, and emotional requirements of healthful living. Therefore, social marketers must advocate on both sides of the exchange equation so that non-profit leadership, policymakers, and philanthropists develop a different vantage point from which to view the individuals they seek to help. They must work with constituencies who share the desire to serve, so that accumulated efforts recognize and empower poor citizens in ways that are consonant with the treatment of equals rather than an extension of paternalism. Anything less must be deemed unacceptable by the parties involved.

Therefore, the task of social marketing mirrors that of public–private partnerships. These cooperatives negotiate with a dual marketplace that often has radical differences of opinion and criteria for success. Work in Portland, Oregon by the author is an interesting case in point (Hill, 2002a). The city faced a crisis when 1,500 homeless teenagers took up residence in a section of the downtown, prostituting themselves, dealing and using illegal drugs, and panhandling for money. To solve the problem, Portland policymakers called together a collection of people who represented various constituencies, including business people, clergy, social workers, academics, and community activists. The initial meetings revealed stark differences in perspectives and approaches that formed serious roadblocks to consensus-seeking by local government leadership.

In the end, successful resolution required the infusion of the homeless themselves, allowing each constituency to interact with, and experience vicariously, their lives on the streets. Over time, a significant shift occurred, whereby the focus on differences between groups based on preconceived notions moved to a shared viewpoint built upon first-hand knowledge. The system designed to resolve this situation was less about compromise and more about serving the interests of youths whose lives left them with few alternatives.

Social marketers should take note of such community-based accomplishments as they ponder suitable strategies and tactics. The people they hope to reach may have very different goals and behaviors in mind when juxtaposed against funders for societal initiatives, and this gap must be closed for a truly successful conclusion to occur.

Step-by-step application

Let us examine this particular social marketing issue within the context of the consumer cycle of poverty noted earlier. This process begins with loss/lack of familial/friendship love that often leaves impoverished consumers without recourse. Clearly, the homeless teenagers in Portland are no longer in contact with their parents or extended family, or with adult supervisors and other guardians. They were often described as 'throwaway' and 'runaway' youths who were not welcome to return to previous housing options. Firms with social marketing interests, including non-profits and government entities, need to find ways to encourage at-risk families to reduce interpersonal stresses and avoid such separations from occurring in the first place, to support transitional housing options when young people naturally mature but may lack the resources to make the leap to complete independence, and to promote constructive methods of continual contact between these teens and the positive adults in their lives.

Regardless, some subset of these youths will eventually end up homeless and fall into impoverished conditions that spiral out of control until they have few options to sleeping under bridges, in wooded areas, or out in the open near enclosed structures. The social marketing task is to encourage these youths to enter the shelter system instead of engaging in illegal and illicit behaviors on the streets. One of the major roadblocks to action is their fear that they will be forced to receive rehabilitation or various forms of treatment for substance abuse and mental health problems, or be reunited with parental figures/guardians or face outstanding warrants for their arrests. In order to smooth the way, social marketing can be employed to create messages that recognize their various stages of willingness to address such circumstances, and to present information that allows for entry into the system on their terms rather than those of business owners or government officials.

In a similar vein, the decision to remain on the streets rather than seek or have access to appropriate shelter leaves them with little more than the clothes on their backs and a few possessions that they can keep on their persons at all times or find secure hiding places for in out-of-the-way environs. Such circumstances leave these youths with few reasonable opportunities for safe and secure housing, adequate health care, and food and clothing. The social marketing challenge, then, is to help these teens see that the availability of basic commodities exists in a fashion that is consistent with their current willingness to enter into a new set of relationships with adults. Such messages give credence to their perspective of why they went on the streets in the first place and their lack of trust for the legal system of support that has failed them in the past. Thus, the provision of a basic bundle of goods and services must be given with no strings attached, and because of the inherent dignity of the person rather than as a type of reward for their capitulation.

Standard media portrayals of family life and nearly unlimited access to goods and services make for additional sources of alienation for these homeless teenagers. They see clearly what is available for some and count themselves as among the unfortunate 'other' who must find satisfaction using different and often unorthodox paths. As a result, their perceptions of their behaviors do not include either the guilt or shame society hopes they might experience, culminating instead in a form of 'sneaky thrill' that is justified based on their misfortunes of birth. While the ability of social marketers to challenge media portrayals is limited at best, targeted messages to youths that demonstrate recognition of the hardships associated with their lives, the unconventional nature of their relationships with adults, and the importance of connections on the streets may signal greater empathy.

Finally, the tenuous nature of their circumstances and poor future prospects are difficult to overcome. The typical homeless youth is less focused on long-term growth and prosperity and more focused on short-term survival and immediate gratification. Accordingly, they often make decisions that sacrifice their future health and options in lieu of the here and now. Social marketers may hope to change this decision calculus by showing them the negative consequences of short-run thinking, providing them with a clear path to change that is consonant with their needs and abilities, and demonstrating appropriate adult role modeling in a consistent and caring environment. At some level, messages must communicate the inherent value of these teenagers to our society in ways that help them rise above well-worn negative self-images that keep them ensconced in a cycle of poverty. A difficult and novel task indeed!

KEY WORDS: Global poverty; consumer behavior; social marketing; restricted consumption; culture of poverty.

Key insights

- Despite the difficult circumstances of global poverty experienced by much of humankind, the culture of poverty myth does not hold true for most impoverished consumers who actively manage the meager resources at their disposal to survive in the material world.
- The negativity associated with extreme poverty is exacerbated by the media, which often portrays the cornucopia of goods and services available within the larger global material culture as if it is, or should be, available to all citizens.
- The most important task for social marketers is to counter the belief that self-worth and consumption are co-related, so that the poor can recognize that their real value as human beings is not contingent upon material abundance that is beyond their current economic capabilities.

REFERENCES

Andreasen, A.R. (1975) *The Disadvantaged Consumer*. New York: The Free Press.

Bahram, A., Dhanda, K. and Hill, R.P. (2004) 'A model of consumption and environmental degradation: Making the case for sustainable consumer behavior', *Journal of Human Development*, 5(November): 417–432.

Caplovitz, D. (1963) *The Poor Pay More*. New York: The Free Press.

Chossudovsky, M. (1998) 'Global poverty in the late 20th century', *Journal of International Affairs*, 52(Fall): 293–311.

Dollar, D. (2005) 'Globalization, poverty, and inequality since 1980', *The World Bank Research Observer*, 20(Fall): 145–175.

Hill, R.P. (1991) 'Homeless women, special possessions, and the meaning of "Home": An ethnographic case study', *Journal of Consumer Research*, 18(December): 298–310.

Hill, R.P. (1992) 'Homeless children: Coping with material losses', *Journal of Consumer Affairs*, 26(Winter): 274–287.

Hill, R.P. (2001) 'Surviving in a material world: Evidence from ethnographic consumer research on people in poverty', *Journal of Contemporary Ethnography*, 30(4): 364–391.

Hill, R.P. (2002a) 'Service provision through public–private partnerships: An ethnography of service delivery to homeless teenagers', *Journal of Service Research*, 4(May): 278–289.

Hill, R.P. (2002b) 'Stalking the poverty consumer: A retrospective examination of modern ethical dilemmas', *Journal of Business Ethics*, 37(May): 209–219.

Hill, R.P. and Bahram, A. (1999) 'Global poverty and the United Nations', *Journal of Public Policy & Marketing*, 18(Fall): 135–146.

Hill, R.P. and Jeannie, G. (2007) 'The consumer culture of poverty: Behavioral research findings and their implications

IMPOVERISHED CONSUMERS AND SOCIAL MARKETING

in an ethnographic context', *Journal of American Culture*, 30(March): 81–95.

Hill, R.P. and Stamey, M. (1990) 'The homeless in America: An examination of possessions and consumption behaviors', *Journal of Consumer Research*, 17(December): 303–321.

Hill, R.P. and Stephens, D.L. (1997) Impoverished consumers and consumer behavior: The case of AFDC mothers', *Journal of Macromarketing*, 17(Fall): 32–48.

Holloway, R. and Cardozo, R.N. (1969) *Consumer Problems and Marketing Patterns in Low Income Neighborhoods: An Exploratory Study*. Minneapolis, MN: Graduate School of Business Administration.

Irelan, L.M. and Besner, A. (1966) 'Low income outlook on life', in L.M. Irelan (ed), *Low Income Lifestyles*. Washington, DC: US Department of Health, Education, and Welfare, pp. 1–8.

Lee, R.G., Ozanne, J.L. and Hill, R.P. (1999) 'Improving service encounters through resource sensitivity: The case of health care delivery in Appalachia', *Journal of Public Policy & Marketing*, 18(Fall): 230–248

Milanovic, B. (2007) 'Global income inequality: What it is and why it matters', in K.S. Jomo and J. Baudot (eds), *Flat World, Big Gaps: Economic Liberalization, Globalization, Poverty & Inequality*. New York: Zed Books, pp. 1–23.

Ozanne, J.L., Hill, R.P. and Wright, N.D. (1998) 'Juvenile delinquents' use of consumption as cultural resistance: Implications for juvenile reform programs and public policy', *Journal of Public Policy and Marketing*, 17(Fall): 185 -196.

Richards, L. (1966) 'Consumer practices of the poor', in L.M. Irelan (ed), *Low Income Lifestyles*. Washington, DC: US Department of Health, Education, and Welfare, pp. 69–83.

Sturdivant, F.D. (1969) *The Ghetto Marketplace*. New York: The Free Press.

UNDP (1998) *Human Development Report 1998: Changing Today's Consumption Patterns for Tomorrow's Human Development*. New York: Oxford University Press.

UNDP (2001) *Human Development Report 2001: Making New Technologies Work for Human Development*. New York: Oxford University Press.

Wasson, R.R. and Hill, R.P. (1998) 'The process of becoming homeless: An investigation of families in poverty', *Journal of Consumer Affairs*, 32(2): 320–332.

22

Social Marketing and International Development

Georgina Cairns, Bruce Mackay and
Laura MacDonald

INTRODUCTION

This chapter describes some of the ways in which social marketing has contributed to international development. The chapter outlines how social marketing practice in the developing world has, in turn, been shaped by the context of international development, as well as the social and economic conditions of the countries involved. The content is presented predominantly from the perspective of the practitioner, as it draws mainly from the authors' own experiences of working in developing countries.

The chapter begins with a brief outline of what, for the purposes of this chapter, we mean by international development and poverty. This is followed by an introduction to the origins and evolution of social marketing in developing countries.

Five key context-specific influencers that have shaped the nature and scope of social marketing are highlighted. We call these influencers the '5Bs'– *Benefactors*, *Branding*, *Benefits*, *Barriers* and *Behaviour Change Communications*. Each of the 5Bs is briefly described, and discussed using examples mainly drawn from the authors' own experiences. We suggest that the influence of the 5Bs has resulted in some differences between typical developing and developed world social marketing approaches and practice. We suggest there has been limited sharing of these different experiences as well as the insights that may be gained from such exchange. More specifically, there is limited dissemination in the developed

world of information about social marketing practice in developing countries. We suggest this creates an asymmetric knowledge base, and is a lost learning opportunity. Greater awareness and understanding of social marketing practice and thinking in the developing world offers insights that can contribute to social marketing thinking and practice in general.

The chapter concludes with recommendations for more efforts to explore, analyze and assimilate the experiences of social marketing in international development among the international social marketing community and its shared knowledge base.

A DEFINITION OF INTERNATIONAL DEVELOPMENT

International development is generally understood as policies, strategies and interventions supported by foreign assistance and intended to alleviate poverty among countries that are collectively described as the 'developing world'.

The developing world is as heterogeneous and diverse as the developed world, and there are many ways to understand and characterize those parts of the world where substantial proportions of the population live in extreme poverty. Two globally recognized methods of monitoring poverty are the World Bank poverty thresholds based on daily expenditure and the United Nations (UN) composite poverty indices.

The World Bank (2008) estimates there are more than 2.5 billion people living on less than $2 per day. At income levels of less than $2 per day, there are many dimensions to the deprivation experienced, but all of those living at this level of subsistence are subject to insecurity of livelihoods, periods of hunger, limited or no access to health care or education and reduced life expectancy. For example, life expectancy in the UK for children born in 2008 is estimated to be 80 years. In India, this falls to 64, and in the most populous country in Africa, Nigeria, life expectancy is 49 years. Adult HIV prevalence rates on the African continent average 4.9%, compared with 0.5% in the European region (World Health Organization, 2010).

The UN uses a composite indicator that reflects the multi-dimensional nature of poverty. This indicator is based on access to education and health care, living standards, as well as ability to participate in the life of the local community and decision-making processes that affect personal well-being and autonomy. A revised version of the UN's composite measure, the Multidimensional Poverty Index (MPI), was introduced in 2010. Using the MPI criteria, 1.7 billion people living in 104 countries live in extreme poverty (UNDP, 2010).

International development became established as a concept after the Second World War. International development is a dynamic, multi-disciplinary and complex subject area in its own right and we do not attempt to systematically explain or explore this. Instead, observations on how and where social marketing practice fits with contemporary international development themes and activities are used to explore the unique characteristics of social marketing practice in developing countries.

International development is the term used to describe foreign assistance intended to alleviate poverty in countries and regions of the world where large proportions of the population live in absolute poverty. International development may be delivered as a single, transformative project to address a specific problem or may comprise a program of related activities aimed at alleviating poverty or specific contributory factors. International development is distinct from crisis management activities such as disaster relief and humanitarian aid, although closely linked under the broader banner of international aid.

In developing countries, infrastructure and public services such as sanitation, utilities and roads are usually underdeveloped, and poor people, especially, may have little or no access to them. Extreme competition for, and inadequate management of, natural resources and weak governance and judiciary also tend to be prevalent and exacerbate the challenges associated with the lack of basic public utilities and services. International development is concerned with sustainable poverty alleviation strategies that build infrastructure and human capacity to improve life chances. Development initiatives may address systemic, structural barriers to development progress as well as providing grassroots support aimed at empowering and enabling poor people to take action to improve their daily lives and future prospects.

The causes of poverty are complex and many factors are both symptomatic of, and causal to poverty. Suboptimal health coupled with poor standards of health care; low levels of economic growth; lack of public investment; as well as livelihood and income insecurity among the working age population all contribute to the poverty trap. The targeting of one or more of these factors (as well as others such as governance, equality and sustainability) is one of the ways that international development works to disrupt the poverty cycle. Historically, most (but not all) social marketing in developing countries has focused on improving poor people's health. Most of this chapter therefore will focus on the health issues, where social marketing has been most active and made most impact, namely: family planning, HIV/AIDS prevention and control and malaria prevention and control interventions.

International development is also characterized by at least partial funding and/or other forms of assistance, from foreign sources, such as cooperative expert initiatives. Historically, these foreign sources of assistance have been direct aid from developed countries (bilateral aid) multilateral agencies, such as the World Bank and non-profit organizations such as Population Services International (PSI) who may raise funds and other support resources from public, private and/or civil society sources.

Early in the post-war period, international development often emphasized technical solutions, 'modernization' of poor country infrastructure and economic growth. This paradigm is now outdated within the international development community and has been replaced by an emphasis on building human capacity and measuring development progress by gains in life expectancy, literacy, education, human rights and living standards, as well as economic growth. This paradigm strongly emphasizes the overarching goal of expanding the range of things that people *can do* or *be* in life, and is embodied in the United Nations Human Development Approach. The Human Development Approach envisions four important broad objectives for effective poverty alleviation: equity, sustainability, productivity

1. Eradicate extreme poverty and hunger
2. Achieve universal primary education
3. Promote gender equality and empower women
4. Reduce child mortality
5. Improve maternal health
6. Combat HIV/AIDS, malaria and other diseases
7. Ensure environmental sustainability
8. Develop a global partnership for development

Figure 22.1   Millennium Development Goals summarized

Source: http://www.un.org/millenniumgoals/.

and empowerment. The eight Millennium Development Goals (MDGs) adopted by the United Nations in September 2000 provide specific indicators and time-bound focus for the aims of the Human Development Approach to development. Summaries of the MDGs are provided in Figure 22.1.

In addition to paradigmatic conceptions of poverty's causes and solutions, and prevailing socio-economic and political conditions in developing countries, international development initiatives are also shaped by the motives of those who fund and deliver development assistance. Common drivers for international development projects and programs are:

*   A commitment to the general emancipation of women, and the specific idea that 'children by choice' and good health are human rights to which all are entitled.
*   A belief that 'development' can, indeed should, be actively encouraged rather than be left to happen of its own accord.
*   A commitment to 'transitional assistance': that is, aid from rich to poor countries that have recently emerged from colonialist rule.
*   Science and technology innovation – a very familiar driver of change at all levels of national socio-economic status.
*   The motivation of individuals determined to 'do something' about the plight of others, be it due to famine, disease, oppression or any other root cause.
*   Concerns about population growth in poor countries, and misperceptions that this is the root cause of poverty.[1]

In summary, the working context of this chapter is the application of social marketing that contributes to contemporary international development goals and approaches which aim to improve the lives and life chances of those living in extreme poverty.

THE FOUNDATIONS OF SOCIAL MARKETING ARE IN THE DEVELOPING WORLD

The concept of social marketing as an approach for social change was 'born' in the developing world in 1967 when the Nirodh condom intervention was launched in India. The government was committed to family planning, and Indian and the US experts at the Indian Institute of Management partnered with FMCG (fast moving consumer goods) companies to distribute condoms alongside their own products. This large-scale, successful intervention used segmentation, mass media communications and strategic distribution methods to promote acceptance and access to family planning (Chandy et al., 1965; Walsh et al., 1993).

Social marketing's naming ceremony occurred in the developed world after this when Kotler and Zaltman (1971) famously used the term to describe the application and potential power of commercial marketing methods to achieve social change. Five years later came the first report of social marketing in Africa by Black and Harvey (1976).

Development professionals in bilateral and multilateral donor organizations started using and reporting on the outcomes of social marketing approaches in the 1980s and momentum slowly grew. In January 1995, the British Overseas Development Agency advertised in *Marketing Week* for consultants who could advise on contraceptive social marketing. One of the authors of this chapter entered the sector via this route.

The UK's Department for International Development (DFID), the German-owned development bank KfW and the United States Agency for International Development (USAID) are some of the bilateral agencies using social marketing approaches to support their development strategies. The United Nations organizations UNFPA and UNAIDS have also been proactive in the adoption of social marketing for international development. Some of the largest non-governmental organizations (NGOs), including Population Services International (PSI), DKT International, Marie Stopes International and the Academy for Educational Development (AED), specialize in social marketing approaches in their strategic planning and operational delivery. Local NGOs such as the Ghana Social Marketing Foundation, the Greenstar Network in Pakistan, the Society for Family Health in Nigeria and the Social Marketing Company in Bangladesh also use social marketing approaches.

In 2003, DFID published its first review of social marketing (Meadley et al., 2003). The review estimated British government expenditure on social marketing to be £20–30 million per annum, and estimated that this represented 10–15% of donor funding for social marketing worldwide.

Despite the significant scale of funding that donors and development agencies are committing to marketing orientation in projects and programmes, many health and development practitioners and planners are only just beginning to embrace marketing principles such as the 4Ps and exchange theory. Ten years ago they would have been more suspicious, or even downright sceptical. 'But you can't sell the pill like paint', said a horrified in-country adviser, whose head office had awarded the company of one of the chapter authors a $7 million contract to do just that. But just as social marketing has gained increasing recognition in developed countries, so it has become an increasingly popular framework for facilitating behaviour change in the developing world. HIV and AIDS have put condom social marketing firmly on the map. Similarly, dramatic and visible health impacts of a consumer-centric approach to the promotion of mosquito nets and substantial improvements in the distribution and quality of family planning products and their accessibility to women have generated much interest in the application of marketing techniques to public health challenges.

UNIQUE CHARACTERISTICS OF SOCIAL MARKETING IN DEVELOPING COUNTRIES

Social marketing in developing countries most often involves the promotion of, and improved access to, products such as condoms and mosquito nets and services such as family planning advice and screening for malaria, rather than primarily marketing of ideas and lifestyle changes. Messaging is therefore shaped around a key product or service. Supplementary activities, particularly Behaviour Change Communications and Branding strategies, underpin core behavioural benefits. Typical supplementary benefits, highly valued by users, are quality assurance, sustainability and lower prices or free products and services. Some initiatives are described as social marketing and some are not. Regardless of labels, those which adopt a user-centred approach to planning, delivery and evaluation, drawing on the principles of exchange theory, supported by marketing tools such as insight research, segmentation and competition analysis to achieve their goals, clearly have underlying social marketing principles.

The evolution, delivery and impacts of social marketing in developing countries are a little different to social marketing practice in developed industrialized economies. We suggest this can be best illustrated using the 5Bs, so we have organized the chapter around these headings. We hope this helps explain in what ways and why social marketing in developing countries has developed unique characteristics, while retaining the core principle of voluntary behavior change as a driver of large-scale social change for public good.

An estimate of a typical breakdown of a social marketing budget by one of the authors of this chapter (who has been designing, managing and evaluating social marketing projects in the developing world for over 15 years) illustrates how social marketing in the developing world is organized by and around the 5Bs:

- A typical *Benefactor* budget is likely to be in the range of $0.5–10 million, for 3–5 years of work. Typically, this will split down to approximately 25% on each of the other 'Bs' as follows:

  ○ delivering *Benefits*, through the large-scale procurement and packaging of products and services that enable positive behavior choices;
  ○ tackling *Barriers* to access – for example, by establishing or improving distribution logistics of products and services;
  ○ using *Behavior Change Communications*, most commonly through mass media channels, to promote new behavioral norms and appropriate use of products and services; and
  ○ developing and sustaining *Branding* by investing in technical activities such as quality control, and relational marketing activities such as follow-up customer care.

Although many individuals working in international development still have limited knowledge and experience of marketing, they are interested in using it for the same reasons that social marketing has become increasingly popular in developed countries. They will have learned for themselves or heard from colleagues that socially marketing products and services seems to work – or, at least, work better than alternative methods such as distribution through government clinic or short-term availability of free products. The application of the 4Ps in family planning for example has demonstrated how proven communication (promotion) and segmentation (product choice and targeted promotions) techniques can efficiently and safely (price) provide (place) the support their clients need and want.

Development workers know that the underpaid staff at government clinics are often overwhelmed with patients, and have little time to counsel a woman worried about the side-effects of taking the pill. They may also remember they had the opposite problem in the 1970s and 1980s when many of the specialist family planning clinics they used to fund had highly trained but underemployed staff. Additionally, they are aware that marketing can play a highly effective role in scaling up outreach activities to bring about large-scale access of services. Public health professionals know that commercial distribution of drugs to privately owned, often unlicensed 'medicine shops' works pretty well, even in the poorest countries, and that public sector supply is likely to be erratic. The profit-led commercial distribution system, for example, provides access for millions of Pakistani women who want to use modern contraception but who cannot walk further than the local shop unless accompanied by a male relative. Similarly, if a quarter of all adults in a country have HIV, it makes sense to ensure that a man is never more than 5 minutes from a condom, and that means persuading every little shop and kiosk and bar to stock them.

In other words, social marketing in developing countries is based on the same marketing principles as social marketing in the developed countries. However, the dynamics of the commercial marketplace, unmet consumer demand and competitive factors including those impacting funding decisions play a very direct and visible role in strategy and roll-out of social marketing activities in developing countries. The following sections explain a little more about how and why.

Benefactors

Foreign aid is the most common source of funding for social marketing interventions in developing countries. The donor as the benefactor is inevitably a highly influential stakeholder. As the gatekeeper to significant resources, the donor ultimately determines for what, and how much, support is available, whether it is financial or other forms of support such as expertise or cooperative activities.

Decisions on methods, priorities, timelines and evaluation measures are also determined by the donors. Decisions on foreign aid will be guided by donors' own rationale and strategies for international development spending as well as shared international goals such as the MDGs.

For example, donors usually place great emphasis on financial sustainability, and/or support for programs are usually for fixed time periods. An exit strategy and/or a route to a self-financing model may be a specified program objective and a critical indicator of success for the funder. Local government officials in developing countries may also be concerned that interventions are not sustainable without continued donor funding. Socially marketed goods or services even when heavily subsidized may be unaffordable to the 'poorest of the poor' after the program ends. They may also be concerned that foreign funding does little to strengthen the local health system, that is, government facilities, not the shopkeepers, private doctors and local 'healers' who actually provide 50–90% of the health care in most developing countries (Mills et al., 2002).

In the box are observations from one of the authors of this chapter on typical responses encountered in the first stages of planning a social marketing project which illustrate how influential the funding source can be.

Additionally, integration of social marketing with private sector partners in market research, promotion, distribution and quality improvement also significantly influences strategy, operational approaches and their implementation.

Defining, scoping and determining levels and forms of support are clearly complex, negotiated

---

When meeting an official in the Ministry of Health in a developing country expect the discussion to centre on contraceptives, condoms or mosquito nets or maybe oral rehydration salts or iodized salt. Government health services such as family planning, HIV/AIDS, malaria or child health departments may be interested to hear about market research, segmentation, promotion, pricing and distribution strategies and the budget line for each of these activities. First, however, the discussion will be about who is the donor, and the likely budget available. Discussions on social marketing in the country office of a foreign donor will focus on the same health topics and is likely to be centred on products and services but will also need to take into account its own government's preferences and priorities for human development. Under George Bush's administration US-funded AIDS/HIV projects and programs were required to include the promotion of ABC (Abstinence, Being Faithful and Condoms). A development bank funder on the other hand, may want to talk about vouchers which poor people can use to purchase health services, and about 'social franchising' of the clinics to deliver them. Other donors may seek confirmation that money will not be used toward abortion services, while others may want to talk about scaling-up a clinic network which can deliver safe abortions.

processes, demanding exceptional planning expertise and political sensitivity. So what are the
drivers for the flow of funds, and the decisions
to support social marketing rather than other
methods?

Development workers intuitively like the idea
that people will surely use a product they buy for
themselves with their own money – nobody can
be sure what happens to all those condoms distributed free by government clinics. They like the
can-do attitude and work ethic of the people –
Indian, Nigerian and Cambodian, as well as
American and others from the head office – who
say they can do this thing called 'social marketing'. Their CVs are different to more traditional
health professionals, with experience perhaps in
FMCG companies or advertising agencies and an
MBA (Master of Business Administration) rather
than an MPH (Master of Public Health). The language they use may also be different, but their
goals are the same as those from more conventional international development or health sector
backgrounds. Furthermore, with donors rightly
requiring evidence of impact, sales figures which
provide some indicator of return on investment
and how this translates into the number of infant
deaths averted by a mosquito net, or measures of
the number of married couples using contraception and the link to birth-rate changes, provide
very welcome metrics that can help secure future
support and continued support for positive behavior change.

Benefits

Positive behavior change is not easy to initiate
and sustain in any circumstances, but in conditions of extreme poverty there are a myriad of
challenges. Social marketing in the developing
world was partially triggered by the recognition
that marketing and markets might be able to
address some of these challenges and enable poor
people to take action to improve their own well-
being and livelihoods. Early advocates of marketing theory and practice in development assistance
recognized various advantages such an approach
could bring. Linking with commercial markets
offered more efficient distribution networks as
well as the capacity and incentive for commercial
operators to scale up. The strong emphasis marketing placed on two-way communications and
engaged, relationship-based exchange offered an
alternative framework to old-style, elite-led public
information services.

Underpinning all of this was, however, a commitment to and investment in the hitherto elusive
but critical benefits of quality assurance and
continuity of supply that could support positive

behavior choices. It is fundamentally disempowering and may even be life-threatening to a woman
who wishes to space the birth of her children to
find her local supplier is out of stock of her regular
contraceptive product or she is sold a product
that is substandard or even fake.[2] Consistent availability of safe, reliable products or services is a
fundamentally necessary condition to making and
sustaining positive behaviors.

Additional benefits that may be critical to the
successful impact of improved availability of
products and services have also been delivered
using social marketing techniques. A subsidized
mosquito net aimed at protecting pregnant women
and under-5s is not much use if only the man of
the house sleeps under it. Similarly, if the net
needs to be dipped in insecticide regularly to
retain its protectiveness, but understanding or
ability to do this is absent, improving access will
not deliver any net benefit to the end-user.
Enjoyable and entertaining informational event
and field-based support services have been used
to promote and sustain regular net dipping, as
well as reinforce consistent and constant use of
bed nets.

Pre-purchase behaviors and behavior determinants can also be critical to the effectiveness of
socially marketed products. For example, the best
predictor of contraceptive uptake is that a couple
have actually talked about limiting their family
size (Bandura, 2002). Communications that raise
awareness that encourage open discussion and a
shift in cultural norms alongside enhanced access
to products have the potential to generate very
large-scale social change by creating an enabling
and empowering social climate. In Thailand, for
example, the promotion of condoms, along with
their mass distribution and improvements in product quality by the NGO Population Development
Association (PDA), strengthened the success of
the country's national strategy to slow the growth
of HIV and AIDS infection rates and reduce birth
rates. From the late 1980s, socially marketed condoms, and the de-marketing of the sex industry in
Thailand by the PDA contributed to a much lower
prevalence of HIV and AIDS than might have
been expected. The use of condoms in commercial
sex increased from 25% in 1989 to 94% by 1993,
and HIV prevalence among Thai military con-
scripts declined from 4% in 1993 to 2% in 1996,
reflecting a national trend of improved awareness,
as well as a change in sexual behavior trends
(Nelson et al., 1996, cited in D'Agnes, 2001:
350–351)

Bangladesh has seen a rapid increase in use of
modern contraception despite remaining one of
the world's poorest countries (the reader is probably aware that, in general, fertility rates tend to
fall as incomes rise). The total fertility rate fell

from 6.3 births per woman in 1970 to 2.3 in 2008, while the percentage of women using modern contraception has increased more than six fold, from 8% in the mid-1970s to 50% today (World Health Organization, 2010). PSI started social marketing condoms in 1975, with what is described by Phil Harvey, its first director, as 'lavish funding' from USAID. This evolved into the now indigenous Social Marketing Company (SMC), which became the largest social marketing program in the world. SMC provides access to oral contraceptives and condoms at thousands of non-clinical, commercial outlets across Bangladesh, and from saleswomen who go door-to-door. More than 30% of pill users and 7 out of 10 condom users buy socially marketed brands (Harvey, 1999).

Social marketing organizations such as PSI have extended their activities into serviced products such as the three-monthly contraceptive injection, and healthcare services such as HIV counseling and testing (see http://www.psi.org for examples and more details). Social marketing has also been used to successfully increase demand for and acceptance of public health initiatives such as vaccination (McKee, 1992).

Barriers

Lack of information, substandard quality of goods and services in the commercial marketplace, patchy delivery of public sector health care and a lack of accountability and practice are just some of the recognized long-standing barriers to human development progress for poor people in poor countries.

Identifying and tackling barriers to individual and community access to opportunities for self-determined improvements in livelihoods, well-being and freedom to engage in social, political and economic decision-making processes are key contemporary goals in international development. The Capabilities Approach has been highly influential in strengthening and refining the paradigm of human development as a process that extends individual choice and supports human capabilities and freedoms to pursue self-determined goals. The Capabilities Approach was first conceived by Amartya Sen (1999), the Nobel laureate, economist and philosopher, and has subsequently been developed by Sen and others. It has informed and strongly shaped the UN's Human Development Approach and the Human Development Index, and most recently the MPI (UNDP, 2010).

The Capabilities Approach defines poverty as a deprivation of 'freedoms' to realize goals, aspirations and the potential of latent individual capabilities. The Approach emphasizes the sovereignty of the poor in framing the problem, and determining the solution(s), and the most appropriate steps to reduce or alleviate poverty and its effects. Although the Capabilities Approach frames poverty as a much wider experience than material deprivation, it explicitly recognizes that lack of income is a major barrier to self-determination and progress for poor people. The cost of products and services, for example, are a primary barrier to accessing family planning, health care and other basic services and goods for many poor people.

The Capabilities Approach casts 'substantive freedoms' that allow people to realize their own unique potential and self-determined goals as key to alleviation of poverty. Substantive freedoms, such as the opportunity to fully participate in democratic and economic processes that impact one's life, to have a 'voice', to live into old age ordinarily and to use these freedoms to pursue self-determined aspirations are often unavailable to those living in extreme poverty. Poor people are thus marginalized by society and its institutions. The Capabilities Approach places social institutions such as markets, democracy, the judiciary and the media as central to the existence and eradication of poverty. It highlights their power to support or block individual freedoms. The Approach emphasizes the simultaneous importance of freedom of choice, the heterogeneity and diversity of human development and the critical role and responsibility of society's powerful institutions to support both.

In rich and middle-income countries, programs can sometimes fail because logistics do not work properly, or front-line personnel are untrained or supervised by managers unsuited to the task. In many developing countries, weaknesses may be compounded by a host of additional problems related to chronic underfunding of public infrastructure. Poor roads and a lack of telecommunications make logistics more difficult, and high levels of illiteracy, or instructions printed in languages not spoken locally, mean that even if the product or service is available to the end-user, it may not deliver any benefit. Substandard quality, and socio-cultural factors, such as restrictions on women's freedom of movement, are also common barriers experienced by poor people in developing countries. Demand for products and services therefore may be strong, but remain unmet because of socially embedded barriers.

The social marketing conceptualization of structural barriers to voluntary behavior change has much in common with the conceptualization of poverty as institutionally mediated deprivation of substantive freedoms. Social marketing tools such as user-focused research, and competitor analysis intended to identify and address barriers, are practical tools that can support the Capabilities Approach to development. Social marketing explicitly recognizes the importance of structural influences in constraining or expanding individual choice sets. Qualitative consumer research that aims to identify and give voice to user views on priority benefits and the barriers to realizing these benefits, for example, can be a supporting tool for translating research and theory into action. For example, only 60% of Africa's population have access to safe, treated water. It is estimated that women in rural Africa use 26% of their time to collect water, walking many miles each day to draw water from sources which may be untreated and irregular (WaterAid, 2007). Through the lens of the Capabilities Approach, this is clearly a significant deprivation of women's freedoms to pursue other aspirations and goals. The Rural Africa Water Development Project in Nigeria has used a combination of social marketing, partnership with women's groups and investment in simple filtration technologies and training to make water sources, previously unusable because of contamination, safe to use. The initiative has transformed the daily lives and future prospects of the women, their families and their communities (see http://www.rawdp.org for more details).

The effects of poor availability of safe and sanitary utilities and environments are often compounded by direct costs for even the most basic services and utilities. The very poor regularly face difficulties in meeting basic food, shelter or sanitation needs. This inevitably means the few resources available to them are used to meet urgent immediate needs, leaving little or no money to invest in products delivering longer-term benefits such as anti-malarial bed nets or family planning. By contrast, in the developed world, the principle of universal access to at least basic medical and social care for all citizens is seen as public responsibility. The UK, for example, spends 8% of its gross domestic product (GDP) on health care and more than 80% is paid for by the government. In Nigeria and India, about 4% of GDP is spent on health care, but in both these countries only 25% is paid for by the government. The rest comes directly from people's pockets. To make matters worse, much of this private expenditure is spent on informal, unregulated services and products of uncertain efficacy or even safety (World Health Organization, 2010).

Social marketing of safe reliable products and services at subsidized rates is more common than free distribution. There are a various reasons for this, but one is that charging for products and services creates opportunities to use private sector distribution chains instead of inefficient public sector distribution systems. At the time of writing this chapter, socially marketed condoms are for sale in Zimbabwe at 10 cents for a pack of three, but PSI sells them to trade buyers at just 1 cent. This ensures that margins are sufficient to incentivize efficient delivery through the commercial distribution chain to local shops. Market research can help to determine price elasticity of demand and set a price that is deemed affordable by users. The founder of PSI, Phil Harvey, suggest that for a family planning program to work, a year's worth of contraception should not cost more than 1% of average income (Harvey, 1999: 131).

Critics of the subsidized approach suggest charging the very poor anything at all for products that offer benefits to the whole society is both morally questionable and doomed to fail. Sachs (2005), for example, favours large-scale foreign-funded assistance to build infrastructure, and population-level change through massive subsidy, in preference to change led by 'consumer choice'. Critics of the subsidized product interventions argue that free distribution is the only way to reach the poorest individuals and families. Furthermore, a strategy of near 100% population saturation offers collective benefits and thus supersedes the logic and ethics of a strategy that is dependent on individual behavior choices (Teklehaimanot et al., 2007). Cohen and Dupas (2007), reporting on a controlled quasi-experimental intervention, found subsidy to be less effective than free distribution of insecticide-treated bed nets in reducing malaria infection rates.

A counterargument to this is that massive-scale intervention is associated with top down planning which is unable to anticipate and respond to the realities of poorly performing institutions and infrastructures of developing countries. The net result of such large-scale intervention may be dependency on development assistance and inefficient distribution of resources, with the most disadvantaged receiving least benefits and those in positions of power and influence accruing the most. Cohen and Easterly (2009), for example, argue that market-based systems are more effective as a development strategy than large-scale aid projects.

Currently, both subsidy and free products and services models are used in social marketing in developing countries. Consultation with target groups, the analysis of options and learning from practice on a case-by-case basis can be used to determine which is most appropriate to the prevailing needs and circumstances.

Branding

A critical success factor in effective social marketing interventions in the developing world has been to identify, design and deliver relevant consumer choices to a consistently safe and reliable standard.

Most poor people in most poor countries get most of their health care by handing over their own money in exchange for drugs, advice and services, but traditionally with little or no 'consumer rights' safeguard (Hanson and Berman, 1998; Travis and Cassells, 2006). Mackay (2008) describes the difficulties poor people in developing countries experience in assessing and managing the intangible aspects of the healthcare provision. Private healthcare markets are predominantly informal and unregulated and government provision is patchy and rarely called to account. Decision-making for the poor 'consumer', therefore, is characterized by uncertainty and risk due to the lack of information, lack of redress and, ultimately, a lack of any meaningful voice or choice. Branding, underpinned by the development and delivery of quality-assured, consistently 'fit-for-purpose' products and services, has been used in social marketing interventions to reduce the uncertainty and risk. Branding therefore creates opportunities for consumers to engage in beneficial behaviors by offering greater certainty of outcome in an environment where

information-sharing and accountability have traditionally been significant barriers to positive health behavior decisions.

Two models of social market branding are the 'manufacturers' model' and the 'own-brand model'. The 'manufacturers' model' involves commercial manufacturers and distributors who work with development organizations to develop ready access to products. The product or service is socially marketed by the development organization, and the commercial partner commits to low-cost availability, either through subsidy and/or reduction in profit margins. Increased sales volume helps to offset reduction in marginal profit levels, and the backing of the social marketing organization reduces commercial operator risk. The 'own-brand model' is based on the social marketing organization using direct procurement and price setting for the product or service. The social marketing organization builds its own brand identity and associated communications. Efficient distribution may still be achieved by leveraging existing commercial distribution systems.

In general, in the poorest and smallest countries the own-brand model, based on heavily subsidized or even free distribution, appears to be the most effective approach to increasing consumer uptake (an example is given in the box). The downside for donors is that program costs rise as demand grows. The manufacturer's model, where products

---

In the 1990s in Pakistan the manufacturers' and own-brand models were both deployed country-wide, providing an opportunity to compare the two models and better understand their relative strengths and weaknesses.

The Futures Group followed the manufacturers' model, which was to over-brand a contraceptive pill (Nordette), which was already being marketed with a new name, 'Chabbi' (which means 'key' in Urdu). A hormonal contraceptive already widely available was also over-branded. The manufacturers committed to supporting their products with face-to-face technical advice to those prescribing and dispensing pharmacological products, known as 'detailing'. The Futures Group used donor funds for training several thousand private doctors, paramedics and Lady Health Visitors, and shopkeepers, described as 'chemists' (although none had any formal pharmacy training). Signage to reinforce the TV advertising message 'for birth spacing you can trust, go to the sign of the key' was provided to suppliers' premises. The Lady Health Visitors were each responsible for the delivery of a dozen or so small educational and motivational meetings for women in their neighborhood. No donor money was used for price subsidies.

PSI used the NGO own-brand model. Efforts were devoted to supporting its existing own-brand (Nova) products with TV advertising, by training doctors, pharmacists and health visitors, and by subsidizing the price. PSI also supported its network of private GPs, pharmacists and health visitors who could offer family planning advice and services under the Green Star brand with detailing, supply logistics, branding materials and promotions, public education and evaluation. A non-profit organization, Social Marketing Pakistan, was established to coordinate and manage the activities and network of private clinics and practitioners, and the distribution logistics.

Ultimately, the combined efforts of the two NGOs increased access, choice and quality assurance for consumers, but the own-brand model has emerged as the more dominant in Pakistan. By 2008, Green Star was the largest provider of modern contraception methods in Pakistan, with a successful strategy of meeting the needs of the hardest-to-reach groups. The Futures Group also continues to provide to other (mainly more affluent) sectors of the market (http://www.greenstar.org.pk; Gardiner et al., 2006).

and services are offered at discounted rates, seems to work for lower- to middle-class communities and middle-income countries such as Jordan or Turkey with consumers willing or able to pay a higher price for modern contraceptives. In both models, companies invest in promotion, further boosted by donor-supported social marketing of the products. Greater sales volume to counterbalance reduced profit margins provides the incentive for price reduction and partnership working. Determining the optimum balance between financial sustainability and maximizing access can be achieved through situation analysis. As well as taking into account consumer's ability to pay, mapping and understanding existing infrastructure and relationships can help to determine in advance which model is likely to be most appropriate.

Professional branding strategies, underpinned by commitments to international safety and quality standards, and consumer rights have helped to improve service quality and accountability. Branding strategies also bridge information gaps through relationship management and ongoing evaluation.

Behavior change communications

As well as support from donors and other agencies for social marketing projects, donors also started funding mass media organizations, such as the radio station Soul City in South Africa, and the BBC's World Service Trust TV channel. These could deliver large-scale professional campaigns, usually described as *Behavior Change Communications*.

In most developing countries the social marketing of condoms and their correct use has been a key element of the response to HIV/AIDS. Social marketing organizations adopted classic techniques and methods such as consumer research, segmentation, a mix of media channels and platforms, and follow-up monitoring to measure change. Early evaluation found limited success. The task of changing sexual behaviour proved a lot more challenging than just marketing condoms. Behaviour Change Communications (BCC) was found to be an essential added ingredient. BCC are usually developed at local and national mass media communication levels. Their objectives are to promote beneficial behaviors and determinants of those behaviors as the norm, and to enhance the benefits by ensuring consumers know how to access, how to use appropriately and what to expect as a result. Common characteristics are consumer insights, individual- and community-focused messaging and the use of multiple channels and communication networks. The PSI website dedicates a whole section exclusively to BCC resources (go to http://www.psi.org/resources/bcc/).

An example of the value of BCC can be found in the marketing of bed nets. Across the African continent, mosquito nets are available through multiple sources. One of the authors of this chapter describes in the box below how social marketers found that, in some countries, encouraging the purchase of a subsidized anti-malarial bed net could be achieved if pricing and distribution were pitched correctly, but in order for the purchase to result in sustained health benefits, users required post-purchase information and support.

Malaria is endemic in many parts of the developing world, and kills millions every year, especially children. Researchers and pharmaceutical and net companies developed liquid pyrethroid insecticide formulations into which an ordinary bed net could be dipped. After drying, a mosquito that landed on it would die before it could deliver its malarial bite, so there were high hopes when the results showed that this method worked, even though the nets had to be re-treated approximately every six months. During tests in the Gambia, researchers gave the nets and the insecticide away for free, but donors were wary of committing themselves to permanently funding a recurrent expenditure such as six-monthly insecticide treatment, so initially follow-up support was not offered. However, it became apparent that failure to regularly treat nets was a significant threat to the success of the initiative. The chain of activity – buying a single-use sachet of insecticide, reading the instructions, donning the latex gloves enclosed in the packet, measuring out the right amount of water into a bucket, dipping then drying in the shade, then doing it all again in six months time and then again – was found to be an unsustainable behavior without post-purchase BCC. Mass dipping events provided a platform for BCC and reinforcement of the necessary post-purchase behavior. Furthermore, mass dipping made great promotional sense – offering something for free, a one-off event with banging drums and razz-a-mat-tazz, and plenty of on-the-spot peer pressure to negate the doubters saying it does not work or it causes cancer. In fact, newer technologies have now come to the rescue with the development of 'permanent' nets, made from yarn which has been impregnated with the insecticide, rendering the tedious task of re-treatment unnecessary.

There are concerns that BCC using mass media promotion is a form of top-down communications. These concerns may be based on perceptions of BCC as a persuasion tool in diffusion of innovations approaches (Rogers, 2003). This criticism is obviously not confined to BCC, but it is particularly relevant to communications in international development. It is argued by some that externally influenced language and imagery can act as 'Trojan horses' for alien cultures and values, however well intentioned, and pose a risk to the social capital of those it aims to benefit (Freire, 1970). Participatory research and communication methods advocated and developed by Robert Chambers (1983) for international development and now used by many in the field aim to reduce this risk. Participatory research methods used in international development and in social marketing can capture and reflect oral culture and community consciousness of poor and marginalized peoples and inform and shape BCC.

In her review of development communications strategies and methodologies, Waisbord (2001) concludes that many communication methods, including those used in social marketing, and participatory development approaches are complementary. Waisbord (2001) suggests that combining methods represents real opportunities to integrate bottom-up social change and technology-supported individual behavior choices and that their selection and application should be guided by an assessment of which is most 'fit for purpose'. Mass media and traditional belief systems are both influencers of community and individual behaviors. Understanding and building on their respective roles, while maintaining a clear vision of target audiences as the agent of change, can usefully be supported by techniques and paradigms from both.

CURRENT AND FUTURE TRENDS IN SOCIAL MARKETING

A commitment to engaging with the poor and marginalized and to understanding their experiences, aspirations and the barriers they encounter, is core to contemporary international development practice and social marketing. Participatory approaches used in both provide insight on the nature and scale of deprivation, and also its social and economic context, from the perspectives of poor people.

Until about 10 years ago, social marketing in developing countries was seen as a distinct, rather separate, activity to other international development activities. This view was shared by social marketing evangelists, and by government officials (in donor and recipient countries), who were suspicious of its 'commercial' aspects. These barriers are now breaking down. The advantage of greater efficiency of commercial distribution, even in the poorest countries, is now recognized by donors, as is the effectiveness of research-based marketing communications. Social marketing organizations and programs have also come to realize the greater coverage they can achieve by cooperating more closely with the public sector. In Kenya, for example, PSI have started selling own-brand mosquito nets through government clinics as well as retail shops, and now work with government distribution and promotions systems to encourage wider use of free nets.

Social marketing approaches, however, are still rarely applied in development initiatives concerned with broad-based social issues such as gender equality, governance reform and redistribution of economic assets such as property rights, public financing, etc. Social marketing could both contribute to, and gain from, more involvement with these issues.

The DFID 2003 review of social marketing concluded:

> Social marketing represents an extremely valuable tool to induce behaviour change of public health significance and to improve access to health goods and services ... but performance is not always matching potential; changes in existing practice are recommended to social marketing programme design and management, strengthening national ownership and DFID capacities and procedures (Meadley et al., 2003).

Although, these remarks are focused on health care, the sentiments are relevant to more general principles of improving the application of social marketing in developing countries. Historically, social marketing evaluative research in developing countries has tended to focus on outputs and reach.

More emphasis on the qualitative aspects of evaluation, as well as measures of outputs in process evaluation, and more focus on behavioral impacts to complement the measures of 'reach' would help in understanding how to do this.

The evaluative research that has been done is not widely published in the peer reviewed literature. Kotler and Lee (2009) report comments by Bill Smith of the AED that few if any of the first bold, large-scale social marketing public health interventions in the 1970s in the developing world are known to social marketers in the USA. Websites devoted to international development practice, policy and research, such as PSI's (http://www.psi.org), Eldis (http://www.eldis.org/go/

about-eldis) and AED's (http://www.aed.org), are excellent sources of data and case studies on social marketing in the developing world. They are largely unknown among the social marketing communities working in the developed world. By contrast, social marketing formative process, and summative evaluation of interventions in the developed world, enjoy significant visibility in international public platforms for social marketing. A quick tally of papers published from 2006 to 2010 in the peer reviewed journal *Social Marketing Quarterly* counted 93 papers reporting on social marketing in developed economies, six in developing economies and two that reported on both.

CONCLUSION

Social marketing began in the developing world and has since been at the forefront of innovation and development in social marketing practice.

Social marketing interventions, like other international development initiatives, may be planned both as an adjunct to public service provisioning, and as a remedial response to market failures. Multilateral and bilateral donor agencies, not-for-profits and commercial sector partners commonly deliver services, products and programs for behavior change alongside, or separate from, government-funded services. Social marketing in developing countries is often integrated with commercial marketing functions and systems.

Social marketing fits with market-oriented approaches to development and with the Capabilities Approach. These approaches place sovereignty of voluntary choice, as well as respect and support for self-determination and diversity in human development, as necessary conditions for poverty reduction.

There is a substantial body of knowledge and experience of using social marketing in developing countries. The experience and learning available from this is valuable but would benefit from more critical evaluation. The practice of social marketing in developing countries and its evaluation is somewhat unknown to the wider international social marketing community. These are lost learning opportunities for the global social marketing community in the developed and developing worlds. Social marketing in the international development setting supports behavior change in difficult and demanding circumstances. Poverty alleviation is one of the most radical and challenging goals for social marketing. We suggest that social marketing within this context

deserves more visibility than it has received to date.

KEY WORDS: International development; poverty alleviation; foreign aid; behavior change communications; developing countries; subsidized condom marketing; social marketing.

Key insights

- The practice of social marketing has its origins in the developing world.
- It is most commonly organized around the marketing of products, and frequently leverages commercial product market infrastructures such as distribution systems and promotion channels.
- Behavior Change Communications are frequently used to enhance the impact of improved access and availability of products and services.
- Social marketing principles are increasingly being used to improve availability, access and acceptability of essential healthcare services.
- Principal funders of social marketing interventions in the developing world are bilateral and multilateral donors. This influences scope, objectives and evaluation criteria.
- The social marketing of products and services is perceived and used as a strategic and operational response to market failures.
- The social marketing of products and services is perceived and used as a strategic and operational response to inadequate and/or insufficient public sector service provision.

NOTES

1 The fear that numbers will grow and outstrip the means to support them has a long history. From Thomas Malthus's *An Essay on the Principles of Population* in 1798 through to Paul Ehrlich's *Population Bomb* in 1968, each generation views this debate through the lens of its own time and place. Typically, those most privileged fear that they will be 'swamped' by those disadvantaged and of another class, color, tribe or religion.

2 Estimates of the prevalence of fake drugs are difficult to validate but are thought to be 10–30% of all medicines distributed in developing countries. See, for example, Wellcome Trust, American Pharmaceutical Group Opinion Formers' Conference on Counterfeit Medicines: Perspectives and Action. London: Wellcome Trust, 2009. Available at

http://www.wellcome.ac.uk/stellent/groups/corporatesite/@policy_communications/documents/web_document/WTX057518.pdf

REFERENCES

Bandura, A. (2002) 'Environmental sustainability by socio-cognitive deceleration of population growth', in P. Schmuch and W. Schultz (eds), *The Psychology of Sustainable Development*. Dordrecht, the Netherlands: Kluwer.

Black, T.R.L. and Harvey, P.D. (1976) 'Report on a contraceptive social marketing experiment in Kenya', *Studies in Family Planning*, 7(4): 101–108.

Chambers, R. (1983) *Rural Development: Putting the Last First.* New York: John Wiley.

Chandy, K.T., Balakrishman, T.R., Kantawalla, J.M., et al. (1965) 'Proposal for family planning promotion: A marketing plan', *Studies in Family Planning*, 1(6): 7–12.

Cohen, J. and Dupas, P. (2007) *Free Distribution or Cost-Sharing? Evidence from a Randomized Malaria Prevention Experiment.* Washington, DC: The Brookings Institution. Available at: http://www.brookings.edu/~/media/Files/rc/papers/2007/12_malaria_cohen/12_malaria_cohen.pdf (accessed 2 December 2010).

Cohen, J. and Easterly, W. (2009) *What Works in Development? Thinking Big and Thinking Small.* Washington, DC: The Brookings Institution.

D'Agnes, T. (2001) *From Condoms to Cabbages.* Bangkok: Post Books.

Freire, P. (1970) *Pedagogy of the Oppressed.* New York: Continuum.

Gardiner, E., Schwanenflugel, D. and Grace, C. (2006) Market development approaches in Pakistan: A case study. Extracted from Market Development Approaches Scoping Report. Available at: http://www.eldis.org/index.cfm?objectId=82A43EC1-0209-60B4 (accessed 24 January 2011).

Hanson, K. and Berman, P. (1998) 'Private health care provision in developing countries', *Health Policy and Planning*, 13(3): 195–211.

Harvey, P. (1999) *Let Every Child be Wanted: How Social Marketing is Revolutionising Contraceptive Use Around the World.* Westport, CT: Auburn House.

Kotler, P. and Lee, N.R. (2009) *Up and Out of Poverty: The Social Marketing Solution.* Upper Saddle River, NJ: Wharton School Publishing.

Kotler, P. and Zaltman, G. (1971) 'Social marketing: An approach to planned social change', *Journal of Marketing*, 35: 3–12.

Mackay, B. (2008) 'From life insurance to safer sex: Reflections of a marketing man', *Social Science and Medicine*, 66: 2168–2172.

McKee, N. (1992) *Social Mobilization & Social Marketing: Lessons for Communicators.* Penang, Malaysia: Southbound Press.

Meadley, J., Pollard, R. and Wheeler, M. (2003) *Review of DFID Approach to Social Marketing.* London: DFID Health Systems Resource Centre.

Mills, A., Brigha, R., Hansen, K. and McPake B. (2002) 'What can be done about the private health sector in low income countries?' *Bulletin of the World Health Organization*, 80: 325–330.

Rogers, E.M. (2003) *Diffusion of Innovations*, 5th edn. New York: Free Press.

Sachs, J. (2005) *The End of Poverty: Economic Possibilities for Our Time.* New York: Penguin Books.

Sen, A. (1999) *Development as Freedom.* Oxford: Oxford University Press.

Teklehaimanot, A., Sachs, J.D. and Curtis, C. (2007) 'Malaria control needs mass distribution of insecticidal bednets', *Lancet*, 369(9580): 2143–2146.

Travis, P. and Cassells, A. (2006) 'Safe in their hands? Engaging private providers in the quest for public health goals', *Bulletin of the World Health Organization*, 84(6): 427.

UNDP (2010) *United Nations Development Report 2010. The Real Wealth of Nations: Pathways to Development.* New York: Palgrave Macmillan. Available at: http://hdr.undp.org/en/media/HDR_2010_EN_Complete_reprint.pdf.

Waisbord, S. (2001) Family tree of theories, methodologies and strategies in development communication: Convergences and differences. Prepared for the Rockefeller Foundation.

Walsh, D.C., Rudd, R.E., Moeykens, B.A. and Moloney, T.W. (1993) 'Social marketing for public health', *Health Affairs*, 12(2): 104–119.

WaterAid (2007) *Women and WaterAid Issues Sheet.* Available at: http://www.wateraid.org/documents/plugin_documents/women_and_wateraid_issue_sheet_1.pdf (accessed 2 December 2010).

World Bank (2008) *Poverty Data: A Supplement to the World Bank Development Indicators.* Washington, DC: International Bank for Reconstruction and Development.

World Health Organization (2010) *World Health Statistics 2010.* Geneva: WHO Press.

23

Social Marketing for a Sustainable Environment

Sue Peattie and Ken Peattie

INTRODUCTION

This chapter considers the important role that social marketing can play in promoting a more sustainable economy and society. It particularly focuses on social marketing's potential role in changing our relationship with the physical environment to prevent the erosion of humanity's future quality of life due to overexploitation of the planet's resources. Despite many years of emphasis on education, better regulation and harnessing market mechanisms to protect the environment, policymakers and communities globally are still struggling to arrest or reverse its degradation. Behaviour change will also be crucial to achieve substantive progress towards sustainability, including change among consumers, householders, citizens, businesses, communities, voters, investors and decision-makers. Social marketing's efficacy in moving people beyond raised awareness and good intentions to secure and maintain pro-environmental behaviour change, and in building partnerships for change among key stakeholders, make it a tool that policymakers and communities are increasingly turning to.

THE ENVIRONMENTAL FOUNDATIONS OF WELL-BEING

The goals that social marketers pursue generally involve efforts to enhance or protect the well-being and quality of life of individuals or communities. There are four main behavioural spheres to which social marketing interventions are applied (Kotler and Lee, 2007):

- **Health improvement**, including healthy eating, physical activity, substance abuse, sexual behaviours and a range of behaviours linked to particular conditions such as asthma, diabetes and depression or health behaviours such as immunisation, breast-feeding or oral health.
- **Safety/injury prevention**, including road safety, domestic violence prevention, gun safety and the prevention of domestic accidents.
- **Community involvement**, including volunteering, charitable giving, blood or organ donation, voter participation or participation in education.
- **Environmental protection**, including waste reduction, water and energy conservation, anti-littering, wildlife habitat protection, safe pesticide use and wildfire prevention.

Although often treated as discrete categories of behaviour, the boundaries between them are permeable and sometimes crossed: for example, by volunteering for a community scheme to protect the environment.

Health behaviours have tended to dominate within social marketing practice and scholarship, yet protecting the physical environment plays an important role in our well-being, quality of life and health. However, this is not always immediately apparent to many living in Western industrialised economies, whose lifestyles are somewhat insulated from environmental realities by technology and relative wealth.

The fundamental role of the environment in human welfare is expressed scientifically through the concept of 'ecosystem services', the benefits that humankind enjoys from the physical environment which sustains life (WRI, 2005). These services include our food, water and fuel, and materials such as wood and fibres that we derive from the environment to provide shelter, clothing and products such as medicines. Ecosystems also protect our well-being by regulating climate and temperature, preventing flooding and diseases, and managing water quality and waste. They also provide less tangible, but still vital, recreational and spiritual benefits that contribute to our well-being and health (Aron and Patz, 2001; Corvalán et al., 2005).

The 20th century witnessed unprecedented increases in global population and in the average material standard of living that individuals enjoy. During the final quarter of the century, gross domestic product (GDP) per capita, measured in real terms, roughly doubled (World Bank, 2004), and yet this did not prevent the century ending with almost three billion people living on under US$2 per day and an estimated 30,000 daily child deaths directly related to poverty (UNICEF, 2000). This economic growth also came at a significant environmental cost. In 2005, the United Nations' four-year Millennium Ecosystem Assessment research project (WRI, 2005) concluded that 60% of global ecosystem services have been degraded through the unparalleled economic growth of the latter half of the 20th century, which had 'resulted in a substantial and largely irreversible loss in the diversity of life on Earth' and that 'gains in human well-being and economic development, ... have been achieved at growing costs in the form of the degradation of many ecosystem services ... and the exacerbation of poverty for some groups of people. These problems, unless addressed, will substantially diminish the benefits that future generations obtain from ecosystems' (p. 1).

It is perhaps curious that our understanding of promoting health from a social perspective has developed largely in isolation from our understanding of environmental health, when the two are inextricably linked in practice (Kelly and Doherty, 2003). Air and water quality are two of the key determinants of health and welfare globally (Corvalán et al., 2005), and an environmental issue such as climate change provides health challenges because it alters the living conditions and geography of many pathogens such as mosquitoes, which spread disease (McMichael et al., 1996). Promoting and protecting human health and well-being across the globe and into the future will depend to a significant extent on our ability to improve and protect the health of the planet and the ecosystems on which we all depend (Aron and Patz, 2001). This is a task that social marketing has the potential to contribute greatly to (Maibach, 1993), yet it is a potential that we are only really beginning to properly exploit.

SUSTAINABLE DEVELOPMENT AS A SOCIAL GOAL

During the 20th century economic growth was the predominant public policy goal, reflecting a belief that it would solve social problems caused by poverty, and would also fund solutions to other social and environmental problems. By the final quarter of the century it was becoming evident that this belief was somewhat over-optimistic, and that the nature of our economic growth was in practice generating new social and environmental problems. In 1983, the UN established the World Commission on Environment and Development, chaired by Dr Gro Harlem Brundtland. Its remit was to address growing concern 'about the accelerating deterioration of the human environment and natural resources and the consequences of that deterioration for economic and social development'. The Commission's findings, *Our Common Future* (WCED, 1987), known as the Brundtland Report, popularised the concept of 'sustainable development', which was encapsulated as 'meeting the needs of the present without compromising the ability of future generations to meet their needs' (p. 43). It promoted a new approach to development which took an intergenerational view, placed a greater emphasis on meeting the needs of the global poor rather than the wants of the global consumer class, and recognised the planet as a finite and vulnerable environmental system upon which we all depend.

For many people working in social marketing, the term 'environment' will be more familiar in the sense of the influences in the external social environment that they work within, and the relationships between the stakeholders within it, rather than as the 'green' physical environment. Similarly, the term 'sustainable' will be most familiar in relation to sustaining the funding streams which will ensure the future security of their programmes, or sustaining the behaviour change and impact of a campaign.

From a broader socio-environmental perspective, the concepts of sustainability and sustainable development have been subject to a bewildering variety of post-Brundtland definitions and interpretations (Hopwood et al., 2005). There has also been frequent misappropriation of the term 'sustainable', most notably by economists promoting the notion of sustainable growth (ultimately an impossibility on a finite planet).

Despite this, a general acceptance has emerged that the term 'sustainable development' refers to the goal of achieving 'a high, equitable and sustainable quality of life by integrating the social, economic and environmental activities, outcomes and impacts of human society' (Eckersley, 1998, p. 9).

The pursuit of an integrated and balanced pattern of social and economic development that does not destroy the environmental resources on which we all depend is the essence of sustainable development. Questions about exactly how it will be achieved, and how priorities, responsibilities and timescales should be determined, has produced 30 years of controversy across Earth Summits, Climate Change Conferences and World Economic Fora. What is not disputed is that it will require substantial changes to many types of human behaviour, which suggests an important role for social marketing. Data from ecological footprint research suggest that humankind's exploitation of environmental resources is already running at around 30% above a level that the planet can sustain without environmental degradation (Hails et al., 2008). Reversing this, and creating a pattern of human activity that the planet can sustain indefinitely, is unlikely to be achieved by consuming, producing, living and learning in the ways we have become used to. To paraphrase Einstein, you cannot solve a problem by thinking in the same way as you did when you caused it, and much the same goes for behaviour.

Since social marketing's inception, it has been used in campaigns related to environmental behaviours like recycling (Zikmund and Stanton, 1971), or promoting eco-literacy (Taylor and Muller, 1992). However, such campaigns have remained something of a minority sport compared with the application of social marketing to health behaviours. In the 21st century this looks set to change as the negative social, health and economic consequences of climate change and other environmental crises have become clearer and more pressing. In the future, the natural environment looks set to become more important for social marketing and vice versa.

TOWARDS ENVIRONMENTALLY SUSTAINABLE BEHAVIOURS: A 'TWO WORLDS' AGENDA

The social and environmental challenges which sustainable development addresses are global, but priorities vary among countries. This is partly rooted in the inequitable distribution of the costs and benefits of industrialisation and economic growth. In very general terms the richer countries with relatively mature and stable social, political,

educational and economic systems have provided most of the technologies and financing that underpinned economic growth and industrialisation. Many of the human, and particularly natural, resources that have driven industrialisation and economic growth have come from relatively poor countries, with less mature and stable social, political, educational and economic systems (with both sets of factors often linking back to the history of imperialist strategies amongst the richer nations in previous centuries). The economic benefits of industrialisation have accrued disproportionately to the richer nations, while the social and, particularly, the environmental costs have accrued disproportionately to the poorer countries.

As Cairns et al. (Chapter 22) demonstrate, the international development agenda provided some of the early impetus for social marketing's development. Although the growth in social marketing practice has since mostly been through applications in richer countries, there are still many successful interventions within poorer nations from which useful lessons can be drawn. Dholakia and Dholakia (2000) highlight the potential value of social marketing for tackling the social, economic and ecological crises in many poorer countries and its successful use on issues such as family planning, the provision of micro-credit, disease prevention and literacy. Ironically, however, although many poorer nations could benefit greatly from further social marketing interventions that deliver better environmental protection, health promotion and poverty alleviation, they often lack the stable and enabling institutional frameworks that social marketers depend upon for successful campaigns (Dunhaime et al., 1985).

There are many issues for which social marketing campaigns are required, whatever the level of wealth and development of a country. Combating the spread of HIV/AIDS, dealing with alcohol abuse, promoting smoking cessation, reducing carbon emissions or coping with water shortages are just some of the quality of life challenges that social marketers have tackled which straddle the wealth divide. Other behaviour change and social marketing priorities reflect the differences in lives on either side of the divide, with behaviours linked to both poverty and affluence each playing a potential part in environmental degradation (Leiserowitz et al., 2005). Social marketing interventions in richer countries frequently tackle quality of life and well-being problems linked to affluence, including obesity, sedentary lifestyles and mental ill-health associated with overwork, stress and the pursuit of materialist lifestyles (often collectively referred to as 'affluenza'; James, 2008).

In poorer countries social marketing priorities frequently reflect the realities of poverty and the struggle to access the basic means of well-being, such as sufficient nutritious food, clean water, education and basic health care. By contrast, such things are routinely taken for granted by the majority of people in richer nations. In consumer economies, social marketing to protect the environment is focused on campaigns to reduce individuals' indirect environmental impacts: for example, by promoting involvement in recycling or reducing home energy use (Barr et al., 2006). In poorer countries environmental protection often involves changing behaviours which more directly impact on the environment such as discouraging poaching or the over-exploitation of wild food sources, the overcutting of wood resources for fuel and charcoal, or farming practices that lead to soil erosion (Corvalán et al., 2007; Regmi and Weber, 2000).

For those working on health interventions within wealthy countries it is perhaps tempting to dismiss sustainable development and environmental protection as not being a priority for social marketers. The scale and nature of the changes needed seem to call more for strong regulation, new technology to provide alternative resources and energy sources, and better trade and aid policies to tackle global poverty, rather than for marketing campaigns. The reality is that social marketers have a potentially vital role to play in environmental protection because the unsustainable interaction between humankind and the planet reflects a range of human behaviours (Leiserowitz et al., 2005).

KEY BEHAVIOURAL SPHERES FOR ENVIRONMENTAL SUSTAINABILITY

In wealthy and poor countries alike, exactly which environmentally related behaviours could and should be a focus for social marketing interventions is an important question. It is complicated by the nature of the sustainability agenda, which means that the implications of, and motivations for, a particular behaviour can become distinctly entangled. A simple behaviour change such as switching from driving a car to pedalling a bicycle is one that social marketers have sought to promote (e.g. see James, 2002). It provides health benefits to the individual, environmental benefits through reduced carbon emissions and community benefits through traffic reduction, yet for one individual it may be motivated purely by a desire to save money or even (for those living in areas subject to gridlock) time. Whether or not cycling constitutes an environmental behaviour therefore

depends on whether you define such behaviours by motivations (in which case it may or may not be) or consequences (in which case it is, but only among other things).

At the broadest level, key behaviours are suggested by the IPAT formula proposed by Ehrlich and Ehrlich (1990) that humankind's environmental Impact is a function of Population, Affluence (the average material standard of living people enjoy) and the Technology involved in providing those living standards. This generates several key behaviour spheres at a macro level, with significant implications for environmental sustainability.

Reproductive behaviours

Between 1930 and 2000 the global population roughly tripled to exceed six billion (UNPF, 2007), a process which contributed greatly to the mounting ecological stresses revealed in the Millennium Ecosystem Assessment report. A widely agreed approach to progressing towards sustainability is to curb population growth rates, particularly among relatively poor but populous nations. This is an area where social marketing has traditionally been active (often in combination with condom-based strategies to combat HIV/AIDS). The extent and effectiveness of this application of social marketing led Harvey (1999) to describe it as having revolutionised contraceptive use around the world. It is an important part of a success story in behaviour change, which by the turn of the millennium had 62% of married women of reproductive age worldwide using contraception (UNPD, 2001).

Migration behaviours

It is not only absolute population numbers that impact on the environment and human quality of life, since the spatial distribution of population is also important. Since 2000 the balance has shifted so that, for the first time in history, more people live in urban than rural settlements (UNPF, 2007). Recent trends in births and migration patterns, if continued, will see two billion people living in urban slums by 2030, which will profoundly challenge the ability of social marketers working in poorer countries to deliver improvements in health and poverty alleviation. The growth of 'megacities' of over 10 million people (of which there were 18 by the year 2000) will also severely challenge the hinterlands of those cities to provide the necessary water and food and absorb the wastes they produce. This highlights the importance of managing future migration behaviours, and particularly rural-to-urban migration in poorer countries. Whether social marketing could be effective in stemming or reversing the flow of population from rural communities and into urban slums may become an important question in the future.

Consumption behaviours

It is behaviours linked to the overall level of affluence that we enjoy, particularly in Western industrialised consumer economies, which will arguably require the greatest change if we are to establish environmentally sustainable economies and societies. This is not to say that changing consumption behaviours is an entirely developed country agenda. Rising living standards in poorer countries leads to the 'nutrition transition' effect in which populations shift away from consumption of traditional foods based on grains, roots and tubers towards increased consumption of meat and dairy products, refined and processed food, and sugars, oils and fats (Popkin, 2002). The demand for meat in developing countries, for example, doubled between 1986 and 2007 (Steinfeld et al., 2006). Concern about this transition is usually focused on diet-related health issues, but it also has substantial environmental implications (Lang, 2002). These are linked to the often dramatic differences in relative energy and water intensity, and contribution to greenhouse gases, of meat and dairy production compared with providing similar levels of human nutrition through grains and vegetables (Carlsson-Kanyama and González, 2009).

There is a general recognition that consumption patterns are important drivers of both social inequalities and environmental degradation (Burgess et al., 2003). However, the majority of policy initiatives have focused on trying to change production technologies and methods, rather than attempting to tackle the social drivers of consumption or move away from a strongly materialist culture in industrialised economies (Mont and Plepys, 2008). Possibly the most challenging aspect of progressing towards sustainability will be a move away from a culture in which increasing economic growth, and growth in consumption, represent largely unchallenged expectations and social norms. Jackson (2009), in his monograph *Prosperity without Growth*, makes a detailed and compelling case for a global transition to targeted growth as a mechanism to pursue sustainable development. This involves only targeting strategies of economic growth at poor countries where poverty is the major threat to well-being and sustainability. For the already-wealthy countries the emphasis is instead on managing economic contraction and pursing quality of life improvements

that are not dependent on economic growth. Such a radical change in public policy and in social norms and expectations is obviously going to face an uphill battle for acceptance, regardless of the amount of environmental science and economic evidence supporting the need for it. Reducing expectations in economic and consumption growth in already-rich countries will require considerable upstream and downstream social marketing to stand any chance of being adopted (or even discussed as a feasible alternative) as a matter of strategic choice rather than through environmental, social or economic necessity.

In some cases technological fixes can successfully bypass stubborn behaviours. For example, leaving large electrical appliances on standby can consume considerable amounts of energy for relatively minor convenience benefits. The annual standby power consumption of a typical Japanese household in 2000 was estimated as 398 kWh, or approximately 9.4% of domestic electricity (Sasako, 2001). Manufacturers have therefore sought to reduce the standby power consumption of appliances. In the case of Sony's new generation of Eco-sense TVs, they have bypassed the need to change consumer behaviour through a standby power consumption close to zero and a 'presence sensor' which will switch off the TV if viewers leave the room.

Technological improvements are unable to overcome all forms of environmental impact, and are frequently counterbalanced by other types of change. Having more fuel-efficient cars does not constitute progress if we own more of them and drive them further. Where steps have been taken to change consumer behaviour to reduce environmental impacts, they have mostly focused on relatively unchallenging changes involved in product substitutions by consumers or increasing recycling rates for discarded products and packaging (Belz and Peattie, 2009). Achieving the type of transformational change within consumer economies which will deliver progress towards sustainability will need to involve far more challenging types of change. As Jackson (2005) noted in his wide-ranging literature review with an emphasis on consumer behaviour, achieving behaviour change is 'Fast becoming the "Holy Grail" of sustainable development policy' (p. 105).

Cultivation behaviours

Although the word 'technology' in the IPAT formula may suggest industrial processes and 'high tech' solutions, it refers more broadly to the means by which we generate that which we consume. Under this broad definition, the technology with one of the greatest sets of environmental impacts is agriculture. This means that behaviours in rural agricultural communities and economies will play an important part in determining whether or not environmental quality is preserved or destroyed (Regmi and Webber, 2000). Over one-third of the planet's surface is already used for agriculture, and there is little prospect for expanding this without destroying other valuable environmental resources such as forest or peat bogs (WRI, 2005). Agriculture already uses 70% of available global freshwater and is responsible for 14% of greenhouse gas emissions (with a further 18% linked to land-use change mostly driven by the conversion of land for agriculture; Steinfeld et al., 2006). Improved farming practices have the potential to reduce energy usage and greenhouse gas emissions, protect biodiversity, preserve water and avoid pollution.

Ironically, changing time-honoured farming practices was used as an example of a tough behaviour challenge for marketers in Kotler and Zaltman's seminal article back in 1971 (although in the context of existing commercial marketing rather than the new discipline of social marketing they were outlining). The potential value of social marketing to promote sustainable agricultural land management has been recognised (Duxbury, 2003) and involves encouraging farmers to adopt practices that:

- Prevent soil erosion or exhaustion, or the contamination of water resources through leaching due to the overuse of chemical fertilisers and pesticides.
- Protect biodiversity by avoiding monocultures, adopting organic methods or protecting natural wildlife refuges such as hedgerows.

However, compared with health interventions, such applications are relatively uncommon, although some examples do exist (e.g. Jacobson et al., 2003). In practice, social marketing interventions on farms have generally focused on health and safety of farm workers, food safety for consumers, or water quality protection for human health, rather than on protection of environmental quality through farming practices.

Technology adoption behaviours

The technologies we use are an important determinant of environmental impacts, but this is usually regarded as the province of regulators or those concerned with socially responsible business strategies, rather than of social marketers. However, social marketing has a role to play in the adoption of greener technologies, because successful technological innovation has a strong behavioural component. In countries such as the UK, we have for example seen public campaigns to encourage the uptake of more energy-efficient domestic boilers, including financial incentives through a scrappage scheme, to complement the commercial marketing efforts of manufacturers.

New greener technologies will not succeed in the market without addressing behavioural issues such as resistance to change, perceived risk, ease of use, aesthetics and fashion. Technologies which are significantly more environmental sustainable are likely to challenge existing consumer habits and routines and may require them to reconsider their values and priorities. This is exactly the type of innovation most likely to prompt consumer resistance (Garcia et al., 2007), yet consumer resistance to green innovations remains a significantly under-researched and poorly understood issue.

Sustainability will require different strategies for encouraging innovation and technology adoption for different types of economy, to reflect their stage of development and level of affluence. Tukker (2005) outlines strategies for three types of economy:

1. **Industrialised consumer economies** will require significant reductions in the resource intensity of consumption while maintaining economic activity levels. Sustainability would require at least a 'Factor 4' reduction, which delivers the same level of economic benefit from one-quarter of the material and energy resources.
2. **Emerging industrial powers** such as China, India and the major economies of South America need to avoid following the unsustainable development paths of the richer nations, and instead to 'leapfrog' to more sustainable technologies and patterns of production and consumption.
3. **Poor 'base of the pyramid' economies** within Africa and parts of Asia will be encouraged to develop and adopt innovative and dedicated technologies and solutions which improve the quality of life for individuals and communities, but without dramatically increasing their resource consumption.

At this macro level, the behaviours which social marketers can seek to address often concern significant, conscious decision-making processes, rather than habitual, lifestyle-based behaviours. Migrating from a rural community to a town, changing the planting scheme on a farm, 'downshifting' to a lower-consumption lifestyle, installing a low-energy boiler, or having a child are all likely to be the product of a decision-making process which the social marketer can seek to influence (with the caveat that the latter may be the product of no decision at all and may instead reflect habit or chance). Other behaviours, particularly relating to the cumulative impacts of consumption, may relate more to low-involvement 'everyday' behaviours. These behaviours may involve little sense of conscious choice and are typically governed more by history, convention, circumstance and habit (Shove and Warde, 2002). Which type of behaviour is most difficult for social marketers to influence is an interesting point to debate, but it is important to recognise that they are likely to require different types of approach.

MOTIVATING PRO-ENVIRONMENTAL BEHAVIOURS

At the level of individual behaviour, the majority of academic research into pro-environmental behaviour (PEB) can be roughly divided to reflect two distinct roles that individuals adopt. The first concerns our behaviour as consumers and our willingness to change the products that we buy, how they are used and consumed, and what we do with any used product or waste that results (Jackson, 2005). The second concerns our behaviour as citizens and our willingness to contribute to the public good through political action, charitable donations and direct voluntary contributions to the environmental quality of the communities we live within (Turaga et al., 2010). Although initially largely separate and reflecting different disciplines, these streams of research are increasingly becoming intertwined through the rise of concepts like the 'citizen consumer' and consumer activism (Kozinets and Handelman, 2004), and a recognition that the motivations for engaging in the two types of PEB may be far more similar than researchers originally realised (Turaga et al., 2010).

Social marketing is relevant to the adoption of both forms of PEB because it can influence the behaviour of individuals operating in a number of different roles. Many campaigns target individuals' behaviour in the context of their personal consumption and lifestyles, but others target them in their role as parents, or as citizens (e.g. campaigns to encourage voting) and 'upstream' campaigns may focus on individuals in their roles as influential members of organisations (Andreasen, 2006).

Of the two forms of PEB, research data suggest that consumption-orientated behaviours are more widely practiced within societies worldwide than citizenship/political behaviours (Leiserowitz et al., 2005). They also, arguably, have the greater direct environmental impact. Key contributions concerning consumption PEB come from

management and marketing, where the emphasis is strongly on consumer purchasing of products such as organic food, renewably sourced energy and low-energy appliances. Consumer willingness to pay price premiums is a major focus of the research, particularly relating to the consumption of energy (see, e.g., Banfi et al., 2008). Some of this research takes a wider view of consumption to also include alternative strategies for meeting consumer needs (such as product-to-service substitutions or communal product sharing), behaviour during the use phase of products and household waste management and product disposal strategies. This broader view of consumption and its focus on the physical as well as economic impacts of products is also adopted by disciplines such as ecological economics and industrial ecology.

People might naturally assume that commercial marketing targets individuals as consumers, whereas social marketing addresses them in other roles (such as parent or citizen). The reality is far more complicated. Both personal health and environmental health are impacted by our purchasing and consumption behaviours, particularly in spheres such as food and transport. Policymakers have therefore become interested in promoting consumer behaviour change, both through their own campaigns, and through policies which influence commerce such as food labelling regulations or vehicle taxation. Similarly, these concerns can prompt companies to proactively engage in marketing activities to pursue social goals related to better personal and environmental health. Such strategies could represent an expression of corporate social responsibilities and underlying values, or simply reflect the opportunities or perceived threats linked to operating in an environmentally sensitive market (Belz and Peattie, 2009). Encouraging domestic energy-saving behaviours, for example, began with the 'switch it off' public information campaigns during the oil crises of the early 1970s, and has since become the subject of social marketing campaigns. It has also become a key aspect of commercial marketing strategies of energy providers and manufacturers of many energy-using (and saving) products.

There is also an interesting parallel between the fields of health behaviours, which have been the predominant sphere in which social marketing has developed, and PEB. Both have suffered in the past through an overemphasis on the role of information and knowledge in driving behaviour. Social marketing's emergence is partly a reflection of the weaknesses of earlier intervention approaches based on the health belief model and its information-deficit-based approach to encouraging people to adopt healthier behaviours (Janz and Becker, 1984). This is remarkably similar to the field of sustainable consumption where models of consumer behaviour such as the theory of reasoned action or the theory of planned behaviour have placed a similar overemphasis on tackling any information deficits and addressing peoples' beliefs and attitudes (Jackson, 2005). A key feature of the research literature on PEB is the weak relationship (and often significant gap) between attitudes and knowledge and actual behaviour (Peattie, 2010). This forms another reason why the application of social marketing, with its ability to move people beyond awareness in order to achieve behaviour change, has such potential value in motivating PEB.

SETTING PRIORITIES FOR PRO-ENVIRONMENTAL BEHAVIOURS

Another important aspect of pursuing more sustainable consumer behaviour is setting priorities for which behaviours to influence through social marketing interventions. This can be difficult because our total environmental impacts as consumers reflect the sum outcomes of a complex, diverse and interrelated set of behaviours which make up our lifestyles. It reflects the big decisions of our lives about where we live, the homes we choose to live in and how many people we share them with. It also reflects the myriad of habitual everyday behaviours we adopt. The environmental impacts of a particular behaviour can also have significant variations across time, space and circumstance. The relative balance of energy and climate change merits of someone in Britain eating a British apple from cold storage, or a New Zealand apple transported by sea, will change throughout the year according to the season. Energy-saving behaviours which are significant in the UK mean far less in a country like Norway which, despite being a major oil producer, relies almost entirely on renewable hydroelectric power.

In some cases attempts to encourage pro-environmental behaviours using an appeal on the theme of 'every little helps' have promoted behaviours with a relatively trivial impact, which has tended to obscure, rather than clarify, behavioural priorities. Mackay (2008) analysed the energy-use impacts of different behaviours, and in commenting on the relative worth of the popular consumer advice to switch off mobile phones chargers when not in use, noted that 'All the energy saved in switching off your charger for one day is used up in **one second** of car-driving....The energy saved in switching off the charger for **one year** is equal to the energy in a single hot bath' (p. 68). The risk is that by encouraging consumers to change

certain behaviours which contribute relatively little, they still get the impression that they have made significant progress towards a sustainable lifestyle. It is the equivalent of the obese person feeling they eat sensibly because they have added some salad into their diet.

The environmental impacts of individuals' consumption in industrialised economies is mostly accounted for by a relatively small number of product categories. This is helpful in terms of focusing social marketing efforts on those behaviours with the most impact. The European Environmental Impact of Products (EIPRO) project (Tukker et al., 2005) rigorously analysed the evidence base on the environmental impacts of products consumed by households. It assessed 255 domestic product types against a wide range of environmental impacts and concluded that 70–80% of total impacts of European consumer lifestyles related to only three consumption spheres:

- Food and drink;
- Housing (including domestic energy); and
- Transport (including commuting, leisure and holiday travel).

These consumption spheres were translated into a potential portfolio of behaviours as part of a scooping study into social marketing approaches to promoting sustainable behaviours conducted for the UK government's Department for Environment, Food and Rural Affairs (Defra, 2007). Consumer workshops conducted by the Green Alliance were then used to identify those behaviours that combined significant environmental impacts with likely public acceptability, and which had the potential to act as catalysts for future change. The short list produced from this process included the following behaviours, many of which have already been the subject of social marketing campaigns:

1. **Conduct a household environmental audit**: this was a key component of the 'Eco-Smart' social marketing programmes run in Australia.
2. **Tackle energy efficiency in the home**: including

   - Install microgeneration;
   - Insulate;
   - Buy energy efficiency appliances;
   - Install a smart energy meter.

Home energy efficiency has been a popular target for social marketing interventions such as Canada's community-based Residential Energy Efficiency Program (Kennedy, 2001). Since it targets behaviours which provide financial as well as environmental benefits, campaigns tend to focus on facilitation of behaviour change, for example, by providing financial subsidies for domestic insulation.

3. **Tackle water efficiency in the home**: including the installation of a water meter. This is even more of a behavioural priority in the many parts of the world that are considerably more water stressed than the UK, and has been a key focus for the successful community-based social marketing campaigns pioneered by McKenzie-Mohr (2000); also, see Chapter 10.

4. **Seek alternative transport for short trips (of less than 3 miles)**: this was a fundamental objective of the highly successful TravelSmart social marketing campaign in Australia (James, 2002). It is worth noting that transport behaviours tend to be very complex and tend to be more strongly influenced by location, local infrastructure and lifestyle than by specific choices. This can make transport behaviours particularly difficult and complex for social marketers to influence (Cao and Mokhtarian, 2005).

5. **Use low carbon vehicles**: although this might logically appear to be commercial marketing territory, there are a number of behaviour issues that can deter consumers from switching to a low carbon vehicle based around their lack of knowledge about clean vehicle technologies and concerns about refuelling, reliability, servicing and insurance. Social marketing approaches have therefore been examined as a strategy to encourage the uptake of low carbon vehicles (Kurani and Turrentine, 2002).

6. **Avoid short-haul domestic and regional (intra-EU) flights**: attempts to de-market short-haul flights have so far been a focus for NGO campaigns more than for specific social marketing campaigns. However, in the Ipsos MORI report *Tipping Point or Turning Point: Social Marketing & Climate Change* (Downing and Ballantyne, 2007) this was highlighted as a potentially viable target for behaviour change campaigns because feasible alternatives existed which consumers could be encouraged and incentivised to use.

7. **Buy local and seasonal food (certified where possible)**: this is also associated with commercial marketing, and particularly the produce marketing strategies of retailers. There are, however, examples of social marketing campaigns to promote this type of consumer behaviour, such as within the on-campus 'slow food' campaign at Marquette University in Wisconsin.

8. **Waste less food**: in the UK the 'Love Food, Hate Waste' social marketing campaign sought to motivate householders to reduce the UK's £8 billion food waste bills by encouraging behaviours such as forward meal planning to reduce ingredient wastage and showing how to create appetizing meals from leftovers (Smithers, 2007).

9. **Rely less on animal protein**: reducing the level of animal-based protein in diets has been the focus of social marketing campaigns with an emphasis on reducing obesity and heart disease, but it also has the potential to contribute to significant reductions in greenhouse gas emissions (Downing and Ballantyne, 2007).

Behaviour change such as reducing the use of short-haul flights or the consumption of animal protein highlight an important distinction between social marketing for sustainability and conventional commercial approaches to marketing more sustainable goods and services. Achieving real progress towards sustainability will require the 'de-marketing' of certain products, technologies and forms of consumer behaviour. Applying social marketing to promote a behaviour such as consumption reduction takes social marketers into territory in which the potential lessons to be learnt from commercial marketing will be comparatively few (Peattie and Peattie, 2009). It is also territory in which the social marketing mix based around the concept of 'Social Propositions' (see Chapter 10) makes more sense than talking about consuming fewer products as the 'product'. Ultimately, the key lessons for social marketers seeking to promote consumption reduction are likely to come from the experience of other social marketing applications such as smoking cessation or tackling obesity. Essentially, the challenge is to overcome a societal addiction to over-consumption in industrialised economies, and lessons from tackling other forms of addiction may be valuable.

An emphasis on consumption reduction is also likely to put commercial and social marketers on something of a collision course. Although commercial marketers in many key sectors are seeking to reduce the environmental impacts of their products, there is a continuing emphasis on growth within commercial organisations (and society) that makes consumption reduction a difficult societal goal for both producers and consumers to accept. This can create conflict between the commercial marketers of products associated with sustainability challenges (such as air travel), and social marketers seeking to reduce or change consumption activity (e.g. to prevent disruptive climate change). Again, the lessons from existing social marketing efforts involving 'critical social marketing' to counteract the influences of commercial marketers (see Chapters 6 and 16) – for example, involving the tobacco companies – will be an important source of insight.

SEGMENTING MARKETS FOR PRO-ENVIRONMENTAL BEHAVIOURS

Once key behavioural priorities have been identified, segmenting markets allows the different potential motivators of, and barriers to, behaviour change to be understood across distinctive groups within the general population (see Chapter 8, for more on segmentation and targeting). Part of the success of social marketing campaigns is that they target the behaviour of specific types of people (like women, teenagers, parents, smokers or the overweight) and customise interventions to meet their needs. Although public environmental campaigns can target specific groups (such as drivers), they have more often attempted to influence the consumption behaviours of all consumers using a single message. The effectiveness of this has increasingly been called into question as evidence has accumulated that people differ in how they relate to the environment, which environmental issues concern them, what connections they make with their lifestyles and how they perceive responsibilities for causing and tackling environmental problems (Barr, 2007).

In relation to environmental sustainability, commercial marketers have led efforts to group consumers into meaningful and measurable market segments according to their attitudes, knowledge, behaviours and other characteristics (Straughan and Roberts, 1999). Rose et al. (2007), for example, suggest using a psychographic segmentation to understand and target social status and fashion-conscious 'outer directed' consumers since they are the ones most prone to overconsumption.

One of the only comprehensive segmentation exercises to approach the subject from a social marketing perspective was produced by the British Market Research Bureau for Defra (2007). This used demographics, psychographics, behaviours and barriers faced to divide the UK population into the following seven distinct segments:

1. **Greens**: who are driven by a belief that environmental issues are crucial. They are well-educated on green issues, feel involved with and connected to the issues and arguments and do not view environmentally orientated people as strange or eccentric.
2. **Consumers with a conscience**: who want to be *seen* to be green. They are motivated by environmental concern and seek to avoid feeling guilty about environmental damage. They are focused on consumption and making positive choices.
3. **Wastage focused**: who dislike waste of any kind and seek to avoid it. They have good knowledge about wastage and local pollution, but lack awareness of other issues and behaviours. This group see themselves as ethically distinct from the greens.
4. **Currently constrained**: who would like to be green, but who don't think there is much they can do in their current circumstances. They have a focus on balance, pragmatism and realism.
5. **Basic contributors**: who are sceptical about the need for behaviour change. They tend to think about their behaviour relative to that of others and are driven by a desire to conform with social norms. They have relatively little knowledge of, or interest in, environmental issues and behaviours.
6. **Long-term restricted**: who have a number of serious life priorities to address before they can begin to consciously consider their environmental impacts. Their everyday behaviours often have relatively low impacts, but for reasons other than environmental concern (e.g. through ill health, old age or relative poverty).
7. **Dis-interested**: who display no interest or motivation to change their current behaviours to make their lifestyle more pro-environmental. They may be aware of climate change and other environmental issues, but this has not entered their current decision-making processes. This is a group for whom other types of intervention will be required through regulation, fiscal measures, 'choice editing' or structural measures.

The results of this segmentation exercise highlighted the importance of a social marketing approach to encouraging PEB within society. There was considerable variation in the attitudes, behaviours and the motivating factors and barriers among the different segments. Mass communication strategies to encourage PEB are unlikely to succeed, since a message that appeals to and motivates one segment could well have the opposite effect on another. This segmentation was then cross-referenced with the behaviour priorities short list (from the previous section) to create a map of sustainability-orientated behaviour change opportunities (Figure 23.1), most of which are self-explanatory.

PARTNERSHIPS FOR PRO-ENVIRONMENTAL BEHAVIOURS

The process of trying to promote more sustainable lifestyles and consumption behaviours creates an interesting blurring of the boundary between social and commercial marketing (and marketers). The ultimate goals are primarily social, yet the key context of consumption behaviours is essentially (or at least traditionally) commercial.

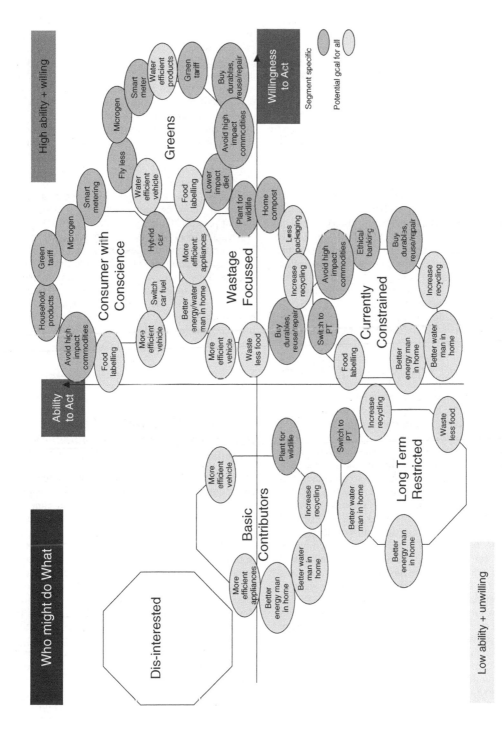

Figure 23.1 Sustainable consumption behaviour opportunities (Defra, 2007). PT = public transport

Social marketing generally involves taking the micromarketing philosophy, tools and techniques of the commercial marketer and applying them in social contexts to meet macromarketing social goals. Influencing consumer behaviour in pursuit of environmental sustainability often has a reciprocal dimension that involves taking the societal goals of the social marketer and seeking to apply them within a commercial consumption context.

As companies seek to adopt corporate social responsibility and sustainable marketing strategies, so the distinction between commercial and social marketers seeking to encourage PEB among consumers becomes less clear. This creates a new situation in which the commercial marketer seeking to pursue more sustainable marketing strategies can learn valuable lessons from the social marketer (Belz and Peattie, 2009). Although the consumption reduction agenda can place social and commercial marketers in opposition, the overall sustainability agenda can also often encourage them to join forces to promote the adoption of an environmentally superior technology, product or consumption behaviour.

The marketing strategies of social enterprises (organisations which pursue primarily social goals through commercial means) and environmental cause-related marketing strategies involving commercial and social partners are just two areas where the worlds of social and commercial marketing are becoming more intertwined. Another example of the boundary-blurring process comes from commercially based campaigns to influence domestic behaviours. For example, companies such as Proctor & Gamble (manufacturer of Ariel detergent) and Marks & Spencer developed campaigns to encourage consumers to machine wash their clothes at 30°C, a simple behaviour change which creates laundry energy savings of around 41%. IPC Green Matters Research in 2007 showed that 88% of those who had changed their behaviour to wash at 30°C had been influenced by the Ariel campaign. P&G had a commercial vested interest in encouraging this change, because it was linked to their product claims of effective washing performance at lower temperatures. For M&S the campaign was not product-linked but was one part of their 'Plan A' corporate sustainability strategy to improve the social and environmental performance of all aspects of its business, including its customers' behaviour. The message about the environmental (and money-saving) benefits of washing at 30°C was reaching consumers from manufacturer, retailer and government campaigns with little clear delineation between what was commercial, and what was social, marketing.

A final example of the blurring process is Fairtrade, in which a product is promoted to consumers in (mostly) industrialised nations on the basis of the social and environmental benefits derived for the producer and producer communities in poorer countries by patronising a brand which pays a defined minimum price for commodities such as coffee or sugar (through standards which also incorporate environmental protection of biodiversity). This is a commercial operation in which the marketer promotes both the benefit to the consumer (which typically combines an emphasis on product quality with the 'warm glow' from a socially responsible purchase) and a wider social benefit to the producer and environmental benefits. Although the context may be conventional commercial marketing, the mindset is much closer to social marketing in promoting a social proposition to consumers, linked to choosing and purchasing a particular type of product (Golding and Peattie, 2005).

These blurred boundaries suggest that there are considerable opportunities for partnership activities between commercial, public and third-sector organisations to promote PEB within peoples' consumption behaviour and lifestyles. This has implications for social marketing since it has proved itself an effective mechanism for developing partnership initiatives that integrate efforts across these sectors (Andreasen, 2006).

CONCLUSION

Integrating the social marketing and the environmental sustainability agendas

More than 20 years have passed since the Brundtland Report was published and, despite many laudable initiatives, policies and innovations, humankind's destruction of the natural environment continues to accelerate. It was at about the time of the Brundtland Report's publication that human society's demands on the planet went beyond what could be sustained without environmental quality becoming degraded and less productive, according to ecological footprinting data (for more details, see Hails, 2008). In other words, for the past 20 years we have been living beyond our environmental means, and scientific evidence is mounting that the eventual cost of this particular debt will be an impact on our economy and quality of life that will make the 2008/2009 'credit crunch' seem insignificant. It has also placed the environmental health and public health agendas on a collision course, which means that for the next generation of social marketers, 'sustainability' will be about much more than the continuation of funding.

Attempts to promote more sustainable behaviours have often suffered from the same problems as early health promotion campaigns of an over-reliance on the provision of information, awareness raising and trying to promote positive attitudes. Research has gradually revealed that the links between information, awareness, attitudes and actual PEB are frequently very weak (Jackson, 2005). Social norms, the symbolic importance of consumption activities, habit, time constraints and situational factors are also crucially important and help to explain the commonly appearing gap between peoples' pro-environmental attitudes and their consumption behaviours. Jackson's conclusions from his review of the evidence base reads like a clear call for both upstream and downstream social marketing interventions in pursuit of sustainability:

It is clear that achieving pro-environmental behaviour change demands a more sophisticated policy approach. A concerted strategy is needed to make behaviour change easy: ensuring that **incentive structures and institutional rules** favour pro-environmental behaviour, **enabling access** to pro-environmental choice, **engaging people** in initiatives to help themselves, and **exemplifying the desired changes** within Government's own policies and practices (p. xii).

It could be assumed that the challenge of securing environmental health through pro-environmental behavioural change would be similar to promoting behaviour change for personal health. Indeed, some of the behaviours coincide, and the social marketing process applied to influence them could be almost identical. Walking or cycling instead of driving, reducing red meat consumption, consuming fresh local produce and avoiding pre-packaged and pre-prepared foods all contribute to protecting both the health of individuals and the environment. The concept of the LOHAS (lifestyles of health and sustainability) market has emerged to describe those consumers who combine a pursuit of a healthier lifestyle with environmental concern (Belz and Peattie, 2009). However, environmental sustainability campaigns involve collective, long-term benefits in which the connection between the behaviour and the contribution to sustainability are often complex and difficult to prove (in other words they mostly operate at the right-hand side of the context for social marketing propositions; see Figure 10.1).

Environmental behaviours frequently lack the obvious direct and personal benefits that most health-related social marketing campaigns can use as motivators. Social marketers have therefore often had to be creative to uncover the less obvious direct and personal benefits within

environmental campaigns to make them appeal to people. One of the more creative campaigns was the Chesapeake Bay 'Save the crabs, then eat 'em' campaign (Landers et al., 2006). This campaign sought to reduce the use of fertilisers on domestic lawns and the resulting environmentally damaging run-off which polluted the local waterways. It appealed to householders to reduce fertiliser use in order to protect the local blue crabs, which were also a prized delicacy in local restaurants – hence, the campaign strapline.

For some key environmental behaviours, there are also direct and personal benefits that can be used to leverage behaviour change. Reducing household use of energy and other resources can bring direct economic benefits. The highly successful TravelSmart campaign was aimed at promoting more sustainable travel behaviours among Australian city dwellers, but did so by stressing that substituting walking or cycling for short car journeys can bring benefits of health, economy and convenience (James, 2002).

As social marketing has evolved as a discipline, so it has become better suited to behaviours linked to environmental sustainability as well as to the conventional health agenda. Social marketing, taking its cue from commercial marketing, originally had a tendency to focus on a specific type of behaviour (such as smoking or consuming a high-fat diet) and its impact on the health of the individual. Sustainability challenges are less easy to understand and tackle from such a perspective. The environmental sustainability of any behaviour depends upon the sustainability of the lifestyle it is part of, and the sustainability of both the society in which it occurs, and of any resources used (and how they are provided) to support it. A simple illustration of the need for a holistic lifestyle perspective is the so-called 'rebound effect' of economic savings that arises from energy-saving interventions. Successful domestic energy reduction programmes generate financial savings for households, but their overall environmental impact depends on what other form of consumption is accounted for by the savings (Herring, 1999). A household that uses the money it saves on energy bills for a long-haul flight for a cheap holiday is unlikely to have reduced their overall environmental impact.

Over time a greater understanding has emerged within social marketing of the importance of understanding health behaviours from a more collective perspective of a household or a community, and of considering a behaviour as part of a lifestyle rather than in isolation. These insights will also be important in relation to environmental sustainability and the promotion of environmentally sustainable lifestyles and communities (Barr et al., 2006). The importance of communal behaviours and of community-led social marketing solutions for sustainability challenges has been widely recognised, particularly through the work of McKenzie-Mohr (2000) and his colleagues working in the field of community-based social marketing.

The need to understand the collective impacts of our lifestyles, rather than of individual behaviours, also operates at a societal level. Imagine for a moment that the government of the Seychelles achieved a change in its citizens' behaviour so that they all consumed no more resources than their islands could produce, and produced no more waste and pollution than their local environment could absorb. This would do nothing to hold back the rising sea levels that they must endure as a result of the climate impacts caused by consumption and production behaviours in other societies.

Climate change is not the only important sustainability issue that social marketers can help to tackle, but it is the one which most powerfully demonstrates the connection between our collective behaviours, environmental sustainability and human well-being. It is also the challenge we cannot afford to get wrong. A failure to change our behaviours to reduce our climate impacts will undo much of the good done by policymakers trying to pursue sustainable development, and all the social marketing efforts to improve our health, well-being and environmental quality.

The sustainability challenge will ultimately require transformative changes to the norms, attitudes, lifestyles and behaviours of individuals and organisations worldwide. Maintaining current patterns of consumption and production, and existing inequalities in health, wealth and environmental quality, is neither morally defensible nor physically possible. Progress will require a mix of regulation, investment and innovation being applied to policy, technology and education in the search for transformative change. Ultimately, however, the importance of behaviour change as the 'Holy Grail' of sustainable development policy means that social marketers will have a vital role to play in this particular crusade.

KEY WORDS: Sustainable development; environmental protection; ecosystem services; pro-environmental behaviours; consumption reduction.

Key insights

- Sustainable development represents an approach which balances economic development with social welfare and environmental protection with the aim of improving and sustaining the quality of life for both current stakeholders and future generations. Social marketing has the potential to contribute across a broad range of issues within the sustainable development agenda which tackle poverty, health inequalities and environmental protection. Two important but controversial behavioural spheres to tackle are population control among poorer countries and reducing over-consumption and inefficient use of resources in richer countries.
- The human health and environmental health agendas have traditionally been considered separately, but environmental challenges such as the health impacts of climate change are demonstrating that environmental quality has a very direct impact on human health and quality of life.
- A range of behavioural issues are key to environmental protection. Pro-environmental behaviours relate to our roles as consumers, and as citizens, but these roles are beginning to merge. Key behaviours can include significant life changes such as having children or relocating, and 'everyday' behaviours relating to our household consumption and domestic routines. Many environmental impacts relate to the running of our homes, the food we eat and our transport and travel behaviours.
- As social marketing has evolved beyond a focus on specific behaviours or individuals to include more holistic approaches, taking into account lifestyles and social context (particularly the influence of communities), so it has become increasingly well suited to influencing environmental behaviours.

REFERENCES

Andreasen, A.R. (2006) *Social Marketing in the 21st Century*. Thousand Oaks, CA: Sage Publications.

Aron, J.L. and Patz, J.A. (2001) *Ecosystem Change and Public Health: A Global Perspective*. Baltimore, MD: Johns Hopkins Press.

Banfi, S., Mehdi, F., Massimo, F. and Martin, J. (2008) 'Willingness to pay for energy-saving measures in residential buildings', *Energy Economics*, 30(2): 503–516.

Barr, S. (2007) 'Factors influencing environmental attitudes and behaviors: A UK case study of household waste management', *Environment and Behavior*, 39(4): 435–473.

Barr, S., Gilg, A. and Shaw, G. (2006) *Promoting Sustainable Lifestyles: A Social Marketing Approach*. London: Department for Environment, Food and Rural Affairs.

Belz, F.-M. and Peattie, K. (2009) *Sustainability Marketing: A Global Perspective*. London: Wiley.

Burgess, J., Bedford, T., Hobson, K., Davies, G. and Harrison, C. (2003) '(Un)sustainable consumption', in F. Berkhout,

M. Leach and I. Scoones (eds), *Negotiating Environmental Change: New Perspectives from Social Science*. Cheltenham: Edward Elgar, pp. 261–291.

Cao, X. and Mokhtarian, P.L. (2005). 'How do individuals adapt their personal travel? A conceptual exploration of the consideration of travel-related strategies', *Transport Policy*, 12(3): 199–206.

Carlsson-Kanyama, A. and González, A.D. (2009) Potential contributions of food consumption patterns to climate change', *American Journal of Clinical Nutrition*, 89(5 Suppl): S1704–S1709.

Corvalán, C., Hales, S. and McMichael, A.J. (2005) *Ecosystems and Human Well-Being: Health Synthesis*. Millennium Ecosystem Assessment (Program). Geneva: World Health Organization.

Defra (2007) *Survey of Public Attitudes and Behaviours toward the Environment*. London: Department for Environment, Food and Rural Affairs.

Dholakia, R.R. and Dholakia, N. (2000) 'Social marketing and development', in P.N. Bloom and G. Gundlach (eds), *Handbook of Marketing and Society*. Thousand Oaks, CA: Sage Publications.

Downing, P. and Ballantyne, J. (2007) *Tipping Point of Turning Point: Social Marketing & Climate Change*. London: Ipsos MORI.

Dunhaime, C.P., McTavish, R. and Ross, C.A. (1985) 'Social marketing: An approach to Third-World development', *Journal of Macromarketing*, 5: 3–13.

Duxbury, L. (2003) 'Communication and its role in bringing about sustainable land management', *Environmental Health*, 3(2): 85–94.

Eckersley, R. (1998) 'Perspectives of progress: Economic growth, quality of life and ecological sustainability', in R. Eckersley (ed), *Measuring Progress. Is Life Getting Better?* Collingwood: CSIRO Publishing, pp. 3–34.

Ehrlich, P.R. and Ehrlich, A.H. (1990) *The Population Explosion*. New York: Simon and Schuster, pp. 58–59.

Garcia, R., Bardhi, F. and Friedrich, C. (2007) 'Overcoming consumer resistance to innovation', *MIT Sloan Management Review*, 48(4): 82–88.

Golding, K. and Peattie, K. (2005) 'In search of a golden blend: Perspectives on the marketing of fair trade coffee', *Sustainable Development*, 13(3): 154–165.

Hails, C., Humphrey, S., Loh, J. and Goldfinger S. (eds) (2008) *Living Planet Report*. Gland, CH: WWF International.

Harvey, P.D. (1999) *Let Every Child be Wanted: How Social Marketing is Revolutionizing Contraceptive Use around the World*. Westport, CT: Greenwood.

Hastings, G. and Saren, M. (2003) 'The critical contribution of social marketing: Theory and application', *Marketing Theory*, 3(3): 305–322.

Herring, H. (1999) 'Does energy efficiency save energy? The debate and its consequences', *Applied Energy*, 63(3): 209–226.

Hopwood, B., Mellor, M. and O'Brien, G. (2005) 'Sustainable development: Mapping different approaches', *Sustainable Development*, 13: 38–52.

Jacobson, S.K., Sieving, K.E., Jones, G.A. and Van Doorn, A. (2003) 'Assessment of farmer attitudes and behavioural intentions towards bird conservation on organic and conventional Florida farms', *Conservation Biology*, 17(2): 595–606.

Jackson, T. (2005) *Motivating Sustainable Consumption: A Review of Evidence on Consumer Behaviour and Behavioural Change*. London: Policy Studies Institute.

Jackson, T. (2009) *Prosperity without Growth*. London: Sustainable Development Commission.

James, B. (2002) 'TravelSmart, large-scale cost-effective mobility management: Experiences from Perth, WA', *Municipal Engineer*, 1: 39–48.

James, O. (2008) *The Selfish Capitalist*. London: Vermillion.

Janz, N.K. and Becker, M.H. (1984) 'The health belief model: A decade later', *Health Education Quarterly*, 11: 1-47.

Kelly, G. and Doherty, M. (2003) 'Healthy, wealthy and wise: A systematic approach to environmental and social health', *Environmental Health*, 3(20): 11–25.

Kennedy, R.D. (2001) 'Social marketing of the Residential Energy Efficiency Project: Effective community implementation of a national program', *Environments*, 28(3): 57–72.

Kotler, P. and Lee, N.R. (eds) (2007) *Social Marketing: Influencing Behaviors for Good*. Thousand Oaks, CA: Sage Publications.

Kotler, P. and Lee, N.R. (2009) *Up and Out of Poverty: The Social Marketing Solution*. Philadelphia, PA: Wharton School Publishing.

Kozinets, R.V. and Handelman, J.M. (2004) 'Adversaries of consumption: Consumer movements, activism, and ideology', *Journal of Consumer Research*, 31: 691-704.

Kurani, K.S. and Turrentine, T.S. (2002) *Marketing Clean and Efficient Vehicles: A Review of Social Marketing and Social Science Approaches*. Davis, CA: Institute of Transportation Studies, University of California.

Landers, J., Mitchell, P., Smith, B., Lehman, T. and Conner, C. (2006) '"Save the crabs, then eat 'em": A culinary approach to saving the Chesapeake Bay', *Social Marketing Quarterly*, 12: 15–28.

Lang, T. (2002) 'Can the challenges of poverty, sustainable consumption and good health governance be addressed in an era of globalization?' in B. Caballero and B.M. Popkin (eds), *The Nutrition Transition: Diet and Disease in the Developing World*. London: Academic Press, pp. 51-70.

Leiserowitz, A.A., Kates, R.W. and Parris, T M. (2005) 'Do global attitudes and behaviors support sustainable development?', *Environment*, 47(9): 22-38.

Mackay, D. (2008), *Sustainable Energy – Without the Hot Air*. Cambridge: UIT.

McKenzie-Mohr, D. (2000) 'Promoting sustainable behavior: An introduction to community-based social marketing', *Journal of Social Issues*, 56(4): 543–554.

McMichael, A.J., Haines, A., Slooff, R. and Kovats, S. (1996) *Climate Change and Human Health*. Geneva: World Health Organization.

Maibach, E. (1993) 'Social marketing for the environment: Using information campaigns to promote environmental awareness and behavior change', *Health Promotion International*, 8(3): 209–224.

Mont, O. and Plepys, A. (2008) 'Sustainable consumption progress: Should we be proud or alarmed?' *Journal of Cleaner Production*, 16(4): 531–537.

Peattie, K. (2010) 'Green consumption: Behavior and norms', *Annual Review of Environment and Resources*, 35: 195–228.

Peattie, K. and Peattie, S. (2009), 'Social marketing: A pathway to consumption reduction?' *Journal of Business Research*, 62(2): 260–268.

Popkin, B.M. (2002) 'An overview on the nutrition transition and its health implications: The Bellagio meeting', *Public Health and Nutrition*, 5: 93–103.

Regmi, P.P. and Weber, K.E. (2000) 'Problems to agricultural sustainability in developing countries and a potential solution: Diversity', *International Journal of Social Economics*, 27(7–10): 788–801.

Rose, C., Dade, P. and Scott, J. (2007) *Research into Motivating Prospectors, Settlers and Pioneers to Change Behaviours that Affect Climate Emissions*. Norfolk: Campaign Strategy Ltd.

Sasako, M. (2001) Standby power consumption of household electrical appliances in Japan. *Third International Workshop on Standby Power*, Tokyo, 7–8 February.

Shove, E. and Warde, A. (2002) 'Inconspicuous consumption: The sociology of consumption, lifestyles and the environment', in R.E. Dunlap, F.H. Buttel, P. Dickens and A. Gijswijt (eds), *Sociological Theory and the Environment: Classic Foundations, Contemporary Insights*. Lanham, MA: Rowman & Littlefield.

Smithers, R. (2007) *Campaign Launched to Reduce UK's £8bn Food Waste Mountain*. Available at: www.politics.guardian. co.uk, November 2.

Steinfeld, H., Gerber, P., Wassenaar, T., et al. (2006) *Livestock's Long Shadow – Environmental Issues and Option*, Rome: FAO.

Straughan, R.D. and Roberts, J.A. (1999) 'Environmental segmentation alternatives: A look at green consumer behaviour in the new millennium', *Journal of Consumer Marketing*, 16(6): 558–575.

Taylor, D.W. and Muller, T.E. (1992) 'Eco-literacy and environmental citizenship: A social marketing challenge for public sector management', *Optimum*, 23(3): 6–16.

Tukker, A. (2005) 'Leapfrogging into the future: Developing for sustainability', *International Journal of Innovation and Sustainable Development*, 1(1/2): 65–84.

Tukker, A., Huppes, G., Guinée, J., et al. (2005) *Environmental Impact of Products (EIPRO) 2005: Analysis of the Life Cycle Environmental Impacts Related to the Total Final Consumption of the EU25*. Brussels: European Commission Joint Research Centre.

Turaga, R.M.R., Howarth, R.B. and Borsuki, M.E. (2010) 'Pro-environmental behaviour: Rational choice meets moral motivation', *Annals of the New York Academy of Sciences*, 1185(1 Ecological Economics Reviews): 211–224.

UNICEF (2000) *Progress of Nations Report*. Paris: UNICEF.

UNPD (2001) *Majority of World's Couples are Using Contraception*. New York: United Nations Population Division.

UNPF (2007) *State of the World's Population 2007*. New York: United Nations Population Fund.

WCED (1987) *Our Common Future* (*The Brundtland Report*). World Commission on Environment and Development. Oxford: Oxford University Press.

World Bank (2004) *World Development Indicators*. Washington, DC: International Bank for Reconstruction and Development.

WRI (2005) *Ecosystems and Human Well-being: Synthesis Report (Millennium Ecosystem Assessment)*. Washington, DC: World Resources Institute/Island Press.

WWF (2008) *Living Planet Report*. Gland, Switzerland: WWF International.

Zikmund, W.G. and Stanton, W.J. (1971) 'Recycling of solid wastes: A channel-of-distribution problem', *Journal of Marketing*, 35(3): 34–39.

24

Business as Unusual: The Contribution of Social Marketing to Government Policymaking and Strategy Development

Jeff French

Social marketing is not about telling people what to do or coercing them into doing it, but the art of understanding what will help people make choices and take action which will lead them to better lives. In short, politicians and public officials who seek to serve the public and make the world a better place have to learn how to make positive life choices the easy and natural choices for people. This means that they will need to embrace social marketing principles as a core approach to policy and strategy development as well as a powerful tool for developing specific interventions.

INTRODUCTION

The world faces a number of key challenges as we move into the 21st century. We face a huge growth in chronic disease associated with both an ageing population and behavioural choices such as overeating and smoking (World Health Organization, 2008). There are growing threats to the environment and sustainable development (Stern, 2007). we also face massive economic challenges resulting from poor economic management (Marmot et al., 2008).

The last hundred years of human development has seen remarkable progress in the well-being, and material circumstances of much of the world's population. Governments, non-governmental organisations (NGOs) and the private sector in a growing number of countries are dealing with populations with characteristics that have simply not existed until this point in human history. In short, governments and their agencies, as well as the private sector and the NGO sector, are dealing with populations that are very different to those of even 30 years ago. Reduced absolute poverty, increased education (literacy and numeracy), mass access to information and growing expectations are not universal, but they are becoming the expected and desired norm. Figure 24.1 illustrates some of the main contextual challenges and uncertainties faced by civil society and some of the possible outcomes.

Factors such as obesity, smoking, energy use and civic disengagement have substantial behavioural components and governments are now seeking to tackle these issues.

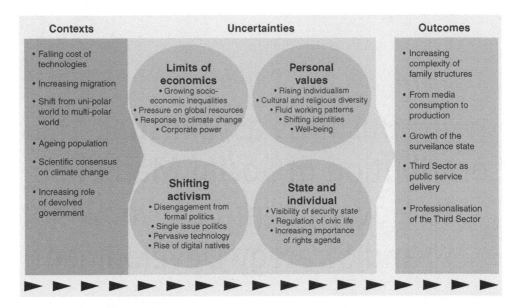

Figure 24.1   Some of the main contextual challenges and uncertainties faced by civil society and some of the possible outcomes. Source: Henley Centre HeadlightVision for The Carnegie Trust

WHY SOCIAL MARKETING SHOULD BE ADOPTED BY GOVERNMENTS?

Until now social marketing has been the province of a relatively few dedicated academics and practitioners. However, we are now witnessing the slow but steady adoption of social marketing by many public sector organisations, agencies and governments. Why is this happening now?

There are a number of drivers that have come together to create more interest in the application of social marketing to key policy and behavioural challenges across government. In a tautological and literal sense, human behaviour sits at the heart of all politics and subsequent policy formulation, strategy development and operational delivery in the public sector. Owing to the triumph of increasingly empowered populations, governments who want to stay in power or parties seeking power will in future focus more on the development of policies and interventions that are not only supported by the electorate but also are increasingly defined by, involve and meet the needs of citizens.

Social marketing, with its emphasis on understanding people as the starting point for developing intervention, is a powerful tool that needs to be more systematically applied and it is one that is usually easily understood by politicians as the political process itself is increasingly being influenced by marketing and politicians are increasingly having to become marketing experts. As a recent report makes clear, much of what has been done to date to assist people to change behaviour has not been as effective as it could have been if more systematic approaches had been taken to applying social marketing and the use of geodemographics. Social marketing can

> Give commissioners insights into the needs and behaviours of different kinds of people. Investment should be made in developing these skills among PCT [Primary Care Trust] staff and in improving both the quality and the quantity of data on local public health needs that they use in their work. Understanding how to use social marketing tools and having reliable data on local needs are vital first steps to finding solutions (Boyce et al., 2008: vii).

The fact of increasingly empowered citizens has huge implications for state-sponsored interventions intent on making the world a better place. It means that increasingly a focus on enabling and empowering people to do the right thing for themselves and others is a key part of the way forward. This means services and interventions being driven by a desire to meet citizens needs and not needs defined solely by experts or politicians.

A further driver is the increasing significance of behavioural challenges linked to major policy areas. For example, health is increasingly acknowledged to be a basic human right and also a marker for success in many governments. Good health also conveys economic advantage to states and promotes a more effective and sustainable healthcare system. The balance of current evidence suggest that tackling chronic disease will require a balanced programme of both clinical intervention and primary prevention focused on behaviour change. Health distribution and social inclusion are also increasing challenges for the majority of governments – people who most need services and are most often disproportionately at most risk and those who are in most need of support of behaviour change are least likely to have access to services to support them. We also know that the long-term costs and sustainability are key issues. Most governments are experiencing increasing growth in healthcare budgets as a percentage of gross domestic product (GDP). This trend is probably not sustainable in the long term and represents a significant challenge for all countries. However, there is good evidence that well-planned and executed behavioural change programmes can be highly cost-effective and reduce demand on healthcare systems and costs:

> This review suggests that a 10% improvement in outcomes as a result of prevention and social marketing could save families £7b, reduce public expenditure by £3b, reduce employer costs by £1.5b and would generate social values of over £8b (Lister et al., 2006: 11).

> Four out of five deaths in the UK of people under 75 could probably have been prevented. Existing public health campaigns are not currently reaching those who continue to smoke, take little exercise, eat poorly and drink too much. The financial cost of preventable ill health ranks alongside our economic stability and international security. Our economic analysis estimates that the total annual cost to the country of preventable illness amounts to a minimum of £187 billion. In comparative terms this equates to 19% of total GDP for England (NSMC, 2006: 3).

> Prevention can be much more cost-effective than cure. Especially when targeted at groups with high risks, prevention can be substantially more cost-effective (Belot, 2006: 19).

> The evidence shows that some 25–30% percent of the burden of disease in Canada can be attributed to the following four risk factors:

- Smoking
- Physical inactivity
- Unhealthy eating patterns

- Immoderate use of alcohol (Ministry of Health Planning, 2003: 9).

The underutilisation and misinterpretation of marketing in government policy and strategy development and what can be done about it

Many government policies that try to change behaviour are not effective or have such weak evaluation that is difficult to tell if they are effective or not (French and Mayo, 2006; Hills, 2004). However, there has been significant growth in knowledge about what works and what does not in the field of behaviour change and how to plan and deliver such interventions over recent years but often this knowledge is not always used to shape national interventions or local community interventions. Worse still is the practice of some governments running media-based promotional programmes that they know will have little effect other than to create a sense that a government is acting. In this situation, governments and their officials and the agencies that work with them seem to be trapped in a situation in which they all know that what is being delivered has little chance of success but they still invest time and effort in it. There is often political and policy pressure to 'be seen to be acting' on behavioural challenges and for action to happen rapidly. This often means that advertising and other media promotions are seen as a quick way of demonstrating that action is being taken. This situation can be described as a *conspiracy of passive failure*.

This conspiracy is not driven by a wish for programmes to fail or as a way to fool the public that solutions are known but rather by more positive and understandable motivators such as a desire to do something and to do it quickly, or a belief that people need encouragement and information. There is also often a very real political need to be seen to be acting to give confidence to people that something can be done and it can be done by the government. Clearly, media promotions and advertising and other forms of mass communication are extremely powerful tools that social marketers will want to deploy and in the right circumstances, as part of the right marketing and policy mix, can play a major role (Hornick, 2002; Lannon, 2008). However, the point is that they should be used as part of planned and coordinated marketing strategy not as the default solution.

Much government communication and marketing is also bedevilled by six further misapplications of marketing in support of policy-making and strategy development. These issues relate to:

1. Silo working.
2. Short-term planning and budgeting and insufficient investment in scoping and development.
3. Lack of outcome-based budgeting.
4. Poor or incongruent evaluation.
5. A lack of strategic social focus.
6. Poorly articulated aims and objectives.

Silo working results from different government departments and agencies having responsibilities for distinct policy areas focused on behaviour change such as smoking reduction, transport safety, recycling, energy use, etc. Often, even within single departments or agencies, related behavioural issues are dealt with by different policy and communications and marketing teams such as illegal drug misuse and alcohol misuse or sexual health. This approach to marketing in the public sector results in both friendly fire competition and potential inefficiencies. Government agencies can often be found competing with each other for citizen's attention or to influence behaviour change among the same target groups. This often happens even when issues could potently be tackled from the citizen's perspective as a single issue such a safe alcohol use and safe sex, these two issues being often very closely associated in actual decision-making and subsequent behaviours.

There is often a perceived need to act quickly not only for political reasons but also for reasons of departmental pressure associated with annual budgeting rounds for programmes. The phrase 'use your budget or lose it' is one known to many public sector managers. Historic budgeting encourages people to spend funds quickly, especially towards the end of financial years, to ensure that their budgets are not cut in the following year. One of the few ways that large amounts of funding can be spent in a short period of time is on mass media advertising, and it is well known in the advertising industry that the last quarter of public service spending years is generally a bumper time. These pressures result then in media or even marketing programmes being less effective than they could have been if sufficient time had been invested to thoroughly develop the programme.

A lack of outcome-focused budgeting is a further example of why many public sector communication and marketing programmes do not succeed. Outcome-based budgeting involves the adoption of a three-phase approach to budgeting. First, budgets are sought for a thorough scoping phase to gather research, data and evidence and develop preliminary hypothesis about possible forms of intervention. The second phase of budget allocation is the construction of a development phase budget to pretest and refine and evaluate possible forms of intervention. This stage culminates in the development of a full business case and the time-scale for the application of the recommended budget that will be required to deliver measurable outcomes across the designated target group. Rather than this form of outcome-based budgeting, many public sector 'campaigns' start with the allocation of a fixed sum of money. So, rather than start with the question 'How much do we need to invest over what time to hit the targets we wish to achieve?' marketers and communication staff in the public sector are faced with the question 'What can you do with this much money during the next three months?'

One of the most effective tactics for getting social marketing taken more seriously and attracting funding of sufficient size and duration is to recommend and move towards the three-step approach to outcome-focused budgeting described above.

Poor evaluation is also common in public sector communication and marketing. Evaluations often focus on awareness or knowledge increase when the real test of a programme is behaviour change. The development of more comprehensive evaluation strategies is another key tactic for convincing governments to take up social marketing interventions. Evaluation strategies should involve process, impact and outcome evaluation elements. Process evaluation should track the efficiency of the programme: that is, Is it reaching the number of people anticipated for the costs predicted? Impact evaluation should capture the immediate or short-term effects of the social marketing programme: that is, Are more people calling the help line that is part of the programme. Outcome evaluation should focus on and provide evidence that people are actually changing their behavior: that is, How many people are now consistently recycling to the level anticipated?

Behaviour change programmes also require a set of clear measurable and achievable behavioural objectives that can be delivered over a designated time-scale. Often, many governmental programmes have unrealistic, or, in the opposite extreme, poorly articulated objectives.

According to Bill Novelli of AARP, picking the wrong goal is one of the mistakes nonprofits repeat the most. 'Too often, people create an elegant plan around the wrong premise or the wrong goal.' 'A successful programme, no matter how we define it, has got to begin with very clear, realistic, measurable goals,' says Barbara Beck of the Pew Charitable Trusts (Fenton Communications, 2009: 4).

Time for social marketing to get strategic

In addition to issues discussed above, one of the biggest weaknesses in public communication and marketing interventions is a lack of strategic focus. Much of the social marketing literature and examples of practice currently lie at the 'operational social marketing' end of the spectrum, where social marketing programmes or campaigns are developed to address specific topic such as condom use. A 'strategic social marketing' approach, by contrast, is increasingly being developed to look at ways in which a stronger customer understanding and insight approach, aligned with more strategic audience segmentation work, and whole systems planning, can inform policy development and strategic planning. As R. Craig Lefebvre suggested:

> We need social marketers to be at the policy table when options are being discussed and presented, not just sat at the sidelines. There are glimmers visible of people in policy areas asking for social marketing viewpoints for policy analysis and creation stages. We need to ensure they know and understand the social marketing viewpoint – be part of the discussions. This is about having an upstream focus, not just advising for the policy status. Change needs to be part of the discussion (Lefebvre, 2008).

A key challenge for social marketing then is to focus 'upstream' to influence policy that, in turn, can impact on factors that affect individual behaviour, such as fiscal policy, food policy and transport policy.

Figure 24.2 illustrates the three levels of social marketing policy, strategy and implementation. Social marketing can be used to inform all three levels and is most effective when it works at all three levels simultaneously to ensure that social programmes are based on common understanding of evidence, citizens' views and a common and mutually reinforcing hierarchy of objectives and programmes of action.

THE CONTRIBUTION OF SOCIAL MARKETING TO POLICY AND STRATEGY FORMULATION IN GOVERNMENT

The 5th 'P' in social marketing is the 'P' in Policy. Many of the challenges which are faced by governments are reflected in transnational and global trends. The connections between people, government and the wider global economy are evolving rapidly, reflecting new challenges in the development of policy. Influences on political policy are many: see Figure 24.3.

Applying social marketing approaches means recognising that in any given situation there are a range of such influences on policy and also a range of possible intervention options that could be used to achieve a particular goal with different groups of people. Evidence indicates that single interventions are generally less effective than multilevel interventions; the point is to make reasoned judgements about the relative balance or mix between the interventions selected. Where this is done at

1: Policy development and scoping
   informed by social marketing
   e.g. citizen/customer/consumer insight

2: Strategic intervention scoping
   a: Informing selection of interventions to achieve goals
   b: Included as an intervention option in its own right, alongside others, i.e. including a social marketing intervention in *the mix*

Operational social marketing:

3: Applied as a planned social marketing process
   either as
   • Social marketing initiative
   • Social marketing campaign
   • Social marketing programme

4: Also able to directly inform development of:
   – other interventions and/or
   – service development and delivery

Figure 24.2   The three levels of social marketing policy, strategy and implementation

- Political ideology and opinion
- Evidence about plausible interventions
- Evidence about the effectiveness of current interventions
- Public opinion
- Expert opinion
- Pressure from vested interest groups
- Pressure from the media
- Observational data
- Technological breakthroughs
- Financial and budgetary opportunities and constraints
- Macroeconomic influences
- Demographic changes
- Global, national and local cultural and social influences
- Systems failures
- Environmental changes, threats and opportunities

Figure 24.3 Some key influences on policy

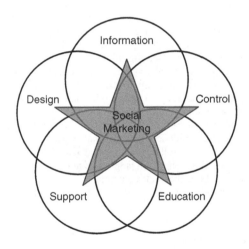

Figure 24.4 The strategic intervention mix

the strategic level it can be described as the 'strategic intervention mix', which is different from the social marketing mix of the 4Ps.

The marketing mix commonly known as the 4Ps, which consists of price, place, product and promotion, is a useful mnemonic for some of the key principles used to develop and deliver social marketing interventions. The strategic intervention mix refers to the mix of five key public sector policy tools that governments can use to improve peoples' lives. All liberal democratic societies use these five tools and combinations of them to deliver a better life experience for citizens (see Figure 24.4).

These tools can be understood as follows:

1. **Control**: using the power of the law and regulations as a body of rules and having binding force to incentives and penalise the behaviour of individuals, organisations and markets for social good.
2. **Information and persuasion**: informs and communicates facts and attitudes and may seek to persuade and suggested behaviours.
3. **Education**: informs and empowers critical decision-making, creates awareness about benefits and develops skills for change and personal development.
4. **Design**: creates the environment and procedures that support self and community development, and safety.
5. **Support**: state and other collectively funded goods and services provided to support mutually agreed social priorities.

Each tool has its strengths and weaknesses, but all five tools are needed to build an integrated strategy of social improvement. A good example of such an approach is the national tobacco control campaign in England. *Go Smoke Free* 2000 used a sustained approach and a wide range of interventions to reduce smoking (www.gosmokefree. co.uk). These included cessation services run alongside a national ban on smoking in public combined with educational programmes and tax disincentives on the purchase of tobacco products. The *Go Smoke Free* strategy also makes use of the marketing mix, by offering different 'products', at the right 'price' (addressing costs and sacrifices, as well as savings), in different 'places' (online, by telephone, through primary care facilities), which are promoted appropriately (through integrated marketing and media programmes). Social marketing can make a significant contribution to the development and application of all of these forms of intervention, as described in the following section.

POLICY COHERENCE AND INTEGRATION

It is vital that behaviour change programmes are also planned and implemented across sector borders; most behavioural challenges facing governments will require the development of delivery coalitions with private sector organisations and NGOs to ensure that sufficient weight of effort and resources can be brought to bear on the issue over a sustained period of time. A multifaceted approach, where a number of sections of government and stakeholder partners combine with a joint vision of what they want to achieve, has a much higher chance of success than single initiatives developed in silos. It is always critical to ensure policy coherence; there are numerous examples of programmes across government which have contradictory aims and objectives.

It follows from the evidence presented here that there is no single intervention, and no simple remedy, that can reduce the burden of chronic diseases. As we have learned from our experience with tobacco, it requires a prolonged commitment of skills and resources in a multi-setting, multi-factor, multi-strategy approach (Ministry of Health Planning, 2003: 10).

The most successful interventions in reducing smoking rates have involved combinations of policies, including price increases, advertising restrictions, smoking site restrictions, consumer education and smoking cessation therapies (Goodman and Anise, 2006: 12).

All successful behavioural programmes utilise a combination of strategies across governments/NGOs/stakeholders to achieve change. Part of this approach is the development of stakeholder coalitions. It is 'vital that any behaviour change programme should be developed in partnership with stakeholder organisations' (NICE, 2007: 20). Working with external stakeholders can provide:

- Useful insight into consumer behaviours: for example, the development of the Obesity Social Marketing Strategy in the UK involved many retail organisations who contributed valuable insight into behaviours of key groups of consumers/target groups.
- Strategic advice and support within the wider political environment: often stakeholders circumnavigate the hierarchical processes of government by their direct access to ministers.
- Organisations close to target group – providing 'main message givers': for example, UK tobacco campaigns fronted by charities to avoid perception of 'stop smoking'.
- In the Netherlands a 'Fat watch' campaign run in partnership with supermarkets and other private sector allies, brought favourable changes in consumption of saturated fats.

Government cannot act alone to actively involve both citizens and the private sector (Department of Work and Pensions, 2009, pp. 36).

Good policymaking and social marketing

We know that in any area of policy where there is a strong knowledge base, and broad consensus about what to do, a high degree of central policy specification can work, so long as it focuses on a few key priorities. Where there is less knowledge about what works, management by setting out broad policy objectives is more likely to succeed, leaving more freedom for front-line managers and staff to develop and test new approaches (The Prime Minister's Strategy Unit, 2006). We also know that involving practitioners in policymaking and ensuring that their knowledge is used early in the policy process improves effectiveness. Both of these areas of policy understanding lend themselves to the application of social marketing to help with setting agreed behavioural objectives and to engaging people and service delivery workers in the development of programmes of action. We also know that effective policymaking results when horizontal networks are developed to assist in the capture and sharing of best practice (The Prime Minister's Strategy Unit, 2006). In essence, effective policymaking should involve (Bullock et al., 2001; Mulgan and Lee, 2001):

1. Designing policies around outcomes.
2. Policy should be informed by end-user wants and needs.
3. Policies should be (and be seen to be) inclusive and fair.
4. Policy should be evidence-based.
5. Policy should avoid unnecessary burdens on delivery agencies or other sector.
6. All relevant stakeholders should be involved in policymaking.
7. Policymaking should be forward- and outward-looking.
8. Policy should have systems in place to learn from experience.

The core policymaking process is essentially about understanding the problem, the context and the stakeholders who are affected by the issue and who might be part of the solution, then going on to develop solutions based on a deep understanding of the evidence and experience that exist. On the basis of this knowledge, the next phase of the policymaking process is to formulate and test possible interventions and combinations against agreed criteria and risks. Next, follows the selection of strategies and agreeing achievable objectives and how they will be measured. As discussed above, social marketing concepts and principles may be used strategically to ensure that a strong customer focus directly informs the identification and selection of appropriate interventions.

Developing policy that can have an impact on many of the big behavioural challenges faced by governments also requires simultaneous short-, medium- and long-term strategic thinking – at least

Table 24.1 Policy matrix

	Short (1–2 years)	Medium (2–5 years)	Medium to Long (5–10 years)	Long (>10 years)
Individual				
Group				
Community				
Locality				
Regional, State or Province				
National				
International Region (IE EU)				
Global				

eight levels of action – as indicated in the policy matrix in Table 24.1.

This framework indicates the need to develop a comprehensive policy spanning different levels of intervention. In addition to developing and sustaining a consistent and coherent policy, there is a need for the policy to be supported by congruent strategies, programmes and projects. This requirement sets out considerable challenges for national governments and even more challenges for international organisations. It requires the development of a long-term vision, and the tenacity to stick with it often over time frames that span more than one administration. Given the nature of politics in democratic countries, governments will change and policy directions will shift. However, to tackle complex social challenges, to shift social norms and support behaviour change at a population level requires the development of a consensus about what the evidence and market research indicates is the correct strategy. This represents a challenge to politicians, for it requires the building of as much cross-party consensus as possible. Such consensus is possible and has been achieved in areas such as energy supply and transportation and health protection involving long-term projects such as nuclear building programmes, but this is not an easy task. A broad consensus still allows for different political approaches to be developed and enacted at the level of strategy development and implementation. For example, the World Health Organization has done much to build a consensus about the policy for health while still leaving individual countries to develop their own interpretations of this broad policy (World Health Organization, 1974). Social marketing can assist with this broad consensus development about the best way to tackle large behavioural issues by helping to bring together both target audience insights and through the development of systematic plans that can be tracked and evaluated over time to demonstrate progress or the need to change programmes in the light of evaluation.

Social marketing can be used strategically to ensure that understanding about target audience behaviour and presences directly informs the identification and selection of appropriate policy and interventions. The power and utility of applying citizens' understanding of their views, beliefs and needs when developing policy and strategy is illustrated in Figure 24.5.

Policy that does not have broad support of the public and strategy that does not meet the needs of the target audiences at which it is directed are unlikely to be successful. There is a need then to engender a sense of ownership for policy intended to improve public health among recipients or effected communities and by those who are developing, delivering and monitoring progress of the policy. Policy that can't or won't be implemented is counterproductive, as it serves only to distract and create cynicism. The creation of public policy is the responsibility of elected officials supported by professionals who are able to advise on the evidence and organisational issues that will inform the policy. Public policy should set out a clear aim to be achieved and supported by an equally clear evidence-based rationale for the policy and its intended interventions.

Developing the strategy for delivering policy needs to involve the widest possible coalition of interests if ownership is to be created and if all available expertise is to be used to inform the development of the strategy. Social marketing has a role to play in supporting the informing of policy and strategy development and, in so doing, creating a sense of ownership and buying into the policy. Social marketing can also help politicians and public officials to test the policy and refine it through a process of target audience engagement. The use of focus groups, surveys, interviews, observational studies and other forms of gathering citizens' views can be powerful tools for ensuring

Figure 24.5   **Understanding citizens' requirements for developing policy and strategy**

- Setting clear, measurable policy objectives, targets and behavioural objectives (individual and organisational).
- Collection and analysis of user and citizen understanding, support for, views and needs, to inform policy selection and development.
- Review of evidence and experience regarding the intended policy.
- Behavioural modelling based on theory, evidence and practice.
- Audience and stakeholder segmentation.
- Understanding and formulating targeted strategies.
- Development and pretesting of services, products, campaigns and other interventions.
- Modelling and projecting impact, outcomes and potential gains.
- Budget development and modelling of return on investment.
- Identifying stakeholders and partners and other asset analysis and development that contribute to delivery.

Figure 24.6   **Examples of how social marketing can assist in the policy development process**

that policy and strategy is developed in such a way that it will be supported and taken up by those whom it is designed to help. The application of this kind of citizen-focused approach to the development and testing of policy and strategy is being increasingly used by governments and political parties to help them develop manifestos that carry popular support.

Figure 24.6 provides examples about how social marketing can assist the policymaking process.

Developing a strategic approach to social marketing

Strategy is the coordinated application of all an organisation's resources to achieve its goals

strategy and is not the same as operational social marketing planning; it involves strategic analysis, strategic choice and strategic implementation and these three tasks are iterative in nature. Strategy is focused on both how an organisation, service or department is structured and operates as well as how it develops specific plans and applies its resources to achieve specific goals. The development of strategy involves the following seven steps:

1. Determine and codify, explicitly, current mission goals and objectives.
2. Agree criteria for selecting a new strategy.
3. Describe the current strategy and assess its strengths and weaknesses.
4. Assess current and future external opportunities and threats.

5. Summarise results of analysis and conclusions.
6. Generate new options and analyse each against results and conclusions of the internal and external analysis.
7. Select a new strategy.

Public sector strategy will set out clear objectives, time frames and the resources that will be applied in the delivery of the strategy. The strategy will be delivered through a series of action and intervention programmes within which there will be specific projects. It is essential to ensure that this simple set of management processes is well understood if the policy is to have any chance of achieving its aims. There needs to be internal consistency between all of these elements along the policy-into-practice continuum. As discussed above, there is often a short-term political driver in developing public policy to jump from policy-making directly into the establishment of a number of pilot projects or even full-scale intervention programmes without having fully developed a long-term strategy that includes a well-developed evaluation strategy capable of capturing both process and outcome data. The development of effective policy requires that each of these planning stages is addressed systematically.

There is also a need to ensure that there is consistency between policy development and delivery and that all learning opportunities are maximised in order to ensure that future strategy and policy development can become increasingly effective over time and that the mistakes of the past are not repeated.

How to promote the uptake of social marketing in government

The key challenge for social marketers is ensuring that the benefits of adopting a social marketing approach are fully understood by politicians and public officials. This is not, in many respects, about selling empirical evidence of the effectiveness of social marketing: rather, it is about constructing a narrative that helps policymakers and planners to understand the rationale for social marketing and the value of its application across policy formulation, strategy development and implementation. The first duty and task for any social marketers is to market social marketing to policymakers and planners. A number of examples of how this can be done are now emerging (French and Blair-Stevens, 2006; Kotler and Lee, 2008). There are a number of tasks that social marketers need to consider when seeking to influence policymakers and planners. These tasks include asking and answering the following two questions:

1. What are policy and planners needs?
2. What will convince them that applying a social marketing approach will enhance the impact of their programme?

To answer these questions it is necessary to bear in mind that, just like all behaviour change programmes, there is in effect what is known as an 'exchange' for policymakers when considering the application of a social marketing approach. The costs for policymakers are focused on the need to invest time in research and gathering users' views. There are the costs of developing and synthesising a more comprehensive array of different forms of evidence and influence on the policymaking process and the possible delay in being able to deliver high-profile visible action, often in the form of a social advertising programme, if this is not supported by the evidence gathered.

On the benefits side of the 'exchange', politicians get a more defendable programme of action because it is based on sound evidence and support from the intended audience. A programme of action more likely to be effective and one that due to its explicit measurable objectives can be used to inform the development of future interventions. Politicians and planners also get a programme of action that is not only fit for purpose but also one that can be tested for its utility because it has clear aims and objectives, known input costs and outcome measures and, through a process of rigorous evaluation and cost–benefit analysis, can add to knowledge about what works and at what cost. The accumulation of this kind of knowledge is a key benefit of taking a social marketing approach.

We all know it pays to plan before executing a big programme. But let's define 'good' planning:

1) Spend time and money planning. Plan for the best-case and worst-case scenarios. Look at the issue from every angle. Understand the problem backwards and forwards. Review potential solutions. Who are your allies in pushing a specific solution? Who are your enemies? It does cost money to plan, but thorough planning means clearer goals, more concise messages, the right target audiences, and a road map leading to success.

2) Think strategy before moving to tactics. Jon Haber of Fleishman-Hillard says the 'laziest thing people do is go right to tactics.' A press breakfast is a tactic. You have to start with what you are trying to get done, who can get it done for you, what you have to tell them, and who has to tell them to persuade them (Fenton Communications, 2009: 10).

Experience in the UK when developing a national social marketing strategy (Department of Health, 2007, 2008) showed that there were four basic subgroups or segments of public officials and politicians in terms of their attitudes and beliefs with regard to social marketing (see Figure 24.7). Different strategies and tactics are required to influence and inform these four groups of politicians and four groups of public officials.

The 'It doesn't work and its wrong' group needs compelling evidence that social marketing can help tackle social issues and convincing that social marketing does not involve the manipulation of people or placing undue responsibility on individuals for what some of this group perceive to be political economic drivers to social problems. While working to convince this group of the merits of social marketing can involve confrontational meetings and strong challenges, the tactics and approach for convincing this group of the merits of social marketing are relatively straightforward.

This group need to be helped to develop a full understanding of social marketing's principles, which are based on a deeply respectful relationship with the target audience and ethical principles that are opposed to manipulation. This group also need to understand that social marketing is not just slick media advertising and emotional appeals that work on peoples' vulnerabilities. This group should be provided with evidence in forms that meet their criteria to convince them that social marketing is a good investment. This means collating and synthesising evidence and providing it in forms and through channels that are credible to this audience such as professional peer-reviewed journals, presentations at conferences and having

independent academic institutions review and synthesise evidence reviews. This set of tactics is also the principal means of convincing the 'It's OK but does it work?' group.

The 'It might work but it's not right' group do not need convincing about the power of social marketing and, if anything, they are more worried that it does work and so is even more dangerous because they believe it is manipulative or has unethical elements. For this group the key tasks for the social marketer are two fold.

The first actions are to set out clearly, in ways that are unambiguous, the principles that underpin social marketing practice. The customer triangle is an example of this kind of tool (NSMC, 2007; see Figure 24.8).

The second set of actions is to develop, if possible, sets of national and local ethical guidance and codes of conduct for social marketing and relate social marketing practice to existing professional codes of practice (Eagle, 2009).

It is also worth considering developing strategies for all groups to address the accusation that social marketing places undue responsibility on individuals to adopt a certain types of behaviour (Maibach and Holtgrave, 1995). It could rightly be argued that social marketing could place an inordinate amount of responsibility on individuals and, in so doing, does not recognise the wider social and economic determinants of particular individual behaviours. An approach to consider when confronting this criticism is to make it clear and give examples about how, when developing social marketing programmes, it is usually necessary to address the social, political or physical barriers that enable or inhibit individual health behaviour. It should also be emphasised that

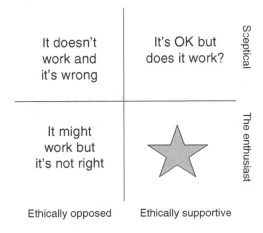

Figure 24.7   The four basic subgroups in terms of their attitudes and beliefs with regard to social marketing

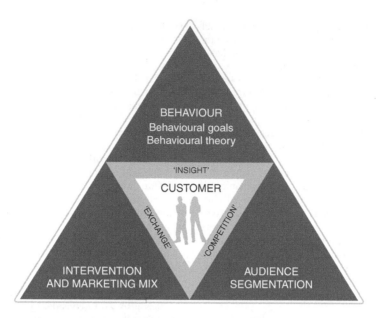

Figure 24.8   The 'customer triangle' © NSMC

social marketing principles can and are being applied to inform the decisions and actions of socio-economic and political decision-makers and service providers. Social marketing has the potential to be a key tool for convincing decision-makers and individuals who are in a position to influence overall social determinants and risk conditions: for example, the 2000 Perth Travel-Smart metropolitan transport strategy 2000. This strategy has set the direction for transport for 35 years in Perth, Australia, based on extensive user research and clear behavioural goals to model travel demand management as part of the transport solutions (http://www.dpi.wa.gov.au/travelsmart).

The 'Star group' are in many ways the most important group, and a group that needs particular effort rather than just leaving them because there are already might be on your side. This group of politicians and public officials can be supported to promote the uptake of social marketing with other groups and to act as very credible advocates to other politicians and public servants and practitioners. This group needs to be nurtured, supported and connected. Putting members of this group in touch with each other through seminars, conferences, briefings and launches can help to build a sense of momentum and a community of interest that can have powerful effects on the policymaking machine. This group can also help to normalise the language of social marketing and help to get social marketing considered as a

possible element in new policymaking and strategy development.

Stars can be further subdivided by the power and interest they have. The power matrix illustrated in Figure 24.9 is a helpful tool for further analysing and developing tailored strategies for influencing politicians and public officials who are generally supportive of social marketing.

Although all of these groups could be described as 'low hanging fruit' (i.e. people who it is possible to influence), the really important group are those who have power to influence the system. Public sector managers and politicians who are generally supportive, but do not have high levels of interest and are powerful, need to be engaged but not over-communicated with, as this may be counterproductive. They need to be briefed and kept informed but do not expect them to act as proactive champions. The 'key players' segment are the people to focus most supportive effort on: for this group, the tactics in Figure 24.10 can be applied.

There are many other ways to seek to influence all groups of politicians and public officials to take an interest in social marketing. These forms of influence are fairly universal: a non-exhaustive list of possible actions is set out in Figure 24.11.

In addition to the list of approaches set out in Figure 24.11, there are many other ways to lobby and seek to influence and inform politicians and public officials, such as writing to elected officials

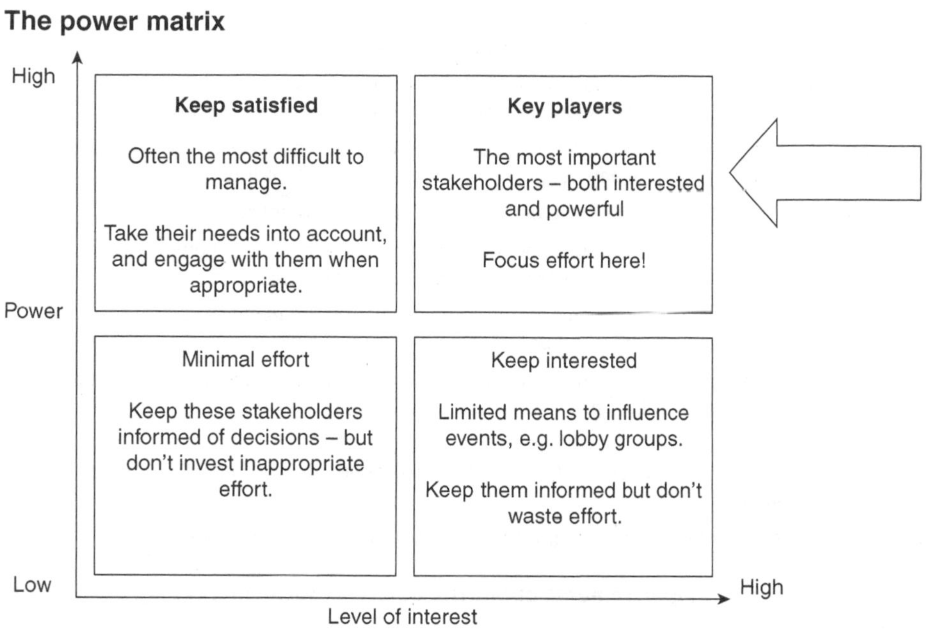

The power matrix

High

Power

Low

	Keep satisfied	**Key players**

Keep satisfied

Often the most difficult to manage.

Take their needs into account, and engage with them when appropriate.

Key players

The most important stakeholders – both interested and powerful

Focus effort here!

Minimal effort

Keep these stakeholders informed of decisions – but don't invest inappropriate effort.

Keep interested

Limited means to influence events, e.g. lobby groups.

Keep them informed but don't waste effort.

Level of interest   High

Figure 24.9   The power matrix

- Build a compelling story about the power of social marketing that key players can understand and use.
- Build supportive networks among these key players.
- Supply key players with examples of good practice and evidence, and give them stories they can tell to others.
- Provide key players with opportunities to experience first-hand the power of applying a social marketing approach (take them on field trips or bring real practitioners to them).
- Provide key players with constructive criticism of current practice and suggestions that they can use to improve performance.
- Take every opportunity to celebrate and promote success with them: for example, set up award ceremonies and invite these politicians or senior public servants to talk at these events or give the awards to great social marketing projects.

Figure 24.10   Key players supportive action checklist

about particular policies and how they might be improved by the application of social marketing, writing letters or making personal contact with the editor of relevant TV, radio, newspapers and magazines, appearing at hearings and committees and other public functions where policy is debated and making points about the relevance and need for the application of social marketing to the issue being considered. The proactive development of policy papers and discussion papers about

how social marketing can help tackle behavioural challenges or public service reform is also a useful tactic.

CONCLUSION

In summary, when seeking to influence politicians and public officials who make up the machinery

1. Scan for and respond to policy proposals and strategies that are put out for consultation and that could benefit from the application of social marketing.

2. Inform politicians and public officials about the positive effects of social marketing by running seminars, conferences, debates and workshops, and producing briefing packs.

3. Arrange for social marketing experts and people who have led successful social marketing programmes to speak at events for politicians and senior public officials.

4. Provide summaries of the evidence of the impact of social marketing.

5. Encourage social marketing practitioners at local and regional level to communicate with their elected officials and senior public servants about social marketing.

6. Work with special interest groups such as charities who are interested in social marketing or are already applying it to influence politicians and public officials.

7. Work with public policy research institutions, academic institutions and policy think-tanks on joint papers or joint events to promote the benefits of applying social marketing in the policy arena.

8. Brief and offer training to public officials and professional associations in the application of social marketing.

9. Approach the businesses community and trade federations and coalitions.

Figure 24.11   Influencing governments about the power of social marketing: a checklist of possible actions

of governments to support the uptake of social marketing, four key elements of the positive exchange resulting from a commitment to apply the disciplines of social marketing can be used to convince them that they should promote and support the uptake of social marketing as a central mechanism for policy and strategy formulation. These four elements have been discussed above, but can be synthesised as the political and policy benefits of:

*   Setting out of clear aims and objectives
*   Cross-departmental and sector coordination
*   Outcome-based budgeting
*   Evaluation and learning.

Politicians and public officials are interested in efficiency and effectiveness but also in generating popular support for their programmes. The benefits of setting out clear aims and objectives from a political perspective are related to an ability of politicians to demonstrate that they are having a positive effect on the well-being of society. Many governments are also attempting to bring about a fundamental shift in the business model of public sector service providers and government institutions. Moving from an approach where solutions are derived principally by policy analysts working with subject experts utilising limited forms of evidence and data towards a model that is also influenced by a deep contextual

understanding about what target audiences know, believe, value and say will help them and is a further political benefit that many politicians can relate to.

This fundamental shift also includes the coordinated use of all forms of intervention that will help engage communities and enable people to change. In this context, it is probable that social marketing will be adopted by increasing numbers of governments and public sector agencies as it is a highly systematic approach to social improvement that sets out unambiguous success criteria in terms of behaviour change alongside thorough and transparent planning about how to achieve it based on deep customer insights. This focus on measurable return on investment is a feature that many governments and other organisations trying to bring about change will value. Social marketing will also be attractive to governments because of its emphasis on developing deep customer insight, and population segmentation, enabling governments to develop interventions that can respond to a broad diversity of needs and target specific subgroups often at most need (The Prime Ministers Strategy Unit, 2006).

At a time of declining trust in civic institutions, fragmentation of society and rising consumerism, social marketing offers a well-developed approach for tackling key behavioural challenges faced by many governments. Social marketing offers a methodology that embraces the reality of markets, choice and mutual responsibility. Social marketing also offers a way to balance the rights and responsibilities of individuals and the rights and responsibilities of wider society through the exercise of choice, and the provision of incentives and penalties, to behave in a way that maximises personal advantage and the well-being of others.

Social marketing is not about telling people what to do or coercing them into doing it, but the art of understanding what will help people make choices and take action which will lead them to better lives. In short, as stated at the start of this chapter, politicians and public officials who seek to serve the public and make the world a better place have to learn how to make positive life choices the easy and natural choices for people, and this means that they will need to embrace social marketing principles as a core approach to policy and strategy development as well as a powerful tool for developing specific interventions.

Social marketing will also be attractive to governments because it is a deeply democratic approach to delivering social justice and is well matched to the sophisticated cultural, social and political environment of the 21st century. Politicians, public servants and practitioners will need to invest time and effort in developing their understanding of social marketing's principles so that they can become stronger champions for the communities they serve.

KEY WORDS: The 5th P policy; misinterpretation of marketing in government; policy and strategy development; outcome-based budgeting; social marketing programmes; strategic social marketing; policy coherence and integration; the conspiracy of passive failure.

Key insights

- When working to influence politicians and senior government officials or to persuade them to apply a social marketing approach it is necessary to apply social marketing principles to developing your understanding about what will move and motivate them, how to communicate with them and what you can offer that will help them deliver on their priorities and commitments.
- Governments, politicians and senior officials in liberal democratic countries generally seek to serve the people they represent in a way that reflects the needs of the people and their wishes as expressed through the democratic process. Social marketing, as an approach to developing social change programmes, embodies many

principles such as developing insight, customer orientation, segmentation and systematic planning that reflect not just effective evidence-based process but also many of the principles of engagement and understanding that politicians and senior officials are familiar with as part of representative democratic processes. Social marketing is then a harmonious fit with such processes.

- Governments also face key challenges about not only being more responsive to peoples needs but also making sure that every penny of public funding is well spent and results in a measurable public benefit. Social marketing's systematic planning process and focus on measurable outcomes also makes it a natural choice of those charged with developing and delivering social change programmes.

REFERENCES

Belot, M. (2006) *Prevention in the Curative Sector. CPB Memorandum.* The Hague: CPB Netherlands Bureau for Economic Policy Analysis.

Boyce, T., Robertson, R. and Dixon, A. (2008) *Commissioning and Behaviour Change: Kicking Bad Habits Final Report.* London: The King's Fund.

Bullock, H., Mountford, J. and Stanley, R. (2001) *Better Policy Making.* London: Centre for Management and Policy Studies.

Department of Health (2007) *Small Change Big Difference.* London: Department of Health.

Department of Health (2008) *Ambitions for Health: A Strategic Framework for Maximising the Potential of Social Marketing and Health-Related behaviour.* London: Department of Health.

Department of Work and Pensions (2009) *Communicating with Customers.* London: Department of Work and Pensions.

Eagle, L. (2009) *Social Marketing Ethics: Report Prepared for the National Social Marketing Centre. Technical Report* London: National Social Marketing Centre.

Fenton Communications (2009) *Now Hear This. The 9 Laws of Successful Advocacy Communications.* Washington, DC: Fenton Communications.

French, J. and Blair-Stevens, C. (2006) 'From snake oil salesmen to trusted policy advisors: The development of a strategic approach to the application of social marketing in England', *Social Marketing Quarterly*, 12(3): 29–40.

French, J. and Mayo, E. (2006) *It's Our Health!* London: National Consumer Council.

Goodman, C. and Anise, A. (2006) *What is Known about the Effectiveness of Economic Instruments to Reduce Consumption of Foods High in Saturated Fats and Other Energy-Dense Foods for Preventing and Treating Obesity?* Copenhagen: WHO Regional Office for Europe. Online: http://www.euro.who.int/document/e88909.pdf

Hills, D. (2004) *Evaluation of Community-Level Interventions for Health Improvement: A Review of Experience in the UK*. London: Health Development Agency.

Hornick, R.C. (ed) (2002) *Public Health Communication Evidence for Behavior Change*. New Jersey: LEA.

Kotler, P. and Lee, N.R. (2008) *Social Marketing: Influencing Behaviors for Good*, 3rd edn. Thousand Oaks, CA: Sage Publications.

Lannon, J. (2008) *How Public Service Advertising Works*. Henley-on-Thames: COI, IPA WARC.

Lefebvre, R.C. (2008) *Interview for the National Social Marketing Centre*, February 27.

Lister, G., Fordham, R., Mugford, M., et al. (2006) *The Societal Costs of Potentially Preventable Illnesses: A Rapid Review*. Healthy Futures 2. Cambridge: Palgrave.

Maibach, E. and Holtgrave, D.R. (1995) 'Advances in public health communication', *Annual Review of Public Health*, 16: 219–238.

Marmot, M., Friel, S., Bell, R., Houweling, T.A.J. and Taylor, S. (2008) *Closing the Gap in a Generation: Health Equity Through Action on the Social Determinants of Health. Final Report of the Commission on Social Determinants of Health*. Geneva: World Health Organization.

Ministry of Health Planning (2003) *Prevention that Works: A Review of the Evidence Regarding the Causation and Prevention of Chronic Disease. (Consultation Draft).*

Chronic Disease Prevention Initiative: Paper #2. Victoria, BC: Prevention and Wellness Planning, Population Health and Wellness, Ministry of Health Planning.

Mulgan, G. and Lee, A. (2001) *Better Policy Delivery and Design*. A discussion paper. London: Performance and Innovation Unit, Cabinet Office.

National Social Marketing Centre (2006) *It's Our Health! Realising the Potential of Effective Social Marketing*. Summary. London: National Consumer Council.

National Social Marketing Centre (2007) *Social Marketing Works*. London: National Social Marketing Centre, National Consumer Council.

NICE (2007). 'Behaviour change at population, community and individual levels', *NICE Public Health Guidance 6*. London: National Institute for Health and Clinical Excellence.

The Prime Minister's Strategy Unit (2006) *The UK Government's Approach to Public Service Reform*. London: Cabinet Office.

Stern, N. (2007) *The Economics of Climate Change: The Stern Review*. Cambridge: Cambridge University Press.

World Health Organization (1974) *ALMA–ATA Declaration*. Geneva: World Health Organization.

World Health Organization (2008) *The World Health Report 2008 – Primary Health Care (Now More Than Ever)*. Geneva: World Health Organization.

Social Marketing in Practice: Case Studies

25. SOCIAL MARKETING AND ADVOCACY – W.D. NOVELLI AND B. WORKMAN

The combination of public policy advocacy and social marketing is the topic of this chapter. Drawing on their experience at AARP (the non-profit membership organization in the USA that helps people of 50 years and over improve the quality of their lives), the authors discuss the synergistic benefits they have realized by blending these two social change strategies. The chapter focuses on two detailed case studies: (1) the *'Don't Vote....until you know where the candidates stand on the issues'* campaign, which used grassroots activities and national ad campaigns; and (2) their efforts to influence the development and enactment of the Medicare Part D drug plan using citizen advocacy. While the chapter is designed to demonstrate the effectiveness of blending social marketing with advocacy to influence upstream factors and change social norms and laws, the authors also discuss the challenges of using this synergistic approach to social change.

26. SOCIAL MARKETING AND TOBACCO CONTROL – T. DEWHIRST AND W.B. LEE

Tobacco use is the highest risk factor for ill health and premature death in high-income countries.

Given that tobacco use is a preventable risk behavior, the authors examine social marketing in practice within the field of tobacco control. They describe how target markets for interventions have been segmented along a number of dimensions, in line with either smoking prevention or smoking cessation approaches, and how the marketing mix elements should be developed synergistically. To demonstrate the key principles underlying the production of effective campaigns, the authors examine the extent to which de-normalization messaging, fear appeals and social and cultural norms contribute to these. The emerging use of new media and Web 2.0 technologies and the importance of continuous evaluation of social marketing tobacco control campaigns are emphasized.

27. SOCIAL MARKETING AND THE HEALTH EDUCATOR – R.J. MCDERMOTT, K.R. MCCORMACK BROWN AND R. THACKERAY

Social marketing is a relatively recent concept for health education and health promotion practice, compared with its four decades within the social and behavior change fields. The authors note that, despite demonstrably successful social marketing community programs and initiatives around the world, there continues to be challenges for health educators applying social marketing.

These are identified as a lack of understanding, an incompatible ideology and difficulties with addressing competition and audience segmentation and targeting. It is critical for higher education institutions to create academic certificates and programs about social marketing and how to use it to effect and sustain change. A global professional association for social marketing and associated competencies for health educators is anticipated by the authors.

25

Social Marketing and Advocacy

William D. Novelli and Boe Workman

INTRODUCTION

AARP is in the business of leading positive social change. Experience has taught us that in order to do that we need the synergy that comes from combining social marketing and policy advocacy.

In this chapter, we will show that social marketing and public policy advocacy are complementary, and when combined can create a synergistic approach to achieve positive social change. On the marketing side, we need to expand our thinking. As robust as it is, social marketing theory is still not broad enough. It does not fully incorporate policy advocacy, for example, and only recently began to incorporate legal sanctions. Also, marketing places a lot of emphasis on the individual. While this is very important, we need to think not just of changing the individual's behavior, but of environmental change as well.

So, at AARP, when we talk about leading positive *social change*, or creating social impact, we are referring to the development and implementation of activities and programs:

1. To influence our members (and others) to change their behavior in ways that will improve the quality of their lives as they get older.
2. To change the whole environment, including social norms, so that the desired behavior becomes the *expected* behavior and change is sustained.

Influencing the environment often involves: changing public policy at the national, state and community level; influencing the private policies and practices of business and other organizations; and changing long-held norms and expectations.

The social problems we are concerned with are so difficult that it takes all the tools we can muster to bring about change – advocacy, legal action, communication, pricing and distribution strategies, services and products and other offerings. That's why the synergy that comes from combining social marketing and public policy advocacy is so important. It's a powerful combination. It's the way to change individual behavior – which is often the province of social marketing – and to change the environment in which people function – which usually is achieved most effectively through public policy advocacy (Brownson et al., 2006; Frieden, 2010).

In this chapter, we will demonstrate how we combine social marketing and public policy advocacy at AARP to lead positive social change. Following a brief historical perspective of social marketing as an approach to social change, we will provide an overview of AARP to establish a context for social marketing and advocacy at work. We will then offer two examples of social marketing and advocacy work, followed by an example of an application where we believe a synergistic approach to social change integrating social marketing practices and policy advocacy can make a significant difference. We will conclude by summarizing some key learning from our experiences.

SOCIAL MARKETING AND SOCIAL CHANGE: A BRIEF HISTORY

The notion that marketing can be applied to ideas, issues, and causes has been around a long time. In 1969, Philip Kotler and Sidney Levy argued that 'marketing is a pervasive societal activity that goes considerably beyond the selling of tooth-paste, soap, and steel'. Since that time, social marketing has developed into a robust and effective discipline for achieving social change, as evidenced by Sage's decision to commission this Handbook and the Department of Health and Human Services' inclusion of objectives to increase the use of social marketing as part of their goals for *Healthy People 2020*.

Social marketing was defined by Kotler and Zaltman in 1971 and reconfirmed by Kotler and Roberto in 1989 as:

> A social change management technology involving the design, implementation, and control of programs aimed at increasing the acceptability of a social idea or practice in one or more groups of target adopters. It utilizes concepts of market segmentation, consumer research, product concept development and testing, directed communication, facilitation, incentives, and exchange theory to maximize the target adopter's response (Kotler and Roberto 1989: 24).

Initially, the practice of social marketing was closely identified with marketing *products* involved in social change – for example, contraceptives and oral rehydration salts to control infant diarrhea. Then, in 1994, a significant shift occurred when Alan Andreasen argued that social marketing is not a theory or a unique set of techniques, but a *process* for developing social changes programs modeled on processes used in private sector marketing (Andreasen, 1994). He further said that 'increasing the acceptability of a social idea or practice' should not be the goal of social marketing. Instead, the ultimate objective of social marketing should be *behavior change*, and he offered the following definition:

> Social marketing is the application of commercial marketing concepts and tools to programs designed to influence the voluntary behavior of target audiences where the primary objective is to improve the welfare of the target audiences and/or the society of which they are a part (Andreasen, 1994).

He later noted that social marketing can be carried out by non-profit and public sector organizations (Andreasen, 2002), but cautioned, drawing upon the work of Bloom and Novelli (1981) and Fox and Kotler (1980), that the non-profit and for-profit worlds differ in important ways. These differences must be taken into account in applying for-profit tools in the non-profit sector.

Andreasen's view of social marketing was widely accepted and, in essence, established that the fundamental objective of social marketing is not just the marketing of ideas, but the *influencing of behavior*.

- Getting people to start and maintain a positive behavior: for example, physical activity.
- Persuading people to stop, or not to start: a negative behavior, such as tobacco use.

With behavior change established as the ultimate objective of social marketing, scholars and practitioners began to define how social marketing fit into the landscape of other social change approaches. Andreasen (2002) established six benchmarks for social marketing which have now been adapted by the National Social Marketing Centre (Blair-Stevens, Slater, and French (2006) and others (e.g., the *Social Marketing Quarterly*) as standards of practice and criteria for differentiating social marketing from other social change interventions and programs:

1. The behavior change bottom line.
2. Consistent use of audience research.
3. Careful segmentation of target audiences.
4. Creation of attractive and motivating exchanges with target audiences.
5. A strategy that attempts to use all 'Four Ps' (Products, Price, Place and Promotion).
6. Attention to the competition faced by the desired behavior.

A common view in the literature on social change identifies three levels of societal intervention which can be instrumental in bringing about effective social change (Stokols, 1996; McLeroy et al., 1988).

The first level of intervention is at the individual level. The foundation of this approach is that in order to address major social problems, individuals must ultimately behave differently. So, these interventions focus on getting individuals to change behavior. Since social marketing is focused on individual behavior change, this is its primary niche.

The second level of intervention is at the community level. Proponents of this approach believe that social change is more effectively brought about by changing the standards of acceptable behavior in the community, rather than focusing on the individual. They argue that when the norms and values of the community change, individuals will change their behavior as well, and the change will be more sustainable.

The third level of intervention occurs at the structural level. The argument here is that the ability of individuals and communities to change is constrained by social structures: that is, laws, public policies, institutions, availability of technology, etc. Proponents of this approach tend to focus on media advocacy, public policy advocacy, and legal and legislative means to achieve social change (Wiener and Doescher, 1991).

Within these intervention levels, Rothschild (1999) has identified three categories of intervention tools: education, marketing, and the law.

Education refers to 'messages of any type that attempt to inform and/or persuade a target to behave voluntarily in a particular manner but do not provide, on their own, direct and/or immediate reward or punishment' (Rothschild, 1999).

Marketing refers to 'attempts to manage behavior by offering reinforcing incentives and/or consequences in an environment that invites voluntary exchange' (Rothschild, 1999). Unlike education, marketing offers a direct and timely exchange for a desired behavior.

While education and marketing involve voluntary behavior, law involves the use of coercion to achieve behavior in an involuntary manner. It is also used 'to increase or decrease the probability of transactions that might not develop as desired through free-market mechanisms' (Rothschild, 1999).

For those involved in leading social change, this framework provides a useful paradigm for program development. Practitioners must first determine the appropriate intervention level. Should the focus be on individual change, community-level change, or structural change? Then, they must determine if the social change goal can be met through voluntary individual behavior change or whether changing the law is more appropriate. If voluntary behavior change is deemed most appropriate, they must decide whether it is best accomplished through education or by developing a social marketing program built around the accepted benchmarks.

Our experience at AARP has taught us that success in leading social change often requires a combination of these approaches. Some behaviors – or non-behaviors – are much more resistant to change than others. The goal is to get individuals (and organizations), usually on a large scale, to change their behavior in ways that will lead to positive social change and benefit the individuals and society as a whole. One health insurer put it this way in an ad: 'When one person

exercises, it impacts his or her health; but when one million people exercise, it impacts the healthcare system.' It's about changing society.

Our experience has led us to conclude that social marketing can be most effective when used in conjunction with other approaches to facilitate change. This has also been argued by Andreasen, who observed that 'social marketing can also grow to the extent that it can be seen as complementary to community and structural approaches rather than competitive. To the extent that the latter two approaches require some actions of individual people (e.g., community activists or politicians), social marketing can help' (Andreasen, 2002).

AARP: A PLATFORM FOR SOCIAL CHANGE

In order to provide a context for understanding how social marketing practices and policy advocacy complement each other to help AARP lead positive social change, it is useful to understand something about AARP's history, structure, mission, and the environment in which we operate.

At AARP, we are at the forefront of one of the greatest societal changes in modern history – the aging of the population in America and throughout the world. It's a paradox. On the one hand, our increased longevity and vitality are tremendous accomplishments. More people are living longer, and generally are in better health than ever before. On the other hand, increased longevity, combined with the fundamental change in age distribution resulting from the aging of the baby boomers, is putting increasing strain on our social structures, institutions, and programs, raising questions about their affordability and long-term viability.

It is also making us realize that aging just doesn't happen to older people. It's a process that begins at birth. The behaviors we exhibit and the decisions we make as we move along life's continuum have a tremendous impact on the quality of our lives when we get older. So to improve the lives of people as they age, we can't just look at behaviors and policies that affect older people. We have to address them throughout the life span. For example, osteoporosis has been called a pediatric disease with geriatric consequences. If individuals don't build their bone mass when they are teens – especially women – they may experience the disease when they are much older. Likewise, it takes a lifetime of saving to build an adequate retirement nest egg. A person can't start saving at age 60 and hope to have enough money to live through his or her retirement years. The behavior of setting money aside for retirement must start much earlier in life.

This is an exciting period, an opportunity to be part of influencing events and social change in the unfolding drama of an aging population, not just in the USA, but throughout the world.

In his book, *Social Marketing in the 21st Century*, Alan Andreasen writes, 'Social Marketing is about making the world a better place for everyone...' (Andreasen, 2006). In essence, this is our mission at AARP – 'to enhance the quality of life for all as we age.' We lead positive social change and deliver value to our members through information, advocacy and service. As such, we are concerned both with influencing individual behaviors and large-scale social (environmental) change – creating a society where all people can age with independence, dignity, and purpose.

Our roots in social change go back to our founder, Dr Ethel Percy Andrus. She was a true social innovator. After she retired as principal of Lincoln High School in Los Angeles, she realized that many teachers, after a lifetime of devoted service, did not have access to affordable health insurance and received pensions that barely sustained them and prevented them from living out their lives with a sense of dignity. So in 1947, Dr Andrus founded the National Retired Teachers Association to give retired teachers a national voice on legislative and social issues and to advocate for pension reform, tax benefits, housing improvements, and health insurance, and to continue their support for education.

One of the most immediate and critical issues she addressed was the lack of group health and accident insurance for people past the age of 65. After years of persistent efforts, she finally located a company willing to risk a pilot program of health insurance for the elderly, and NRTA began offering low-cost health and accident policies to its members.

Dr Andrus recognized that millions of older Americans, from all walks of life, lived in constant fear of financial disaster from a ruinous illness or accident and needed these same benefits. So, in 1958, she formed AARP as a vehicle for social change. She saw AARP as doing more than working for pension reform and providing group health insurance. It was a way to spread her philosophy that the retirement years should be seen as an opportunity for new growth and involvement with society – not as a time for withdrawal from life.

Her vision was that aging Americans could maintain their personal dignity and continue their social usefulness by recognizing their own individual worth through a commitment to service. She gave AARP the motto that still guides our organization today, 'To serve, Not to be served.'

Today, AARP has more than 40 million members age 50 and over. We are dedicated to making life better for people as they age and championing the future of our members and every generation. And, we lead positive social change and deliver value to our members through information, advocacy, products and services. We do this by focusing on the core needs that every generation shares: the need for health and financial security; the need to feel connected to family and community; the need to give something back; and the need to simply enjoy life.

Meeting these needs and ensuring the quality of life for all as we age are no small tasks. They require a unique, three-part organization:

1. AARP, the parent, is a strong, non-profit, non-partisan advocate for consumer rights that provides trusted information through publications, voter education, research, television and radio programs and a website, which cover the issues our members care about most. In addition to our national office in Washington, DC, we have staffed offices in every state, the District of Columbia, Puerto Rico, and the US Virgin Islands.
2. The AARP Foundation is our charitable arm. It provides services to both members and non-members – especially the most vulnerable in society. Our foundation delivers direct services, such as the nation's largest free, volunteer-run tax assistance program, and legal advocacy work to support the rights of older people across the country.
3. AARP Services, Inc. (ASI) endorses and makes available products and services designed specifically for the 50+ consumer – many of whom might otherwise be excluded from the market. We do this by working with leading businesses to identify and respond to the ever-changing needs of Americans as they age. These relationships not only help shape the marketplace but also earn revenue that helps us achieve our mission of leading positive social change and delivering value to our members. We refer to this as our 'triple bottom line': social impact, member value, and revenues to reinvest in the enterprise.

To achieve social impact, we work to influence public policy, the marketplace, and corporate, societal and individual practices and behaviors to bring about change. We focus on financial security, health care, and supportive services, and livable communities. We also understand that we can learn a lot from the experiences of other countries, so we have become a major force in global aging issues. We also want to make sure that our members receive value for the $16.50 they pay each year to be a member of AARP. Member value comes primarily in two forms: economic value and social value.

Economic value includes products and services ranging from travel discounts, insurance products and discounts on prescription drugs to financial products and independent financial counseling, information on how and where to retire, opportunities for community involvement and volunteering, educational and fun events like AARP's Life@50+ National Event and Expo, and information on how to make the most of life after 50.

AARP members also consider our work in leading social change as a member value because it provides them with an opportunity to make a difference and leave society better than they found it, which is a high priority for many of our members.

We use six tools to achieve our social impact and member value goals:

1. Products and services.
2. Strategic alliances.
3. Advocacy.
4. Information and research.
5. Philanthropy.
6. Volunteers.

Some of these – products and services, strategic alliances, and some of our information – are managed by our taxable subsidiary, ASI, and its own subsidiary, AARP Financial. The others are managed by AARP. Our AARP Foundation manages our philanthropic efforts as well as our national community service programs that are staffed primarily by volunteers.

AARP, the parent, oversees our advocacy, program and research efforts. We regard research as essential to achieving our triple bottom line, and we invest in it. Much of it is basic consumer research to better understand the marketplace, understand and segment our target audiences and learn how to appeal to people. We engage in competitive analysis because we want to try to stay ahead of our competitors. We also do as much benchmarking as possible to assess our progress.

We track our brand and our image to see how we are regarded, with a set of attributes that we measure on a periodic basis. We conduct tracking studies to measure the level of trust people place in AARP, as well as their perception of relevance, their intention to join, and to renew their membership.

We also partner with other organizations, because we realize that we can't succeed alone. We are able to leverage our resources and increase our reach through these strategic alliances.

Of course we have to have resources to fund all of these activities. We generate revenue from a variety of sources, including membership dues, royalties on products and services, advertising in our publications, grants to the AARP Foundation and other sponsorship, and exclusivity fees associated with our National Event and Expo and other events, activities, and relationships.

Our business model makes us somewhat of a hybrid. Unlike many others in the non profit sector, we have a well-functioning for-profit arm. But unlike those in the for-profit sector, those profits aren't designed to pay dividends to the owners, but to gain capital to fund social change and to fund our social mission. It's important to note that this social mission is the driving force behind all of our activities, just as it was when Dr Andrus started offering low-cost group health insurance and mail order pharmaceuticals to AARP members nearly 50 years ago.

Many of the products and services we offer through ASI are a differentiating force in the marketplace. They are designed to be consumer friendly, to raise marketplace standards, to provide high-quality alternatives – some of which cannot be found elsewhere in the marketplace – and to influence companies to offer new and better choices for our members to help them meet their needs and live the way they want to live. In other words, we strive to meet a social need as well as an individual one – to change individual behavior and enhance the public good.

This structure and triple bottom line business model provide AARP with a powerful platform from which to lead positive social change on a wide scale. As the following examples will illustrate, we routinely use Andreasen's six benchmarks of social marketing. We intervene at the individual, community, and structural levels. And, we use education, marketing, and law – in the form of policy advocacy – to achieve our social change goals. We also use legal advocacy in the courts to achieve social change, but it is not included here because it is beyond the scope of this chapter.

Let us now explore how AARP employs social marketing practices and policy advocacy to achieve social change within its triple bottom line business model. The goal in each of the examples described below is to influence the individual behavior of the target audience and to change the environment (including social norms) so that the desired behavior becomes the expected behavior and the change is sustained.

AARP'S 2006 'DON'T VOTE' CAMPAIGN

In the third edition of *Social Marketing: Influencing Behaviors for Good*, authors Philip Kotler and Nancy Lee recognize that social marketers often place too much of the burden for improving the status of social issues on individual behavior change and that they should direct some of their efforts to influence upstream factors (Kotler and Lee, 2008). Andreasen concurs, noting that 'the same basic principles that induce a 12-year-old in Bangkok or Leningrad to get a Big Mac and a caregiver in Indonesia to start using oral dehydration solutions for diarrhea can also be used to influence…other individuals whose actions are needed to bring about widespread, long-lasting positive social change' (Andreasen, 2006). Because our advocacy and social change model at AARP relies heavily on citizen engagement, we do a lot of work to influence upstream factors. Our 2006 'Don't Vote' campaign (which is chronicled in more detail in Kotler and Lee, 2008) is one such example.

Situation

AARP is a non-profit, non-partisan organization that neither endorses nor contributes to any candidates for public office. We work with elected officials from across the political spectrum to address issues important to people over 50 and their families. We also educate the candidates and the voters on these issues, so that they become part of the election debate, and so that voters can choose the candidates that best represent them. We do not support or oppose candidates themselves.

We've been doing this for many years, and our focus is always the same: to serve as a resource for educating our 40 million members and everyone else on important public issues, and to make sure our members know where the candidates stand. Likewise, we strive to make sure that issues of importance to our members and their families, such as the long-term strength and solvency of Social Security and making health care affordable for all Americans, are addressed by the candidates.

Voters aged ≥55 years old lead all other age groups, both in percentage of those registered to vote and those who do vote. In the November 2004 election, nearly 70% of voters aged 55–64 went to the polls, as did over 70% of those aged 65–74. As such, we viewed the federal and state elections in 2006 as an excellent opportunity to advance our issue agenda by encouraging our members (and others 50+) to vote, and to help them make informed voting decisions based on the candidates' positions.

Target audience

Our target audience was the members of AARP and all other people 50+. One of our program goals was to get candidates to adopt our positions and campaign on them, thus elevating our issues in priority. Moreover, we wanted to make the process transparent and visible so it would be difficult for candidates to later back off from a position they had once taken. So in that sense, we were also targeting the candidates themselves.

Behavior objectives

The primary behavioral objective of our campaign was for our members and people 50+ to vote in the 2006 federal and state elections. And our goal was for them to make informed voting decisions based on their knowledge of the issues and the candidates' positions on them. We also wanted voters to view AARP as an organization working for change on their behalf.

Our objective with the candidates was for them to see our issues more prominently. We also wanted to influence the candidates directly, to put our issues onto their platforms, and to state their positions on our issues clearly.

Strategy

Our 2006 election strategy was designed to frame issues with a clarity that creates real distinctions between candidates, and to take full advantage of our credibility with the public. We accomplished this through expanded grassroots activity and a multi-channel communications program using paid and earned media, including traditional and non-traditional media, to ensure that AARP's issues were deciding factors in voters' candidate choices. Two key components of this were our 'Don't Vote' national advertising campaign and our 'Frontrunner Race' strategy.

The 'Don't Vote' ad campaign was conceived as a fresh, intrusive way of conveying AARP's perennial election message that candidate choices should be based on where the candidates stand on the issues, not on personalities. In this case it translates to: 'Don't vote – until you know where the candidates stand on the issues.' That was the theme of the campaign, and it got to the heart of why we get involved. We ran full-page ads in newspapers, had a billboard truck winding through the streets of Washington, DC (primarily to let Congress know what we were up to) and ran television ads telling people, '**DON'T VOTE . . . until you know where the candidates stand on the issues.**' Our most effective TV spot was our 'Song 'n Dance' ad which featured an attractive candidate with the perfect blow-dried image at a community event singing about why voters should vote for him. After running off a litany of superficial reasons, he says, 'You can vote for me with assurity, just don't ask about Social Security.' This approach not only made our point effectively but also broke through the cluttered landscape of political ads and captured people's attention.

Everything we did was aimed at getting voters to focus on the issues that were most important to them personally and helping them learn where candidates stood on those issues. Our elections website **dontvote.com** gave voters all across the country access to the information and resources they needed to cast an informed ballot on the elections in their state and district, including AARP voters' guides, links to candidate websites, and information on voting.

The campaign was thoroughly tested to ensure that registered voters from age 40 to 75, with household incomes ranging from $25,000 to over $100,000 and from a variety of ethnic groups understood the message. We test virtually all our advertising as a matter of course, and these ads received some of the most positive responses we have ever received. The message of the campaign was clearly understood by all, and respondents recognized that the purpose of the campaign was to encourage them to make an informed choice and vote.

Our staffed offices in every state, the District of Columbia, the Virgin Islands and Puerto Rico, all work to educate voters in their own communities, neighbor to neighbor, about where candidates stand on the issues that matter to them. At the same time, in 2006, we sought to have a higher level of outreach activity in a smaller number of races. Thus, we initiated our 'Frontrunner Race' strategy as part of our continuing effort to find new ways to get the issues our members care about in front of the candidates and the voters.

We selected six races to test our Frontrunner Race strategy – two gubernatorial races (Arkansas and Colorado) and four federal races (Colorado Congressional District 7, Iowa Congressional District 1, Ohio Congressional District 6 and the Tennessee Senate contest). These were races where we tested new strategies to elevate AARP's issues in the elections – laying the foundation for future legislative campaigns and raising the profile of AARP and 50+ voters. The races were selected based on a number of criteria, including how competitive the races were projected to be, the fact that they were open seats in swing states and districts, and whether there had been a history of bipartisan cooperation in the states involved. Table 25.1 outlines the key strategies for each race.

Results

Some 52% of all voters in the 2006 national elections were aged ≥50 years old, and about 25% of all those who voted were AARP members. An analysis of the campaign produced the following results:

- In five of the six races, the candidate most closely aligned with AARP's policy positions in our voters' guides was elected.
- Despite an environment in which Iraq dominated much of the debate, AARP issues were central to the campaign debate in five of the six races.

Table 25.1 Frontrunner Race strategies, 2006

Race	Key Strategies
Arkansas Gov.	Test emphasis on African-Americans; candidate forums, voter guides, issue brochures, etc.; newspaper advertising including African-American papers; direct mail with emphasis on African-Americans; van tour
Colorado Gov.	Test emphasis on Hispanic and low-involvement voters; candidate forums, voter guides, issue brochures, etc.; advertising in Hispanic media; direct mail with emphasis on Hispanics and low-involvement voters; absentee voter outreach; phone banking; expanded State Member Update distribution
Colorado CD 7	Test emphasis on Hispanics and presidential voters; candidate forums, voter guides, issue brochures, etc.; advertising in Hispanic media; direct mail with emphasis on Hispanics and presidential voters
Iowa CD 1	Test television/newspaper media mix targeting broad range of members; candidate forums, voter guides, issue brochures, etc.; general market television and newspaper advertising; direct mail
Ohio CD 6	Test television/newspaper media mix targeting broad range of members; candidate forums, voter guides, issue brochures, etc.; general market radio and newspaper advertising; direct mail; phone banking
Tenn. Senate	Test emphasis on baby boomers; candidate forums, voter guides, issue brochures, etc.; advertising in general market media; direct mail with emphasis on boomers; dedicated website; phone banking

- AARP's campaign encouraged voters to focus on issues rather than personalities in making candidate decisions. Pre- and post-election surveys show that the percentage of members reporting that candidates' issue positions were the key factor in their voting decisions increased from 29% to 42% over the course of the campaign.
- The percentage of AARP members who reported turning to AARP for information to help them make voting decisions increased from 9% to 16% over the course of the campaign.
- The percentage of members who viewed AARP as the most trusted source of information to make voting decisions increased from 6% to 13%, making AARP *the most trusted source* for voting information of all sources, including churches or other religious organizations, unions, fraternal organizations, universities or alumni associations, professional organizations, and political parties.
- A majority of members believed that the information AARP provided about political candidates was important in helping them understand where candidates stood on issues of interest to them and said the information from AARP was important in helping them make distinctions between political candidates' positions.
- Awareness of AARP voters' guides among members increased 20 percentage points over the course of the campaign, from 30% to 51%.
- TV ads (61%), newspaper ads (54%), and voters' guides (51%) generated the highest awareness.
- The three most informative tactics –candidate forums (62%), van tours (59%), and the voters' guides (54%) – were also the three most helpful (56%, 47%, and 42%, respectively).
- The voters' guides had a good reach (measured by awareness) and provide informative and helpful information. The TV and newspaper ads generated more of their impact because of their relatively wide reach rather than because of informative and helpful content. The *Issues* brochures and State Member Update provided better content than the newspaper and TV ads, but had a less extensive reach.

Media tracking showed that Frontrunner-related media accounted for about 20% of all AARP-related media in the five test states from 1 July through 1 December 2006. However, the nature of the stories was very different from media attention traditionally received by AARP, as it was much more state-focused. Frontrunner-related articles were on state survey results, AARP advocacy activities related to the state election and the senior vote and on various candidates' positions as framed by AARP voter guides.

Conclusion

Our 2006 'Don't Vote' campaign was effective. Moreover, we learned a great deal from our strategies and execution which we used to prepare an even more extensive voter education program for 2008.

PRESCRIPTION-DRUG COVERAGE IN MEDICARE

For many people, and certainly for older Americans (our members), the lack of access to and the high cost of prescription drugs are difficult and frustrating problems: on one hand, they need and value the drugs their doctors prescribe, but on the other hand, many people simply can't afford them. The cost of brand-name prescription drugs has been rising faster than the rate of inflation for many years. As we approached what was to become the debate over the Medicare Modernization Act in 2003, we faced a serious problem. The marketplace was out of balance, and our members and their families couldn't afford or sustain rising drug costs.

A study by Harris Interactive found that higher out-of-pocket drug costs were causing massive non-compliance in the use of prescription drugs. Millions of Americans were not asking doctors for the prescriptions they needed, did not fill the prescriptions they were given, did not take their full doses and took their drugs less often than they should. Moreover, the higher people's out-of-pocket costs for drugs, the more likely they were to be non-compliant.

We were hearing from our members every day on this. It was affecting not just low-income seniors, but middle-class people on fixed incomes as well. It was a huge and persistent problem that would not go away by itself. And, efforts to provide relief through pharmaceutical industry discount cards and other means were laudable, but were simply not enough. The problem was much bigger than that and had to be solved systemically, by achieving affordable and sustainable prescription drug coverage in Medicare.

Helping our members, and all older Americans, to cope with this was one of our highest priorities. So, we embarked on an all-out campaign to win support for affordable drug coverage in Medicare, with cost containment so that a Medicare benefit could be 'sustained. We felt that if we could help make prescription drugs more affordable for our members and others, compliance would improve among individuals and society would benefit.

This was a problem calling out for a public policy solution – changing Medicare to include prescription drug coverage – but we knew that citizen advocacy would play an important role in the outcome. As such, we developed a dual strategy: one for 'Inside the Beltway' and one for 'Outside the Beltway.' Our 'Inside the Beltway' strategy targeted members of Congress and their staffs, opinion leaders and influentials, and the major media. Our 'Outside the Beltway' strategy targeted the grassroots – our members and others who wanted an affordable prescription drug benefit in Medicare. We wanted to get the point across to legislators that there is strength in numbers. We believed that by mobilizing in force behind promoting one big idea – a prescription drug benefit in Medicare – we could persuade Congress to act.

These two strategies were highly integrated and played off each other. As part of our 'Outside the Beltway' strategy, we launched a drive to collect hundreds of thousands of signatures on petitions demanding the drug benefit in Medicare. We mobilized our network of volunteers to collect them at county fairs, mall events, baseball games, voter vans and AARP chapter meetings. We also generated more than 200,000 contacts with Congress (through emails, letters, and phone calls) urging them to pass a drug benefit.

We held 'kitchen table' events (where people, as if sitting at their kitchen tables, figured out what their drug costs were and how to go about meeting them) in targeted states to drive home the idea that the high cost of drugs was having an adverse effect on families. The purpose of these events was two fold: to raise consciousness among people that a drug benefit was truly possible and to focus on states that had members of Congress who would be especially involved in any drug legislation.

The 'Outside the Beltway' strategy not only created public demand for the Congress to act in passing legislation but also gave us our policy direction. We did extensive polling and focus group research to find out what our members needed and expected in terms of a Medicare drug benefit and found that: (1) the premium should be no greater than $35 a month (anything higher would drive people away from a voluntary benefit); (2) the maximum deductible that most people would accept would be $250; (3) the co-pay would have to be less than 50%; (4) everyone hated the idea of a gap in coverage (the doughnut hole, as it was called); and (5) protection against catastrophic costs was essential.

We were able to use this information with Congress as part of our 'Inside the Beltway' strategy to advocate for a policy our members and the public would accept. In most large-scale social legislation, policy discussions are fierce and compromises are eventually reached when possible, or rejected. This was no exception. Congress and the administration had set aside $400 billion over 10 years to pay for drug coverage in Medicare. We realized that this was not enough to cover all beneficiaries completely, so the dollars would have to be targeted to those most in need – the poor and those with catastrophically high costs. There were also financial incentives built in to persuade companies with retiree coverage not to drop the coverage. To spread the money to cover these objectives, there would have to be some gaps: hence, the doughnut hole.

The final debate over the Medicare Modernization Act (MMA) was contentious and hard-fought, made more so by the process for writing the legislation and the bitter political environment in Washington. After tough negotiations and fierce debate in both houses of Congress, the legislation passed. It was not perfect, but the good substantially outweighed the problems with the program. While we didn't get everything we wanted in the bill, we believe it did make Medicare stronger and better for older Americans and their families, and for the boomers to follow when they reach beneficiary age.

Many pundits, politicians and others have said that the MMA would not have passed without AARP's support. We fought and negotiated hard to get all the improvements we could in the legislation. Then, we not only endorsed it but also went out to our members and the public and promoted its passage as strongly as we could, once again calling on our grassroots to advocate on its behalf.

Undoubtedly, our advocacy on this issue had a significant and measurable social impact. By the end of the 2006 enrollment period, more than 22.5 million Medicare beneficiaries were enrolled in Part D plans, and an estimated 38.2 million Medicare beneficiaries had some source of drug coverage. Moreover, a study by the Kaiser Family Foundation reported that approximately 80% of those enrolled in Part D plans were happy with the program. The average participant is saving about $1200 a year.

Getting the MMA enacted into law was only half the battle. Because the MMA created a voluntary benefit (or product), it created an environment for change but did not mandate individual behavior change. Unlike a law requiring people to wear seatbelts, for example, there was no requirement for Medicare beneficiaries to sign up for Medicare Part D (the prescription drug benefit). Likewise, it did not require any specific companies to offer a Medicare Part D product: it only set the parameters for doing so. So, we mounted a major campaign to educate people about the new law and persuade them to enroll in the program. We were a primary source of credible, accurate, and actionable information that helped Medicare beneficiaries make informed decisions about the program and choose the most appropriate Medicare Part D plan.

In keeping with our triple bottom line business model, we also wanted to see if there were other ways we could positively impact the lives of our members and others and provide them with even greater value. So, ASI tackled the issue with its strategic partner, UnitedHealthcare. They assessed the needs of AARP members and developed the AARP Medicare Rx Plan to address those needs.

The AARP Medicare Rx Plan offers the widest range of covered drugs by offering each drug on Medicare's recommended list of options. It is the only Part D plan in *every* zip code in all 50 states and the five territories. And, of the 3.2 million members enrolled in the plan, 35% are low income and eligible for Medicaid. So we are serving over 1.2 million vulnerable Medicare beneficiaries and helping them gain access to critical prescription drugs.

The AARP plan offers the most to the most – value through coverage and price to virtually all Medicare beneficiaries. Through the AARP Medicare Rx Plan, we have contributed to our social impact goal of reducing the cost of prescription drugs, and are improving access to affordable drugs so nearly everyone in the country who has access to Medicare can have access to a solid plan with excellent coverage.

In terms of member value, we're saving our members money – a *billion* dollars in the last 30 months alone through our pharmacy services, including our Medicare Part D plan.

Despite the success of the Medicare Part D program, it didn't solve the whole problem. It helped to make prescription drugs more affordable for people on Medicare, but what about the people who are not on Medicare, including those whose employers have cut back on healthcare benefits?

Our ultimate goal is to make prescription drugs more affordable for everyone. So we're continuing to work on changes in public policy to do that by: supporting measures to legalize the importation of safe drugs from Canada and other countries; to give the Secretary of Health and Human Services the authority to negotiate drug prices; to encourage the use of purchasing pools among states, cities, and other jurisdictions; and to speed generic drugs to market.

And, we're also using marketing practices to help people change their behavior in terms of how they *buy* and *use* prescription drugs. We call this our Wise Use of Medications campaign. It entails educating people on how to get the most out of the drugs they take, encouraging them to ask their doctors for generics where appropriate and providing consumers with information on the comparative effectiveness of drugs.

Our major partner in this program is Walgreens. As part of our work with them, over 3.5 million *Wise Use of Medications* publications have been distributed through 6500 Walgreens stores. Many of our state offices are working with Walgreens and other pharmacies on what we call 'brown bag medication reviews.' Consumers bring all of their medications, supplements and vitamins to a community center where pharmacists consult with them individually about drug compliance and interactions. We are also piloting AARP 'Let's Talk About Meds' seminars to help people manage their medications and realize lower costs by using generics.

The high cost of prescription drugs has been a problem for our target audience (and in fact, Americans of all ages) for many years, causing them not to comply with behaviors (taking medications appropriately) to achieve the health benefit the drugs provide. Having worked on this problem for decades, and conducting extensive research on the target audience as well as drug prices, we determined that the primary cause of noncompliance was cost. It was not that people did not want to comply, it was the high cost of the drugs primarily that kept them from doing so. We believed that if we could initiate programs to reduce the costs, both systemically and for the individual, we could achieve the goal of greater compliance, thus improving the health of individuals and society.

Through our combined advocacy and social marketing efforts, we have been able to move the needle considerably. This could not have happened without an effective advocacy campaign to win a prescription drug benefit in Medicare, or without an effective campaign conforming to the benchmarks for a successful social marketing program. Combined, this social change strategy yielded an outcome that neither could have achieved on its own. At the same time, it has provided us with a pathway for continued success as we work toward broader healthcare reform.

FUTURE APPLICATIONS

The biggest return on investment our nation could ever get from a synergistic combination of social change, including social marketing and public policy advocacy, would be through adopting a national, coherent set of goals and strategies and an effective, coordinated and sustained program on health promotion and disease prevention. This would change America.

The USA has a spotty history in this important area, except for public health interventions like sewage, clean water and other sanitation initiatives that have made a real difference. For decades, probably centuries now, there have been calls for prevention to save lives and save money. Ben Franklin said an ounce of prevention is worth a pound of care. Newt Gingrich wrote a book called *Saving Lives and Saving Money* that had many prevention recommendations. An example of the periodic calls for coming to our senses is the report issued in 2006 by the Partnership for Prevention under the guidance of the National Commission on Prevention Priorities. The report ranked 25 evidence-based *clinical* prevention services. At the top were:

- Discuss the daily aspirin use of men 40+ and women 50+.
- Childhood immunizations.
- Smoking cessation advice and help to quit.
- Colorectal cancer screening.
- High blood pressure screening.

This report states that there is significant underuse of effective prevention care in the USA, resulting in lost lives, unnecessarily poor health outcomes, and inefficient use of healthcare dollars. It goes on to say that expanding access to high-quality primary and secondary services – and improving delivery systems to ensure that these sources are offered – should be a nationwide priority. These are *clinical* prevention services.

When it comes to prevention, we tend to be shortsighted. A good example is the National High Blood Pressure Education Program (Department of Health and Human Services (HHS), 2011), which combined public, patient, and professional education to increase detection and control and decrease stroke and heart attack from hypertension. This was perhaps the most successful national health promotion in American history. But what happened? The National Heart, Lung and Blood Institute of the National Institutes of Health (NIH) phased out the program and went on to other things. Today, high blood pressure is back to being a very serious problem.

Other examples of shortsightedness are the youth tobacco control programs in Florida and Mississippi, funded with money from the settlement between the state Attorneys General and the tobacco industry. Both programs were working, and the Florida program was so successful it was being touted as a prototype for other states. Then the governors and legislatures of both states cut the budgets, and the programs are essentially gone.

Besides being shortsighted, we also excel at fragmenting our US prevention efforts. They're all over the place. Numerous federal and state government agencies are involved. We have little coherence, no synergy, and no home-run power.

HHS tries to track how we're doing, but that's not a real program. A few years ago, a senior administration official talked about progress in discussions with a particular restaurant chain about trans-fat in cheese. That's a good example of fragmentation.

To succeed at health promotion and disease prevention we need to do better than that. We need to do two things:

1. Create *environmental* change, so that appropriate behavior is seen as normative behavior. This means changing the environment in which people actually live and work and play.
2. Focus on individuals' behaviors, to help and inform and educate people to take the proper steps to good health.

This requires both social marketing to create individual change and policy advocacy to create environmental change. A case in point is the Institute of Medicine (IOM) report on tobacco control (Bonnie et al., 2009). It contains two major recommendations:

- First, that state and local officials should redouble efforts to implement proven measures to reduce tobacco use. These include higher tobacco taxes, laws requiring that all workplaces and public places be smoke-free and comprehensive tobacco prevention, and cessation programs funded in every state at levels recommended by the Centers for Disease Control and Prevention (CDC). In this recommendation we see strategies for policy change, legal interventions, and social marketing that go well beyond what we typically think of as a medical model.
- The second IOM recommendation is for Congress to enact bipartisan legislation granting the Food and Drug Administration (FDA) broad regulatory authority over the manufacture, distribution, marketing, and use of the tobacco products. This is clearly a policy strategy. We almost won comprehensive tobacco control legislation with FDA oversight back in 1998, but we didn't get it done.

In 2008, at the Prevention and Health Care Reform Roundtable sponsored by the American Cancer Society, American Diabetes Association, and the American Heart Association, a report was released on 'The Impact of Prevention on Reducing the Burden of Cardiovascular Disease.' It said that:

Aggressive use of nationally recommended *clinical prevention activities*, such as smoking cessation programs, controlling pre-diabetes or lowering cholesterol, could increase life expectancy for U.S. adults by reducing cardiovascular disease (CVD).

The report went on to say that our current healthcare system is not optimally designed to promote health or prevent illness, and that the lesson from these findings is that we need a system in which we can apply these interventions in a way that is efficient and cost-effective.

The report's emphasis is on building a new clinical prevention system for the delivery of services. This is important, to be sure. Smoking cessation, adult and childhood immunizations, colorectal cancer screening, and high blood pressure screening all lend themselves to *clinical* treatment.

But clinical treatment is *only a part* – actually a small part – of health promotion and disease prevention. People don't live in clinical settings. They live in supermarkets, 7-Elevens, playgrounds, classrooms, offices, and factories. Americans also live in a media society – in front of TV sets, video games, movies, and computer screens. They live on cell phones and Blackberries and in restaurants. And, they especially live on couches (Pleis et al., 2008).

The point is that clinical settings are not where normative behaviors are set, where habits are formed and where peer and other influences take place. Even community settings aren't a big enough canvas. What makes someone decide to eat lunch every day at a fast food outlet? Or not? Start or quit smoking? Load up a grocery cart with snack foods and soft drinks? Drive recklessly?

Clinical settings can contribute to both environmental change and individual behavior change. But clinical settings are only a small, although important, part of the whole.

How do we attack the health disparities among and between ethnic groups and socio-economic strata? AARP's Public Policy Institute published a paper on racial and ethnic disparities in flu and pneumonia immunization rates among Medicare beneficiaries. Together, the two vaccine-preventable diseases of influenza and pneumonia represented the seventh leading cause of death in the USA in 2003. Medicare covers these vaccines at no out-of-pocket cost to beneficiaries.

In 2004, 67% of white adults ≥65 years old, but only 45% of older African-Americans and 55% of older Hispanics got a flu shot. There is an even wider gap on pneumonia immunization rates – only 34% of Hispanics and 39% of African-Americans compared with 61% of whites. What accounts for this discrepancy, and how do we correct it? Social marketing is an appropriate approach to help answer this question.

One of the biggest conundrums in dealing with prevention and wellness issues is this: We often know what to do, but we're not very good at getting people to do it. We've got a long way to go in bringing about significant behavior change on a large scale. And it's costing us dearly – in terms of health status, productivity on the job, quality of life, and in terms of our ability to afford a healthcare system where costs are skyrocketing.

We know just what to do to decrease tobacco-related disease, but we're not doing it. The Commonwealth Fund Study, *Bending the Curve*, has estimated that we could save some $200 billion over 10 years if we did. Obesity and hypertension control are two other areas where effective, widespread programs would yield a major cost savings. In fact, the Commonwealth Fund Study also found that by reducing tobacco use and obesity, creating incentives for wellness programs and healthy behavior, and covering preventive services, we could save an estimated $493 billion over 10 years. Achieving this requires a combined approach using social marketing and policy advocacy.

In order to make all of this happen, we need leadership. One leader who has emerged is New York City Mayor Michael Bloomberg. During his tenure, New York City has banned smoking in bars and restaurants and banned trans-fats in restaurants. Today there are an estimated 600,000 fewer smokers in NYC than there otherwise would have been if Mayor Bloomberg hadn't acted. His foundation has given millions for tobacco control in developing countries. He's spoken out for boosting prevention programs as a means of solving our healthcare problems.

Certainly we need presidential leadership, and President Obama is providing it. He has said that the path to fiscal sustainability goes through healthcare reform. And he specifically talked about prevention. As he has pointed out, 'The nation faces epidemics of obesity and chronic diseases as well as new threats of pandemic flu and bioterrorism. Yet less than four cents of every health care dollar is spent on prevention and public health' (Cohen et al., 2008).

We also need a true, public–private partnership, Congressionally mandated, with real money behind it, and with the clout and stature to bring everyone to the table. Putting a national prevention initiative in a government agency or agencies is not working...and will not work. We certainly need government – national, state, and local – in this partnership, but we also need everyone else. By everyone, we mean educators, corporations, including the fast food and processed food industries, those who benefit from and influence our agricultural subsidies, the media, policymakers, insurance, and pharmaceutical groups and all others who can make or break the program. They need to commit and participate.

We also need to get past the narrow focus of whether prevention saves money or costs money. We need to reframe the debate. As Steven Woolf (2009) points out, the better question is how much health the investment purchases.

Imagine how great this could be – an opportunity to change the nation. This is what we need for America's continued success and for the health and well-being of future generations. And a synergistic approach combining social marketing and policy advocacy could make it happen.

We're optimistic. We believe that health promotion and disease prevention can improve the quality of life for millions of people and make health care affordable for government, corporations, employees, and families as our society ages and becomes more diverse. AARP is committed to this. Right now our main prevention focus is on physical activity and wise use of medications. But we see the big picture, and we are committed to wellness and prevention in a big way.

CONCLUSION

As a result of our experience at AARP, we have come to realize that effecting social change on a large scale requires using all of the tools in the social change tool box. That means influencing the environment, including social norms, so that the desired behavior becomes the expected behavior, and influencing individuals to change their behavior in the desired way to achieve the social change goal. Social marketing practices and policy advocacy both have a role to play in this. They should not be seen as competitors vying for superiority in the social change methods hierarchy, but as complementary methods, each having their own strengths and appropriate uses.

Any organization that engages in the strategy and tactics of policy advocacy as part of overall social change must realize that there are potential land mines and other disadvantages.

First, it takes a good deal of resources to become adept and effective. This includes policy research and analysis, including public and thought-leader polling and qualitative research. It also includes outstanding strategic experience, something your opponents (e.g., special interest groups, trade associations, corporations) may have in abundance.

Second, in the rough and tumble of policy advocacy, your organization may become a target of criticism, including through the media. When policy opponents want to come after AARP, they often go directly to our members, to legislators and of course to the press. You may have to fend off criticisms as a normal part of your advocacy work.

Finally, policy opponents may come after individuals, such as your management, your board members, and your donors. This is a no-holds barred business, and not for the faint of heart. In one (semi-) amusing experience at AARP, a group of members stood outside Bill Novelli's window after the Medicare Modernization Act was passed and dramatically burned their AARP cards in front of TV cameras. Then one of the demonstrators walked inside the building and asked for a new membership card. She was going on a trip, she explained, and needed the card to get travel discounts.

As government agencies (e.g., the CDC) and other organizations (e.g., the Robert Wood Johnson Foundation) turn to advocacy to bring about long-lasting social change (Ottoson et al., 2009), new tools are becoming available that will equip social marketers with skills needed to blend advocacy with a marketing mindset. A variety of tools and products are now available on the internet.

In sum, the goal of both social marketing and policy advocacy is to influence behavior to deliver a positive benefit for society. When used together, they can be effective in achieving greater social change than either one can alone, especially when the social change also requires influencing upstream factors and changing social norms and laws.

KEY WORDS: AARP; social change; policy advocacy; individual behaviors; environment; Medicare Modernization Act; social impact; aging; prescription drug coverage; 'Don't Vote' Campaign; triple bottom line; disease prevention.

Key insights:

- Social marketing and public policy advocacy are complementary, and, when combined, can create a synergistic approach to achieve positive social change.
- Effecting social change on a large scale requires using all of the tools in the social change toolbox. This means influencing the environment, including social norms, so that the desired behavior becomes the expected behavior. Social marketing practices and public policy advocacy both have a role to play in this. They should not be seen as competitors vying for superiority in the social change methods hierarchy, but as complementary, each having their own strengths and appropriate uses.
- When used together, social marketing and policy advocacy can be effective in achieving greater

social change than either can alone, especially when the social change also requires influencing upstream factors and changing social norms and laws.

REFERENCES

Andreasen, A.R. (1994) 'Social marketing: Definition and domain', *Journal of Marketing and Public Policy*, Spring: 108–114.

Andreasen, A.R. (1995) *Marketing and Social Change: Changing Behavior to Promote Health, Social Development, and the Environment*. San Francisco, CA: Jossey-Bass, p. 7.

Andreasen, A.R. (2006) *Social Marketing in the 21st Century*. Thousand Oaks, CA: Sage Publications.

Andreasen, A.R. (2002) 'Marketing social marketing in the social change marketplace', *Journal of Public Policy and Marketing*, 21(March): 3–13.

Bloom, P.N. and Novelli, W.D. (1981) 'Problems and challenges of social marketing', *Journal of Marketing*, 45(Spring), 79–88.

Brownson, R.C., Haire-Joshu, D. and Luke, D.A. (2006). 'Shaping the context of health: A review of environmental and policy approaches in the prevention of chronic diseases', *Annual Review of Public Health*, 27, 341–370.

Fox, K.F.A. and Kotler, P. (1980) 'The marketing of social causes: The first ten years', *Journal of Marketing*, 44(Fall), 24–33.

Frieden, T.R. (2010). 'A framework for public health action: The health impact pyramid', *American Journal of Public Health*, 100(4), 590–595.

French, J. and Blair Stevens, C. (2005) Social Marketing Pocket Guide (1st edn). National Social Marketing Centre for Excellence. Available at: www.nsms.org.uk.

Institute of Medicine, Committee on Secondhand Smoke Exposure and Acute Coronary Events (2010). *Secondhand Smoke Exposure and Cardiovascular Effects: Making Sense of Evidence*. Washington, DC: National Academies Press.

Ottoson, J., Green, L.W., Beery, W.L., et al. (2009) 'Policy-contribution assessment and field-building analysis of the Robert Wood Johnson Foundation's Active Living Research program', *American Journal of Preventive Medicine*, 36(2S):S34–S43.

Pleis, J.R., Lucas, J.W. and Ward, B.W. (2009). 'Summary health statistics for U.S. adults: National Health Interview Survey, 2008', *Vital Health Statistics*, 10(242): 1–157.

Kotler, P. and Lee, N.R. (2008) *Social Marketing: Influencing Behaviors for Good*, 3rd edn. Thousand Oaks, CA: Sage Pulications.

Kotler, P. and Levy, S.J. (1969) 'Broadening the concept of marketing', *Journal of Marketing*, 33(January): 10–15.

Kotler, P. and Roberto, E. (1989) *Social Marketing: Strategies for Changing Public Behavior*. New York: The Free Press.

Kotler, P. and Zaltman, G. (1971) 'Social marketing: An approach to planned social change', *Journal of Marketing*, 35(July): 3–12.

McLeroy, K.R., Bibeau, D., Steckler, A. and Glanz, K. (1988) 'An ecological perspective on health promotion programs', *Health Education Quarterly*, 15, 351–377.

Rothschild, M.L. (1999) 'Carrots, sticks, and promises: A conceptual framework for the management of public health and social issue behaviors', *Journal of Marketing*, 63(October): 24–37.

Stokols, D. (1996). 'Translating social ecological theory into guidelines for community health promotion', *American Journal of Health Promotion*, 10, 282–298.

Wiener, J.L. and Doescher, T.A. (1991) 'A framework for promotion of cooperation', *Journal of Marketing*, 55(April): 38–47.

Woolf, S.H. (2009) 'A closer look at the economic argument for disease prevention', *JAMA*, 301(5): 536–538.

26

Social Marketing and Tobacco Control

Timothy Dewhirst and
Wonkyong Beth Lee

INTRODUCTION

With the emergence of social marketing in the late 1960s and early 1970s, as part of the push to expand how marketing was conceptualized, it was argued that the tools and concepts of the marketing discipline were increasingly applicable to non-profit and public organizations, as opposed to being limited to those in the for-profit sector (Kotler and Zaltman, 1971). Demonstrating that marketing concepts and techniques could be useful towards addressing social, environmental, and public health concerns, such as reducing instances of drinking and driving or encouraging energy conservation practices, the discipline could also be seen as responsive to pressures of being more socially relevant.

Tobacco use has received considerable attention from social marketers, given that it represents the single most important cause of preventable illness and premature death in most industrialized countries. During the mid-1990s, smoking was identified as the leading preventable cause of death and disability in developed countries, with roughly 3 million people estimated to die from smoking each year and about 1.5 million of them before the age of 70 (Peto et al., 1996; Wald and Hackshaw, 1996); moreover, the death toll from smoking is forecasted to reach 10 million per year by 2020, with 70% of those premature deaths occurring in developing countries (Mackay et al., 2006). In the USA, for example, it is estimated

that approximately 440,000 people die prematurely each year as a result of smoking. Tobacco use is responsible for a greater number of deaths among Americans than the total caused by motor-vehicle crashes, suicides, murders, AIDS, and illicit drug use combined (USDHHS, 2004). From a global public health standpoint, particular concern has increasingly become directed toward tobacco use in emerging economies such as Russia, Indonesia, and China, given their notable populations, less stringent political and regulatory environments, and that the majority of men smoke in these countries (70%, 62%, and 60%, respectively). At present, there are an estimated 1 billion smokers globally, with one-third found in China alone (Byrnes and Balfour, 2009).

Because illness and premature death caused by smoking is preventable, tobacco control efforts have attempted to educate those 'at risk' (i.e., both current and potential smokers) about the harms of tobacco use and to dissuade them from smoking. In this chapter, we provide an overview of social marketing efforts relating to tobacco control, and, in doing so, attempt to offer a global perspective with the case illustrations presented. First, we provide a definition of *social marketing*, which provides the scope for what is covered in the chapter. Second, the chapter clarifies how target markets are commonly specified through market segmentation and the processes by which marketing and promotion objectives are established. Third, we offer that mass media anti-smoking campaigns have traditionally been classified broadly as either prevention or cessation focused, with target markets being established accordingly. We then discuss the emergence of campaigns relating to tobacco industry de-normalization that have coincided with the public release of internal corporate documents from the tobacco industry as a result of litigation. The chapter also provides an overview of additional themes that are commonly used for anti-smoking programs, including insight about the viability of using fear appeals and social norm messages. In doing so, the chapter provides an overview of the key principles that underlie the production of an effective promotional campaign. Finally, the chapter identifies emerging trends in social marketing practices, suggests areas for future research, and provides a summary of main findings.

SOCIAL MARKETING DEFINED

Providing a definition of social marketing helps provide scope for which programs are typically classified as social marketing and which ones are not. A prevailing definition has been put forward by Andreasen:

> Social marketing is the adaptation of commercial marketing technologies to programs designed to influence the voluntary behavior of target audiences to improve their personal welfare and that of the society of which they are a part (1994: 110).

In this definition, Andreasen urges non-profit and public organizations to incorporate and apply marketing principles for reaching their desired objectives. For example, this commonly involves examining marketing environment factors and thereby identifying internal strengths and weaknesses and external opportunities and threats facing the organization, as well as utilizing the principles of market segmentation to identify target markets and a related marketing mix.

In further explaining his definition of social marketing, Andreasen points to the importance of designing 'programs', which is distinctive from 'campaigns': campaigns have a fixed termination point, often lasting a year or two, whereas programs may include several campaigns and take decades to implement. The organization's goals, he advises, should be oriented toward a program rather than an isolated campaign, given that it often takes considerable time to influence societal attitudes and behavior. Additionally, Andreasen discusses the importance of attempts to 'influence' behavior, which qualifies that social marketing programs do not necessarily involve behavior change. Many social marketing initiatives are prevention-oriented, and as such are encouraging the status quo to target audiences (i.e., if an individual is a non-smoker, the social marketer hopes that the individual will remain a non-smoker).

In referring to influencing 'voluntary' behavior, Andreasen identifies that coercion is not part of a social marketing initiative. Thus, whereas legislation might be used as a substitute for social marketing or be combined with social marketing efforts and share complementary goals, legal solutions are considered separate from social marketing. As a result, despite their importance toward reaching tobacco control objectives, legislative measures such as taxation, health warnings on cigarette packages, and smoke-free environments in the workplace, restaurants, and other indoor or public spaces are not covered in this chapter.

Finally, Andreasen specifies that the objectives of a social marketing initiative seek to benefit target consumers and the society as a whole, rather than the marketer. A profit-seeking imperative and consequent self-serving notion, from the perspective of those engaged in marketing, serves as a major distinction between the for-profit, private sector's activities and social marketing. Many marketing initiatives from for-profit firms, which might at first glance appear like social marketing, are more accurately described as a public relations function, corporate social responsibility, or cause-related marketing. In the USA, for example, Philip Morris ran prominent US$100 million promotional campaigns during the late 1990s that communicated the philanthropic and social activism activities of the company, relating to social issues such as feeding the hungry and supporting domestic violence crisis centers. Although the causes, issues, or charities in question were undoubtedly important, a controversial element to the program was that the money spent toward promoting Philip Morris' charitable donations considerably exceeded what was contributed to those in need, suggesting that their efforts were more prominently focused on enhancing the image of the firm (Dewhirst, 2005). Internal tobacco industry documents made public from litigation reveal that the overriding objectives of these programs, along with those promoted as preventing underage tobacco sales or youth smoking generally, is often to avoid or defer regulatory measures and advance public opinion about tobacco industry marketing practices (Landman et al., 2002). In accordance with Andreasen's definition of social marketing, tobacco industry-sponsored programs are not regarded as social marketing; thus, they are considered beyond the scope of this chapter for further discussion.

MARKET SEGMENTATION AND KEY TARGET GROUPS

A marketing strategy starts with a clear target market in mind, and *segmentation* is a commonly used approach in which specific audiences are identified by dividing a mass market into subsets on the basis of variables such as demographics, geography, psychographics, and behavioral components (Kotler et al., 2005). Marketing strategists commonly recognize the human diversity of consumers they are attempting to influence, and promotions tend to be directed toward well-defined segments. In recognizing various segments of consumers, social marketing programs and promotions can obviously be better directed toward the specific needs, wants, and desires of target groups. By identifying and understanding the idiosyncrasies, attitudes, and interests of identified targets, a social marketing program is far more likely to elicit favorable consumer responses, in contrast to a single undifferentiated effort aimed at the 'average' member of the mass market.

Demographic segmentation accounts for dimensions such as age, gender, ethnicity, education, socio-economic status, occupation, religion, and stage of the family life-cycle. In terms of age, pre-teens or adolescents are generally identified as the target market for prevention-oriented mass media campaigns, which reflects that in many countries smoking initiation typically occurs around 13 to 14 years old. The American Legacy Foundation's 'truth' campaign, for example, targets youth aged 12–17 years old. In Canada, 'young adults' – aged 20–24 – are another age segment likely to get considerable attention because they have the highest smoking rates among all age groups (Health Canada, 2002).

Geographic segmentation accounts for dimensions such as market density and regional differences of a domestic or international market, which may consequently play a role in the development of promotional strategies. Multi-language anti-smoking programs are a common consideration in many jurisdictions. With Canada being a bilingual country, anti-smoking campaigns that are national in scope would likely need to be prepared in both French and English, and it would be advisable to avoid developing ad copy that was merely translated from one language to the other. Malaysia's first national anti-smoking media campaign, 'Tak Nak' (meaning 'Say No'), was developed with both English and Bahasa Malaysia language versions.

Successful social marketing programs from one country might be adapted for use in additional countries. The Australian TV ad, dubbed 'Aorta', serves as an example of an anti-smoking, fear appeal promotion that has been adapted for use in Norway, Poland, Thailand, and the US state of Massachusetts (Hastings et al., 2004; Hill et al., 1998). When introducing campaigns to new, additional jurisdictions, as was done with 'Aorta', social marketers face challenging decisions in determining to what extent the approach will be adapted and thereby account for unique cultural tastes, preferences, and values apparent in a given country.

Psychographics, also referred to as lifestyle analysis, is another commonly used segmentation approach in which the personality, activities, interests, and opinions of the target market are considered. Personality attributions of adolescent smokers may include rebelliousness, disobedience, and risk-taking (Dewhirst and Sparks, 2003); thus, social marketing programs might be developed in an attempt to counteract the association of these qualities with cigarettes (as commonly seen in tobacco promotions). Social marketing messages designed around the theme of tobacco industry misbehavior and marketing practices, as revealed by internal corporate documents released during litigation, can capitalize on the propensity of youth to rebel by directing their rebellious tendencies toward the tobacco industry. For example, one of the initiatives from the American Legacy Foundation's 'truth' campaign, known as 'body bags', involved filming young people stacking body bags on the sidewalk immediately in front of the headquarters of a major tobacco firm (i.e., Philip Morris in New York City) to symbolize the 1200 people who die daily from tobacco-related illness in the USA (Lavack, 2004).

Behavioral segmentation involves taking into account the usage situation and extent of use. Thus, social marketers may classify consumers into non-users, ex-users, potential users, first-time users, sporadic users, and heavy users of tobacco products. A target group of particular interest for a social marketing program might be identified as 'social smokers', who are commonly defined according to the context of their tobacco use: non-daily smoking, primarily by young adults with other smokers or people (rather than alone), that occurs mostly in bars, nightclubs, or at parties (Gilpin et al., 2005; Moran et al., 2004). Often, social smokers do not identify themselves as smokers (Luoto et al., 2000). Consequently, social smokers may be less motivated to engage in adaptive behavior that minimizes their health risks. Thus, social marketing messages targeting social smokers can enhance their awareness that they are not immune from the dangers of occasional smoking because there is no safe level of cigarette smoking.

MARKETING MIX CONSIDERATIONS

Having specified a target market, the development of a marketing strategy then involves establishing a corresponding marketing mix, which is commonly broken down into four domains known as the 4Ps. A marketing mix consists of strategies relating to product, price, place (i.e., distribution), and promotion. Marketing mix considerations should not be developed in isolation; rather, the 4Ps should be developed synergistically.

The first P, product, involves what is being offered to the consumer and should be capable of satisfying their specific needs and wants. Strategic product decisions often concern which benefits will be emphasized when target consumers engage in a desired behavior or may instead identify perceived costs that can be avoided (Kotler and Lee, 2008). The core product for a tobacco control campaign might emphasize being sick less often (reduced absenteeism from work or school) or saving money as a benefit of not smoking, whereas wrinkling of the skin or becoming addicted and unable to quit might be identified as perceived costs. Serving as an illustration of a campaign that called attention to the addictiveness of smoking, an initiative from the UK Department of Health showed people with fish hooks in their mouths being dragged to a retailer selling cigarettes. Whereas this anti-smoking campaign, utilizing a 'hooked' theme, generated considerable publicity, it also proved to be controversial, with numerous complaints being directed to the Advertising Standards Authority based on the images being offensive, frightening, and distressing, particularly to children that might see the promotions (Sweney, 2007).

An additional product strategy consideration is the use of *branding*, which is defined as a name, term, symbol, or design to identify a product (Aaker, 1996). The Canadian Cancer Society, for example, utilizes a yellow daffodil flower to symbolize living with strength and courage (see fightback.ca).

The second P, price, involves social marketers determining the cost as well as how much value targeted consumers attach to adopting the desired behavior. Pricing goes beyond the financial costs of assuming a behavior and also includes consideration about the time, effort, and energy required from consumers (Kotler and Lee, 2008). If a cessation advertisement offers a smoker's helpline, for example, it is important that the necessary resources are in place to field incoming calls and queries; in other words, it is critical that smokers using the helpline do not face undue waiting times and consequent hassle costs. Nicotine replacement therapy exemplifies a financial cost that many smokers incur in attempts to quit. Research from Canada reveals that, with a price increase in tobacco products (i.e., de-marketing tobacco through tax increases), a one-month lagged effect is apparent regarding the increased use of nicotine replacement therapies (Inness et al., 2008). However, this effect is temporary – dissipating after three months – suggesting that there is a brief window of opportunity for the heightened implementation of cessation-oriented tobacco control campaigns. 'Quit and Win' contests also illustrate a price-oriented anti-smoking approach, in which incentives, usually financial, are provided to promote smoking cessation.

The third P, place, involves how the product reaches the consumer and the convenience in which it is acquired. According to Kotler and Lee, 'place is where and when the target market will perform the desired behaviour, acquire any related tangible objects, and receive any associated services' (2008: 247). An aim is to make services easily available (e.g., establishing suitable times and locations for smoking cessation classes). Alternatively, social marketing has been used to make smoking more difficult, unpleasant, and non-normative by influencing the public acceptability of smoke-free indoor air policies. During the mid-1990s, when a California-wide smoking ban was being implemented in enclosed workplaces (bars were initially exempted), 10-second television ads from the California Department of Health Services aired which labeled half of the screen as 'Smoking Section' and the other half as 'Non-Smoking Section', yet both sides of the screen were virtually indistinguishable with thick smoke depicted. The image was complemented by a male voice-over remarking, 'No matter what they tell you, smoke doesn't stay in the smoking section' (cited in Reid, 2005: 92).

The fourth P, promotion, involves communicating information and lifestyle dimensions to targeted consumers, with a goal of influencing their perceptions, opinions, attitudes, and behavior. Effective promotional planning typically involves strategically consistent brand communication and a clear determination of the target audience. There are several ways to communicate with consumers, including advertising (mediums such as TV, radio, newspapers, magazines, billboards, and websites), event sponsorship, celebrity endorsements, coupons, sampling, contests, direct marketing, publicity, product placement, and public relations.

The aforementioned fish hook campaign from the UK Department of Health included television commercials and posters, as well as magazine, newspaper, and internet advertising. Promotional planning also involves determining which strategies will be utilized regarding message content and tone.

PREVENTION VERSUS CESSATION APPROACHES

Numerous mass media anti-smoking campaigns have been undertaken to reduce smoking prevalence, and traditionally these efforts have been broadly classified as either prevention- or cessation-focused. For prevention-oriented ad campaigns, emphasis is commonly placed on the health or social risks of smoking; yet, there is considerable debate about the effectiveness of providing youth with messages about the personal, physical health consequences of smoking. Biener (2002) and Biener and Taylor (2002) argue that anti-tobacco ads portraying the serious consequences of tobacco use in an emotionally evocative manner are highly effective, and they present the promotions produced by the Massachusetts Tobacco Control Program as a case in point. Additional researchers have concluded that anti-smoking health messages can be effective with adolescent target markets (Henley and Donovan, 2003; Smith and Stutts, 2003; White et al., 2003). Nevertheless, other evaluations of anti-smoking ad campaigns have led to the conclusion that emphasizing the long-term, personal health consequences of smoking to youth typically has little impact (Goldman and Glantz, 1998; Pechmann et al., 2003; USDHHS, 2000). According to marketing research prepared during the early 1980s for Canada's largest tobacco firm, Imperial Tobacco Ltd. (ITL), adolescents who start smoking do not disbelieve the health implications of smoking, but they almost universally assume these risks are non-applicable because they do not anticipate becoming addicted (Kwechansky Marketing Research Inc., 1982). Thus, it is conceivable that many health messages are largely dismissed because adolescent 'experimenters' do not foresee themselves being committed smokers in the long term.

Although prevention-oriented ad campaigns are likely to have a well-defined target group in terms of age segmentation (i.e., pre-teens or adolescents), it is comparatively more challenging to determine the priority target group when undertaking a cessation approach. Cessation-oriented ad campaigns have potential relevance to a broad range of existing smokers. Addiction, for example, is apparent among adolescent smokers (Moffat and Johnson, 2001), and McVea et al. (2009) found that 'inescapable quit reasons' and 'emotionally compelling' messages were the only truly motivating ones for adolescents experiencing smoking cessation attempts. Obviously, to be persuasive, different messages and executions are needed to appeal to adolescents as opposed to established smokers in their 40s or 50s.

Gender and stage of the family life-cycle are additional demographic attributes often used for segmentation purposes, and cigarette smoking has been identified as a 'gendered' practice in multiple jurisdictions and contexts (Amos, 1996; Chollat-Traquet, 1992; National Cancer Institute, 2008; USDHHS, 2001; Waldron, 1991; Waldron et al., 1988). General market research findings show that, compared with men, women more often smoke to relax and relieve stress, and they more frequently use smoking as a weight control strategy. Thus, a social marketing program directed toward women smokers would need to account for potential weight gain concerns being a more prominent deterrent to quitting smoking. The program might also offer substitute activities for trying to relax and relieve stress. In terms of family life-cycle approaches, cessation approaches may target women smokers at the time of pregnancy, communicating that smoking is harmful to both the expectant mother and her unborn baby. Meanwhile, for tobacco cessation messages targeted at new fathers, Johnson et al. (2009) caution that many new fathers continue their smoking, and disregard smoking cessation messages, in an attempt to maintain context- and age-specific masculine ideals.

A potential theme of cessation-oriented approaches concerns the harmful health consequences of secondhand smoke. It is worthwhile noting that public awareness about the harmfulness of secondhand smoke did not generally become evident until the mid-1980s, at which time the US Surgeon General released a landmark report linking the exposure of secondhand smoke to lung cancer in adults and respiratory problems in children. The emergence of social marketing programs, communicating the accumulating evidence relating to secondhand smoke, had a profound influence on the social acceptability of tobacco use, as people gained a better understanding that the combination of smoke produced by the burning of tobacco and the exhaled smoke from a smoker was also debilitating to non-smokers. Smoking could no longer be considered merely an individual right or personal choice, and non-smokers began taking more active roles, arguing for their interests in tobacco-related issues.

DE-NORMALIZATION CAMPAIGNS

Pro-tobacco and anti-tobacco promotions can be seen as opposing communications that contribute to whether or not smoking is commonly perceived as 'normal' behavior. A norm is defined as:

a rule that governs a pattern of social behaviour… On the one hand, a norm may encapsulate the usual behaviour within a society (and is thus a norm in the sense of being statistically normal behaviour). On the other hand, the norm is a pattern of behaviour that is desired or prescribed, whether or not actual behaviour complies with this ideal (Edgar and Sedgwick, 1999: 261–262).

It is important to be mindful about context, however, because a norm can be culturally, geographically, or demographically specific. For example, in Canada, it is normal to be a non-smoker, yet in many Asian markets such as Korea, roughly two-thirds of men smoke. Thus, for this particular Korean demographic, it remains normal behavior to be a smoker (Mackay and Eriksen, 2002).

The definition of a norm also points to the fact that a norm may be behavior that is preferred or favored, and this is applicable to smoking, considering the health consequences of tobacco use. To normalize behavior refers to efforts towards influencing consumers to conform to a standard or norm. The 'de' prefix, meanwhile, refers to opposing efforts that attempt to reverse whether a given behavior (or industry, for that matter) such as smoking is considered normal.

An important objective of pro-tobacco promotions historically has been to reaffirm the social acceptability of smoking, which can contribute to consumers overestimating the proportion of people that smoke in a given society. According to internal documentation of ITL, for example, lifestyle imagery is to be maintained for each of the firm's Player's cigarette brands, with ads continuing to:

reflect the brand's popularity among young people, to demonstrate the social acceptability of these brands among the target consumer's peer group, and to place the products in scenarios and settings which invite the target consumer to easily associate a Player's brand with a pleasant lifestyle to which he will identify (Chacra, 1980: 1).

Yet, communication efforts pertaining to the de-normalization of tobacco are commonly undertaken to reinforce that smoking is not normal or mainstream behavior in Canadian society (in fact, during 2005, roughly 20% of Canadians aged 15 years and older were regarded as current smokers; thus, non-smokers clearly represent the majority), and to emphasize that the observed downward trend of tobacco use is desirable (Health Canada, 2005; Lavack, 1999).

Some de-normalization campaigns focus on smokers and smoking behavior: consequently, they seem to 'blame the victim' to persuade smokers to change their behavior. The stupid.ca campaign (Figure 26.1), which is supported by the provincial government of Ontario, Canada's most populous province, seemingly serves as such an example, despite the program's website claims that the objective is to demonstrate that the tobacco industry manipulates youth, as well as illustrate the potential consequences of tobacco use. The program is also supposedly a social commentary about the decision to smoke and it is not meant to be an insult to smokers or convey that smokers are stupid. Nevertheless, the ad copy of the 'Rat Poison' promotion seen in Figure 26.1 states that, 'Arsenic has been banned in rat poison. But it's still in some cigarettes. Good thing rats are too smart to smoke'. Several researchers have cautioned against using an approach that blames the victim, owing to the resulting loss of self-esteem that may be apparent among vulnerable groups who are addicted, and question the effectiveness of public health interventions that serve to stigmatize smokers (Bayer and Stuber, 2006; Poland et al., 2006). Such messaging can pit non-smokers against smokers – an 'us versus them' mentality – and contribute to the observation that, in many instances, tobacco control practitioners do not have a particularly good understanding or relationship with smokers (Poland et al., 2006). Even so, the stupid.ca campaign has been praised in some circles for recognizing that youths are a distinct target market (i.e., speaking in their own language) and for emphasizing the potential social risks of smoking (i.e., appearing un-cool or silly) (George, 2005).

Litigation against the tobacco industry has facilitated the release of internal corporate documents, thus prompting an additional stream of anti-tobacco ads that are commonly referred to as *tobacco industry manipulation* campaigns in the USA and *tobacco industry de-normalization* campaigns in Canada (Lavack, 2004). According to Canada's Non-Smokers' Rights Association (2004), tobacco industry de-normalization (TID) is a public health strategy designed to inform consumers about tobacco company corporate fraud and negligence, the failure of tobacco companies to sufficiently warn smokers about the dangers of smoking, and how tobacco companies target their marketing efforts at youth populations. The focus of TID campaigns is on using social marketing and social activism to increase consumer awareness about the marketing tactics and business

Figure 26.1   Ads that circulated during 2005 as part of the stupid.ca counter-marketing campaign from the government of Ontario, Canada. Used with permission

decisions of the tobacco industry. Reviews of internal corporate documents from the tobacco industry have revealed unethical and manipulative marketing tactics, including the apparent targeting of adolescents (Carter, 2003; Cummings et al., 2002; Dewhirst, 2004, 2008; Hastings and MacFadyen, 2000; National Cancer Institute, 2008; Pollay, 2000; Pollay and Lavack, 1993), misleading and deceptive product claims or advertising (Hammond et al., 2006; Pollay and Dewhirst, 2003), and public relations and lobbying efforts to impede smoke-free bylaws in public places (Drope and Glantz, 2003; Landman, 2000).

The premise behind TID is that being exposed to facts and the truth about tobacco industry practices will alter consumer attitudes toward smoking, which will in turn change their smoking behavior or prevent them from starting to smoke. One reason TID campaigns are becoming popular for population-level smoking prevention programming is because the approach appears to be effective at changing smoking-related attitudes and behaviors among youth populations (Bauer et al., 2000; Farrelly et al., 2002, 2005; Hersey et al., 2005b; Sly et al., 2001a; Thrasher and Jackson, 2006; Thrasher et al., 2006). The truth® campaign of the American Legacy Foundation (Figure 26.2) exemplifies a TID initiative that uses edgy and hard-hitting TV and print media ads, promotional items (e.g., t-shirts), social activism, and a website to target youth with facts about tobacco and tobacco industry marketing practices.

Evaluation of the truth® campaign demonstrates that the program has effectively changed youth perceptions of the tobacco industry and intentions to smoke among youths (Farrelly et al., 2005; Healton, 2001; Hersey et al., 2005a; Sly et al., 2001b; Thrasher et al., 2004).

Overall, the findings on the effectiveness of the TID counter-marketing approach are mixed. Goldman and Glantz (1998) contend that the most successful TID campaigns have messages designed around the theme of tobacco industry misbehavior and marketing practices. The approach appears to offer benefits by helping smokers redirect their guilt about smoking into anger concerning the thought of being manipulated (Lavack, 2004). Additionally, the approach appears to be effective at increasing anti-tobacco attitudes and beliefs among adolescents (Bauer et al., 2000; Farrelly et al., 2002, 2005; Sly et al., 2001a). For TID campaigns to remain effective, however, consideration must be given to the possibility of a ceiling effect in which existing messages lose their impact over time (Pechmann and Reibling, 2006). This phenomenon requires program planners to change TID messages periodically to remain novel, up-to-date, and contemporary with the needs of youth (Farrelly et al., 2003), as well as complement TID campaigns with other approaches. Pechmann and Reibling (2006) contend that anti-smoking programs using only TID tactics are not sufficient and there is a need to include other themes relating to negative emotions or social norms.

Figure 26.2   Print advertising from the American Legacy Foundation's truth youth smoking prevention campaign. The ad circulated during the early 2000s. Courtesy of the American Legacy Foundation

THE USE OF FEAR APPEALS

Fear appeals are commonly used in anti-smoking campaigns, yet there is considerable debate about the optimal level of fear appeals to be used in mass communications. Fear appeal messages typically utilize a consequences – recommendation format. Such messages present the physical health consequences of unhealthy, risky behaviors, and seek to increase the audience's arousal level and motivate them to seek solutions. Following the depiction of possible health consequences, in a graphic manner, recommended strategies follow, which are meant to reduce the audience's aroused fear by providing solutions (Keller, 1999). When people experience threat, they typically feel fear and are motivated to avoid it. Morand and Mullins (1998) found that ex-smokers' concern about the potential 'scary' health consequences of smoking was the primary motivation for smoking cessation.

The general conclusion from the fear appeals literature is that moderate-level fear appeals tend to increase behavioral intentions, whereas low-level fear appeals are unlikely to change behavioral intentions, and high-level fear appeals can boomerang (Keller and Lehmann, 2008). Overall, fear appears to mediate attitude changes

and actions of desirable health-related behaviors (Leventhal et al., 2003).

A mass media anti-smoking campaign launched in Australia in 1997 serves as an example of fear appeals being used effectively (Hill et al., 1998). The campaign was described as 'the mother of all scare campaigns' and 'Aorta', one of three television ads used, showed fatty deposits being squeezed by a surgeon's hand from a smoker's aorta. Hurley and Matthews (2008) evaluated the cost-effectiveness of the campaign and they concluded that the campaign prevented a considerable number of deaths caused by smoking and saved sizable healthcare costs.

Nevertheless, researchers have raised concern about the apparent predominant use of fear appeals in tobacco control (see Pechmann and Slater, 2005, for a comprehensive overview of social marketing messages that may prompt adverse effects). According to the tone of a given message, highly threatening 'health and fear' oriented messages that target youth may be ill-advised and counterproductive to the stated goals of tobacco control advocacy groups, with conceptual explanations including boomerang or reactance effects. Brehm's (1966) reactance theory suggests that when individuals perceive an unfair threat to their freedom of action, they are likely to experience a state of reactance, in which there is a heightened motivation to perform the threatened behavior and reassert their freedom. Fishbein et al. (2002), for example, advise that televised US anti-drug public service announcements (PSAs) should account for the negative health consequences of drug use behavior rather than merely focusing on the essence of the tagline, 'Just say no'. Henriksen et al. (2006) test the boomerang effect for tobacco industry-sponsored anti-smoking ads (i.e., youth smoking prevention promotions put forward by Philip Morris and Lorillard), and although such an effect was not demonstrated, they did conclude that adolescents scoring high on psychological reactance measures expressed the strongest intention to smoke and were least responsive to anti-smoking ads from any source (including ads from the American Legacy Foundation).

Hastings and MacFadyen (2002) argue that the use of fear appeals in tobacco control have proven less effective than what was initially thought. They contend that the public in many developed economies already largely know that smoking is dangerous. Thus, when consumers receive information (i.e., smoking is dangerous) that is inconsistent with their behavior (i.e., I still smoke), they are motivated to reason against the information and justify their behavior by questioning their susceptibility as well as the severity of the consequences (Keller, 1999). As a result, fear appeals in anti-smoking campaigns may no longer be effective to those who are targeted (e.g., smokers) relative to those who are already persuaded by the messaging (e.g., ex-smokers).

Hastings and his colleagues also point to the ethical implications of using fear appeals (Hastings and MacFadyen, 2002; Hastings et al., 2004). When people experience fear, they can show maladaptive responses to avoid fear (Hill et al., 1998). In fact, smokers already demonstrate a maladaptive response by *rationalizing* their smoking behavior (Lee et al., 2009). When smokers are exposed to messages conveying fear appeals, they may become more motivated to rationalize their smoking behavior, and consequently may not engage in adaptive behavior that minimizes their risks.

Biener and Taylor (2002) contend that fear is only one of many different emotions that smokers experience related to smoking (e.g., regret, sadness, anger toward tobacco companies, and empathy for smokers). Understanding the diversity of smokers' emotional reactions about smoking is considered important towards creating effective interventions. For example, Lee et al. (2009) found that smokers who are regretful about their smoking are more likely to have quit intentions within six months. Consequently, it is recommended that anti-smoking campaigns focusing on regret about the possible future consequences of smoking may be as effective as those focusing merely on rational reasons concerning why smokers should quit smoking.

Although the use of fear appeals in anti-smoking campaigns is controversial, themes that evoke smokers' emotional arousal remain important. In the US state of Massachusetts, anti-tobacco television advertisements that evoked strong negative emotions were seen as most effective by people who had quit smoking during the course of the campaign, followed by smokers who were more ready to quit and smokers who were less ready to quit (Biener et al., 2000). Also, media messages evoking disgust by focusing on young victims suffering from serious, tobacco-related disease appear to effectively target youth by enhancing anti-industry motivation and reducing intentions to smoke (Pechmann and Reibling, 2006).

THE IMPORTANCE OF SOCIAL AND CULTURAL NORMS

Several researchers have argued that the most effective ads targeting youth should involve enhancing youths' perceived social norms (Pechmann and Reibling, 2006; Pechmann et al., 2003). For example, Pechmann et al. (2003) conducted a large-scale study, in which youths were randomly assigned to view either anti-smoking advertising or advertising unrelated to smoking from the USA, Canada, and Australia. The ads conveying the physical risks of smoking, as well as the TID ads, were found to influence adolescents about the perceived severity of smoking risks and also served to increase their knowledge about smoking. These ads, however, were found to have little impact on behavioral intentions. Rather, it was the ads conveying social disapproval risks that bolstered youths' intentions not to smoke.

One reason why using social norms may be so crucial for effective anti-smoking campaigns, targeted at youths, is that youths, compared with adults, are more sensitive and need to accommodate the conformity pressure coming from social norms (Gibbons et al., 1995). This reasoning is consistent with the results from a recent meta-analysis of various health communications, which showed that messages emphasizing social consequences are more effective than physical consequences among youth populations (Keller and Lehmann, 2008).

Overall, mass media campaigns have been a demonstrated useful tool for community-based tobacco control in the USA, Canada, Australia, the UK, and Western Europe (Logan and Longo, 1999). Nevertheless, most research on advertising fear appeals, for example, has been conducted in the USA, and thus little is known about any differences in the possible effectiveness of fear appeals by cultural context (LaTour, 2006). Research on social marketing in tobacco control also has been limited primarily to individual determinants of smoking, despite the fact that many public health problems originate from environmental and social structural factors (Grier and Bryant, 2005; Wallack, 2002). Despite tobacco use being universal, it occurs in particular social and cultural contexts, with social norms and cultural values shaping people's smoking-related attitudes, beliefs, and behavior (Nichter, 2003; Unger et al., 2003).

Hastings and MacFadyen (2002) urge social marketers to consider a paradigm shift in tobacco control in which the cultural determinants of smoking (i.e., the importance of symbolism and cultural meaning to consumption) are recognized in addition to the individual determinants. Moreover, considering that national anti-smoking campaigns remain relatively novel in many developing and non-Western countries, there is a need to understand how culture might play a role in whether the implemented campaigns are likely to be effective or not. Indeed, cross-cultural research has informed that different ad appeals are commonly adopted in various cultures, and the effectiveness of particular promotions often varies from one culture to another (Han and Shavitt, 1994; Kim and Markus, 1999). Individualistic ad appeals, which focus on individual benefits and preference, personal success, freedom, and independence, might be utilized to a greater extent in the USA, whereas collectivistic appeals that focus on in-group benefits, connectedness, harmony, and family integrity might be employed more often in countries such as China, Japan, and South Korea.

CONCLUSION

Providing a definition of social marketing, as put forward by Andreasen (1994), provided scope for what would be covered in this chapter, and pointed to the need for non-profit and public organizations to incorporate and apply marketing principles to reach their desired objectives. Grier and Bryant (2005), for example, have recognized that many social marketing efforts focus on the development of advertising messages, but they urge those in public health to integrate each of the marketing mix elements. The development of a marketing strategy typically involves specifying target markets, through market segmentation, and establishing a related marketing mix (i.e., strategies relating to product, price, place or distribution, and promotion).

This chapter also specified how target markets are commonly established by taking into account strategically relevant variables relating to demographics, geography, psychographics, and behavioral aspects. When tobacco control efforts are first introduced to a particular jurisdiction, however, a mass market approach is usually taken without a well-defined segment in mind. The rationale for such a mass market approach reflects that the prevalence of tobacco use likely remains relatively high when social marketing programs are initially being implemented. Moreover, for non-profit and public organizations, it is often politically more feasible to generate and sustain program funding if the tobacco control objectives are meant to appeal to a widespread and diverse group. However, as overall smoking prevalence continues to decline in many developed countries, adopting market segmentation variables for establishing particular target groups is recommended. It is anticipated that such an approach will yield more efficiency (economical use of resources) and effectiveness (realizing desired results) than would be the result of a single undifferentiated effort aimed at the 'average' member of the mass market. Nevertheless, some researchers have cautioned that tobacco control efforts exclusively targeting youth are ill-advised because this may send the message that smoking is okay for adults and, consequently, position smoking as 'forbidden fruit' and a rite of passage into adulthood (Lynch and Bonnie, 1994; Siegel, 1998).

As indicated earlier in this chapter, mass media anti-smoking campaigns have traditionally been classified broadly as either prevention- or cessation-focused, although campaigns relating to the harmful health consequences of secondhand smoke started to gain momentum during the mid-1980s in some jurisdictions, and tobacco industry de-normalization campaigns emerged with the public release of internal corporate documents from the tobacco industry as a result of litigation. Anti-smoking media campaigns may place relevant issues on the public agenda, stimulate public discussion, and ultimately serve to shape social norms against the acceptability of tobacco consumption (Wallack, 1990). A cornerstone of social marketing efforts is attempts to influence behavior with an outcome that is driven by benefiting target consumers and society as a whole.

A rich body of literature, from both a theoretical and practitioner perspective, is evident on the discipline of social marketing and tobacco control. There is a wealth of research pertaining to a variety of anti-smoking approaches commonly utilized, including the use of testimonials (e.g., someone speaks about the personal impact of losing a family member or friend from smoking) as well as those that account for overall death toll figures, the likely physical consequences of tobacco use (i.e., health-related, such as lung cancer, or cosmetic-related, such as wrinkling of the skin and stained teeth), cigarette content and its cancer-causing ingredients (e.g., arsenic, benzene), secondhand smoke, and addiction (the difficulty of quitting). However, it is also apparent that much of the existing research is situated in the USA and other developed, Western countries, and thus there is clearly a need for additional research that is sited in less-developed countries, prompting an understanding that is more international in scope. Quite simply, a better understanding is needed about which message themes, tones, and executions are likely to be most effective on the basis of cultural context. Cahill and Perera (2008), for example, note that 'Quit and Win' contests were first developed during the 1980s by the Minnesota Heart Health Program and that international contests now take place in an estimated 80 countries. It would be particularly illuminating to examine whether the efficacy of such an approach is largely dependent on underlying cultural values and the extent that country is economically developed or industrialized.

There are two additional issues, relating to social marketing and tobacco control, that seem to warrant the special attention of researchers. First, the importance of online media, for those in tobacco control, has been identified by Freeman and Chapman (2008) and the National Cancer Institute (2008). Evidence-based practice for utilizing new media and Web 2.0 technologies, as part of an integrated and comprehensive approach, would surely be fruitful. Second, it is recognized that social marketing campaigns need to be evaluated continuously (i.e., both pre-testing and post-testing) and should be designed so that they can work synergistically with additional, ongoing tobacco control initiatives. When evaluating the efficiency of media messages, advertisers commonly account for wear-out, which is defined as the point at which the advertising gets stale or trite, and message receivers become less responsive because they are tired or irritated about seeing the given ad too many times (Wells et al., 2006). On the other hand, the mere exposure effect suggests that when people are exposed to stimuli repeatedly, it becomes familiar, and they come to perceive it more favorably (see Zajonc, 1968, for a comprehensive overview). The mere exposure effect helps explain why multiple exposures of self-help materials, targeting smokers, are more effective than a single exposure (Dijkstra et al., 1999). Ultimately, advertising repetition is a double-edged sword. The message should be repeated for the audience to register and remember, but not to the extent that the audience finds the message boring. Research that attempts to identify the tipping point of repetition and wear-out effects would be captivating.

Speaking to the trans-national and trans-border dimensions of tobacco control, the World Health Organization (WHO) created the Framework Convention on Tobacco Control (FCTC), which is the world's first public health treaty. To date, 174 parties have signed and ratified the WHO FCTC, which 'requires parties to adopt a comprehensive range of measures designed to reduce the devastating health and economic impacts of tobacco' (see http://www.fctc.org for details). Article 12 of the FCTC emphasizes the education, communication, training, and public awareness of tobacco control issues in their agenda. The most vivid development and future direction of social marketing programs in tobacco control will be the global scope that is undertaken.

KEY WORDS: Social marketing; tobacco; smoking; prevention; cessation; market segmentation; marketing mix; de-normalization; social norms; fear appeals.

Key insights

- A marketing strategy involves clearly identifying a target market and establishing a corresponding marketing mix (i.e., strategies relating to product, price, place, and promotion). A mass market approach is often utilized when tobacco control efforts are first introduced to a particular jurisdiction, but market segmentation should be adopted over time, accounting for relevant variables related to demographics, geography, psychographics, and behavioral aspects.
- Tobacco control efforts have traditionally been classified broadly as either prevention- or cessation-focused, whereas programs highlighting the harmful health consequences of secondhand smoke emerged in some jurisdictions during the 1980s and tobacco industry de-normalization campaigns appeared with the release of internal corporate documents from litigation.
- A variety of approaches and communication content and tones have been utilized, including the use of fear appeals and enhancing perceived social norms. Although there is debate about which approaches are likely to be most effective, it is necessary to consider the target audience as well as the particular social and cultural context of social marketing efforts.

REFERENCES

Aaker, D.A. (1996) *Building Strong Brands*. New York: The Free Press.

Amos, A. (1996) 'Women and smoking', *British Medical Bulletin*, 52: 74–89.

Andreasen, A.R. (1994) 'Social marketing: Its definition and domain', *Journal of Public Policy and Marketing*, 13: 108–114.

Bauer, U.E., Johnson, T.M., Hopkins, R.S. and Brooks, R.G. (2000) 'Changes in youth cigarette use and intentions following implementation of a tobacco control program: Findings from the Florida Youth Tobacco Survey, 1998–2000', *Journal of the American Medical Association*, 284(6): 723–728.

Bayer, R. and Stuber, J. (2006) 'Tobacco control, stigma, and public health: Rethinking the relations', *American Journal of Public Health*, 96: 47–50.

Biener, L. (2002) 'Anti-tobacco advertisements by Massachusetts and Philip Morris: What teenagers think', *Tobacco Control*, 11(Suppl 2): ii43–ii46.

Biener, L. and Taylor, T.M. (2002) 'The continuing importance of emotion in tobacco control media campaigns: A response to Hastings and MacFadyen', *Tobacco Control*, 11: 75–77.

Biener, L., McCallum-Keeler, G. and Nyman, A.L. (2000) 'Adults' response to Massachusetts anti-tobacco television advertisements: Impact of viewer and advertisement characteristics', *Tobacco Control*, 9(4): 401–407.

Brehm, J.W. (1966) *A Theory of Psychological Reactance*. New York: Academic Press.

Byrnes, N. and Balfour, F. (2009) 'Philip Morris unbound', *Business Week*, (May 4): 38–42.

Cahill, K. and Perera, R. (2008) 'Quit and Win contests for smoking cessation', *Cochrane Database of Systematic Reviews*, 4(October 8): 1–30.

Carter, S.M. (2003) 'From legitimate consumers to public relations pawns: The tobacco industry and young Australians', *Tobacco Control*, 12(Suppl III): iii71–iii78.

Chacra, A. (1980) 'Player's trademark F'81 advertising'. Prepared for Imperial Tobacco Ltd. Exhibit AG-35, *RJRMacdonald Inc. v. Canada (Attorney General)* (May 5).

Chollat-Traquet, C. (1992) *Women and Tobacco*. Geneva: World Health Organization.

Cummings, K.M., Morley, C.P., Horan, J.K., Steger, C. and Leavell, N-R. (2002) 'Marketing to America's youth: Evidence from corporate documents', *Tobacco Control*, 11(Suppl I): i5–i17.

Dewhirst, T. (2004) 'Smoke and ashes: Tobacco sponsorship of sports and regulatory issues in Canada', in L.R. Kahle and C. Riley (eds), *Sports Marketing and the Psychology of Marketing Communication*. Mahwah, NJ: Lawrence Erlbaum Associates, pp. 327–352.

Dewhirst, T. (2005) 'Public relations', in J. Goodman (ed), *Tobacco in History and Culture: An Encyclopedia*. Farmington Hills, MI: Charles Scribner's Sons, pp. 473–479.

Dewhirst, T. (2008) 'Tobacco portrayals in U.S. advertising and entertainment media', in P.E. Jamieson and D. Romer (eds), *The Changing Portrayal of Adolescents in the Media since 1950*. New York: Oxford University Press, pp. 250–283.

Dewhirst, T. and Sparks, R. (2003) 'Intertextuality, tobacco sponsorship of sports, and adolescent male smoking culture: A selective review of tobacco industry documents', *Journal of Sport and Social Issues*, 27(4): 372–398.

Dijkstra, A., De Vries, H. and Roijackers, J. (1999) 'Targeting smokers with low readiness to change with tailored and nontailored self-help materials', *Preventive Medicine*, 28(2): 203–211.

Drope, J. and Glantz, S. (2003) 'British Columbia capital regional district 100% smokefree bylaw: A successful public health campaign despite industry opposition', *Tobacco Control*, 12(3): 264–268.

Edgar, A. and Sedgwick, P. (1999) *Key Concepts in Cultural Theory*. New York: Routledge.

Farrelly, M.C., Healton, C.G., Davis, K.C., et al. (2002) 'Getting to the truth: Evaluating national tobacco countermarketing campaigns', *American Journal of Public Health*, 92(6): 901–907.

Farrelly, M.C., Niederdeppe, J. and Yarsevich, J. (2003) 'Youth tobacco prevention mass media campaigns: Past, present, and future directions', *Tobacco Control*, 12(Suppl 1): i35–i47.

Farrelly, M.C., Davis, K.C., Haviland, M.L., Messeri, P. and Healton, C.G. (2005) 'Evidence of a dose–response relationship between "truth" antismoking ads and youth smoking prevalence', *American Journal of Public Health*, 95(3): 425–431.

Fishbein, M., Hall-Jamieson, K., Zimmer, E., von Haeften, I. and Nabi, R. (2002) 'Avoiding the boomerang: Testing the relative effectiveness of antidrug public service announcements before a national campaign', *American Journal of Public Health*, 92(2): 238–245.

Freeman, B. and Chapman, S. (2008) 'Gone viral? Heard the buzz? A guide for public health practitioners and researchers on how Web 2.0 can subvert advertising restrictions and spread health information', *Journal of Epidemiology and Community Health*, 62(9): 778–782.

George, L. (2005) 'Light(en)ing up: Anti-smoking lobbyists have suddenly developed a sense of humour in their fight to get kids to butt out', *Maclean's* (August 22): 38–39.

Gibbons, F.X., Helweg-Larsen, M. and Gerrard, M. (1995) 'Prevalence estimates and adolescent risk behavior: Cross-cultural differences in social influence', *Journal of Applied Psychology*, 80: 107–121.

Gilpin, E.A., White, V.M. and Pierce, J.P. (2005) 'How effective are tobacco industry bar and club marketing efforts in reaching young adults?' *Tobacco Control*, 14(3): 186–192.

Goldman, L.K. and Glantz, S.A. (1998) 'Evaluation of antismoking advertising campaigns', *Journal of the American Medical Association*, 279(10): 772–777.

Grier, S. and Bryant, C.A. (2005) 'Social marketing in public health', *Annual Review of Public Health*, 26: 319–339.

Hammond, D., Collishaw, N.E. and Callard, C. (2006) 'Secret science: Tobacco industry research on smoking behaviour and cigarette toxicity', *Lancet*, 367(9512): 781–787.

Han, S.-P. and Shavitt, S. (1994) 'Persuasion and culture: Advertising appeals in individualist and collectivistic societies', *Journal of Experimental Social Psychology*, 30(4): 326–350.

Hastings, G. and MacFadyen, L. (2000) 'A day in the life of an advertising man: Review of internal documents from the

UK tobacco industry's principal advertising agencies', *British Medical Journal*, 321(7257): 366–371.

Hastings, G. and MacFadyen, L. (2002) 'The limitation of fear messages', *Tobacco Control*, 11: 73–75.

Hastings, G., Stead, M. and Webb, J. (2004) 'Fear appeals in social marketing: Strategic and ethical reasons for concern', *Psychology and Marketing*, 21(11): 961–986.

Health Canada (2002) *Canadian Tobacco Use Monitoring Survey (CTUMS)*. Available at: http://www.hc-sc.gc.ca/hc-ps/tobactabac/research-recherche/stat/_ctums-esutc_fs-if/2002_overview-apercu-eng.php.

Health Canada (2005) *Long-Term Trends in the Prevalence of Current Smokers*. Canadian Tobacco Use Monitoring Survey. Ottawa, ON.

Healton, C. (2001) 'Who's afraid of the truth?' *American Journal of Public Health*, 91(4): 554–558.

Henley, N. and Donovan, R.J. (2003) 'Young people's response to death threat appeals: Do they really feel immortal?' *Health Education Research*, 18: 1–14.

Henriksen, L., Dauphinee, A.L., Wang, Y. and Fortmann, S.P. (2006) 'Industry sponsored anti-smoking ads and adolescent reactance: Test of a boomerang effect', *Tobacco Control*, 15(February): 13–18.

Hersey, J.C., Niederdeppe, J., Evans, W.D., et al. (2005a) 'The theory of "truth": How counterindustry media campaigns affect smoking behavior among teens', *Health Psychology*, 24: 22–31.

Hersey, J.C., Niederdeppe, J., Ng, S.W., et al. (2005b) 'How state counter-industry campaigns help prime perceptions of tobacco industry practices to promote reductions in youth smoking', *Tobacco Control*, 14(6): 377–383.

Hill, D., Chapman, S. and Donovan, R. (1998) 'The return of scare tactics', *Tobacco Control*, 7: 5–8.

Hurley, S.F. and Matthews, J.P. (2008) 'Costeffectiveness of the Australian National Tobacco Campaign', *Tobacco Control*, 17(6): 379–384.

Inness, M., Barling, J., Rogers, K. and Turner, N. (2008) 'De-marketing tobacco through price changes and consumer attempts quit smoking', *Journal of Business Ethics*, 77(4): 405–416.

Johnson, J.L., Oliffe, J.L., Kelly, M.T., Bottorff, J.L. and LeBeau, K. (2009) 'The readings of smoking fathers: A reception analysis of tobacco cessation images', *Health Communication*, 24(6): 532–547.

Keller, P.A. (1999) 'Converting the unconverted: The effect of inclination and opportunity to discount healthrelated fear appeals', *Journal of Applied Psychology*, 84(3): 403–415.

Keller, P.A. and Lehmann, D.R. (2008) 'Designing effective health communications: A meta-analysis', *Journal of Public Policy and Marketing*, 27(2): 117–130.

Kim, H. and Markus, H.R. (1999) 'Deviance or uniqueness, harmony or conformity? A cultural analysis', *Journal of Personality and Social Psychology*, 77(4): 785–800.

Kotler, P., Armstrong, G. and Cunningham, P.H. (2005) *Principles of Marketing*, 6th Canadian edn. Toronto, ON: Pearson Prentice-Hall.

Kotler, P. and Lee, N.R. (2008) *Social Marketing: Influencing Behaviors for Good*, 3rd edn. Thousand Oaks, CA: Sage Publications.

Kotler, P. and Zaltman, G. (1971) 'Social marketing: An approach to planned social change', *Journal of Marketing*, 35(July): 8–12.

Kwechansky Marketing Research Inc. (1982) 'Project plus/minus'. Prepared for Imperial Tobacco Ltd. Exhibit AG-217, *RJR-Macdonald Inc. v. Canada (Attorney General)* (May 7).

Landman, A. (2000) 'Push or be punished: Tobacco industry documents reveal aggression against businesses that discourage tobacco use', *Tobacco Control*, 9(3): 339–346.

Landman, A., Ling, P.M. and Glantz, S.A. (2002) 'Tobacco industry youth smoking prevention programs: Protecting the industry and hurting tobacco control', *American Journal of Public Health*, 92(6): 917–930.

LaTour, M.S. (2006) 'Retrospective and prospective views of "fear arousal" in "fear appeals"', *International Journal of Advertising*, 25(3): 409–416.

Lavack, A.M. (1999) *Tobacco Industry Denormalization Campaigns: A Review and Evaluation*. Prepared for Health Canada. Available at: http://www.nsra-adnf.ca/DOCUMENTS/PDFs/lavackpaper.pdf (March 10).

Lavack, A.M. (2004) 'Ads that attack the tobacco industry: A review and recommendations', *Journal of Nonprofit and Public Sector Marketing*, 12: 51–71.

Lee, W.B., Fong, G.T., Zanna, M.P., et al. (2009) 'Regret and rationalization among smokers in Thailand and Malaysia: Findings from the International Tobacco Control Southeast Asia Survey', *Health Psychology*, 28(4): 457–464.

Leventhal, H., Brissette, I. and Leventhal, E.A. (2003) 'The common-sense model of self-regulation of health and illness', in L.D. Cameron and H. Leventhal (eds), *The Self-Regulation of Health and Illness Behavior*. New York: Routledge, pp. 42–65.

Logan, R.A. and Longo, D.R. (1999) 'Rethinking antismoking media campaigns: Two generations of research and issues for the next', *Journal of Health Care Finance*, 25(4): 77–90.

Luoto, R., Uutela, A. and Puska, P. (2000) 'Occasional smoking increases total and cardiovascular mortality among men', *Nicotine & Tobacco Research*, 2(2): 133–139.

Lynch, B.S. and Bonnie, R.J. (1994) *Growing Up Tobacco Free: Preventing Nicotine Addiction in Children and Youths*. Washington, DC: National Academy Press.

Mackay, J. and Eriksen, M. (2002) *The Tobacco Atlas*. Geneva: World Health Organization.

Mackay, J., Eriksen, M. and Shafey, O. (2006) *The Tobacco Atlas*, 2nd edn. Atlanta, GA: American Cancer Society.

McVea, K.L.S.P., Miller, D.L., Creswell, J.W., McEntarrfer, R. and Coleman, M.J. (2009) 'How adolescents experience smoking cessation', *Qualitative Health Research*, 19(5): 580–592.

Moffat, B.M. and Johnson, J.L. (2001) 'Through the haze of cigarettes: Teenage girls' stories about cigarette addiction', *Qualitative Health Research*, 11(5): 668–681.

Moran, S., Wechsler, H. and Pigotti, N.A. (2004) 'Social smoking among US college students', *Pediatrics*, 114(4): 1028–1034.

Morand, M. and Mullins, R. (1998) *Evaluation of the Excuses Campaign: Results of a Telephone Survey Conducted Immediately After the 1996 Media Campaign*. No. 9. Melbourne: Victorian Smoking and Health Program.

National Cancer Institute (2008) *The Role of the Media in Promoting and Reducing Tobacco Use*. Tobacco Control

Monograph No. 19. Bethesda, MD: US Department of Health and Human Services, National Institutes of Health, National Cancer Institute.

Nichter, M. (2003) 'Smoking: What does culture have to do with it?' *Addiction*, 98(Suppl 1): 139–145.

Non-Smokers' Rights Association (2004) *Tobacco Industry Denormalization: Telling the Truth about the Tobacco Industry's Role in the Tobacco Epidemic.* Toronto, ON: Non-Smokers' Rights Association, Smoking and Health Action Foundation.

Pechmann, C. and Reibling, E.T. (2006) 'Antismoking advertisements for youths: An independent evaluation of health, counter-industry, and industry approaches', *American Journal of Public Health*, 96(5): 906–913.

Pechmann, C. and Slater, M.D. (2005) 'Social marketing messages that may motivate irresponsible consumption behavior', in S. Ratneshwar and D.G. Mick (eds), *Inside Consumption: Consumer Motives, Goals, and Desires.* New York: Routledge.

Pechmann, C., Zhao, G., Goldberg, M.E. and Reibling, E.T. (2003) 'What to convey in antismoking advertisements for adolescents: The use of protection motivation theory to identify effective message themes', *Journal of Marketing*, 67(2): 1–18.

Peto, R., Lopez, A.D., Boreham, J., et al. (1996) 'Mortality from smoking worldwide', *British Medical Bulletin*, 52: 12–21.

Poland, B., Frohlich, K., Haines, R.J., et al. (2006) 'The social context of smoking: The next frontier in tobacco control?' *Tobacco Control*, 15: 59–63.

Pollay, R.W. (2000) 'Targeting youth and concerned smokers: Evidence from Canadian tobacco industry documents', *Tobacco Control*, 9(2): 136–147.

Pollay, R.W. and Dewhirst, T. (2003) 'A Premiere example of the illusion of harm reduction cigarettes in the 1990s', *Tobacco Control*, 12(3): 322–332.

Pollay, R.W. and Lavack, A.M. (1993) 'The targeting of youths by cigarette marketers: Archival evidence on trial', *Advances in Consumer Research*, 20: 266–271.

Reid, R. (2005) *Globalizing Tobacco Control: Antismoking Campaigns in California, France, and Japan.* Bloomington, IN: Indiana University Press.

Siegel, M. (1998) 'Mass media antismoking campaigns: A powerful tool for health promotion', *Annals of Internal Medicine*, 129(2): 128–131.

Sly, D.F., Heald, G.R. and Ray, S. (2001a) 'The Florida "truth" anti-tobacco media evaluation: Design, first year results, and implications for planning future state media evaluations', *Tobacco Control*, 10(Spring): 9–15.

Sly, D.F., Hopkins, R.S., Trapido, E. and Ray, S. (2001b) 'Influence of a counteradvertising media campaign on initiation of smoking: The Florida "truth" campaign', *American Journal of Public Health*, 91(2): 233–238.

Smith, K.H. and Stutts, M.A. (2003) 'Effects of shortterm cosmetic versus long-term health fear appeals in anti-smoking advertisements on the smoking behaviour of adolescents', *Journal of Consumer Behaviour*, 3(2): 157–177.

Sweney, M. (2007) 'Anti-smoking ads hooked off air', *MediaGuardian*, http://www.guardian.co.uk/media/2007/ may/16/advertising.uknews, posted 16 May 2007, accessed 31 December 2010.

Thrasher, J.F. and Jackson, C. (2006) 'Mistrusting companies, mistrusting the tobacco industry: Clarifying the context of tobacco prevention efforts that focus on the tobacco industry', *Journal of Health and Social Behavior*, 47(4): 406–422.

Thrasher, J.F., Niederdeppe, J., Farrelly, M.C., et al. (2004) 'The impact of anti-tobacco industry prevention messages in tobacco producing regions: Evidence from the US truth® campaign', *Tobacco Control*, 13(3): 283–288.

Thrasher, J.F., Niederdeppe, J.D., Jackson, C. and Farrelly, M.C. (2006) 'Using anti-tobacco industry messages to prevent smoking among highrisk adolescents', *Health Education Research*, 21(3): 325–337.

Unger, J.B., Cruz, T., Shakib, S., et al. (2003) 'Exploring the cultural context of tobacco use: A transdisciplinary framework', *Nicotine and Tobacco Research*, 5(Suppl 1): S101–S117.

US Department of Health and Human Services (2000) *Reducing Tobacco Use: A Report of the Surgeon General.* Atlanta, GA: US Department of Health and Human Services, Public Health Service, Centers for Disease Control and Prevention, National Center for Chronic Disease Prevention and Health Promotion, Office of Smoking and Health.

US Department of Health and Human Services (2001) *Women and Smoking: A Report of the Surgeon General.* Washington, DC: US Government Printing Office.

US Department of Health and Human Services (2004) *The Health Consequences of Smoking: A Report of the Surgeon General.* Atlanta, GA: US Department of Health and Human Services, Centers for Disease Control and Prevention, National Center for Chronic Disease Prevention and Health Promotion, Office on Smoking and Health.

Wald, N.J. and Hackshaw, A.K. (1996) 'Cigarette smoking: An epidemiological overview', *British Medical Bulletin*, 52: 3–11.

Waldron, I. (1991) 'Patterns and causes of gender differences in smoking', *Social Science and Medicine*, 32(9): 989–1005.

Waldron, I., Bratelli, G., Carriker, L., et al. (1988) 'Gender differences in tobacco use in Africa, Asia, the Pacific, and Latin America', *Social Science and Medicine*, 27(11): 1269–1275.

Wallack, L. (1990) 'Media advocacy: Promoting health through mass communication', in K. Glanz, F.M. Lewis and B.K. Rimer (eds), *Health Behavior and Health Education: Theory, Research, and Practice.* San Francisco, CA: Jossey-Bass, pp. 370–386.

Wallack, L. (2002) 'Public health, social change, and media advocacy', *Social Marketing Quarterly*, 8(2): 12–31.

Wells, W., Moriarty, S. and Burnett, J. (2006) *Advertising: Principles and Practice*, 7th ed. Upper Saddle River, NJ: Pearson Prentice-Hall.

White, V., Tan, N., Wakefield, M. and Hill, D. (2003) 'Do adult focused anti-smoking campaigns have an impact on adolescents? The case of the Australian National Tobacco Campaign', *Tobacco Control*, 12(Suppl 2): ii23–ii29.

Zajonc, R. (1968) 'The attitudinal effects of mere exposure', *Journal of Personality and Social Psychology Monographs*, 9(2): 1–27.

27

Social Marketing and the Health Educator

Robert J. McDermott, Kelli R. McCormack
Brown and Rosemary Thackeray

HISTORY

If social marketing's presence in the social and behavioral change literature is only about 40 years old (Kotler and Zaltman, 1971), then its occupancy of the public health literature, particularly as it relates to health education and promotion, is even more recent. In one initial example, Freimuth and Greenberg (1986) reported on the pretesting of television advertisements to promote family planning products in developing countries (*Family of the Future* program) as part of the Egyptian Contraceptive Social Marketing plan. Later, Hubley (1988) reflected on the health education challenges and the social marketing of condoms in Africa to address the AIDS epidemic. Other 1980s-era researchers described the use of social marketing to advance an oral rehydration therapy effort in rural Haiti (Cayemittes et al., 1988). These illustrations notwithstanding, noted authorities (Kotler and Lee, 2008; MacFadyen et al., 1999) recognize an article written by Lefebvre and Flora (1988) as the first of its kind in the peer-reviewed, mainstream public health literature to advocate for a larger presence of social marketing in health education. Lefebvre and Flora (1988) argued that after experience with large-scale community-based health education programs – namely, the Stanford Three-Community Study (Meyer et al., 1977), the National High Blood Pressure Education Program (Ward, 1984), and the Pawtucket Heart Health Program (Lefebvre et al., 1986, 1987), all taking place in the USA, the potential utility of social marketing as a tool or resource should be clear.

Kotler and Lee (2008, p. 12) identify several other milestones emanating from the final decade of the 20th century and the first years of the 21st century that contributed to the development of social marketing as a public health tool: (1) the work of Prochaska et al. (1992) that presented the organizing framework (i.e., the transtheoretical model) often used in health behavior change campaigns; (2) the creation of the *Social Marketing Quarterly* (a practitioner and researcher journal) by the former Best Start Social Marketing, Inc., of Tampa, Florida (USA); and (3) the growth of two professional conference activities – the *Social Marketing in Public Health Conference* sponsored initially by the University of South Florida College of Public Health, and later, co-sponsored with the Academy for Educational Development (Washington, DC, USA), and the *Innovations in Social Marketing Conference* promoted by various scholars and practitioners. Other 'early' contributions of note for health education, either supportive or cautionary, come from Manoff (1985), Walsh et al. (1993), a litany of papers published in *Health Promotion International* (Buchanan et al., 1994; Hastings and Haywood, 1991, 1994; LeFebvre, 1992; Maibach, 1993) and a 2000 issue of the *American Journal of Health Behavior* (Brown et al., 2000; Bryant et al., 2000; Forthofer and Bryant, 2000; Lindenberger and Bryant, 2000; McDermott, 2000; Parvanta and Freimuth, 2000; Rothschild, 2000; Smith, 2000).

An important visible emergence of social marketing in health education, and its recognition as having a distinctive role in research and practice, came arguably with the appearance in 2005 of a recurring feature column in *Health Promotion Practice*. Whereas 'social marketing' is clearly a part of the health education and promotion lexicon today, and several notable examples of successful initiatives hold up to scrutiny – from the UK (Eadie and Cohen, 2007; McDermott et al., 2007; McLean, 2007), from Australia (Donovan et al., 2007; Jones and Hall, 2007; Previte, 2007), from New Zealand (Milne et al., 2007), from Canada (Lagarde et al., 2007), from the USA (Bryant et al., 2007), and from other countries (Deshpande, 2007; MacArthur and Tharaney, 2007; Smith, 2010) – social marketing has both its detractors and advocates among health education professionals, as well as practitioners who think they are 'doing' social marketing when, in fact, they are not.

THE PROMISE OF SOCIAL MARKETING AND HEALTH EDUCATION

Social marketing has been criticized by some skeptics as not being new, not being better than other health behavior change approaches, and not being ethical (Buchanan et al., 1994). These dismissals are not unlike ones levied against social marketing in general in the 1970s (Laczniak et al., 1979; Luck, 1974). Laczniak and Murphy (1993) have proposed a set of questions that can help practitioners determine the extent to which ethical concerns exist with respect to a social marketing intervention. Truss and White (2010) have illustrated ways in which misunderstanding about the ethical basis for social marketing occurs and also responded to a number of the common criticisms levied against it. Andreasen (2001) has devoted an entire book to the explication of ethics in social marketing. It is not our purpose in this chapter to examine perceptions about the ethics of social marketing in detail; rather, our treatment of the subject is simply to suggest it as one factor as to why social marketing has not been deployed more extensively by mainstream health educators.

Andreasen (1995) described social marketing as '...the application of commercial marketing technologies to the analysis, planning, execution, and evaluation of programs designed to influence the voluntary behavior of target audiences in order to improve their personal welfare and that of their society' (p. 2). Because of social marketing's 'roots' in commercial marketing, more traditional health behavior change specialists may disdain it or may be less inclined to see how altering certain purchasing preferences (e.g., selecting a particular brand of cola drink over another brand) and altering health behavior (e.g., choosing a smoking policy, seeking acceptance of a designated-driver program, or adopting 'safer sex' practices) share certain traits (McDermott, 2000). In part, what separates commercial and social marketing is the latter's '...emphasis on so-called 'nontangible' products – ideas, attitudes, lifestyle changes – as opposed to more tangible products and services that are the focus of marketing in the business, health-care, and nonprofit sectors' (Lefebvre and Flora, 1988, p. 3).

Whereas health educators' philosophical skepticism about social marketing might be at least partially understood, the absence of a greater commitment to its teaching in professional preparation programs is more difficult to comprehend. In the USA, for example, where health education is represented as an area of university study in approximately 199 baccalaureate, 139 master's, and 43 doctoral programs (American Association of Health Education, 2005), the number of institutions in which social marketing is a subspecialty probably can be counted on one hand. This dearth in emphasis is incomprehensible given the lack of success that traditional prevention approaches in the USA have had in changing the status of key youth and adult risk and protective behaviors (smoking, binge drinking, leisure time physical activity, fruit and vegetable consumption) in the past two decades (McDermott, 2008; US Centers for Disease Control and Prevention, 2006, 2007a–e). Health behavior issues that continue to baffle health educators and other prevention specialists have demonstrated responsiveness to social marketing interventions at the level of 'community' – among them – hypertension (National Heart, Lung, and Blood Institute, 1993), high cholesterol (Lefebvre et al., 1986, 1987), youth smoking (Social Marketing Institute, 2000), alcohol-impaired driving (Rothschild et al., 2006), and youth physical activity (Bretthauer-Mueller et al., 2008; Bryant et al., 2007, 2010; McDermott et al., 2010; Wong et al., 2004) to name a few representative examples.

CHALLENGES FOR HEALTH EDUCATORS IN APPLYING SOCIAL MARKETING

With so many opportunities to effect change in health behavior, why is social marketing not more thoroughly embraced by health educators? It is possible that social marketing continues to be only superficially understood by some, impeding comprehension of its systematic approach to examining consumer behavior and, in turn, in crafting responsive interventions. Health educators who view social marketing as just persuasion, behavior modification, or altering the environment with a myriad of different social influences miss its sophistication. Likewise, health educators who see it as simply social advertising, media advocacy, or the design and dissemination of appealing health messages miss the richness of the research that underlies the product, price, place, and promotion mix.

Part of the reluctance of health educators to engage social marketing more fully also might be attributed to ideology. For persons professionally prepared as pro-health ideologues, the notion of promoting consumer behavior change that does not necessarily have 'health' as its central or underlying value may arouse a dissonance that is, on first analysis, incompatible with or unsuitable for, the traditional health educator mindset. This dissonance may be clearer if one examines the following characteristics of marketing (McDermott, 2002):

- Marketing teaches who or what the competition is and what it offers to people that is appealing.
- Marketing teaches the importance of adopting a consumer orientation.
- Marketing assumes people are driven by self-interest. Being pleased and satisfied drives health behavior as it does purchasing behavior.
- Marketing assumes negative health behaviors are not inherently superior (or inferior) to other health behaviors – but merely ones that compete in the marketplace.
- Marketing initially targets the low-hanging fruit – not engaging every person and not attacking every problem or audience segment concurrently or with equal vigor; instead, it seeks out people who are more ready to change, thereby increasing return on investment, a strategy that is almost always defensible given public health's limited resource environment.

In reference to these bulleted items, it is possible that the 'competition' is, in fact, more appealing than what health practitioners 'offer.' For example, the woman or man who comes home after a hard day of work may have children to care for, meals to prepare, and other household chores to address an hour later. Presently, she or he has the option of spending the next hour walking or jogging to meet 'health objectives' or investing that same hour in a reclining chair, elevating the feet, and taking a nap. If one does not understand the appeal of the competition, no behavioral negotiation or compromise is likely. The consumer's perceived value of the relaxation may have some health benefit, but indeed, the appeal of its non-health benefit is probably just as enticing, if not more so. Getting this same weary individual to choose a brisk walk over a nap requires understanding what these other benefits provide for her (or him) – for example, clearing the mind, providing some social distance between work demands and family demands, altering the environment, or recharging one's spirit. A marketer may be able to motivate the brisk walk over the nap but not necessarily by promoting the 'health benefits' of reducing risk of stroke, diabetes, cardiovascular disease, or osteoporosis. The marketer, perhaps unlike the health educator, does not feel as much need to 'win' the health principle. If well-meaning health educators dwell only on promoting what is 'good for us,' without consideration of what mediates the behavior, both the message and the targeted behavior are likely to be lost in the struggle.

For the US-based *VERB*^{TM} (Bretthauer-Mueller et al., 2008; Wong et al., 2004) and *VERB*^{TM} *Summer Scorecard* (Bryant et al., 2007, 2010; McDermott et al., 2010) initiatives, health educators and social marketers used an extensive literature review as well as other confirmatory formative research to design the interventions to increase youth participation in physical activity. These interventions leveraged factors known to appeal to the target audience – 'tweens' (9–13 year olds) – the need to 'belong or fit-in' with friends, the desire for power and self-determination, the wish to develop skills through trying new things, and the overarching goal of 'having fun' (Marketing VOX: The Voice of Online Marketing, 2010). Even more to the point, market (formative) research demonstrated that tweens placed little or no value on exercise's health benefits (SpencerHall, 2003). Thus, in the latter project, whereas the *actual product* was physical activity, the *core product* consisted of 'having fun,' 'spending time with friends,' and 'trying new things' – a focus that promoted 'health' without actually ever making a reference to health. In the social marketing plan, physical activity became positioned as a way to have fun with friends and master new skills. Moreover, the primary audience segment was tweens who were moderately active – neither ones who were already participatory in numerous other activities (and therefore, not in need of intervention) nor ones who wholly rejected physical activity and had neither the support systems nor the resources to be participatory. This segmentation strategy is one that health educators and other public health authorities often reject – selecting instead to focus on everyone – or on the most needy, a group in the present case that could easily have exhausted available resources without altering behavior beyond a negligible degree. The techniques of segmentation and carefully planned audience targeting engage available resources to maximize the return (i.e., the proportion of the potential audience that adopts the behavior change). A more difficult audience to reach is not ignored; it becomes the next priority group, but one that might be addressed via an entirely different milieu of marketing strategies.

ERRORS COMMONLY MADE BY HEALTH EDUCATORS IN APPLYING SOCIAL MARKETING

Hill (2001) notes that health educators have traditionally viewed social marketing as a collection of promotional activities or an approach limited to a set of communication initiatives. Grier and Bryant (2005) provide further evidence of this narrow perspective in their description of abstracts submitted to the *Social Marketing in Public Health Conference* and manuscripts submitted to the *Social Marketing Quarterly*. Andreasen (1995) identifies at least seven features that programs should have to be considered 'social marketing' endeavors:

- Consumer behavior is the bottom line.
- Programs must be cost-effective.
- All strategies begin with the customer.
- Interventions involve the Four P*s*: Product, Price, Place, and Promotion.
- Market research is essential to designing, pre-testing, and evaluating intervention programs.
- Markets are carefully segmented.
- Competition is always recognized.

Although social marketing has not been adopted universally as an intervention-building strategy in health education, some practitioners have claimed it as an approach while making significant errors in attempting to apply it. Using Andreasen's criteria, we can illustrate some examples of how well-meaning health education practitioners sometimes have failed to leverage social marketing's full potential or have taken ill-advised shortcuts with marketing's conceptual framework.

First, programs or campaigns for which knowledge or attitude change is the principal endpoint do not even require a marketing framework because they do not necessarily seek alteration in behavior. Moreover, social marketing involves the principles of exchange theory (Bagozzi, 1978) in which consumers act in their self-interest as they attempt to gain benefits for the least cost possible. In exchange theory, the offer to the audience must yield benefits that the consumer (and *not* the health educator) finds attractive. The cost of behavior change also must be weighed with respect to certain intangible costs that the

consumer is asked to 'pay' – perhaps in terms of time, convenience, pain, abandonment of established and long-standing behavior rituals, or various other psychic sacrifices.

In addition, many so-called social marketing interventions start and end with the *promotion P* without regard to other important features such as the framing of the *product*, the consideration of both monetary and non-monetary costs associated with *price*, and appropriate exploration of the *place* in which the behavior is performed or the behavioral decision is made. If shortcut approaches not involving formative research *do* happen to succeed, their creators are indeed fortunate. A more likely result, however, is that the programmers will be left wondering why so few people participated when the *promotion* seemed so right to them. Whereas conducting formative research cannot absolutely guarantee that programs will succeed, doing so can greatly reduce the likelihood that planners will be disappointed in the outcome of their efforts. It also should be pointed out that formative research cannot be reduced in scope to hastily gathered focus group data or a handful of intercept interviews of persons who seem to 'fit' the target audience profile. Although one can argue that some data are better than none at all, a non-systematic 'quick and dirty' approach to acquiring data can easily lead to poor marketing decisions and inappropriate resulting strategies. Using inadequate data for formulating the 'marketing mix' is unwise and clearly inconsistent with good social marketing practice.

As indicated previously, some health education practitioners struggle philosophically with the creation of programs that fail to target *all persons* who could potentially benefit from a behavioral intervention. Sometimes this dilemma is fueled further by persons who oversee public health efforts and are holders of the belief that they must serve the entire public or demonstrate benefit for everyone that comprises the tax-paying citizenry (Quinn et al., 2005), or supervisory personnel who fail to grasp social marketing altogether (Marshall et al., 2006). Fortunately, an important asset of the marketing framework is its use of strong behavioral theory such as that contained in the transtheoretical model (Prochaska et al., 1992). Because the transtheoretical model, with its stages of change feature, notes that all persons are not equally ready to alter their behavior, it is an excellent match to marketing's philosophy of segmenting audiences and trying to make headway first with those most ready to adopt the desired behavior (i.e., the 'low-hanging fruit'). Furthermore, the transtheoretical model 'stages' persons based on their *current*, *recent*, or other *prior* behavior, a notable departure from public health epidemiology's typical strategy for grouping people on the basis of age, sex, race/ethnicity, and other demographic factors – and the presumed 'risks' that are thought to accompany these traits. Therefore, the model has additional properties that make it a good fit for the marketing mindset and marketing's use of formative research to understand consumer decisions relevant to behavior. Consequently, health educators should find solace in the blending of these two approaches for achieving desired behavior change.

Finally, if health educators are going to succeed better as marketers, they are going to have to improve their understanding of what competes against the behaviors they are attempting to change. Doing so requires a critically important cognitive shift away from viewing some behaviors as being 'healthier' than others, and replacing that view with the perspective of seeing all behaviors as simply competing in the same environment (or marketplace). For example, if health educators want both youths and adults to eat more servings of fruits and vegetables each day, then they must understand how the attraction of fast food competes for their attention and palate. If health educators want children and youths to be more physically active, then they must understand the appeal of television viewing, the entertainment that comes from 'surfing' the internet, and the sense of fulfillment that comes from having an enviable reputation as a skilled videogame player. If health educators want young sexually active individuals to use condoms and practice other safer sex behaviors, then they must understand the rewards of feeling sexually attractive, being sexually spontaneous, and the 'psychic costs' of always being prepared or interrupting a romantic moment. Traditionally, health educators have either ignored or only superficially paid attention to the behavioral competition. Moreover, they have attempted to argue the health benefits of 'good nutrition,' 'proper exercise,' and 'safer sex' as worthwhile endpoints in and of themselves. The health educator of the future will need to understand the competition and adopt more of a marketing mindset that views behaviors as being essentially 'neutral' except in the context in which they are applied.

CURRENT INITIATIVES TO PROMOTE SOCIAL MARKETING AMONG HEALTH EDUCATORS

CDCynergy is an interactive decision support tool for health communication that was originally developed by the Robert Wood Johnson Foundation Turning Point Initiative, the Academy for Educational Development, the Centers for Disease Control and Prevention (CDC) National Center for Health Marketing, and the Oak Ridge Institute for Science and Education (ORISE). Developers designed *CDCynergy* to assist CDC employees in creating public health-based health communication interventions.

In March 2007, developers released the CDCynergy Social Marketing Edition. The social marketing version is similar to its health communication counterpart; it enables health professionals to walk through the steps of planning a social marketing intervention, answering questions as they go along. The end result is an outline for a social marketing plan. In addition, CDCynergy Social Marketing is rich with examples, case studies, and videos that explain various social marketing phases. CDCynergy Social Marketing is available on the web through Oak Ridge Institute for Science and Education at http://www.orau.gov/cdcynergy/demo/.

At least three academic journals applicable to health educators have a dedicated focus on social marketing. The first of these journals to come into existence was the *Social Marketing Quarterly*. The journal was founded as a newsletter in 1994 by Best Start Social Marketing, Inc. (Tampa, Florida, USA) and transformed into a bound publication a few years later. The *Social Marketing Quarterly* is a scholarly, internationally circulated journal that addresses theoretical, research, and practical issues relevant to social marketers. In addition to social marketers, the journal targets health educators and public health, communication, marketing, and social change professionals. Its content includes original research, applications of theory, case studies, conference notices, essays, editorials, interviews, book reviews, and other relevant news regarding social marketing efforts worldwide. Its comprehensive approach makes it an invaluable resource for practitioners, academicians, program developers, and public policymakers.

In October 2005, *Health Promotion Practice*, one of the journals published under the auspices of the Society for Public Health Education (SOPHE), added a recurring feature section having a social marketing focus. Since its inception, the section has offered overviews of social marketing for the health educator, as well as examination of exchange theory, consumer orientation, competition, audience segmentation, formative research, product definition, price and placement strategies, materials pretesting, and other relevant topics.

Finally, in December 2010, Emerald Group Publishing Limited launched the *Journal of Social Marketing*. Its future volumes are expected to include empirical research, literature reviews, and conceptual papers.

Charter certification of health education specialists began in the USA in 1989. *A Competency-Based Framework for Graduate-Level Health Educators* (National Commission for Health Education Credentialing, Inc., 1999) outlined general work responsibilities performed by entry-level health educators. Within this document, social marketing was identified as a sub-competency under the umbrella of advanced practice within the responsibility of administering health education programs. It specifically stated, 'Apply social marketing principles and techniques to achieve program goals.'

The 2004 Competency Update Project resulted in a revision of these entry-level health educator responsibilities (Gilmore et al., 2005). Unfortunately, social marketing was not included in the updated list of *Responsibilities and Competencies of Health Educators* (National Commission for Health Education Credentialing, Inc., n.d). However, in Area II, planning health education strategies, interventions, and programs, competency A states: 'Involve people and organizations in program planning.' Sub-competencies include: (1) identify populations for health education programs; (2) elicit input from those who will affect or be affected by the program; (3) obtain commitments from individuals who will be involved; and (4) develop plans for promoting collaborative efforts among health agencies and organizations with mutual interests. Consequently, the strengths of social marketing can still be utilized in fulfilling these responsibilities and competencies.

HEALTHY PEOPLE 2020

Healthy People provides a science-based, 10-year blueprint for strategic national objectives to promote health and prevent disease in the USA. First published in 1979, *Healthy People* has set and monitored national health objectives as well as the impact of prevention activity. In short, it is the foundation of public health efforts in the USA. However, not until the release of *Healthy People 2020* has there been recognition of the use of social marketing as a strategy for behavior change. In the most recent blueprint for health in the USA, social marketing is included as one of 13 Health Communication and Health Information Technology objectives (HealthyPeople.gov, 2010):

HC/HIT-13: (Developmental) Increase social marketing in health promotion and disease prevention.

- HC/HIT-13.1 *Increase the proportion of State health departments that report using social marketing in health promotion and disease prevention programs.*
Potential data source: The National Public Health Information Coalition (NPHIC/CDC Cooperative Agreement Healthy People 2020 Survey), CDC.
- HC/HIT-13.2 *Increase the proportion of schools of public health and accredited master of public health (MPH) programs that offer one or more courses in social marketing.*
Potential data sources: National Survey of Public Health Competencies in Social Marketing: Survey of Association of Schools of Public Health (ASPH) member schools and accredited MPH programs (Florida Prevention Research Center, University of South Florida).
- HC/HIT-13.3 *Increase the proportion of schools of public health and accredited MPH programs that offer workforce development activities in social marketing for public health practitioners.*
Potential data sources: National Survey of Public Health Competencies in Social Marketing: Survey of ASPH member schools and accredited MPH programs (Florida Prevention Research Center, University of South Florida).

Having social marketing as an objective within *Healthy People 2020* sets the stage for schools and colleges of public health (and other disciplines such as business and public policy) to provide training in social marketing and to demonstrate further how it can be used effectively to translate theory into practice and scale up evidence-based health intervention approaches.

CURRICULA AND TRAINING NEEDS

Currently, there are few social marketing degrees worldwide being offered. Some universities provide concentrations or specializations in social marketing. Others offer post-baccalaureate certificates in social marketing. Depending on the university, social marketing as a course is taught in a school of public health as part of a social and behavioral science sequence, in a business school as a not-for-profit marketing course, in a communication department as an emphasis in health communication, and possibly, in a public policy or environmental sciences department. It is not surprising that social marketing is taught in a variety of different university structures as these structures vary widely across and within countries. Anecdotally, social marketing courses are often taught in the academic department within which a faculty member has an interest in using social marketing as a systematic approach to changing behavior – public health, health education and behavior, marketing, communication, environmental sciences, and others. Those who teach social marketing are challenged, as there are no formal or codified 'social marketing competencies' or defined skills that can be used to guide a social marketing curriculum or the content within a social marketing course, especially as it relates to the needs of health educators.

As with most skills and competencies, one course in social marketing does not a social marketer make! The need for more in-depth training is why it is critical for institutions of higher education to create academic certificates and programs for people wishing to learn more about social marketing and how to use it to effect and sustain change (McKenzie-Mohr and Smith, 1999). Deshpande and Lagarde (2008) identified the social marketing training needs of 477 social sector professionals across 33 countries and discovered 23 topics of interest (Table 27.1). As can be gleaned from this list, a single course in social marketing cannot provide the breadth and depth of requisite knowledge and skills to use social marketing successfully.

So what might an advanced-level (post-baccalaureate) certificate or minor in social marketing look like? Appropriate courses may include an overview course in social marketing, one or two courses on consumer behavior research that include techniques for audience analysis and segmentation, a course on strategic planning, a course on data collection techniques, including use of emerging technologies (e.g., social media) as well as individual and focus group interviewing, a course on how to use social marketing at the level of community, training in program evaluation and measurement, and a capstone course that allows the participant the opportunity to put into practice the knowledge and skills learned. This latter course is crucial to take marketing and social science theory and put into practice when working with individuals and groups.

Given advanced technology and the increased understanding of how to use it for teaching and training purposes, it is not inconceivable that a social marketing certificate could be offered by the world's premier social marketing experts. The world is no longer bound by bricks and mortar, only by the imagination of how best to translate marketing and social science theory into effective social marketing practices. As universities continue to embrace globalization and economies become more knowledge-based (Wildavsky,

Table 27.1 Social marketing (SM) topics preferred at a training event

- Audience analysis
- Ensuring sustainability of change
- Evaluation research methods
- SM 'product'
- Competitive analysis
- SM 'price'
- Conducting social marketing with limited resources
- Formative research methods
- Applying social marketing at the community level
- Managing stakeholders
- Positioning and branding
- SM 'promotion'
- Identifying the target market
- Understanding the exchange process
- Audience segmentation
- Using new technologies
- Ethical issues faced by social marketers
- Budgeting of SM programs
- Funding of SM programs
- SM 'place'
- Advocacy initiatives
- When to use SM
- Reviewing SM basics

Source: Deshpande and Lagarde (2008).

2010), it is possible that universities from different countries will partner to provide the necessary skills and knowledge to train social sector professionals and community members alike. Ultimately, how social marketing techniques influence desired and sustainable change will be embraced more thoroughly by health education practitioners and other public health professionals up and down the programming hierarchy.

GROWING AWARENESS OF SOCIAL MARKETING

During the past decade those working in social marketing have seen an increase in academic centers of social marketing in the UK, Australia, the USA, and elsewhere. These centers are potentially valuable for increasing awareness of the utility and applicability of social marketing in the areas of environment, transportation, education, health care, and housing – all of which come to bear on public health. During the first decade of the

21st century social marketers have seen governments build and fund agencies to increase and enhance the use of social marketing (e.g., the National Social Marketing Centre in the United Kingdom and the National Center for Health Marketing at the CDC in the USA).

As the need for social marketing training increases, so does the need to share social marketing best practices and scholarship. To this end, several milestones have occurred that celebrate social marketing's past successes and raise expectations for improving practice. In 2008, the *1st World Non-Profit and Social Marketing Conference* was held in Brighton, England. Given the overwhelming success of the first conference in bringing marketers, social section professionals, and academicians together, the *2nd World Non-Profit and Social Marketing Conference* was held in Dublin, Ireland in 2011. In 2010, the *Social Marketing in Public Health Conference* celebrated its 20th anniversary. This conference has had more than 6000 attendees in its history and has trained more than 4000 participants through its annual training academy.

There has been an enhanced desire to create a professional association for social marketing as demonstrated through a survey of public health professionals (Marshall and Sundstrom, 2010). A professional organization for social marketing is not a new idea. Almost 20 years ago the legal paperwork was filed in the USA to create such an entity; although the initiative stalled, new momentum to create a global social marketing association has emerged. Health education should take note, because such an association will be stabled with the following principles in mind (Marshall and Sundstrom, 2010):

- A systematic approach to large-scale behavior and social change.
- A well-established professional discipline with a strong academic and practical foundation.
- A community of practice that is open to varied disciplines and practitioners.
- An association that is inclusive of the views of practitioners, organizations, academicians and researchers, donors, policymakers, and others who advocate for, practice, and support social marketing.

CONCLUSION

In conclusion, the evidence for social marketing to advance health education practice is strong and growing. Therefore, the reticence of the health education profession in subscribing to social marketing seen in recent decades is likely to subside as this evidence base mounts, and as theory and practice become interwoven in professional preparation programs around the globe.

KEY WORDS: Transtheoretical model; risk behaviors; protective behaviors; pro-health ideology; competition; consumer orientation; actual product; core product; audience segmentation; return on investment; social marketing competencies.

Key insights

- Social marketing's use in health education and promotion is no more than 25 years old.
- Several milestones in the 1990s and early 21st century contributed to the development of social marketing for health promotion.
- Social marketing has been criticized as not being new, not being better than other health behavior change approaches, and not being ethical.
- The lack of emphasis on social marketing as a sub-specialty in health education professional preparation programs is puzzling given the lack of success that traditional prevention approaches have had on key youth and adult behaviors.
- Social marketing may be poorly understood by some health educators.
- Some health educators may disdain social marketing, in part, because its approach may not necessarily have "health" as its underlying theme.
- The first decade of the 21st century has seen governments in the United Kingdom and the United States fund agencies to increase the use of social marketing for health behavior change.
- The creation of a professional association for social marketers may expand social marketing's use in public health.

REFERENCES

American Association of Health Education (2005) 'Directory of institutions offering undergraduate and graduate degree programs in health education', *American Journal of Health Education*, 36(6): 345–360.

Andreasen, A.R. (1995) *Marketing Social Change*. San Francisco, CA: Jossey-Bass.

Andreasen, A.R. (2001) *Ethics in Social Marketing.* Washington, DC: Georgetown University Press.

Bagozzi, R.P. (1978) 'Marketing as exchange: A theory of transactions in the marketplace', *American Behavioral Scientist*, 21(2): 535–556.

Bretthauer-Mueller, R., Berkowitz, J.M., Thomas, M., et al. (2008) 'Catalyzing community action within a national media campaign: VERB™ community and national partnerships', *American Journal of Preventive Medicine,* 34(6): S2110–S221.

Brown, K.R.M., Bryant, C.A., Forthofer, M.S., et al. (2000) '*Florida Cares for Women* social marketing campaign: A case study', *American Journal of Health Behavior,* 24: 44–52.

Bryant, C.A., Forthofer, M.S., Brown, K.R.M., Landis, D.C. and McDermott, R.J. (2000) 'Community-based prevention marketing: The next steps in disseminating behavior change', *American Journal of Health Behavior,* 24: 61–68.

Bryant, C.A., Courtney, A., Baldwin, J.A., et al. (2007) 'The VERB™ summer scorecard', in G. Hastings (ed), *Social Marketing – Why Should the Devil have All the Best Tunes?* Oxford, UK: Butterworth-Heinemann, pp. 272–278.

Bryant, C.A., Courtney, A.H., McDermott, R.J., et al. (2010) 'Promoting physical activity among youth through community-based prevention marketing', *Journal of School Health,* 80(5): 214–224.

Buchanan, D.R., Reddy, S. and Hossain, Z. (1994) 'Social marketing: A critical appraisal', *Health Education Research,* 9: 49–57.

Cayemittes, C., Ward, W., Obanor, N., et al. (1988) 'Marketing oral rehydration solution in rural Haiti', *Health Education Research,* 3(4): 421–428.

Deshpande, S. (2007) 'The challenges of using social marketing in India: The case of HIV/AIDS prevention', in G. Hastings (ed), *Social Marketing – Why Should the Devil have All the Best Tunes?* Oxford, UK: Butterworth-Heinemann, pp. 297–301.

Deshpande, S. and Lagarde, F. (2008) 'International survey on advanced-level social marketing training events', *Social Marketing Quarterly,* 14(2): 50–66.

Donovan, R.J., James, R. and Jalleh, G. (2007) 'Community-based social marketing to promote positive mental health: The Act-Belong-Commit campaign in rural Western Australia', in G. Hastings (ed), *Social Marketing – Why Should the Devil have All the Best Tunes?* Oxford, UK: Butterworth-Heinemann, pp. 335–342.

Eadie, D. and Cohen, L. (2007) 'A marketing strategy to increase awareness of oral and bowel cancer', in G. Hastings (ed), *Social Marketing – Why Should the Devil have All the Best Tunes?* Oxford, UK: Butterworth-Heinemann, pp. 236–244.

Forthofer, M.S. and Bryant, C.A. (2000) 'Using audience-segmentation techniques to tailor health behavior change strategies', *American Journal of Health Behavior,* 24: 36–43.

Freimuth, V.S. and Greenberg, R. (1986) 'Pretesting television advertisements for family planning products in developing countries: A case study', *Health Education Research,* 1: 37–45.

Gilmore, G.D., Olsen, L.K., Taub, A. and Connell, D. (2005) 'Overview of the national health educator competencies update project, 1998–2004', *Health Education and Behavior,* 32(6): 725–737.

Grier S. and Bryant, C.A. (2005) 'Social marketing in public health', *Annual Review of Public Health,* 26: 319–339.

Hastings, G. and Haywood, A. (1991) 'Social marketing and communication in health promotion', *Health Promotion International,* 6(2): 135–145.

Hastings, G.B. and Haywood, A.J. (1994) 'Social marketing: A critical response', *Health Promotion International,* 9: 59–63.

HealthyPeople.gov. (2010) *Topics and Objectives Index – Healthy People.* Retrieved 22 December 2010 from: http://www.healthypeople.gov/2020/topicsobjectives2020/pdfs/HP2020objectives.pdf.

Hill, R. (2001) 'The marketing concept and health promotion: A survey and analysis of "recent health promotion" literature', *Social Marketing Quarterly,* 7(1): 29–52.

Hubley, J.H. (1988) 'AIDS in Africa – A challenge to health education', *Health Education Research,* 3: 41–47.

Jones, S.C. and Hall, D. (2007) 'Be well, know your BGL: Diabetes Australia's diabetes awareness campaign', in G. Hastings (ed), *Social Marketing – Why Should the Devil have All the Best Tunes?* Oxford, UK: Butterworth-Heinemann, pp. 322–328.

Kotler, P. and Lee, N.R. (2008) *Social Marketing – Influencing Behaviors for Good,* 3rd edn. Thousand Oaks, CA: Sage Publications.

Kotler, P. and Zaltman, G. (1971) 'Social marketing: An approach to planned social change', *Journal of Marketing,* 35(3): 3–12.

Laczniak, G. and Murphy, P. (1993) *Ethical Marketing Decisions: The Higher Road.* Boston, MA: Allyn and Bacon.

Laczniak, G.R., Lusch, R.F. and Murphy, P.E. (1979) 'Social marketing: Its ethical dimensions', *Journal of Marketing,* 43(2): 29–36.

Lagarde, F., Tremblay, M. and Des Marchais, V. (2007) 'Physicians taking action against smoking', in G. Hastings (ed), *Social Marketing – Why Should the Devil have All the Best Tunes?* Oxford, UK: Butterworth-Heinemann, pp. 293–296.

Lefebvre, R.C. (1992) 'The social marketing imbroglio in health promotion', *Health Promotion International,* 7: 61–64.

Lefebvre, R.C. and Flora, J.A. (1988) 'Social marketing and public health intervention', *Health Education Quarterly,* 15(3): 299–315.

Lefebvre, R.C., Peterson, G.S., McGraw, S.A., et al. (1986) 'Community intervention to lower blood cholesterol: The 'Know Your Cholesterol' campaign in Pawtucket, Rhode Island', *Health Education Quarterly,* 13(2): 117–129.

Lefebvre, R.C., Lasater, T.M. and Carleton, R.A. (1987) 'Theory and delivery of health programming in the community: The Pawtucket Heart Health program', *Preventive Medicine,* 16(1): 80–95.

Lindenberger, J.H. and Bryant, C.A. (2000) 'Promoting breastfeeding in the WIC program: A social marketing case study', *American Journal of Health Behavior,* 24: 53–60.

Luck, D.J. (1974) 'Social marketing: Confusion compounded', *Journal of Marketing,* 38(4): 70–72.

MacArthur, C. and Tharaney, M. (2007) 'Development of a primary school curriculum for the control of trachoma in Tanzania', in G. Hastings (ed), *Social Marketing – Why Should the Devil have All the Best Tunes?* Oxford, UK: Butterworth-Heinemann, pp. 329–334.

McDermott, L., Stead, M. and Hastings, G. (2007) 'A marketing strategy to review the effects of food promotion to children', in G. Hastings (ed), *Social Marketing – Why Should the Devil have All the Best Tunes?* Oxford, UK: Butterworth-Heinemann, pp. 254–259.

McDermott, R.J. (2000) 'Social marketing: A tool for health education', *American Journal of Health Behavior*, 24: 6–10.

McDermott, R.J. (2002) 'Our proud heritage in school health', *Journal of School Health*, 72(10): 429–431.

McDermott, R.J. (2008) 'If health education had *vital signs*, then where would we take its pulse?' *The Health Educator*, 40: 3–9.

McDermott, R.J., Davis, J.L., Bryant, C.A., Courtney, A.H. and Alfonso, M.L. (2010) 'Increasing physical activity levels in children 8 to 12 years old: Experiences with VERB™ Summer Scorecard', *Perceptual and Motor Skills*, 111: 1–9.

MacFadyen, L., Stead, M. and Hastings, G. (1999) *A Synopsis of Social Marketing*. Retrieved 27 August 2010 from: http://www.ism.stir.ac.uk/pdf_docs/social_marketing.pdf.

McKenzie-Mohr, D. and Smith, W. (1999) *Fostering sustainable behavior – an introduction to community-based social marketing*. Gabriola Island, BC: New Society.

McLean, N. (2007) 'QuitandSave Scotland: Linking social marketing and social enterprise', in G. Hastings (ed), *Social Marketing – Why Should the Devil have All the Best Tunes?* Oxford, UK: Butterworth-Heinemann, pp. 284–291.

Maibach, E. (1993) 'Social marketing for the environment: Using information campaigns to promote environmental awareness and behavior change', *Health Promotion International*, 8(3): 209–224.

Manoff, R.K. (1985) *Social Marketing: New Imperative for Public Health*. Westport, CT: Praeger.

Marketing VOX: The Voice of Online Marketing (2010) *How-to: Tips for Targeting Tweens*. Retrieved 20 December 2010 from: http://www.marketingvox.com/how-to-tips-for-targeting-tweens-040147/.

Marshall, R.J. and Sundstrom, B. (2010) 'Determining the level of interest in a professional association for social marketing in the United States: Results of a national survey', *Social Marketing Quarterly*, 16: 21–30.

Marshall, R.J., Bryant, C., Keller, H. and Fridinger, F. (2006) 'Marketing social marketing: Getting inside those "big dogs' heads" and other challenges', *Health Promotion Practice*, 7(2): 206–212.

Meyer, A.J., Maccoby, N. and Farquhar, J.W. (1977) 'The role of opinion leadership in a cardiovascular health education campaign', in B.D. Ruben, (ed), *Communication Yearbook I*. New Brunswick, NJ: Transaction Books.

Milne, K., Walker, S. and Porter, I. (2007) 'QuitandWin New Zealand', in G. Hastings (ed), *Social Marketing – Why Should the Devil have All the Best Tunes?* Oxford, UK: Butterworth-Heinemann, pp. 278–283.

National Commission for Health Education Credentialing, Inc. (1999) *A Competency-based Framework for Graduate-level Health Educators*. Allentown, PA: NCHEC.

National Commission for Health Education Credentialing, Inc. (n.d.) *Responsibilities and Competencies of Health Educators*. Retrieved 22 December 2010 from: www.nchec.org/credentialing/responsibilities/.

National Heart, Lung, and Blood Institute (1993) 'The fifth report of the Joint National Committee on detection, evaluation, and treatment of high blood pressure', *Archives of Internal Medicine*, 153(2): 149–152.

Parvanta C.F. and Freimuth, V. (2000) 'Health communication at the Centers for Disease Control and Prevention', *American Journal of Health Behavior*, 24: 18–25.

Previte, J. (2007) 'Using the Internet to reach upstream and downstream in social marketing programmes', in G. Hastings (ed), *Social Marketing – Why Should the Devil have All the Best Tunes?* Oxford, UK: Butterworth-Heinemann, pp. 315–321.

Prochaska, J.O., DiClemente, C.C. and Norcross, J. (1992) 'In search of how people change: Applications to addictive behaviors', *American Psychologist*, 47(9): 1102–1114.

Quinn, G., Albrecht, T., Marshall, R. Jr and Akintobi, T. (2005) '"Thinking like a marketer": Training for a shift in the mindset of the public health workforce', *Health Promotion Practice*, 6(2): 157–163.

Rothschild, M.L. (2000) 'Ethical considerations in support of the marketing of public health issues', *American Journal of Health Behavior*, 24: 26–35.

Rothschild, M.L., Mastin, B. and Miller, T.W. (2006) 'Reducing alcohol-impaired driving crashes through the use of social marketing', *Accident Analysis and Prevention*, 38(6): 1218–1230.

Smith, W.A. (2000) 'Social marketing: An evolving definition', *American Journal of Health Behavior*, 24: 11–17.

Smith, W.A. (2010) 'Social marketing in developing countries', in J. French, C. Blair-Stevens and R. Merritt (eds), *Social Marketing and Public Health – Theory and Practice*. New York: Oxford University Press, pp. 319–330.

Social Marketing Institute (2000) '*Success Stories – Florida "Truth" Campaign*'. Retrieved 20 December 2010 from: http://www.social-marketing.org/success/cs-floridatruth.html.

SpencerHall (2003) *Inspiring Children's Physical Activity – Exploratory Research with Parents*. Retrieved 20 December 2010 from: http://www.cdc.gov/youthcampaign/research/PDF/InspiringPhysicalActivity.pdf.

Truss, A. and White, P. (2010) 'Ethical issues in social marketing', in J. French, C. Blair-Stevens, D. McVey and R. Merritt (eds), *Social Marketing and Public Health – Theory and Practice*. New York: Oxford University Press, pp. 139–149.

US Centers for Disease Control and Prevention (2006) *Healthy Youth! YRBSS Trend Fact Sheets 1991–2005*. Retrieved 22 October 2007 from: http://www.cdc.gov/HealthyYouth/yrbs/trends.htm.

US Centers for Disease Control and Prevention (2007a) *BRFSS – Turning Information into Health.* Retrieved 30 October 2007 from: http://www.cdc.gov/brfss/.

US Centers for Disease Control and Prevention (2007b) *BRFSS Data.* Retrieved 10 October 2007 from: http://apps.nccd.cdc.gov/brfss/Trends/trendchart.asp?qkey=10000andstate=US.

US Centers for Disease Control and Prevention (2007c) *BRFSS Data.* Retrieved 10 October 2007 from: http://apps.nccd.cdc.gov/brfss/Trends/trendchart.asp?qkey=10100andstate=US.

US Centers for Disease Control and Prevention (2007d) *BRFSS Data.* Retrieved 10 October 2007 from: http://apps.nccd.cdc.gov/brfss/Trends/trendchart.asp?qkey=10020andstate=US.

US Centers for Disease Control and Prevention (2007e) *BRFSS Data.* Retrieved 10 October 2007 from: http://apps.nccd.cdc.gov/brfss/Trends/trendchart.asp?qkey=10150andstate=US.

Walsh, D.C., Rudd, R.E., Moeykens, B.A. and Moloney, T.W. (1993) 'Social marketing for public health', *Health Affairs*, 12(2): 104–119.

Ward, G.W. (1984) 'The national high blood pressure education program: A description of its utility as a generic program model', *Health Education Quarterly*, 11(3): 225–242.

Wildavsky, B. (2010) *The Great Brain Race: How Global Universities are Reshaping the World.* Princeton, NJ: Princeton University Press.

Wong, F., Huhman, M., Asbury, L., et al. (2004) 'VERB™ – A social marketing campaign to increase physical activity among youth', *Preventing Chronic Disease*, 1(3), 1–7. Retrieved 20 December 2010 from: http://www.cdc.gov/pcd/issues/2004/jul/pdf/04_0043.pdf.

Afterword

SOCIAL MARKETING: A FUTURE ROOTED IN THE PAST – W. SMITH

The Handbook concludes with an afterword that attempts to look forward and ask what lies ahead for the field of social marketing. Drawing on the experience of 35 years in social marketing as an author and a program manager, Bill Smith proposes that we look for the future in our most basic roots. The afterword begins by outlining some of the more recognizable achievements of social marketing and then asks what really led to these achievements. The answer to this question is the central dilemma of the afterword. While some argue that marketing should focus on its uniqueness and its differences from communication and regulation, Bill Smith argues the opposite. He sees the management capacity of social marketing to integrate regulation, education and facilitation as the best promise for its future. Using the metaphor of a home contractor, he illustrates that the field is both a series of specializations and a management process that holds them together. He makes the case that marketing is unique in the depth of its experience and in its ability to absorb lessons from other disciplines. He ends by suggesting four steps the field must take in the future if it is to live up to this promise. Bill Smith places the future of social marketing in the hands of Adam Smith, who was the first to teach us that the needs of the producer should be considered only with regard to meeting the needs of the consumer.

Social Marketing: A Future Rooted in the Past[1]

William Smith

INTRODUCTION

The enormous array of ideas about social marketing presented in this book can be difficult to navigate. Many of the authors have years of practical experience and have developed strong opinions about what works. Others are leading academics whose lives have been dedicated to understanding and teaching social marketing. The purpose of this afterword is to propose a future for social marketing that integrates many of their seemingly contradictory views into a single unified process of social change: a management process driven by the fundamental belief expressed by Adam Smith that 'the interest of the producer ought to be attended to, only so far as it may be necessary for promoting that of the consumer' (Smith and Cannan (ed.), 1904).

THE ACHIEVEMENTS

I have been privileged for more than 30 years to work on social marketing teams from around the world. Like many of the social marketers of my generation I spent years in the villages of Asia, Latin American and Africa trying to understand why mothers gave enemas to children with diarrhea, why men refused to allow their wives to use contraceptives, and why whole villages melted into the hills when immunization teams arrived. It is hard to believe sometimes how far we have come. The icon of that day was the barefoot doctor of China. Public health was training tens of thousands of villagers to act as surrogate health systems, where no health system existed. The word 'behavior' was nowhere to be found. The idea that millions of illiterate rural mothers could manage the complex process of rehydrating a child was considered absurd. At the same time men and women in India, Bangladesh, and Thailand were launching a new era in family planning. The notion that people deserved a choice when it came to planning their families was iconoclastic. The marketing of contraceptives – hundreds of millions of contraceptives – was emerging as a viable and exciting alternative to forced sterilization and the 'rhythm' method. With the emergence of AIDS, 'behavior change' and social marketing became popular instruments to fight a disease that stigmatized, disfigured, and killed.

During the past 30 years, social marketing has helped to reduce fertility rates, promoted widespread condom use among gay men, saved millions of children from dehydration, improved the quality of immunization services, dramatically reduced smoking, promoted education for girls, and helped a generation in their battle to conserve energy, protect biodiversity, and save the planet.

THE DILEMMA

But exactly what has been responsible for all these achievements? What is social marketing? This has been the most difficult question of all, and many views are expressed by the authors in this Handbook. For some it is anything that human beings do to change other human beings. So, it is not a hurricane, a new disease, a war or a lobotomy, but apparently it is a new law, or a message from the government, a tweet from a friend, or a new contraceptive. Novelli et al. (Chapter 25) articulate a sensible argument for this notion in their excellent discussion of how one of the great advocacy organizations of the world uses social marketing and advocacy together.

Other authors define social marketing by its motivation, and not its effects. So Anker and Kappel (Chapter 19) discuss what happens when social marketing is undertaken by commercial marketers – and the dangers from the mixed priorities that can occur when the 'primary' goal is corporate profit. They do not argue against commercial social marketing, just for caution. This balance seems wise given that the R&D and marketing of commercial products and services such as automobiles, medicines, houses, and the internet can be demonstrated to have an infinitely more positive influence on human life than anything we social marketers can claim. So the fact that their goal is profit does not put commercial marketers beyond the pale – although Dewhirst and Lee (Chapter 26: tobacco), Hoek (Chapter 16: food), and Jones (Chapter 17: alcohol) each remind us that commercial marketing is complicit in many public health problems.

There is a third view that avoids the issue of how marketing is different from anything else, and simply lists its characteristics: exchange, segmentation, competition, consumer focus, etc. This is helpful, but not really definitional, because many other disciplines use these tools.

Perhaps the clearest articulation of social marketing has come from our academic leaders who are concerned with the question: 'What is unique about social marketing?' They argue convincingly that to define social marketing too broadly dilutes its special power to contribute to social change. Rothschild (1999) described marketing as part of a triad of intervention strategies – education, regulation, and marketing. He describes *marketing*'s unique contribution as facilitation, making it easier for a person to change, versus *education*, which provides information, and *regulation*, which uses social control. He argues that all three are important, but if we are to develop our discipline, he says, we must be clear about what we contribute and not be seduced into becoming communicators or regulators.

If we look at the history of our achievements, however, we see that the tobacco wars were dominated by education and regulatory strategies and the creation and marketing of alternatives like the 'patch' were less important. Indeed, almost all of the achievements we claim in social marketing had within them some use of education and regulatory activities. Even the marketing of subsidized contraceptives, which of all our interventions most closely parallels Rothschild expectations, had to deal with importation duties and local advertising and distribution policies to be effective.

To be honest, when marketing leaves the classroom and enters the real world it becomes a much messier thing. This is just as true of commercial marketing as it is of social marketing. Great companies are very concerned with regulations and policy. They educate and lobby, as well as market. In a small business 'marketing' may mean 'sales', while at P&G or NIKE it is a philosophy that permeates the entire organization.

So what then is it?

ROOTS AND MISSION

For 3000 years kings and priests talked to God and told the people what he said. It is not a coincidence that democracy and capitalism emerged at the same time. The notions that 'all men are created equal' cannot survive without the conviction, stated by Adam Smith in 1776 that 'the interest of the producer ought to be attended to, only so far as it may be necessary for promoting that of the consumer' (Smith and Cannan (ed.), 1904). As long as the king controls consumption, he controls equality – or the lack of it.

If marketing is the instrument through which Adam Smith's assertion is to be achieved, then social marketing is the mechanism to achieve that goal for problems which commercial marketing has abandoned. There are yet no products that compete with alcohol, or cigarettes or heroin, so social marketing must find a new way to fight them. There are populations who will not pay full price for condoms, so we must market them at subsidized prices. For those who can afford a condom, there is no condom which provides the pleasure of barebacking it, so we must make condoms seems important in other ways. Social marketing exists to repair flaws in the marketplace that make the commercialization of products or services insufficiently rewarding to pursue.

In the hullabaloo about the practice of our profession, we cannot lose sight of our purpose. We are here to remind powerful people that Adam Smith was right and help them meet the needs of the consumers as well as the needs of science. I want to argue that the definition and practice of social marketing should be rooted in this principle.

Today, the new kings and priests are in the legislatures and laboratories. Laws enforce what science discovers. Governments regulate, cajole, pronounce, and nudge. Evidence-based interventions have become our new icons. These interventions are tested as though they were drugs or vaccines to be distributed and injected in populations to protect them from themselves. The new kings believe that awareness of their magic is enough to make people desire it, and that laws are enough to make people tremble before them. Social marketing is here to remind those powers that the people, even people ignorant of their scientific 'truths' and their patronizing laws, are there to be served.

The initial contribution of social marketing to the field of social change was to frame the individual as a consumer with rights, rather than (1) a citizen with obligations, (2) a student to be taught or (3) an audience to be entertained. When you are an irresponsible 'citizen' you are fined or jailed, as we rightly do with drunk drivers. When you are a student you are taught the value of fruits and vegetables and expected to give up the saliva-producing depth of your grandmother's pulled pork sandwich. Regulatory and education strategies work, but they have limitations. We cannot regulate all human behavior in a democracy. As for education, people know how to do a great many things that they refuse to do despite their knowledge.

Our first job was to make it easier for people to change. We produced new products and services that helped people reduce barriers or experience benefits they care about. When a program in Texas blessed car seats to overcome the fears of Hispanic mothers who don't trust *gringo* technology, when 1 million young women in Madagascar are given a 'red card' to open conversation with a boyfriend who is pushing for sex before she is ready, when Honduran mothers are given a life-saving 'tonic' which prevents dehydration in babies, or when a limo service offers men who refuse to stop drinking and driving a free ride to the local bar, that's facilitation, driven by the design of products and services which consumers want and can get.

But, today, there are many of our greatest challenges where facilitation is too expensive and often just not possible. Are we to abandon these challenges to educators and regulators alone or is there still some important thing we can contribute, even when facilitation is too expensive and too difficult?

Humans are flawed, and so are their systems: so, traffic laws must be obeyed; our food must be protected; our children must be immunized against diseases that affect others; and our environment must be protected against its destruction. Education may fail, but it also works. Mothers told to protect their child from SIDS (sudden infant death syndrome) by laying him on his back, did so without

government regulation or new products to make it easier. Millions stopped smoking as they learned about its risks. And, yes, millions more stopped when cigarettes were taxed, distribution systems limited, and tobacco executives demonized.

In the real world we need regulation, education, and facilitation if we are to interfere with our species tendency toward self-destruction. But how are we to know which we need, at what time in history, and with what other combination?

A NEW PERSPECTIVE ON THE SOCIAL MARKETING PROCESS

I believe that this is our new mission. I will define social marketing as:

> Our most experienced management system for balancing and integrating the application of regulation, education, and facilitation tactics to meet the desires of large-scale populations as they change over time.

It is an approach which argues that people act on what they know. They obey rules. And they like things to be easy. But no one strategy is sufficient to deal with the complex array of social problems confronting us. Social marketing has taught us that if we listen to people, we can orchestrate our programs and ourselves as facilitators to accelerate and maximize the efficiency of behavior change.

In marketing circles this will not be a popular view. Marketing academics are right to worry that if we make marketing too broad it will become nothing at all. They argue that marketing should be limited to facilitation strategies and that while communication and regulation work, they are distinct categories. Among practitioners of social marketing the belief that we need regulation, education, and facilitation is very popular, but actual programs too often default to communication or education strategies alone.

I believe that by focusing on marketing as a management system rather than a discrete tactic for behavior change, we recognize what is already happening and we lay the groundwork for improvements that matter. After 30 years in the field I think social marketing is and ought to be the general contractor for building effective behavior change interventions that serve both society and the individual.

Social change is like building a house or a community. We need specialists such as carpenters, electricians, and masons. We also need an architect, a plan, a homeowner, and a general contractor (or clerk of works). This is my metaphor to help describe my conviction that we must now be more than a mechanism to facilitate change.

In this metaphor, the *architect* is the funding agency. The *homeowner* is the population who is to benefit from the construction. Did I mention this is public housing? Yes, the homeowner is not actually paying for the house. This impoverishment places them at considerable disadvantage. The *specialists* include advocates, communicators, researchers, designers, and a plethora of other talents and professions. The *plan* is often developed by the architect well in advance of contracting the general contractor and often it is not what the homeowner wants. Oh, and he architect under-budgets fundamentals like market research and plows lots of money in accessories to help 'sell' the houses.

An effective social marketer is a *general contractor (GC)*. The GC is the person who understands what professions are needed, when they are needed, how much they cost, and choices that she has in using them to improve efficiency and save money. Most important, the GC is responsible for understanding and pleasing both the architect and the homeowner.

Many problems of definition stem from the fact that for years we have had electricians or carpenters playing the role of general contractor. An electrician spends a lot of time talking about electrical, the advocate talking about advocacy, the communicator talking about communication, and the designer talking about designing a new condom or a new dating service. It is a rare specialist that makes a great general contractor.

WHY IS MARKETING SO SPECIAL?

Marketing is special for several critical reasons. Marketing is eclectic and assimilates knowledge from any discipline that meets the needs of the consumer. It is experienced, with vast resources dedicated to studying its effectiveness. It is ubiquitous and adapts itself to whatever problem is important. And it is disciplined when it is applied professionally.

Social problems vary tremendously in their complexity, their level of readiness to respond to influence, and the tools we have available to address them. New theories, new tools, and new technologies are emerging all the time. Many of these new tools are marketed as 'the answer' to all the complexities of social change. Social media is the latest fad promising unparalleled advantages in networking and sharing. Tools are not the answer. But systems that integrate them are. And what other systems do we have?

In the 1970s and 1980s, health promotion emerged as an integrating system for public health. Environmentalists have focused on 'system theory' as an integrating function. Transportation and law enforcement talk of the 'Three Es': education, enforcement, and engineering. Each sector reflects the needs of the particular clusters of behaviors they address.

But none of these have the history, discipline, or experience of marketing, the core discipline from which social marketing pulls its strength. No other discipline has invested the vast sums of money and talent in understanding how people behave and how to efficiently influence their behavior. So pervasive has marketing become in modern life, that it is often mis-used to manipulate rather than serve. Like democracy itself, it may be terrible, but it is better than '*all those other forms that have been tried from time to time*'.

As I pointed out, this is a controversial view in the community of social marketers. It rejects the classical definition of social marketing so eloquently described by Mike Rothschild as decidedly distinct from both communication and regulatory strategies. Mike is right to worry that a broad definition will lead to sloppy and undisciplined interventions. But I want to propose we reconsider that narrow, if valuable, distinction, in favor of an emphasis on what Adam Smith's concept of marketing really means: organizing around the needs of consumers rather than the producers.

I want to argue that our true competitors are not education, regulation or participatory strategies, but the individuals who propose that any one of them, working alone, can achieved complex behavior change. For some, the idea that marketing is the engineering function of capitalism is abhorrent. But that is what I believe it to be. And social marketing, in all modesty, should become the engineering, or the contractor, function of social change.

I don't worry like many others that marketing is often manipulative. Like any system, social marketing can be used ethically or unethically. We can execute programs like professionals or amateurs. When we behave unethically or like amateurs we should be brought to task. But there is nothing inherently evil about using all we know about human behavior in an integrated, constantly improving process to make society better and give individuals a chance at happiness.

I do worry that we seemed trapped in an endless series of social experiments in which behavior change has become an infectious disease to be fought with a never ending array of behavioral medicines and 'vaccines'. I worry that few managers ask themselves how to integrate what we know about human behavior into a continuous, self-conscious system of innovation, and instead are driven to try the novel and abandon the 'done that, been there' alternative.

WHERE DOES THIS VISION LEAD US?

I believe that the greatest challenge we face in the future is to live up to this promise. Today, too much of what we call social marketing is dominated by advertising, communication, and messages. Too many of us who call ourselves social marketers have little or no background in the fundamentals of our profession. Our political systems are not organized like our economic systems and so policymakers have a hard time understanding our jargon. Attempts like reinventing government, to make our government services entrepreneurial, have demonstrated the possibility of success, but failed to produce widespread change.

This vision requires we change in at least four fundamental ways.

Focus on the managers of social change

Social marketing, to bring us a back to my metaphor, is in the *public* housing business. Some portion of the social marketing process is *paid for by someone other than the consumer.* This is not true of successful commercial marketing and it presents a particularly complex dilemma. The presence of a third, financing party, results in the social marketer having two masters of remarkably different character: the piper who pays the bill and the consumer or public it is designed to serve.

The actual process is much more complicated. Our social marketing 'housing' project is staffed by four, not just two, key players: (1) the social marketing expert (general contractor); (2) the donor; (3) the team of specialists who actually does the work; and (4) the homeowner. Each of these players brings to the social marketing process different degrees of understanding, different experiences and bias, and different kinds of power.

To misunderstand this complex dance of interests is to misunderstand why social marketing fails or succeeds. Success depends not upon the quality of the research, the amount of the budget, the sophistication of the advertising or the design of the service. Success depends upon how cleverly the competing interests of this team are managed. French (Chapter 24) offers an excellent discussion of why social marketing should be important to

government and how these relationships can be effectively managed.

I am proposing a future in which we broaden our perspective from the consumer and focus more attention on the donor, who controls so much of the process. We must offer donors more than facilitation strategies: they need an organizing system, not just another tactic.

Replace the 4Ps with the four cells of competitiveness

I have argued forcefully that the 4Ps are the fundamentals of our profession. I still think they are, but that with a broader perspective, we need a broader platform. What if we were to think in terms of four alternative strategies organized around the idea of competitiveness? Something like:

Increase benefits to the desired behavior	Make smoking not socially rewarding
Reduce barriers to the desired behavior	Improve quitting technologies
Increase barriers to the competing behaviors	Tax cigarettes, limit distribution
Decrease benefits to the competing barriers	Close bars to smoking

There is nothing original here. Competiveness has been one of our most powerful contributions to the process of social change. But a refocus in some way may strengthen and renew our commitment to multiple avenues to achieve competitiveness.

Respect our specialists as specialists

Social marketing today permits too many specialists to act as general contractors. We need an organizational structure that reflects our dependence upon the specialization of our profession, without communicating that you are a researcher, a creative, an advertiser, a media buyer, or a designer who is somehow not a full-fledged social marketer. At the same time, we need to train a cadre of general contractors, who are no more superior to an advertiser than a general contractor is superior to a carpenter, but who are schooled in the management of integration. This will take time, but if we begin to create interest groups of specialists among us, we can begin to recognize the importance of all our disciplines.

Actively populate our profession with new players

Today our profession is populated largely by communication and advocacy specialists. For reasons of history and mission, these professions have been attracted to social marketing. There exists a growing and powerful design community that still remains largely outside our profession. There is also a community of social entrepreneurs who could add tremendously to our ability to understand and manage social change. If we actively reach out to those communities, ally or merge with them, we can redress the imbalance in our programming which worries so many of us.

CONCLUSION

After reflecting on the excellent chapters in this book and on my own experience across many countries and many social marketing challenges, I have concluded that our future lies is opening up rather than closing down. The fears that we have abandoned marketing in favor of too much communication are well founded. But I don't believe the answer is to convince people to focus. Instead, if we bring in new people, think of ourselves as the specialists we are, and add a cadre of integration manager, we have a better chance not only of improving the quality of our work but also of living up to the mission set for us by Adam Smith: 'the interest of the producer ought to be attended to, only so far as it may be necessary for promoting that of the consumer' (Smith and Cannan (ed.), 1904).

NOTE

1   This chapter was written immediately after an intensely exciting four-month conversation with Michael Rothschild and Nancy Lee that occurred at the end of 2010. We were trying to distinguish between social marketing and other endeavors that compete with it for the attention of change actors. We arrived at a two-page Declaration and a positioning statement for social marketing. That statement may be published before this Handbook is released. We did not agree on everything, but the process was intellectually exciting. It is impossible to disentangle the effects of that conversation on the conclusions of this afterword, so I wish to recognize their contribution in challenging and enlightening my position, and express my gratitude for their friendship and patience with my own often convoluted thinking process. I wouldn't have gotten here without them.

REFERENCES

Rothschild, M. (1999) 'Carrots, sticks and promises: A conceptual framework for the management of public health and social issue behaviors', *Journal of Marketing*, 63(4): 24–37.

Smith, A. (author) and Cannon, E. (editor) (1904). *An Inquiry into the Nature and Causes of the Wealth of Nations, Vol. II*, 5th edn. London: Methuen and Co.

Index